PENGUIN BOOKS

CITIZEN SAILORS

'A moving and evocative story of the war at sea' N. A. M. Rodger, author of *The Command of the Ocean*

'This impressive human history of the Royal Navy begins the long overdue process of putting it back at the heart of the war effort' *Independent*, Book of the Week

'Prysor does for the sailors of the Royal Navy what Patrick Bishop did for the RAF in *Fighter Boys* . . . He reminds us of their extraordinary contribution to our survival' *Daily Express*

'An absorbing read' *Literary Review*

'Full of terrific stories' *Sunday Times*

'This excellent book . . . captures the soul of the men who were there' *Navy News*

'Skilfully weaves together a coherent "people's history of the sailors' war" . . . Fresh and compelling' *Times Literary Supplement*

'Breathtaking skill . . . freshness and force . . . Prysor makes the Navy of the Second World War intensely personal, vivid and vital' *Military Times*

'Reads extremely well, with a gripping narrative that explains the unfolding of the war whilst weaving in moving and vivid personal accounts . . . This is a book that manages to fuse the strategic with the human and the social with consummate skill, and in so doing it delivers a multifaceted understanding of the war at sea as well as a poignant reminder of the way in which society has lost its "sea vision"' *Nautilus International Telegraph*

**ABOUT THE AUTHOR**

Glyn Prysor was educated at Oxford University, where he completed a doctorate and taught modern history. He lives in Sussex. This is his first book.

# Citizen Sailors

*The Royal Navy in the Second World War*

## GLYN PRYSOR

PENGUIN BOOKS

PENGUIN BOOKS

Published by the Penguin Group
Penguin Books Ltd, 80 Strand, London WC2R ORL, England
Penguin Group (USA) Inc., 375 Hudson Street, New York, New York 10014, USA
Penguin Group (Canada), 90 Eglinton Avenue East, Suite 700, Toronto, Ontario, Canada M4P 2Y3
(a division of Pearson Penguin Canada Inc.)
Penguin Ireland, 25 St Stephen's Green, Dublin 2, Ireland
(a division of Penguin Books Ltd)
Penguin Group (Australia), 250 Camberwell Road,
Camberwell, Victoria 3124, Australia (a division of Pearson Australia Group Pty Ltd)
Penguin Books India Pvt Ltd, 11 Community Centre,
Panchsheel Park, New Delhi – 110 017, India
Penguin Group (NZ), 67 Apollo Drive, Rosedale, Auckland 0632, New Zealand
(a division of Pearson New Zealand Ltd)
Penguin Books (South Africa) (Pty) Ltd, Block D, Rosebank Office Park, 181 Jan Smuts Avenue,
Parktown North, Gauteng 2193, South Africa

Penguin Books Ltd, Registered Offices: 80 Strand, London WC2R ORL, England

www.penguin.com

First published by Viking 2011
Published in Penguin Books 2012
002

Typeset by Palimpsest Book Production Limited, Falkirk, Stirlingshire
Printed in England by Clays Ltd, St Ives plc

ISBN: 978-0-141-04632-7


www.greenpenguin.co.uk

ALWAYS LEARNING                    **PEARSON**

For Hester, with love

# Contents

# Illustrations

# Great Britain and Northern France

SHETLAND ISLANDS

ORKNEY ISLANDS

Scapa Flow

OUTER HEBRIDES

*Loch Ewe*

N

100 miles

Tobermory

Greenock · Rosyth *Firth of Forth*

·Glasgow

*Firth of Clyde*

Newcastle

NORTH SEA

Londonderry

Belfast

Barrow-in-Furness

Hull

Liverpool

Grimsby *Humber Estuary*

Skegness

IRELAND

Great Yarmouth

Lowestoft

Harwich Felixstowe

Milford Haven

LONDON

Cardiff ·Bristol

Chatham

Dover

Dunkirk

Southampton Portsmouth

Calais

Plymouth & Devonport

*Lyme Bay* Portland

*Isle of Wight*

Newhaven

Boulogne

SCILLY ISLES

ENGLISH CHANNEL

Cherbourg

Dieppe

Le Havre

PARIS

Brest

FRANCE

St Nazaire

↓ Bordeaux (150 miles)

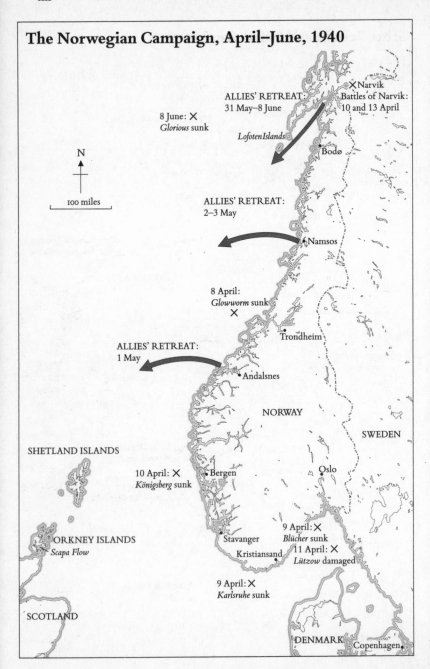

# The Norwegian Campaign, April–June, 1940

ALLIES' RETREAT:
31 May–8 June

Battles of Narvik:
10 and 13 April

✕ Narvik

8 June: ✕
*Glorious* sunk

*Lofoten Islands*

● Bodø

**N**

100 miles

ALLIES' RETREAT:
2–3 May

● Namsos

8 April:
*Glowworm* sunk
✕

● Trondheim

ALLIES' RETREAT:
1 May

● Andalsnes

NORWAY

SHETLAND ISLANDS

SWEDEN

10 April: ✕
*Königsberg* sunk

● Bergen

● Oslo

ORKNEY ISLANDS
*Scapa Flow*

9 April: ✕
*Blücher* sunk

● Stavanger

11 April: ✕
*Lützow* damaged

● Kristiansand

9 April: ✕
*Karlsruhe* sunk

SCOTLAND

DENMARK
● Copenhagen

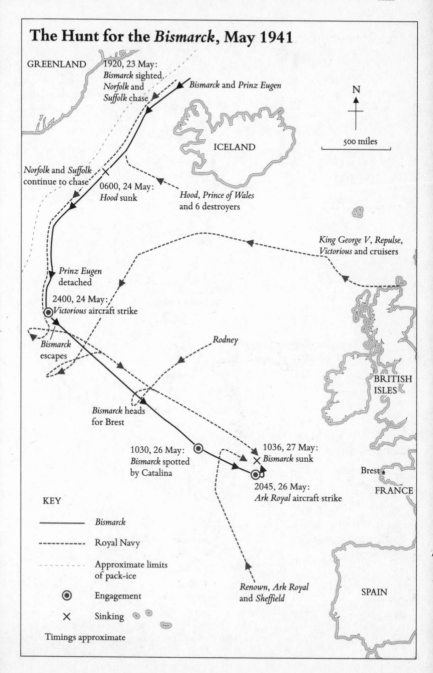

# The Hunt for the *Bismarck*, May 1941

GREENLAND

1920, 23 May:
*Bismarck* sighted.
*Norfolk* and
*Suffolk* chase

*Bismarck* and *Prinz Eugen*

N

ICELAND

500 miles

*Norfolk* and *Suffolk*
continue to chase

0600, 24 May:
*Hood* sunk

*Hood*, *Prince of Wales*
and 6 destroyers

*King George V*, *Repulse*,
*Victorious* and cruisers

*Prinz Eugen*
detached

2400, 24 May:
*Victorious* aircraft strike

*Bismarck*
escapes

*Rodney*

BRITISH
ISLES

*Bismarck* heads
for Brest

1030, 26 May:
*Bismarck* spotted
by Catalina

1036, 27 May:
*Bismarck* sunk

Brest

2045, 26 May:
*Ark Royal* aircraft strike

FRANCE

KEY

———— *Bismarck*

-------- Royal Navy

- - - - - Approximate limits
of pack-ice

◉ Engagement

✕ Sinking

Timings approximate

*Renown*, *Ark Royal*
and *Sheffield*

SPAIN

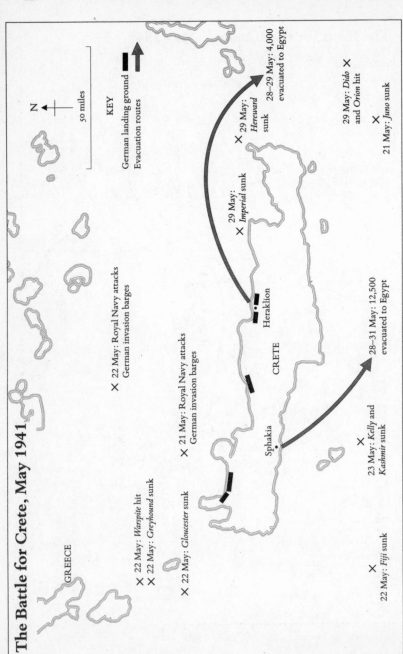

# The Battle for Crete, May 1941

GREECE

X 22 May: *Warspite* hit
X 22 May: *Greyhound* sunk

X 22 May: *Gloucester* sunk

X 22 May: Royal Navy attacks German invasion barges

X 21 May: Royal Navy attacks German invasion barges

CRETE

Heraklion

Sphakia

X 23 May: *Kelly* and *Kashmir* sunk

28–31 May: 12,500 evacuated to Egypt

28–29 May: 4,000 evacuated to Egypt

X 29 May: *Imperial* sunk

X 29 May: *Hereward* sunk

X 29 May: *Dido* and *Orion* hit

X 21 May: *Juno* sunk

X 22 May: *Fiji* sunk

N

50 miles

KEY

German landing ground
Evacuation routes

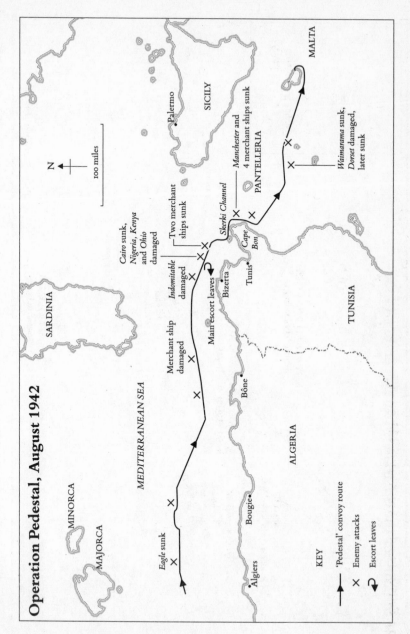

Operation Pedestal, August 1942

N

100 miles

MEDITERRANEAN SEA

MINORCA

MAJORCA

SARDINIA

SICILY

*Palermo*

*Manchester* and
4 merchant ships sunk

*Cairo* sunk,
*Nigeria, Kenya*
and *Ohio*
damaged

Two merchant
ships sunk

*Skerki Channel*

*Indomitable*
damaged

*Waimarama* sunk,
*Dorset* damaged,
later sunk

PANTELLERIA

MALTA

Cape
Bon

Merchant ship
damaged

Main escort leaves

*Bizerta*

*Tunis*

*Eagle* sunk

*Bône*

*Bougie*

ALGERIA

TUNISIA

*Algiers*

KEY

⟶ 'Pedestal' convoy route

✕ Enemy attacks

⟳ Escort leaves

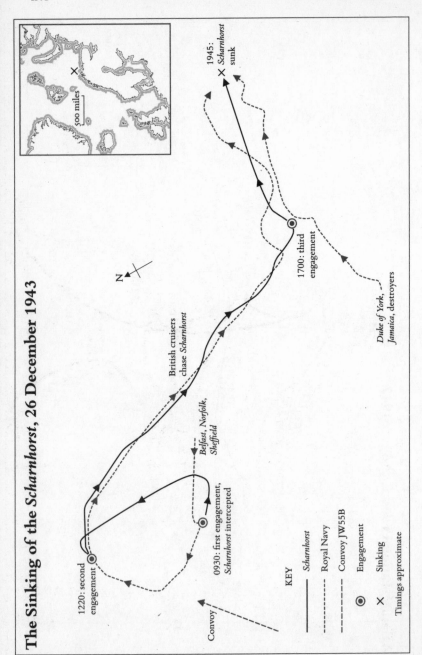

# The Sinking of the *Scharnhorst*, 26 December 1943

1945: *Scharnhorst* sunk

1700: third engagement

British cruisers chase *Scharnhorst*

*Belfast, Norfolk, Sheffield*

0930: first engagement, *Scharnhorst* intercepted

1220: second engagement

N

*Duke of York, Jamaica, destroyers*

Convoy

500 miles

KEY

*Scharnhorst*

Royal Navy

Convoy JW55B

Engagement

Sinking

Timings approximate

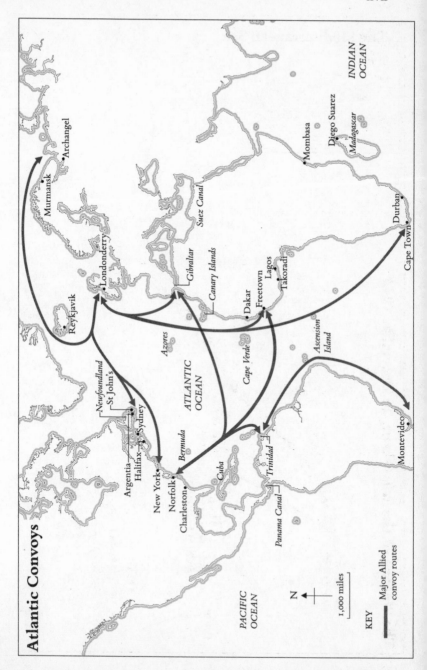

# Atlantic Convoys

INDIAN
OCEAN

Diego Suarez
Mombasa
*Madagascar*

Durban
Cape Town

Archangel
Murmansk

Londonderry

Gibraltar
*Canary Islands*

Lagos
Takoradi
Dakar
Freetown

Reykjavik

*Azores*

ATLANTIC
OCEAN

*Cape Verde*

Ascension
Island

*Newfoundland*
St John's
Sydney

Bermuda

Montevideo

Argentia
Halifax

New York
Norfolk
Charleston

*Cuba*

*Trinidad*

PACIFIC
OCEAN

*Panama Canal*

N

1,000 miles

KEY

—— Major Allied
convoy routes

# The Mediterranean Sea

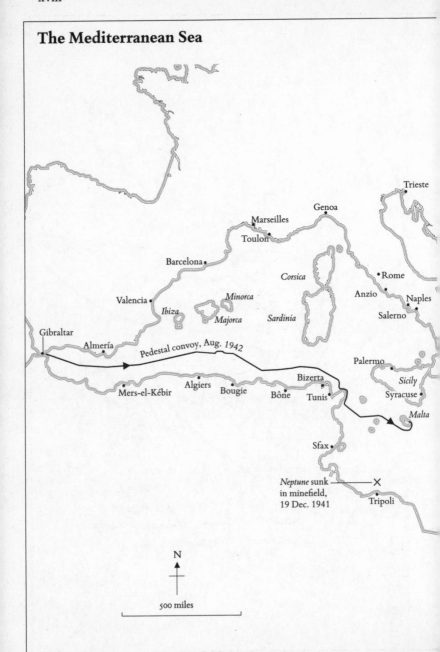

Trieste

Genoa

Marseilles

Toulon

Barcelona

*Corsica*

• Rome

Anzio

Naples

Valencia

*Minorca*

*Ibiza*

*Majorca*

*Sardinia*

Salerno

Gibraltar

Almería

Pedestal convoy, Aug. *1942*

Palermo

*Sicily*

Mers-el-Kébir

Algiers

Bougie

Bône

Bizerta

Tunis

Syracuse

*Malta*

Sfax

*Neptune* sunk
in minefield,
19 Dec. 1941

✕

Tripoli

N

500 miles

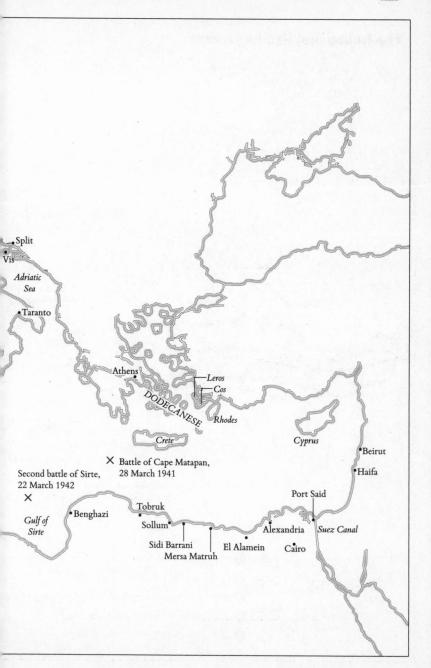

Split

Vis

*Adriatic Sea*

Taranto

Athens

Leros

Cos

DODECANESE

Rhodes

Crete

Cyprus

Beirut

Haifa

✕ Battle of Cape Matapan, 28 March 1941

Second battle of Sirte, 22 March 1942

✕

*Gulf of Sirte*

Benghazi

Tobruk

Sollum

Sidi Barrani

Mersa Matruh

El Alamein

Alexandria

Cairo

Port Said

*Suez Canal*

# The Indian and Pacific Oceans

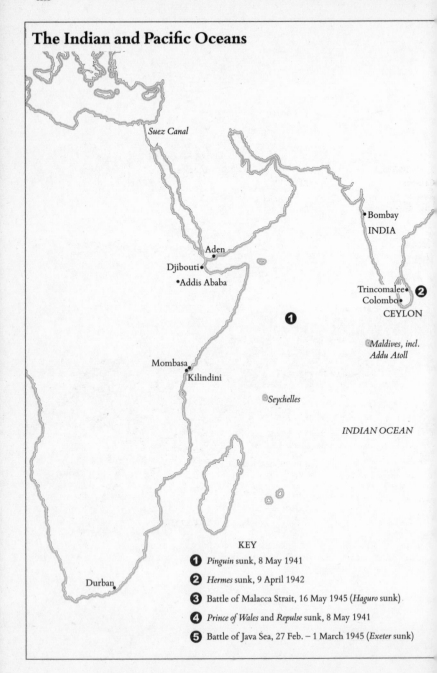

Suez Canal

Bombay
INDIA

Aden
Djibouti
Addis Ababa

Trincomalee ❷
Colombo
CEYLON

❶

Maldives, incl.
Addu Atoll

Mombasa
Kilindini

Seychelles

INDIAN OCEAN

Durban

KEY

❶ *Pinguin* sunk, 8 May 1941

❷ *Hermes* sunk, 9 April 1942

❸ Battle of Malacca Strait, 16 May 1945 (*Haguro* sunk)

❹ *Prince of Wales* and *Repulse* sunk, 8 May 1941

❺ Battle of Java Sea, 27 Feb. – 1 March 1945 (*Exeter* sunk)

# 1. Introduction

In the early morning mist of 3 May 1940, the cruiser HMS *Carlisle* was slipping out of a Norwegian fjord. Able Seaman Charles Hutchinson manned his anti-aircraft gun, hungry and tired after a long and sleepless night. Since the previous evening, British and French ships had been rescuing 5,700 soldiers from the besieged port of Namsos. With the town now abandoned to German forces, *Carlisle* was part of a small convoy making a break for home. Lookouts strained their tired eyes. On the exposed upper deck, the gunners waited for the inevitable alarm.

Shortly before nine o'clock, the first German bombers were spotted swooping over the mountains which lined the fjord. It was the beginning of six hours of sustained attack as the convoy made its way out to sea. 'Hell's pandemonium started,' wrote Hutchinson soon afterwards, 'planes attacking from all angles, and I couldn't describe it if I wanted to. No-one except those taking part could ever realise it . . . It was like Hell let loose.'

Junkers 88s dropped their payloads from high altitude while ships veered from side to side, near misses sending torrents of water into the air. Stuka dive-bombers screamed as they flew down towards their targets. Some aimed for a French troopship directly ahead of *Carlisle*, while Hutchinson and the other gunners put up their barrage, empty shell casings piling up on the deck beside them. It was not long before the nearby French destroyer *Bison* was hit and sinking rapidly. Hutchinson watched as some of her sailors managed to scramble aboard the British destroyer HMS *Afridi*. They enjoyed little respite: *Afridi* was struck later in the afternoon, capsizing and taking ninety-two souls to the bottom of the Norwegian Sea.

Safely back at the naval base of Scapa Flow, nestled at the heart of the Orkneys, the sailors could reflect on their experiences. 'Now, when I think of the episode I marvel at it,' wrote Hutchinson in a battered notebook, 'how everyone on the ship and particularly on the guns stuck it without any panic during the heavy raids, as really I don't think it would have surprised anybody if some of them had panicked and run as it was a Hell of an experience.' The gunners had managed to fend off the attacks on the troopships, saving thousands of lives, and had destroyed several bombers in the process. 'I'll never forget the sight,' wrote Hutchinson of one ill-fated enemy plane. 'It was high in the air and it wobbled and then down it came. We watched it with a fiendish delight. We must be funny creatures – in peace-time one wouldn't harm a fly, then taking a delight in seeing them crash to their doom.'

Charles Hutchinson was twenty-six. From East Yorkshire, he had volunteered for the Humber Division of the Royal Naval Volunteer Reserve before the war, and had been mobilized in August 1939. He began writing his diary at the start of 1940, filling notebooks with his thoughts during idle moments in quiet corners, and even scribbling beside the gun up on deck while trying to protect the paper from the elements. This was an entirely new habit for a man with an ordinary working-class background, and the enthusiasm with which he took to it caused him some surprise. 'I certainly have written some of these lines in queer places and positions,' he noted. 'I don't know what's come over me to write all this, but I should never remember it all so I thought if I wrote just what I thought each day it would be more natural.'

In his cramped mess, where men lived and slept shoulder-to-shoulder, Hutchinson's constant writing was soon noticed. 'Look at old Hutch digging out,' he recorded one of his shipmates saying, 'Old H. G. Wells hasn't a bloody look-in.' Most of his friends believed he was composing long letters home, but in fact his new-found hobby was driven by an almost obsessive desire to record his experiences:

This has caught hold of me and now it seems to fascinate me into writing, as even when the raids were on I used to be thinking: 'I shall have to remember this one', and trying to keep in my mind the wording of it, but often it is a few hours after before I have the opportunity of writing it down. I usually tear a few pages out and keep them with me and I fill my pen and sit in a quiet place and write, but I have to be quick and unseen or I should be rushed in as insane.

On 10 May 1940, only a few days after *Carlisle*'s return from Norway, rumours began to pass through the ship that German troops and tanks had invaded Belgium and Holland. One man from each mess was granted permission to visit the wardroom to listen to the six o'clock news on the radio along with the officers. Neville Chamberlain had resigned, to be replaced as Prime Minister by Winston Churchill. The French army and the British Expeditionary Force had mobilized to meet the German advance. Here, finally, was the confrontation expected since the declaration of war in September 1939. 'Everyone seems certain it will be for the best,' wrote Hutchinson, 'and the war will soon be over now. I hope so, but I hope the civil population hasn't to go through the same experience as us.'

* * *

The war at sea appears at first glance to have been somehow less human than other campaigns, shaped more by technology and intelligence, strategy and firepower, than by people. Much of the sailor's experience of war was unfamiliar: an array of complex machinery and novel technology; an alien environment matched by a unique culture and language; battles fought in far-flung locations, many entirely foreign to those without sea-going experience. All this has resulted in an almost unavoidable anthropomorphism: ships, not their sailors, are too often seen as the main characters. Yet ships were weapons, not protagonists.

In September 1941, the social survey organization Mass Observation asked people what they thought about the Royal Navy. The public held the navy in high esteem, it reported, but considered the service 'an anonymous and efficient organisation'. One interviewee said that 'the navy is doing a tremendous job with its usual silence and courage'. Sailors, another commented, did 'lots of dull, dangerous work bravely and well'. The problem, suggested the Mass Observation report, was that the navy was more remote than the army or the air force. 'People know less about the Navy than the other Forces,' it stated. The experiences of sailors were more difficult to identify with. People thought about the navy in a 'less personal way'. Epitomizing the public mood, one respondent admitted, 'I know no sailors but I think they are heroic.'

Some sailors felt that the general population would never truly understand their experiences. 'I don't think anyone could realise what sort of a life we lead,' wrote one rating in 1939, 'even if you told them the facts.' Over the course of the war, writers and film-makers attempted to portray life at sea in a manner which would capture the public's imagination. Nicholas Monsarrat's *H.M. Corvette* and Ludovic Kennedy's *Sub-Lieutenant* vividly depicted the duties of an officer in a small warship. Noël Coward's acclaimed film *In Which We Serve*, released in 1942, told the personal stories of the officers and men of a destroyer sunk in the Mediterranean. In his 1944 novel *Very Ordinary Seaman*, J. P. W. Mallalieu used his own experiences of the lower deck to write from the perspective of the average rating. He warned his civilian readers not to romanticize the sailor, but rather to see him as an ordinary man with a duty to uphold:

You may think that sailors are always what they seem to be when they're ashore: carefree, happy-go-lucky, and clean. But at sea they are dirty, unromantic, and damp. Forget the sailor with the navy-blue eyes and remember the one with his stomach torn out by a red-hot tracer shell. But don't think of sailors as heroes, either. They are not heroes – not in any storybook sense. They 'drip', they 'chuck their hands in', they are afraid. Think of us as we really are – boys and young men who want to come home, but who go on going to sea and meeting the horrors which the sea can bring, partly because we have to, partly because we feel instinctively that there is not room in the world for both us and for the Nazis.

Personal diaries were strictly forbidden, but this did not prevent many sailors – both officers and ratings – from recording their thoughts on paper. Some, like Charles Hutchinson, wrote every day in pocket diaries, notepads or loose sheaves, storing them in their lockers and 'ditty boxes'. Some officers used typewriters. A few produced reams, others jotted down the occasional line. Many transcribed their notes more expansively once home on leave, or while their ship was in port. Midshipmen – teenaged trainee officers – were required to keep a journal detailing their professional and personal responses to what they witnessed at sea and ashore. In their letters home, usually censored to remove any sensitive information, sailors reported back to their loved ones and acquaintances. Some were reticent, unwilling or unable to express their emotions. Others were effusive, freely explaining their thoughts and fears.

This book is a people's history of the sailor's war, inspired by these writings. It draws upon the experiences of individuals to create a human panorama. It seeks to explore everyday concerns as well as to describe extraordinary experiences; to capture the emotional and personal responses of sailors and naval personnel to the situations in which they found themselves.

The Royal Navy was an immensely diverse organization. Sailors served in towering battleships and aircraft carriers, fast cruisers and versatile destroyers. Some crewed small motor launches which operated around the coasts, others manned converted fishing trawlers. Submariners formed a distinctive caste, as did the Royal Marines and the aircrew and pilots of the Fleet Air Arm. The Women's Royal Naval Service was a vital part of the wartime organization, even if only a few women went to sea. The Commonwealth also provided personnel: Canadians, South Africans, Australians and New Zealanders all served aboard British ships. Any one vessel required a multitude of talents: from stokers and artificers in the engine room to teams loading and firing guns; from wireless operators, coders and signalmen to galley cooks; from electrical specialists to administrative staff; from officers versed in engineering or navigation to those expert in torpedoes or gunnery.

Over the course of the war the career regulars of the peacetime navy were joined by tens of thousands of mobilized reservists – many from the merchant navy – and then by the wartime volunteers and draftees who eventually formed the bulk of the navy's personnel. Distinctions continued for some time between these groups, on a psychological as well as a practical level. Ultimately, however, these differences were less significant than the fact that every member of the Royal Navy shared a common duty. Perhaps most importantly, every sailor retained an emotional link with Britain or the Empire. This was a central part of the sailor's psychological condition. Whether home was romanticized or criticized, pined for or escaped from, it was a defining feature of a sailor's everyday concerns. But whether they were regulars, reservists, volunteers or draftees, each was ultimately serving the same society with the same purpose. Just as they were all sailors, so were they all citizens.

Sailors shaped the nature of Britain's war. Great Britain was a maritime superpower. It presided over an empire of 530 million people and 13 million square miles. It could exploit the resources of the Dominions, of islands in the West Indies, of much of sub-Saharan Africa, of India, and of territories in south-east Asia and the Far East. Britain governed the mandated territories of Palestine and Transjordan in the Middle East, as well as having interests in Egypt and Iraq. Britain was a financial powerhouse and a global trading behemoth, a status made possible by control of the world's largest merchant fleet, which carried goods and passengers all over the world. The sea was the foundation of Britain's power, but reliance on the oceans also left it vulnerable.

The Royal Navy was central to British strategy. It enabled the evacuation of armies, the invasion of foreign territories, and the supply and maintenance of forces in diverse regions from the deserts of North Africa to the jungles of Burma. It provided and protected material links with vital strategic resources: steel and soldiers from the United States, oil from South America, rubber from the Indian Ocean. British sailors fought a campaign unprecedented in its geographical scale, in every ocean of the world and along every major coastline from America to Australia, from the Arctic to South Africa. In this global struggle, ships formed the sinews of industry and of empire. The Royal Navy helped to protect the merchant sailors whose cargo vessels fed the population and fuelled the factories, linked imperial and international cohorts, and formed the foundation of Britain's very survival.

Yet sailors were significant not simply because of what they witnessed, but also because of what they represented. Their war was one in which aggression was matched by humanitarianism, and in which individual exertions relied on collective efforts. It was fought in the shadow of national history, in which a constant struggle with the fear of death was often played out in mundane routine, punctuated only rarely by moments of exhilaration and high drama. Over time, concepts of bravery and heroism would come to be defined not only by actions but also by attitudes. Ordinary men and women and their social superiors negotiated a clash of classes, and had to balance demands for a new vision of the future with the immediate necessities of fighting a world war. A crisis of imperialism precipitated tensions amongst the great powers: the decline of Britain's global supremacy in the face of American economic might, Soviet ruthlessness, and colonial disintegration. Ultimately, the experiences of Britain's citizen sailors epitomized the nation's experience of war.

## 2. Flashes of Fire

'I don't want to frighten you darling,' wrote John Evans to his fiancée Moyra, 'but I've always been frank with you, so I may as well tell you that Mussolini is liable to declare war on Britain without any notice at any moment now. We are prepared for it however, and searchlights are shining across the straits all night long, gun crews closed up on the Rock and one ship ready for immediate action.' It was September 1935, and Evans was serving aboard the battlecruiser HMS *Renown*, which had been sent from the Home Fleet to Gibraltar. His shipmates joined many others in celebrating their last moments of freedom before full mobilization: 'The tense situation is sending the lads ashore in hundreds, and the cabarets of Gibraltar are crowded to overflowing. I must own up and admit I was one of them last night . . . we all had a queer feeling this morning and decided not to get "blotto" again.'

Two thousand miles away, at the south-eastern edge of the Mediterranean, sailors at the Egyptian port of Alexandria were also preparing for hostilities. 'We are as ready as we can be for war,' wrote Lieutenant Vere Wight-Boycott of the destroyer HMS *Encounter*. Reinforcements had been sent to Port Said, around the coast to the east, which served as the gatehouse to the Suez Canal: the vital strategic artery which led to the east coast of Africa and the Indian Ocean. Royal Navy vessels from far and wide congregated in anticipation of action. Alexandria harbour, wrote Wight-Boycott, was 'packed with men of war and Air Arm aircraft buzzing over it like flies . . . Ships from all over the world are here or hereabouts, having made sudden rushes from West Indies, round the Horn, China and Home.'

The reason for such alarm lay in the modest east African country of Abyssinia, known to its inhabitants as Ethiopia. The international crisis which followed would herald the rise of a new wave of aggressive Fascist militarism and would fatally undermine the peacekeeping efforts of the League of Nations. It would be followed by appeasement, rearmament and, ultimately, by the outbreak of war in Europe.

It had begun in December 1934 with a clash at Walwal, on the border between Abyssinia and Italian Somaliland. This was unfinished business for the Italians: a perfect opportunity for the Fascist regime to establish its military prestige by overturning a humiliating colonial defeat which had led to the establishment of Ethiopia as an independent state in 1896. During the summer of 1935, Italian forces prepared to invade. Britain's commitments to the League of Nations were limited, but international sanctions might ultimately require military involvement if Italian aggression was to be confronted. If this were to happen, British sailors would be on the front line.

For those in Gibraltar and Alexandria, a confrontation seemed imminent. Yet it was not a palatable option for senior commanders. Military briefings for Prime Minister Stanley Baldwin advised caution before implementing economic sanctions or closing the Suez Canal. 'Everything possible should be done to avoid precipitating hostilities with Italy until we are more ready,' suggested the chiefs of staff. 'It would be a dangerous prospect for us to go to war with Italy with the British Fleet unmobilised.'

Many in Whitehall felt that Italy should be groomed as a possible ally against Germany, already developing its own military ambitions. The Admiralty therefore attempted to balance deterrence and conciliation. Naval units had been moved away from Malta, too close to Italian airbases for comfort, and Alexandria had been established as the centre of operations in the eastern Mediterranean. Reinforcements were to be sent only under the auspices of training, with senior officers anxious to avoid, as the First Sea Lord Admiral Chatfield put it, 'touching off the excitable Iti'.

Italian troops launched their invasion of Abyssinia at the start of October 1935. At the mouth of the Suez Canal, British sailors watched as troopships loaded with reinforcements passed through unchallenged on their way to east Africa. Midshipman Manisty of HMS *Sussex* had some sympathy for them. 'Today was the hottest day we have had,' he wrote on 6 October. 'One could fully realise what a terrible time the Italian soldiers must be having.'

Sailors soon settled into a regular war routine, with constant drills and manoeuvres, restrictions on leave and strict discipline. Exercises were conducted in accordance with the expected character of a war with Italy: coping with gas attacks, abandoning ship and, above all, anti-aircraft defence. Small radio-controlled planes were flown as targets for the High-Angle guns. These 'Queen Bees' were slow and unwieldy and, despite some initial difficulties, were soon obliterated with ease. John Evans reflected the optimism fostered by this shallow success: 'I feel perfectly safe on a battleship in the event of an attack from the air – in day-light anyway. I cannot possibly imagine one plane getting through a barrage such as we put up.'

Douglas Woolf joined the battleship HMS *Ramillies* as a cadet, and was assigned to gunnery control, calculating the required range and direction of fire. At first, he found his new role impossible. 'I am in charge of a whole lot of gadgets, indicators, arrows here, dials there, and god knows what else,' he wrote in a letter home. 'I have not got the faintest idea of how they work!' He relied entirely on the gun-nery ratings who operated the machinery: 'I just repeat orders that come down . . . Some hope we have got if we go to war and we are raided by aeroplanes when I am down there. The first shot will prob-ably go through the funnel!'

Soon, however, Woolf was confident of his ship's ability to repel an air attack. 'I say in all seriousness an aircraft bombing attack on any battleship will fail under the present anti aircraft system,' he wrote. 'Pom-Poms are easily the most effective weapons ever invented against aeroplanes. You cannot conceive what they are like until you have seen them working.' Aside from the smaller dedicated guns, *Ramillies* had been firing broadsides with her huge 15-inch guns. 'My gosh,' wrote Woolf, 'when they go off you are just blown off your feet the whole ship gives a heave.'

After the initial rush of mobilization, expectations of action oscil-lated as successive rumours swept across the fleet. 'The situation is still grim,' wrote John Evans from Gibraltar on 16 October. 'One or two people think we shall "get stuck into" the Italians before long if they insult us much more – but I don't think so.' Air attack remained a concern for senior officers, as did the threat from Italian submarines, which heavily outnumbered their British counterparts in the region. Yet few were truly troubled. 'The modern Italian is an unknown quantity,' wrote First Sea Lord Chatfield, 'but I cannot believe he is a greatly different fighter than in the past.' He was not alone in believing that 'the final outcome of a conflict with Italy cannot be a matter of doubt'.

Such confidence was replicated throughout the ranks. Aboard HMS *Ramillies*, reported Douglas Woolf, 'the matelots are still quite confident we are going to give 'em bloody Italians a smack in the eye!!' 'The Navy's description of the Italian sailors is that they are a crowd of macaroni eating yellow rats,' wrote Charles Thomas of the cruiser HMS *Leander*. There was also animosity, fuelled by the prospect of an interminable stay in the Mediterranean, away from home and with increased duties. When a rumour passed through HMS *Renown* that she was to be sent to the international port of Tangier, one sailor remarked 'that he was going to visit the first "bag shanty", pick out an Italian girl and get "torn into it" and so get his own back on Mussolini'.

Over the following weeks, sailors remained on high alert. As 11 November 1935 passed with more manoeuvres and drills, Midshipman Manisty recorded his thoughts in his journal: 'Armistice Day – it seemed odd to be commemorating those killed in the last war while we are waiting here all ready for another.' Douglas Woolf reported that 'the two minutes silence was kept on the quarterdeck and a short service held'. Others were less introspective. John Evans and his messmates played a game of 'Cowboys and Abyssinians'. He informed his fiancée that 'one chap picked up the only sharp knife in the mess and cut a chunk out of his finger. We were about to lash him up to a stanchion and burn him. We stopped playing immediately after the accident!'

Three days later, British parliamentary elections were held, with the Conservative-dominated coalition aiming to hold on to power under Stanley Baldwin. 'Pray hard that the National Government get back into office darling,' John Evans had written to his fiancée, 'another Labour Government will force me to kill somebody.' Lieutenant Vere Wight-Boycott was responsible for organizing proxy votes aboard HMS *Encounter* at Alexandria. Only two men from a total of one hundred ratings completed their forms. 'The rest say their wives will only vote for the best looking man,' he told his father. 'I hope you will poll a sterling Conservative vote (for more and bigger navies) for me on the day,' he wrote. 'I am not sure what it is all about but I would like to exercise my electoral prerogative in favour of arms, ammunition, wine, women and song, and everything that good old Stanley with his pipe and pips stands for.'

It was not only Stanley Baldwin who could decide the fates of British sailors. The League of Nations remained nominally capable of encouraging collective action. But after seemingly endless debates which had resulted only in the imposition of modest economic sanctions on Italy, the organization enjoyed little popularity on the lower deck. 'We don't think much of the League of Nations in *Leander*,' reported Charles Thomas. 'We must build a bigger navy,' wrote John Evans, reflecting the general mood of his messmates, few of whom seemed to trust international arbitration: 'Dispense with all pacts with these weak-kneed Latin races and so make them sit up and listen to us when we talk . . . let's build a *Hood* with the money wasted on the League of Nations.'

While they waited for news, sailors had the opportunity to explore. Many recent recruits found themselves in the Mediterranean for the first time. 'The town itself is typically Spanish,' wrote Charles Thomas in Gibraltar. 'White and yellow many-windowed red-roofed houses. Spanish is spoken more than English – all the newspapers being in that language. Quite a lot of the shops are owned by Moors from across the Straits who wear brilliant clothes and the inevitable fez.' The local population was, to Douglas Woolf, 'a most motley crowd'. He described 'Indians, Moors, Spaniards and matelots all mixed up in one'. Poverty was never far from the surface. Local scavengers were usually allowed on board ships to collect leftovers after mealtimes. Sailors nicknamed them 'Rock scorpions'.

If Gibraltar was foreign, Alexandria was positively alien. Douglas Woolf thought it 'the strangest place I have been so far – so different from the European countries. The one thing that strikes you first ashore here is the variety of smells, one minute you get a smell like a monkey house at the zoo and the next a smell of that sickly incense that all these Eastern peoples seem to like so much.' Alexandria and Port Said, at the mouth of the Suez Canal, provided plenty of leisure opportunities for officers. 'The International Sporting Club has made all officers honorary members and there are always tennis and squash courts for the asking,' wrote one midshipman in his journal. 'The police have offered to lend horses morning and evening and there is always golf and shooting if one likes to arrange it.'

Recreational activities were an opportunity for ambitious young officers to ingratiate themselves with superiors, whose patronage could be critical to their professional advancement. Vere Wight-Boycott was excited by the prospect of playing doubles tennis on the centre court of the Alexandria Sporting Club, with its stands and scoreboards, particularly when he was partnered with Admiral Raikes, the port's senior naval officer. The young lieutenant was hoping to impress, but things did not go entirely smoothly: 'I served and promptly hit him in the back at the net, not once, but twice in the same game.'

Sailors exploring northern Africa beyond the British enclaves found little opulence and far greater poverty. 'We must thank our lucky stars that we are English,' wrote John Evans. 'Tangier is alive with brothels, dirty films (called blue pictures), beggars, children, blind and snake charmers. The houses are terribly dirty and almost falling down for want of care.' Charles Thomas visited Tetuan, the capital of Spanish Morocco and around thirty-five miles from Tangier. He found the usual snake charmers and jugglers, but also visited a school for orphans and wandered through an Italian school surrounded by 'mosaic work, gardens, orange groves and marvellous flower gardens'. As for the local population, he found it 'quite strange to see the Arab women wearing yashmaks or white veils obscuring their faces', but was impressed by the 'courteous' men. He bought a hashish pipe from a street trader as a souvenir.

By December 1935, despite such diversions, many were becoming disillusioned after weeks of restrictions on leave and perpetual exercises. As the prospect of spending Christmas abroad became a certainty, some of the frustrations began to show. 'I think we are going to fight the Italians with paper (darts perhaps),' wrote Vere Wight-Boycott. HMS *Leander* remained at Gibraltar. Despite terrible weather, the festivities were largely successful. 'Every ship flies Christmas trees at the mast heads and yard arms,' wrote Charles Thomas. 'The majority of the crew wear either fancy dress or some one else's uniform . . . It is the custom for the youngest boy in the ship to wear the Commander's uniform complete with war medals and do the round of the ship with the Captain.' Afterwards, the Royal Marines band played dancing music, and sailors partnered each other for turns across the floor. Then came a show by the ship's concert party, a dramatic troupe made up of ratings and officers, who 'gave the first performance of "The Road to Addis Ababa" which as you may guess consisted chiefly of a skit on Mussolini and on the Cabinet'.

Early in the new year, on 20 January 1936, King George V died. He was succeeded by his son, Edward VIII. The following day, a royal message was read aloud to ships' companies by their commanding officers, in which the new monarch emphasized his personal affinity with the navy and informed his sailors that 'my visits to many parts of the Empire have enabled me to note with pride that loyalty and devotion to duty remain the watchword of the Royal Navy wherever it is called upon to serve'.

Any serious political appetite for intervention over Abyssinia had long since faded. The Hoare–Laval Pact, a poorly conceived Anglo-French attempt to broker a peace deal, had been leaked to the newspapers, damaging British prestige in America and making global agreement on more effective sanctions even more unlikely. And with Italian victory in Abyssinia imminent, the new Foreign Secretary, Anthony Eden, was reluctant to make further international commitments. Few in the Admiralty retained any confidence in the League of Nations or in collective security. First Sea Lord Admiral Chatfield even expressed the hope that 'the Geneva pacifists will fail to get unanimity and the League will break up'. He also wondered whether the best approach might still be to take pre-emptive unilateral action against Italy, 'to re-assert our dominance over an inferior race'.

Plans for war against Italy formed during the crisis would remain in place. Malta was now considered indefensible, so Alexandria would serve as a permanent base. Key targets in Italy were identified, including the naval base at Taranto, which would be attacked by torpedo-bombers launched from aircraft carriers. The robust programme of exercises conducted during the crisis had left the Mediterranean Fleet a far better-prepared fighting force. Several of its commanding officers, amongst them Andrew Cunningham and Max Horton, would later become instrumental in leading the Royal Navy through the Second World War. Yet the navy's recovery from the savage budgetary cuts of the 1920s would take some time. When warships in Alexandria were joined by a group of trawlers hastily fitted with minesweeping equipment, John Evans was unimpressed. 'The crews are made up with reservists and chaps off the dole,' he wrote. 'Of the latter people, very few have been to sea before. There is a great shortage of men these days!'

By the spring of 1936, another European threat had emerged. In March, German troops entered the demilitarized zone in the Rhineland, marking the debut of a newly strident military power. British planners had already attempted to limit German strength at sea. The 1935 Anglo-German Naval Agreement had made significant concessions to German maritime ambitions, despite its headline clause limiting the Kriegsmarine to 35 per cent of the Royal Navy's total tonnage. This undermined whatever credibility remained of the Treaty of Versailles, which had established far greater restrictions after the First World War, but it was above all a concession which illustrated British insecurity.

Yet while the Admiralty grappled with the strategic conundrum posed by the growing German threat, some ordinary sailors were not greatly concerned. 'I do not attach any importance to the German affair, and feel mighty confident that it will fizzle out,' wrote John Evans. Others were more circumspect. 'It was too much to expect Versailles to be fair to Germany after the grimmest four years of war ever known,' wrote Midshipman Geoffrey Carew-Hunt of

HMS *Kent*, far away in the East Indies. 'A lot of Germany's restive-ness is due to being kept under too much.' But he also noted that some commentators were suggesting 'that it would be better to fight before Germany is ready'.

On 4 May 1936, HMS *Enterprise* entered harbour at Djibouti in the east African colony of French Somaliland. Upon arrival, the ship's commanding officer, Captain Charles Morgan, proceeded directly to the French governor's residence, where he had been instructed to meet a small group of passengers. He found rather more than he had been expecting: 150 people, fifteen tons of luggage, several cases of silver bullion, one dog and two lions. This was the entourage of Emperor Haile Selassie I, the ruler of Abyssinia.

'My first impression on being presented to his Majesty on Monday morning was how very tired he looked,' wrote Morgan in an official report of his mission. 'I felt somehow that he was almost at his last gasp and from his first few remarks knew he was a very frightened man. He had a hunted look in his eye . . . Such beautiful hands too, I have never seen such delicate hands on any man, and I should think his fingers must have been nearly twice as long as mine.'

Morgan informed Haile Selassie that the maximum number of passengers *Enterprise* could carry was fifty, along with the baggage and silver, and that 'I could not take the lions, but that I would accept the dog'. As the message was transmitted through interpreters, 'all held up their hands in horror . . . The Emperor looked so weary and fragile that I felt a perfect brute for screwing him down.'

The party was received on board while the ship's band played. Haile Selassie inspected the ranks of sailors and was shown to the rear of the quarterdeck, where a curtained space had been prepared with furniture, carpets and tables. Morgan led him to a comfortable chair, and the Emperor fell fast asleep. The passengers disembarked at Haifa, bound for Jerusalem. Soon afterwards, Haile Selassie travelled to Britain, where he would remain in exile for the next five years, resid-ing at Fairfield House in Bath. During the crisis, his eloquent, emotional, and ultimately fruitless appeals for support from the international community won him many admirers. 'I have been sel-dom so impressed with any man, black or white,' stated Captain

Morgan in his report, 'and his consideration, courtesy and above all his dignity has left a very deep impression on every officer and man in my ship.'

As *Enterprise* passed through Alexandria on her way to Palestine, a message for the Emperor was delivered to the ship which read: 'You put your faith in the Great White Nations and they have let you down. Sincerest sympathies and heartiest congratulations on your splendid efforts . . . A crowd of Britishers.' By now, Italian forces had captured Addis Ababa. Haile Selassie would eventually return in triumph in May 1941, on the anniversary of his departure, with a force of African soldiers under the leadership of British officers.

Even before Addis Ababa had fallen, the Royal Navy had shifted its attention to another developing crisis in Spain. Charles Thomas had visited Cadiz in February: 'Judging from the posters and numerous uniforms I should imagine that a revolution is very imminent in Spain in favour of a Royalist return to power.' HMS *Orion* was sent to Tangier as a result of civil unrest amongst Spanish workers. Douglas Woolf described the scene:

> As usual these damned bolshy Spaniards were causing trouble – all on strike and generally breaking the place up – not to mention the large population of Italians, who were celebrating their stupid little victories, flags everywhere, Mussolini this – Mussolini that – Even the Italian houses were festooned with placards – 'down with the English Pigs!' and I think the height of insolence considering this is a neutral port was the following in a huge coloured lighting sign as one might see in Piccadilly Circus – 'ADDIS ABABA ITALIANA'!

* * *

The summer of 1936 brought turmoil to Spain after General Francisco Franco launched an attempted military coup in July. It failed to overthrow the government and a bloody internecine struggle was developing between the rebels and those loyal to the government. The scale of the potential humanitarian disaster of the Spanish Civil War was not immediately clear. 'We knew little of the Spanish question, and cared less,' wrote Midshipman David Leggatt of

HMS *Devonshire* to his uncle the following month. 'There were so many situations that seemed more important to us – the Italian-Abyssinian one, the Russo-Japanese one, the Chinese, the Danzig, and all the rest of them. So far as I was concerned there was a very left and very incapable government in Spain and minor disorders seemed imminent, and that was about all.'

*Devonshire* was sent to Majorca. 'All was amazingly quiet,' wrote Leggatt, 'and the whole thing seemed to be quixotic. We eventually discovered that the rebels were in command and were running things very nicely, thankyou. The army had killed a dozen or so officers with Communistic ideas, and had four left to finish off on our arrival. They would all be done by midday, we were informed.' After sailing to Minorca and Ibiza to check on the condition of the expatriate British communities, *Devonshire* returned to Majorca. 'Once back there we prepared to enjoy ourselves,' wrote Leggatt. 'The place is ideal – beautiful weather and scenery, and very cheap for a holiday they say – and we prepared for a "quiet number", or else to see an interesting bombardment should the loyal navy turn up.'

On the Spanish mainland, refugees began to flood into the coastal ports. Gibraltar soon became an enclave. Douglas Woolf described it as 'crowded with refugees and the hotels absolutely unbearable with Spaniards, unhappy Spaniards'. The Royal Navy was soon mobilized, evacuating people of all nationalities. The destroyer HMS *Basilisk* took refugees from Almería to Gibraltar. 'As well as Britishers,' wrote her captain, Francis de Winton, 'we had Germans, Swiss, Italians, Danes, Swedes, Dutch and maybe a few more. A number were put in my cabin quarters, the remainder were in the wardroom and a spare cabin. My officers saw that all were well treated and fed.'

Sailors did everything they could to accommodate the hundreds of desperate men, women and children in cramped messdecks. In the destroyer HMS *Express*, reported Captain Casper Swinley, 'babies, slung in canvas cots, were fed on condensed milk out of ginger beer bottles'. Douglas Woolf interviewed every civilian coming aboard HMS *Orion*, inspecting their paperwork and making sure they signed official documents. 'It is pathetic and I can't help feeling bad for them,' he wrote in a letter home. 'Not only have they lost their money, their homes, everything that meant anything to them but they have lost their country.'

In July 1936, several Royal Navy ships that had been due to return to Britain were instead sent to Barcelona. 'We are being diverted, Spain being in a state of internal revolution,' wrote Paymaster Commander Wright of HMS *London* in his diary. He had been told to expect up to 1,000 refugees, but found this hard to believe: 'I rather suspect we will find a damp squib when we arrive.' *London* reached Barcelona the following morning. 'Found the city fairly quiet,' wrote Wright. 'All churches have been looted and gutted and some shops looted. General shortage of food. Cars driving around laden with folk bristling with rifles. Most of the Communists and syndicalists appear to be young men and women.'

Refugees soon began to arrive at the quayside. Many of those fleeing the fighting were foreign nationals: some were tourists and travellers, others were workers or expatriates from all over the world. Two hundred appeared on the first day, including 'one complete troupe of chorus girls, and a fair number of children; three sweet little girls wearing green pyjamas and red sashes were on deck in the evening'. Two days later, a large group of Swiss refugees came aboard: 'decent, orderly folk with whom it was a pleasure to deal – a great contrast to many of our own nationals'. After this, instructions were 'to evacuate Danes, Turks and Persians. We have already had eighteen nationalities on board.' Even after a week of evacuation, the numbers of people arriving continued to increase. Wright did his part: 'Gave up my cabin to an expectant mother and slept on the gun deck.'

Between 23 July and 21 August, *London* evacuated 1,960 refugees in twenty-three shiploads, many of whom were then transferred to destroyers including *Douglas*, *Gallant*, *Gipsy* and *Maine* for transport to the French coast. After a short spell at Malta, the ship returned to Barcelona in mid-September. Over 200 people passed through on 20 September, 'nearly all Spanish, travelling as Cubans and South Americans . . . only one British!' The end of the operation came in early October. The Admiralty had been warned that rebel warships were preparing to fire on coastal towns from Malaga to Barcelona. *London* retreated to an anchorage on the outer edge of the local waters, and left the area altogether a few days later. Wright's initial annoyance at the mission had by now transformed into anxiety that he was unable to do more to help. 'Personally,' he wrote, 'I feel we should have remained inside.'

In July, Mrs J. E. Larios and her husband had been rescued by HMS *London* and then taken to Marseilles aboard the destroyer HMS *Douglas*. Describing her experiences in a letter to her father, she advised him:

> I do think publicity should be given to the amazing care, kindness and unselfishness of the Navy over this. From the Admiral down to the sailors who carried our bags on board and the stewards who cooked coffee and sandwiches all night. Everybody slaved for us all, and we must have made an infinity of work and trouble and discomfort for them all. I have never in my life received more kind hospitality with thought and organization behind it.

HMS *Devonshire*, meanwhile, had been sent to Valencia. 'It's a grim spot,' wrote David Leggatt, 'especially with burnt churches, barricades and occasional corpses.' Refugees from Madrid congregated in the harbour before being subjected to customs searches by Spanish troops, and boarding small boats to be ferried to the warships. Leggatt thought them 'poor wretches', arriving 'wet and terrified – in some cases – up a gangway which was so smashed by every wave that it frightened me badly. Luckily only one person went in, an old lady; a sailor jumped after her and by the grace of God got her back before a wave broke her against the ship's side. She came up the gangway unaided and laughing!'

Nearly 400 British and 200 European or South American men, women and children were housed below decks. Some slept in hammocks, young families were given the ship's lifeboats, the injured were accommodated in cabins, along with 'old women, cripples, two stretcher cases, seventeen babies under eighteen months old, and several pregnant women . . . everybody was stowed away somewhere'. Leggatt praised the ship's company: 'They gave up everything for the civilians, and never murmured at all. Their great delight was carrying babies around . . . One, who was well under a year old, was found gurgling over chocolate biscuits and lemonade in one of the mess-decks, surrounded by admiring matelots.'

As Franco's forces closed in on the Basque ports of Santander and Bilbao in northern Spain, American and German ships left with their own countrymen. Only the British destroyers *Exmouth*, *Escort* and *Esk* remained in Bilbao to evacuate civilians. Refugees had been assembled in the early morning by Spanish soldiers, as small boats from the three British ships waited alongside the jetty. Before they could leave, the civilians had to be checked, registered and searched by the troops. Twelve men from *Esk* had been landed, and Lieutenant Commander Bill Wilson reported that 'hot coffee, liberally laced with rum' was offered to the Spaniards in order to expedite matters.

Eighty-one refugees were waiting. Wilson described how they were let through the barriers 'only with the greatest reluctance, and much flourishing of shotguns and pistols'. Baggage was ransacked, suitcase linings ripped open, and money confiscated. Men and women alike were searched with little regard for their dignity. One elderly lady arriving on board *Esk* was asked if she had been mistreated: 'No,' she replied, 'they only tickled me.'

In early 1937, the fighting around Bilbao became more intense and rumours circulated amongst sailors of devastating air raids throughout the Basque region. Vere Wight-Boycott heard that a Nationalist pilot who had baled out over the town had been confronted by a lynch mob: 'He shot two men with his pistol before being captured and dying a horrible death, in which many women took part.' As Franco's forces prepared a final offensive against the city in the spring, the German Condor Legion was used to target several important strategic locations in the area. One of these was the town of Guernica.

Some areas of Spain were more peaceful than others. HMS *Encounter* was sent to assist the small number of British consular administrators in the ports of the north-west. Sailors were allowed to explore ashore, and several took the opportunity to visit a small nineteenth-century Royal Navy cemetery in Arosa. Ever the keen sportsman, despite his tennis mishap in Port Said in 1935, Vere

Wight-Boycott arranged a football match against the local professional side in Vigo. 'They are called the Celta,' he explained in a
letter home. 'They had 6 of their proper team playing including 2
internationals, the remainder were fighting for Franco. You will be
hardly surprised to hear they beat us 12–1 (and even then they were
not trying very hard). Owing to the war they have no opponents
and are keen to get a game with anyone.'

Meanwhile, Royal Navy ships were also present around the Spanish
island possessions: the Canary Islands off the coast of Morocco to the
south-west of Spain, and the Balearic Islands off the east coast. Before
the outbreak of the insurgency, the Spanish government had posted
General Franco to Tenerife, with its sparsely vegetated mountains and
expanses of banana plantations, in a futile attempt to limit his influence. It became one of the first places to fall to Franco's rebels.

In the town of Santa Cruz de Tenerife, every house displayed the
red and yellow colours of the new rulers. In the harbour, an oil spill
had blackened the water. Las Palmas appeared equally unappealing. 'I
don't see why people pay so much to see these places,' wrote Charles
Thomas of HMS *Leander*, sent to Tenerife to ensure the safety of British expatriates. Ashore, there were few disturbances, but the violence
had not quite ended. 'Yesterday the former Governor of Tenerife was
executed,' reported Thomas, 'the event being celebrated by a salute of
blank shot. It seems rather strange and perhaps a little incongruous to
see such a display of militarism in a sleepy town like Santa Cruz.'

In contrast, the Balearic Islands became an important forward base
for the Italian air force, the largest foreign contingent supporting
Franco's troops. Douglas Woolf of HMS *Orion* now found himself at
Palma. The Majorcans, he believed, were 'quite content whichever
side wins, as long as the Iti's don't get in'. He noticed the 'terribly
pathetic' fortifications: cannons with wooden barrels painted grey
and patrol vessels armed with wooden guns.

> In some ways it's like a game of toy soldiers: the women are in
> uniform, the children are in uniform, yet it is absolutely impossible
> to find any two uniforms alike . . . Unhappy Spain – brother killing
> brother; sister, sister; and yet half of them don't know what they are

fighting for except the one slogan they are continually having driven into their ears 'Viva Franco'. God what folly it all is – we just look on and mother them while the other countries are all waiting to grab something.

In Tenerife, sailors from *Leander* were warned not to go out alone after dark and 'not to speak to foreigners especially not the Italian sailors'. When the old German battleship *Schleswig Holstein* arrived at Las Palmas, however, attitudes were very different. A training vessel for cadets, she was visiting the Canary Islands as part of an Atlantic cruise. 'A lot of the men have been aboard *Leander* and they are quite interesting to speak to,' wrote Charles Thomas. 'One I was speaking to – he spoke perfect English – told me that after leaving school he was sent to a "labour training camp" and was selected to be trained in the Navy, to become an officer . . . This seems to be a good idea, education and not social standing being the qualifying condition.'

Fraternization was widespread. At Cartagena, HMS *Basilisk* was joined by the pocket battleship *Admiral Scheer*. Captain Francis de Winton wasted little time in visiting his German counterpart: 'He was a pleasant sort of chap and spoke good English . . . He had no hesitation in saying that he supported Franco's lot.' In Tenerife, a football match was organized between the German ratings and sailors from *Leander*, and was played on a pitch high up in the hills. According to one member of the crowd, 'Before kicking off, the German team lined up in the centre of the pitch and gave three "Sieg Heils" with the Nazi salute, after a pause our team responded with three cheers accompanied by clenched fists. We lost by the odd goal.'

Majorca became a magnet for the warships of the European navies: British, French, German, Italian and Spanish sailors mixed freely on the streets and in the bars and cafes of Palma. In February 1937, Douglas Woolf wrote to his parents describing one encounter:

Perhaps the one visit of interest to you will be our call on the German pocket battleship the *Graf Spee*. We went over [to] her on Saturday for drinks etc. I was personally very much impressed by the whole business. It's incredible how friendly they are and how trustful they are as far as we are concerned. Of course the main topic of conversation with us all were politics. Why they were out here etc. They say that if Franco should lose, the Communist movement will spread to France and they will be locked between Spain, France and Russia. They all spoke perfect English. Ashore it was really funny as the Italians could obviously not understand why the German and our matelots were so friendly going about the place arm in arm! It was beyond their comprehension especially as they had a military alliance with Germany!! In fact it amuses me the French matelots band together with the Italians, and we and all our alliances with France pay friendly calls and have drinking parties in the *Graf Spee* – it amused us too as every time they enter the mess, up goes their arm – Heil Hitler, nobody takes any notice, it's quite automatic.

Woolf and the midshipmen of HMS *Rodney* enjoyed several parties and suppers with their counterparts in *Admiral Scheer*'s sister ship the *Deutschland*, invariably 'consuming lots of beer'. The fraternity was not confined to officers: ratings had an equal enthusiasm for socializing. Woolf overheard one inebriate declare loudly that the lower deck were 'the best --- diplomats in this --- world'. One occasion 'ended in a complete riot, we going ashore with these fellows over to the *Deutschland* where we stayed until 3.30 in the morning. As for the troops, they were just the same. I saw one fellow of ours rather under the weather arm in arm with two Germans who were taking him back to his ship.'

The Spanish Civil War encouraged direct comparisons between the naval capabilities of the great European powers. Sailors themselves were increasingly preoccupied with their position in the hierarchy. 'The Italians are easily the worst,' wrote Douglas Woolf to his parents, 'dirty ships, dirty boats, dirty men and filthy officers! The French not much better, except their officers are somewhat better mannered. The Germans absolutely marvellous, clean ships, well disciplined and clean men and charming officers.' Yet there was little doubt in Woolf's mind which navy was superior: 'I think without boasting that it still takes something to beat the English matelot ashore and afloat.'

Yet by the summer of 1937, German and Italian support for Franco was obvious to every British sailor. It was not merely confined to air support. At the end of May, the *Deutschland* was attacked by Republican aircraft off the coast of Ibiza, killing more than twenty of her crew. In retaliation, German ships bombarded the government-held coastal town of Almería. Not long afterwards, when the cruiser *Leipzig* appeared to have been attacked by Spanish submarines, both the German and Italian navies took the opportunity to withdraw in protest from the maritime patrols that had been introduced by the Non-Intervention Committee, an international body established to ensure neutral arbitration.

'At present Franco is receiving help wholesale from Germany and Italy,' wrote Douglas Woolf. 'Their warships are shelling the coast and all the planes are of Italian make and piloted by Italians . . . Of course we as usual look on and stay neutral and do nothing.' As the war progressed over the following years, Britain's position would remain ambiguous. Humanitarian work continued, but aside from a handful of flashpoints – most involving British warships being summoned to warn off potentially hostile seizures of merchant vessels – sailors were resigned to observing the fighting without participating. The British government's approach was intended to protect trade at all costs. Certain senior officers privately approved of the Nationalist cause, as did some at Westminster, but for many ordinary sailors Britain's acquiescence was frustrating. Their passive role contrasted sharply with the hundreds of volunteers travelling from Britain to join the International Brigade, fighting for the government against Franco.

Events elsewhere also distracted from the situation in Spain. The abdication of Edward VIII on 11 December 1936 had been as much of a shock to sailors as to the rest of society. He had been seen as a monarch with an inherent knowledge and love of the service, a natural successor to his father. Midshipman Geoffrey Carew-Hunt was serving in Hong Kong at the time of the announcement. 'Personally I feel it is a great misfortune to Great Britain and the Empire,' he wrote in his journal. 'The new King has the hardest task ever set before any King.' Partly to allay these concerns, a message from the newly crowned George VI was read to ships' companies all over the world:

> It has been my privilege to serve as a naval officer both in peace and in war; at Jutland, the greatest sea battle of modern time, I saw for myself in action the maintenance of those great traditions which are the inheritance of British seamen. It is my intention always to keep the closest touch with all ranks and ratings of the naval forces throughout the Empire and with all matters affecting them. I shall do so in the sure knowledge that they will be worthy of the implicit trust placed in them by their fellow countrymen and that, in their hands the honour of the British navies will be upheld.

On 20 May 1937, the Coronation Review took place off Spithead. Alongside the Royal Navy's finest, a handful of foreign warships were present as guests of honour. At the head of the inspection queue was the American battleship USS *New York*, followed by the modern French battleship *Dunkerque* and the German pocket battleship *Graf Spee*. Representing Japan was the *Asigara*. Rear Admiral George Campbell Ross had been Assistant Naval Attaché in Tokyo between 1933 and 1936, and was appointed as the liaison officer to the ship during the celebrations. When he went aboard, he noticed that most of her brand-new equipment had been covered up with freshly painted canvas.

The Review was a success. The weather was glorious, the press reports gushing. But here was a physical manifestation of a global naval power struggle: the Americans given pride of place, the Germans and Japanese impressive, the British indulgent hosts. The BBC's evening radio programme employed the veteran expert Lieutenant Commander Thomas Woodrooffe as a commentator. As he began his broadcast it became obvious that he was a little the worse for wear. 'At the present moment, the whole fleet is lit up,' he began, creating a national catchphrase in the process. 'It's fairyland. The whole fleet is in fairyland.' All the lights on the ships were then extinguished in unison, described in slurred commentary. He managed one more line before the producers tactfully cut to dancehall music: 'There's nothing between us and heaven. There's nothing at all.'

\* \* \*

John Evans had married Moyra in the summer of 1936 and spent a few weeks in a shore job at Portsmouth. Yet he had little opportunity to enjoy life with his new wife. In March 1937, he was transferred to the China Station to serve aboard the small gunboat HMS *Scarab*. Along with a handful of other gunboats, *Scarab*'s role was to patrol the Yangtze upriver of Shanghai, keeping order and protecting British merchants from pirates. 'Before I came to China I had seen one dead person in my life,' wrote Evans in July 1937. 'Now I have seen about three dozen in three weeks.' Bodies floated past regularly amid filth and detritus. The hygiene regime was strict: carbolic soap and Izal medicated toilet paper were constant companions. Armed with only a couple of small guns, *Scarab* was not designed to fight a war, but she was destined to become embroiled in one.

Japanese forces had been advancing gradually into northern China since the spring. Geoffrey Carew-Hunt, now serving aboard the cruiser HMS *Cumberland*, followed the progress of the campaign. 'The struggle seems to consist of staccato rather than continuous fighting,' he wrote in his journal. 'It really appears that no agreement can be reached and that fighting will continue until the Japanese have gained control over as much more land as they want at the moment.'

Japan had first invaded Chinese territory back in 1931, seizing the province of Manchuria, and the following year Japanese troops had outraged foreign powers by attacking Chinese forces in the international settlement of Shanghai. Such aggression was troubling for British strategists. Japan had been an ally in the First World War, and the Imperial Japanese Navy and the Royal Navy had close links. The Japanese had modelled their naval customs on British examples, adopting language, uniforms and traditions from their mentors during the heyday of the Anglo-Japanese alliance. But the partnership had been abandoned by Britain in favour of placating the Americans, and by the 1930s the position of the British Empire in China – from

Hong Kong in the south to Shanghai in the north – was becoming increasingly tenuous.

This was an empire of business: an informal arrangement of companies and diplomatic outposts united by the vast potential of the Chinese market. Contemporary statistics estimated the value of British investments to be comfortably double that of Japan, the closest competitor, and six times that of the USA. Many of the most successful companies involved in China were British-owned to some degree, including several merchant firms and the Hong Kong and Shanghai Banking Corporation. Protecting such disparate British interests in this volatile part of the world was difficult. 'We are always rather sitting on a box of fireworks,' wrote Admiral Sir Howard Kelly, commander-in-chief of the China Fleet in the early 1930s.

Finance, not fighting, was the foundation of British power, and so the navy's role was primarily the protection of investments and citizens. Away from Shanghai and Hong Kong, a small group of old warships patrolled the coastal treaty ports such as Amoy and Swatow, and the gunboats carried out their anti-piracy operations in the small harbours inland along the Yangtze up to Wuhu and Hankow. Gunboat sailors were employed in peacekeeping and posturing, not enforcement. As Sir John Pratt, advisor on Far Eastern affairs to the Foreign Office, put it: 'Gunboats are very convenient aids to policy so long as you are not driven to using them, but the moment you are then the spell is broken.'

By the time Japan launched its 1937 offensive in China, British attention was firmly fixed on the European dictators, and Prime Minister Neville Chamberlain was far from alone in his views when he told the Cabinet that he 'could not imagine anything more suicidal than to pick a quarrel with Japan at the present moment when the European situation had become so serious'. A simultaneous war in the east and west was the great fear of British strategists. 'We cannot foresee the time when our defence forces will be strong enough to safeguard our territory, trade and vital interests against Germany, Italy and Japan simultaneously,' advised the chiefs of staff, emphasizing the need to use diplomacy 'to reduce the numbers of our potential enemies and to gain the support of potential allies'. Yet by the autumn of 1937, Germany and Japan would be bound by a pact of mutual aid, bringing this nightmare scenario a step closer.

Meanwhile, sailors were witnesses to the escalating violence. Japan's diplomatic euphemisms were a cause of particular disdain. John Evans explained the irony to his wife, who had sent a concerned letter fearing for his safety: 'With regards the "major war" out here, you've got it <u>all</u> wrong! There is no "war", merely local "<u>incidents</u>".' Those stationed around Shanghai and the treaty ports were effectively in the front line, albeit neutral observers in what one officer called 'a strange sort of twilight war'. Sailors were warned in the starkest possible terms of the repercussions of quarrels with the new invaders. Guidance to officers stated that the Japanese were 'officious and suspicious' and that there was a 'necessity for care, tact and self-restraint' when dealing with them.

Action seemed a real possibility. 'There seems to be considerable unrest in the Fleet,' wrote Geoffrey Carew-Hunt in July 1937. 'Everyone is in doubt as to whether ships will have to proceed suddenly to Shanghai, Tsingtao or some other place. It is extremely hard to gather the facts of the situation from the Press News and so those who do not see all the secret reports which come in cipher have rather a hazy notion of what is going on.' The following month, the war began to envelop Shanghai and the Yangtze region. 'The situation in Shanghai has become very grave,' wrote Carew-Hunt. 'Fighting is imminent and the presence of a large Japanese fleet at Woosung does not improve matters. The Chinese have blocked the Yangtze about 15 miles above Woosung and are mobilising.' Four thousand British women and children were evacuated. Sailors were sent ashore to guard key positions and utilities, including the waterworks and power station.

HMS *Cumberland* entered the area two days later and her crew witnessed the first attacks. 'The Japanese fleet had arrived and had commenced bombarding immediately,' wrote Carew-Hunt. 'The bombarding ships presented an impressive sight. They were streaming round an elliptical course with battle flags flying and all quarters cleared for action.' The fighting was not all one-sided. Japanese anti-aircraft guns had to fend off Chinese planes and, in the confusion, *Cumberland* became a target. A dive-bomber attacked the British ship, but its double payload drifted in the wind and exploded just beyond the starboard beam. 'Neither bomb landed near enough to cause real fear,' wrote Carew-Hunt. 'I personally felt very exhilarated though I did think that more accurate attacks would have been more alarming than interesting.'

Soon, the Japanese advance turned towards the Chinese capital city: Nanking. John Evans and HMS *Scarab* arrived there in early December 1937, as Japanese forces closed in. 'Nanking is in a state of panic just now,' he wrote. The harbour began to swell with crowds of Chinese refugees. *Scarab* sent armed guards aboard private steamers and launches to prevent their seizure by civilians and soldiers. The atmosphere aboard the British vessels, however, remained relatively calm. On 4 and 5 December, sailors continued their usual activities: men from *Scarab* played a football match against their counterparts from the French warship *Admiral Charnier*. Rear Admiral Reginald Vesey Holt of HMS *Bee*, the senior British officer on the Yangtze, went ashore with other dignitaries. 'After the usual air-raid warnings, we played golf at a charming club in the Sun Yat Memorial Park and again the next day, starting early and taking lunch,' he wrote to his son. 'The weather was glorious and we watched the aerodrome being bombed. I gave a cocktail party at the Club for English residents and German and American.'

Japanese bombers began a concentrated offensive on the city the following morning. 'The air was littered with Japanese war planes,' wrote John Evans, 'and the bombs dropped did quite a lot of visible damage, causing fires in many places.' No damage was sustained by *Scarab*, but shrapnel was retrieved from the deck. Self-preservation was the order of the day. When a boatload of Chinese officers attempted to shelter astern of the gunboat, it was quickly shooed away.

Within a few days, the Japanese blitz had obliterated large parts of the capital. Outside the walls of the city, the Chinese resorted to desperate scorched-earth tactics. 'Today has been very hectic and disastrous for Nanking,' wrote Evans on 9 December:

> The noise has been both deafening and terrifying . . . It's just getting dark and huge fires are raging all round the city wall . . . These fires

must extend on this side about 10 miles. It is a most awe-inspiring, wonderful, terrible and tragic sight. It makes me feel sick. It is impossible to describe, but just imagine huge fires raging from the Houses of Parliament to Tilbury Docks, along the banks of the river Thames . . . Just now terrific reports can be heard all over the harbour and flashes of fire illuminate the heavens . . . This scene will be forever in my memory . . . The Japanese are so close now that we can see the flash of gunfire and hear the rat-tat-tat of machine guns. Four Japanese destroyers have got through the boom at Kiangyim and are expected at Nanking any time now. They will do a lot of damage.

On 11 December *Scarab*, her sister gunboat *Cricket* and the American oil tanker USS *Panay* were anchored with other foreign merchant ships when Japanese artillery guns opened fire at point-blank range. 'For the first time in my life I have actually been in action,' wrote Evans. 'Shrapnel fell all around us and it was a miracle that nobody was hurt . . . The whine of the shells and crack of the explosions were most frightening. Anyway no white people were hurt but a few Chinese in sampans were blown to pieces. These sampans had taken refuge under the "much respected" Union Jack.' This was merely confirmation that British and American flags no longer meant immunity from Japanese attack. The only positive, as far as Evans was concerned, was that 'the Japanese are hopelessly inefficient – these shore batteries should have blown us out of the water'.

The flotilla escaped upriver, with the gunboats helping to tow several merchant ships including one enormous hulk owned by the trading firm Butterfield and Swire. The following morning several senior British officers left for Wuhu in a tugboat, and the American vessels proceeded a few miles further upriver. Japanese soldiers appeared in motor launches, adorned with the flag of the Rising Sun, circling the British ships and attacking Chinese fishing boats as they went. 'They set fire to every junk and sampan in the vicinity,' wrote Evans, 'and I suppose considered themselves very clever.' After lunch, most of the gunboat's crew were napping when a lookout shouted an alarm:

Everybody scrambled up on deck in a panic. As I looked up I saw
three planes turn into diving formation, and to my horror saw a bomb
drop. I ducked down behind a coal bunker . . . There was a deafening
crash and as I looked up I saw a junk and a couple of sampans blown
into the air. The occupants must have been killed instantly . . . everybody was dashing around after Lewis guns and ammunition . . . There
was no order to open fire but everybody did – self-preservation I suppose. Anyway the third plane had the shock of its life as the bullets
peppered the fuselage unfortunately without hitting a vital spot.

Fortunately for *Scarab*, the Japanese bombs had landed around fifteen yards away. The sailors were ready when the next wave of planes
appeared. 'I was at my proper action station this time,' wrote Evans,
'and as the planes turned in our direction I yelled out "open fire" and
the shell from the 3-inch gun exploded right under the tail of the first
plane. Oh boy! You ought to have been here just to see the scattering
match . . . all guns were blazing merrily away and it would have
meant certain death so they turned tail and made off in the direction
of the *Panay* and the oil tankers.'

A few minutes later, *Scarab*'s crew heard several huge explosions,
and clouds of smoke began to billow over the horizon. *Panay* had
been destroyed. Yet there were more pressing concerns for the gunboat sailors, as a third wave of Japanese raiders appeared. John Evans
'had a mouth full of cake' and struggled to bring his gun to bear:
'This time they dived straight at *Scarab* [and] with a feeling of relief I
saw the bombs pass overhead . . . The firing was not so good this time
but good enough to save the lives of every white person and no ships
were lost. I'm sorry to say that the water was full of dead chinks and
debris from sampans and junks.'

Further along the river in Wuhu, the British consul, the flag captain
and the other senior officers in *Ladybird* had been fired upon by shore
batteries. The ship was hit four times, killing one man and injuring a
further two, including the flag captain. As HMS *Bee* arrived she was
also targeted, and Rear Admiral Holt went ashore, incandescent. 'I
put on my protest face,' he wrote to his son. 'Colonel Hashimoto had
not much to say except that he thought it must be his fault, and admit-

ted that his men did not know one flag from another.' Nevertheless, Japanese weapons stayed trained on the British vessel. *Scarab* soon arrived in Wuhu to relieve *Ladybird*. Because of the delicate diplomatic situation, John Evans and his shipmates were not allowed on shore, but they were able to trade cigarettes with visitors. 'We had a few Japanese soldiers on board,' he wrote. 'Quite pally too!'

After the fall of Nanking, Chinese civilians and soldiers suffered unimaginable violations at the hands of Japanese troops. Hundreds of thousands of people were tortured and killed. Tens of thousands of women and girls were systematically raped and mutilated. Thousands more were subjected to other unspeakable atrocities. British citizens, embassy staff and some civilians had already been evacuated. Aboard one ship, HMS *Capetown*, a plaque was installed in the sick bay commemorating the birth of a Chinese baby during the voyage to Hong Kong.

With Japanese forces now in control of much of north-eastern China, Shanghai was strategically redundant. Hong Kong, some 750 miles to the south-west and as yet relatively untouched by the fighting, would now become the cornerstone of British influence. Charles Thomas had arrived from the Mediterranean in July 1937. He joined the staff of the naval wireless station, located offshore on Stonecutter's Island. In a letter to his parents, he described an abundance of plant and animal life – a 'naturalist's paradise' – and the relative comfort of the living quarters, complete with tennis and badminton courts, billiard tables, bar, and swimming pier. His duties involved two days in the main transmitting station followed by two days on watch at the hillside receiving station, from where he could enjoy a view of the harbour: 'The twinkling lights of the peak seem to meet the stars and it is hard to find the dividing line.'

Life at the wireless station was unusual in many ways. 'There is nothing of the Navy about it,' wrote Thomas to his aunt. It was effectively 'a civvy job with sensible hours'. Uniform regulations were relaxed. Most wore shorts, shirts and sun hats in the daytime, and at night 'pajamas tucked inside stockings, and shorts worn outside, as a guard against bites'. Pay went further here than elsewhere. Food was so cheap that each man received around twenty Hong

Kong dollars per week in savings from the mess allowance, of which four dollars paid for Chinese servant boys: 'They do all the "housework", wait on you at meals, bring tea in the morning before getting up, bring tea whilst you are on watch and make your beds spreading the mosquito nets before you turn in at night.'

Hong Kong was well known for its highly stratified colonial set. Sailors referred to the numerous club and society balls of the Far East as 'snobbery parties'. This was a feature of life in the British colony which particularly antagonized Thomas, a young man who was already beginning to form strong opinions about the ills of the British class system: 'Every European here is waited upon hand and foot. I am, myself, I admit. It must go to the heads of these people who have created a caste which is nauseous to say the least.'

The Chinese, however, were a source of perennial fascination. On the streets, while men had 'adopted English dress', women still wore 'picturesque and gaily coloured dresses in Chinese style'. Shopkeepers tallied by abacus. Order was maintained in many of the rougher areas by Sikh policemen, installed by the British to maintain order, 'armed with huge wooden truncheons'. Poverty was unavoidable. 'There are hundreds of homeless Chinese and they sleep on the pavements even in the main streets,' wrote Thomas. 'Little boys of from four to ten years of age work all day blacking shoes and girls of the same age sell newspapers at night.' Cholera was rampant, and the staff of the wireless station received regular inoculations and booster shots. For Thomas, there was an inescapable conclusion: 'This colony is very nice for the British residents but the Chinese population is just left to carry on as best they can. The filth and poverty is appalling and I should not wonder at any epidemic breaking out.'

Sailors were drawn to the Wanchai district, which contained the China Fleet Club and other servicemen's bars and hostels. It was crowded and rowdy. Prostitution was rife, as were venereal diseases. Official estimates put the rate of infection ashore at around 60 per cent of the local population. One in five of the ship's company of HMS *Delight* fell victim during a six-week stay for repairs in 1938. John Evans felt strongly about the issue: 'I don't think the average

Englishman at home realizes the horrible and disgusting, not to mention degrading, things that go on in these foreign places.'

By early 1938, the British naval base at Hong Kong began to move towards a war footing, with enhanced security procedures and improvements to defences. 'Things are being tightened up here,' Charles Thomas wrote to his brother. 'I would not be surprised if this colony was attacked. Naturally they will be out of hand altogether and I can't imagine our being in a position to stop them because an attack by Germany and Italy in the west would be certain.'

News of the Japanese advances on the mainland and tales of the ensuing atrocities led to large-scale anti-Japanese demonstrations throughout Hong Kong. In the cinemas, images of the nationalist military leader Chiang Kai-shek were greeted with raucous cheering by the Chinese audience members. As the multitude of refugees from the north grew, increasing numbers of Japanese shops in the settlement were forced to close by a combination of boycotts and protests. British servicemen were warned 'not to join crowds or throw crackers'.

The upheaval led to demands from the British business community for guarantees of protection in the event of violence. Charles Thomas was not impressed: 'If Hong Kong was attacked all these business men would move to Macao and if Macao were attacked then to Saigon. They are all right making money in a country but my stars when it comes to any trouble! They howl for warships at the least sign of any trouble as in Spain.' Nevertheless, the businessmen were right to be concerned. British strategy was unequivocal: in the event of a Japanese attack, Hong Kong would be abandoned. Singapore would be the last British bastion in the Far East.

The Singapore naval base was officially opened on 14 February 1938 'with much fuss and pomp' according to Lieutenant Ian Anderson, serving in the submarine HMS *Olympus*: 'The dock was opened by the Governor who sailed into it in his yacht standing on the prow with the Sultan of Johore, saluting, which looked most impressive, though it would have been more so if the Chinese pantry staff of the yacht had not been lounging on the deck below blowing Woodbines and looking completely bored.' There was an RAF fly-past followed by speeches consisting, in Anderson's words, of the 'usual Government flannel'.

A band played 'God Save the King', which ended with a 'mad rush by all the guests to get to the marquees'.

Lieutenant Vere Wight-Boycott passed through a few weeks later, on his way to join HMS *Delight* at Hong Kong. 'The naval base at Singapore, although from the *Daily Express* you would imagine was completed, is far from it,' he wrote to his father. 'They have got no further than building some of the shops, but none of the machinery is installed. This is of course a long way to have got, as they have had to remove a hill, cut down a jungle, and drain a swamp to get as far as they have.'

By the summer of 1938, the Japanese were firmly in the ascendancy. Although Shanghai itself remained nominally international, the changing power dynamic was clear. Sailors visiting the nearby island of Wei Hai Wei found the British clinging to their foothold. 'The situation ashore is quite incomprehensible,' wrote Wight-Boycott to his mother in June 1938. 'Though the island appears almost entirely British, just like Malta, it is rented from the Chinese. But it has been captured by the Japanese.' Submariner Ian Anderson recorded in his diary that 'the Japanese flag flew proudly on Centurion Hill'. Yet he noticed that the remaining British residents were attempting to assert their rights: 'Most of the island was labelled "British Property" in large white noticeboards, and there was a liberal sprinkling of Union Jacks on houses and gates.'

On the mainland, there was no shortage of evidence of the character of the Japanese occupation. 'Their army is quite mad and believe they are divine, which after all is one of the usual symptoms,' wrote Rear Admiral Holt, in charge of the gunboats of the Yangtze. Ian Anderson reported one example of the treatment of the local Chinese population which particularly attracted his opprobrium: 'A disgusting and uncivilised order that they should bow low before all Japanese when passing them in the street, a regulation enforced without hesitation by a blow in the face from a rifle butt.' Nevertheless, he also noted that Chinese resistance fighters were said to be killing one Japanese sentry at random every night. John Evans told his wife that 'the Chinese are being used as slaves . . . They shoot them when their services are no longer required.' He had heard many reports of Japanese atrocities: 'A French nun and a Russian girl were raped in the Yangtzepoo Road a few days ago by seventeen Japanese soldiers, both victims have since died.'

It was against this backdrop of a brutal and relentless Japanese advance in China that sailors in the Far East learned of the crisis over German moves on Czechoslovakia. Press reports were devoured and details pored over. 'I expect you are listening to the news pretty carefully these days to see whether we are at war or not,' wrote Lieutenant Vere Wight-Boycott to his father on 25 September. 'I don't myself think G.B. will be involved. We will stand aside as usual and let Germany do what she likes, and "Perfidious Albion" will be the cry again. Still, by the time you get this you may be dusting off your Truncheon.' That evening he gave a short lecture to the ratings in HMS *Delight* on global geopolitics: 'I found there were a number of large gaps in my knowledge of what had happened to date so I did a bit of inventing to fill them in.'

In response to Germany's actions, Chamberlain ordered the Royal Navy to prepare for war. It was a widely publicized move, and the most substantial deterrent Britain could muster. In Hong Kong, there was little appetite for a European conflict, despite the sense of impotence and frustration at the inability of the British government to impose itself. 'During the past week, everybody in the Colony has been in a state of tension fearing that Japan might attack us if war was declared on Germany,' wrote Charles Thomas in Hong Kong. 'This place is not expected to hold out and Singapore would be the centre of operations.'

The news of the Munich Agreement was greeted with relief. Although Chamberlain's 'piece of paper' would later become infamous, it was seen by many as a timely reprieve. On 2 October 1938, submariner Ian Anderson received a letter from his father:

We are living here through anxious and historic days. Till the last day of September war with Germany seemed almost inevitable. Then came a wonderful change . . . war staved off for a time and we hope and pray for all time. Chamberlain is the hero of the hour for the great fight he made for peace. He showed splendid courage and determination. It is however not an ideal peace. Czechoslovakia has had to make great sacrifices and much sympathy is felt for her . . . At any rate peace pleases the people . . . one couldn't help thinking of the terrible slaughter amongst women and children that modern weapons would bring.

Not everyone was so pleased. 'It is the duty of every able bodied man and woman in the Empire to make himself or herself prepared to accept the challenge of the dictators if and when it is offered,' wrote Charles Thomas. 'At present they seem to be very busy showing their strength on the weakest opponents they can find. It sickens me to read the hypocritical speeches of Hitler and Mussolini . . . Religious and racial persecution do not belong to this century and it appears to me that this will prove their undoing.' He had a firm opinion about what Britain required: 'another William Pitt or Palmerston to dictate to the dictators. A quadruple alliance of Great Britain, France, U.S.S.R., and the U.S.A. plus the smaller European democracies could do this.'

The Munich Agreement gave fresh impetus to rearmament and plans for war. Training exercises attempted to prepare for the defence of Singapore. One event in February 1939 involved twenty-five warships and over 10,000 troops. These efforts did little to enhance morale. Vere Wight-Boycott wrote to his father describing a simulated defence of the base in April 1939: 'In spite of headlines "Attack on Singapore Repulsed" the Combined East Indies Squadron and China Fleet exercise resulted in the absolute failure of the defence to prevent air attack and naval bombardment . . . This is the second year in succession that the defence has failed.'

The Royal Navy's foothold in the Far East appeared increasingly precarious. Japan was a dangerous new enemy: brutal, relentless and expansionist. Few sailors doubted that they would come under attack sooner or later. Midshipman David Leggatt, now of the submarine HMS *Regent*, wrote to his aunt back in Britain: 'The Japs know that they can beat up our fleet here due to a vast numerical superiority and can force our hands to no mean extent. So far we are sliding, and I have no idea as to what will eventually happen . . . The only solution at the moment seems to remove the Empire to an ice-floe and somebody would probably bomb us out of that!!!'

Sailors were frustrated that more was expected of them than was possible given the circumstances. Vociferous criticisms from the expatriate communities were the cause of much resentment. 'I think the trouble is that the Navy guarantees to protect the lives of British Subjects but <u>not</u> their property,' wrote Vere Wight-Boycott. When Hankow fell in October 1938, Rear Admiral Holt was annoyed by criticism from the business community. China, he stated, had been 'occupied by the Japs, and this rightly or wrongly by martial law and there is nothing I can do about it . . . The British Navy is not much use to anybody here now.'

As the Japanese advanced through northern China, the crews of the gunboats on the Yangtze were the last remnants of British influence in the region: isolated, ancient, and soon to come under serious threat of elimination. John Evans described the scene:

A harmless gunboat anchored in the Yangtze-Kiang, dirty brown water swishing by, the only scenery being the ghostlike appearance of Pukow and Nanking two miles astern, a few Japanese warships, and on either bank rice and paddy fields. At night, everywhere in darkness, and not a sound can be heard except for the throb-throb of *Scarab*'s dynamo.

# 3. Total Germany

Charles Thomas was brought back to Britain from his job in the wireless station at Hong Kong during the summer of 1939. He was drafted into the light cruiser HMS *Capetown*, which was about to depart for the Mediterranean. In August, he spent his last few days in England at Devonport. One evening, a week before war was declared, he decided to explore Plymouth, and recorded his thoughts in his diary:

> Tonight I am visiting the pictures after a walk round the Hoe and the Barbican. Whenever I visit this part of the town, I think of the thousands of sailors from Drake's time until now, who have trodden the same stones. It is impossible not to be stirred by the thoughts that along these narrow lanes the men went to join the ships which fought the Spanish Armada, with Blake against Van Tromp, with Rodney at the 'Saints', with Howe on 'The Glorious First of June', at Trafalgar, and not so many years ago at Jutland. I wonder if in years to come, other sailors will think of us?

In March 1939, German troops had occupied Czechoslovakia, destroying what credibility remained of the Munich Agreement. The following month, Italian forces moved into Albania and subsequently concluded a 'Pact of Steel', which formalized the alliance between Italy and Germany. Over the course of the summer, Poland became the focus of a fresh crisis. Britain made guarantees to Warsaw that she would intervene in the case of German aggression, now made more likely by a pact between the Nazis and Soviet Russia. By the end of August, thousands of reservists had returned to service in the Royal Navy. New documents of war doctrine had been issued. Coastal Command aircraft had begun to fly reconnaissance missions.

Merchant shipping had been brought under the nominal control of the Admiralty. As German tanks and troops moved into Poland, the Fleet began to mobilize. An ultimatum was sent from London to Berlin demanding the withdrawal of German soldiers from Polish soil. At 11.17 a.m. on 3 September, not twenty minutes after the deadline had passed, a message was sent to every ship in the navy stating simply: 'TOTAL GERMANY repetition TOTAL GERMANY'.

The Royal Navy had long been prepared for the possibility of war. Nella Last, a housewife living in Barrow-in-Furness, recorded her reaction to the news in the diary she was keeping for Mass Observation. 'When the Prime Minister spoke so solemnly and said "WAR" I thought the shock would kill me,' she wrote, recalling a trip to Portsmouth:

> Eighteen months ago I was in Southsea and saw the Fleet come in. Hundreds of young 'ratings' walked on the Prom and I gradually became conscious of a look they all had – a mixture of detachment, gravity and 'purpose'. I could have rushed up to one and begged him to tell me what he saw that I could not. My husband got vexed at me for what he called my silliness but when I heard the P.M. I knew what they saw.

The day before the outbreak of war, Lieutenant Commander George Blundell of HMS *Kent* recorded that 'the men are very cheerful and listen to any announcements with terrific keenness'. *Kent* was the flagship of the China Fleet, and the distance from home did little to dampen the patriotism of her sailors. The next day, Blundell noted in his diary, the men 'sang "God save the King" rather louder than usual . . . At 1905 the boy bugler, Kennedy, piped "War has been declared against Germany".' Blundell was not quite so enthusiastic: 'I can't say I felt very thrilled. In fact I have no wish to fight anyone except I'd like to scupper that fool Hitler.'

Winston Churchill, the new First Lord of the Admiralty, arrived back at the office he had vacated during the First World War to find his old desk and maps just as he had left them. Before long, the first slips of paper detailing his suggestions and demands were making their way through the corridors, as they would in their hundreds each day of his incumbency, terrorizing the six Sea Lords who headed each administrative section of the Admiralty. The flurry of wartime paperwork also began for naval commands, from the major depots of Devonport, Portsmouth and Chatham, to the many smaller stations which covered the entirety of British territorial waters: from Rosyth to Dover, Portland to Belfast, and Grimsby to Milford Haven.

Across the navy, sailors settled into wartime routine proper: in the Home Fleet based at Scapa Flow, tucked away in the chilly Orkneys; aboard the ships of the Mediterranean Fleet, from Gibraltar to Suez and thence to the Red Sea; around the tropical harbours of the Indian Ocean and the African coastline; amongst the ships and bases dotted around the Americas and West Indies, from Bermuda to Buenos Aires; and in the small, aging, isolated China Fleet. Aboard the Yangtze gunboats, captains gathered their men and told them the news. In HMS *Ladybird*, ancient cutlasses were passed around and the crew practised repelling boarders.

'It is difficult to believe and supremely depressing,' wrote Lieutenant Commander Frank Layard in his diary on hearing the news of the declaration of war. Only a few hours later, the passenger liner *Athenia* was sunk 250 miles north-west of Ireland by the German submarine U-30. More than 1,400 passengers and crew were aboard, of whom 128 were killed, including 28 American citizens. The U-boat's commander, Fritz-Julius Lemp, would testify that he had attacked the vessel in error, mistaking it for a legitimate target. Indeed, there were strict instructions for U-boat commanders in the first weeks of the war to avoid civilian casualties. Nevertheless, the public reaction on both sides of the Atlantic was inevitably vociferous, echoing the furore which had followed the sinking of the liner *Lusitania* during the First World War. 'A very stupid thing for the Germans to have done,' noted Layard, 'considering the effect likely to be made in America.'

Convoys were soon organized, and over the course of September the routes were established which would become the highways for the delivery of food and fuel, machinery and munitions, troops and tanks. Coal tramps and steamers began to travel together along the east coast, from the Firth of Forth to the Thames. Destroyers escorted groups of merchant vessels just west of Ireland to start their passage across the Atlantic. On the western side of the ocean, the first convoys set off eastwards from Jamaica and Halifax, Nova Scotia, bound for Britain while others headed south from the Scilly Isles to Gibraltar, then on to Cape Town.

John Adams was a junior officer in the destroyer HMS *Walker*, one of a ship's company made up largely of reservists, drawn together at short notice from the pool of available manpower. On 4 September, *Walker* was escorting a group of merchant ships including the SS *Corinthic* when a lookout raised the alarm. Depth-charge teams were told to stand by as the ship manoeuvred to attack. 'One rating in his excitement took the pin out of the hand release gear and fired a depth charge,' wrote Adams in his diary. 'The *Corinthic* heard the explosion, thought she had been attacked by a submarine, and lowered both boats, terrified niggers jumping into them as they were being lowered together with their suitcases! She then raised the Red Ensign upside down and blew off steam.'

There was no U-boat, and the merchant sailors soon regained their composure. A few days later, however, the confusion of those first days would cause far more serious damage. The night of 11 September was pitch black, and *Walker* was part of an escort group some 300 miles south-west of Land's End. Manoeuvring was difficult and communications became garbled. In the darkness, *Walker* careered towards another destroyer, HMS *Vanquisher*. Before any evasive action could be taken, the two ships collided. 'Our bows went into *Vanquisher*'s port side like a knife and must have killed ten men immediately in the mess decks,' wrote Adams in shaky handwriting afterwards. Sailors from *Walker* boarded *Vanquisher* to assist. Adams helped to carry a heavy chest full of confidential books up to the main deck. 'All the lighting was out and how we carried it I don't know,' he wrote. 'We also rescued the ship's kitten.'

All the men from *Vanquisher* who were mobile were transferred to *Walker*. The collision had crumpled the two ships together and several men were trapped. Adams described their fate:

The two ships remained locked while we tried to get the other men out, but in the end the First Lieutenant shot them with a revolver as it was hopeless. We then went full astern and after lots of tugging got clear. *Vanquisher*'s side was a ghastly sight and we could see one signal-man climbing up inside. He had been clinging on to one of his friends, but when the ship went astern, both his (the friend's) legs were torn off, and he had to let go. The whaler rescued him safe and sound . . . Several on board are badly injured and suffering from oil fuel poisoning . . . The mess decks were an indescribable chaos of men in all stages of undress and injury. An able seaman has his foot half torn off and his leg badly fractured; I don't think he will live.

Petty Officer Edward Records was serving aboard HMS *Keith*. On 13 September, at the port of Milford Haven in South Wales, he and his shipmates were on twenty-four hours' leave. The dark September nights were also causing him problems. 'Last night it was black ashore,' he wrote in his diary. 'Came off and lost my way. Walked all around the blinking Dockyard tripping over wires, walking up sand dumps, looking down docks and then it slightly rained. Drunk as a Lord. Bad head this morning.'

*Vanquisher* was brought to the docks for repairs the following day. Records was amongst the large crowd of onlookers who witnessed the extent of the damage before a makeshift screen was erected. 'I got a look at her,' he wrote. 'Cutting plating away to retrieve bodies. One body taken out as I looked.' There were plenty of stories to share between the survivors and the men on the quayside. Records was told about the signalman whom Adams had seen inside the wreck: 'Sig seeing his mate in water caught hold of him and held him for an hour and a half. Found out when assistance arrived he was holding half a body . . . One hand had to be shot I believe. Wrapped round with steel plating, crushed and impossible to extract him and his case absolutely hopeless and mad with pain. A better death poor fellow if it is so.' This was a supremely shocking episode. 'WAR,' wrote Records. 'I saw plating being drawn away and ratings working on it turning their heads. Ambulance leaving ship at 1600 and she's been in since 0900.' There would be many more self-inflicted casualties in the first months of the conflict.

For the Royal Navy, complacency was as great a threat as any enemy. Before the war, the Kriegsmarine had been viewed as the European rival most closely matching the Royal Navy's own values: technical skill, strong discipline, strategic strength and high morale. Yet a worthy rival was not necessarily an equal. Admiralty assessments of the German naval system highlighted 'a lack of that indefinable quality derived from centuries of familiarity with the sea that we call seamanship'. Its personnel were thought to be 'soldiers on water, not true sailors'.

Admiral Erich Raeder, the head of the Kriegsmarine, had planned to construct a fleet which could match the Royal Navy, but the schedule was for completion by 1944. In 1939, the German surface fleet consisted of two battleships, three weaker 'pocket battleships', and two old and obsolete First World War-vintage battleships, along with only five smaller cruisers and seventeen destroyers. It had no aircraft carriers and scant air resources of its own. The Royal Navy's Home Fleet alone was more than a match for this force, with five battleships, two battlecruisers, a modern carrier and fourteen cruisers. The Royal Navy quickly re-established its blockade between the Faroe Islands and Iceland, enforced by the small ships of the Northern Patrol which brought hundreds of vessels into harbour to be searched for contraband. At the outbreak of war, Raeder despairingly admitted that, if drawn into a pitched battle, his fleet of warships could 'only demonstrate that it knows how to go down with dignity'. Germany's best chance for success at sea lay under the surface.

The submarine was the chief weapon of the underdog. Britain was the world's merchant shipping superpower, directly controlling or having the option to lease around a third of global cargo-ship capacity. An imperial war effort ultimately depended on maritime supply routes. Admiral Karl Dönitz, commander of the Kriegsmarine's U-boat arm, despaired with good reason at Hitler's negligence of his branch. But although only thirty-five of his fifty-seven boats were operational at the start of the war, they had an immediate impact. It was not until November that U-boat commanders were permitted to sink suspected enemy ships on sight, but the Allies still lost forty-one merchant vessels in the first month of the war. In a misguided early attempt to take the fight to the submarines, the air-craft carriers *Ark Royal* and *Courageous* were each given a small escort of destroyers and sent out to hunt for U-boats.

It was a questionable plan: with only rudimentary underwater detection technology the carriers were highly vulnerable. On 14 September the *Ark Royal* had a narrow escape when she was caught to the west of the Hebrides by U-29. The submarine's torpedoes failed to detonate and it was promptly sunk by the escorting destroyers. On 17 September the predictable consequence finally came to pass. 'Learnt that *Courageous* has been sunk by a torpedo,' wrote George Blundell of HMS *Kent*. 'This is a serious loss and we are all very depressed to-night about it.' Sinking in barely fifteen minutes, the carrier took 518 men with her. It was the first major warship loss of the war, and the details spread quickly through the fleet. 'So many rumours that one does not know what to believe,' wrote Edward Records of HMS *Keith*, who reacted in a familiar fashion: 'Ashore the evening and got well drunk.'

The carrier hunter groups were quickly withdrawn, but the vul-nerability of British warships continued to trouble sailors and the Admiralty alike. Only a few days after the sinking of *Courageous*, a German bombing attack missed *Ark Royal* by little more than twenty feet. In October, the Kriegsmarine claimed an even greater scalp. 'I think I ought to record the sinking of the *Royal Oak* at Scapa Flow,' wrote Able Seaman I. G. Hall of HMS *Glasgow* in his diary. 'She lost 800 hands which is pretty tragic. Imagine in four and a half years of the last war no submarine got through . . . and yet after two months of this they get in and sink the *Royal Oak* and even get out. Some-thing wrong somewhere I'm thinking.'

Lieutenant Commander Günther Prien had taken U-47 through a gap in the defences of the Home Fleet's base and hit the anchored battleship in two separate torpedo strikes, before negotiating strong currents and avoiding the depth-charge attacks which followed. Despite the deaths of 833 men, there was widespread respect for Prien's achievement. 'The news of the *Royal Oak* disaster upset us all, I knew several of them,' wrote Douglas Woolf. 'One can't help prais-ing the submarine's crew for great bravery in the exploit.' For

Lieutenant Commander Frank Layard it was 'a marvellous bit of work by the U-boat one must admit but scandalous that it should have been possible'.

For Ian Anderson, junior officer in the British submarine HMS *Odin* in the Far East, the sinking of the *Royal Oak* was 'an amazing performance'. Regardless of the fact that they were now enemies, he had considerable sympathy for his counterparts in German submarines: 'Poor devils, I don't envy them; the cry at home is "Exterminate the U-boats" as though they were poisonous insects; a vile means of warfare I know, but it's rough on the chaps inside to be looked on as if they were the scum of the earth.'

November brought the first Armistice Day of the war. 'Only a hollow mockery 20 years after,' noted Anderson in his diary on 11 November. Able Seaman Hall had similar sentiments. 'Another Armistice day and this one finds us in the grips of a long war with the old enemies once more,' he wrote. 'Strange it is to hear the patriotic songs and think over what they mean. It seems to inspire me with a certain spirit and camaraderie I must admit.' HMS *Glasgow* had been relocated to Immingham, on the Humber, and Hall could not resist recording his thoughts on possible future events: 'I'd like to know what the idea is as I think there is something in the wind. Perhaps they are suspecting Germany will soon be moving through Holland, and want us near at hand. What a life . . .'

Twenty-three-year-old Richard Walker was a volunteer officer in the armed merchant cruiser HMS *Scotstoun*, a pre-war passenger liner hastily fitted with guns and manned by a motley mix of regular sailors, ex-merchant crew reservists, and men freshly recruited from seafaring communities including a group of Newfoundland fishermen known as the 'Newfies'. *Scotstoun* was part of the Northern Patrol, blockading the entry to the Norwegian Sea in the waters between Iceland and Scotland. Walker found himself off the southern coast of Iceland, watching the effect of the early sunlight on the icy water. 'The water is covered with a thin film,' he wrote in his diary, 'patterned rather like millions of Nazi swastikas.'

Conditions were tough. The crew endured gale-force winds and heavy waves which reduced the speed of the ship to a crawl. 'The forward guns cannot be manned at times, spray coming over the crow's nest, and drowning us on monkey island and control,' he wrote. 'One sea hits us such a crack that half the ship's company appear on deck thinking it a torpedo at least.'

In the autumn of 1939 *Scotstoun* seized three German merchant vessels in the Denmark Strait, including one named *Eilbeck*, which was brought into the Clyde. By the time she was handed over to naval authorities, she had been thoroughly looted. 'Binoculars, barometers, torches, clocks, sextants, charts, books, all disappear by stealth,' wrote Walker. 'However, it all belongs to the Hamburg [shipping] company, none of it being the men's personal property, so we do not feel guilt.' Nevertheless, these minor spoils of war did little to abate the frustrations of the ship's officers, most of whom were career navy men and eager to see action. 'The whole ship's company apart from the Royal Navy – the Captain, No. 1 and the POs, who all thirst for blood – are the least militant crowd you could imagine,' complained Walker. 'No. 1 and the Chief Gunner's Mate are pining for a scrap and the Midshipmen are longing to cover themselves with blood and glory, but the rest of us are far too cowardly for warfare and prefer a life of ease. "Drink, drink, Lead a Life of Pleasure", that's me!'

The waters to the north of Britain were the scene of one of the most dramatic incidents of the early months of the war. On 23 November 1939, the Armed Merchant Cruiser *Rawalpindi*, another converted civilian ship, came across the powerful German battleships *Scharnhorst* and *Gneisenau* to the north of the Faroe Islands. Although his vessel was no more than a fortified passenger liner, and faced with overwhelming odds, Captain Edward Kennedy refused to surrender. Before the *Rawalpindi* finally succumbed, he managed to signal the locations of the German warships to the Home Fleet, thus ensuring they were unable to break through into the Atlantic. The cost was 238 sailors killed, with another 37 rescued and captured by the Germans, and a handful rescued by HMS *Chitral*.

'She never had a chance,' wrote Ian Anderson, submariner in the Far East, after hearing the news. 'She fought till every gun was out of action and the ship on fire from end to end and went down with colours flying and 250 odd of her crew of reservists and pensioners. A fine show.' In the Mediterranean, Lieutenant Vere Wight-Boycott of HMS *Delight* recorded his reaction:

> We heard about the *Rawalpindi* a few days ago – fair enough and nobody could have asked or expected anything else when a big clumsy P&O liner meets a squat, powerful, armoured war ship. Somehow though it seems more tragic than the *Oak* or *Courageous*, because they were mostly Reservists, and the skipper must have been pruning his rose garden a few months ago.

Captain Kennedy, who died in the attack, was sixty years old. His son, Ludovic, a junior officer at the time, later wrote a wartime autobiography in which he described his last memories of his father, who had been a reservist for eighteen years before being recalled to serve once again:

> I have never seen him so happy; he was like a child who has been given a new toy . . . His enthusiasm was unbounded, his pride immense. I knew then that the disappointment which had been rankling for the past eighteen years had vanished. They were forgotten in his passionate interest and pride in his new command. Before I left, he showed me the guns lying on the jetty, waiting to be fitted. Big, powerful creatures they looked, their snouts pointing threateningly to the sky. Across the shield of each gun was scribbled in thick white letters RAWALPINDI.

The story was quickly mythologized as a symbolic act of British naval heroics. 'They must have known as soon as they sighted the enemy that there was no chance for them,' declared Winston Churchill in the House of Commons. 'But they had no thought of surrender. They . . . went to their deaths, and thereby carried on the great traditions of the Royal Navy. Their example will be an inspiration to those who come after them.' To some outsiders, however, the mindset epitomized by the *Rawalpindi* seemed strange, even perverse. Jock Colville, Private Secretary to Prime Minister Neville Chamberlain, wrote in his diary soon after the incident:

I cannot help feeling that there is something very wrong with a code of honour which, as in the case of the *Rawalpindi*, prescribes that a ship must go down with all hands fighting to the last when cornered by a bigger vessel and unable to escape. Why should not the crew scuttle their ship and take to the boats? The effect would be the same except that hundreds of lives might be saved from a fate of flames and impotent horror. Codes of honour are often relics from a barbarous age, and it is tragic that modern opinion should remain so obscurantist on these matters. But it is undeniably true that if the *Rawalpindi*'s crew had scuttled their ship and saved themselves, their action would have been represented as disgraceful at home and abroad.

While the waters around Britain witnessed the worst of the war, there were far fewer opportunities for those in the Mediterranean to participate. 'We are having our own little private war,' wrote Vere Wight-Boycott to his family in November 1939. 'It's hellish hot. In fact I think I shall have to join the bearded party (we have 5 on board at the moment) as the sun has burnt all the skin off my upper lip and I can't shave it.' During the first week in September, the destroyer HMS *Delight* had travelled through the Indian Ocean to Aden. 'The ship is caked with salt from stem to stern,' he wrote, 'You can chip salt off the funnels with a knife.'

For the sailors of *Delight*, and those in other ships operating around the Mediterranean, the autumn of 1939 was a difficult time. Italy was not yet an active protagonist, but the area remained strategically vital. Sailors kept in close touch with developments at home. Newspapers brought reports of the ignominious end of the first phase of civilian evacuation, with mothers and children returning to London, as Wight-Boycott put it, 'having fallen out with the people billeting them. I am not surprised as I wondered how on earth it could work, unless the Germans kept up an unceasing bombardment of London, thereby demonstrating to refugees how lucky they were.' Censorship was another annoyance. Wight-Boycott found it 'maddening as all sorts of things have happened lately here which would amuse you'. One of these was a German report that *Delight* had been sunk:

'If this is true (censorship prevents me from giving an opinion) it proves I am a good swimmer I think you'll admit.'

The autumn of 1939 continued to bring rumours, theories and feverish predictions. 'We have heard of Russia's invasion of Finland in the last day or two,' wrote Wight-Boycott. 'This is an unexpected sort of war. I have heard people saying that within two years England, France, Germany and Italy will all be fighting on the <u>same</u> side against Russia. Somebody will have to bump Hitler off first I think though.' Charles Thomas of the nearby HMS *Capetown* echoed this prediction: 'No doubt we will soon be supporting Germany against the inroads of Communism.'

Alec Dennis was a junior officer in the destroyer HMS *Griffin*. Since the Italian invasion of Albania, *Griffin* had been operating from Alexandria. 'I found it a fascinating place,' he wrote. 'The approach from the sea is difficult, the shore-line flat and of a uniform ochre colour with few distinguishing marks. Sometimes in hazy weather you could locate the city in a general way from the smell – a mixture of raw sewage and tannery effluent.' Above all, it was the sense of age that most struck Dennis; the Ras el Tin lighthouse and the remains of the ancient Pharos gave him 'an overwhelming feeling of the past'. Wartime routine prevailed, as it had done in some form since 1935, but much time was taken up with training. *Griffin* took part in a landing exercise in Aboukir Bay – 'the site of Nelson's victory', as Dennis put it – in which a small force of saboteurs tested the defensive capabilities of local militia fighters.

*Griffin* was sent back to British waters in November 1939 to join the 1st Destroyer Flotilla. Soon afterwards, the flotilla was operating off the Dutch coast when it strayed into a minefield. HMS *Gypsy* was hit and sank rapidly. 'We spent a dismal few hours trying to pick up survivors in the dark with the brown foamy current flowing by and the pervasive smell of oil fuel,' wrote Dennis. 'Mingled with the cries of the drowning men was the mournful tolling of the channel bell buoy. A fitting requiem for the first of our flotilla to go.'

Back ashore at West India Docks on the Thames, Dennis was struck by the contrast between the civilian attitude to the war and his own experiences in the first few weeks of the conflict. 'Apart from the blackout and the plethora of uniforms London still seemed to be on a peacetime footing,' he recalled. 'Food and drink were plentiful, nightclubs full of people and blue smoke. It was irritating to hear them talking about the "phoney war". I wished some of them could try a few wet cold nights off the Gabbard, get blown up and go for a swim.'

But while some sailors met with adversity from the very start of the war, others saw plenty of hard work and little action. HMS *Glasgow* spent most of October on escort duties in the Atlantic. Able Seaman I. G. Hall confessed in his diary that 'most of us are getting fairly fed up with Defence Watches' with the ship 'steaming around' but seemingly doing little else. 'Life's pretty dreary and rather hard at times.' Despite the tension of wartime routine and the expectations of action, the autumn remained a relatively calm period for *Glasgow*. 'This war is one of nerves and boredom,' wrote Hall, 'without a doubt in common with a lot of wars, in fact all wars.'

By the start of December, he was looking forward to the end of his twelve-year service stint: 'I certainly thought we'd be firing some angry shots. Roll on my twelve.' Only a few days later, however, there was a sharp reminder that even if the violence of the enemy did not pose a threat, the dangers of the sea still could: 'The captain of "A" turret was killed to-day, a wave swept him whilst on the fo'castle, against a fan and a rib pierced his lung. We were doing no speed, practically stopped in fact. However with a powerful sea like this running it is dangerous. Roll on my twelve.'

For those naval officers employed in shore jobs, rather than serving in warships, there was a moral dilemma to address. Within a few days of hostilities, Lieutenant Commander Frank Layard, working at a desk in Portsmouth, had begun to worry. 'Sitting in an office ashore,' he wrote in his diary, 'a pretty poor way of fighting a war for an N.O. [Naval Officer] . . . I can't bear to think of our chaps being killed especially when I am sitting here doing nothing.'

Expectations of the proper behaviour of a naval officer weighed heavily on Layard's shoulders, as they did for most of the officers in the service. Imbued with the imagery of the age of sail, when British seamen braved shot and storm to win famous victories, the officers of the Second World War struggled to reconcile their duties with those of their forebears. The first weeks of the conflict nevertheless provided examples that bore comparison. Layard described one incident in which Dick Jolly, Captain of HMS *Mohawk*, did his duty in a manner reminiscent of the glory days:

Apparently Jolly in the *Mohawk* although mortally wounded by splinters from the bomb with one arm shot away and terrible body wounds sent for a chain on the bridge and continued to take the ship up harbour and it was not until the ship was secured that he collapsed and died before he reached hospital. It seems that hardly a soul on the upper deck or bridge escaped death or wounding. Stories of that sort make an enormous impression on me. It makes me wonder if I could ever be heroic like that. I hope I could.

Layard felt strongly that he should be at sea, but this sense of duty was tempered with tortured self-doubt. After having volunteered for 'Special Service', through which he might be sent to serve in a ship at very short notice, he wrote: 'I hope I'm not required as I don't think I'm nearly brave enough but I feel I must make an effort.' He was worried that many years ashore had made him obsolete. 'The 1st Lieutenant should be a man of ability, personality and tact,' he wrote. 'It is a job that should not be given to somebody who has been out of the service for as much as 17 years but I suppose they have no others.' Layard's fortieth birthday brought news of the sinking of the *Rawalpindi*. 'With every fresh Naval disaster I get a return of this awful complex "how would I have been?",' he confessed. 'Should I have done my duty bravely or should I have disgraced myself?'

Some officers decided to take matters into their own hands. Twenty-five-year-old navigator Graham Lumsden was serving aboard HMS *Albatross*, an elderly seaplane carrier, which was operating out of Freetown, Sierra Leone. The climate was difficult and the mundane routine aboard *Albatross* was trying. Periodic refuelling stops by larger and more glamorous warships made the ship's company restless. Lumsden became increasingly troubled by the lack of activity. 'The Navy is used to living in ships for long periods,' he explained, 'but the moist heat, the cramped environment, the repetitive routine, and above all, the lack of action for all except our airmen were worse enemies than our German foe. Every few weeks we raised steam and sighted our anchor to ensure that it was not too deeply buried in the changing mud: a small event which braced our minds and reminded us that we were all seamen and mobile.'

For an ambitious young officer, this was not a situation conducive to advancement. At the end of 1939, Lumsden decided to engineer a solution and petitioned his captain for a transfer, 'on the grounds that inaction was bad for me as a young specialist navigating officer and for the Navy, because any talents I possess in that direction were being wasted'. Not only did the captain agree, but 'he considered my arguments applied also to young Captains! We were both relieved and returned to Liverpool.'

Across the Atlantic, the cruiser HMS *Ajax* guarded the coast of South America. Junior officer Douglas Woolf, who had joined the ship from HMS *Orion*, was more content with his lot than Lumsden but, even so, Britain seemed very far away. *Ajax* had spent much of the previous year based at Bermuda and touring the Caribbean, where the young officers made the most of the leisure opportunities in tropical waters, fishing for exotic catches. On one occasion, Portuguese men-of-war jellyfish were fired upon with revolvers. On another, an octopus was brought up the gangway, spilling ink across the quarterdeck. Then one summer's day Mr and Mrs Woolf of Wembley, Middlesex, received a telegram sent from *Ajax* delivered via Portishead:

HAPPY RETURNS MUMMY DARLING HAVE NOT
WRITTEN OWING TO TEMPORARY LOSS OF FACUL-
TIES RIGHT HAND THROUGH SLIGHT INCIDENT
WITH SHARK LOVE DOUGLAS.

Patrolling the coasts of South America over the course of 1939, *Ajax* and her sailors had become well known in the major ports. After a devastating earthquake in Chile in January, *Ajax* had been sent to Concepción to help with relief efforts. Before the outbreak of war, a Chilean girlfriend had sent Woolf a newspaper cutting with the headline: 'HMS *Ajax*: The Terror of the South Seas'. Yet the cruiser's achievements during the first weeks of the conflict scarcely seemed to justify such a reputation. On 3 September *Ajax* came across the small German merchant vessel *Olinda* off the coast of Uruguay. An armed party was sent over to bring back the German crew of forty-three, then the ship was sunk. 'There was something terribly pathetic about the whole business,' wrote Woolf. 'The crew were definitely not aware that war had been declared . . . However we had no trouble from them at all and I think most of them are glad to be out of the war.'

Events at home were at the foremost of every mind. 'We are all well,' wrote Woolf to his parents at the end of September, 'which is practically all the news I can tell you – I myself am my usual self and try not to worry. I expect you have just the same feelings as we do – not knowing when an Air Raid is coming, as we think of a blasted tin fish coming into us. But we've got used to it already and just trust to luck.'

South American waters had been the stage for the most famous confrontations between German raiders and British ships in the First World War: a group commanded by Admiral Graf von Spee had won a famous, if minor, victory against Royal Naval forces at the Battle of Coronel, only to be destroyed soon after in the Battle of the Falklands. *Ajax* was now Britain's vanguard in the region, and her sailors fully expected an imminent confrontation with the enemy, perhaps even the warship which bore the name of the German hero of the previous war. 'We are all keyed to meeting a pocket battleship!' wrote Woolf in late October.

The 'pocket battleships' were heavily armed but compact warships, several of which were sent across the oceans at the outbreak of war to attack Allied shipping. Although they had some success in capturing and sinking merchant vessels, far more important was their psychological impact on the British. One, the *Deutschland*, had since returned to Germany, slipping undetected through the Denmark Strait to the north of Iceland. She would be renamed *Lützow* to avoid the potential trauma of losing a warship named after the Fatherland. Another remained at large, and she was very familiar to Douglas Woolf. In February 1937, he had visited the *Admiral Graf Spee* on several occasions at Majorca during the Spanish Civil War and witnessed the cordiality between British and German sailors. After meeting the ship again in December 1939, his mood was rather different:

> To have really felt the fear of death for the first time in my life, to have seen War in all its ghastliness, to have seen courage, reckless bravery, the unselfishness of placing one's Country before all, all these things conjured up before one in the living hell we endured an hour and three quarters. Such is War and sufficient to say perhaps we did our duty and fought a glorious and gallant battle against odds that to us all appeared suicide. Only a miracle saved us and even more miraculous is that we won. I am thankful to God that I still have my life . . . Dec 13th – A day that for evermore will be vivid in my memory.

*Graf Spee* had been intercepted off the South American coast by HMS *Ajax*, along with fellow cruisers HMS *Exeter* and HMNZS *Achilles*, the latter manned chiefly by sailors from New Zealand. Commodore Henry Harwood, commanding the cruiser force from *Ajax*, had not hesitated to take the initiative. 'Everything happened so quickly that one wasn't given any time to think,' wrote Woolf. As soon as the alarms were sounded he 'struggled into a jacket, trousers and shoes and scrambled hell for leather up to my Action Station on the Bridge'.

On a clear morning, shortly after 6 a.m., and with the advantage of range, *Graf Spee* could open fire before the cruisers could return it. The German guns first found *Exeter*, which had split off from *Ajax* and *Achilles* in an attempt to straddle the enemy. Despite several direct hits, with fires below deck and communications cut, *Exeter* nevertheless kept up her own fire for forty minutes until forced to break off and escape south. *Graf Spee*'s commanding officer, Captain Hans Langsdorff, then turned his attention to *Ajax* and *Achilles*.

Aboard *Ajax*, Douglas Woolf described 'explosion after explosion bursting all round us, the roar of our guns raking the enemy'. Two turrets were put out of action, and the bridge was hit. Yet, under constant fire from the cruisers, Langsdorff decided to take *Graf Spee* west: retreating rather than confronting the weaker ships. 'She fought a good fight,' wrote Woolf, 'but I don't think she ever bargained for such resolute action, as we took two little cruisers with a chance of one in ten of ever getting away with it, let alone winning against a battleship with armour four to five times thicker than ours. It was a miracle and we have with no boast added another page to British Naval History.'

*Graf Spee* was forced into the Uruguayan port of Montevideo, at the mouth of the River Plate. Here she remained, the crew attempting repairs with little help from local Anglophile craftsmen, while Langsdorff assessed his options. Despite her reputation, the so-called 'pocket battleship' had not been designed for a fleet action and would struggle to defeat a larger force. The British began a disinformation campaign of false signals and local rumours to convince the Germans that Royal Navy reinforcements were close at hand.

As the news spread, sailors in other ships around the world pondered the stand-off. 'The *Graf Spee* has been given 72 hrs to leave port,' wrote Able Seaman Hall of the Home Fleet cruiser HMS *Glasgow* in his diary, repeating the now-ubiquitous rumours. 'There are about half a dozen of our ships including the *Renown* and *Ark Royal*. Poor devils they won't stand a chance, it must be like waiting to be executed. War is pretty bad I guess.' Aboard *Ajax*, waiting outside Montevideo with repairs ongoing, the atmosphere was one of 'even greater strain on the nervous system' according to Woolf:

So for 86 hours we went with sickly chaos in our tummies – grabbing a few minutes sleep here and there, and biscuits and chocolate to eat – perhaps those hours were the worst – the awfulness of uncertainty and waiting. At last, last night she came out and forward once again we went off to have our final smack at her – only to see her go up in smoke before our eyes. The anti-climax was terrible, relief and then the realisation of victory – the cheering of the men.

Captain Langsdorff had committed suicide rather than face ignominy; the German ship had been scuttled. The international press corps reported the dramatic events with gusto in articles that would be syndicated worldwide.

Aboard *Ajax* the elation and relief were short lived for Woolf: 'now the depressing job of cluing up the killed and writing letters to their relatives. How we escaped with so few killed I don't know – seven in all.' After the encounter, however, *Ajax* would be seen as a 'fighting ship' with both her captain Charles Woodhouse and Commodore Harwood garnered official and popular praise. 'I think this crew would follow our Captain now through anything,' wrote Woolf, 'as I think we have him to thank for our lives for the splendid way he handled the ship and out-manoeuvred the *Graf Spee*. Instead of our title South American Squadron we call ourselves the Suicide Squadron!'

The Battle of the River Plate galvanized the navy, and the British press did its best to ensure that it excited the nation. 'From the accounts in the newspapers it appears that the British light cruisers were "all over" the German ship in gunnery and tactical manoeuvring,' wrote Charles Thomas, in the Mediterranean aboard HMS *Capetown*. 'H.M.S. *Rawalpindi* – an armed merchant cruiser – did not run away from the *Deutschland* yet the latter's sister ship would not face the issue with our two light cruisers which proves the finer quality of our officers and men. The news of the war at sea has been more cheerful during the past few days.'

On the day that *Exeter* returned home to Plymouth in early 1940, her arrival was noted by Ivor Turner, a signalman in the minesweeper *Sunlight*. 'I wonder what Drake and Nelson would have said could they but have been there,' he wrote in his diary. 'It's a funny thing but some people don't realize that there's always a loser . . . I wonder what the wives and mothers of the sailors killed on the *Graf Spee* are thinking. Much the same as the British wives and mothers . . . Where is the victory?'

While the *Graf Spee*'s nemeses were garnering praise, others looked on jealously. Aboard HMS *Kent*, the British flagship in the Far East, the summer of 1939 had been difficult. A newly instigated war routine of watches, drills and practice proved taxing for officers and men alike, and morale sank. In August, Captain Leslie Ashmore suffered a nervous breakdown and was sent ashore to recover after being relieved of his command. Ashmore had been known as 'Happy' to his fellow officers. 'I've never seen a man look so miserable,' wrote newly appointed executive officer George Blundell after his departure.

Despite the positive reaction to news of the outbreak of war aboard *Kent*, a sense of detachment soon set in. 'We get no news from home,' complained Blundell in his diary, 'and I keep wondering when we are going to wake up.' Over the course of the autumn and winter, mechanical problems were frequent. Discipline began to fray. 'I had to read three warrants on the quarter deck,' he recorded on one occasion, 'two of them on the two leading stokers caught in an indecent act on the golf course at Wei Hai Wei.' When one able seaman left his post without permission, he was put under arrest. Blundell was worried: 'This apathetic attitude on the part of some of the men – even the good ones – is rather disturbing. It is chiefly because it is so difficult to realize there is a war on out here and also due to boredom.' During a stay in harbour at Fremantle, Australia, in January 1940, there were a record number of men late back from shore leave, and Blundell was astounded to discover that one sailor had been caught with twenty-three pairs of stolen tropical shorts in his locker.

A similar ennui had set in aboard HMS *Odin*. The submarine had been due to return to Britain in September 1939, but after the declaration of war it was instead sent to Penang, to the north of Singapore on the west coast of the Malayan peninsula. Junior officer Ian Anderson had been looking forward to going home after several years on the China Station. 'We are still ignored,' he wrote, 'and shall soon have to resign ourselves to spending the war at Penang.' He was incredulous at how little seemed to have changed. 'It's impossible to realise we're at war in this place,' he wrote. 'The same invitations to become honorary members of the Penang Club, the Penang Sports Club, the Penang Swimming Club, the Penang Flying Club etc.; I feel almost guilty in writing polite acceptances while at home people are at war in deadly earnest, patrolling in the North Sea.' Anderson spent most of his time in Malaya with girlfriends, including one memorable trip to 'one of Singapore's three enormous open air funfair-cum-cabaret-cum-circus-cum amusement parks. It is a long time since I've been to one and I'd got into the habit of thinking them rather vulgar and rough but this evening I enjoyed more than any at the Raffles.'

In November 1939, *Odin* began a tour of the Indian Ocean which lasted until April 1940. These five months began with a four-week patrol of the Maldives to search for German vessels which might be hiding amongst the coral reefs and small islands. This had happened in the First World War: notices were displayed for the benefit of the men detailing the story of the infamous German raider *Emden*. Senior officers were required to go ashore and 'interrogate the natives as to ships seen'. There was a problem: 'As they speak no known language this is unlikely to be of much use . . . We have got a large bag of rice for trading with the natives who have no other form of currency, but are said to be delighted to give one a large fish in exchange for a cupful of rice.'

*Odin* visited the tiny atoll of Peros Banhos, near the Maldives. It was barely inhabited, but there was a 'small settlement in real outpost of the Empire style'. As the landing party approached the shore, the British red ensign was seen flying, which, wrote Anderson, was 'most gratifying'. The British sailors received a warm, if confusing welcome, as the handful of inhabitants spoke only French: 'Very affable though conversation was a trifle difficult.' Many of the men were excited by tales of the island's pirate past, and stories about buried treasure abounded. 'It is really astonishing,' wrote Anderson, 'to think that some people can, and do, spend almost their entire lives in a place like this.'

The submariners spent the first weeks of 1940 in Ceylon at a naval retreat at Diyatalawa, '5000 feet up in the hills,' wrote Anderson, 'where the air is pure and powerful and already I feel a new man'. In contrast to the nearby internment camp for German prisoners, the British barracks were comfortable. 'One sleeps in a bed with a spring mattress, and one has admirable Sinhalese servants to do everything for you. There is a golf course, a squash court and tennis courts; hockey and football grounds; shooting, fishing and riding so what more could one ask for.' Anderson also spent time at the 2,000-acre estate of a tea magnate. He was impressed: 'I feel tea planting is a life I could thoroughly appreciate myself in this country – a healthy and wealthy existence.'

In March 1940 *Odin* visited Diego Suarez, the French naval base on the island of Madagascar. It was, wrote Anderson, 'undoubtedly one of the world's fouler cesspools . . . rotten with dirt and disease, everything is shoddy and nothing works properly. Even the cars look as though they've been rescued from the scrap heap. The houses are practically all tin-roofed shacks or mud huts, and the natives are the seediest collection of scoundrels I've yet seen. If this is a typical example of a French colony then they're not fit to have an Empire.' His main gripe was that a British colony would have built 'proper roads . . . a golf course and a club' whereas Diego Suarez boasted only 'two cracked concrete tennis courts in a piece of waste ground behind the barracks; the netting round has long since ceased to be of any use; the net has holes in it; there are no drinks to be had; there isn't even a ball boy'.

Next stop was the Seychelles and the isolated coral atoll of Aldabra. It was known for its beautiful and rare giant tortoise, which was very nearly extinct. Ian Anderson recorded in his diary that the crew were given a present by the local fishermen: 'a large turtle which was hauled on board with some difficulty . . . the revolting job of butchering it and cutting it up performed on deck by a black man . . . the shoulders and flippers were hacked off to be made into steaks, the more advanced eggs, which are exactly like ping pong balls, were fried for breakfast, the shell was returned to the donors, the guts chucked over the side, and we were off again, all in under 50 minutes'.

Meanwhile, closer to home, the Admiralty had obtained information that a German vessel carrying merchant sailors captured by the *Graf Spee* was lying off the coast of Norway. A rescue plan was hatched and, on 16 February 1940, a Royal Navy task force seized the *Altmark*, freeing the prisoners with the subsequently immortalized cry: 'The Navy's here!' The violation of the territorial waters of a neutral country was controversial, but soon overwhelmed by propaganda. Able Seaman Hall, of HMS *Glasgow*, was sceptical. 'They say the destroyer was the *Cossack*,' he wrote in his diary. 'I'm glad she caught the *Altmark* but expect there'll be a deal too much laudatory writing and neverending self praise about England and so forth instead of quiet praise of the actual people who took part.' 'The wireless has just given us the first news of the boarding of the *Altmark*,' wrote Vere Wight-Boycott, first lieutenant of HMS *Delight*. 'The wireless mentioned four Germans killed. I wonder if it includes the Captain. He was a swine most certainly, though skilful and brave.'

Some sailors attempted to retain a semblance of normality, even into the spring of 1940. On Friday 5 April, the Grand National took place. John Adams, sub-lieutenant in HMS *Walker*, had an idea: 'I took my wireless up to the bridge and broadcast the race via our loud speaker for shouting at merchant ships. Quite a success.' The winning horse was Bogskar. It would be the last time the race was held until 1946. News of the German invasions of Denmark and Norway came only a few days later. 'Words absolutely fail me about the German invasions,' wrote John Carter, a young reservist in HMS *Ilex*. 'Still, things are well in hand and we are making those Huns very, very uncomfortable . . . My only ambition now is to kill off as many Germans as possible.'

For those who remained beyond Europe, the sense of detachment was now overwhelming. 'Any number of wild rumours were flying around to-day,' wrote George Blundell of Ceylon-bound HMS *Kent* in April 1940. 'First, that six destroyers had entered Narvik; second that there was a fearful battle going on in the Skagerrak; third that we'd captured Trondheim and Bergen; and finally that the *Blücher* and *Karlsruhe* had been sunk. This latter was broadcast and there was a cheer throughout the ship.' When it became clear that these were not rumours, and that German forces had indeed invaded Denmark and Norway, Blundell despaired at being denied the opportunity to prove his mettle. HMS *Kent* was destined to remain at Ceylon for the rest of the spring, and he was bereft: 'I felt to-day that I could lie on the deck, roll and scream like a disappointed child at not being in the show going on in the North Sea. The day I was appointed to this ship I count as the worst day of my life. Here we sit and do nothing and the only German I shall see the whole war will be the pasty faced ones from the Diyatalawa internment camp.'

While a hastily prepared defence of northern Norway began, the British Expeditionary Force continued to reinforce defensive positions alongside the French army in anticipation of a German offensive into the Low Countries. Midshipman David Leggatt, serving in the submarine HMS *Regent* in the Far East, wrote to his uncle on 12 April:

What a world. News rushes in every minute: actions at sea, in the air, maybe even on land; marches into Norway, Denmark and heaven knows what next. It is all too big for me, far too big, so I won't even comment on it, since by the time you get this it will all be ever so much clearer too and perhaps Holland, Belgium and the rest will no longer exist. How horrible it all is, and how unnecessary.

The English Channel and the North Sea were already battlefields. In April 1940, volunteer officer Ronald Middleton was on the bridge of the destroyer HMS *Malcolm* as the ship made her way through the Dover Straits. He was the son of a Labour MP and had practised as a solicitor before joining up just before the outbreak of war. Middleton was in the chart room when *Malcolm* was bombed by German aircraft. He rushed out to see the damage:

The upper deck had been sprayed with shrapnel from bursting bombs and shrapnel had pierced the ship's side and there were many casualties. We cleared the mess deck and laid out our dead and dying. Men were screaming. It was harrowing to hear a man screaming with pain, gradually becoming quieter and quieter until he was silent. The doctor was on leave and we had no pain killing drugs. One man screamed for his 'Mummy' until he died. One man had had his head blown off – a horrid sight.

Paul Chavasse was the torpedo officer of the minelayer *Princess Victoria*. On 18 May 1940, as the ship was approaching the Humber estuary, he left the bridge and settled into his bunk for a well-earned rest. Expecting to be woken, he had removed only his boots, keeping on his clothes and his inflatable life jacket bought specially from the military outfitters Gieves.

*Princess Victoria* hit a magnetic mine. Chavasse was thrown into the bulwark and briefly knocked unconscious. He came to in the dark, on the floor, with the ship starting to heel over and sink. Feeling his way through the door, he tried desperately to inflate his life jacket, but in vain. As the angle of the ship steepened alarmingly, he felt his way along the corridor, making for the upper deck. His wife Elizabeth explained his fate in a letter to her father:

Suddenly the door he was leaning on gave way, and he fell into a cabin. There he was and four huge waves landed in before he really came to his senses. He then found himself swimming round and round rather like Alice in the Pool of Tears, looking for the door. When he told me this I felt as though I was living again through this nightmare.

Chavasse was trapped against the top of the cabin with the water rapidly rising. Taking a final breath, he dived deep down and made for the open door. Only afterwards did he realize that an inflated life jacket would have made this impossible. 'It is not unlike a Cinema escape,' wrote Elizabeth.

His lungs held out long enough for him to escape the ship and emerge into the sea. The strength in his limbs sustained him until rescuers in a boat from the destroyer *Ivanhoe* pulled him from the water. He was battered and bruised but safe. Elizabeth was the first family member to visit him in hospital, back ashore at Grimsby. 'He has lost everything he ever possessed,' she wrote. His wrist watch – a wedding present – was gone, as were his binoculars, his favourite fine ivory hair brushes and some 'rather super fur gloves'. There was, however, one extraordinary recovery. A few days later, another ship was sent to the site of the sinking to check that no secret documents kept aboard had surfaced. The only thing they found was a framed photograph of Elizabeth Chavasse in her wedding dress, the frame smashed but the picture still recognizable. 'The utter thankfulness and the shock of it all has I think knocked me a bit,' she wrote. 'It will be wonderful having him home soon . . . The more I think of it the more wonderful it is he is still alive.'

# 4. Daniel and the Lions

In late March 1940, the trawler *Northern Spray* was patrolling off the remote Scottish island of North Rona, some forty miles north of the Outer Hebrides. 'Heavy snow and rain,' wrote William Robertson in his diary. 'This is the worst weather I have been in. One lifeboat and a Carley Float smashed to bits by heavy seas, deck rails and ventilators twisted and bent, doors torn off, depth charges broken adrift from moorings and rolling about on deck. Mess flooded, and galley dinner ruined with salt water.' The patrol was abandoned and the trawler returned to Stornoway.

On 1 April, recorded Robertson, it was still 'snowing like hell'. Yet the following morning brought glorious sunshine, and the sailors 'went swimming over the side'. Over the following week, instructions were received to take on stores and food to last several months. 'We begin to wonder where we are going,' wrote Robertson. 'Duffle coats, extra blankets, gloves, waterproofs and extra underwear are issued to us . . . With the laying of minefields and increased tension in Norway it seems probable we may go out there.'

At dawn on 9 April German forces launched an invasion of Denmark and landed troops along the Norwegian coastline from Kristiansand to Narvik. Denmark fell quickly. Norwegian forces initially resisted in the south: shore batteries in Oslo sank the cruiser *Blücher*, helping King Haakon and his government to escape. Yet the capital was soon overwhelmed. British sailors had observed the invasion force but were powerless to stop it. Confronted by the German cruiser *Admiral Hipper*, Lieutenant Commander Gerard Roope of the destroyer HMS *Glowworm* decided to ram his enemy, tearing his ship apart in the process. One hundred and eleven men were killed and several dozen more rescued and taken prisoner. Roope received a posthumous Victoria Cross.

French and British troops were landed at several points along the coast to aid Norwegian forces. The campaign centred on the crucial port of Narvik, the gateway to local iron-ore supplies, tucked away in the winding fjords of the far north. The day after German mountain troops seized the town, a destroyer force led by Captain Bernard Warburton-Lee in HMS *Hardy* swooped into the fjord at dawn during a heavy snowstorm and attacked the ill-prepared German destroyer flotilla. *Hardy* torpedoed the *Wilhelm Heidkamp*, destroying the flagship and killing her commander. Four other destroyers were sunk or severely damaged, along with six enemy merchant ships. As they attempted to escape the fjord, Warburton-Lee's flotilla was attacked by another group of German destroyers. *Hunter* was hit by shellfire and sank. *Hardy* sustained heavy damage: on the bridge, only one man escaped death or serious injury. She was beached and her crew fled ashore, while Captain Warburton-Lee died from a severe head wound. He, too, would receive a posthumous Victoria Cross.

'I felt a little proud,' wrote Vere Wight-Boycott to his brother, 'when I read in the stop press in a newspaper that the crew of *Hardy* were seen landing in a boat, fully armed "like a little military incursion intent on the capture of Norway".' He was particularly impressed by Warburton-Lee: 'a moneyed chap, played polo, expert at racquets . . . the type I think that usually does pretty well when courage and sacrifice are required'.

The battleship HMS *Warspite* was on patrol in nearby waters when the ship's company was informed by the captain over the loudspeakers of the destroyer battle in Narvik fjord. As wireless operator Donald Auffret recalled, they were told that 'we were going in the next day to clear the mess up'. Amongst the men, the mood was 'very sombre'. Narvik fjord was bounded by snow-covered mountains, the skies were grey: 'A very, very grim place. The sea was the colour of lead – it looked very forbidding.'

The Second Battle of Narvik, three days after the first, resulted in yet more German casualties: eight destroyers lost and dozens of deaths. *Warspite* was able to use Swordfish biplanes to find enemy destroyers hiding in the fjords, before attacking them with heavy guns. Auffret described the effect of one broadside on an enemy destroyer: 'She was literally lifted out of the water, up onto the beach – and then slid down again. She must have been hit by about six 15-inch shells simultaneously.' A Swordfish from *Warspite* also sank U-64: the first successful air strike against a German submarine in the war.

Despite eliminating yet more enemy destroyers, the British task force was unable to secure Narvik, which remained in German hands. *Warspite* also came perilously close to being sunk by U-boats in the fjords. Submariner Erich Topp recalled sighting the battleship: 'a giant among giants, steaming inevitably into our sight. The atmosphere on board was electric.' It was a critical moment. 'If we could destroy the *Warspite*,' wrote Topp, 'Allied resistance would collapse and with it the belief in the invincibility of the British Navy.' But just as the submarine was about to fire its torpedoes, it hit a submerged rock and was knocked out of position.

Hunting German warships in the maze of waterways appeared to be the ideal opportunity for commanding officers to prove themselves in true Nelsonian style. But while a daring captain might inspire some sailors, others were deeply unsettled. Able Seaman I. G. Hall recorded his thoughts on 12 April, as HMS *Glasgow* made her way towards Narvik: 'What we'll do there I don't know but if it is left to the Captain no doubt we'll go right in and make a name for ourselves.'

There were reports that the German battleship *Scharnhorst* was nearby. Ammunition had been prepared and aircraft launched. Hall was troubled. He updated his diary after an address from the captain: 'He said that if the aircraft reported that the *Scharnhorst* was in we should go right in and attack and if possible he would ram her. He said it would be a fine scrap and that our chance had come at last. He also said that it would not be frightening but merely exciting. Well the way he spoke had every one just about ready to die even before the battle.' In the event, reports of the sighting were proved false. 'I don't think I've ever seen people so relieved,' wrote Hall. 'Anyhow it is evident that the captain will stop at nothing to achieve fame, come what may.'

When William Robertson's trawler *Northern Spray* finally reached Narvik on 24 April, she joined a naval attack on German land forces. Robertson described *Warspite* and *Vindictive*, along with cruisers and destroyers 'formed in a semi-circle . . . pouring broadside after broadside into the town one after the other'. The *Spray* 'went in firing', along with sister ship *Northern Dawn*, to help blockade the port and prevent enemy soldiers from escaping in boats.

It was not all one-way traffic. 'German snipers were picking off men on the ships,' scribbled Robertson. The following day was dominated by attacks from German bombers. Casualties were slight, but the psychological effects far outweighed the material damage. 'Crew badly shaken with this experience,' wrote Robertson. 'One man also put ashore with shell-shock.' *Northern Spray* returned to the safer haven of Skjel fjord, in the Lofoten archipelago to the west, to rest and recuperate. The men from the trawler were invited to the repair ship HMS *Vindictive* to watch a screening of the pre-war musical satire *Wake Up and Live*.

A few days earlier, on 20 April, the cruiser HMS *Carlisle* had arrived at the central Norwegian port of Andalsnes. It lay to the south of Trondheim, hidden at the end of a series of branching fjords guarded by snow-covered mountain ranges. *Carlisle* was charged with providing anti-aircraft cover. 'You can't see the path of the fjord as it turns round sharp bends,' wrote gunner Charles Hutchinson in his diary. 'We just seem to be in a basin with us in the middle, or, the way I could describe it better, as a mouse trap with us taking the part of the cheese in the centre.'

Shortly before midday, the expected air attack began, and Charles Hutchinson had his first taste of dive-bombing:

All one could hear was the powerful engines of the plane diving flat out through the low clouds and over the mountain top. It seemed to fill the whole sky. I then looked death, stark death, in the face for the first time in my life. I saw it release two wicked looking black bombs – they seemed small at first and then got larger and larger – they kept on in a straight dive at us after he pulled out – straight for the bows of the ship they came whistling, and then it got into a shriek – my God, the noise chilled you.

Men threw themselves to the deck all around him, but Hutchinson remained transfixed at his post. 'I don't know whether I was petrified or what, but I kept on looking,' he admitted. The bombs hit the water just off the port side, the explosions covering the deck with mud and water. For more than six hours waves of bombers continued to swoop down from the mountains. Hutchinson and the gunners continued their barrage, braving further torrents of mud, water and splinters. *Carlisle* suffered several more near misses, but no serious damage. Eventually, the ship raised anchor and withdrew down the fjord. 'They still came,' wrote Hutchinson, 'but we literally blasted our way out . . . We were ready for dropping – my eyes ached that much that they seemed to make my neck ache, and every bit of my body. We strained our eyes over the mountains and into the sun and the snow seemed to sparkle and dazzle you.' The experience had been exhilarating at times, petrifying at others, but few were eager to repeat it. 'That was our first Christening,' he told his battered and discoloured notebook, 'and we can't have anything worse now, whatever happens.'

Soon, every sailor would have a similar story about devastating air attacks. Trawler crews shared tales of the *Aston Villa*, crippled by bombs from Stukas near Namsos, which was rumoured to have 'sunk herself so as the Germans could not collect any details of the submarine detecting gear'. Whenever bombers were sighted on the horizon, wrote William Robertson, there was a collective intake of breath, followed by 'many sighs and thank Gods' should a confrontation be avoided.

'I think most of us agree that air attacks are a very demoralizing sort of attack to the nerves,' wrote Able Seaman Hall of HMS *Glasgow*. 'I must say I would rather be on land for a raid than in a ship,' wrote John Adams of HMS *Walker*. 'One feels so naked and exposed on the upper deck and unable to dodge, and also one knows that the plane is attacking you.' In the narrow enclosed fjords, aircraft could appear with little warning. Stukas dived out of the dazzling sun, meaning lookouts often had to rely on their hearing. Many were only alerted to an attack by the sound of engine roar and the whistling of incoming bombs. The usual defensive manoeuvre was simply to increase speed and constantly alter course. Bombers at high altitude were beyond the range of small ships, although gunners could rarely resist trying their luck. When two distant aircraft drew machine-gun fire from *Northern Spray*, William Robertson noted that 'our Lewis gunners were told off for wasting ammunition'.

Over the course of April, German infantry with strong support from the air swept north from Oslo towards the ports of central Norway, and recently landed battalions of British troops began to retreat. Allied ships were sent to rescue them. HMS *Carlisle* was at Namsos and, on the evening of 30 April, HMS *Walker* entered Romsdal fjord as part of a force which was to evacuate soldiers from Andalsnes. 'We went in amongst the high mountains all covered in snow,' wrote John Adams in his diary, 'several fishermen and their wives watching us from the shore.' The late evening twilight allowed him to see that the town was 'in indescribable ruins – not a wall standing and fires everywhere'. Nearly 600 soldiers were embarked and taken to a cruiser to be transported home. 'They were in a completely demoralised state,' wrote Adams, 'and had been machine gunned and bombed the whole day.' *Walker* returned to the docks to collect more passengers. By now, many of the sailors had had an opportunity to hear first-hand accounts of the campaign from their compatriots. 'There were only 120 men left from 1200 of the Sherwood Foresters,' wrote Adams, 'and they had only been ashore a week!'

While relieved soldiers crammed below decks, German divebombers caused havoc in the enclosed fjords. At Namsos, the sloop HMS *Bittern* suffered a direct hit and survivors were brought aboard HMS *Carlisle*. 'I've never seen such a grim sight in my life before,' wrote Charles Hutchinson. 'We are like a hospital ship – men wounded and bandaged lying everywhere – the ship is packed. If we stop much longer I reckon the lot of us will go – it's sheer madness and everyone thinks so . . . there is one poor fellow with his face badly cut and he is blind, and all he keeps saying is: "When will I be able to see?" There are a lot that look in a terrible state.'

With German troops closing in on Andalsnes, *Walker* stayed to cover the last of the rescue force the following night. As the last ships of the convoy were leaving the fjord, German aircraft appeared from behind the mountains and attacked. 'I could see the bombs coming the whole way,' wrote Adams. The destroyer escaped with a near miss, making for the open sea as fast as the engine room could manage. Looking back to the fjord, Adams could see neither ships nor aircraft, only 'shells bursting up in the sky'. It had been a narrow escape. Fearing that his shaken comrades needed reassurance, Adams reached for his bible: 'I read the lesson about Daniel and the Lions on the quarterdeck.'

On 10 May German forces finally launched their long-expected invasion of the Low Countries and France. Meanwhile, the struggle for Narvik continued unabated. *Walker* was sent to assist and suffered yet more air attacks and several near misses. 'The ship's company's nerves are in a terrible state,' Adams admitted. *Walker* spent the final week of May on patrol around the fjord, helping to protect ships heading out to sea and searching for elusive enemy submarines. 'There were German planes around us the whole time,' wrote Adams. 'Where are our fighters?!' *Walker*'s time with the destroyer force at Narvik culminated in an attack by Heinkel bombers, small groups coming in waves over the course of two hours. The result, wrote Adams, was 'absolute pandemonium. Eight ships zigzagging like fury, everyone blazing into the sky and almost impossible to see planes. We had 52 bombs dropped on ourselves alone.'

Narvik was briefly recaptured at the end of May, but by this time the situation in France was becoming critical, as resistance began to crumble in the face of the relentless advance of German tanks. The decision was made to withdraw British and French troops from Norway altogether, and by the beginning of June another hasty evacuation was underway at Narvik. *Northern Spray* headed for the Lofoten archipelago, to the west of Narvik and away from immediate danger. But first she had to negotiate the Nordstrandskir minefield at night. 'We were ordered on deck wearing our lifebelts, while the ship's speed was reduced to dead slow,' recorded William Robertson. A minesweeper only a few hundred yards ahead hit a magnetic mine, which exploded. 'We had a hell of a shock,' he wrote.

As ships laden with evacuated soldiers traversed the Norwegian Sea they were harried and harassed by enemy forces. 'We trudged home at 7 knots,' wrote John Adams of HMS *Walker*, 'with enemy ships and aircraft all around, but – thank God – never seen.' Six vessels were lost during the escape, and the warship carrying the

Norwegian government only narrowly avoided being hit. By far the most devastating and controversial sinking was the aircraft carrier HMS *Glorious*, overtaken by the German battleship *Scharnhorst* and pounded by her guns. The signal to abandon ship caused immediate chaos. Marine Ronald Healiss recalled 'a flood of humanity, pressing through the shell debris and the wreckage, running with the ugly current of a crowd'. Men gathered at their appointed positions, 'in flocks, sheep-like', just as they had during emergency drills. Several immediately leapt overboard, condemning themselves to being stranded in the open seas as the doomed carrier steamed on.

*Glorious* listed dramatically, sailors ascending to the edge before summoning the courage to leap off. 'Little knots of men clawed each other round the waist as they clambered up the rails,' wrote Healiss, 'laughing and swearing as they stripped off their boots and trousers and prepared to jump.' Healiss described the moment he reached the brink: 'I saw the ship's screw on the starboard side still churning beneath me. It was going to be one hell of a jump. I didn't want to hit that ruddy great green bronze screw, nor any of those oily black bobbing heads in the water.' He survived, and endured four days and nights in a damaged lifeboat before being rescued, one of only three officers and forty ratings from the ship's company of 1,200 men.

Many sailors were proud of their achievements, particularly the sinking of so many German destroyers at Narvik. A young rating in the battlecruiser HMS *Hood* wrote a letter home describing his disappointment at missing the campaign: 'I should have loved to have been in that.' German forces sustained 5,550 casualties in total during the campaign and the Luftwaffe lost over 200 planes, despite its aerial superiority. Crucially, the German navy had lost four of its most useful cruisers, and so many precious modern destroyers had been sunk or seriously damaged that Raeder was left unable to contemplate any significant naval operation, including support for a cross-Channel invasion of Britain.

Norway had brought many British matelots face to face with their counterparts for the first time since the war's outbreak. In HMS *Warspite*, which had sunk eight enemy destroyers at Narvik, the reaction to prisoners of war was one of good-natured sympathy.

Despite official discouragement, fraternization was common, and gifts of cigarettes and chocolate changed hands readily. One rating explained: 'They didn't have two heads, nor had they horns or cloven hooves. They were just seamen like ourselves, doing a job they had been ordered to do.'

Yet Norway had also been a traumatic experience. Including the casualties from *Glorious*, the British lost 4,500 men, eclipsing even the 1,800 Norwegian deaths. For sailors, the apparent inability of the Fleet Air Arm to impose itself was a serious failing, and their exposure to air attack was a new and uncomfortable experience. To Able Seaman Hall of HMS *Glasgow*, Norway seemed to consist of 'mental strain but not much else'. There was little doubt that morale had been shaken. One young stoker in HMS *Warspite* recalled having to step over the bodies of wounded men who had been laid out on the messdeck: 'You knew this was definitely for real, especially when a young fellow asked me to cover his legs as they were cold, and you had to make believe, as he had lost both of them.' Although the bravery of officers such as Warburton-Lee of HMS *Hardy* had been widely praised, for many ordinary sailors the pattern of posthumous Victoria Crosses was troubling. As Able Seaman Hall noted: 'Guess the saying they have about "Bloody war and quick promotion" about sums up their outlook on life.'

For sailors arriving home from Norway the news of the German advances in France came as an unwelcome shock. 'Events have been happening so quickly that it is almost impossible to put them down on paper,' wrote John Adams. On 23 May, the talk in HMS *Walker* was that 'the Germans have captured Boulogne, and raided Yorkshire and Kent. Lots of Fascists have been arrested. The Government have made a bill turning over everyone's property to the state.'

In fact, Boulogne was not quite lost. Transport ships supported by navy destroyers had been sent to evacuate civilians and British soldiers on the verge of capture. As German forces neared, the operation became more frantic, with destroyers firing at enemy troops and aircraft alike. Refugees were embarked only at the discretion of commanding officers, and many desperate French civilians were turned away. Meanwhile, discipline amongst soldiers waiting to depart was occasionally precarious. One man was shot by a young subaltern after breaking ranks and rushing towards the gangway of a waiting ship.

Near the end of the evacuation, on 23 May, the destroyer HMS *Keith* was embarking troops when she came under heavy attack both from the air and from inland. Splinters from mortars and bombs pierced the exposed bridge and the captain was killed by a sniper's bullet. The first lieutenant took over, despite being wounded, and ordered every man on the bridge to take cover.

Lieutenant Graham Lumsden, who had engineered his own transfer away from a quiet post in Sierra Leone, was now *Keith*'s navigator:

It was a bitter experience for men of the Royal Navy to lie down under fire for several long minutes while the bombs crashed all round us and expecting any second to be hit . . . As the seemingly endless bombing continued I, no doubt like many others, found that lying on the deck while under fire was an undignified, unsuitable, indeed unacceptable position for a professional officer . . . So I got to my feet, remarking to the First Lieutenant that I had had enough of it.

He managed to steer *Keith* out of the harbour, and eventually back to Dover. She was patched up and sent to Dunkirk. By the end of 26 May, nearly 30,000 men had already been brought home from northern France, mostly support staff and other so-called 'useless mouths'. Thereafter, it was Dunkirk and the beaches to the east of the town that became the focal point for the next rescue.

Operation Dynamo – the British code name for the Dunkirk evacuation – competed for resources with the ongoing campaign in Norway, not to mention the Atlantic and Britain's other global maritime commitments. Yet a total of thirty-eight destroyers, one anti-aircraft cruiser and one hundred minesweepers were sent to embark the Allied troops pushed back to the coast of northern France by the German advance, and to protect the escape routes across the English Channel. After an appeal from the Admiralty for assistance, more than forty converted passenger ferries and several hundred tugs, trawlers, barges, dredgers, yachts and small craft were put at the disposal of Dover Command and made their way across the Channel. Some estimated that as many as 700 civilian 'little ships' aided the evacuation. Some were borrowed, some were commandeered, and many others were crewed by ordinary citizens. There was also a strong international element to the rescue fleet. Nineteen French destroyers and torpedo boats, one Polish destroyer, several Belgian tugboats and dozens of French civilian craft took part. More than forty Dutch *schuyts* – motor boats known to British sailors as 'skoots' – gave sterling service in the shallow waters.

Dunkirk itself was a modern working port with several miles of quayside and docks. Heavy damage from incessant bombing meant that the harbour's eastern mole became the focal point of the operation. Little more than a narrow wooden jetty, exposed and difficult for ships to manoeuvre alongside, it became the main embarkation point for the thousands of British and French soldiers who were to be evacuated. Soldiers arriving at the coast around Dunkirk also congregated along a few miles of sandy beaches to the east of the port, many queuing for boats, some wading and swimming out to waiting vessels.

In J. B. Priestley's memorable phrase, the 'little holiday steamers made an excursion to hell'. Burning oil produced a thick pall of black smoke which billowed ominously over the port. The explosions of bombs and shells could be heard in Dover. Fires raged incessantly, burning through buildings and the remnants of the transport and equipment of the British and French armies. 'Piles of French dead were stacked on the pier,' wrote one soldier after his return home. Men swarmed on the surrounding beaches, as one contemporary account had it, 'like some mighty ant heap upturned by a giant's foot'. 'Down on the beach you immediately felt yourself surrounded by a deadly evil atmosphere,' wrote one soldier. 'A horrible stench of blood and mutilated flesh pervaded the place. There was no escape from it.'

The sight of ships and naval uniforms proved exhilarating for many soldiers. 'My first reaction was incredible contentment,' wrote Arnold Johnson of reaching the beaches at La Panne on 28 May. 'The Navy is in charge! What a relief to escape from the confusion and chaos on the road to Ypres and find ourselves in the hands of the

Navy.' 'The first thing I noticed when looking out,' wrote one army medical officer, 'was the reassuring shapes of our navy ships steaming up and down in the channel. I felt a wave of comfort at their presence.' On board the destroyer HMS *Malcolm*, army chaplain Ted Brabyn wrote in his diary: 'Never was a prayer more heartfelt than the one "Thank God we've got a Navy".'

If sailors at Dunkirk were seen as saviours, their practical roles were as organizers, transporters and protectors. At the mole, the logistics of embarkation proved relatively straightforward. Lines of troops were easier to organize here, and despite several moments of confusion and one occasion when the jetty was erroneously reported to be unusable, the physical movement of men was carried out with remarkable efficiency.

Lifting soldiers from the beaches proved far more problematic. Small boats and coastal craft that could run in close to the sand ferried small groups of men out to the larger ships offshore. Some soldiers were able to make their own escape from the beaches, but most were lifted off by lifeboats, rowing boats, yachts and smaller craft. Many struggled to find the energy to get aboard, let alone to help row back to the ships. Lieutenant Robert Hichens, working to ferry troops from the beaches, wrote in his diary that 'the unfortunate soldiers were the most awkward ham handed stiffs I have ever seen near a boat, poor things. I was so sorry for them. They were so tired and so pathetically helpless with the sea, with all their equipment.'

Sub-Lieutenant Bill Hewett of the minesweeper HMS *Sutton* took a lifeboat to the shore and ferried men back and forth to the ship. On 28 May, the ship embarked over 500 soldiers between 9.30 p.m. and 2 a.m., most in groups of no more than twenty-five. 'It was rather a desperate business at times,' wrote Hewett, 'in the boats crammed with troops, trying to handle them in the swell and the wash of bombs.' When a nearby whaler overturned, he reported, 'we pulled out all the fellows we could reach – some sank with all the ridiculous ironmongery tied on to them.'

Some soldiers had been given strict instructions by superiors not to discard their equipment. If a soldier slipped into the sea in full gear, obedience would be fatal. 'I saw lots of men drowned wearing overcoats and packs,' recalled gunner Bill Richardson. 'They were wading up to their necks with all this gear and carrying rifles over their heads. I screamed at them to throw away their rifles, do anything, save themselves. I watched them pulled over backwards by the tide and drowned. Lots and lots of them.' Others worried that they would have to pay for any equipment lost in France. Lawrence Vollans lugged his heavy anti-tank gun all the way to a ship: 'When it came to my turn, I handed [the sailor] the anti-tank rifle first. "What's this?" he asked, grasping it by the barrel. "It's a Boyes anti-tank rifle," I replied. "You won't be needing that any more," he said, and promptly dropped it into the sea.'

Getting from the sea onto a ship was perhaps the most arduous task of all. 'In the blackness we could hear the shouts of the sailors encouraging the men as they swam to the boats,' recalled Sergeant Bill Brodie. 'Now it was so near doubts began to creep in, it did not look so easy to reach the tenders and in the phosphorescent glow of the breakers we could see the bodies of men who had not made it being gently washed ashore on the rising tide.'

Overloading was a constant danger. Karl Engler had managed to get aboard a small crowded vessel. 'Everyone in the boat made an effort to get rid of the chaps hanging on,' he recalled. 'They had to kick their hands until they let go. Unfortunately, some of them could not swim and as by now we were in fairly deep water some just struggled away. It was an experience I was not proud to be a part of but it was the only chance of survival we had.' Sergeant Leonard Howard of the Royal Engineers described the actions of an officer in charge of one overcrowded boat: 'He ordered one man who was hanging on the side to get away – but he didn't, so he shot him through the head. From the people around, there was no reaction at all. There was such chaos on the beach that that didn't seem out of keeping.'

In the early part of the operation, the priority was to evacuate British soldiers before their French counterparts. 'My instructions are that the safety of the B.E.F. is the primary consideration,' wrote Lord Gort, the army's commander-in-chief, on 29 May. 'Every Frenchman embarked is in place of one Englishman.' Rear Admiral

Frederic Wake-Walker, the navy's senior officer at Dunkirk, had similar orders: 'Refuse them embarkation if the British troops are ready to embark.' It meant that drastic measures were occasionally taken to deal with frustrated French soldiers. Sergeant Bill Brodie described how one group 'made a rush to the shore and grabbed a rowing boat. They clambered aboard and started to row. They did not get far for a burst of fire from a Bren gun manned by a naval rating stopped them immediately and we saw the boat floating upside down and some more bodies in the sea.'

'Some difficulty experienced through persistent attempts of large masses of French troops to intercept boats and demand passage,' reported the commanding officer of the minesweeper HMS *Sutton* on 29 May. 'Assisted by British troops in heading off French swimmers by rifle fire from 50 yards further along beach.' Lance Corporal Peter Wells was waiting to board a destroyer when 'a French officer started to rush up the gangway, and the naval lieutenant on the bridge told him to stop. This bloke wasn't standing for it – he carried on running up. So the lieutenant drew his pistol and shot the Frenchman dead.'

Despite so many traumatic incidents, a total of 98,780 men were evacuated from the beaches during the operation. Meanwhile, over 239,000 – more than double the total taken from the beaches – boarded ships from the mole at Dunkirk. Yet if embarkation here was logistically easier, it was by no means safer. The mole was a target for air bombardment, and reaching the larger ships – sometimes involving passage in a smaller craft – remained fraught with peril. Many soldiers were forced to leap onto scramble nets, or reach for the hands of sailors or friends already on board. When ships were full, sailors left in a hurry. 'They just got hold of the gangways and pulled them away,' recalled Private Samuel Love. 'They got hold of the rope ladders and started shaking men off.'

Most of the troops lifted from Dunkirk and the beaches were taken home on big ships: ferries designed to carry large numbers of passengers, and the destroyers which supported them. Once on board, relief was the overriding emotion. Many soldiers fell asleep instantly. Most of those arriving at Dunkirk had been without regular rations for some time, surviving instead on food looted or scrounged from civilian homes and farms. Major Pat McSwiney remained desperate for food even when safely on board HMS *Shikari*: 'The ship's dog seemed to be gnawing a bone with some meat still left on it. I decided my need was greater, so I stole the bone and gnawed it myself.'

In comparison with vulnerable ferries, destroyers were less comfortable but appeared to be safer havens. 'The ship kept vibrating with the eruption of explosions,' wrote Gregory Blaxland, evacuated in HMS *Icarus*, 'and I assumed they were caused by her own gunfire. I had made up my mind in a most uncharacteristic manner that the enemy could not possibly harm us.' Richard Doll recalled that 'though whilst we were waiting to start several shells fell quite near us I never really appreciated that we might be sunk'.

For sailors it was a very different matter. To remain stationary and clustered under air attack was, of course, counter to every captain's deepest instincts and required no little nerve. One soldier described the sight of a destroyer being attacked: 'The bomber swooped, there was a cloud of smoke and spray, and when this cleared there was no sign of the ship.' Although Stuka dive-bombing attacks were not always as deadly as they appeared to be, ships at Dunkirk were certainly not safe.

RAF fighters did what they could, but they were precious weapons and their numbers were restricted to preserve them for the imminent German assault on Britain itself. The first day of severe naval losses was 29 May. Bombing raids on the east mole caused near-panic. Barely half of the men aboard the paddle steamers *Waverley* and *Crested Eagle* were saved when they were hit. Humphry Boys-Smith, a reservist naval officer, had commandeered a small Dutch *schuyt* on the Thames, and replaced its crew with six British seamen. He was watching when the paddle steamer *Gracie Fields*, packed tight with troops, was attacked by a dive-bomber. One explosion caused damage to the steering cables, making the vessel 'career along at full speed in a circle'.

'The carnage was horrifying,' Boys-Smith continued. 'The ship's decks resembled an abattoir or a butcher's shop. Ribbons of human flesh festooned the rigging . . . The survivors could scarcely keep their feet, so slippery were the decks with blood.' They helped to transfer some of the injured to the *schuyt*, and other ships came to help before *Gracie Fields* finally sank. On his return to Ramsgate after the operation had ended, Boys-Smith 'was met by an infuriated Dutch officer who accused me of stealing his craft. I could not be bothered with him and went to bed.'

On the same day, the destroyer HMS *Wakeful* had just embarked a full load of soldiers when she was attacked by a German *Schnellboot*, a fast motor craft known to the British as an E-boat. A torpedo hit the forward boiler room, causing *Wakeful* to split in two and sink within seconds. Soldiers had been packed into the engine room, the boiler room, the store rooms, and any spare space below decks. Only one of the 640 soldiers survived, and no more than twenty-five of the ship's company were picked up by minesweepers which arrived at the scene shortly afterwards. In the chaos and confusion which followed, another destroyer, HMS *Grafton*, was hit by two torpedoes from a German submarine. The hundreds of soldiers she was carrying below decks had to be controlled at gunpoint. Ships attempting to assist ended up firing on one another, and the commanding officer of *Grafton* was killed in the melee. Eventually, the troops from *Grafton* were transferred to other vessels, soldiers and sailors singing 'Abide With Me' in harmony as they waited.

Fifteen British and four French ships were sunk on 29 May, along with three vital personnel carriers. So severe were these losses that the naval authorities insisted on the temporary withdrawal of precious modern destroyers from the operation. The first appeal for 'little ships' was broadcast that evening. Yet the losses continued. James Stevenson, of the Grenadier Guards, was on board a hospital ship with seven pieces of shrapnel in his leg. 'I was lying on deck when Jerry bombed us,' he recalled. 'The blast of one bomb took the skin off my hands and face, set me alight and blew to pieces several of the men near me. I rolled over to the side of the ship and jumped into the sea because I was alight. I swam back to Dunkirk and as they pulled me out on the beach I remember hearing somebody say "Poor bastard." My eyes and mouth had been stuck together by the blast wave and I could just about breathe through one nostril.' He passed out and eventually came to in a hospital ward in Dover.

On 1 June the extra destroyers were returned to Dunkirk. It led to another day of terrible damage. Nine warships and personnel transports were sunk or put out of action, and the destroyers were removed once again. When HMS *Ivanhoe* was immobilized, she had to be towed by tug across the Channel with the captain's steering instructions relayed verbally from man to man through the ship, so that sailors could move the rudder by hand. Soldiers had to stretch waterproof material over a waterline hole in the hull. During the passage, the tow rope broke several times and the ship survived air attacks to limp into harbour.

The sea was not an inevitable means of salvation. Of the thirty-eight destroyers involved in Operation Dynamo, six were sunk and twenty-six were damaged. Of forty-six personnel carriers, nine were sunk and eleven damaged. Overall, nearly one in five of the ships that took part was sunk, and nearly half were damaged. Of the eighty-four 'big ships' involved, fifty-two were sunk or sustained damage.

Yet despite the Luftwaffe's supremacy over the course of the evacuation, it was unable to prevent the Royal Navy and its allies from rescuing 338,226 men by 4 June, including around 225,000 British and 120,000 French soldiers. From a total of 68,111 British servicemen killed, wounded and captured during the retreat and evacuation, there were 7,000 casualties from the Royal Navy. Around 40,000 Frenchmen who remained were captured, many of whom had contributed to a vital rearguard defence. 'They were fine fellows, those soldiers,' wrote Sub-Lieutenant Hewett, 'they deliberately stayed behind while the last of the B.E.F. got out, holding back the Germans in the streets of Dunkirk.'

Operation Dynamo required a monumental effort of organization. A total of 848 vessels of all descriptions had come under the control of Vice-Admiral Bertram Ramsay's naval headquarters in Dover. Although many of the small craft commandeered by the Admiralty were operated by naval officers and manned with navy personnel, merchant sailors played a central role in the evacuation, and ordinary individuals provided far more than moral support. That such an armada could be formed was testament to stoic service and civilian sacrifice. That it could be monitored, managed and manoeuvred was a matter of bureaucracy and administration. From Ramsay's operations rooms beneath Dover Castle, to the staff at Ramsgate who handed out thousands of charts and instructions to little ships, to Admiral Wake-Walker and Captain Bill Tennant, in command on the ground at Dunkirk and along the dunes, Dynamo was an achievement of improvisation and organization. Ramsay wrote to his wife after the end of the operation:

> The success is mostly due to the first class direction and management of the show equally with glorious courage, skill and endurance of the personnel of all the ships. The one without the other would have been ineffective. We can always count on the glorious deeds but less often on good direction and management. This may sound as self praise but it is nevertheless the plain truth.

Exhausted troops arrived back at Dover and Ramsgate, many wearing uniforms still saturated with seawater. Naval officials, civilian aid workers and local residents helped to treat, refresh and organize the returning troops before they were whisked away to remote camps in packed trains. In Dover, any Wrens that could be spared from the naval headquarters were sent down to the docks. First Officer Nancy Currie described their efforts:

> We grudged the time we had to eat and hardly slept for more than an hour or so at a stretch. We helped to deal with men coming ashore. We undid the boots of those lying along the seafront. We improvised pillows for some who were too weak to tell us their next-of-kin. We drove any car anywhere – to and from the hospitals and back to the pier heads to fill them up again with men too exhausted to walk. We cut sandwiches and poured cocoa; we rolled bandages. Meanwhile work at the Castle and the base went on . . . and I never once heard a Wren say that she was tired.

Although it was unprecedented in scale and strategically critical, Dunkirk was merely the latest evacuation conducted by the Royal Navy, and several more soon followed. Further to the west, near

Dieppe, an attempt was made to rescue the 51st Highland Division from the exposed beaches of St-Valéry-en-Caux. Just over 2,000 were picked up, before the remaining 6,000 surrendered to German forces. At Le Havre, rescue efforts were more successful, with some 11,000 men evacuated. Even after Dunkirk, more than 100,000 British soldiers remained in France, many of them support staff, and at the end of May even more infantry troops had been landed in a short-lived attempt to bolster the French army. In mid-June there were frantic evacuations from Cherbourg in Normandy and several locations in Brittany including St Malo, Brest and St Nazaire. Over 144,000 British troops were rescued in these operations, more than half the total embarked at Dunkirk, along with over 18,000 French and nearly 30,000 Polish and Czech soldiers.

Lieutenant John Mosse was helping to direct the evacuation at St Nazaire. His ship, HMS *Havelock*, had been sent directly from Norway to France and on 17 June she was one of many destroyers and smaller vessels shuttling troops and stores from the quayside to larger ships offshore. He was on the bridge of the destroyer *Highlander* when the converted passenger liner *Lancastria* was struck by bombs. 'She had just embarked five thousand troops,' wrote Mosse. 'We watched her roll over and sink. For a while the side of her hull remained above water with hundreds of men sitting on it singing lustily before they floated off.'

The weather was good and the sea was calm, but thousands were trapped below decks with little chance of survival. Many of those who made it safely into the water became victims of oil, debris and exhaustion. Small boats rescued as many as they could. Of those brought aboard *Highlander*, wrote Mosse, 'half a dozen "corpses" were brought round by artificial respiration of which I claim a couple'. On hand to help were several 'women of the Church Army whose quiet calm as they attended the wounded and shocked was an example to all'.

It was a traumatic incident, the full details of which were kept secret. Between 3,000 and 4,000 were estimated to have been killed: the single greatest loss of life from a British vessel in the entire war. Mosse described a tugboat which came alongside *Highlander* 'with some survivors who had been picked up out of a large patch of oil fuel. They had discarded their clothing, and their gleaming bodies were black to the last detail. Some wag started singing negro spirituals and we all felt better.'

Despite such a tragic end to the evacuations, sailors were unanimously proud of their efforts. Although Dunkirk produced a sense of foreboding for British civilians, next in line for the German onslaught, it also encouraged a feeling of relief. 'When the last Allied soldier is withdrawn from Dunkerque,' wrote Charles Thomas to his father at the end of May, 'the enemy can be said to have lost the war. A country is not defeated until its army in the field is defeated and the enemy have not succeeded in doing this yet.' His ship, HMS *Capetown*, was now in the Mediterranean, and he was eager to see action: 'At the time of writing unfortunately we belong to those "who also serve who only stand and wait" – not a pleasant job when our one ambition is to have a smack at the enemy.'

While troops were being rescued from the French coasts, the Mediterranean had remained relatively peaceful. Officers continued to enjoy the usual leisure pursuits. At Alexandria, Lieutenant Henry Hackforth of HMS *Orion* kept a daily chronicle of tennis matches, horse racing, dinner parties and cocktail functions. It ended abruptly. On 10 June, he wrote 'ITALY DECLARES WAR ON ALLIES AND BOMBS MALTA.'

Italy's declaration of war was fully expected but, combined with the continued German advance into the heart of France, it was still an unwelcome development. 'Today's news says Germans have crossed the Seine and the Wops are against us,' wrote Vere Wight-Boycott, first lieutenant of HMS *Delight*, on 10 June. 'We seem really up against it now . . . We have fought worse odds before I think, and still won the last battle.' 'I suppose the news of the last few days shook you a bit,' wrote the recently evacuated soldier L. G. Baylis in a letter to his parents. 'Perhaps we finally realise what the German army is like. Thank God we've got a Navy and pray that the French fleet stays on our side.'

The French government signed an armistice with Germany on 22

June. HMS *Kent* was at Ceylon, preparing to sail for the Mediterranean. The news was met with stoic defiance. 'After the first shock and a slight general depression,' wrote George Blundell in his diary, 'the general feeling in the ship is "Fight to the Death", and the sailors mostly think it is bound to come right in the end . . . England against Europe! How magnificent! Now the fight's on. I pray for our folk at home. Can they take it? I'm afraid the women and children may squeal.' Blundell was in little doubt as to what would now be the critical factor: 'As I see it, the immediate future hangs on whether the Germans or ourselves get hold of the French Navy.'

Despite the assurances of Admiral Darlan, a member of the newly formed Vichy government and in command of the French fleet, that he would not allow his ships to be commandeered by the Kriegsmarine, there were grave fears within the Admiralty of this potential outcome. Although the Royal Navy enjoyed an overwhelming numerical and material advantage over its enemy, the addition of France's modern and powerful warships, not to mention her numerous other ships and submarines, would more than even the odds.

A plan known as Operation Catapult was put into action to eliminate the threat. Around the world, French ships were confronted with ultimatums. The submarine *Surcouf* was seized at Plymouth, and the battleship *Richelieu* was disabled at Dakar. In Alexandria, British warships surrounded the French. The odds were overwhelming: HMS *Warspite*, *Malaya* and *Royal Sovereign* faced the French battleship *Lorraine*; a swarm of British destroyers and cruisers covered three French heavy cruisers; HMS *Orion* with *Neptune* and *Calcutta* were alongside the cruiser *Duguay-Trouin*. Smaller French ships were swamped by a host of other British vessels. Guns were trained on each other at point-blank range, a throwback to the days of sail. 'Hostilities at that range were too terrible to contemplate,' wrote Lieutenant Henry Hackforth of *Orion*.

Admiral Andrew Cunningham was charged with securing the submission of the French forces. He was able to convince his counterpart to stand down without resorting to fire. French sailors disabled their ships, and oil flowed freely into the harbour. Hackforth was relieved but recorded that, by common consensus, the

British sailors 'were quite ready if necessary to "knock hell out of those Frogs"'. John Smith of HMS *Neptune*, who had just turned seventeen, described the stand-off in a rather different way in his diary: 'French ships in harbour gave a lot of trouble. Boarding parties. All want to go home but we will not let them.'

Many of the most powerful French warships were in the port of Mers-el-Kébir, near Oran in Algeria. Here, Admiral James Somerville was tasked with securing their surrender. The ultimatum put to the French gave them the choice to sail with the British, to sail to ports in Britain or the West Indies in order to neutralize themselves, or to scuttle their ships within six hours. There was mounting pressure on Somerville to resolve the situation quickly, with messages from London demanding news and urging action. Ultimately, with no French response forthcoming, he was ordered on 3 July to destroy the resisting French warships using every means possible. 'We have seen our first action,' wrote Bernard Williams, anti-aircraft gunner in HMS *Hood*, 'although I regret to say it was against the French fleet. We went down to Oran to try and make the French come to a reasonable agreement to prevent them falling in the hands of the enemy but they refused all our offers although we allowed them all day to make up their minds so we had no alternative but to open fire.'

'What a bombardment!' recalled one sailor. 'I had never seen anything like it.' The roar of the broadside was ferocious, as shells from the line of British battleships cascaded into the harbour. There was short-lived resistance from the guns of French warships and shore batteries. Destroyers guarding the battleships were straddled by French shells, some of which contained coloured dyes intended to aid accuracy. 'Blue, green and yellow – very colourful,' wrote Captain Francis de Winton, commanding the 13th Destroyer Flotilla from HMS *Keppel*.

Bernard Williams and his fellow anti-aircraft gunners had an excellent vantage point, but were also exposed. 'Things got a bit warm,' he wrote, 'and as we couldn't do any good we took cover as shrapnel from the French shells was beginning to get too close for comfort and we were expecting to get a salvo inboard any minute but we had a charmed life.' For many of the young men aboard *Hood*, this first taste of action was not without fear. Seventeen-year-old Bill Crawford wrote home: 'For a while there was Hell and I do not know yet how we were not hit, except for the shrapnel that was flying around everywhere.' In a letter to his brother Jim he admitted, 'It was pretty hot there for a while . . . as we were the Flagship their fire was concentrated on us. You could see most of the shells coming, and I can tell you I did not feel so good.' Williams was also honest in his letter home: 'I must admit I felt a bit funny in the stomach when I heard the shells whistling over the top of our heads, the only pity is that it wasn't the Italians.'

Compared to a mere handful of British casualties, there were nearly 1,300 French deaths. The battleship *Bretagne* was engulfed by an explosion, two other battleships and several smaller warships were seriously damaged, including *Dunkerque*, which had graced the Coronation Review of 1937. Yet despite the carnage, the battleship *Strasbourg* and four destroyers managed to escape, evading pursuing ships and aircraft from *Ark Royal*, eventually reaching the safe haven of Toulon. It was far from the end of the Vichy French threat in the Mediterranean.

Before the war, British admirals and sailors alike had harboured hopes of a fleet action, a face-to-face confrontation between the major battleships of the opposing sides, in the tradition of Trafalgar or Jutland. It was a bitter irony that when this fleet battle occurred it involved the decimation not of an enemy, but of a former ally. 'It was a fine sight,' wrote Captain Francis de Winton of the attempt to catch *Strasbourg*, 'and must have been rare in the war, to see two destroyer flotillas ahead of a battle squadron in full pursuit of the enemy . . . The only thing was, this was the wrong enemy, at the wrong place and the wrong time.'

'We all feel thoroughly dirty and ashamed that the first time we have been in action was an affair like this,' wrote Admiral James Somerville to his wife. 'I feel I will be blamed for bungling the job and I think I did. But to you I don't mind confessing that I was half-hearted and you can't win an action that way.' Nevertheless, the ruthless operation was a sign of the sincerity of British resistance, and was acknowledged around the world, not least in the United States.

British public opinion, according to Home Intelligence reports, was marked by 'general relief'. Within the armed forces, a similar feeling was evident. 'To many of us here,' wrote Charles Thomas in HMS *Capetown*, 'the action taken against the French fleet was a surprise. A heartening surprise because it dispelled our fears that the Govt were a crowd of washerwomenish humanitarians.'

Mers-el-Kébir was also the first major operation for Force H, a rag-tag collection of cruisers, battleships, an aircraft carrier and destroyers drawn together from four flotillas, and proved the first act of a new phase of the war in the Mediterranean. British squadrons immediately set off to seek out Italian warships. As Bernard Williams of HMS *Hood* explained in a letter, 'We steamed down the Med. in the hopes of "testing the quality of the ice-cream" as the Admiral put it but all we saw of them was their air-force who gave us rather a warm welcome.'

*Hood* managed to avoid being hit by bombs, but there were some near misses which had an unsettling effect on the ship's company. 'It was most unpleasant to hear the bombs whistling down,' wrote Williams. 'The slightest bang for a couple of days afterwards made the blokes jump. It is a bit nerve racking but everybody did his job without any panic and we are getting used to alarms now.' Young Bill Crawford was philosophical about the threat: 'May the Itie's and Gerry's bombs make holes in the sea as it doesn't cost much to fill those kind of holes in.'

A month earlier, submariner Ian Anderson had finally entered the war proper. After having spent the first ten months in the Far East and touring the Indian Ocean, HMS *Odin* had moved to Malta and was scheduled for her maiden patrol in the Mediterranean. On the evening of 4 June, the crew prepared for their first taste of action. There were rumours that Italy might soon be entering the war. Anderson took a moment to record his thoughts in his diary:

Tonight we sail, just in case, so that we shall be all set to do our worst at the earliest opportunity. I don't think I shall take this diary with me; it would be a pity for it, as well as myself, to be fish food if the worst occurred. Personally I still feel optimistic and believe that

Musso is merely putting up a gigantic bluff and that it won't be long before the excitement of the moment will have died down and be a thing of the past. And then perhaps I'll get home. There is no time for more now as there is much to be done and so, for the time being, I bid farewell to myself, and, incidentally, to anyone who has waded through the monotonous monologue of these pages.

Ten days later, the submarine was attacked by Italian destroyers in the Gulf of Taranto and hit by a depth charge. It sank with the loss of all fifty-five men. Ian Anderson had been away from home for three years, and the outbreak of war had postponed his return to Britain. Shortly before his final patrol, he had written a letter for his family, as had many of his fellow submariners. It was left ashore along with his diary to be sent home in the event of his death. He wrote:

I sincerely hope you will never receive it but I should hate to die without making a farewell of some kind to you all . . . I hate this finish to everything as much as you do especially as there has been no chance of seeing you first. It is a little hard after three years to be robbed of the leave I had so much looked forward to. But I do hope you won't be sad . . . And in a few years time no doubt we shall all meet again and the things which have seemed so important on this earth, which have made us sad or glad or happy or angry or bored or excited or disappointed will all have been forgotten in the content of that new place.

And so good-bye and remember: No Tears!

With my love to you all

Ian

## 5. The Sea Will Run Red

'All one discusses is the situation at home,' wrote Charles Hutchinson on 18 June 1940. HMS *Carlisle* was in the Red Sea, escorting convoys between Aden and Port Sudan. At ten minutes to four that afternoon, Winston Churchill stood at the Dispatch Box in the House of Commons to make one of the great speeches of the war. The Prime Minister discussed the catastrophe in France, and sought to reassure his fellow politicians, his public and the wider world that Britain was nevertheless prepared to defend itself.

Hundreds of thousands of troops had been rescued, he insisted, and although equipment was in short supply, half a million Local Defence Volunteers were ready to serve. The forces of the Dominions were standing alongside 'the Mother Country', along with Czechs, Poles, Norwegians, Dutch, Belgians and French. The fighter pilots of the air force were ready to repel the Luftwaffe. And to invade Britain would require a monumental effort of transportation, protection and supply under continuous attack. 'Here is where we come to the Navy,' growled Churchill. 'After all, we have a Navy. Some people seem to forget that. We must remind them.'

'There are a few Jonahs on board with the "all is lost" stuff,' wrote Hutchinson of his shipmates in *Carlisle*, 'but there are plenty who can still make fun out of imagining us in Hitler's Navy. Most of us are positive we will not submit to him, and I don't think we have lost, but I hope they don't invade England. We have yet to see the reaction of our forces if this should come about and our own homes getting the same treatment as the other countries under German rule.'

'I expect that the battle of Britain is about to begin,' said Churchill, concluding his speech. 'The whole fury and might of the enemy must very soon be turned on us. Hitler knows that he will have to break us in this island or lose the war . . . Let us therefore brace ourselves to our duty and so bear ourselves that if the British Commonwealth and Empire lasts for a thousand years men will still say, "This was their finest hour."'

'Only Britain left against the lot,' wrote John Adams of HMS *Walker* the following day, as the destroyer patrolled the Western Approaches. 'Intense feeling that we've got to smash them all the more now. Very hot. Wish I were home, bathing at Howick or Bamburgh . . . All B.E.F. and R.A.F. evacuated from France. Canadians, Aussies etc. all in England now. All signposts down. Local Defence Volunteers to guard against parachute troops.'

'I do hope this letter arrives home under more hopeful circumstances than it is written,' wrote Charles Thomas to his brother from the Mediterranean a few days later. 'There can, for a Britisher, be no surrender – I will not go home to an England under German domination . . . Before a German soldier reaches the English shores the sea will run red from Scapa Flow to Dover Straits and you will have shot quite a few of the b—s. We are in a somewhat difficult position – going to be pretty grim I guess.'

Despite Churchill's assurances, the invasion seemed imminent. Even for sailors far away from the English Channel, the country appeared to be in desperate peril. 'I wish to hell I was at home to receive those Goddam, blasted Huns,' wrote John Carter, a young reservist serving aboard the destroyer HMS *Ilex* in the Atlantic. 'If I get hold of one of them, it is going to have its bowels ripped out and hung before its nose while it slowly dies, with slow fires round its limbs. I don't care whether it is man, woman or child. If it's German, it gets what it deserves – death by torture.'

Soon after Churchill's speech, the French government finally capitulated. In Britain, there were demands from some quarters to negotiate a truce. Some sailors doubted whether the home front could hold out, or that politicians could be trusted to continue to resist. 'I pondered on what action I should take if our Government also came to terms with Hitler,' wrote Ridley Waymouth, then in command of the sloop HMS *Leith*. 'I sent for my engineer officer and told him to work out whether we could reach Canada with the fuel remaining so that, if necessary, I could continue the war from there.'

At the outbreak of hostilities, the Admiralty had encouraged officers to submit any suggestions they might have to improve the prosecution of the war. In June 1940, Captain Alfred Duckworth submitted a document entitled 'Schemes for Baffling and Defeating the Hun', which set out his ideas for defeating the German invasion. He suggested, amongst other things, that enemy parachute troops might be countered by 'the employment of light aerial nets, to act as traps . . . nets being either stationary or airborne . . . towed by suitable aircraft'. Enemy aircraft, meanwhile, could be prevented from landing by 'long metal stanchions between 10 and 20 feet long . . . carrying barbed arrows'. Retaliation would also be necessary, Duckworth argued, suggesting several targets in Germany for bombing. Finally, he emphasized that if the Germans used gas or chemical weapons, Britain should respond immediately: 'We must be ready now, and exact plans prepared to return the blow in kind – with knobs on.'

Duckworth's ideas on preventing invasion were in keeping with the tone of several other proposals put forward. One officer suggested the use of 'infra-red ray cameras' to detect enemy landing craft at night. There was serious discussion of using a so-called 'Bullfrog' loudspeaker system, based on an American design, to demoralize invaders with ear-splitting shrieks, particularly if they happened to be 'Italian native troops'. Other suggestions which were considered or trialled included burning oil slicks and a 'sea-flame barrage'. Lord Louis Mountbatten, then commanding a destroyer flotilla, suggested that a section of coastline 'could be contaminated with mustard gas by a low-flying aircraft spray'.

A system was in place to identify the invasion when it came, and to coordinate the efforts of the army, navy and air force in defence. 'Cromwell' would be the general code-word signifying an invasion. Coastal forces would be the first line of defence at sea, and were provided with various codes to use when the enemy was sighted: 'Blackbird' for enemy ships, 'Gallipoli' for landing craft, 'Caterpillar' for tanks, 'Parasols' for parachute troops, and 'Starlings' for landing aircraft.

A scheme was formulated known as Operation Lucid, in which

burning oil tankers would be drifted into Boulogne and Calais in an attempt to destroy the barges that were being accumulated in preparation for the German seaborne assault, which Hitler's staff had code-named Operation Sealion. Chief Petty Officer Ronald Apps trained aboard the tanker *War African* at Sheerness in July 1940. The plan was for the unwieldy vessel to be set on course and then left to drift towards her target while the crew escaped into speedboats alongside. While the training continued, the tanker was filled with fuel oil ready to be ignited, despite frequent nearby air raids. 'Those four weeks were a bit hairy,' recalled Apps. When Bomber Command took on the challenge of attacking the invasion barges, there was some relief in Sheerness.

Government documents initially referred to home defence as the 'Battle for Britain'. In July 1940 this battle seemed to depend heavily on the navy. Home Intelligence reports described a general cheerfulness amongst the public but also a degree of apprehension, with fears that the apparent delay in the expected invasion might signify some new and devious plot or novel weapons. Yet the reports also suggested that 'determination to challenge and meet this surprise is widespread'. Central to this attitude was that 'confidence in the Navy is at a high level'. Sailors continued to provide reassurance, and there was a general belief that 'the Navy will win the war for us in the end'.

On 4 July Ronald Walsh was scrubbing out his mess in the anti-aircraft ship HMS *Foylebank*, anchored in Portland harbour. His work was cut short by the alarm for action stations, and as he ran for the upper deck the ship was rocked by an explosion and he was knocked off his feet. 'I got up,' he recalled, 'went back to the mess and saw the hammock nettings burning, the double ladders twisted with blokes inside and the tables I'd been scrubbing with their legs twisted. It was a terrible sight.'

By the time Walsh reached daylight, *Foylebank* had suffered further devastating damage from bombs dropped by German Stuka bombers. Holes were torn through the hull, and the deck was covered with injured bodies and smouldering metal. As the surviving men began to abandon ship, Walsh passed 'a mass of dead men piled up'. Later, he saw the ship's doctor 'sitting on a bollard with his guts in his hands'. Casualties were high: 176 of the 300-strong crew had been killed, and many more had sustained injuries.

One of Walsh's shipmates, Jack Mantle, remained strapped into his pom-pom gun, which had been damaged by a blast. Despite serious injuries, Mantle proceeded to operate the broken weapon, attempting to bring down a Stuka. 'He was cursing and swearing at it as it went out over the bay and approached him again,' Walsh recalled. 'He managed to move the lever and he fired four barrels of pom-pom into the Stuka just as it machine-gunned him. He flaked out over his gun, hit in the chest by bullets. The Stuka blew apart.' Mantle was awarded a posthumous Victoria Cross. 'Between his bursts of fire,' stated the citation, 'he had time to reflect on the grievous injuries of which he was soon to die but his great courage bore him up till the end of the fight, when he fell by the gun he had so valiantly served.'

The attack on Portland formed a prologue to the confrontation between the Luftwaffe and Fighter Command which became known to the British as the Battle of Britain. But the German name for the early phase of the offensive was *Kanalkampf*: the Channel War. At this time, there was no more significant body of water in the world. From mid-July, attacks on coastal convoys and southern ports began in earnest. Although the German strategy was ill-defined, the Luftwaffe sought to dominate the English Channel by attacking exposed convoys and drawing out British fighters to be picked off.

After returning from Norway, HMS *Delight* was immediately sent to Rosyth for repairs. When they were complete, the destroyer sailed south and on 31 July passed into the Channel. 'We were well pleased with ourselves,' wrote Lieutenant Vere Wight-Boycott soon afterwards. 'The refit had been very complete . . . We had a harmonium in the wardroom and a piano on the messdeck . . . The ship was painted and clean and the ship's company in good humour.' Wight-Boycott, the ship's executive officer, was in his cabin when *Delight* was shaken by explosions. He scrambled out towards the bridge just before another blast: 'Glass and paint chips were flying about and I was blown on to my back.'

*Delight* had been detected by German radar at Cherbourg and attacked by bombers twenty miles off Portland Bill, suffering a direct hit on the forecastle. By the time Wight-Boycott had recovered, the bridge was 'a shambles, with every bit of glass in the screens splintered, holes in the deck, and fittings twisted'. Lights had been extinguished, and the switchboard fell silent. Fires raged below decks and the smoke impaired the eyes and lungs of damage control teams. Wight-Boycott saw a sailor who 'had been nearly cut in half by a splinter and his body was in the flames'.

The engine room personnel had been decimated, leaving no steam to power emergency systems. Before long, it became clear that ship would have to be abandoned. A small group was despatched to Portland in a powerboat to seek help. Others had to wait until the last moment before boarding the ship's whaler and Carley floats as *Delight* slipped beneath the waves. 'This was perhaps the most trying time of all,' wrote Wight-Boycott. 'One young Ordinary Seaman, normally a rather tough fibred type, suddenly broke down, saying he was blind. He seemed absolutely unhurt, and presumably it was due to shock.'

Motor launches from Portland arrived with plentiful supplies of whisky, which was gratefully gulped by the survivors. One normally teetotal officer, 'a careful and abstemious man', became utterly drunk. 'When we reached harbour,' wrote Wight-Boycott, 'it was decided that he had better be put on a stretcher and sent up to hospital with the wounded.' Another man, a veteran rating 'who had been a tower of strength', was lying under a blanket. Wight-Boycott comforted him with the promise of a quiet job in the Commodore's garden: 'He answered, "What, with only one leg?" and died shortly after we got ashore.'

From 13 August, the Luftwaffe began to concentrate its attacks on the Royal Air Force. Targeting airfields and inland bases, as well as bombing ports, German aircraft were met by squadrons of British fighters, flown by an international coalition of pilots, which engaged them in dogfights over land and sea. By now, most Channel convoys had been withdrawn, but those travelling down the east coast and into the Thames continued to suffer attack from the air. Ordinary Signalman Ivor Turner had joined the minesweeper HMS *Sunlight* in May 1940, and was thrown immediately into an intense schedule of work. *Sunlight* operated out of Sheerness, clearing mines from the mouth of the Thames estuary out into the North Sea and around the Kent coast. Throughout July, Turner and his shipmates were subjected to attack from German bombers and E-boats. 'Why I volunteered for this mine-sweeping I don't know,' he wrote after one particularly stressful day. 'Perhaps I like the danger ... Yet every time we are attacked I think my stomach has dropped.'

On 13 August, *Sunlight* had a narrow escape after being sent out to sea at 4.30 a.m. to clear enemy mines in Barrow Deep. 'We went after them and exploded one just behind us,' wrote Turner. 'The stern of our ship was lifted out of the water and the sweep broken in 3 places.' Other minesweepers in the flotilla fared much worse after being attacked by enemy bombers. '*Tamarisk* and *Pyrope* were sunk today ... Only 12 survivors all told ... What can you do with about 30 planes!' *Sunlight* continued to sweep constantly throughout August and September, with air raids and dogfights overhead. By October, the crew was exhausted. 'Four ships from here lost in the last 2 days,' wrote Turner. 'Let's hope we get our leave before our turn!'

In July 1940, Geoff Dormer was made sub-lieutenant and drafted into the anti-submarine trawler *Cape Argona*, about to begin duties on the east-coast convoys. Dormer arrived in Harwich to find the harbour damaged by air attacks. Parkeston Quay was 'lined with blackened, burnt-out, bullet-riddled trawlers'. Escorting a north-bound convoy near Shipwash, *Cape Argona* was called upon to fend off a Stuka attack. 'I pressed the Alarm Bells,' wrote Dormer, 'then, in accordance with orders, scrambled into the Bridge shelter, a sort of vertical steel coffin, designed to protect at least the Officer of the Watch from machine-gun fire ... I was paralysed with fright, but once in the coffin, one could see little and do less, though it was equipped with a voice pipe.'

Not long afterwards, *Cape Argona* rescued survivors from a sinking passenger liner, the *Empress of Britain*. Dormer described how 'the Maltese wife of a Serviceman, heavily pregnant, had both arms broken, both legs badly cut and burned, and a couple of bullets in her body ... A man with both legs broken, and a bullet through his foot, sat propped against our bulwarks, bleeding gently as he smoked a cigarette. He was surrounded by children, amused at the funny shape of his legs.' The mother survived and eventually gave birth to a healthy baby.

The summer of 1940 was a psychologically draining experience for those on the east-coast convoys. Dormer suffered from extreme fatigue. When he slept, he had nightmares in which he was still on the bridge, facing overwhelming air attacks. 'I would turn in, fully clothed, life-belt and all, of course, and immediately dream that I was back up there, facing yet worse problems. Once I dreamed that I had been called, and I was back on the Bridge, all ready to take over, only a few minutes after I'd been relieved.'

By September, the confrontation between the RAF and the Luftwaffe was reaching its climax. Meanwhile, an invasion still seemed a very real threat. Mock seaborne assaults were staged, to prepare defences and improve tactics. One overnight exercise at Southend on 11 September produced the recommendation that sentries should wear rubber-soled boots to ensure stealth and that 'trip wires with bells might prove useful'. Such training produced bouts of rumours. A few days after the invasion of Southend, Able Seaman Hall – aboard HMS *Glasgow* at Scapa Flow – recorded the latest in his diary: 'I have heard from a very good source that the coast of England has been invaded by the Germans on three occasions in the last week but have been repulsed. The Germans have used gas and have inflicted casualties. However there is nothing about it on the wireless which is I suppose politic.'

Naval shore establishments around the British Isles prepared for the forthcoming battle. At the training establishment HMS *Royal Arthur*, Derric Breen and his cohort of new recruits practised infantry combat and coastal defence. 'We were waiting for invasion,' he explained. By day, they learned advanced Morse and telegraphy. In the evenings they settled down in the Skegness sand dunes. Equipment shortages meant that their weapons were positively archaic: a few old Lee Enfield rifles and some First World War-vintage machine guns, 'two ancient water-cooled Maxims on heavy tripods'.

Puck Duvall was one of around 350 women working at Hatston naval air station – designated HMS *Sparrowhawk* – near Kirkwall in the Orkneys. Her husband, a pilot, had been killed in June 1940 when his

Skua aircraft was shot down over Trondheim fjord. She recalled that Wrens regularly visited the rifle range for target practice. On one occasion the naval officer in charge, Captain St John Fancourt, made an impassioned speech about the threat of invasion, declaring that RNAS Hatston would be defended to the last man, 'and the last Wren'.

By mid-September, it was becoming clear that the Luftwaffe was struggling to overcome the stern resistance of Fighter Command. Overstretched and fatigued German pilots were suffering increasingly heavy losses against their well-organized, well-supplied and intensely motivated enemies. Sunday 15 September proved a decisive day, with the defeat of a strong Luftwaffe attack, and the destruction of sixty German aircraft for the loss of twenty-six British planes. Five days later, Hitler postponed Operation Sealion, and the proposed invasion would later be suspended indefinitely.

The RAF had won a significant victory, with the pilots of the Spitfires and Hurricanes of Fighter Command, as well as those of Bomber Command and Coastal Command, proving the most potent aggressive deterrent in Britain's armoury. But the difficulties involved in mounting a seaborne invasion were also the result of German weakness at sea. Attempts to congregate the required mass of landing craft in continental Channel ports were disrupted by British naval and air forces. The Royal Navy's Home Fleet remained a vastly superior force to any the Kriegsmarine might be capable of amassing to support the vulnerable troop carriers. The absence of the German destroyers and warships eliminated in the Norwegian campaign was keenly felt.

In the early evening of 7 September, 364 German bombers accompanied by fighters attacked London, with another hundred returning later in a second wave. It heralded the start of eight months of intensive bombing raids which became known as the Blitz. 'Directly above me were literally hundreds of planes,' wrote eighteen-year-old Colin Perry in his diary, after watching the attack from a hillside in Surrey. 'The sky was full of them. Bombers hemmed in with fighters, like bees around their queen, like destroyers round the battleship.'

Maritime communities were at the heart of the German strategy to force Britain into submission by eroding its economic capabilities and public morale. London was the first major target, with the docks in the East End suffering greatly. Devastation ashore was mirrored in the waterways. One sailor recalled seeing along the Thames 'the skeletons of dead ships; masts, stems, sterns and, here and there, a lonely bridge protruded from the water'.

As the bombing campaign was extended across the country, it was industrial centres which bore the brunt of the damage. Along with conurbations such as Coventry, Birmingham and Sheffield, major maritime cities such as Southampton, Bristol and Liverpool were specifically targeted. From early 1941, the Luftwaffe was ordered to focus its attentions on shipping centres across the British Isles. Besides London, ports and dockyard towns suffered many of the biggest raids: Cardiff and Bristol in January; Swansea in February; Portsmouth, Clydebank and Plymouth in March; Bristol, Belfast and an eight-day blitz on Devonport and Plymouth in April; Liverpool, Belfast and Greenock in May. Smaller raids also hit shipbuilding zones at Barrow-in-Furness, Hull and Newcastle.

While it was civilian areas which suffered most from the bombing, barracks and dockyards were also threatened. During the raids on Devonport in April 1941, ninety-six sailors were killed when a bomb hit an accommodation block. At the height of the Blitz, John Somers was at the Chatham depot waiting to be assigned to a ship. In a parallel of the scenes of civilians huddling together in the London Underground, sailors took shelter in the tunnels under the base. 'The best bomb shelter in the world,' recalled Somers. 'Every air raid alert and the tunnels were filled. We slept in them every night.'

Before the onset of the Blitz, Charles Thomas had written to his father, comparing the attitudes of some of his messmates with what he perceived to be the mood back in Britain:

It is pleasant and encouraging to read how determined the people at home are . . . Some of the men are horrible pessimists – especially those married. One said there would be nothing left in England soon so I worked out on paper for his benefit that at the present rate of air attack, after two years the population would be diminished by only about 1/50th of 1%. I am not dismayed at all.

But as the scale of the bombing became clear, sailors serving away from Britain were naturally increasingly anxious about conditions at home, and the safety of their loved ones. John Evans, brought back from China and now aboard HMS *Southampton* in the Mediterranean, wrote to his wife who was living in Gillingham:

> I guess you are having a tough time of it just now but you must keep cheerful and hope for the best! I know it must be a very trying time for you and the babies and I only wish that I could do something to help you, but there is nothing I can do except write you as often as possible, and that I will do dear! I do love you so much darling, please look after yourself!

Others were more circumspect. Midshipman David Leggatt, in the Far East with the submarine HMS *Regent*, wrote to his uncle: 'The last news we got tonight was of the big raid on London (by the time you get this it will doubtless have become the first big raid). It all sounds perfectly horrible, but I suppose it will help to clear up the slum problem after the War.'

Officers were advised by the Admiralty to reassure their men, emphasizing 'courage and patience and the attitude of mind which says that no news is good news'. But the issue became one of the driving forces behind the development of welfare services within the navy. Sailors were assured that in the event of a death in the family they would be notified as soon as possible wherever they were in the world. Notices in ships stated that 'relief services are now very thoroughly organised throughout the country', and that the Royal Navy Benevolent Trust charity 'gives immediate assistance to dependants . . . wherever the need requires'. Details were also provided on emergency billeting arrangements, financial aid, compensation payments, the War Damage Act and dependants' grants.

Far from feeling detached from the civilian experience, many sailors were all too aware of the psychological effects of bombing. One naval chaplain wrote a letter in early 1941 to four nurses at King's College Hospital in London:

You will never know what an inspiration you who are carrying on in London, and all other places that are being bombed, are to those in the fighting forces – especially to those in the Navy. Everyone of us has remarked how we were absolutely scared stiff on the occasions when we were in houses during a raid. I know I was, and was thankful to be back in the comparative safety of a ship. At least we feel we can keep our nautical home moving about and stick our porcupine quills up when the 'wicked' enemy is about!

On 16 May 1941, the Blitz came to a conclusion. It was far from the end of German bombing campaign, but there was at least some respite from the intensity of nightly raids. Noël Coward visited Plymouth and was impressed by what he saw. He described the scene on Plymouth Hoe in a letter to his lover and collaborator Jack Wilson:

The other day I went to a certain very badly blitzed coastal town . . . In the evenings between 7.30 and 9.30 there is a band on the front and the whole of the town, or what is left of it, come out and dance in the sunlight. The girls put on their bright coloured frocks and dance with the sailors and marines and soldiers. The fact that they were dancing on the exact site of a certain historic game added a little extra English nostalgia to what was one of the most touching and moving scenes I have ever seen.

The Blitz was a direct attack on Britain's economy and morale, but it was conceived in tandem with blockade. Alongside strikes on shipping and ports, the waters around the British Isles became increasingly threatened by mines and submarines. Many of the ships employed to combat these weapons were part of the Royal Naval Patrol Service. Often small and fragile, they were usually converted fishing trawlers or other practical vessels, and required a particular hardiness to operate.

'It is thoroughly unpleasing,' wrote Richard Walker, 'to brush a dewdrop from one's nose and take a lump of skin with it because the drop has frozen.' He was serving in the anti-submarine trawler *Northern Reward*, patrolling the waters to the north of Scotland. She was a small boat, her high bows useful for breaking ice. The *Reward* had been built in Bremerhaven in 1936 and, along with the twelve other trawlers with the name *Northern*, had been given to Britain as part of the German First World War reparations. 'Our main job is to hunt the U-boat,' wrote Walker in his diary. 'We listen to the ASDIC endlessly until the remorseless "ping" of the transmission gets on our nerves.'

Along the east coast, coal tramps travelled from Scotland and the north-east of England to London, delivering thousands of tons of essential fuel for the factories and industries of the south. Many of the escort ships working along this vital route were old and battered. Derric Breen joined the sloop HMS *Egret* in late 1940. A veteran of the Middle East, her hull was peppered with splinter holes. Life aboard was far from comfortable. The wireless telegraphy office, where Breen worked, was below decks and claustrophobic. 'Our links with the world at war were via a voice-pipe and a little canister on the end of a string, through which messages could be passed to and from the bridge,' he recalled. 'We were unaware of the causes of the screeches, bumps and thumps which came to us through the ship's tin-foil hull.'

By the end of 1940, the Battle for Britain had already begun to take its toll on the sailors of the Patrol Service. Two hundred and thirty-four vessels of all descriptions had been sunk in the Thames estuary and the English Channel. For those defending the coasts, the pattern of the war was set. Geoff Dormer, by now a veteran of the east-coast convoys, spent Boxing Day of 1940 in the Firth of Forth. He found himself alone, the only man on board save for a drunken rating on watch duties. He admitted that he was in a 'profound depression, and seriously considered suicide'. He took out and loaded a revolver. After a moment of contemplation, he fired at several empty gin bottles.

Frustrations were also evident in the Home Fleet. At the start of the war, the force had been the most powerful and modern in the Royal Navy, with five battleships, two battlecruisers, the aircraft carrier *Ark Royal*, fourteen cruisers and several destroyers and submarines. After the outbreak of hostilities, some ships were detached to serve in other parts of the world, most notably the Mediterranean. But the main purpose of the Home Fleet was simple: to contain and confront the German navy in the North Sea.

The early part of the war had not been straightforward. Losing *Royal Oak* to a torpedo in Scapa Flow itself was an embarrassment, and prompted a rapid reassessment of anti-submarine defences. The campaign in Norway had been costly and controversial. The sailors of most of the larger warships had been spectators during the evacuations from France and continued to be so. Serving aboard a Home Fleet destroyer, Ludovic Kennedy had ample opportunity to pursue his nascent writing career during long stretches in port. 'I would sit down there,' he recalled, 'and I would start writing *Autobiography of a Sub-Lieutenant* by Ludovic Kennedy, Chapter One. It was ridiculous but it was fun.'

When ships of the Home Fleet were mobilized, their efforts to contain the few German warships attempting to break out of the North Sea often proved futile. Commerce raiders, such as *Deutschland*, were able to escape through the Denmark Strait, between Greenland and Iceland, and return to German ports after sinking merchant shipping. In October 1940 *Admiral Scheer* escaped from the North Sea and sank sixteen ships, including three in the Indian Ocean, before making her way back to Norway in March 1941. Another, *Admiral Hipper*, also managed to evade detection and enter the Atlantic. In February 1941, the battleship *Scharnhorst* along with *Gneisenau* managed to break out into the Atlantic, eventually reaching Brest.

The Admiralty had to make conscious efforts to sustain morale in the Home Fleet in the face of such apparent failures. Later in the war, the Cabinet minister Stafford Cripps addressed the men of HMS *Renown*. 'He stressed the fact that really we were playing a very important part in the war,' noted Midshipman J. B. T. Davies in his journal, 'though it appeared that we could be much better employed. Furthermore he stated that although we did not receive the publicity others were having our part was greatly appreciated at home.'

At the end of 1940, however, there appeared to be little to appreciate. Time spent in harbour at Scapa could be dangerous for morale.

One of the chief problems for the commanders of the Home Fleet was that operational necessity did not always permit a great deal of leave. Those in distant parts of the world might not expect regular trips back, but those in the Orkneys or the Clyde, being so tantalizingly close to their families, often expected to be able to travel home more frequently. This could cause problems aboard even the most prestigious of warships.

Since Mers-el-Kébir, the battlecruiser HMS *Hood* had been largely employed patrolling in northern waters, occasionally providing distant cover, but often cruising between Scapa Flow, Loch Ewe on the north-west coast of Scotland, and the Clyde. Seventeen-year-old Bill Crawford kept a diary tracking the mood on the messdecks. 'Painting superstructure and funnels to-day,' he wrote on 10 December, after *Hood* had returned to the Clyde. 'There sure is unrest as regards leave. The Captain spoke to us about it to-day, he said nothing could be done.'

The painting was in preparation for a visit the following day by the commander-in-chief of the Home Fleet, Admiral William Whitworth. Crawford wrote: 'There is open talk about mutiny, especially among the stokers, who have already had one bit of trouble.' Worse was to come on 12 December. 'Things came to a head to-day,' he reported. 'The stokers practically mutinied, locking up officers and saying they wouldn't work. The Captain asked them all to come up into the battery, he told them he could do nothing about leave and asked all the ship's company to stand by him.'

After this intervention, it appeared to Crawford that 'things have kind of eased off'. The captain had admitted that 'he was doing all he could but he did not think we would get leave till next year'. All was quiet until Christmas, when *Hood* went to sea again. 'To-day of all days,' wrote Crawford, 'Everybody is fed up.'

While the sailors of the Home Fleet felt underemployed, the burden of protecting the front line of British waters fell on the navy's coastal forces. The so-called Narrow Sea between the south-east of England and the enemy-occupied coasts of France, Belgium and Holland was the scene of a struggle which continued throughout the war. German E-boats fought a raiding campaign to disrupt convoys, causing havoc along the east coast – which became known as E-boat Alley – and in the English Channel. The Royal Navy's equivalents were motor launches (MLs), motor gunboats (MGBs) and motor torpedo boats (MTBs), which were tasked with dealing with the E-boat threat.

Ordinary Seaman Stan Bowman was drafted to ML 144, part of a flotilla based at Newhaven in the summer of 1941. In August, the flotilla was searching for E-boats near the French coast. Bowman had been on watch until midnight, before turning in. He was awoken an hour later by explosions. 'I find myself on deck with only socks on,' he wrote in his diary. 'Many salvos of shells are sent over and we get one so near that the splash drenches us. The shore batteries have got our range and shells burst astern, above and in between the boats.' Rather than manning their close-range gun, he admitted, 'Howlett and myself are terrified and trembling, and find ourselves on deck in the prone position, hoping and praying for the best.' After a brief lull, the motor launch made for home at top speed. 'Heavy seas raging now,' wrote Bowman, 'and we are lucky to be alive.'

The dangers of service in small boats produced a distinctive sense of camaraderie. G. W. Gillett was the radar operator in MTB 350, part of the 11th MTB Flotilla, organized from the shore establishment HMS *Beehive* at Felixstowe. The flotilla's duties were to attack enemy convoys off the Dutch coast and patrol the North Sea coast. 'Sometimes we would go to sea on exercise and do a spot of fishing on the way home,' wrote Gillett. 'A depth charge would be set to explode while we were travelling at high speed . . . we would return to the scene to find a lot of good sized fish floating on the surface. After collecting them on board, they would be delivered to the base galley where the Wrens would prepare a fish dinner for us.'

This was one of the more respectable perks of the job. On occasions when bad weather kept them ashore, the daily rum ration would sometimes be supplemented: 'the Coxswain would ask us if we would like tomorrow's tot, and after that, shall we have the next day's as well? The answer was always "Yes". Afterwards, the Coxswains would sometimes get together to have a few more drinks and would definitely not be in a fit state to go to sea.' Gillett was under-age, and therefore ineligible for a tot, but nevertheless he was 'looked-after' by the senior men. On one occasion the weather suddenly improved and the MTB was due out, but the Coxswain was incoherent. 'Panic stations ensued,' wrote Gillett. 'Our only course of action was to get him to the Sick Bay where he would have to undergo the stomach pump, and with time to spare he was able to take his place on the wheel.'

Amongst the sailors of convoy ships and their escorts, there was some concern that the British coastal forces were unable to match their German counterparts. John Adams was the first lieutenant of the destroyer HMS *Cleveland* in the summer of 1942, a time when coastal forces were coming under increasing pressure from E-boats. In June *Cleveland* was escorting convoys in the Channel which came under sustained attack, after which Adams was honoured for his efforts by being Mentioned in Despatches. 'We had been expecting E-boat attacks for months,' he wrote, 'and now they've come. Of course Admiralty wants to know what we are doing and the answer is that we have nothing to fight back with. MLs are no bloody good.'

Over the course of the campaign in the Narrow Sea, several coastal forces commanders proved that, in fact, they were able to match their enemies, given the appropriate weapons and support. An offensive attitude was critical. Many coastal forces personnel viewed themselves as part of an elite, more akin to aircrew than warship sailors. Later in the war, John Wilson was made acting sub-lieutenant of MTB 738, one of three officers and three senior ratings in a crew of six. His boat was tasked with finding enemy shipping to sink, minelaying, and fighting off E-boats. It was uncomfortable work, and the men were given an extra tuppence a day as 'hard-lying' pay. Crews would spend their days ashore then, as Wilson put it, 'like R.A.F. bombers, go out on operations at dusk'.

Regardless of the diminishing strategic threat of invasion throughout 1941, fears of an assault persisted for many years. Coastal forces remained on alert for possible enemy incursions. Training exercises continued in earnest. 'A mock invasion has just been held here,' wrote Wren Charlotte Dyer, working at Western Approaches in Liverpool, in September 1942. 'As usual the "invaders" wore forage caps, and the defenders steel helmets. Hostilities began, on a mild scale, on Friday night, but only started in earnest on Saturday afternoon. By Saturday evening half Liverpool seemed to be in flames.' Dyer found it all rather annoying, and worried that the exercise would disturb her normal duties and leave her with more paperwork to complete. Sure enough, while she was working in her office, a stern-looking senior Wren arrived and pinned a large notice to the door: 'DEAD. Place Burnt to the Ground.'

Although the direct threat to Britain's shores was contained, and the intense immediate reaction amongst sailors short lived, the country remained in a desperate situation by the spring of 1941. If the Blitz had failed to destroy public morale, fears remained that a blockade could. It was not invasion but supply which became the chief concern for sailors. Petty Officer Edward Records, having survived the sinking of HMS *Keith* at Dunkirk, was now serving in the destroyer HMS *Eskimo*. 'Apparently we are still short of material,' he wrote in April 1941. 'The stuff isn't getting through from America as should be. As I go from place to place and see the fellows walking round with a rifle on their shoulder I wonder what real weapons we have got . . . It makes me wonder if our crowd really could withstand an invasion. All things seem to point that our mob are still playing at War and trusting to Providence.'

# 6. Working Up

'How nice it would be,' wrote eighteen-year-old Geoff Dormer in his diary in September 1938, 'to be a Swede, or a South Sea islander! People are queuing outside the shops where the latest news is posted up. Peace or War? Life or Death? The scales seem to be slowly tipping the wrong way. The suspense is monstrous.' He had heard that the army was preparing for civil disturbances, predictions that air-raid panics would cause 'riot and revolution', and that Westminster Abbey was open all night to accommodate people praying for peace. He listened to demonstrations in Hyde Park, where political agitators and pacifists spoke to crowds of tens of thousands. A few days later, he was 'shaken by the sight' of anti-aircraft guns being installed 'among a flock of sheep', and 'men digging trenches where yesterday children were playing ball'. 'War is inevitable,' he decided. 'That is the sickening truth . . . I am going to find out about joining the Navy.'

Dormer came from a well-to-do family, and wanted to join the Royal Naval Volunteer Reserve. He had been inspired by a painting he had once seen depicting a few small trawlers of the Auxiliary Patrol guarding the Strait of Otranto against Austrian cruisers during the First World War. The caption quoted Drake: 'I must have the gentleman to haul and draw with the mariner, and the mariner with the gentleman.' But before he could volunteer, there was a development:

Friday. Every newspaper hoarding, every headline this morning, carries, in enormous letters, the one word, 'Peace' . . . when I went to the News Cinema, [Chamberlain] was clapped and cheered, at every appearance on the screen. 'News Review' claims that our defences are grossly inadequate, and that, if we had gone to war, London would have been in ruins by now.

After Munich, Dormer decided to postpone joining up. The following year, in August 1939, he was with a group of students hiking in the mountains of Yugoslavia. They returned to the coast as Germany invaded Poland and, on 3 September, Dormer was aboard a passenger ship travelling from Dubrovnik to Trieste. During the voyage he met several uniformed members of the Hitler Youth and struck up a genial conversation. One told him, 'If we meet on the battlefield, I'll shoot over your head.' In December 1939, Dormer volunteered for the navy 'knowing well that I was not nearly brave enough to be a soldier'.

The Royal Navy was not merely the foremost of Britain's armed forces: it was the most prestigious military organization in the world. Its ships were represented in popular culture as the apogee of national virility. Battleships such as HMS *Hood* were not simply national symbols but physical manifestations of industrial might, of technological advancement and of imperial strength. For British society, the navy was a vital element of national identity.

Many young men were eager to wear the gold braid on the sleeve of a deep blue officer's jacket, or bell-bottomed trousers and a flat round hat with the name of a warship embroidered around it. Such an ingrained aura of history and national duty gave the navy a very different appeal from the glamorous novelty of the RAF, while the army was not only widely viewed as mundane and workmanlike, but was still tarred with the collective memory of the trenches of the Great War. Naval recruiters enjoyed a steady supply of men for whom navy blue was the most attractive option, as a government report on recruitment highlighted, encouraged by 'both the personal prestige of the man concerned, and the feeling that the Navy is the Senior Service and has a high reputation for successful action'.

Unlike in the army, every conscripted naval recruit had specified a preference for the service on his draft documents. Some were eager to avoid infantry duties; others had particular skills in engineering that could be put to good use. Many prospective pilots decided that the Fleet Air Arm might provide a better chance of flying than the RAF. Civilian doctors sometimes chose the navy because of its reputation for professionalism and the opportunity to play a full role as part of a fighting unit aboard ship.

Those signing on just for the duration of the conflict were given the label 'Hostilities Only'. As the numbers of 'regulars' – career sailors – dwindled below 100,000, wartime recruits came to predominate. Over half a million 'Hostilities Only' ratings were serving by 1945. Some 40,000 temporary officers were commissioned: four times the number of regular officers. From a total strength of less than 200,000 regulars and reservists before the war, the navy had grown to a force of more than 800,000 by 1945.

Maintaining the standard of this new intake became the main challenge for Admiralty officials. Sustaining an adequate skill-base within the service was essential, and specialist knowledge and experience were at a premium. A potential deficit of skilled manpower led to the upper age limit for volunteers being raised from thirty-six to forty, then forty-five, for those with appropriate seafaring experience or technical skills, particularly engineers such as artificers, mechanics and artisans, and communications personnel such as writers and coders.

Traditionally, the navy had often focused on qualities that were not always subject to quantitative analysis. As Lord Moran put it, 'selection is a search for character'. Yet as the war progressed, more scientific methods of selection, often involving psychologists and later psychiatrists, attempted to sift potential candidates and identify their most appropriate roles. This was the navy as an industrial operation: skills and aptitudes were as applicable to the departments of a ship – mechanical, communicational, managerial – as to any factory production line.

Yet even before the outbreak of war, thousands of men had already been called into active service from the navy's reserves. This was a vital pool of experienced manpower made up of pensioners – officers and men who had retired from the navy – merchant mariners who were part of the Royal Naval Reserve, and many other veteran seafarers. Teenage Midshipman John Carter, RNR, who had volunteered to transfer into the navy from a merchant vessel, wrote to his parents in late September 1939 expressing his enthusiasm for the move: 'It is a great change from the Merchant Service. Here I am definitely an officer whereas there I was simply nobody, of less importance than the deck boys and treated accordingly.'

This influx of reservists was essential to the navy's ability to fight the war, particularly in the first few years, but it was not without controversy. In August 1939, Charles Thomas described his fellow sailors aboard HMS *Capetown*: 'The ship's company is made up of reservists with a small percentage of active service ratings . . . It would be no understatement to say that thirty per cent of the ship's company are between forty and fifty years of age.' Initially, he was optimistic about the fresh intake: 'The spirit of the reservists is somewhat different from the active service ratings and one can discuss life outside the Services without meeting the foolish ideas of men who have never been outside the Service.' Before long, however, the problems associated with such a proportion of rusty ratings became clear: 'The fighting efficiency of the *Capetown* is nil . . . The living conditions on board are worse than on Nelson's ships – overcrowded messes and inadequate arrangements for washing and such like.'

Captain Ridley Waymouth, commanding officer of the sloop HMS *Leith*, visited an armed merchant cruiser, a converted civilian vessel, being fitted out in Malta dockyard. He was impressed by the captain and executive officers, both reservists, but less so with the rest of the wardroom:

> The large mess was dim with the fumes of duty free tobacco and duty free drink. Perhaps 20 old officers of the First War vintage were sitting round the small tables swilling whisky and talking of nothing but old times and how wonderful to get duty free drink again. They were a drink-sodden lot and many none too sober. It was a sickening sight and, after blasting them, I left. I told some of them we had weeded their type out of the service after the last war and we did not intend to be submerged by them again.

It was not only men who were urgently required. The recruitment of women was an essential part of the navy's ability to organize itself and operate effectively. The Women's Royal Naval Service was an attractive prospect for potential recruits and, having existed since 1917, was a relatively well-established organization. When an initial government call for volunteers was made in 1939, there were ten applicants for each of the initial 1,500 places. In July 1940, there were 6,000 'Wrens' but by July 1944 there were nearly 74,000. By 1945, there were almost twice as many Wrens than temporary male officers in the navy.

Wren Elizabeth Hodges believed that the 'snob appeal' of avoiding service in industry or on farms aided recruitment to the navy's women's branch. The uniform for females, she stated, was 'rather more attractive' than those of the other services. Of course, this was equally true for men. Yet the navy was far from an easy option for women. Wrens were seldom mollycoddled. Elizabeth Gibson attended Greenwich Naval College for two weeks of training in January 1941. 'We lived in spartan conditions with snow on the ground,' she recalled, 'and slept in a cellar where there was a hole blown out at one end in a previous air-raid.'

Wrens were assigned a vast array of tasks throughout Britain: from Fleet Air Arm stations on windswept Scottish islands to bustling depot bases, from administrative offices in London to heavy harbour work preparing ships for sailing. Many served abroad as communications staff, by the end of the war travelling as far afield as Canada, the Middle East, Ceylon and Australia. A few trained as mechanics for the Fleet Air Arm; a handful served as test pilots. One of their most crucial roles was in organizing the complex system of convoys at the headquarters of Western Approaches in Liverpool. In November 1939 John Adams visited the Liver Building and noted in his diary that it was 'lousy with W.R.N.S., knitting and polishing their nails'. The outward appearance of female service in the navy was not always of emancipation. Posters encouraged women to 'Join the Wrens and Free a Man for the Fleet'. Although many women worked at docks, operating harbour launches and handling torpedoes, there was a sharp divide between support roles and fighting.

Admitting greater numbers of women into the navy might have proved controversial at times, but this was nothing compared to the difficulties of expanding the officer cadre. With such a rapid expansion of manpower, and the increasing numbers of vessels required for convoy duties, the flow of officers from Dartmouth's Britannia Royal Naval College quickly ceased to be sufficient.

The usual procedures for career advancement nevertheless continued to function during the war. Richard Campbell-Begg decided to join the Royal Navy in 1941. He was seventeen and a child of the Commonwealth: born in New Zealand and living in South Africa. He was fortunate enough to receive one of only two places reserved for boys from the Dominions at Dartmouth, as part of the Special Entry Scheme. 'The office job was proving a little boring,' he wrote, 'the war was on so I decided on a nautical career.' In contrast to the truncated period of intensive training that most new wartime recruits received, his was relatively relaxed: six months at Dartmouth followed by twenty months as a midshipman – a trainee probationary officer – in cruisers and a destroyer.

Midshipmen were assigned to warships for their practical training. Once the initial excitement of finally being part of a working ship had abated, the banality of routine usually took over. Midshipman John Roberts described in his training journal the aftermath of joining HMS *Renown* in October 1941. Three and a half days were 'spent in drawing plans of all the decks. This turned out to be more tedious than I had thought, but it certainly made us learn our way about.' What every teenage officer cadet wanted, having been imbued at Dartmouth with the legacy of the glorious days of old, was real experience of battle. As Roberts reached the end of fifteen relatively quiet months in *Renown*, he yearned for 'blood and thunder'.

If Dartmouth was creating officers steeped in the spirit of the past, the Royal Naval Volunteer Reserve was very much of the present. This new breed of civilian officer was absolutely crucial to the navy. As early as 1942, temporary officers formed half of the total officer corps. They served all across the navy, but played a particularly critical role in the small warships which escorted convoys and in the small craft that would eventually shepherd the Allied invasion troops back across the Channel.

Before the war, volunteer officers – then mostly part of what was properly called the Royal Naval Volunteer Supplementary Reserve – were widely characterized as upper-class leisure yachtsmen. Richard Walker had joined the reserve in 1938. He had been educated at Harrow and Cambridge, and his experiences exemplified the image of the RNVSR. Training largely consisted of sailing boats off Harwich with several establishment figures and well-off gentlemen, including the wealthy Arctic explorer August Courtauld.

Arthur Prideaux was an Oxford-educated solicitor working in the City, and was thirty-six at the outbreak of war. Having had some experience of yachting, he had decided to join the reserves in October 1938 because of what he termed 'a prudent desire to get in on the ground floor'. He duly presented himself at HMS *President*, the headquarters of the London Division of the RNVR on Victoria Embankment. After being shown into a room with a panel of senior officers, he began to worry as they outlined the maritime basics he would be required to know: navigation, manoeuvring, etiquette. 'Elementary stuff to you of course,' one officer exclaimed, 'we can take that as read.' After five weeks of rudimentary training, Prideaux was given command of an anti-submarine trawler, freshly fitted with the latest technology and weaponry. He later recalled that 'only painstaking bluff and some quick thinking concealed the depths of one's bewilderment and ignorance during those first few weeks at sea'.

In truth, 'yachting experience' was an unusual skill-set for the average civilian, and usually meant at least a rudimentary grasp of navigation and seamanship which was highly desirable in naval service. Despite the popular image, the campaign to recruit sailing gentlemen lasted only a few months, after which the intake of temporary officers required more rigorous testing of aptitude and new interview protocols. Geoffrey Hobday appeared before an Admiralty selection board in May 1940 following his application for a temporary commission. He recalled that the four senior officers were 'very efficient and bombarded me with questions designed to test my grasp of seamanship, engineering and navigation as well as my general knowledge'.

Officer candidates were often required to undergo a probationary period of several months on the lower deck, serving as ordinary sailors. This was partly a form of training and induction into the navy, partly an opportunity for observation and assessment, and also provided a rudimentary form of psychiatric screening. Spending time working and living with ratings could be an invaluable experience. There was little better preparation for understanding the mentality of the ordinary sailor than to be one. 'The officers are the ones who have Nelson etc. on the brain, cling to out-of-date ceremonial, and evolve weird methods of wasting time,' wrote John Wilson after his period as an ordinary rating, before progressing to full officership. He had far more respect for non-commissioned officers who had worked their way through the ranks: 'The Petty Officers are progressive. On the whole they have less education but more brains. The trouble with officers is that they are out of touch.'

Class remained a pernicious issue in the navy, and the recruitment and selection of officers was one of the most controversial examples of the consequences. Promotion from the ranks of experienced sailors of the lower deck was never truly embraced by the Admiralty. The way in which lower-deck men could apply for promotion was through the 'CW' scheme, so called because it was organized through the Commission and Warrant Branch. During the war it was mainly applied to 'Hostilities Only' ratings with educational qualifications, and effectively provided an opportunity for middle-class recruits to obtain a commission. Admiralty instructions referred to 'intelligent men who can quickly absorb instruction and have the required character and personality'.

Official statements laboured to argue that making permanent ratings into temporary officers was too disruptive. Spending a few months as an ordinary seaman before being commissioned was thought to be very different from spending years rising through the ranks. There was also a strong argument that experienced senior ratings and petty officers were just as crucial to the efficient operation of warships as commissioned junior officers. The CW scheme did produce some broadening of the social criteria for officers. Yet this remained a potent potential grievance and, to many spurned internal candidates, a strong impression of class discrimination remained.

One of the most cynical, angry and eloquent critics of the system was Charles Thomas. As a teenager, he had been fascinated by wireless telegraphy. By the late 1920s he was a committed hobbyist, putting together and operating wireless communication sets and spending hours sending messages through the developing technology. He was well educated, having won a scholarship to Chorlton High, a new secondary school in Manchester. When a branch of the RNVR dedicated to wireless experts was established in Manchester, he was one of its first recruits. After a short time working as a laboratory assistant, he transferred into the Royal Navy proper as a wireless telegraphist in 1934, for a standard term of seven years in the main fleet and five more as a reservist afterwards.

Thomas was in an unusual and unenviable position. If he had volunteered at the outbreak of war, there might have been a good chance of a commission in the RNVR on account of his secondary education. As it was, he was an experienced specialist in a critical branch of the navy and far too valuable where he was, or so it seemed, to be allowed to advance beyond the rank of petty officer to a full commission. Even before the war, Thomas had strong views on the issue. 'The administration of our Fighting Services seems to me to be a fine example of blockheaded stupidity,' he wrote to his brother in 1938. 'How much longer are they going to recruit officers from the chosen class? How much longer are they going to put money and social position before efficiency?'

Thomas had plans after the war 'to get a movement going amongst the younger people to force the throwing open of the Services and the abolition of the Society side of it all'. He became increasingly frustrated, bitter and depressed about his situation. 'If I voiced these opinions openly (that is more than I do) I would have the pleasure of being dismissed from the Service as a communist agitator,' he complained, adding poignantly, 'Nobody is interested however and I am laughed at by anybody I mention my ideas to.'

While experienced men like Charles Thomas discovered fresh challenges after the outbreak of war, the new intake faced an even steeper learning curve. Fresh recruits were introduced to naval life in 'stone frigates': naval barracks and training centres around Britain.

Each was given the HMS prefix and run as if it were a ship. The kitchens would be the 'galley', the medical room was the 'sick bay', the dining area was the 'mess', even the floor would always be called the 'deck'. There were different shore establishments for each of the various branches of the navy. HMS *Dolphin* at Gosport catered for the submarine service. In Portsmouth, HMS *Vernon* specialized in torpedoes. HMS *Excellent* on Whale Island, Portsmouth, was the specialist gunnery centre. HMS *King Alfred* in Hove trained prospective officers.

Wartime recruits and signals ratings were initially welcomed at HMS *Royal Arthur* near Skegness. It was a perfect example of naval pragmatism, being based at the Butlin's holiday camp. Morning parade was held on a wide concrete road alongside putting greens, a swimming pool, theatres and the dance hall. The accommodation was, unfortunately, better suited to summer holidays than winter drill. Sid France entered the navy in January 1940, and arrived at *Royal Arthur* amid snow and freezing temperatures. He and his fellow recruits were led to the holiday chalets where sailors were billeted. Each wooden hut housed two men, and contained a double bed with a partition down the middle. France suggested to his bedmate that they remove the partition. The other man gladly agreed, and so 'the newest additions to the world's greatest Navy committed their first breach of King's Rules and Admiralty Instructions by removing the boards and snuggling together under six blankets'.

Vincent Shackleton had worked as a clerical assistant in a wool mill near Bradford before joining the navy, and a very different world:

We came together, clerks, refuse collectors, bank managers, mechanics, teachers, fitters and others representing a whole gamut of occupations. Within a month we had been sorted into some category or trade. We learned a new language, came to accept the discipline without question, were conditioned to carry out orders without questioning their validity and accepted an unvarying routine. Some of the lads had never made a bed in their lives, others were incapable of sewing on a button. They came from the far north of Scotland, from Dawlish in Devon, from the slums of Liverpool, and fifteen of them came from 'the smoke' with every variety of cockney accent. We had to learn to communicate, to get on together, to eat and sleep as a community, to accept the principles of fair shares for all, and the preservation of a high standard of cleanliness and appearance which was gently, but very firmly, forced upon us. There were some rebels, but they were few and far between.

The other main training centre for 'Hostilities Only' ratings was HMS *Ganges* at Shotley, near Ipswich. Before the war, it had been infamous as the navy's preparatory establishment for boys. Shivering youths ended swimming lessons with a jump from the high diving board, simulating the leap from the high bows of a warship in the event of abandoning a vessel. Any boy refusing to jump voluntarily was simply thrown unceremoniously from the board. Kenneth Rail attended *Ganges* in 1938 when he was fourteen. 'Wisdom it is Strength . . .', went the *Ganges* motto, which was imprinted on his memory. 'Tho' you flogged us, and you flayed us, you took us on as boys, and made us men.'

During the war, naval training could be exceptionally tough. Stan Bowman was at the RN Barracks in Portsmouth in September 1940. Drills were frequent and arduous: '14 collapse on parade ground out of 30,' he recorded in his diary after one session. *Ganges* remained, for some, a grim experience. 'Any difference between it and a concentration camp is purely coincidental,' wrote John Wilson in his letters home. 'One spends six days a week being sworn at by petty officers and one being told by the chaplain not to swear.'

Wilson was the son of Churchill's personal physician, Lord Moran. He volunteered for the navy in 1943, at the age of eighteen. As a clear candidate for officership, despite his youth, he was put through the basic training process before being fast-tracked to a commission. For young men like Wilson, this mixing of men was eye-opening. 'This was the first time I had met the urban working class in large numbers,' he recalled. 'I was struck by the number of unnecessary words they used . . . and astonished by the foulness of their language.'

Distinct elements of the navy had their own training procedures.

Convoy escort vessels trained at Tobermory on the Isle of Mull in the Inner Hebrides, the Fleet Air Arm had specific training programmes for pilots and aircrews, and those new to the Submarine Branch had to learn the rudimentary aspects of operating a new kind of vessel. For those transferring into submarines from surface ships, even simple aspects of shipboard life could prove frustrating. Patrick Mullins recalled one particular problem encountered during his submarine instruction in HMS *Elfin*, in Northumberland:

> We had to master the intricacies of a submarine's 'heads'. The success-ful discharge of the contents of a W.C. depended on the proper operation of a five-position lever and a correct calculation of how much air pressure to build up in the system in order to overcome the external sea-pressure. If you put the lever to 'Blow' with insufficient pressure you suffered the indignity of 'getting your own back'. As the operation naturally brought air bubbles to the surface it was necessary first to hail the officer of the watch and ask him for permission to 'blow'.

Specialist training sought to make practice as realistic as possible, including the use of makeshift equipment, projectors and simulators. Charles Friend trained for the Fleet Air Arm in 1939 at Whale Island. There were simulators to aid prospective fliers: in 'mock-up cockpits which bumped, yawed and generally gave a realistic impression of flying, we looked at a green floor through binoculars. Model ships manoeuvred on it and spots of light were projected down around them as shell splashes.' They were known to trainees as 'seasick-making platforms'.

For some of the less technical branches of service, specialist train-ing was largely absent. R. B. Buckle became a cook in HMS *Warspite*. His qualification for the role was little more than perfunctory. He was asked to prepare a 'test menu' of potato soup, roast beef and Yorkshire pudding, and apple tart. All that was required was to cut two slices of meat from a joint that was already roasting for the ship's evening meal, ladle some cabbage, potatoes and gravy from pots onto plates, and let the Wren assistants finish the remainder.

There were also limitations imposed by the contingencies of wartime. John Wilson trained for a time in HMS *Foudroyant*, a ragged hulk used to instruct new sailors in the basics of seamanship. He described her as a '5th rate 46-gun frigate built at Bombay in 1817 . . . We lived almost exactly as seamen did in Nelson's time.' Geoffrey Hobday recalled that, due to a shortage of boats, trainee officers in Portsmouth had to use ice-cream vendors' tricycles to practise sailing manoeuvres.

Training for new officers could be just as tough as for ratings. John Wilson had already been through ordinary training at the infamous HMS *Ganges*, but he found *King Alfred* equally trying. 'Life is frightful,' he told his family in a letter. 'My hair is turning white under the strain . . . My work is good. I drill with such enthusiasm that I cut my hands to bits on the rifle. I can do no more. I'm doing my best, and more, and if they don't like it that's that. The tension grows every day. Everybody is jumpy and fed up, and we work like fiends. But I'm damned if I'll let them do me in without a hell of a fight.'

Geoff Dormer attended HMS *King Alfred* in May 1940. He was dismayed by the amount of bayonet training: 'exactly what I had joined the navy to avoid'. There were, however, other attractions to young men in sleepy Hove. Many frequented nightclubs such as Rector's or Maxim's, hastily populated by women of ill repute from London. Such establishments were quickly put out of bounds to recruits, but it did little to stop determined clients.

After their initial training was over, ratings and officers would be assigned new jobs, either in ships or shore establishments. A rudimentary medical examination was usually part of the drafting process. John Somers described the procedure:

A long line of men would file past the doctor, usually seated. A bright light strapped to his forehead, or a torch in his hand. Your turn came. 'Drop 'em.' i.e. drop your trousers. Down they went. He shines his light on your privates. 'OK!' Takes knackers in the other hand. 'Cough,' he says. They bounce. 'You're OK. NEXT!' You pull up your trousers and shuffle away. You have passed.

Second Officer Elizabeth Hodges, a young Wren from Yorkshire, worked in a depot drafting office during 1942 and 1943. Her chief duty was to assign new Wrens to jobs and locations throughout Britain. She dealt with a wide variety of young women, including 'a large consignment of girls from the "red light" districts of Cardiff, Liverpool and Glasgow'. She found that interviews were the most useful tool at her disposal. Some women had one particular motive for joining up: 'MEN, in capital letters, would be their ultimate goal.' Hodges sent more streetwise women to cities or convoy hubs, where they would have to deal with the incessant attentions of sailors, whereas the less experienced girls would go to quieter establishments where they would be mainly in the company of other women.

Variety was the hallmark of naval service. A newly drafted sailor might receive any number of possible postings. Aside from the network of 'stone frigates', shore bases and administrative centres, Admiralty offices and foreign bases, a vast array of seagoing craft plied their trades across the world. The most prestigious were the 'capital' ships: the gargantuan battleships, such as HMS *Hood*, that were regarded as the pinnacle of naval endeavour. Known as 'battle wagons' to men in smaller vessels, these giants were manned by over 1,000 sailors and armed with monstrous guns which had the potential to destroy a ship with a single shot. Of a similar size but a very different nature were the aircraft carriers. Up to 1,500 men might be required to operate one of these floating hangars, which were used either as launching pads for offensive strikes or to provide air cover for ocean convoys.

Cruisers were regarded as the equivalents of the Napoleonic frigates: faster and more flexible than the battle wagons, but smaller and with less powerful guns. Smaller still were the destroyers. These were the workhorses of the fleet, involved in everything from protecting battleships to conducting torpedo attacks on enemy battleships or hunting U-boats with depth charges. Destroyers were the classic small ship, with only a couple of hundred men on board. Known as 'boats' rather than 'ships' to some of the more derogatory battleship sailors, they were nevertheless a vital part of the navy's organization.

Corvettes, which became the main escort vessels of the Atlantic, might be manned by barely a hundred sailors, minesweepers even fewer. Submarines were a special case: their crews close-knit and elite. Sailors might also serve in coastal forces, where motor torpedo boats carried perhaps a dozen men. Aside from the warships and escort vessels, the navy managed all manner of vessels, many of which were makeshift or irregular. There were vast depot ships providing logistical support, small sloops and barges, minelayers and frigates, launches and cutters, anti-aircraft gunships and bombardment monitors.

When they joined a new ship, sailors were thrown into a new environment with unfamiliar associates. Officers might have the luxury of a cabin. Ratings would have to search for a place to sling their hammock, with all the best spaces usually already taken, locate a locker in a cramped mess, and find a seat at the right table. Some newcomers made friends quickly, others were regarded with ambivalence by their messmates until they proved themselves. Every ship was different; every group of sailors had its own character. Not everyone was happy with his initial posting. Sid France was sent to the Admiralty Guard in Bath: one of a small group of ratings serving as an armed guard for naval staff. 'I was disgusted,' he wrote, 'I had volunteered for the Navy to go to sea and they'd made me a bloody soldier!' For those who found their particular role unsatisfactory, hopes of escape rested on a transfer or, in the worst-case scenario, sinking.

For a newly commissioned ship and a newly formed ship's company, the process of 'working up' was the key to efficiency and morale. This was the period before the start of active operations, during which training, trialling and testing would take place, in order to ensure that both the mechanical and the human elements of the ship were fully prepared and in good working condition. Ideally, this was not merely a time for practice, but of pushing a ship and its crew to the limits of their capabilities.

Men would arrive at a dockyard from all over the country. Officers would have gathered beforehand, to be briefed by the commanding officer. When the newly commissioned ship was ready, it would be signed over to the captain. Midshipman John Roberts eventually got his wish for 'blood and thunder' and was transferred to a destroyer in

1. 'I don't want to frighten you darling . . .' John Evans and Moyra.

2. Emperor Haile Selassie, travelling through Ethiopia with an armed guard,
January 1935.

3. Charles Hutchinson, photographed in 1944.

4. Aircraft recognition training on board HMS *Rodney*, 1943. Sailors examine a selection of model planes on the deck.

5. The wrecks of German supply ships in Narvik harbour, after the attack by British destroyers on 13 April 1940, photographed by the Fleet Air Arm.

6. A stoker fuelling the furnace on board the armed trawler HMT *Stella Pegasi*, June 1943.

7. Cleaning the guns on board HMS *Mauritius*, August 1942.

8. Washing down the decks of HMS *Rodney*, August 1940.

9. Two young ratings from HMS *Hood*, pictured early in the war with the ship's mascot.

10. British sailors from HMS *Malaya* read about the sinking of the *Hood* at Brooklyn Navy Yard, New York.

11. On their return to Gibraltar after helping to sink the *Bismarck*, sailors from HMS *Sheffield* raise their caps to acknowledge the cheers from crowds ashore.

12. The assembled ship's company of HMS *Prince of Wales* with Winston Churchill and his staff, upon their return to Scapa Flow after meeting President Roosevelt in Newfoundland, August 1941.

13. Sailors from *Prince of Wales* abandon ship, with HMS *Express* alongside, 10 December 1941.

14. Commander George Blundell (*right*) pictured with Captain the Honourable Guy Russell, on board HMS *Nelson*, November 1943.

15. HMS *Penelope* under repair in Malta, January 1942. The shell splinters on her hull led to the nickname 'HMS *Pepperpot*'.

16. Lashed to HMS *Penn* and HMS *Ledbury*, the stricken tanker *Ohio* nears Malta, 15 August 1942.

17. Paul and Evelyn Chavasse, during their investiture at Buckingham Palace. Paul (*left*) survived the sinking of his minelayer in 1940, and was torpedo officer of HMS *Jamaica* at the Battle of North Cape in 1943. Evelyn (*right*) commanded destroyers in the Atlantic, including HMS *Broadway* which sank U-89. Their elder brother (*centre*) was a colonel in the army.

18. An ex-American destroyer drops a depth charge during an Atlantic convoy, May 1941.

19. After their U-boat is sunk by British ships, German submariners are helped aboard a destroyer.

20. Another mark is added to the tally of U-boat kills on board the destroyer HMS *Hesperus*, December 1943.

October 1943. He described the day that HMS *Serapis* was finally ready for duty:

> At last we commissioned. On the 13th according to plan, but there was still work to do in the ship. The ship's company arrived in the morning and in the afternoon we took in all our stores. It was a busy day; the workmen still trying to finish off jobs, and we trying to sort ourselves out. Dust and smoke from recent welding hung everywhere; the smell of new paint mixed with that of the first meals being cooked in the galleys. Just before midnight things quietened down, exhausted but contented we turned in, testing the springs in our new untried bunks carefully . . . The ship was alive, she was ours, no longer the centre of clattering of pneumatic drills, riveters and cutters . . . No, our home was our own.

Seasickness was ubiquitous in the first days at sea. Working up *Serapis* in Scottish waters over the winter of 1943, John Roberts commented on the problem in his journal: 'About a hundred of our seamen had never been to sea before and their tummies completely gave it up! The wheelhouse stank like a pig sty and there was hardly anybody fit enough to steer the ship.' Petty Officer C. C. Young, an old hand, described how he and the other veterans took new recruits 'from the messdeck on our shoulders up to the wings of the bridge, hung them over and said "Now lookout – or else". Hard medicine, but it worked and in two days they were doing their work well. One of the finest cures for seasickness was work, it took your mind off it and you had no time for self pity.'

Time at sea was essentially battlefield training. Midshipman Davies of HMS *Renown* recorded the details of a training exercise in October 1942: 'It was assumed that we, in company with two other capital ships, four cruisers and destroyers were bombarding an enemy shore base. This gave the 15-inch [guns] opportunity for exercise, also the 4.5-inch which were constantly in action repelling air attacks. During the forenoon we were hit twice by torpedoes on the port side, in addition we received a small bomb hit on the after deck, which started a fire.'

Although realism was a central ambition of naval practice, there were limits. 'There appeared to be some chivalry on both sides for this operation,' wrote Davies, 'as a truce was called for lunch.' In the afternoon, *Renown* was again 'attacked' by bombers and several 'German ships': 'During the course of the action we received two 11" shell hits, and one 8" all starting large fires. The enemy lost the "Lutzow" and "Scheer". Survivors were picked up and instructions were given that "the hands of prisoners were not repeat not to be bound" . . . A commentary was given over the broadcaster throughout the whole exercise, on the whole sounding quite convincing and lending a far more realistic atmosphere to the whole thing.'

The value of such training was varied. An earlier damage control exercise in the battleship had been less successful, as John Roberts explained: 'The damage control and fire parties failed to imagine the conditions under which a real torpedo hit would force them to work. Thus the real value of the exercise was lost and there were people calmly walking through "flooded" compartments, or using water to put out electrical fires.'

One celebrated example of wartime working up was the corvette training establishment HMS *Western Isles*, at Tobermory, which prepared ships for escort duty. It was run by the indomitable Commodore Gilbert 'Monkey' Stephenson, also known to the corvette crews as the Terror of Tobermory. His emphasis on the test, the ruse and the trick was intended to produce initiative amongst officers and men. One sailor recalled that 'he'd allocate a ship to raid another ship during the night and pinch anything they could find, like the log books or gun off the bridge or something like that, and woe betide the officer [commanding the raided vessel] next morning'. In another well-known episode, Stephenson dropped his cap onto the deck of a corvette and announced that it was a bomb. When the quartermaster kicked it into the sea, 'Monkey' paused before stating that the cap was now a man overboard that needed to be saved. Geoff Dormer attended Tobermory in 1941. 'When displeased,' he recalled of Stephenson, 'he would bounce up and down, and literally froth at the mouth.'

Combat on land and in the air was subject to any number of variables. For the average sailor in a warship, however, the experience of battle was, in theory, far more predictable. The aim of naval training was to ensure efficiency under any circumstances. This might not always have been successful, but it could be invaluable. One junior officer recalled his response when his frigate was hit by 'friendly fire' from an American ship: '[Y]ou're disciplined in the sense that you know what to do if this sort of thing happens. This is what naval discipline's about. It's not a question of standing up and saluting but, in this situation, you do it by numbers, it comes to you automatically . . . It's not parade-ground stuff, it's survival, because you know what to do next.'

At sea, the need for purposeful training manoeuvres was acute. In the Indian Ocean in May 1940, Captain Blundell complained that aboard HMS *Kent*, 'The tragedy is that we are <u>never</u> allowed to carry out proper realistic practices in case somebody should faint, or the ship should get off course, or the log stop. Better this, say I, than we should all die in action through lack of having practised it when we had the chance.'

Although the ultimate goal was to produce efficient ships' companies who could perform their duties under pressure, the process of working up did not apply only to ships. Practical training was but one part of the initiation of a new sailor. 'The first two weeks on board were probably the worst two weeks of my naval career,' recalled Ken Nodder of joining the aircraft carrier HMS *Furious* in January 1940. 'Everything was strange; finding your way around the ship was bewildering, the talk was "foreign" (nicknames for equipment and procedures, parts of the ship were confusing and the language was "blue"), the routine was strict, amenities were primitive and the ship was crowded.' To become a true sailor meant embracing a new kind of society.

# 7. Memor Es Tuorum

When Captain Angus Nicholl took command of the cruiser HMS *Penelope* in October 1941, he gathered the ship's company and explained his philosophy:

> In my eyes every man on board is of equal importance. It is obvious that a gunlayer is an important man but before he presses his trigger he has to know that the rest of the gun's crew have done their job properly. And none of the gun's crews can work properly unless they are kept properly fed by the ship's cooks. Our job is to fight the enemy, to destroy his warships with our shells and torpedoes; but to enable the ship to do this the engine room staff, the signalmen and the wireless men have a vital part to play in seeing that the ship gets to the right place at the right time.

Each ship, boat or base had a distinctive character, shaped by the attitudes of leaders, the nature of its personnel and their shared experiences. To imbue each individual with a sense of this character was fundamental in establishing the cohesion to which Nicholl aspired. Several institutional cultures existed beneath the umbrella of the Royal Navy. The code of the submarine service was shaped by its extreme operational demands. The Fleet Air Arm was a nascent organization quickly building its own ethos, distinct from that of both the RAF and the wider navy. Coastal forces had their own colourful character. Wrens often had very different attitudes from their male counterparts.

But alongside the divisions within the service was a strong institutional identity which was at the heart of the navy's character. Sailors entered a unique community, with its own venerated culture and history. Despite the influx of new recruits and the changing demands on the service during the war, this collective identity endured. Everyday life in the Royal Navy was irrevocably shaped by the nature of naval society.

The famous bell-bottoms of the rating and the officer's tailored suit were visible representations of the Royal Navy's culture and historic identity. Yet uniform also provided one of the most explicit means of differentiating between ranks, classes and departments. Officers' uniforms were a particularly obvious example. Coloured features integrated into the standard suit signified areas of expertise. Engineers, for instance, were designated purple, paymaster administrators were white, medics had an appropriate scarlet. Embroidered rings on the sleeves of regular and reserve officers distinguished their status: straight rings for Royal Navy regulars, crossed lines for those from the Royal Naval Reserve, and 'wavy' lines for the Royal Naval Volunteer Reserve.

Although they were eventually phased out, the longevity of such obvious distinctions reflected a corporate resistance to their abandonment. A familiar adage claimed that regular RN officers were gentlemen attempting to be sailors, RNR officers were sailors attempting to be gentlemen, and RNVR officers were neither attempting to be both. Many regular officers were initially unenthusiastic about reservists, particularly if they failed to live up to the high standards expected of them. 'These RNVR officers do not realize the prestige and behaviour the RN confers on them,' wrote George Blundell of HMS *Kent*, after a disciplinary transgression by a volunteer.

Parity of respect between regulars and reservists was difficult to achieve. While regulars might have looked down on their 'amateur' counterparts, reservists too resented the attitudes of some 'careerists'. Alex Hughes, an RNR officer serving in an elite reconnaissance unit in 1944, complained in his diary about the ambitious arrogance of some of his regular navy counterparts who wanted to pick and choose their assignments:

I think that some of these permanents came into this racket as a short cut to the limelight and 'gongs' which would be of use to them after the war . . . Actually right through the Navy one finds the same thing – the permanents always have an eye to the future – even if that may be to the detriment of the present execution of the war. Most of the Reserves

feel as I do I think. We are trained and will be needed at short notice –
therefore sit back, keep fit and carry out development where possible . . .
my pride will not let me refuse to do a job when it does turn up.

Successful officers sought to reduce divisions. In his inaugural address,
Angus Nicholl told his officers that he was 'only concerned with the
way each of them did their job. They had equal responsibility for the
efficiency of the ship; and so far as I was concerned all gold stripes
looked the same and I was completely colour-blind to distinction cloth.'

Such was the scale of civilian entry into the service that traditional
assumptions were naturally challenged by force of numbers. While
some officers retained their prejudices, many more were greatly appreciative of the efforts of their volunteer colleagues. It was significant
that the crucial campaign in the Atlantic was fought largely by junior
or middle-ranking officers, many of whom were volunteers by the
end of the war. 'Naval wardrooms are properly defended against the
incursions of uncouth and unfamiliar types,' wrote RNVR officer
Lieutenant H. F. Hooper in 1944. 'The Navy imparts a precious fla-
vour to the life of anyone who joins it, but in the exigencies of war, it
has had to tolerate the peculiarities of outsiders who, like myself, are
not willing to surrender their souls to it unconditionally.'

The distinction between regulars and reservists was by no means
confined to the wardroom. The influx of 'Hostilities Only' draftees into
ships manned by regular ratings could cause mutual resentment. One
volunteer, Signalman H. Osborne, described his new messmates as 'a
poor crowd of active service ratings who I'm afraid turned me against
Naval life . . . They seemed solid from the neck up and all you could get
out of them was the blaming of Hostilities Only men for everything.'

Class distinctions endured throughout the war. Conditions aboard
ship reflected the social divide. Officers usually ate in the wardroom,
waited on by a steward, often a working-class petty officer. Submariner Ian Anderson described in his diary how one steward had
asked for 'a rub up over which knives and forks to use as he usually
found he had two or three left over after one of them slap up din-
ners . . . So we spent the evening gin session in drawing out a neat
diagram illustrating the proper order of implements, enough for a City

dinner, with note on etiquette to match.' The note included the proper method of eating asparagus, and the appropriate uses for finger bowls.

Perceived injustices resulting from social standing were the cause of much resentment. At the height of the conflict, Charles Thomas remained frustrated at the commissioning of upper-class civilians over internal candidates: 'I have no faith in a Navy which, at a time when the fate of our Empire hangs in the balance, prefers to give commissions as officers to civilians whose only qualifications for such are social position and approved education, in preference to trained and educated seamen.'

As such complaints became ever more pressing, they developed into a wider radicalism. 'What I've seen of this war so far has opened my eyes for the rest of my life,' wrote Charles Hutchinson in his diary, 'and I'm convinced that most of the men who are supposed to be educated and act as leaders are no better than any working man in England – just appearance, that's all – and when it calls for anything else it's lacking.' 'It seems that all the elite, providing they work their cards right become "Officers" in the forces,' wrote Petty Officer Edward Records in 1942. 'I feel that in the Navy it isn't so much what one can do but how you can speak. If you can talk well it goes further than working well.'

Although shipboard life reflected certain aspects of wider society, it also encouraged a peculiar form of social interaction. Descriptions of personal relationships aboard British naval vessels often evoked familial metaphors: 'brother sailors', 'brother officers', the 'brotherhood of the sea', or the inevitable Shakespearean 'band of brothers'. Older mentors were known as 'Sea Daddies'. When commanding a cruiser, wrote Admiral Sir Angus Graham, 'one is the father of a British family of nearly a thousand officers and men, with closer ties than any other family because we are confined together almost continuously in the steel hull of a ship'. Geoffrey Hobday wrote that, on his motor gun-boat, 'we resembled a large family, with myself as the father figure'. Many sailors felt, as one corvette crewman put it, a 'family feeling'.

Yet there were many who described their shipmates not as brothers, but as pals, mates, or simply friends. 'One sometimes made good friends aboard ship,' recalled veteran rating Leonard Harris, 'but more often than not the friendship would last only for the duration of the ship's commission. Such was the drafting procedure, it was certainly possible that two close friends, after a ship had been paid off, might never serve together again.' For some, this became a significant feature of life at sea. One medical officer wrote that 'there was friendship but no real comradeship'.

There were no platoons in the navy. Small groups did not, as a rule, train and go into the front line together. Basic training was short and, although several men might be drafted en masse to form a new ship's company, individuals were often transferred alone in order to fulfil particular operational requirements. Even once established in one ship, sailors might easily be drafted away to join another, subject to the requirements of the service. Midshipman J. F. W. Weir had spent barely a month in HMS *Kingston* in July 1941 when he received a draft chit for a transfer to *Ajax*. 'No sooner am I settling down and getting names and the like weighed off than I have to move on,' he wrote in his journal. 'It is all in the game.'

Friendships between sailors were therefore entirely dependent on circumstances. On many larger vessels sailors might only rarely socialize with those from other parts of the ship. Engine-room artificers, for example, might know little about the wireless operators. Friction between different 'professions' was common. Men with more technically skilled roles guarded their privileged positions jealously. Yet it was not simply the physical mechanics of friendship that were influenced by naval service. Telegraphist Donald Goodbrand, who served in the destroyer *Obdurate*, described social relationships based solely on professional association, rather than personal intimacy:

> People didn't talk much about their private lives, the world of their wives, sweethearts, parents, children or domestic circumstances; the non-naval insights were usually kept in a private compartment of the mind . . . The magical quality of the here and now, the present, took over and thrust all other elements into the background, even photographs of loved ones. Nobody's business but one's own.

For Charles Thomas, separated from many of his working-class peers by a secondary education and subsequent social detachment, personal relationships were even less rewarding. He was a loner, preferring his own company to that of his more raucous messmates. 'I have no friends,' he wrote in a typically cynical yet melancholic letter home. 'Acquaintances are useful, friends a nuisance because in the Navy the "lending money" capability of a person is the criterion of friendship and I neither borrow nor lend. I go ashore with my shadow, he is the most intelligent man on the ship.'

Unloading his unhappiness onto the page was undoubtedly a coping mechanism – not all of his letters were quite so downbeat – but Thomas struggled to engage with the community aboard ship, and his frustration at the class-bound hierarchy served to cement his disaffection. On Boxing Day 1940 he wrote to his sister: 'I am very much alone and am very loathe to write about this life because for me it is becoming a hideous nightmare . . . I am only depressed on odd days of the week – on the even days I am bored – the variation keeps me going.'

Naval service could be a deeply troubling experience on a personal level. Periods of loneliness, melancholy and depression were seldom admitted to, but undoubtedly common. Separation from family and friends, from the comforting fabric of British society and from the intellectual freedoms of peacetime life, combined with war-weariness, contributed to Richard Walker's thoughts on the fifth anniversary of the outbreak of war in September 1944:

> The chief drawback of warfare is not so much the long periods of inaction, not even the infliction of discipline, but intellectual isolation. You can't go to a concert or look at a picture. If you want a book your choice is limited . . . You can't think because it's time for 'hands fall in' or you must go on watch. You can't talk sensibly because the main subjects are either sport or naval personalities. Your sense of values falters and loses its balance and you do not know what is worthwhile and what is not.

A ship was not only a war machine: it was a home. Despite the upheaval inherent in wartime service, many sailors formed an emotional attachment to their vessels. In June 1942 Geoffrey Dormer described the reaction of one man who had to leave the trawler *Cape*

*Argona*: 'One of our nicest ratings, who had been on board since the beginning of the war, was drafted and left the ship in tears.'

Yet it was relatively uncommon for a sailor to remain in one ship throughout the war, a result not only of damage to ships and subsequent redrafting, but also the purposeful rotation of personnel to ensure the efficient allocation of skilled men. Transferring from a big ship to a small ship, perhaps from a battleship to a destroyer, or vice versa, often required considerable readjustment. Many of those who served on destroyers believed that they engendered a closer kind of community. C. C. Young, a veteran of destroyers, described 'the absolute trust we had in each other . . . there was this great atmosphere of comradeship, <u>one never let his shipmate down</u>, and this spirit extended to the officers as well'.

Collective identities were built on shared experiences and on tribal loyalty. Competitive sports between ships' companies were common. Sailing races, athletics, football and hockey, and many other activities served to cement team spirit. Inter-ship rivalry was actively encouraged, and could be a useful method of maintaining morale. Even bar-room brawls between groups of sailors from different ships were sometimes seen as indicators of admirable social bonding.

The names of warships were occasionally utilitarian, but those which were more evocative – British towns, imperial territories, naval heroes – could often provide a focal point for group identity. After transferring to HMS *Nelson*, George Blundell noticed one line in a letter he was censoring: '"We are bound to do something big as the spirit of 'Nelson' hovers over this ship." A nice thought!' Ludovic Kennedy was a junior officer in HMS *Tartar*, part of a destroyer flotilla including several ships of the Tribal class: *Eskimo*, *Mashona*, *Matabele*, *Ashanti* and *Bedouin*. He recalled that on the cold winter nights at Scapa Flow, 'we entertained each other dressing up as whatever [tribe] we were and got fairly pissed, and we sang lovely songs'.

Alcohol played a significant role in social interaction. The rum ration was becoming a contentious issue by the Second World War, and was often underplayed in contemporary descriptions of naval life which intended to portray the service in a positive light. 'A remarkably abstemious body is the Navy,' claimed one wartime book.

'Many men prefer nowadays to draw a small amount of pay "in lieu of" their daily rum.' Some did opt out, receiving an extra threepence per day. But the overwhelming majority continued to take the rum ration. Along with mealtimes, the drawing and measuring of the daily tot for every eligible man – 'up spirits' – was a carefully observed fixture of the naval routine. Donald Goodbrand described it being 'portioned out like a holy oblation'.

Along with the daily tot, rum was used to celebrate special occasions – known as 'splicing the mainbrace' – and to galvanize men before battle, or reward them afterwards. It also had many different purposes on the lower deck. As an unofficial currency, it enabled sailors to reward favours and pay debts without having to rely on money, instead using an age-old system of 'denomination' involving 'sippers', 'gulpers' and 'tots'. Saving and storing the rum ration, although illegal, enabled sailors to celebrate after good news, commiserate after bad, or apologize after a squabble. There is no doubt that the ration was immensely popular, and not only with the old hands. But rather than merely acting as an anaesthetic, it was the social and psychological aspects of the grog ration that gave it such potency.

Food also shaped relationships aboard ship. The daily routine was largely organized around mealtimes. A typical schedule might begin with 'heave out' at 5.30 a.m., with morning duties followed by breakfast. Between eleven and noon men would receive their rum, then would come 'dinner', the main meal of the day. In the afternoon there would be 'tea' and the evening 'supper' would be at around 7 p.m., with 'pipe down' at around 10 p.m. This meal routine tended to be far more important than the work schedule in providing stability and reassurance for sailors, making food an emotive subject which had a great impact on day-to-day life.

Impromptu fishing was common aboard destroyers and small craft, whose crews could take advantage of depth-charge exercises to collect a fresh meal. Yet for men so familiar with the sea, the finer points of fishing were sometimes lost. Richard Campbell-Begg recorded one incident in October 1942: 'The steward, who has been fishing out of the gun-room porthole, has just caught a fish which looks like a cod and a large one too. There has been some argument about the best way of killing it but it finally succumbed after being hit half a dozen times on the back of the head with a large spoon.'

The availability of food was shaped by geography, which meant that there was rarely a standard naval menu. A dazzling array of dishes and drinks were consumed during the war, ranging from artificial creations to local delicacies: Bombay oysters, a combination of raw eggs and Worcester sauce; pineapples and bananas from the Azores; Takoradi Club lager, made from groundnut oil, from the Gold Coast; Manchester tart with custard; 'Chinese wedding cake', otherwise known as rice pudding. There were some staples. Pot mess, a stew made with whatever ingredients happened to be available, was perhaps the most familiar. Tins were also ubiquitous, ranging from McConnochie's herrings in tomato sauce to Carnation milk.

The connection between food and social interaction was fundamentally altered by a gradual shift from 'canteen' to 'general' messing arrangements. Canteen messing divided men into small groups, each responsible for its own food budget with which to purchase additions to the staples of bread, potatoes and tea. Each mess would nominate one of its members to take raw ingredients to the galley to be cooked, and back again to the mess table. It ensured choice and variety, but not always in a positive sense. Men then had to pay for any supplements to their meals out of their own pockets at the NAAFI counter. As HMS *Glasgow*'s hard-up Able Seaman Hall wrote: 'You can't help spending a bit on something decent to eat.'

Larger warships were more likely to have general messing, with a centralized budget managed by the paymaster commander and a more sizable communal eating area. Not only did this desegregate sailors, it also removed one potential cause of stress by taking over meal budgets. Catering on such a scale required a substantial commitment of space and technology. Aboard the battleship *Prince of Wales* in 1941, the journalist H. V. Morton was struck by kitchens which baked 1,500 loaves each day, and 'where electrical ovens and every kind of aluminium device challenges comparison with the kitchens of the Ritz'.

It was not only sailors who had to be fed. During service in the Arctic over the summer of 1943, one of HMS *Kent*'s petty officers rescued a baby seal during a storm. 'Horace is now installed in his special quarters in the foc's'le locker,' noted Richard Campbell-Begg in his diary. The crew took care of Horace's every need, feeding him with diluted tinned milk and even providing a regular evening bath: 'He is carried down the gangway and, after some hesitation, takes to the water, swims around for a while and then returns to the gangway to be picked up.' Horace died when an ignorant rating fed him catfish. Happily, a replacement was found within weeks: a female baby seal, which was named Daphne.

In an environment moulded by metal and machinery, it was not surprising that animals should have been so welcome in warships. Before the war, ships often housed a menagerie of wildlife. Dogs and cats were commonplace but bears and lion cubs were not unknown. In tropical waters, monkeys, mynah birds and parrots might be acquired. Locals took advantage of inebriated sailors on shore leave to offload chameleons or lame donkeys. Leonard Harris recalled that in the 1920s and 1930s, most requests for pets were granted by officers. The only exception that came to mind was a mongoose, which was refused on the grounds that it 'did not really come into the pet category'.

In wartime, ships' mascots became minor celebrities, taking centre stage in communal photographs, featuring heavily in press reports or pictured on celebratory greetings cards. Several were rescued or liberated from the Germans. When the men of the destroyer *Orwell* rescued a dog from a U-boat along with prisoners of war, it was adopted and named 'Little Nazi'. When a black cat and her kitten managed to sneak aboard HMS *Orion* in 1940, they were adopted at the instant they were discovered. Sailors were smitten with the kitten, a 'lovely little thing', as Henry Hackforth explained: 'Unfortunately when he was a week old he was stepped on and killed by someone in the darkness during an exercise night action.'

Pets were central to collective identity, but pests could also provide bonding experiences. In 1941, Charles Thomas and the sailors of *Capetown* cooperated to catch rats coming aboard up the ropes when in dock, baiting traps with banana and aniseed. Seagulls were even less popular. They were far more of a nuisance than cockroaches, which were unpleasant but harmless and could at least be raced for gambling purposes.

Sailors were fond of traditional games, and particularly those which involved a wager. Playing for money was strictly forbidden, but this did not prevent tombola or bingo being sanctioned on occasion by officers. Card schools were rife, although the rum tot was a more common stake than the coin. One of the most infamous games in the navy was 'Crown and Anchor': a straightforward dice game in which the odds were heavily against the players. Leonard Harris was an old hand:

Crown and Anchor is played by means of a board marked off in six sections and each being marked with a symbol, these being a crown, anchor, heart, club, diamond and spade; there are also three dice which have the same symbols. To play, the mugs would back their fancy, the operator would roll the dice, and then pay out on the three symbols which were showing. Take for example, the diamond; one showing would pay even money, two would pay two to one, and all three up would pay three to one.

There was one game which epitomized the collective character of the navy at leisure above all others. 'The great game in the boat just now is Uckers,' wrote submariner Ian Anderson in November 1939. 'This is better known as Ludo, but of course it would be too childish to play that so a more grown up name is given to it in the Service.' Uckers was a colourful communal pastime, and leagues and tournaments proliferated throughout the fleet. 'What excitement you can have playing uckers,' wrote John Somers, now serving aboard the cruiser *Dauntless*. 'We have an enlarged version of this: a four foot square board on deck, dice three inches square shaken out of a bucket, the players all dressed in fancy dress made out of the signal flag bunting. Usually one mess deck plays another. Seamen v Stokers or Marines v Torpedo men or the petty officers' mess will put out a team. All helps to relieve the tedium.'

Uckers would be played with whatever equipment was available. At its most spectacular, the board might be a large canvas sheet covering the deck, with an empty bucket or oil drum containing oversized dice, and a cheering crowd of participants. The champion usually wore a special hat, but outlandish attire was a minimum expectation for players. Some might wield bongo drums, whistles or any number of odd utensils. Derric Breen described it as 'fancy dress gone wild; the gear was each player's prized possession'.

Naval life involved a level of intimacy between males that would have been unusual to most civilians at the time, and sailors were far from squeamish about appearing to flout traditional gender roles: from taking part in all-male dancing partnerships in the absence of women to performing and watching male stripteases during raucous naval variety concerts, known as Sod's Operas. Richard Campbell-Begg described a 'glamour boy' contest, held by sailors in the Indian Ocean in early 1945, in which 'five muscular seamen, dressed as girls, and wearing the shortest of shorts were judged on the beauty of their legs'.

Female involvement in such events was rare. Yet the influx of women into the navy did provide other opportunities which were eagerly seized. Charlotte Dyer and some of her fellow Wrens in Liverpool visited the aircraft carrier HMS *Attacker* in February 1944. The sailors suggested a game of deck hockey on the flight deck. It was seven-a-side, with yellow petrol cans for goalposts and a rope-ring for a puck. 'I thought that was a bit thick,' reported Dyer in her diary, 'not to say dangerous, but we agreed to play . . .'

When we started playing, all the girls, with memories of real hockey, obeyed some of the rules, but we soon got wise to the game, and started picking up the puck and throwing it, kicking it, turning and using the backs of our sticks to our heart's content . . . We played for about half an hour each way, the score being about 6–4 to the men at the end of the game. Then we mixed up the teams and had one final scuffle. I think there were more and harder knocks in that part than any other . . . Still, we all enjoyed it very much . . . Next day most of us were so stiff that we could barely walk, and felt as if we were bruised from head to foot. I'm sure we must have looked very funny, hobbling round the place, like wooden dolls!

Sailors were not excluded from the efforts of the British singers, comedians and entertainers employed by ENSA – the Entertainments National Service Association – to amuse the armed forces. Personal performances were common, initially at Scapa and the other home

bases and later abroad. In the spring of 1943, Noël Coward entertained the sailors of HMS *Warspite* at Malta by performing his
repertoire on the catapult deck. Other musical events were less successful. RNVR officer Patrick Mullins recalled the crowd's reaction
to one concert in Rosyth dockyard, featuring the classical singer Iso-
bel Baillie and pianist Kendall Taylor. The matelots 'whistled and
stamped disapproval as each item was announced'. It was, he wrote,
'one of the most embarrassing occasions I have witnessed'.

The everyday elements of life in the navy – whether in a destroyer
or a battleship, a minesweeper or a motor launch – had implications
for the sense of friendship and community which sailors experienced. But underpinning the daily routine was a wider sense of
collective identity based on history and tradition. The motto of
HMS *Glasgow* was 'Memor es tuorum': 'Be mindful of your ancestors'. This could easily have been a mantra for the entire navy.

Language was a key part of the sailor's inheritance. Regular ratings
and officers used a dialect which was an essential tool in constructing
collective sensibilities amongst recruits, as well as representing a historic heritage. For the uninitiated, there were the nautical basics: port
and starboard, leeward and windward, the forecastle and the stern.
Expletives were ubiquitous and colourful, and there was a host of
impenetrable service abbreviations and technical jargon. But sailors
also had to learn a new vocabulary: 'Jackspeak'. The kitchen became
the galley; toilets became the heads. Clothes were dhobeyed, and there
were punishments for wearing the wrong rig. Orders were piped, lazy
men swung the lead, dinner was served from a fanny, and if a new
recruit struggled to learn the ropes he might feel a little chocker.

Aided by an exclusive vernacular and sense of shared culture, sailors across the navy were also possessed of a collective imagination.
Gossip, stories and anecdotes spread quickly between ships and were
carried all over the world. Seventeen-year-old Midshipman Anthony
Ditcham was serving aboard HMS *Renown* in 1940. He described the
rumours that 'a Royal Marine from *Rodney* was arraigned by Court
Martial on a charge of conduct unbecoming, with a sheep', and the
resulting scenes at Scapa Flow:

True or false, the other ships' companies taunted *Rodney* sailors by waggling their fingers under their chins and bleating 'Wa-a-a-a-gh' like a sheep. This never failed to infuriate the Rodneys, and fights would develop . . . A boatful of libertymen each with a skinful would delight in taunting a *Rodney* launch. One boat would list, as they leaned over crying 'Wa-a-a-a-gh!' and the *Rodney* boat would list as the Rodneys leaned towards their tormentors crying 'You bastards, we'll fill you in ashore'.

Three years later, Vere Wight-Boycott and a friend were exploring the small island of Pantelleria in the Mediterranean. He described in his diary how they had passed a local with a 'beautifully clean sheep with a fleece like silk': 'We thought of buying it and sending it to *Rodney* who had a libertyman at Scapa arrested for pursuing a sheep . . . (The story that his defence was that he thought it was a Wren in a duffle coat is not generally credited.)'

Everyday life across the navy was coloured by the traditional practices which helped to evoke an institution founded on history. Timekeeping by 'bells', the naming of watches, messdeck customs and hammocks, were amongst the features of ships' routines and environments which ensured that, whatever their form of service, men were likely to be mindful of their ancestors despite the presence of modern machinery and technology.

Life was imbued with naval custom, and so was death. The burials at sea of wartime victims echoed those of the past: bodies sewn into weighted hammocks and slipped over the side under the Union Jack along with the traditional intonation, 'We commit his body to the deep'. The tradition of 'sale of dead man's effects' was a practice that was religiously upheld by regular ratings and which could serve to integrate new recruits into the ethos of the navy. This was an auction that took place after a death, in which shipmates made bids for the personal possessions of the deceased; the proceeds would be sent to the surviving family. Offers would invariably be much higher than the actual value of the items – fifteen shillings for a block of chocolate worth twopence, or ten shillings for a bar of soap – and the lots might even be returned to the auction after they had been paid for. This 'rollover' could repeat up to three or four times, raising large amounts of money for anything from personal trinkets to valuable uniforms. Such practices continued largely untouched by the naval authorities. Indeed, they were protected and encouraged.

Other more unusual maritime practices were continued during the war, many of which would have been familiar to the eighteenth-century sailor. One was the 'Crossing the Line' ceremony when passing over the equator. In an elaborate piece of macabre theatre, men who had never been into the southern hemisphere were 'tried' by the court of 'Neptune' for invented humorous misdemeanours and subjected to physical punishments, invariably involving shaving and dunking in a tank of salt water. Twenty-one-year-old Able Seaman Donald Butcher of HMS *Nelson* recorded the event in his diary during 1942: 'Crossed the Line. Piped Down at 0900, had great ceremony of all rites due, Commander as King Neptune, Chief Buffer [boatswain's mate] his Wife and all the rest got caught by their Police, so got shaved, ducked very hard by Bears, and presented with a Certificate! Anyway good experience.'

The ceremony was a common occurrence aboard Royal Navy ships throughout the war, purposefully perpetuated by veteran seamen, and inspired both fascination and fear to the uninitiated. Richard Walker, an RNVR officer in the destroyer *Wakeful*, described the event in 1944. It was, he thought, 'an excuse for a brawl':

Neptune holding his Court on a platform rigged up by the torpedo tubes . . . The Court was fully dressed up and painted, the barber using a huge blood-stained razor, an appalling Foamite mixture for soap, and finishing off with filling the victim's mouth, eyes and nose with some noxious liquid made from God knows what. He was finally upset into a canvas tank, soundly ducked, thrown across into another tank, ducked again and then set free. I was caught and dragged to the block but put up a good fight and escaped the shaving, though ducked innumerable times. The sickbay afterwards was crowded with casualties, one man rather serious; he hit his head on a ring-bolt in his efforts to escape and was covered from head to foot with gore. It was discovered, half-way through, that Neptune himself, aka the Cox'n, had been no further south than Gibraltar, so he was given the hell of a time.

At times, such strong adherence to tradition appeared anachronistic. 'The Navy makes me alternately roar with laughter and nearly cry,' wrote Midshipman John Carter to his parents in November 1940. 'Still we seem to get along somehow. The thing is that we are just struggling out of the old traditional era, of red tape and sailing ships, and an institution like this naturally makes rather heavy weather of breaking away and changing over to modern ways of doing things.'

'There's no doubt every ship in the navy takes Nelson to sea with them,' wrote Charles Hutchinson in his diary. 'You do things because Nelson said it was right.' To the journalist H. V. Morton, the warships of the Royal Navy were 'haunted by Nelson'. To some of his fellow commentators, the navy seemed not so much mindful of its ancestors but rather manacled by them. A wartime account attempted to explain:

> Naval history is something more than a record. It is part of the organic means by which naval warfare is conducted . . . This does not mean that the British Admiralty when faced by a new problem say 'What would St. Vincent do now?' It means rather that in dealing with the problem they adopt an attitude of mind instinctively guided by the same ideas as St. Vincent's, not because they are hidebound pedants, but simply because they are practical seamen going about the business of sea warfare in a practical manner.

'Let us not ignore the lessons of the past,' Captain Alfred Duckworth told an audience of junior officers in 1943. 'We can always be learning, and if there are occasions when we can sometimes learn from the mistakes of our seniors there are surely many more occasions when we can profit from their experience and example. It is thus that our great naval traditions have been built up over the centuries. We should be proud to have succeeded to those traditions and proud to maintain them.'

# 8. A Long and Hazardous Journey

'When we was having milk the bells went for evry body to go and put on life belts. I bet Jimmy and Jerry miss us. Goodbye from your loveing daughter Connie. Sorry for merstacs.' Nine-year-old Connie Grimmond finished her letter to her parents with ninety-two 'X's and a final 'goodbye'. She had also doodled a tiny picture of the *City of Benares*, the passenger liner in which she would be travelling, as she prepared to sail from Liverpool on 13 September 1940, bound for Canada.

There were ninety children on board, along with their adult escorts and over 300 other passengers and crew. It was only the latest of several voyages undertaking what was known as 'seavacuation'. Over 200,000 applications from parents had been handled during the first two weeks of the scheme in the summer of 1940, and by September around 3,500 'seavacs' had already been transported to Canada, South Africa, Australia and New Zealand, safely removed from German bombs and even, perhaps, from German bayonets.

Connie was accompanied by four of her brothers and sisters: five-year-old Lennie, eight-year-old Eddie, ten-year-old Violet and thirteen-year-old Augusta, known as Gussie. They had been evacuated from their home in Camberwell, where they lived with their mother and father and seven other siblings. Gussie was in charge. 'Dear Mum and Dad,' she wrote home. 'It is very lovely here on the ship. I wish you were with us. We go into a big room for meals and we have table napkins and three *different* kinds of knives and forks. We have a menu card and we can choose what we like off the card.' Reassuring her mother that everyone was safe, she finished: 'Please mum, don't worry. There are men to guard us at night in case our boat is sunk.'

On the night of 17 September, four days into the voyage and 600 miles out of Liverpool, *City of Benares* was making her way through a storm in a convoy of eighteen ships. Escorting destroyers had turned back as the group passed into the mid-Atlantic, beyond the usual danger zone for enemy submarines. It had been a difficult day for the passengers. The heavy swell had caused seasickness amongst most of the children, who had been sent to bed early. At 10.30 p.m., the liner was rocked by a huge explosion. She had been torpedoed by U-48.

'We were literally shaken out of our beds,' wrote fifteen-year-old Bess Walder from Kentish Town to her schoolfriends soon after-wards. 'This was followed by louder and terrifying detonations.' She leapt from her bunk in the dark, grabbing her dressing gown, life jacket and raincoat. There were two younger girls in the cabin with her. Bess put a lifebelt on one and led her out to the boat deck, before returning for the second child, struggling through a smashed ward-robe to get into the cabin.

> I found that Ailsa had fallen over something and was bleeding to death. I wrapped her in my coat that I wasn't wearing and tried to get out. The cabin was fast filling up with water and I found to my horror that I couldn't get past the wardrobe. Then I yelled and shouted out and one of the escorts came along and managed to get us out.

Bess carried the wounded girl up to the lifeboats, reaching the top of a flight of stairs just before they collapsed. Her allocated raft had been smashed to pieces.

> By this time Ailsa had fainted and was nearly dead. But she was such a brave little kid and game to the end, which mercifully came while she was unconscious. The escort lowered her into the sea and said a prayer for her, and then hustled me into another lifeboat . . . I felt as if I was in a ghastly nightmare.

Bess nestled into the crowded lifeboat, which was lowered into the turbulent seas. 'Then the sailors tried to row away, but the boat was sadly overloaded with children and passengers from the smashed life-boats (about 70 people in all) and in consequence, the boat soon became waterlogged and we were sitting in water up to our chests. You see the poor little children hadn't a dog's chance. It was awful.'

Children and adults were washed away, until only around twenty were left in the lifeboat, by now rolling violently before it flipped over, throwing its passengers into the sea. Bess managed to swim back to the upturned boat. 'I saw my pal Beth Cummings trying to get on. I held out one hand, and by hanging on with the other I fished her up on top of the boat, where we both hung on to the keel with all our might.'

One by one, the other hands clinging on slipped away until, in a brief moment of calm, the girls could see by the light of the moon that their only remaining companions were two Indian crewmen: 'One was dead. The other was half alive and murmuring "Allah, Allah".' Soon, the wind picked up and the lifeboat was thrown around. 'We were flung sky high, our bodies were lifted into the air and we were still hanging on . . . then we were flung down again like a sack of coals.'

At the break of dawn, they could see only the Atlantic. Then, some twenty hours after the sinking, the unmistakable shape of a warship appeared on the horizon. 'Golly,' wrote Bess, 'you don't know what it was to see, and just to look at that Destroyer, it was absolute pure ecstasy.' Boats were sent out to rescue the scattered survivors. Bess and Beth were hauled out of the sea, their salt-encrusted coats cut off and thick sweaters pulled over their heads as they neared HMS *Hurricane*. 'I saw all the sailors lined up on deck ready to receive us,' wrote Bess. 'My goodness if the U-boat commander had heard the cheer they gave us he would have shivered in his ersatz shoes.'

Safely aboard, the girls were bathed by two women who had themselves only just been rescued. Bess was given a mug of diluted rum. The captain took care of her personally: 'He carried me to his cabin, wrapped in a lieutenant's shirt and a first officer's trousers. I bet I looked odd . . .' While she was resting in the captain's cabin, there was a knock on the door and her ten-year-old brother Louis was brought in. He had been rescued from another lifeboat. 'I was so relieved,' she wrote, 'as I was wondering what I should tell mother if he was lost.'

The survivors were eventually landed at Greenock and taken to hospital. Bess and Louis were then driven to a remote house in the

Scottish Highlands to recuperate with their parents. 'I think we are staying here for some time, as my nerves have gone to pot,' Bess wrote to her classmates, 'but it won't take long to pull myself together again.' She thanked them for their letters: 'I am sorry that I haven't answered before, but I have had such a deluge of letters from all parts of Britain that I think I will have to hire a secretary to help me out with them all.' There was a PS: 'Please excuse writing as my hand is a bit wobbly.'

Of the ninety children aboard, only thirteen survived. Neither Connie Grimmond nor any of her siblings were amongst them. German submariners from U-48 later told survivors that many of their crewmates had been deeply traumatized when they discovered that children had been aboard the liner. From the periscope it had simply appeared to be the largest target in the convoy. Over 250 lives were lost in total, including passengers, crew and officers. The *City of Benares* disaster prompted the immediate cessation of the overseas evacuation programme.

The deaths of civilians, including women and children, served as a maritime echo of the onset of aerial attacks on the British public. There was no more gruesome illustration of the precarious balance of the Atlantic. Yet in some ways the stakes at sea were far greater. This was Britain's lifeline. Almost every part of the country's industry, agriculture and military relied on supplies from overseas. Food and fuel, timber and tools, metals and machinery, all had to be delivered by merchant ships carrying their cargoes across the North and South Atlantic from the Americas and from Africa. This may have been a campaign largely unseen by the public, but the Atlantic was Britain's most important battleground. 'The Atlantic is the vital area,' noted Winston Churchill, 'as it is in that ocean and that alone in which we can lose the war at sea.' And as First Sea Lord Admiral Dudley Pound emphasized: 'If we lose the war at sea, we lose the war.'

Submarines had emerged as a potentially devastating weapon during the First World War. To combat the menace, Britain had developed a technology known as ASDIC, an early form of sonar, which could detect submarines beneath the water. But this nascent and largely untested system had led to complacency within the

Admiralty about the scale of the threat. Anti-submarine tactics and training were not well developed in 1940 and when German submarines gained access to the ports of western France in the summer, the number of merchant vessels they sank began to rise dramatically.

Misguided early attempts to hunt submarines using aircraft carriers had proved disastrous, and were stopped after the loss of HMS *Courageous* in September 1939. Another short-lived ruse was to disguise naval vessels as unarmed merchant ships in order to lure submarines into a confrontation. In the summer of 1940, nineteen-year-old stoker P. R. Pragnell was serving aboard one so-called 'Q-ship', HMS *Cape Howe* – renamed *Prunella* – which was trailing behind a convoy in the eastern Atlantic. 'We made sure we acted the part of merchant seamen with conviction,' wrote Pragnell. 'Looking smart was forbidden. We wore old civilian clothes . . . The skipper stood around with his hands in his pockets and a fag on.' *Cape Howe* was promptly attacked, torpedoed and sunk. With the rest of the convoy long gone, Pragnell and a dozen others crammed onto a small wooden raft. More than fifty of their shipmates perished, and Pragnell's group remained adrift for six days before they were discovered and picked up. He had liberated a box of 2,000 Ardath cigarettes from the canteen before abandoning ship, which he donated to the ratings of the rescue ship.

Convoys were the only viable defensive strategy. After having been adopted late in the First World War, a system was quickly introduced in 1939 by which merchant ships would travel across the Atlantic in organized groups. As the war progressed, an increasingly complex organization developed, requiring no small degree of administrative expertise. Convoys labelled 'HX' were fast-moving and east-bound from Halifax, Nova Scotia. 'SC' designated slower-moving groups on the same route. 'ON' convoys travelled west from Britain to America. Sailing southwards, 'WS' convoys – the so-called 'Winston Specials' – journeyed down the west coast of Africa to Freetown in Sierra Leone, then on to South Africa and from there to the Indian Ocean, Suez, India or Singapore. 'SL' convoys travelled in the other direction, from Sierra Leone to Britain. There was also a plethora of amendments, postponements and additional labels depending on operational conditions.

For much of 1940, convoys travelled for most of the voyage with minimal protection. Escort vessels were in short supply, and accompanied the merchant ships only for the last few days into Britain. Even then, most escorts were small and ill equipped. Newfoundlander R. J. Morry was an able seaman in the sloop HMS *Dundee*. In September 1940 she was escorting convoy SC3 from Sydney, Nova Scotia, to Britain, and was the only protection the merchant ships had. It was a slow journey. 'We knew from the start that it would be a long and hazardous voyage,' recalled Morry. 'The larger ships were forced to wait for the slower ones and rounding up strays was continuous.' Frequent submarine scares resulted in confusion and delay. Morry and his shipmates struggled to cope with the upheaval: 'It seemed that every time I went to shower the action alarm would go and I would end up on the after four gun with only a towel around my waist.'

Just after midnight on 15 September, with the convoy still some way off the west coast of Ireland, it was attacked by U-48, the submarine which would sink the *City of Benares* three days later. 'I was about to dress and proceed to my station when the ship jumped and shook under a series of rapid explosions,' wrote Morry. 'The lights went out, but I was on deck in seconds, surrounded by the smell of burnt explosives. Making my way along the deck aft to my action station, I saw there was nothing aft of the main mast but a tangled mess of mangled, twisted and smoking steel. The stern of the ship was gone, along with the officer's quarters.'

There was little choice but to abandon ship. Morry hurried to his appointed position and joined other sailors in one of the boats. As the skiff sat in the water preparing to cast off, it became clear that all was not well. 'I knew we would sink,' he wrote. 'Seated forward, with my feet on the boat's bottom planks, I could feel cold water creeping up my legs. On the rower's second stroke the skiff swamped and then it was swim or drown.' He found himself alone and struggling, his inflatable lifesaver keeping him afloat.

Morry was delirious, but soon found himself 'hanging grimly' onto the bottom rung of a rescue ladder which had been thrown over the bows of a Norwegian timber ship. Yet this was by no means a sure route to survival: 'Every time the ship rolled I would find myself swinging in the air and as she rolled back I would be doused under the surface. Just to my left, at a distance of twenty feet was the tip of the propeller blade, turning very slowly . . . I was suddenly grasped by a large hand and bodily lifted over the ship's rail and dumped unceremoniously upon the steel deck.'

Convoys needed better protection, but with much of the navy occupied in the defence of British shores and fighting in the Mediterranean, there were far too few escort vessels – frigates, sloops, corvettes and destroyers – than were required to cover the expanding convoys and their vital cargoes. There were new destroyers on the production lines, but in the meantime there was only one way in which the urgently needed ships could be acquired.

A few days after the sinking of the *City of Benares*, in a chilly bay in Nova Scotia, the aging American destroyer USS *Foote* was given a new name and a new commanding officer. The name was HMS *Roxborough*, and the officer was Vere Wight-Boycott. He had travelled to Halifax to take command of the ship, which was one of fifty given to the Royal Navy as part of a deal in which America would gain the right to establish military bases on British territory in the Caribbean and western Atlantic. In an attempt to capture a sense of sympathetic cooperation, each destroyer was named after a town located in both the USA and Britain.

This was a seminal moment, and Wight-Boycott described in his diary how many American captains 'had spent some thought in composing a suitable statement of transfer, and had them very carefully typed on good paper so they could keep the carbon copies as souvenirs'. In the case of USS *Foote*, however, Wight-Boycott's counterpart had no such decorum: 'Calling for his fountain pen he scribbled a receipt in appalling American naval or business office language which was scarcely grammatical. This was run off on his typewriter and I duly signed it. It read: Subject – U.S.S. FOOTE (DD169) – Receipt of. I herewith acknowledge receipt of subject vessel and of equipment as listed on inventories I have received copies of.'

'The U.S. trades 50 old warships for control of the North Atlantic,' crowed *Life* magazine. It was indeed a hard bargain. Yet it illustrated the severity of Britain's predicament in the autumn of 1940. Gold reserves were running low. Credit was tightening. For Vere Wight-Boycott, it was difficult to escape the conclusion that America was taking advantage of Britain's plight. He wrote to his mother to report that 'an American NO [naval officer], who had probably never been more than 100 miles from his own coast said to me "What are you doing over here? Why don't you get back and fight?" An <u>American</u> of all people.' Despite the swingeing terms of the destroyer deal, the symbolism of American intervention was significant. 'The pact with America seems a good thing from the propaganda side anyway,' wrote submariner David Leggatt in the Far East, 'though heaven help the poor devils who have to run those 50 destroyers.'

Initial omens were not good. Wight-Boycott's *Roxborough* was forced to return to harbour only days later after a faulty engine used up most of her fuel. During standard preliminary trials, *Chesterfield* and *Churchill* collided, and *Hamilton* crashed into *Georgetown* and grounded at St John's. By the end of 1940, only nine of the destroyers were at sea, and only thirty were in a serviceable condition by the following summer. HMS *Churchill* was, by virtue of her name, one of the most high-profile of the destroyers. Yet like the others she was old, rickety, and top-heavy, leading to an extreme roll in the open seas and an uncomfortable experience below decks. Sid France first went out into the Atlantic aboard *Churchill* in December 1940. He described the sight at 4 a.m. on the first morning at sea:

Icy rain flew horizontally along the deck, threatening to slice the skin from my face. The deck itself had become a vicious living beast, which seemed to roll both ways at once, at the same time lifting her bow and stern together . . . she was thrown around the ocean like a scrap of paper. Again and again she thrust her bow into the waves and I failed to see how she could struggle to the surface, but she did, every time.

These rickety ships were desperately needed. Such was the success of the U-boats in the summer and autumn of 1940 that their crews would refer to the period as the 'Happy Time'. Methods of attack were developed called *Rudeltaktik*, or 'wolf-pack' to the British. Using radio and signals intelligence, groups of U-boats waited along shipping lanes and attacked merchant ships en masse. Focke-Wulf Condor long-range reconnaissance aircraft took advantage of the empty skies to spot convoys and guide U-boats towards them. Striking at night and on the surface to minimize potential ASDIC detection, small numbers of submarines could do serious damage. In October 1940, convoys SC7 and HX79 were the victims of a single wolf-pack. Nine U-boats sank a total of thirty-two merchant ships, twenty from SC7 and twelve from HX79, equating to some 154,000 tons of cargo. The waters of the eastern Atlantic were the most dangerous in the world.

U-boats were not the only danger. On 5 November 1940, convoy HX84 from Halifax was attacked by the German pocket battleship *Admiral Scheer*. The sole escort was the armed merchant cruiser and converted passenger liner HMS *Jervis Bay*. In an echo of the *Rawalpindi*, Acting Captain E. S. Fogarty Fegen had no hesitation in steaming straight for the enemy while the merchant ships scattered and escaped. There was no question that Goliath would destroy David, and *Jervis Bay* was sunk in twenty-two minutes, taking 186 sailors with her. Like the *Rawalpindi*'s Captain Kennedy, Fegen was awarded a posthumous Victoria Cross. *Scheer* escaped into the South Atlantic having managed to sink only five of the thirty-seven ships in the convoy.

One victim, the tanker *San Demetrio*, was seriously damaged with fires spreading. Anticipating the imminent conflagration of 11,000 tons of oil, the crew took to the life rafts. In what became one of the most celebrated stories of the merchant navy, several of the drifting lifeboats happened upon the tanker two days later, still on fire but still floating. *San Demetrio* was reboarded and her diminished crew set about dealing with the damage and restarting the engines. Back underway, they successfully reached the Clyde a week later.

Merchant crews were no passive observers: they were at the heart of the Atlantic struggle. In April 1941, Arthur Potts was aboard the freighter MV *Rookley*, part of a convoy from Newfoundland to Britain which was attacked by a U-boat south of Iceland:

Three tankers and the *Port Hardy* torpedoed in quick succession. Scene indescribable as the tankers immediately became floating hells, while the *Port Hardy* quickly drifted into the mass of flames and smoke. Only one *Port Hardy* lifeboat got away in time and was picked up by rescue ship *Zafaran*. Over 100 men must have met horrible deaths in that inferno. Watching, at close quarters, such a scene, I can only say that while it fascinated the eyes, it will always remain a ghastly memory. This isn't the 'Battle of the Atlantic', it's a 'War of Nerves'. The visible effect on those members of our crew who haven't previously sampled anything is very obvious.

What was collectively called the 'merchant navy' was formed of the various vessels owned by shipping companies which constituted the bulk of Britain's seaborne freight fleet. British companies controlled roughly a third of the world's shipping, and could make use of the services of a great deal more should they wish. In the summer of 1938, British merchant ships were crewed by some 159,000 sailors, with another 34,000 between jobs or otherwise temporarily ashore. Of those employed, around 7,000 were foreign nationals and 45,000 were so-called 'lascars': men from south-east Asia or China recruited locally on a lower rate of pay.

The wartime secondment of men of military age meant that merchant crews were increasingly made up of older veterans and young mariners. By 1941, nearly a quarter of crew members were twenty-one or younger. Their ranks were swelled by the ships and sailors of occupied Europe, from the crews of Dutch coasters to Norwegian trawlermen. Convoys escorted by Royal Navy vessels were often multinational, regularly incorporating American shipping and cargo vessels from a variety of other countries. British and international merchantmen were escorted all over the world, from the Arctic to Africa, and from the islands of the Caribbean to the tropics of the Indian Ocean.

The sailors of the Royal and merchant navies had a symbiotic relationship, which was brought into sharper focus by the close cooperation inherent in the convoy system. Unlike the Royal Navy, built on shared heritage, discipline and ritual, there was no uniform or unifying ethos binding together merchant sailors. Many derided the pomp and pageantry of the Royal Navy, but the distinctions were by no means so simple. Experienced merchant mariners were often also naval reservists, and many crewmen were temporarily brought into the Royal Navy on so-called T124 agreements. Similarly, many RNR officers, who formed an important part of the expanding officer cadre required to lead escort vessels, were called up directly from the merchant fleets.

Warship sailors often had a great respect for their merchant navy counterparts. Merchant ships carried little defensive weaponry of their own, but they were the chief targets for enemy submarines. Destroying thousands of tons of fuel or supplies was the main objective for U-boat commanders; sinking an escort vessel was merely a bonus. 'We can crack on a few revs, fling ourselves about a bit, strike back formidably if the opportunity arises,' wrote Nicholas Monsarrat in his wartime book *H.M. Corvette*. 'But they have to wallow along as if nothing had happened – same course and station, same inadequate speed, same helpless target . . . No amount of publicity, no colourful write ups . . . above all no medals, can do honour to men like these. Buy them a drink ashore, if you like; but don't attempt an *adequate* recompense. You won't get in the target area.'

But such respect did not prevent some disgruntlement about the comparative conditions under which both groups of men laboured. 'We know the merchant men are doing their bit and everyone agrees they are brave,' wrote Charles Hutchinson in his diary, 'but yet we guard them. While they rest or do their Watches they will be earning good money, while we sleep on the deck by the guns for our pay. When one faces the facts, I know which I would choose if only I could.'

Pay was one of the greatest causes of division between warship sailors and their merchant counterparts. At the outbreak of war, the average merchant sailor earned around £10 per month and by 1943 this had risen to £24. The basic daily wage for an average rating in the Royal Navy was barely four shillings, less than £6 per month. This could be supplemented by various extra emoluments, including bonuses for long service and good behaviour, specialist work, and for family men. Royal Navy sailors also enjoyed certain perks, including food and alcohol, as well as reduced travel fares and other domestic benefits. Merchant sailors, meanwhile, were employed to crew a specific ship: if it was sunk much of their pay was suspended. If rescued by a warship, however, they were not obliged to contribute to its efficient working. This was often perceived as ingratitude on the part of ratings, but for many a newly unemployed crewman it was quite logical. No civilian passenger would be expected to work a shift in a destroyer.

Merchant pay was subject to any number of intricacies. Financial incentives varied between shipping firms, unions, duties and international zones. The Merchant Navy Order, part of the government's series of labour controls in the spring of 1941, restricted freedoms but ensured basic principles of leave and off-duty pay; at sea, however, rates were determined on a range of criteria from individual contracts to the specificities of location. In Port Said, a buoy in the harbour demarcated the boundary between the full-pay zone and the reduced-pay sector, and the crews of merchant ships waited in suspense to learn where their berth would be.

In the case of the *San Demetrio*, the crew refused assistance on the final stretch of the voyage into the Clyde because it would have reduced the amount of salvage reward to which they were entitled. When the incident was immortalized in film in 1943, the finale showed the subsequent court case in which the shipping firm's insurance company was ordered to pay nearly £15,000 jointly to the crew, representing the ultimate financial reward for their undoubted heroics.

Regardless of their differences, the fates of merchant sailors and their escorts were bound together in the Atlantic. By the spring of 1941, as the Blitz continued to wreak havoc on British cities, the situation in the Atlantic was becoming critical. In March 1941, Churchill formally named the campaign the 'Battle of the Atlantic' in an attempt to highlight the violent nature of the struggle and, after his similar labelling of the clash between the RAF and the Luftwaffe in the summer of 1940, to indicate its vital importance to British survival. 'This mortal danger to our life-lines gnawed my bowels,' he later wrote.

A Battle of the Atlantic Committee was established in order to coordinate the manifold factors which together formed the basis of British strategy: escort groups, air cover, shipping organization, technological innovation, cooperation with Allies. Information about shipping losses, previously publicly available and published, was now censored. Western Approaches, the command organizing convoy operations, was moved from vulnerable Plymouth to Liverpool and combined with Coastal Command, providing RAF air cover, within a joint headquarters at Derby House. It was led by Admiral Percy Noble, known as 'Uncle Percy' to his subordinates. Here, convoy routes were marked on a wall-sized board with coloured tape. Submarines were marked with symbols: white if their location had been identified by intelligence, black if their whereabouts were unknown. Merchant ship losses were marked in red.

Escort groups were organized, providing teams of destroyers, corvettes and other vessels which worked together to cover incoming and outgoing convoys. Royal Navy ships were supplemented by those manned by the Royal Canadian Navy, which eventually took over sole responsibility for some convoys in the summer of 1941. Groups of merchant ships would be formed, and their captains briefed. As a convoy passed out of the Irish Sea, it would often be joined by escort vessels operating from Derry. As they passed out of Lough Foyle, sailors could see the verdant fields on either side of the waters. 'It seemed you could put out a hand and touch the green and find it velvet,' recalled Sid France. Colours soon turned from green to grey, as the convoy made its way out to sea. 'There was in fact not too much to be frightened of,' wrote Evelyn Chavasse, commanding officer of an escort destroyer and brother of Paul, who had been fortunate to survive the sinking of his minesweeper in May 1940. 'Before the start of every voyage I always got butterflies in my stomach and worried that things might go wrong,' wrote Evelyn. 'The butterflies, however, happily flew away as soon as we had put to sea and the business was on.'

Atlantic convoys might incorporate up to one hundred merchant ships. These were organized in short columns, spanning a width of several miles. The most valuable prizes, particularly those with a volatile cargo of ammunition or tankers containing fuel, were kept in the centre of the group. Keeping the convoy in order was the responsibility of the convoy commodore, carried in one of the merchantmen along with a small radio staff. It was a difficult task, and station-keeping proved beyond many of the more ramshackle ships. Progress was dependent on the speed of the slowest. Initially escorts might constitute no more than six small corvettes and destroyers. Two would cover the rear of the group, with one on either flank, and two would proceed in front of the convoy, searching for U-boats in ASDIC 'sweeps'.

Service in an Atlantic escort was a unique experience. Ships rolled dramatically in rough seas, walking became a stumbling uncertainty, and messdecks were waterlogged. In northern waters, discomfort became a way of life. Many escort destroyers were initially of old and decrepit varieties, such as the V and W class. Many smaller escorts, including the famous Flower-class corvettes, were not designed or intended for service on the high seas. Overcrowding became the norm as both extra equipment and additional personnel crammed between aging bulkheads. An average destroyer's complement of 200 was often bloated to 250 or even 300. Smaller corvettes, sloops and trawlers suffered proportionally.

The seas of the North Atlantic could be wild and unforgiving. Sub-Lieutenant Richard Walker of the trawler *Northern Reward* described in his diary how his small ship was like a 'cork bouncing about among these huge waves':

When you stand on the bridge and watch this ravenous wave, with a crest of foam like a row of teeth, towering above the masthead, you wonder if it is possible for her to survive. We slow down to three knots, just enough to keep steerage way and head on to the sea and, somehow, the gallant little ship manages to struggle to the top, hang poised for a moment while we gaze down into the trough miles below, then she plunges down and we think our last moments have come. I never get used to it and I hope that my terror does not show too blatantly.

Derric Breen was a telegraphist in the sloop HMS *Egret*. 'There was no pattern to the sea,' he wrote. 'One minute we spiralled up to the top of a crest with all the world at our feet, the next we slid or dropped, corkscrewing down . . . restricted to a sight of only mountainous waves . . . we would stagger to a crest, from this peak we could most often see the whole of the convoy.'

Atlantic escorts were invariably small ships. To swap the inherent robustness of a battleship for the apparent fragility of a destroyer could be deeply unsettling. Nineteen-year-old Richard Campbell-Begg transferred from a cruiser to HMS *Orwell*. His new home seemed fraught with danger. 'One creeps along,' he wrote, 'holding on to hand-rails along the lee side and making a dash across the fully exposed portions of deck in between waves. Even so one often arrives on watch fairly drenched.' During one voyage into the Atlantic, he wrote in his diary:

> Not only were we rolling and pitching violently but falling into troughs in the waves and, equally devastating, being hurled up again with no rhythm to the movement at all. When I first staggered out on to the quarterdeck I could only see a small circle of sky above us whilst all around were huge banks of water. Awe inspiring to say the least.

'Gosh, what a life,' wrote Charles Hutchinson in his diary after transferring to a destroyer from a cruiser. 'The messdecks are full of water all the time. You tear along at a hell of a rate, you can't stand up and everything flies all over, you have a job to cling on to anything . . . the guys who have been on them all this time ought to have medals as big as frying pans and I mean it. No one has any idea what it's like, I know I hadn't.'

Telegraphists in small ships had the benefit of working in perhaps the only place guaranteed to be dry, in order to protect the electrical equipment within. Of the wireless telegraphy office in HMS *Egret*, Derric Breen recalled the bucket chairs bolted to the deck, and a constant stream of Morse signals. There was, he stated, 'no escape from our song of the Morse key'. The other essential element of the telegraphists' environment was smoke. In order to stay awake, Breen and his colleagues lit up constantly: 'tins of Balkan Sobranie, Abdullahs and the big Navy Woodbine'.

Leading Signalman C. L. R. Matthews served for over two years in the Atlantic in the destroyer HMS *Fame*. During this time, home for Matthews and twenty or so other signalmen, telegraphists and coders was the communications mess. This was a small space below the waterline, furnished with wooden tables, storage bins and lockers fixed to the bulkheads. Hammocks were slung from hooks or secured to the stanchion columns. Matthews recalled that heating arrangements were basic: 'A two bar electric fire set knee high in the bulkhead. It was rare to have two bars working. The lower one was usually broken by people falling against it and through toasting mouldy bread to disguise the taste.'

Eating and drinking were fraught with difficulty. Storage was primitive, and fresh food did not last long. Aboard some ships, meat was prepared on the open deck alongside the depth charges. Elsewhere, joints were lashed to a messdeck stanchion until they were ready to be moved up to the galley for cooking. Ordinary Seaman F. S. Gardner recalled the difficulties of transporting trays piled with hot food from the galley to the mess in rough weather: 'One would have to walk about eight paces at a time always allowing for that time when the ship steadied up to move on. Passing trays down a ladder needed at least two sailors per tray if we were to deliver the hot meal intact. The mess tea urn which held twelve pints was suspended from a hammock bar and at the appropriate moment one would judge the movement of the ship then half fill their cup with tea.' Sailors were quick to swap the service-issue china for more robust tin mugs and plates.

The necessity of easy transportation, the limitations of the culinary imagination of the average seaman, the restrictions of provisions and galley space, all produced a diet which was conservative, straightforward and largely unchanging. 'The food was pretty awful,' wrote Matthews, 'and providing the weather was reasonable the commonest mid-day meal was "straight rush". This was a lump of meat surrounded by potatoes, followed by boiled rice into which was emptied tins of milk. In rough weather the galley ovens were unworkable and all it could manage was food to be boiled in a deep fanny. We produced a stew with chunks of meat, tinned carrots, swede and tomatoes.'

Despite such hardships, some revelled in the tough conditions. To Matthews, rough weather was exhilarating, and his ability to cope with it a matter of pride. 'Don't mind this weather when I'm up top,' he wrote in his diary, 'in fact glory in it. Love to see her roll and the waves break over the upper deck. You can always see a steady line of horizon and so keep your balance but in the mess, to prepare food and eat is only described by that beautiful naval expression, "It's a bastard".'

Conditions in the western Atlantic were no better than in the east. Newfoundland was infamous for its fog. Vere Wight-Boycott described it as 'a thick white, wet blanket of mist covering the sea'. Matthews explained the phenomenon in his diary, after getting 'all the dope' from his watch officer: 'The Gulf Stream meets the cold Labrador currents and sets up fog. Where there is fog the water is warm, clear patches, the water cold. He knows – he fell overboard off the *Revenge* around here.'

Evelyn Chavasse, commander of the destroyer HMS *Broadway*, described the difficulties of the summer months around St John's: 'In those horrid waters, that is the season of fog and icebergs drifting down from the Arctic. As often as not we had been stumbling along for the last two or three days in a dense fog, with never a sight of sun or stars to fix our position; and to find the harbour entrance, which is a narrow crack a few score yards wide in a wall of rocky cliff, was sometimes a tricky business.'

Newfoundland remained a backwater, despite the rapid expansion of its naval bases. Sailors could pick up local radio stations as they neared land. Signalman Matthews described the 'Saturday night hilarities from St. John's. A fellow is singing "Safe in the arms of Jesus". Newfy radio is a parochial friendly affair. The news consists of items like, "Mr Burrows has finished his business in St. John's and is returning home tonight. Mrs So and so of Princess St has had her baby, a son" etc.'

St John's lay at the eastern tip of Newfoundland. The land itself was inhospitable but, to those with a certain aesthetic interest, extremely appealing as a rugged wilderness. 'It's a wild country,' wrote Matthews, 'only travellable by stony primitive roads, the country being covered with 10 foot scrubby firs, a few inches apart. Impenetrable without the use of an axe. Grand scenery, wild mountains sticking up out of the scrub, beautiful lakes.' He and several messmates went 'camping in the wilds' when their ship was at St John's in September: 'We were under canvas, the weather was very hot and we swam in the adjacent river, played rugby and explored the river by rowing boat.'

The best amenities were available at the St John's YMCA Red Shield Club. 'After booking in,' explained Sid France, 'the first desire of most of us was a hot bath . . . it was heaven to wallow in hot, soapy water, to soak until the bones frozen by the Atlantic gales had thawed out, to dress in clean gear and go down to the dining room and order steak, eggs and chips.'

While the Americans began to develop their newly leased base of Argentia in Placentia Bay, many British sailors found themselves in Halifax, Nova Scotia. According to Midshipman Tom Dowling, the scenery was 'very dull being low pine forests with occasional villages and creeks stretching endlessly and most underdeveloped'. He noted one key detail in his journal: 'The villages, all made of wood, cheered us as we passed and all those on the US side of the border flew the stars and stripes on a tall white flagpole, as all American villages do. The only difference between the Canadian and American villages was the absence of a flag on the Canadian side.'

Halifax was the rich relation to its Newfoundland counterparts. The charms of its ice-cream parlours and local girls were the talk of every escort messdeck at one time or another. Provisions and equipment could also be obtained relatively easily. During one stay, Vere Wight-Boycott bought a 'baby Remington' typewriter, partly to follow the fashion amongst some of his peers – many of whom were eager to own the machine made famous by Ernest Hemingway – but also because 'it is much easier to type at sea than to write'.

Early in the war the main enemy in the eastern Atlantic was the U-boat. In the west, at least at first, it was the weather. The destroyer HMS *Newark* was in Newfoundland from mid-December 1940 until the end of February 1941, snowed in and trapped by the weather and the poor state of the ship. Ordinary Seaman Stan Bowman kept a diary detailing the conditions at St John's in the first weeks of 1941. 'The cold is unbearable,' he wrote on 15 January, 'our blankets are frozen to the ironwork and frost is round the port[hole]s.' The following days brought only rain, 'more snow' and leaking pipes, which made living conditions atrocious: 'The oil in our messes is 2" deep in places and I am utterly fed up with shifting about . . . lockers, kit and everything else smothered.'

At the start of February, an attempt was made to leave Halifax. 'I have 12 hrs out of 24 with blinding snow, icy spray and a gale blowing,' wrote Bowman. 'All around me there's ice, and snow pelts down with the ship over at 50° at times. With Asdics gone, steering busted and one engine failing we are forced to turn back. The messdeck is under water – I have lost count of the days . . . all water is cut off and even drinking water is banned. I have had no food for 22 hrs.' Even the ship's weaponry was not immune from damage. 'Four depth charges were dropped,' noted Bowman. 'We didn't know this until late in the night when a terrific explosion shook the ship and we all grab for lifebelts . . . we find that the storm has cut adrift these charges.'

The storm lasted several days, smashing the ship's whaler. When calm weather did come, the men had to endure a draining limp back to harbour. 'We are now very thirsty, the Ensign is in shreds,' wrote Bowman. With no drinking water, he bought three tins of pears from the NAAFI, merely for their juices. 'At last we reach Halifax at 10 p.m. on Friday,' he concluded, 'with dirty and grimy skin and unshaven faces.'

*Newark* finally managed to leave Newfoundland in the last week of February, arriving at Belfast on 5 March, and Devonport five days later. There was, however, little respite. 'De-ammunition ship – three paltry days leave for each watch,' wrote Bowman in his diary, 'Everyone is disgusted with Royal Navy owing to present conditions – We have to declare our goods to the customs.' Shortly after, he was drafted to a motor launch at Newhaven. As he passed through Portsmouth for a brief spell of training, the conditions he encountered put his hardships into perspective: 'Amazed at the wreckage; station, hospitals, shelters, shops, houses and acres of flat smoking ruins.'

The declaration of the 'Battle of the Atlantic' in the spring of 1941 merely marked a new stage in a continuing struggle between escorts and submarines over the fate of merchant ships. Escort destroyers, corvettes and their smaller counterparts had two chief weapons with which to attack submarines: ASDIC and depth charges. The former enabled escorts to detect the position of a submerged U-boat and the latter exploded underwater with enough force to disrupt gauges, bend metal and, at short distances, entirely tear apart a submarine, sending oil and debris to the surface. When an ASDIC contact was made and confirmed, flags would be raised and the escorts would converge at top speed, attempting to attack before the enemy could escape. If they failed, a lengthy search would ensue, with the Germans attempting to evade detection and escorts maintaining their vigilance for as long as possible.

Leading Signalman Matthews, whose action station was on the upper deck, experienced one particularly dramatic chase:

Our ship trembles in every rivet as we gain speed up to 33 knots. Everyone is saying that the skipper is mad. We just dive right through the waves. The sea is pounding over the ship in a solid wall. Everyone is immediately wet through on going on to the bridge. The chase lasts three hours. At one time (what a horrible few seconds) the ship rolls to port and instead of coming back, stays there. Everyone hangs on with gritted teeth – she goes over a bit further, and then a little more. We are almost on our side, skidding to starboard and she hangs there seemingly an eternity. We can see the water almost level with the bridge. I'm hanging on for all I've got, repeating, 'Get back you Bastard!' Then slowly she comes back. If it wasn't for the noise of the crashing sea and the screaming wind you would have heard everyone's breath come out in a long sigh.

Depth charges were a vital part of the psychology of the escort sailor. 'This was always a spectacular sight,' wrote Sid France, 'when the surface of the sea bulged, then erupted in a vast fountain . . . With good luck, something came up to show that a sub <u>had</u> been there, but more often, especially in our case, there was plenty of fish for supper.' Failure to use this sole means of harming an unseen enemy could be more detrimental to morale than failing to register a hit. 'Wasted an hour messing about after a contact that was lost, just as we were about to attack,' wrote Geoff Dormer after one unsuccessful search. 'It made a bad impression on the crew ... Always attack, always open fire, always drop depth charges, at the slightest excuse. There is probably nothing there, but the lads love making a noise.'

The coordination of detection and detonation required finely honed skills on the part of every sailor involved, both ASDIC operators and depth-charge teams. Neither was effective without the other. Used expertly, these weapons could be deadly, even for the most experienced U-boat commanders. On 10 March 1941 convoy HX122 was attacked and five ships were sunk. 'I was near to despair,' wrote Captain Donald Macintyre, in command of HMS *Walker*, one of the escorting destroyers. When on the surface, U-boats were invisible to ASDIC, and Macintyre searched for the 'tell-tale white wake' that would enable him to attack, forcing the submarine down where it could be exposed to depth charges. When he saw a wake line through his binoculars, he ordered the destroyer to advance at full speed: 'Suddenly, the U-boat spotted us and in a cloud of spray he crash-dived. A swirl of phosphorescent water still lingered as we passed over the spot and sent a pattern of ten depth-charges crashing down.'

The explosions sent 'giant water spouts' high above the destroyer, but the attack had been unsuccessful. *Walker* was joined by HMS *Vanoc* as she continued to search for the U-boat with ASDIC. When another contact was made, the two ships once again attacked with depth charges, churning up the waves to such a degree that underwater detection was impossible, but no hits were registered. After picking up some survivors from a merchant ship who were drifting in a lifeboat, Macintyre saw *Vanoc* increasing speed and moving ahead, before receiving a message over his radio: 'Have rammed and sunk U-boat.' 'What a blissful moment that was for us,' wrote Macintyre, 'the successful culmination of a long and arduous fight. Something in the way of revenge for our losses in the convoy had been achieved.' U-100's commander, Joachim Schepke, was killed during the attack.

But while *Walker* circled *Vanoc*, to which German survivors were swimming, another ASDIC contact was made. Depth-charge teams only just managed to prepare their payloads in time before a pattern was fired. This time, another U-boat surfaced near *Vanoc*, its dark hull immediately illuminated by British searchlights. Guns from both British ships fired wildly: 'Each salvo left one temporarily blinded,' wrote Macintyre. Merchant sailors helped to bring up ammunition shells and 'the decks were piled high with them till the guns' crews were hardly able to work their guns'. Soon afterwards, a signal from the U-boat warned that it was sinking and German submariners began to swim out towards *Walker*, arriving exhausted to be hauled aboard. One British sailor jumped over the side fully clothed to help them up. 'The last to come over the side was obviously the captain,' wrote Macintyre, 'as he swam to *Walker* still wearing his brass-bound cap.' He was Otto Kretschmer of U-99.

March 1941 saw heavy casualties for both sides. British merchant losses were in excess of half a million tons, while Dönitz lost a total of five U-boats, a fifth of the available operational fleet, and three of his elite submariners. The third was Günther Prien of U-47, who had sunk the *Royal Oak* in Scapa Flow, and whose boat had been lost after an attack on convoy OB293. Kretschmer, Schepke and Prien had each been responsible for sinking hundreds of thousands of tons of merchant shipping, and the loss of such talismanic figures came as a serious blow to Dönitz. From here onwards, the wolf-pack became the established strategy and the future pattern of the campaign against convoy escorts began to emerge.

In May, convoy HX129 became the first to be escorted throughout its voyage. Nearly 250 destroyers were now available or under repair, along with another 100 corvettes and almost 350 smaller craft, and the average escort group now totalled five vessels. Air cover from Britain, Iceland and Newfoundland helped to push the confrontation further into the mid-Atlantic. But fifty-eight merchant ships with a total of 325,500 tons were sunk in May, with half destroyed around Freetown. Between March and May, the British had lost, in one way or another, a total of 1.7 million tons. Continued over the year, this rate would amount to a staggering 7 million tons. It was intelligence that would bring this unsustainable state of affairs back under control.

The interception of radio signals, the decryption of ciphers and the effective use of information were vital elements in the unceasing convoy campaign. Aggressive action on the part of escort groups was simply a last resort. Superior intelligence would help to route convoys away from potential confrontations, as well as solving an array of strategic and tactical questions, and contributing to the assessment of the enemy's fleet. Breaking the German naval and U-boat ciphers were perhaps the greatest achievements of the boffins of Bletchley Park, but their intellectual work relied in the first instance on human agency. Deconstructing 'Enigma' required paperwork captured from German vessels in so-called 'pinches'.

On 9 May 1941, the officers of HMS *Bulldog* were even more exhausted than usual. They were short of their full complement of supervisors for watchkeeping during the protection of convoy OB318. The shortage meant extra spells on watch for twenty-two-year-old David Balme, who also happened to be both the navigator and in charge of gunnery control. That day, he had been on watch from 4 a.m. until 8 a.m., before taking a bath, quickly eating breakfast, and returning to the bridge.

'It was a sunny day,' Balme recalled, 'moderate wind but with the usual big Atlantic swell.' The weather was as pleasant as could be hoped for, but there was little time to enjoy the midday sunshine. At noon, two of the ships in the convoy were rocked by torpedo explosions. Escort ships immediately set about their defensive routines. Close to *Bulldog*, the corvette *Aubretia* made ASDIC contact and attacked with depth charges. Suddenly, U-110 surfaced barely 400 yards from *Bulldog*. A wild barrage of fire was directed at the submarine, and it soon had the desired effect: 'The noise was deafening,' wrote Balme, 'and especially from our Lewis machine guns which were being fired from the bridge over our heads by anyone who could pick them up. However, it was undoubtedly the noise of all the shells and bullets hitting the U-boat which panicked the German crew, who all jumped overboard as fast as they could.'

Many of the surviving German submariners made for *Aubretia*, the corvette which had instigated their boat's demise with rapid depth-charge attack. Captain Vivian Funge-Smith described their reception: 'As they came aboard few had much kick left in them. They were promptly stripped and given a blanket. One who either by design or accident spat in the face of a petty officer was promptly pushed back overboard till he should board in a more proper frame of mind.' Notable by his absence was Fritz-Julius Lemp, commander of U-110 and the man who, while commanding U-30, had been responsible for sinking the *Athenia* on the very first day of the war.

Meanwhile, Balme was ordered to lead a boarding party. He and seven others rowed over to the submarine in the ship's whaler and struggled on board in the rough swell, revolvers drawn. The young officer was the first inside. He lowered himself gingerly down the conning-tower ladders. 'Going down bottom first,' he wrote, 'I felt a very vulnerable target to any German still down below.' Yet he found that the submarine was empty of enemies with 'complete silence except for an ominous hissing sound which was either from the batteries or a leak in the hull. The secondary lighting gave a rather dim ghostly effect.' The submarine was listing to port, and the swell of the sea sent echoes through the bulkheads. Outside, the whaler had been smashed against the side. A powerboat was eventually sent from another destroyer, but there was a more pressing concern: 'I felt sure that the scuttling-charges would go off sooner or later, especially as there was the continuous explosions around us from our depth-charge attacks on other U-boats. This was a most unpleasant and frightening noise.'

Balme and his men formed a human chain from the control room, up the ladders of the conning tower and out to the waiting boat. They removed everything they could find: code books, files, charts and equipment. Anything that looked remotely useful was seized. Sailors struggled across the top deck of the submarine with handfuls of vital papers, many of which were soaked in the process. An Enigma machine was unscrewed from a table and sent up. The typewriter-like contraption was used by German sailors to decrypt their own secret signals, and was quickly earmarked for British intelligence.

The boarding party entered the submarine at 12.30 p.m. and remained there for hours. Sandwiches were sent over from *Bulldog*. Still the denotation charges did not ignite. There was even a short debate on whether the submarine could still be operated. Engineers were sent across. 'But,' recalled Balme, 'with everything written in

German and nobody having ever served in submarines, we decided we would do more harm than good by turning the cocks to get her underway.'

A towing cable was attached to *Bulldog*, but soon snapped. Then *Bulldog* made another sonar contact and left to investigate. Balme and his men were left in a submarine which might explode at any moment. 'This was indeed a desolate and awful moment,' he stated. 'There was I, with my boarding party, aboard U-110, in the middle of the Atlantic, alone with no ships in sight with the wind and sea gradually increasing. This must have been about 4 p.m. There were not really any more books or moveable gear we could collect, so I battened down the watertight hatches and we waited.' Finally, at 6.30 p.m., *Bulldog* returned. A new cable was attached, and the boarding party returned to their own ship before setting off for Iceland.

Messages from the naval authorities in Britain ordered that the bounty was to be referred to only as Operation Primrose. A flurry of signals instructed the escort vessels to maintain extreme caution, with instructions that the events were 'to be treated with greatest secrecy and as few people allowed to know as possible'. En route, the submarine finally succumbed and sank beneath the waves, making the maintenance of secrecy somewhat easier. The Enigma machine and the documents, carefully dried out at sea, were sent to Bletchley Park.

Balme's pinch was the latest of several captures over the course of 1940 and 1941, from submarines, trawlers and particularly the weather ship *München*, which allowed Bletchley to develop a fuller understanding of how the German ciphers worked and how they were changed, and laid the foundation for ultimately cracking the codes. Over the summer of 1941, decryption delays were reduced to a minimum, helping to alleviate the effects of extra U-boats becoming available in the Atlantic.

After disembarking in Iceland, Ordinary Seaman Colin Fairrie of *Bulldog* had a conversation with one of the prisoners from U-110. They spoke in Spanish, the only language they shared: 'He had fought with Franco in the Civil War,' wrote Fairrie in his diary. 'Knew San Sebastian, Burgos and Madrid well. Showed him some of my Spanish photos.' He noted the submariner's views on various topics. Jews were 'disliked in Germany because they did not pull their weight in the State – tight-fisted – revenge for the havoc they caused after the World War (1914–1918). Admitted that there were nice Jews and quoted an old German proverb that "Every German knows a good Jew"!'

On the war itself, Fairrie recorded the German's statements with a mixture of sympathy and incredulity: 'A war between politicians . . . The fighting forces and common people are mere pawns in their hands!! The war would of course be over in 3 months time. However England would remain as occupied territory only so long as Anti-Nazi hostilities continued! We being of Nordic descent would be treated as equals! Great ambition was to form a white block versus the coloured races (Chinese and Japs and Russians). French not liked but necessary to have them in the block!' Finally, he noted, 'many Germans very interested in our football matches – admire the English for their skill at the game'. Before he was led away, the German prisoner wrote down his address and asked whether they might correspond after the war, signing off with 'Buen amigo'.

Over the course of the summer of 1941, shipping losses in the North Atlantic would reduce dramatically as intelligence helped Western Approaches to re-route convoys away from known danger areas. In June, a total of 415,000 tons was lost but by July this had fallen by three-quarters to 113,000. It was a welcome reprieve, but did little to diminish the psychological challenge which the Atlantic convoys represented. Nor was this simply a struggle between sailors and submariners. This was a battlefield in which civilians remained in the thick of the action.

In the summer of 1941, British expatriate Vera Boyce said goodbye to her husband, who was working in Canada, and returned home aboard the liner SS *Mendoza*. She kept a journal of the voyage, describing her travelling companions and their activities. Her cabin was shared with two elderly ladies, 'missionaries from Japan. They read the bible and pray every morning.' In the hold, accommodation had been improvised for a posse of lumberjacks, kept entertained by three 'glamour girls' who paraded the upper decks in 'very short shorts'. Most days were spent on a range of activities from bridge to table tennis. There was the 'usual petty squabbling about chairs on deck'. Boyce stayed up until 2.30 a.m. drinking whisky with Americans. She wrote up one entry at a table in the dining room, 'waiting for the bar to open as I am dying of thirst and boredom'. Boyce and her fellow passengers made it to Britain safely, but others were not so fortunate.

In September 1941, the liner SS *Avoceta* was travelling from Lisbon to Liverpool as part of convoy HG73. Aboard was a large group of passengers, many of whom were the wives and children of British nationals who had been stranded in Europe. Despite taking a long detour around the Bay of Biscay in an attempt to avoid U-boats, the convoy came under attack north of the Azores. Ten ships were sunk, and the *Avoceta* was torpedoed. 'She staggered like a stumbling horse,' wrote Rear Admiral Kenelm Creighton, on the bridge as convoy commodore.

> *Avoceta* sat back on her haunches and the bows rose to an ever more crazy angle into the air. No boats could be lowered. There was complete pandemonium; the thunderous bangs and crashes of furniture and cargo being hurled about below decks all mingled with the ghastly shrieks of the sleeping people waking to their deaths. As the bows went higher so did the shrieks. I clung to a stanchion feeling sick and helpless as I had to look on while the children were swept out into the darkness below by the torrent of water which roared through the smoking room.

Forty-nine sailors and seventy-six passengers were killed. Commodore Creighton was one of only twenty-eight crewmen rescued by other ships. Just twelve of the passengers survived. The Atlantic convoys endeavoured to preserve supplies which were vital to the survival of all British citizens. Yet the campaign was far from a soulless statistical equation. To every sailor, merchant crewman and passenger, and indeed submariner, the Atlantic convoys were a very immediate matter of life and death.

For the sailors of the escort vessels in 1941, the struggle was one of psychology as much as aggression. 'War brings to a soldier complete alteration in the everyday details of his life,' wrote the journalist H. V. Morton. 'With a sailor it is different. He fights in what are his barracks and his home . . . the change over from peace to war hardly affects the daily routine of his life at all.' The essence of the Atlantic lay in collective effort, but it was also an intensely individual experience. In his post-war writing, Ludovic Kennedy evocatively portrayed the sense of personal vulnerability and individual peril inherent in the psychological challenge of convoy duty:

> I thought: there are 15 U-boats round the convoy: each U-boat carries about 60 men: that means that within a radius of ten miles from where I am lying there are 900 Germans . . . I thought of it not in relation to the crews of the convoy and escort, which must have been several thousand, but to myself. I saw them collectively, as it were, an army of brutal ruthless men pressing towards me in an ever-narrowing ring. They were the enemy: they were Germans and they hated me . . . I saw them all . . . peering into periscope lenses, setting deflection discs, loading torpedo tubes . . . I thought: *at this moment now, at this moment of thinking*, a torpedo may be racing through the water towards me . . . I had a sudden insane desire to jump out of bed and rush to the top of the masthead. I said aloud to give myself courage, 'I must not panic'. I said it over and over again. It did not help. Another voice, equally loud and insistent, said 'Get me out of here. Now. This minute. Before it's too late.'

The Battle of the Atlantic was a long, gruelling contest of industrial attrition, in which boredom and routine overshadowed gallantry, but one that could nevertheless generate intense action and adrenaline at any given moment. Although it was a vital campaign, there was little sense of overall accomplishment. 'I think we were all a little mad by the time we got in,' wrote Nicholas Monsarrat. 'We'd been at action-stations for virtually a week on end, missing hours of sleep, eating on the bridge or the upper deck, standing-to in the cold and wet and darkness . . . By the end, we'd had enough of it; though if it had gone on I suppose we would have done the same.'

'Properly done, convoy duty was a boring, uneventful task,' wrote Sid France of HMS *Churchill*. 'The escort's purpose is not, as may be imagined from some of the film-maker's ideas, to fight all the way across the ocean, but to be a defence if the enemy finds the convoy.'

It was precisely the relative infrequency of engagements which made tension and anxiety such a problem. Sam Lombard-Hobson agreed that the nature of the Atlantic challenge had been misrepresented:

> Like any new ship to this task we expected, or, rather, hoped for action of some kind immediately, and we remained on constant alert; but after a short while realized that, to do the job properly, men had to be fresh, as well as ready. Sleep is as necessary as food. Documentaries and films on the Battle of the Atlantic have tended to mislead the public into thinking that it was plain bloody murder all the time . . . In actual fact, taken over the whole period, the great majority of convoys got through without interference or mention; and the Atlantic, more often than not, is agreeably kind.

In the Atlantic, the challenge to sailors' morale came from the effects of prolonged stress, rather than fatigue caused by continual fighting. 'I think because we were constantly on the alert, constantly waiting, looking for things, then we came to accept this, what we now call stress,' recalled one corvette rating. 'One day you could get up on the upper deck and accept what you were going to do. But at night-time you could find that it unnerves you completely.' Sailors had to develop psychological barriers. 'Often one had the uncomfortable feeling of being watched by a single eye just above the surface,' wrote C. C. Young of lookout duty in HMS *Hartland*. 'A nerve racking experience. But as always you cannot live with fear all the time, although it returned with a rush and a sickening feeling in the stomach whenever the alarm bells rang.'

Humphrey Tobias Scott was commanding officer of the destroyer HMS *Wishart*. In a letter home, he described the challenges of Atlantic convoy duties:

> Although this job is much better than sitting in the Admiralty there are times one must admit when it rains and it is dark and it is blowing a gale and everything gets capsized and the galley fire gets swamped and you've run out of bread, fresh meat and vegetables, and you've lost your convoy and the chart is wet and you're rolling like hell with

the sea on the quarter and the wind astern and funnel smoke coming over the bridge and the hours go slow and you know that when you do get in to harbour there won't be any eggs, milk or potatoes and that anyway you'll go straight to sea again as soon as you've oiled so why go in anyway and the glass is still falling so there's no hope of the blow letting up, and your steward brings you a cold dinner on a dirty plate on which you can read his thumbprints in the gravy which has dried, and then he's sick just behind you and, your attention distracted, you look round a moment, the ship gives a lurch and your plate slips and your dinner joins the steward's on the deck and then they yell 'Darkened ship right ahead! Sir!' and you fly up to the bridge without your oilskin and its pelting with rain but it doesn't matter because you're wet through already, and it is a false alarm due to the lookout having indigestion and so life goes on and on for a week!

It is then I admit that one pines terribly for Wifey and family and the whiles by the fireside and the day in the garden. Yes, even for the quiet of that room in Whitehall and the Admiralty Luncheon Club tray, and one wonders why one made such a fuss about being ashore and hated the life of a Whitehall limpet.

But come the dawn and the sunlight and you see your convoy and you swell with pride and satisfaction and your heart gives a whoop and you say 'Look at 'em! We're bringing Home the Goods! What a wonderful chap I am! Now I'm doing a job worth doing! And you exult as you let go the Banging Depth Charges on what you hope is a U-boat and you think Hooray! I, Tobias, am winning this war! Life is good and sweet and strong. Then a dollop of spray hits you in the back of the neck to put you in your place and the Midshipman's sight turns out to be right and he shows you the mistake in yours and you realize you're just a worm after all.

# 9. Terrible Punishment

'We are cruising peacefully up and down near the Faeroes, minding our own business,' wrote Sub-Lieutenant Richard Walker of the trawler *Northern Reward* in his diary, 'when at dawn on the horizon a vast battleship appears, clearly the *Bismarck*. Action stations – the First Lieutenant mans the pop-gun on our bows – the ship's company of HMT *Northern Reward* prepare to die at their posts.'

It was 22 May 1941. Every British vessel in northern waters was on the lookout for the German battleship. Intelligence had been received from Norwegian and Swedish sources that *Bismarck* had left Gotenhafen in the Baltic along with her partner ship, the cruiser *Prinz Eugen*, and a British reconnaissance plane had sighted the pair in Bergen fjord. *Bismarck* was the largest battleship in the world, faster than any of her Royal Navy counterparts, and immensely dangerous. With eleven convoys currently under sail in the Atlantic, if *Bismarck* could break out she would wreak havoc that would far outweigh even the *Admiral Scheer*'s successes the previous year. Fortunately, Walker's fears proved unfounded: '"Relax, relax," says the Captain, "It's the *Hood*." General anticlimax and sighs of cowardly relief.'

HMS *Hood* was the *Bismarck* of the Royal Navy. The pride of the fleet, she was regarded as a physical manifestation of Britain's imperial and military prowess, symbolic of centuries of tradition and maritime superiority. Yet unlike *Bismarck*, which represented the pinnacle of technical endeavour, *Hood* was an aging specimen: a battlecruiser commissioned just after the end of the First World War. Technically, she was inferior to her rival, and the outbreak of war had delayed scheduled improvements. Yet, despite this, to serve aboard such a ship was still seen by many sailors as the ultimate honour.

The previous months had not been easy for the ship's company.

An anticipated pitched battle with German warships had not materialized, and the sailors of *Hood*, as well as those of the other capital ships of the Home Fleet, were instead consigned to perpetual patrols. One of *Hood*'s youngest sailors was seventeen-year-old Bill Crawford. After documenting his first experiences of battle in the attack on the French fleet at Mers-el-Kébir, he had noted the open talk of mutiny on the messdecks in December 1940.

In the spring of 1941, Crawford had enjoyed a short period of home leave before returning to the ship at nearby Rosyth. 'Dearest Mum,' he wrote on 18 March:

> Well I got back to the ship and we are now away. Gee I wish you had said for me to stay awhile, I know its wrong to say that, but I sure am fed up . . . I'm going to miss the good cooking, good beds, the black puddings, hot water bottle, and most of all mum I'm going to miss you. Maybe I don't show much appreciation for all these things when I am home, but I do appreciate them, more than I can ever say.

He asked his mother to make enquiries about a transfer to a shore job: 'I wonder if it would do any good mum, if you wrote to the Admiralty . . . If I could only get on a minesweeper or anything at all, so that I could be stationed at either Rosyth, Port Edgar, Kirkcaldy or Leith it would not be so bad.'

Over the next few days Crawford struggled with his post-leave depression. 'I am writing again to-day just because it makes me feel nearer home,' he admitted a few days later. 'Mum I think I am a funny guy because any time I am sorry for things I have done bad to you I want to cry . . . I curse the day I ever joined up and left such a good mother and such a good home.'

Yet towards the end of March, Crawford's spirits had been raised. 'I am beginning to settle down again but it was hard at first,' he wrote. 'Still it was a swell break and I sure enjoyed myself.' By now, a mood of excitement had spread through *Hood*. The long-awaited clash between the greatest capital ships of the British and German navies seemed to be approaching. 'We haven't been away very long, but have had some tense hours since I left,' wrote Crawford, 'And now that Germany has started sending her warships out there looks as if there will be <u>action</u> for the Fleet soon. Anyway, the sooner we get them the better.'

On 23 May 1941, the day after Richard Walker's scare, the cruisers *Suffolk* and *Norfolk* were on patrol in the Denmark Strait. In the wardroom of *Suffolk*, Lieutenant Commander Charles Collett was looking forward to his evening meal. 'We were drinking our pre-dinner sherry,' he wrote soon afterwards, 'when action stations sounded off. The sherry was rather wasted!'

The *Bismarck* had been sighted. Still accompanied by *Prinz Eugen*, she was attempting to break out into the Atlantic. The orders for the British cruisers were clear. Smaller and less powerful than the battleship, they could nevertheless shadow the enemy until help arrived, in the form of a nearby squadron which included *Hood* and the battleship *Prince of Wales*, along with several other warships of the Home Fleet. 'We whipped up the horses and got this (comparatively) old waggon rumbling along in pursuit,' wrote Sub-Lieutenant Basil Smith in *Suffolk*. 'This was a chase – how long it would last and whither the enemy would lead us were very much the unknown factors. We just hoped we were going to be "in on" future Naval History and with a story to tell our grandchildren.'

Stokers and engine-room staff sweated and strained to feed the fires and keep the cruisers at full steam. 'We kept them just in sight,' wrote Smith. 'The enemy was clearly silhouetted against a hard horizon and the advantage lay with us for the horizon to the NE was murky with the snow coming up astern.' After a warning shot to *Norfolk*, there was some surprise in the cruisers that they had been given the opportunity to chase at all. 'They were sighted only 6 miles away skulking along the edge of the ice in a snow-storm,' wrote Collett. 'For some reason best known to himself they did not open fire on us – at that short range they could have blown us out of the water.'

The cruisers shadowed the *Bismarck* along the ice all night until shortly after 5 a.m. on the morning of Saturday 24 May, when smoke from *Hood* and *Prince of Wales* was spotted on the horizon. 'It was a great relief to see these two big ships appear,' wrote Collett, 'as it meant that our main job was completed successfully.' He started to relax a little at his post, high up in the air-defence position, and waited for the action to begin. 'We were mere spectators of this part of the battle,' he wrote, 'and it was thrilling watching those big ships fire at one another at terrific range with such accuracy.'

Midshipman Graeme Allen was celebrating his nineteenth birthday. It was spent at action stations in HMS *Prince of Wales*. Allen was in the upper plot, an office below the bridge with an 'illuminated table with a chart upon it, and the position of one's own ship on the chart was shown by a bright spot of light, the position of which was automatically controlled'. Allen plotted the locations of nearby ships and monitored their movements. Above the plotting table, a square opening allowed the captain to see the tactical situation through 'a 3 foot high pyramid holding a pair of eyepieces'.

It was also Allen's job to keep the ship's log during the action, recording messages from the navigator and captain which were shouted down a voice pipe. After the first salvo from HMS *Hood* at five fifty-two a.m., followed by the first from *Prince of Wales*, the messages became more urgent. At two minutes past six he wrote '*Hood* hit'. At four minutes past six he wrote '*Hood* on fire'. At five minutes past six he wrote '*Hood* sunk'.

Shells from *Bismarck* had penetrated *Hood*'s armour and led to a devastating magazine explosion which tore the ship apart. Only three of her 1,421 sailors survived to be rescued by a destroyer. A few days later, Mrs Crawford received a telegram informing her that her son Bill was missing.

Almost immediately after *Hood*'s demise, *Bismarck*'s guns were briefly turned on *Prince of Wales*. The salvoes were ruthlessly accurate, scoring seven hits and killing thirteen men. One shell struck the bridge, killing two of Graeme Allen's fellow midshipmen and injuring several others, including the captain. 'The shell took off the top of the viewing device,' wrote Allen, now looking up into the devastated bridge, 'and blood began to drip steadily onto the chart table. We caught the drips in a half empty jug of cocoa.'

*Bismarck* had also been damaged, and rather than pressing home the advantage, Vice-Admiral Günther Lütjens decided to withdraw. His instructions from Admiral Raeder were to avoid the Royal Navy, preserving the precious battleship for attacks on vulnerable convoys. *Prince of Wales* dropped back, leaving the pursuit of the *Bismarck* to others. This later caused controversy, with insinuations that her officers had shown excessive caution or even cowardice. But the report of Admiral Wake-Walker, commanding the 1st Cruiser Squadron from HMS *Norfolk*, stated clearly that he had ordered *Prince of Wales* to stay astern of him while she carried out emergency repairs, as well as essential cleaning: 'She was still engaged in washing down her bridge in an attempt to remove the remains of the men killed there.'

Wake-Walker also knew that reinforcements were on their way. The battleship *King George V*, Admiral Tovey's flagship of the Home Fleet, had left Scapa Flow, and was joined by the aircraft carrier *Victorious* and the battlecruiser *Repulse*. Force H had despatched from Gibraltar: the aircraft carrier *Ark Royal*, the battlecruiser *Renown* and the cruiser *Sheffield*. The battleships *Ramillies* and *Rodney* had been redirected from convoys. Admiral Vian's destroyer force was also on its way north from the Mediterranean.

Three hours later, at 9 a.m. on 24 May, Eric Flory and his shipmates aboard the battleship *King George V* eagerly awaited the captain's broadcast concerning the battle off Iceland. Men listened in horrified silence to the announcement over the loudspeakers. 'We must sink *Bismarck*,' wrote Flory in his diary. '*Hood* has gone, our people at home expect great things of us and must be confident in their own minds that *Bismarck* cannot survive. Ships of R.N. converging on enemy from all points. Preparing ship for action – food and casualty stations, all keyed up to high degree ready for battle . . . It's Empire Day – shall we be lucky enough to give those at home a souvenir?' Aboard the cruiser HMS *Dorsetshire* the atmosphere was, as one rating put it, 'electrified'. Emotions were running high: 'We must avenge the *Hood*.'

But the reinforcements were still some way off, and the damaged *Bismarck* was escaping. It fell to *Suffolk* to take the lead in resuming the chase, tracking the battleship with radar, with *Norfolk* and *Prince of Wales* following. All day, sailors remained at action stations. 'I had been standing up straining my eyes to catch sight of the German ships for close on 11 hours without anything to eat or drink and no dinner the night before,' wrote Lieutenant Commander Collett of *Suffolk*. 'I completely lost all count of time.' Sandwiches were brought from the galley to the men at their posts. Sub-Lieutenant Smith was served 'hot sausages in between butterless bread'.

As the light began to fade, the weather deteriorated. Mist descended in patches and squalls of rain began to swirl. *Suffolk* was forced to move in closer for fear of losing her prey in the poor visibility. As the cruiser followed *Bismarck* into one patch of mist she was suddenly confronted with the battleship side-on. 'She appeared out of the mist a huge terrifying monster,' wrote Collett, 'and much too close for our liking!'

Many on *Suffolk*'s upper decks feared the worst. 'Everyone gaped at her expecting to see the vivid orange flashes from her guns,' wrote Collett. As *Suffolk* performed a sharp turn, pounding the engine for every ounce of speed, *Bismarck* fired. 'We could see her 15" shells coming at us – but they all went short. We turned and twisted under full helm and made smoke,' wrote Smith. The salvo fell just behind the escaping cruiser, 'throwing up a tremendous column of water'.

The next salvo came soon afterwards, again falling just short, and the third fell closer still. 'I saw the flash of her guns for the fourth salvo,' wrote Collett, 'and I must admit that . . . I expected us to be hit – I did, in fact, dodge behind our gun director, which is a most flimsy thing and couldn't possibly have protected me against anything but the smallest of splinters!' *Suffolk* made as much smoke as could be mustered to obscure the escape, and fired in defiance at the battleship before returning to position alongside *Norfolk* and *Prince of Wales*. 'We made our thanks for a merciful deliverance,' wrote Smith.

In the confusion, *Prinz Eugen* slipped away alone to the south, while *Bismarck* turned east, heading for the safety of the Bay of Biscay and the protection of the port of Brest. By evening, concerns were growing that the battleship might still be capable of evading the approaching reinforcements. Admiral Tovey, from his flagship *King George V*, ordered an attack on the battleship by aircraft from *Victorious*. The pilots of the rickety Swordfish biplanes braved *Bismarck*'s anti-aircraft guns to drop several torpedoes, killing one German sailor, but causing no significant damage to the ship.

In the early hours of Sunday 25 May, the *Bismarck* went missing. Panic ensued amongst senior officers, and ships were despatched in every direction to search for their quarry. Short of fuel, several had to turn back for home with nothing to report. The *Prince of Wales* was sent to Iceland. Midshipman Graeme Allen had witnessed the preparations for the funerals of his shipmates killed by *Bismarck*'s shells. 'The bodies were sewn up in canvas and laid in a row on the quarterdeck,' he wrote. 'The body of Midshipman Dreyer was just a sort of parcel, as the shell must have passed through him and blown him to pieces.' They were buried at sea, slipped under the Union Jack into the water as the chaplain said the traditional prayers. On reaching Iceland, the ship's company was allowed a few hours ashore at Hvalfjordur. Allen went for a walk. 'I was surprised to see how beautiful the hills were,' he wrote, 'covered with spring flowers.'

It was not until the following morning, at 10.30 a.m. on 26 May, that the *Bismarck* was rediscovered, this time by a Catalina reconnaissance aircraft. As before, the priority was to slow down the battleship until the British hunting party could converge. This duty fell once again to the Fleet Air Arm, and aboard *Ark Royal* aircraft were prepared for a strike. 'The weather was getting worse,' recalled Alan Swanton, 'but we were so wound up about the whole thing that we didn't really feel it'. Swanton was piloting one of fifteen Swordfish biplanes led by Commander James Stewart-Moore. Briefings before the attack had instructed the squadron to ensure surprise by using the cloud cover. 'I was told to attack whichever ship we found first, the cruiser or the battleship,' wrote Stewart-Moore. 'It all seemed straightforward.'

From the flight deck, Swanton's fellow airman Charles Friend could see the daunting weather conditions: 'The waves were so high that even sixty feet tall *Ark Royal* sometimes "took it green" over her bows. *Renown*, plunging along within sight of us was taking it all green; her weather decks were continuously awash, and *Sheffield* could not be seen at all through the spume and spray.' So volatile were the seas that the flight deck of *Ark Royal* was rising and falling by fifty feet with every wave. As Stewart-Moore explained: 'This made landing and taking off, particularly with torpedoes [attached], quite hazardous; it also made handling the aircraft on deck heavy and slow work: twenty men pushing a Swordfish laboriously uphill might suddenly find themselves breaking into a canter as the ship topped a swell and the aircraft rolled happily forward down an ever-steepening slope.'

The carrier reduced speed to allow the aircraft to launch, but with a vicious wind across the deck, taking off was, as Charles Friend put it, 'awesome in the extreme. The aircraft, as their throttles were opened, instead of charging forward on a level deck, were at one moment breasting a slippery slope, and the next plunging downhill towards the huge seas ahead.' Nevertheless, the Swordfish managed to launch successfully, and made for *Bismarck*'s estimated position in formation. The plane being flown by Stewart-Moore's wingman was equipped with a special 'air to surface vessel' radar set, specifically designed for finding ships. Radio communication was unreliable, so the commander had to maintain visual contact with the young midshipman who was operating the device: 'After we had been going for a while, I saw Cooper waving . . . He then semaphored to me that he had a radar contact about twenty miles away to starboard.'

In formation above the clouds, the biplanes made for the contact location and dived, torpedoes ready to be launched. It seemed a perfect attack. 'One after another, torpedoes fell away from the bellies of the Swordfish,' recalled Swanton. 'It was only after 11 weapons had been dropped that the pilots began to realise that something had gone horribly wrong.'

As Stewart-Moore's Swordfish emerged from the cloud, he was looking back for the rest of the formation when his pilot, Hunter, shouted through the voice pipe: 'It's the *Sheffield*.' The squadron were attacking one of their own ships. Hunter pulled out and rocked the plane from side to side, 'waving the wings', but only two others realized the mistake: 'The rest continued their dive, flattened out for the run-in close above the surface, and dropped their torpedoes. They carried out the attack very well, while we watched from above, horrified, and praying for a miracle.'

What occurred was, if not a miracle, certainly a stroke of fortune. Not a single torpedo hit the British cruiser. They were new models, fitted with a magnetic charge intended to guide the missile automatically under the hull of the enemy ship, but the new technology had apparently failed to operate properly. The debriefing session after the erroneous attack was, according to Swanton, 'animated, but lessons were learned'. After some deliberation, it was decided to revert to traditional impact torpedoes.

The next attempt came just after 7 p.m. that evening. This time the Swordfish flew to *Sheffield* and then on through the clouds towards *Bismarck*. 'We ran into a bank of heavy cloud,' recalled Stewart-Moore, 'which proved to be much thicker than we had expected. We flew blind in it for a while, a hair-raising business, but eventually all the aircraft became separated and the squadron completely lost its formation.' Finally, after flying for an hour and a half, they sighted their target. Only a small number of Swordfish were still together. Alan Swanton described the descent: 'In a 4 ship formation behind Stewart-Moore, we descended to 100 ft. There she was, half a mile away, big, black and menacing. She had guns all over her, and they all seemed to be stabbing red flame in our direction. I levelled, 100 ft, 100 knots, heading for her amidships.' It was, wrote Stewart-Moore, 'a rather forlorn attack . . . The run-in was alarming. We had the *Bismarck*'s undivided attention for at least five minutes. The shells we could see seemed to fill the sky; those we couldn't see did not bother us so much.'

At last it was time to release the torpedoes. 'I pushed the "tit",' wrote Swanton, 'the torpedo fell away and the aircraft seemed to jump up into the air.' The Swordfish made their escapes at full speed under heavy fire, as Stewart-Moore described it, 'dodging like snipe as we went. We were only about 150 ft above the sea,' he recalled, 'and the three aircraft were fairly close together, when there was a terrific crash directly below us, as four or five heavy shells struck the water and exploded.' Swanton saw 'a series of flashes, and flak ripped through the underside of the fuselage. "Christ!" I yelled, "Just look at this lot" . . . The shells were hitting the sea in front, but were pushing up 100 ft mountains of water. We continued low and fast until we were out of range . . . It was then that [my observer] Gerry spotted the dark stain on the shoulder of my flying overalls.'

The return to *Ark Royal* could not come fast enough. Swanton had some trouble landing: 'It was a bit of a controlled crash, but I was able to walk away from it.' While he collapsed in the medical room, the other Swordfish pilots and their crews debriefed in the operations room. Stewart-Moore thought it had been 'a sorry tale of small ineffectual attacks'. In fact, a torpedo had hit *Bismarck*'s steering room, crippling the motors which operated the battleship's rudders. Unable to manoeuvre, she was now powerless to evade the closing British warships.

That evening aboard *King George V*, a small service was held in the chapel, attended by a few dozen men. 'Vesper Jesu Lover of my Soul', noted Eric Flory, 'prayers for relatives of *Hood*'s ship's company, they had lost their battle.' The battleship's sailors remained at action stations overnight, with an engagement expected early the following morning. Flory and his colleagues in the galley 'served out pea soup and cakes' and then 'commenced cutting sandwiches for hands to have a bite before action'. At 5 a.m. on Tuesday 27 May, they served tea and sandwiches to 1,000 men. After clearing up, Flory 'sat down on box to hear latest news and have a rest, legs ache, peace and quietness'.

At 7.15 a.m. his peace came to an end. The captain's voice came over the ship's tannoy: 'Hope to engage enemy soon, take it steady and treat it as a battle practice.' 'Tense moments,' noted Flory in his diary. 'Time seems to drag, weather is rough and blowing a gale.' Shortly before 9 a.m. the engagement began. 'Relief at last,' for Flory. 'Our 14-inch guns blaze forth and so we are really in the battle . . . Commander broadcasts: "We are hitting the *Bismarck*" – loud cheers.'

Able Seaman R. J. Morry was a gunner on one of the anti-aircraft 'pom-poms', high up on the starboard side of *King George V*. The Newfoundlander, who had been drafted to the battleship after surviving the sinking of his previous ship in September 1940, found himself with a grandstand view of the action. 'We could see the fall of shot from our position,' he recalled, 'as great clumps of white water rose all around *Bismarck* – much higher than her mast and tower. Then we saw a ripple of fire from *Bismarck* . . . the stern of *Rodney* was lifted out of the water and you could see her propeller turning for a split second, a near miss.'

Morry and the other exposed gunners were, for a brief time, ordered below decks to protect them from these salvoes, but they were soon back up top in time to see the denouement of the battle. By this time, the *Bismarck* was in a terrible state. 'Some of her guns went on firing in an inaccurate manner, her turret guns were drooping over the side, some had barrels blasted off,' wrote Morry. 'She was on fire now from stem to stern; flames could be seen from the apertures in the deck when deck structures were blasted off.' It had taken just half an hour to silence the *Bismarck*'s guns, but it would take another hour to sink her.

*Dorsetshire*'s captain announced, 'I am going to put two fish into the *Bismarck*, one on the Port and the other on the Starboard side.' In *King George V*, Eric Flory decided to improve his vantage point by sneaking onto the bridge. He later recorded the scene in his diary:

> By jove it certainly is rough. A fierce wind is blowing and spray is washing over the bridge. Yes there was the *Bismarck* away to starboard, smoke pouring up her superstructure higher than the foremast, men were still jumping over the side . . . *Bismarck* looked helpless listing to port, guns pointing in all directions. Yes our task was finished. *Dorsetshire* steams up and fires torpedoes to finally sink *Bismarck* . . . The German sailors must have thought that a direct plunge into the sea was far better than the terrible inferno on board. Fires were raging and the steel plates were showing red hot.

Aboard HMS *Tartar* was Ludovic Kennedy, the young officer who had lost his father when the *Rawalpindi* was sunk in November 1939. He would later write his own celebrated account of the sinking of the *Bismarck*, but when interviewed many years afterwards the overwhelming images that remained with him were particularly visceral: 'High seas, very green seas, and then the grey of the British ships and the black of the *Bismarck*, and then these shells exploding and sending up great white fountains . . . and the brown of the cordite smoke.' He recalled 'the fires flickering between the cracks in the decks . . . A group of sailors running down the quarterdeck to jump into the sea.' Kennedy's abiding memory of the *Bismarck* combined awe and empathy: 'I have never seen a more magnificent warship,' he recalled, 'and she sat squarely in the water taking terrible, terrible punishment.'

On the upper decks of the British ships, sailors clamoured for a view of the last moments of this grand enemy as it finally sank. 'The binoculars assigned to the gun crew were very much in demand,' wrote R. J. Morry. For many observers, there were brief, but vivid, moments of human connection. One such instance continued to resonate with Morry: 'I admired the crew of one small gun located on the port waist deck, which kept firing after all her main armaments had ceased. This little gun would fire and you could see a small projectile skipping across the sea to sink a half-mile from our ship.'

There were just 115 survivors from *Bismarck*'s 2,222 officers and men. 'The battle finished, the humanitarian instinct rises above the feeling of revenge and destruction,' wrote A. E. Franklin, a rating in *Dorsetshire*. 'The foe is beaten and hearts go out in succour to them that are in the water.' 'She put up a wonderful fight,' wrote Lieutenant Commander Collett of HMS *Suffolk*, 'and I must say I take my hat off to her ship's company who must have been living in a raging inferno towards the end.'

Others were less forgiving. 'For a moment we feel as if we want to be sorry,' wrote Eric Flory in *King George V*. 'Yes she fought to the last and went down with colours flying, but why be sorry? No we must not have sympathy with such a brutal nation who are killing our families. No that is not warfare, it is brutal murder, so we have just done what should have been done.' Flory's attitude was perhaps as much a reaction to the aftermath of the battle as the destruction of the *Bismarck* itself: on the way back home several British ships were attacked by Luftwaffe bombers. 'The enemy of course would not let us rest,' continued Flory in his diary. 'Planes came . . . *Mashona* was bombed and sank . . . we got back safely and thanked God for victory.' There was, however, little time to savour this victory. Flory had duties to attend to: 'Swept up the dust caused by gunfire and ready for a go at the *Tirpitz* should she venture out.'

★ ★ ★

On 22 June 1941, within a month of the sinking of the *Bismarck*, German troops began their invasion of the Soviet Union. On 21 August, the first convoy set off from Britain bound for north Russia, carrying supplies for the new ally. In the Atlantic, the heavy merchant losses which had caused such consternation since March were beginning to improve. At the start of August 1941, after completing repairs, *Prince of Wales* was sent on a clandestine voyage, carrying the most precious cargo that the country could muster: the British Prime Minister, on his way to a secret summit meeting with the still nominally neutral American President. Churchill came aboard at Scapa Flow along with, as his secretary Jock Colville put it, 'a retinue which Cardinal Wolsey might have envied'. Staff officers, typists, a couple of hand-picked journalists and numerous other additional bodies squeezed into the cramped living quarters.

Churchill was given the admiral's cabin, in the rear of the ship below the quarterdeck: well appointed, comfortable and far removed from the noise and distractions of everyday operations. It did not suit Winston. He soon decided to install himself in the admiral's sea cabin, directly below the bridge, from where he could oversee the running of the ship and the progress of the voyage.

The ship's usual amenities were substantially improved for the benefit of the guests. Additional victuals were provided by Fortnum and Mason, including ninety out-of-season grouse and industrial quantities of sugar and butter. Churchill amused himself by reading C. S. Forester's novels recounting the adventures of Napoleonic naval hero Horatio Hornblower. The wardroom was turned into an impromptu cinema. Churchill sat at the front, along with his staff, in a row of armchairs. The ship's officers improvised. 'We crammed in as best we could,' wrote Midshipman Graeme Allen. The film was *Lady Hamilton*, a biopic of Nelson which was Churchill's favourite. It was his fifth viewing.

Early in the morning of 9 August, *Prince of Wales* arrived at the secluded Placentia Bay, on the southern coast of Newfoundland. At 7.30 a.m. the American cruiser *Augusta* arrived, with several dignitaries on board including President Franklin D. Roosevelt. Churchill was taken across and, in accordance with protocol, presented the

American head of state with a letter of introduction from King George VI. With the preliminaries over, the summit began.

Churchill and Roosevelt enjoyed a relationship based on genuine mutual appreciation, even if the association of their respective nations was not always conducted on equal terms. They shared a connection with the war at sea, both having had responsibility for naval matters during the First World War: Churchill as First Lord of the Admiralty and Roosevelt as Assistant Secretary for the Navy. Indeed, in the secret correspondence with which Churchill had wooed the President since the outbreak of war, his pseudonym had been 'Former Naval Person'.

Their discussions resulted in a joint declaration of mutual principles, the wording of which was thrashed out by the leaders and their staffs. Ronald Middleton, a solicitor before joining the RNVR, was a cipher officer in the *Prince of Wales*. As the talks progressed, he was locked in the cipher room, dealing with a stream of paperwork. 'Churchill's first draft was given to me,' he recalled. 'I cut it up into slices of two lines each so that twelve lines at a time could be ciphered. It was quickly done and transmitted to the Cabinet. The answer was on my desk at the next watch. Drafts passed back and forth, finally one with the Prime Minister's manuscript amendments.'

The result became known as the 'Atlantic Charter'. Rather than a formal treaty, it was an expression of common global aims: democratic freedoms, economic cooperation and free trade, 'freedom from want and fear', disarmament and an international 'system of general security'. Although the promise of self-determination for free peoples would later epitomize the clash between American and British principles of imperialism, the declaration was none the less fêted as a historic moment of cooperation. To the British public, it was a sign that their would-be ally might finally be prepared to intervene on their behalf.

American and British officers and men joined together for a religious service, culminating in a version of the famous naval prayer:

O Eternal Lord God, Who alone spreadest out the heavens, and rulest the raging of the sea; Who has compassed the waters with bounds until day and night come to an end; Be pleased to receive into Thy Almighty and Most Gracious protection the persons of us Thy servants, and the Fleet in which we serve. Preserve us from the dangers of the sea, and from the violence of the enemy; that we may be a security for such as pass upon the seas upon their lawful occasions; that the peoples of the Empire may in peace and quietness serve Thee, our God; and that we may return in safety to enjoy the blessings of the land, with the fruits of our labours, and with a thankful remembrance of Thy mercies to praise and glorify Thy Holy Name; through Jesus Christ our Lord.

On the afternoon of 12 August, *Prince of Wales* left Newfoundland to return across the ocean. During the voyage she altered course in order to pass through a large convoy heading east. Signalmen raised the flags denoting 'church' and 'hill'. Graeme Allen recorded that the Prime Minister was 'hoisted up to the roof of the bridge' and proceeded to wave to the excited crews of passing merchant ships, giving them the famous 'V' sign.

The Charter represented just one element of Atlantic cooperation that contributed to such optimism. Lend-Lease had been ratified by Congress in the spring of 1941, ensuring material aid from the USA to Britain, albeit at a price. In May, the Royal Canadian Navy had begun to take responsibility for convoy escorts to and from Newfoundland. In July, American troops were installed in Iceland, and over the course of the summer US Navy escorts began to provide protection for British shipping in the western Atlantic. German submarines backed away to the east, where they were less likely to provoke intervention from the USA. Many were sent away to the Mediterranean. Much of the Luftwaffe presence in the region was reallocated to the Russian Front, and by 1942 fewer than 10 per cent of sinkings would be attributed to enemy aircraft. Most importantly, continuous escort in both directions across the Atlantic was becoming the norm. Escort forces were building up, and radar and new technologies were being rolled out. By the autumn of 1941, monthly shipping losses were back under control. In November, less than 100,000 tons of shipping was lost in the North Atlantic for the first time since the outbreak of war.

Admiral Dönitz had recognized the opportunity to strike a profound blow against Britain in the summer of 1940. He wanted a fleet of 300 submarines, with 100 operating in the Atlantic at any given time, but this ambition was never close to being realized. The operational total available in this crucial period actually fell from thirty-two to twenty-five and, despite attempts to increase their numbers in the autumn of 1940, there were only twenty-two boats operating in the Atlantic in February 1941. That they were able to sink 2 million tons of shipping between June 1940 and March 1941 was therefore a considerable achievement, but as the convoy system and escort groups began to improve, success became harder to come by. The average number of merchant ships sunk for each U-boat destroyed fell from twenty-two in the first half of 1941 to just seven in the second half. In December 1941, the first British escort 'ace' emerged: the 36th Escort Group, led by Captain Frederic 'Johnnie' Walker, sank five U-boats in five days while protecting convoy HG76.

The autumn also brought one American contribution which would prove decisive above all others. On 27 September 1941 the first 'Liberty ships' were launched. Pragmatically constructed cargo vessels, combining British design and American production skill, they marked a new stage in the shipping war. Eventually, the numbers of lost merchant vessels would be more than made up for by the newly built freighters. The first Liberty ship was officially SS *Patrick Henry*, launched by President Roosevelt at Baltimore, Maryland, and named after the American revolutionary figure most famous for coining the phrase 'Give me Liberty, or give me Death'. This was indeed the beginning of an Atlantic revolution.

# 10. Mare Nostrum

'It is extraordinary,' wrote George Blundell, engineering officer of HMS *Kent*, 'to go from one ocean to another in a day, even less than a day. Here we are at last in the Med.' In August 1940, the former flagship of the China Fleet had passed through the Suez Canal and was finally at the heart of the war. A frantic schedule of work began. The ship was repainted in a more pragmatic grey, and the usual robust routine for a cruiser in an active war zone was adopted. After a Sunday spent in sweat, Blundell overheard one rating proclaim: 'And six days shalt thou labour and do all that thou hast to do, but the seventh is the Sabbath; on it thou shalt work a fucking sight harder.'

Eyes were fixed on the skies. *Kent* adopted a 'lookout bribery system' as an incentive to those responsible for spotting enemy bombers. 'Any lookout correctly reporting an aircraft to the control gets sixpence,' wrote Blundell in his diary, 'and if it is a dive bomber before it dives, he gets a bob.' At first, the danger seemed to have been overstated. 'We expected the Itis to do something,' grumbled Blundell after one successful convoy escort. 'But did we or anybody get any opposition or even see a blooming Iti? Not a bit: it is simply astonishing, the lack of Iti enterprise. Most of us are disgusted at not having met anything or had a scrap, but the Admiral and Captain were both tremendously relieved.'

A scrap was not long in coming. In September 1940, *Kent* was part of a task force bombarding Sollum, to the east of Tobruk in eastern Libya. It was just after eleven o'clock at night, and Blundell was on the bridge, observing the gun flashes and star-shell explosions off the port bow when he heard the sound of bombs dropping:

> We were then firing hard at aircraft . . . we had a low torpedo bomber attack on our starboard beam. I saw the splashes, enormous ones, as

torpedoes were dropped. Shortly afterwards there was a tremendous blow aft. The whole ship reeled, then suddenly felt dead, and we could feel on the Bridge as if her tail had dropped, a sort of bending, dragging feeling and the ship wouldn't steer.

Men were knocked off their feet. Orders were barked down voice pipes for the engines to be stopped. Confidential books were gathered in preparation for possible destruction. Blundell groped his way around the bridge while enemy aircraft machine-gunned the decks. As engineering officer, he realized that any damage to the electrical system would render the steering motors unusable, so sought permission to leave the bridge to investigate. Finding his way by torchlight through the gloom below decks, he took a detour to rescue his film camera and money from his cabin. Just outside the wardroom, he came across a fellow senior officer looking, as Blundell put it, 'pretty squiffy'. A passing sailor was ordered 'to keep an eye on him and sit him down in the wardroom. He looked like a child.'

The rear of the ship was 'in darkness and as silent as the grave as all electric supply had failed'. Blundell checked the emergency cables, moving towards the engine-room hatch in extreme heat. Some engineers had fainted, others were escaping. Blundell ordered one man to find the emergency switches for the engine-room fans and another to accompany him down to the engine room: 'The heat coming up from the hatch was so intense he didn't want to go, so I had to force him down in front of me: I am sure he felt he was going to his death.'

After organizing the situation below, Blundell returned to the wardroom flat, by now filling with smoke and fumes. After putting on his gas mask he staggered through the open bulkhead door, but all he could make out was a fire inside: 'I could see a glow and it was damned hot. I began to feel a bit chokey and sleepy and sat down inside the Flat but realized that the gas mask was pretty well useless. I felt I could sleep for ever and I remember taking a pull at myself and saying internally "No, George Blundell, you're not going to die yet."'

He managed to shut the bulkhead door with the help of another sailor. It was too late for the ship's commander, who was later found dead near where Blundell had collapsed. After isolating the blaze, Blundell made his way up to the quarterdeck, still under machine-gun fire. He arranged emergency steering cables and then found a way down to the steering position with the help of more stokers: 'As I stepped through the cabin door I squelched on something flabby and in the torch saw it was the body of Petty Officer Masters . . . I remember thinking "That's the first dead man I've ever seen," and feeling relieved that it didn't seem at all unnatural.'

Blundell and his men worked for nearly three hours in the emergency steering room, by now on the verge of being submerged, bringing down emergency lighting and pumping a dynamo by hand. They eventually managed to straighten the rudder and at 1.30 a.m. were under tow from HMS *Nubian*. By 5 a.m. the situation was stable enough for breakfast to be served, but the fire below decks was still too intense to retrieve the dead bodies.

Blundell became the de facto executive officer, and had to deal with the aftermath. On 19 September, twenty bodies were extracted, wrapped in hammocks, weighted, and sewn up before being sent over to another ship with an attachment of mourners and the chaplain. 'I wept,' wrote Blundell in his diary. 'So many of my shipmates.' Unfortunately, the following day revealed a problem: 'About 12 of the bodies buried at sea yesterday washed up ashore during the night.' Meanwhile, more corpses had since been retrieved from the ammunition store: 'They were all terribly bloated and the doctors had to cut them up to get them out.' Another funeral service was arranged: 'The later bodies were weighed more heavily . . .'

The war against Italy had begun in earnest. In July 1940, as the Luftwaffe was turning its attentions to convoys in the English Channel, ships of the Mediterranean Fleet had clashed with a large Italian force near Punta Stilo, on the coast of Calabria, the 'toe' of Italy. It was a foretaste of the dangers of air attack. But it would be British, not Italian, air power which struck the first decisive blow in the Mediterranean.

On 11 November Swordfish torpedo-bombers attacked the Italian fleet in harbour at Taranto. It was a plan first mooted during the

Abyssinian crisis and now made possible by arming the rickety biplanes with long-range fuel tanks and modern torpedoes. From the carrier *Illustrious*, some 170 miles away, the Swordfish took off in the moonlight and made their way to attack. Open cockpits meant that the airmen experienced, as one pilot put it, 'the sort of cold that fills you until all else is drowned save perhaps fear and loneliness'.

Two of the most powerful ships in the Italian fleet were hit: the battleships *Littorio* and *Conte di Cavour*, which succumbed to the damage and sank. Several others would require substantial repairs. Although two bombers were lost, it was regarded as an overwhelming success, and was the first part of a wider plan to take the fight to Italian ships and convoys throughout the Mediterranean.

'You will have seen in the papers what a crack our air boys hit the "Wop" fleet in Taranto,' wrote Commander Manley Power, assistant to the local commander-in-chief, Andrew Cunningham, to his wife back home in Britain. 'At the same time some of the light forces were beating up a convoy off Valona well in Musso's "mare nostrum". We are naturally delighted with the results . . . we've struck a big blow this time which may shorten the war a bit, and bring us together earlier. I expect the Top Wop is raving mad, and we shall probably get a lot of bombing back in harbour.'

Mussolini's assertion that the Mediterranean was 'mare nostrum' – 'our sea' – was regarded by some in the Royal Navy as a joke and by others as an affront. Even without the assistance of the French, British dominance over the Italians was a firm expectation. From Gibraltar in the west to Alexandria and the Suez Canal in the east, and with the island of Malta at its heart, the Mediterranean was a vital part of the British maritime system; a crucial imperial artery and a link to India and the Far East.

Gibraltar was Britain's greatest overseas stronghold, the northern of the so-called 'Pillars of Hercules' which formed the natural gateway to the Mediterranean. Charles Thomas had visited in December 1939. 'There is a saying,' he wrote in a letter home, 'which is very true: "You never see a lean priest or a fat cat." Despite the hold of the R. C. Church the place is not as miserable on Sundays as Manchester – the shops and the cinemas are open.' A year later, the town remained as busy as ever. Sailors on shore leave filled the streets, mixing with the multicultural inhabitants and haggling with merchants, wandering through Alameda Botanic Gardens, and queuing for the packed bars and pubs, perhaps even sampling the green-coloured beer at the Rock Hotel.

Gibraltar was home to Force H, commanded by Admiral James Somerville, which consisted of the carrier HMS *Ark Royal*, the battlecruiser *Renown* and the cruiser *Sheffield*, along with a flotilla of destroyers. After Mers-el-Kébir, Gibraltar became a base of operations for sorties and convoys driving east towards Malta. Before the war, Somerville had commanded British destroyers in the Mediterranean, and had been recalled from a brief period of retirement in 1939. He was a popular leader, respected by his subordinates, and took a keen interest in the practicalities of naval warfare, even accompanying Swordfish pilots to learn about their craft. Sailors liked to tell the story of how the admiral would 'pull a skiff round the harbour each morning before breakfast'.

Somerville was also something of an ambiguous personality. In November 1940, he was vilified by Churchill for refusing to risk his forces in an attempt to rout the Italians after a brief encounter at Spartivento. Although the Prime Minister's criticisms were unfair, certainly as far as Somerville's supporters were concerned, the Admiral's letters to his wife reflected a degree of disquiet about his own actions and the wider prosecution of the war. Following the seizure of a handful of weak French ships, an action which resulted in the deaths of several innocent civilians, Somerville wrote: 'It seems to me that we are just as much of a dictator country as either Germany or Italy and one day the great British public will wake up and ask what we are fighting for.'

At the outset of 1941, while enemy bombers continued to terrorize British ports and cities by night, an elite squadron of German Ju 87 Stuka dive-bombers was sent to operate from the airfields of Sicily and southern Italy. They wasted little time in making their presence felt. On 10 January, several ships of the Mediterranean Fleet were escorting a convoy nearby when they were attacked by Italian torpedo-bombers, which drew defensive fighters away from the aircraft carrier HMS *Illustrious*. Forty-three Stukas took the opportunity to launch a surprise attack on *Illustrious*. An anti-aircraft barrage could not prevent damage: six bombs hit and a hundred men were killed. Escaping the Sicilian narrows, she made for Malta, suffering further bombing attacks en route.

Captain Denis Boyd, the commanding officer of *Illustrious*, wrote to a friend soon afterwards, describing the fates of some of his men. One lieutenant 'was hit on the spine by a bomb splinter and fell down . . . He then turned very grey and asked for morphia, knowing he was dying . . . A marine picked him up and his back was heard to break. He was I think already dead.' The master-at-arms had been 'blown to bits in the hangar where a bomb exploded. He was a golden man.' A pilot who had excelled himself at Taranto was 'never seen again. Either he was blown overboard or disintegrated.' A young marine 'was killed by a bomb which did not wound him but just blasted him'. One of the ship's best gunners 'was blown to bits by a bomb which hit the pom-pom just in front of the bridge. He and all the crew were just in an awful mess but were clearly killed instantly. I ordered them to be thrown overboard as these were dreadful sights. Arms, legs, heads and trunks going over the side were awful to see but were better there than lying about the deck where they chilled the stomachs of others.'

Boyd admitted that he had 'felt no sorrow' at the time, as the magnitude of his responsibilities kept him occupied. It was only once the initial bombing attack was over that the full force of emotion descended:

Fear came later when I realised we must have more attacks before reaching Malta. I then felt utterly sick for a while and trembled from head to foot. I went down to my sea cabin, took a good hold of myself, offered up a prayer that I'd do my stuff and then went back and was waggling the engines to steer her for the next 8 hours and through two more attacks without any particular feeling other than an unsatisfied desire for food. From breakfast until 10 p.m. when we secured I only had cocoa and a biscuit.

Once *Illustrious* reached Valletta's Grand Harbour, the island of Malta came under intense attack from the air for the first time, in what became known as the 'Illustrious Blitz'. Canon Nicholls, a priest at St Paul's Anglican Cathedral, described Valletta as 'one great cloud of smoke' in his diary:

> The enemy planes skimmed the roof-tops as they rose out of their dives. The *Illustrious* was hit once and the Captain's cabin demolished. The *Essex*, a fine new P and O [liner], was also hit and had about twenty killed and some injured. The dockyard is badly messed up and probably pretty well finished as a repair shop on any large scale . . . The noise in our crypt was just terrible. There were about 250 people huddled together, many of them crying, but many very brave. The roar was like the loudest thunder one has ever heard, but absolutely continuous, and it was not possible really to distinguish the guns from the bombs.

For those serving in Malta, as for the civilians, this heralded the start of several harrowing days. Lieutenant Commander Michael Blois-Brooke, a young sailor at the time, later described the trauma of helping locals search for missing loved ones, often buried beneath several layers of rubble: 'It was not nice to uncover the smashed body of a child. There is nothing more sad than the sight of a fly crawling over the face of a dead child.'

Aboard *Illustrious*, the psychological effects of the raids began to take their toll. 'My worst job was to see people suffering from strain,' wrote Boyd. 'It was horrible and some got it badly.' One man, 'a fat, cheerful, self-indulgent bachelor', refused to come back to the ship and was sent to hospital. Another, who had been injured during the bombing attacks at sea, 'cried at the least excuse'. Nobody was unaffected, but some were more resilient than others. 'Men I thought tough were no good at all,' wrote Boyd. His closest officers and 'a few sailors and engineers of the quiet nice type' seemed to hold up best. 'Others in varying degrees were looking like death but they stuck it well.' Boyd eventually ordered the abandonment of the ship for three days. Only a small group remained aboard *Illustrious*, with most sent ashore to shelters hidden in hillside caves. 'I think I saved them all from going really potty,' wrote Boyd. 'Had I not done so half of us would have been lunies and in any case we would not have saved the ship . . . they all came back gladly and were able to produce the goods for our awful passage to Alex.'

This was a blitz comparable with that which was terrorizing British cities, but the suffering of the people of Malta had only just begun. Meanwhile, sailors in other ships considered their own efforts to be a form of retribution for enemy attacks on civilians. HMS *Sheffield*, along with other ships from Force H, bombarded Genoa in the early morning of 9 February 1941. Captain Charles Larcom described the operation in a letter to his wife:

> Just back from Genoa where we gave them worse than they gave Portsmouth or Southampton. It was grand . . . Surprise was complete – not a destroyer, trawler, E-boat or aircraft was about and the first that the town knew was the crump of our first salvoes. A Sunday morning, just as the devout were on their way to Mass! I could not help thinking about it that way. For half an hour we plugged shell after shell into the town and docks . . . *Sheffield* gave them 782 high explosive shells in an area about the size of say Gosport. Then we hopped it as fast as our legs could carry us . . . It was terrific. We hit an electric power works with our third shot and something fuzed and we could see blinding flashes running all the way from the works up the light wires in the streets.

After surviving her blitz, *Illustrious* was able to escape to Alexandria, back to the relative safety of the fleet. Egypt was the hub of British activity in the eastern Mediterranean: the gateway to the Indian Ocean through the Suez Canal; a base for operations in the Western Desert and the Middle East. Alexandria itself continued to evoke an intensely foreign atmosphere for British sailors. It was a seedy city: appealingly exotic to some, disconcertingly edgy to others. 'Immorality is very rife,' wrote Charles Hutchinson of HMS *Carlisle* in his diary. 'In most of the cabarets by getting in touch with certain people one can get anything, even drugs . . . I'm talking as if I'm a missionary out to reform, but I'm not . . . With plenty of money you could have a good time, but it's so damned artificial.'

Ratings tended to congregate at the rowdy Fleet Club. Meanwhile, officers enjoyed as many of the trappings of British imperial life as could be sustained in wartime. 'Bars, restaurants, shops and clubs abounded, full of good things and cosmopolitan clientele,' recalled Alec Dennis, first lieutenant of the destroyer HMS *Griffin*. Pastrudi's, the Union Club, or the Ritz would always be well-attended for dinner, followed perhaps by cabaret and dancing at the Monseigneur. Brothels did a roaring trade. Mary's House was one of the better appointed, with dining and drinks as well as other services. 'Later in the war,' wrote Dennis, 'a bomb fell there and certain officers, caught upstairs, were said to have been "killed in action".'

To the east of Alexandria, Port Said also managed to retain some of its charms, at least for officers. Lieutenant John Mosse recalled bathing at the French Club, drinks at the Union Bar (where the head waiter was known as 'Hitler'), and the Eastern Exchange Hotel and cabaret. To beat the early curfew, cans of beer were hidden in an ornamental goldfish pond in the corner of the room. Mosse also enjoyed the services of an Egyptian-hating Sudanese manservant named Mustafa, who had a habit of attacking cockroaches with his feet, 'muttering "King Farouk, King Farouk" as he squelched them'.

The Egyptian enclaves continued to serve as imperial outposts, where officers could enjoy much the same leisure and sporting activities as ever. Indeed, so well known were the habits of senior British officers that enemy spies were able to follow their movements with ease. So inevitable was this surveillance that it could occasionally be used to significant advantage. In the spring of 1941, a round of golf at the Alexandria Sporting Club helped to bring the Royal Navy its first major success of the war in a fleet battle, and ensured the fame of Admiral Andrew Cunningham.

Intelligence sources had revealed an opportunity for a surprise attack on the Italian fleet off the southern coast of Greece. In order to give the impression that his warships would be staying in harbour on the evening of 27 March 1941, Cunningham and his colleagues made sure that they were noticed at the golf club preparing dinner plans, having already made arrangements for the battle fleet to sail. Enemy spies were convinced, and the trap was set.

Guided by reconnaissance aircraft, the British closed in on the Italian fleet to the south of Crete. A few brief clashes followed, in which strikes by Fleet Air Arm torpedo-bombers managed to damage the Italian battleship *Vittorio Veneto* and cripple the cruiser *Pola*, after which the remaining Italian ships were chased towards the Ionian Sea. On the night of 28 March, British radar guided Cunningham towards the Italian fleet which, lacking any similar means of detection, was blind and unprepared. Eighteen-year-old Midshipman T. Ruck Keene was part of the gunnery direction team aboard the battleship HMS *Warspite*. In his journal, he described the moment that the British made visual contact by the light of the moon:

Suddenly a hoarse yell up the voice-pipe, into the 'phones. 'Enemy in sight bearing Green 5.' We were there before we realised, suddenly face to face with two long, dim shapes which filled our glasses with their size, incredibly sinister in the meagre starlight. The 'phones clamped to my head were full of men shouting orders, questions, calculations; everyone was busy . . . Seconds passed and nothing happened. To us in the director the three ships just sat there watching each other, for it was impossible to realise that all the time we were turning round . . . On the bridge the Captain began to speak. He said 'Open . . .' and we did, as four fifteen-inch guns blended their voices into one stunning cacophony of noise, one blinding flash that momentarily paralysed the brain.

Within moments, the Italian cruiser *Fiume* was devastated. 'Three seconds later,' wrote Ruck Keene, 'that long black shape ceased to be a potential menace and became a blazing hull as a magazine exploded; from bridge to stern she was a sea of flame, flame that rose fifty feet into the air surmounted by sparks that rose a hundred.'

Commander Manley Power was at Cunningham's side on *Warspite*'s bridge. 'We had a most terrific show,' he wrote in a letter to his wife. 'It was a wonderful sight. The destroyer ahead of us put a searchlight on them. There one of them was, a lovely graceful ship all silvery in the searchlight. We let drive a broadside and in thirty seconds she was a blazing wreck going off like a Catherine wheel. Then we switched into another and shot her up the same and the other battleships did too.'

It was over in a matter of minutes. Along with *Fiume*, the cruiser *Zara* and two destroyers were eliminated, with several others heavily damaged and scattering. 'The Battle Fleet hauled out at 2230,' noted Ruck Keene, 'and so ended the quickest and most thrilling five minutes of my eighteen years.' For him, it was 'fully revenge' for the sinking of his previous ship, HMS *Southampton*, earlier in the year. Just one Royal Navy aircraft had been lost, along with the lives of its three crewmen. The Italian navy lost more than 2,000 sailors. The British searched for survivors until the morning. 'We collected 900 or so, until some German aircraft started fooling about,' wrote Manley Power. 'So we had to leave the rest and poked off home to celebrate the Battle of Matapan (named by me).'

Newspapers and wireless commentators reported the victory with no little bombast. Cunningham was lauded as a true fighting admiral in the Nelsonian tradition. The imagery of a victory for the British battleship was fully exploited. But the overwhelming emphasis on the role of the big ships led to considerable resentment on the part of sailors from smaller vessels. Charles Hutchinson, in the cruiser *Carlisle*, reported in his diary that in Alexandria a few days later, 'when the lads had had a bottle or two, some of the crowd off *Warspite* had started Blowing, and the fellows off the "boats", that's the destroyers and cruisers that do all the sea time, didn't like it, and told them they hardly ever went to sea . . . One thing led to another and it finished up in a glorious scrap, and then the Fleet Club was closed and beer stopped in a lot of the bars.'

The glow of victory was short lived. Over the course of the summer of 1941, British forces at land and at sea would be put firmly back on the defensive. In North Africa the Italian colonial army had been defeated, and in eastern Africa a multilateral force under British direction was in the process of demolishing the Italian regime built on the ruthless and bloody occupation of Ethiopia. But the seizure of the entire coastline of the southern Mediterranean had been prevented by the introduction of Erwin Rommel as the new commander of a combined German and Italian force based in Tripoli. Then, at the end of April 1941, a German advance into Greece quickly led to the collapse of the British and Commonwealth forces sent to bolster the local resistance.

Another evacuation was soon underway. Civilian men, women and children were rescued from southern Greece. Warships and merchant vessels were once again full of retreating troops. Around 50,000 British and Commonwealth, Greek and Yugoslav forces were embarked, most of whom were taken to the island of Crete.

It was a difficult, dangerous and taxing operation. HMS *Carlisle* was due to transport 500 people, but ended up carrying over 1,200, many of whom were Commonwealth soldiers. Charles Hutchinson was impressed by the New Zealanders, particularly the Maoris: 'the finest lot of fellows I've met'. One Greek soldier also caught his eye: a ten-year-old boy, orphaned and adopted by the unit: 'He was kitted up in battle dress. He did look pitiful, the uniform was miles too big for him, and you could hardly see under his tin helmet, but he was quite cheerful, and I hope he is looked after.'

Below decks in *Carlisle*, there was one grumble which united soldiers and sailors alike. 'It's the same old tale from every one of them,' wrote Hutchinson. '"Where is the air force?" They have had a hell of a time, and when they came on board some of them looked worn out . . . nearly every one of them said as they came on board, "Thank God we've got a navy" or "Good old navy". There's no doubt they do appreciate us.' Everyone agreed that the RAF was stretched to its limits in the region – there were few enough planes even in Britain – but the complaints centred on one particular thing: the reputation of the fighter boys. 'If only the papers and wireless would not blow so much about them,' wrote Hutchinson. 'Everyone in the other two services and people at home get the impression that it's they alone who are fighting the war, perhaps they will later on, but it's not the case at present, and now they only appear to us like glamour girls stealing the limelight.'

Evacuated soldiers told terrifying tales of the front line. German infantrymen were described by the shell-shocked troops as virtual automatons. One widespread rumour aboard *Carlisle*, which Hutchinson was careful to corroborate with several soldiers, was of 'doped' Nazi zombies, immune to fear or fury, marching over piles of their own dead. 'I still can't fathom this dope business,' wrote Hutchinson, 'unless it's these concentrated food pills they take.' It was said that when 'they advance shoulder to shoulder and are shot down they just drop and show no signs of pain, and the rest seem to come on either laughing or sobbing – it seems like a kind of hysteria. Anyhow, I don't believe any human being can just walk into fire and be mown down, and others still come on mechanically.'

There was little doubt that the troops disembarked on the island of Crete did not relish the prospect of another onslaught. But after five days of demoralizing bombing attacks on the island's defences, German forces finally began their assault from the air and sea on 20 May. British ships were tasked with preventing the invasion barges from reaching the shore.

In the darkness of the night of 21 May, signals intelligence and radar helped a British squadron to locate a large convoy of invasion craft including many caiques: shallow wooden skiffs. As the hunters approached their prey, they turned on powerful searchlights, illuminating the enemy transports in a coruscating glare. 'I was hardly prepared for what happened,' wrote Petty Officer Wesley Barker of HMS *Dido* in his journal, after the decimation of a caique packed with German troops. 'The Captain passed the order to the Pom-Poms "let 'em have it". God, what a massacre. Bits of boat and bits of German flew into the air, all this being illuminated by our starboard searchlights and made everything as bright as day. Not a pleasant sight by any means.'

Along with fellow cruisers *Ajax* and *Orion* and the destroyers *Janus*, *Hereward*, *Kimberley* and *Hasty*, *Dido* helped to account for the destruction of a dozen caiques, yachts and other small craft, along with several steamers crammed with invasion forces. It was later estimated that 300 German troops were killed. Barker described the sinking of one steamer:

Our first salvo of shells hit her fair and square amidships, and she immediately burst into flame from stem to stern. The enemy had been waving white flags at us when picked up by our searchlight, but we were out to destroy, not capture. She kept exploding in various places. Then we were down on the caiques again, blasting them and their troops out of the water . . . We ploughed through many in the water shouting 'Kamerad'.

Such was the ruthless ferocity of the attacks on the invasion craft that an amphibious landing was made impossible. But on the following day, the tables were comprehensively turned. While transport aircraft dropped German airborne troops and equipment onto Crete seemingly at will, dive-bombers attacked ships en masse.

On 22 May British vessels protecting the coasts of Crete were subjected to air attacks of a previously unimaginable intensity. German planes seemed to fill the skies. Even Charles Hutchinson, who had experienced 'Hell and no kidding' in Norway, was incredulous at the scale of the action. 'Wherever you looked there seemed to be ships,' he wrote in his diary, 'and they all seemed to be getting attacked and bombed.'

Hutchinson witnessed the destroyer *Greyhound* succumb to bombs: 'She turned and dodged and fired, but it was no good as it was humanly impossible to keep them all off, as they came from every angle, and she got a hell of a hit astern. It seemed to break her stern off and, it seemed, in a very short time she heeled over on one side and then went down stern first. Her bows bobbed above the water for a short period, and then she disappeared.'

After HMS *Greyhound* was sunk, a hastily assembled rescue group, including the destroyers *Kandahar* and *Kingston* and the cruisers *Gloucester* and *Fiji*, was ordered to pick up survivors. Having already fended off several waves of dive-bombers, *Fiji* had less than a third of her anti-aircraft ammunition supply remaining. Stoker Petty Officer Sid Manders overheard one of *Fiji*'s officers complaining that the orders were 'the equivalent of saying "go back, shoot one hundred of your men, drown one hundred and twenty and sink your ship"'. After attempting to rescue as many men as possible, under intense bombing attacks, the four ships were ordered to retreat. It was too late for HMS *Gloucester*, which was sunk by five devastating explosions. After this latest blow, Manders admitted, 'I went down to the mess, got my money and photos of my dear wife, knowing that our turn must come under such conditions.'

'After leaving the *Gloucester*,' wrote Midshipman Robin Owen, on *Fiji*'s upper deck, 'ourselves and the two destroyers became the target for it seemed most of the German air force, and the sky was not clear for one moment.' Owen was manning the starboard air-defence position. 'The action look-outs, who were by now tired out were of little use,' he recalled, 'as most of them were too scared. The ship now had a very scarred appearance as if there were holes everywhere, and the funnels looked like sieves.'

*Fiji* struggled on for several hours until another bomb crippled one of the engine rooms and the ship listed sharply. As stokers escaped the damaged boiler, a few stayed behind. 'No praise would be too high for the men who were still in the after boiler room,' wrote Manders, who had managed to escape to the upper deck. 'They were keeping steam in the system and all the pumps going, knowing that their end was very near.' Wounded men were put into lifeboats and lowered into the sea. Others were throwing makeshift rafts over the sides. Manders noticed that 'two boys came up with a hammock, threw it into the water and followed it'.

Still *Fiji* remained afloat, but yet another attack signalled the end. Midshipman Owen was exposed. 'I lay down hoping for the best,' he wrote. 'The three bombs whistled down, and I saw one pass just overhead and hit us port side again with a thunderous crash. The whole ship lifted out of the water, and I thought that the forward superstructure was falling down. It was lucky that I lay down as a piece of metal crashed through the bulkhead just 2 ft above me.'

By this time, Owen and Sid Manders were two of only a few dozen sailors left on board. 'We could almost walk down the ship's side,' wrote Manders, who managed to reach a Carley float. Owen was also fortunate. Despite losing his lifebelt and his precious camera – 'with which I had taken some fine action shots' – he made it to a raft with a group of twenty others, including the captain, as darkness began to fall. 'Behind us we could just see the vague mass of the ship still floating but upside down, with the four screws sticking out into the air.'

Meanwhile, *Carlisle* had also been attacked. 'The devils started on us,' wrote Charles Hutchinson. 'We fired and fired everything, opened out at them, and then it came – it was hellish, and it's only thanks to God that there are some of us left.' Three Stukas dived from astern, screaming towards the cruiser. The guns' crews poured out their barrage, hitting one of the aircraft, but they could not prevent the bombs from coming. 'They seemed to be crazy,' wrote Hutchinson. 'They came through everything.'

Explosions rocked the ship, sending a tidal wave of water across the deck, smashing into the gun and throwing Hutchinson and his team into the air. 'I was sure,' he wrote, 'and all of us were, that we were being swept into the sea over the side. I didn't seem to have time to think of anything or anyone, only one thought flashed through my mind as I was knocked off the gun and swept away and that was "My God, this is the end".'

Now strewn across the deck, Hutchinson and his drenched crew recovered their senses, inflated their lifebelts, and slipped off their boots, before remounting the gun and continuing the barrage. But the captain had been killed, black smoke was billowing from fires below, and the next gun along had suffered a direct hit, leaving 'just a piece of charred metal'. It was a sobering sight. Later that evening, still at his post, Hutchinson scribbled his thoughts in his notebook:

How the horrors of war are brought to one when your pals [die], well more than pals, as we've lived and slept all as a family for over a year and a half, we've laughed, quarrelled, joked together, all gone ashore together, discussed a lot of our private lives amongst ourselves as we had no one else to confide in. Poor Chas Enderly, married since the war began, always singing . . . Dak Walker, only twenty-one last week, and we gave him sips of our tots and got him drunk out of all recognition, the Gunner's Mate too. I think there are about twelve of our lads [killed] and the rest of them very badly burned and injured . . . Poor old Bob Silvey is still under the gun – I've seen him, but it's impossible to get him out. I was ashore with him the night we sailed . . . The only consolation is that it must have been instantaneous. The gun got a direct hit and wiped out most of them, but in getting it there it certainly saved the ship and the rest of us.

That evening, the captain and seven of the men already identified were buried at sea. Few of their shipmates were able to attend, most having to remain at action stations ready to repel further attacks.

The floats from HMS *Fiji* were still waiting to be rescued. Men had begun to die from exposure. Others swam towards the distant land in desperation. Some sailors were still being pulled from the water. When the Chief Yeoman of Signals was hauled into Owen's float, he 'was discovered to be in possession of a bag containing 500 three-penny bits, which must have been like lead to him in the water'.

After several hours, destroyers were sighted, and guided in by torches and singing. In strong winds, the transfer to HMS *Kingston* was far from straightforward. Owen had to swim forty yards to the scramble nets. 'This,' he wrote, 'was the most dangerous bit as a lot of men too weak to climb the net fell back into the sea and sank.' Some 500 of the 800-strong ship's company were eventually rescued. On the way back to Alexandria, Manders and the other survivors could have a hot shower and were given rum, cigarettes and some makeshift clothing: 'I was in overalls and a pair of sandals made from cardboard and string.'

Every sailor from every ship involved in the defence of Crete had a similar story to tell. The following day, 23 May, the destroyers *Kelly*, *Kashmir* and *Kipling* were attacked by twenty-four bombers as they were preparing to return to Alexandria. Eighteen-year-old Ordinary Seaman F. S. Gardner was a loader in the crew of one of *Kashmir*'s guns. He described the moment the destroyer was hit: 'The ship stopped dead. There was a deafening explosion, fragments were blasted everywhere. The gun's crew instinctively took what cover we could behind ammunition lockers. When I got up *Kashmir* was in two sections both of which began to descend gracefully beneath the waves. We blew up our lifebelts and swam clear of the ship. Fuel oil was everywhere.'

*Kashmir* had sunk in barely two minutes. At the same time, *Kelly* was turning to port when a bomb struck, causing the destroyer to keel over. Survivors faced a gruelling three hours in the water, machine-gunned from the air and struggling to sustain their strength. Eventually rescued by HMS *Kipling* along with 279 others, Gardner described the five hours back to Alexandria on the upper decks of the overloaded ship, during which time no fewer than forty aircraft attacked, dropping over eighty bombs: 'A lone Stuka was spotted on the port beam screaming down towards us much lower than the normal raid. I glanced to my left and there was a stoker who appeared to be badly burned down his left arm. He had some light bandages wrapped loosely . . . He was gripping the side rail and crying. This really unnerved me . . . next to him was another sailor kneeling down with his hands clasped together: he was praying.'

Nerves were frayed throughout the fleet. Midshipman Ruck Keene of HMS *Warspite*, the teenager who had been satisfied by his 'revenge' at Matapan, now found himself severely shaken. He wrote in his training journal of the moment the battleship was hit by bombs which penetrated the messdecks and destroyed two guns, killing their crews. 'To see those awful sights and smell that horrible smell again nearly made me sick,' he wrote. 'And so ended the most costly operation since the war began. To me the loss of life seems far more important than that of the ships.'

Ruck Keene was even more outspoken when commenting on the decision to send *Gloucester* and *Fiji* to assist *Greyhound*: 'Why I cannot think. To detach these two large, heavy cruisers, one of whom was known to be short of anti-aircraft ammunition seems utterly inexcusable madness.' When Captain Douglas Fisher read the journal in his regular inspection, he was furious. 'This is a most improper statement from a young and inexperienced officer,' he scrawled on the page, warning the midshipman against making such 'childish entries' in future.

Ruck Keene spent the morning of 24 May in Alexandria harbour, helping to ferry the wounded from other ships ashore by boat. 'I felt rather bad during the afternoon,' he wrote, 'and was not cheered by the loss of *Hood*, announced that evening . . . After this I felt more depressed and went to see the medical officer on Sunday morning. He told me it was just a natural reaction and recommended me to be sent ashore for a week.'

Meanwhile, German airborne troops were gradually winning the battle for Crete. By 28 May preparations were being made to evacuate defending troops from Heraklion Bay on the north coast and from Sphakia in the south. For those who had already come under attack during the withdrawal from Greece and the defence of Crete, this rescue mission would require a supreme effort of will.

As the cruiser *Orion* made her way to Heraklion, the captain spoke to the ship's company. 'Once again we have another crisis on our hands,' he told them, explaining that they were en route to evacuate 'those same troops we recently landed on Crete . . . It is imperative that we have on board as many as humanly possible, as quickly as possible.' After this, wrote Able Seaman Harry Speakman, 'everyone nursed their own thoughts but the tension was so real it could almost be cut'.

After reaching Heraklion at midnight, several thousand soldiers were embarked in a continuous procession until well after 3 a.m. 'They were stowed in every conceivable nook and cranny,' wrote Speakman, 'where they would not impair the fighting efficiency of the ship during action.' Jim Brooks, a soldier in the Royal Artillery, wrote of his evacuation in a destroyer:

As soon as it was light, and we were on the move, the Luftwaffe was after us, and right until we were only a few miles from Alex, we were continually bombed and machine gunned, many boats were hit and a lot of chaps were killed, hit by a common shell. The Navy saved us again, and we got out just in time. They treated us the usual way, tea directly we were on board, and as much to eat as you wanted.

The appreciation was mutual. Graham Lumsden, who had taken part in the evacuation of Dunkirk a year earlier, was now navigation officer in the light cruiser HMS *Phoebe*. He reflected the sentiments of many when he suggested that 'the soldier has to find a special form of courage, a special hardihood and discipline to carry out his duty: he deserves our great respect'.

As *Orion* and the other cruisers left Crete, they were slowed by a damaged ship, HMS *Imperial*, which eventually had to be sunk after the transfer of soldiers and sailors to other vessels. The delay allowed enough time for the Stukas to find the convoy. Harry Speakman described the chaos:

> Ammunition parties dashed to and fro from the hoists to the guns keeping up with the never-ending demand ... Everyone was too busy to be afraid – the constant demands from the bridge to the engine room to cope with the change of speed whilst manoeuvring kept them busy below, and through all the noise and smoke the Admiral's instructions to the squadron kept everyone on the flag-deck occupied – even some of our weary passengers had a go with their short-range weapons.

*Orion* suffered a near miss, causing 'a shudder that was felt throughout the ship', but the damage was not serious. Others nearby, first HMS *Hereward*, then HMS *Dido*, were attacked before the Stukas returned to *Orion*. This time, a bomb struck the upper deck. Guns were demolished and black smoke began to spread. While repair parties rushed to control the damage as the attack ended, enemy aircraft strafed the upper deck as a parting shot, injuring the captain who later died in the sick bay. 'A period of quiet marked the Captain's passing,' wrote Speakman, 'and whilst the weary gun crews rested the casualties were carried aft in an endless stream ... The dead were laid out on stretchers on the quarterdeck. Instead of the usual burial at sea service, a few short prayers had to suffice because we were still at first-degree readiness.'

It was not the end of *Orion*'s ordeal. Another Stuka attack resulted in a bomb penetrating the bridge, and careering through the decks into the ammunition magazine. Fortunately, it was by now virtually empty. Nevertheless, the cruiser seemed on the verge of oblivion. 'The whole centre of the ship was on fire,' wrote Speakman. 'The ship's side fuel and fresh water tanks had been breached and their contents, plus those of the main fridge and ship's provision stores were all swilling about below. The occasional sight of a body amongst all of this made looking down in the glare from the raging fire like a bird's eye view of Hades.'

As the ship made for Alexandria, a human chain was formed to relay orders from the devastated upper deck down to the sweltering engine room. 'We staggered on,' wrote Speakman, 'outside scarred and filthy, inside broken and warped.' Two hundred and sixty-two men were dead, including 112 sailors, and nearly 300 were injured. 'Every man on board still alive had lost at least one good mate.'

*Dido*, meanwhile, had buried thirty-seven men at sea before arriving back at Alexandria. 'We are living on the *Resource* as our ship is full of water,' wrote Petty Officer Wesley Barker. 'Everyone is suffering a little from reaction. We have had 36 hours almost continuous dive bombing.' It took several days to extricate the dead. 'The gruesome business of cleaning up continues,' wrote Barker. 'Our casualty list continues to mount as they find them, many soldiers among them.'

Charles Hutchinson of HMS *Carlisle* described the long trip back for emergency repairs: 'We spent the night at the gun, cold and miserable and wet . . . all the lads are crashed round the gun looking very weary and dirty and hungry – I suppose I'm the same.' The effects of the experience were pronounced. 'I hope I'm never in anything like it again,' he wrote. 'I don't mind fighting, but I like a bit of a chance. I would like a go at the square heads, hand to hand. I wouldn't feel like giving in then.'

Sailors and their commanders were at the very limits of their endurance. Midshipman Ruck Keene of HMS *Warspite* wrote in his journal: 'I cannot possibly begin to say where one attack began and another ended – someone was always firing.' Arthur Jones, one of *Warspite*'s Royal Marines, explained the effect on the ship's company:

There were plenty of near misses and somehow we were lucky, but it was very wearing. You looked at what happened to the *Illustrious* and wondered how long it might be until it happened to you. Everybody became a bit bomb happy. In fact we were getting so ragged on *Warspite* it became a punishable offence to slam a hatch because it jarred the nerves so much.

Many sailors became resigned to the fact that damage to their ship was likely. Indeed, rather than discuss whether they might be hit, some simply pondered what might be the optimal degree of damage. Aboard HMS *Decoy*, admitted Lieutenant Commander Arthur Prideaux, the prevailing feeling was that moderate damage to the ship would be ideal, as it would necessitate two or three weeks of repairs and 'a most welcome rest'.

This was the ultimate betrayal of the Nelsonian credo – 'engage the enemy more closely' – that the Admiralty worked so hard to perpetuate, yet it was hardly surprising that so many sailors discovered the limits of their endurance under such conditions. 'The anxieties were always present,' wrote one medical officer. 'We were after all in the midst of a war and in fairly regular danger so many men were frightened. Perhaps it would be nearer the truth to say that we were all frightened – at times anyway – but the ones who suffered most were those who were frightened of being frightened.'

Naval medical officers were advised to talk to their ships' companies on the subject of fear. 'The most common cause of anxiety is the fear of the individual that he might be a coward,' sailors were to be told. 'To be afraid is natural – to run away is cowardly. If you are efficient in your job you need have no fear of your behaviour in an emergency.' In the midst of the battle, however, there was little opportunity for medical officers to treat psychological casualties. The cruiser HMS *Ajax*, a respected fighting ship and veteran of the River Plate and Cape Matapan, reported thirty breakdowns from a crew of 800. After thirty-six days of continuous sea time under near-constant air attack, the captain of *Ajax* asked Admiral Cunningham for forty-eight hours' rest in harbour. Cunningham allegedly replied:

> Because you have a fine ship with a fine ship's company which have done magnificent work in the Med., I will come on board your ship and address your ship's company, but, if there is then a mutiny, I shall be no more backward than Lord St Vincent in making you hang your own ring-leaders from your own yard arm.

*Ajax* went back to sea, but without four crew members who leapt overboard as the ship left harbour. They were later tried by court martial and sentenced to three years in prison.

In the last days of May, warships returned to Crete again and again to complete the evacuation. Sailors came under sustained psychological pressure, yet operations continued. In the midst of heated debates about the wisdom of taking such a risk with the fleet, Andrew Cunningham declared to his counterparts that 'the navy had never yet failed the Army in such a situation, and was not going to do so now'. The operation lasted for five days, during which 16,500 soldiers were evacuated while 1,828 sailors were killed and nearly 200 injured. Two battleships and an aircraft carrier were put out of action for weeks of repair work. Three cruisers were lost and five more damaged. Six destroyers were sunk and a further seven would require extensive repairs.

The loss of Crete in June 1941 put Alexandria firmly on the front line. Air raids now became commonplace. Midshipman Ruck Keene described one attack: 'A mighty crash, a great compact cloud of black smoke went up and then came the blast, which was tremendous. It was all most unpleasant and, much as I hate and despise them, it was impossible not to sympathise with the Arabs, or to wonder about the safety of the European section ashore.'

At the same time, the security of the vital oil reserves of the Middle East and British interests in Palestine seemed increasingly precarious. An uprising in the Kingdom of Iraq led by Rashid Ali and supported by Germany had recently been quelled by force. 'British troops reached the suburbs of Baghdad,' explained Ruck Keene, 'where they were met by a request for an armistice from the mayor of the city. The Regent has once more taken over control of the country and a constitutional government has been formed.' Not long afterwards, British and Free French forces moved into Vichy-controlled Syria and Lebanon.

Four hundred miles to the west of Alexandria, the city of Tobruk was under siege. Small, fast convoys had to brave bombers and U-boats to supply the beleaguered defenders. Lieutenant Alec Dennis of HMS *Griffin* emphasized the speed with which the destroyers and their attending minesweeper had to operate in the heavily mined coastal waters: 'You had an absolute maximum of 45 minutes to get all 50 tons of stuff offloaded down wooden chutes, cast off and get out at full speed to be under the fighter umbrella at dawn. If you got caught it was probably curtains.'

Young sub-lieutenant John Carter was based in Mersa Matruh, a small base halfway between Alexandria and Tobruk. 'I hate the desert,' he wrote in his diary, citing everything from the stress of convoy organization and dust sandstorms to the whims of Maltese stewards. Writing was, he admitted, his 'safety valve' against the strain of his situation: 'It is obvious when anybody writes anything at all, those words are written with the sub-conscious idea that they might someday be read. So here! I fully realize that this will be read by other people someday – with what effect it is difficult to tell: interest, sympathy, amusement, or even contempt, although I flatter myself that even if the words mean nothing, they do form rather a lovely symphony of sound.'

Such a safety valve was quite necessary. The Tobruk run was yet another arduous task for the Mediterranean Fleet in the bloody summer of 1941. Even the most experienced mariners were not immune to the physical and mental effects. Engine Room Artificer Clifford Simkin of the sloop HMS *Flamingo* recalled the breakdown of a shipmate: 'One of my mess-mates could not take any more, his nerve had gone, poor fellow. When we were in Greece he was as white as a sheet and would not eat, and now this breakdown. He came from a naval family and had been in the navy since he was 15 years of age.'

Far from being detached from the war at home, many sailors could perfectly understand the suffering of the British civilian population. In 1941 they suffered their own blitz in the Mediterranean. Crete, in particular, became one of the defining experiences of the sailor's war, aided in no small part by Noël Coward's celebrated film *In Which We Serve*. Released in the autumn of 1942, it was inspired by the fate of Lord Mountbatten's HMS *Kelly*. Coward's great achievement was to link the ordeal of sailors clinging to a life raft with their earlier lives at home. Such was the domestic focus that one American movie executive even dubbed it 'Mrs Miniver on a battleship'.

The psychological toll of air attack in the Mediterranean was profound. George Blundell might have had to bribe lookouts in September 1940, but such incentives were certainly no longer required. Sailors were in a position to fight back, and anti-aircraft armaments still inspired a level of confidence far in excess of their actual effectiveness. But ratings and officers alike remained charged with performing their duties stoically and efficiently despite their fears. This was the essence of the sailor's challenge, as John Carter explained in his diary:

> The nervous strain simply grows and grows until you have to exert all your will-power to stop yourself from appearing jittery or nervous. That is courage – the quality of being able to keep from showing your fear in the face of nervous strain: not being able to press a trigger, and keep the sights on what appears to be an enormous aircraft diving into your face, bomb hurtling towards you, and the ping and splintering crunches as his bullets tear through the wood and steel around you. Enduring that is nothing in the heat of battle, behind a gun of some sort. Courage is behaving calmly and normally through the period before such an attack, during the six long hours which never seem to end, and where time seems to stop, when that sudden deadly attack may develop in a moment.

down on his cot to relax, but was roused by the roar of the ship's guns:

> We soon realise something is wrong. The guard is nervous and shaking at the knees. We realise now that action is taking place. We don our White Jackets and caps expecting to be let out on deck . . . The door remains locked. We sit down on boxes near the door and smoke expecting a shell to come bursting through the ship's side any moment and hope for the best. The next moment a titanic explosion takes place. The lights go out and we are thrown to the floor. We did not know what had happened actually, only that we were in complete darkness and that the whole ship shook and the deck lurched at a peculiar angle.

Clarke and the other officers found that their door was open and the guard had vanished. In the gloom, they felt their way to a ladder leading up to the deck and ascended in single file. 'There was no panic,' wrote Clarke, 'but I could feel others pressing up behind me.' They could hear and feel the *Pinguin*'s guns firing as explosions occurred throughout the ship. Escaping from the hatch, Clarke witnessed the full extent of the damage. A store of mines had exploded, splitting the hull in two. The entire rear half of the ship had been blown away, killing many hundreds of prisoners:

> The deck was slippery with gore. We took in the situation at once . . . The deck and the bridge were pointing to the sky at an alarming angle and our thoughts were to get the devil out of it and into the water. Almost in unison we shouted 'for God's sake jump boys'. Seven jumped ahead of me and then I stood poised on the rail for my turn. The bows of the raider gave a sickening lurch which threw me back in-board again. Regaining my feet I saw lying on the deck a German life-belt which I grasped by the tapes in the left hand and again stood on the rails. To me it seemed a question of no more than a few feet to the water. I took a deep breath and jumped. The water closed over my head and I felt my hat float away . . .
>
> I fully expected to submerge a few feet and rise out of the water. To my horror I continued to go down and with a roar of water in my

ears I felt the bridge sink on one side of me and the bows on the other. The bridge and bows passed me very quickly though the pull of the suction was still there. Twice my body turned over and then turned in a flat spin. I thought I had reached the end of my tether and that my lungs would burst . . .

I had been fighting hard with arms and legs kicking out all the time and then to my relief found I was shooting upwards. Down below the water seemed pitch black . . . I broke surface very quickly . . . Still holding the life-belt in my left hand I worked my way to a small piece of wood . . . There was no sign of the raider and I found myself in the midst of oil, floating spars and empty drums. Ahead of me I could see a raft and perched on this was the Mate, an engineer and three Germans.

Clarke was injured, but was pulled onto the raft with the aid of an oar. In the water all around were German sailors and British prisoners scrambling for any floating debris they could reach. Then the ship responsible for sinking *Pinguin* came into view: the cruiser HMS *Cornwall*.

Lifeboats approached the wreckage, as the former prisoners sang songs. Clarke and the others on his raft were dragged into a boat and taken to *Cornwall*. Reaching the side of the ship, they were helped onto the gangway. Clarke's legs gave way and so he began to crawl up on his hands and knees. 'Marines on the Quarter Deck observing my plight came down and helped me up to the deck,' he wrote. 'We must have looked a lovely sight – covered in oil from head to foot and fourteen days growth of whiskers. They thought we were Nazis . . . One Marine gave me a cigarette and when I said "thank you" they exclaimed "Good god he's British".'

Only twenty-seven merchant seamen were rescued, along with sixty German sailors. More than 300 of their Kriegsmarine comrades perished with over 200 of their prisoners. Clarke was checked over by the ship's doctor, given fresh clothes, a tot in the wardroom, and sat down in the doctor's cabin. *Cornwall*'s only casualty had been a lieutenant engineer, who succumbed to the heat after a shell from *Pinguin* damaged an air circulator. He was buried at sea in a service attended by the German prisoners.

'We received the very best of treatment on board the cruiser,' wrote Clarke. 'The Paymaster handed to each of us British survivors £1, a gift from the officers of the cruiser. In addition we received a towel, razor and cream, tooth brush and paste.' Several of the survivors were badly injured, and before *Cornwall* returned to Durban for repairs she disembarked the survivors in the Seychelles. Clarke was taken by taxi to the Empire Hotel in Victoria.

The most seriously injured merchant sailor to be rescued was the second mate of *British Emperor*, whose stomach had been ripped open as he escaped through a shell hole in the ship's side. Not long after arriving in the Seychelles, he died. Clarke described his funeral:

The procession passed along the town's only street which was packed with people and slowly made its way to the cemetery three miles out of town. The cemetery was situated on the mountainside and the site allotted to service men was fully 500 feet above sea level. It took us twenty minutes to climb up the mountain. The bearers had a terrible job. They must have changed bearers about twenty times. On reaching the spot we had a wonderful view of the harbour. Around the surrounding hillsides was a remarkable sight. Hundreds of native girls and men in their Sunday finery. The colours were outstanding. Bright yellow, pink and blue dresses. An excellent service was conducted by the Naval Chaplain followed by firing three volleys and the sounding of the last post by the buglers.

On our return to the hotel we found the street lined with people awaiting the arrival of the German prisoners. These duly arrived in open lorries under armed guards and were jeered at by the crowd. Even native kids of about 6 or 7 years of age shook their little fists at them.

*Pinguin* was the most successful of the German commerce raiders, and her destruction removed a major threat to British shipping in the Indian Ocean. Nevertheless, Royal Navy patrols continued to search between Africa and Ceylon and onwards to Malaya and the East Indies. Ordinary Seaman John Somers had messenger duties in the cruiser HMS *Dauntless*, at least until he shook the captain awake to deliver a note from the bridge. After that, he was posted to the crow's nest. 'The view was terrific,' he wrote. 'Nothing to obstruct your sight and you could see for about 15 miles to the horizon . . . Islands seemed to float in the sky only condescending to join the world as you approached them. Lots of native boats and junks about . . . Every night there was the heat lightning and by day the water spouts not to mention the stars . . . flying fish could be seen. I was surprised to see how far they could glide before dropping back into the sea.'

On 15 June 1941 *Dauntless* was heading to Penang, up the Malacca Strait to the north-west of Singapore. Somers was in his hammock, slung next to a shelf holding stores of food. He was awoken by what he described as 'bumping, crashing, grinding, bashing and bouncing . . . Sugar, rice, tea, bread, butter fall into my hammock.' *Dauntless* had collided with another cruiser, HMS *Emerald*, causing serious damage to the other ship. Fourteen men from *Emerald* were killed, and several injured. There were also casualties in *Dauntless*. An anchor cable had swept across the deck, killing a man. 'The back of his skull was crushed,' wrote Somers. 'They took him away, left his brains behind. The Commander gently pushed them over the side with his foot.'

*Dauntless* returned to Singapore for repairs. Many of the ship's company were housed in the Seaman's Mission and assigned to the local Military Police. Somers went out on foot patrol overnight, armed with a pickaxe handle and wearing a special armband: 'We would wander around the streets of Singapore's red light district but the Raffles Hotel was out of bounds to ratings, no matter how rich you were.'

Little had improved at Singapore since the abysmal war games of 1938 and 1939. It was a naval base rather than a fortress, constructed for accessibility rather than defence. Only the narrow Straits of Johore separated the island from the mainland. Dry docks and warehouses were better supplied than the meagre garrison, with its archaic aircraft and insufficient guns. Nearly a million citizens of multiple ethnicities and nationalities inhabited the city, and few of the locals were truly enamoured of their imperial landlords. The cocktail parties and society functions continued unabated, and ordinary sailors were inevitably alienated. After a short stay in harbour, Charles Thomas – who had experienced a similar atmosphere at Hong Kong before the war –

remained savage in his criticism of the arrogance of the British imperial mentality. He was also struck by one particular practice. 'Persons are allowed to sell clothing in the ship during our short stays in harbour,' he wrote to his sister. 'It is cheap and shoddy and is marked "MADE IN JAPAN". It is sickening and should not be allowed.'

Throughout 1941, Singapore remained somewhat detached from the rest of the war, its colonial society experiencing little of the upheaval seen in the other imperial enclaves of Gibraltar, Malta or Alexandria. By November, David Leggatt's dire predictions of the previous year still remained unfulfilled. But within a matter of weeks, Singapore would be thrust into the heart of a new crisis.

'In the early morning war was declared on Finland, Roumania, and Hungary, and at 2145 on Japan,' wrote Midshipman J. B. T. Davies of HMS *Renown* on 7 December 1941. 'America has now entered the war.' By the following day, more information was available about these pivotal developments. 'News has been coming through all day about the situation in the far east,' wrote John Roberts in his journal:

Japan has attacked several American islands in the Pacific, such as Guam, Pearl Harbor and Manila, as well as Malaya and Thailand. America declared war on Japan this evening and so have Australia, China, and the Dutch East Indies. It seems that the Americans have rather been caught napping because most of the bombing of islands has been done without much show of resistance. The attack on Pearl Harbor was made by planes from an aircraft carrier. I am sure, that if Scapa Flow was four thousand miles from Germany, a German aircraft carrier would never be able to get within range before being attacked by us.

The Japanese offensive was not entirely unexpected, but with the Royal Navy at full stretch in the Atlantic and the Mediterranean, pre-war plans to send a fleet to protect Singapore proved impossible to fulfil. It had been decided in November to despatch the battleship *Prince of Wales*, along with the aging battlecruiser *Repulse*, in an attempt to deter the Japanese. It was a strategy inspired in part by the effect of German battleships on the British. 'We have only to remember all the preoccupations which are caused us by the *Tirpitz*,' argued Churchill in August 1941, fresh from his trip across the Atlantic in *Prince of Wales*, 'to see what an effect would be produced upon the Japanese Admiralty by the presence of a small but very powerful force in Eastern Waters . . . It exercises a vague, general fear and menaces all points at once.'

En route to Singapore, the *Prince of Wales* called at Cape Town. The local civic elite laid on a grand reception for the ship's company, before cars whisked officers away to private homes to be fed and entertained. 'We had an inflated idea of our own abilities,' admitted Midshipman Graeme Allen. He had been below the bridge during the battle with *Bismarck*, and was now assigned to the lower steering position, beneath the reinforced armoured deck and watertight doors. 'Not a place to try to get out of in a hurry,' he remarked. But as *Prince of Wales* continued on into the Indian Ocean, a reorganization of duties left him directing an Oerlikon anti-aircraft gun high on the starboard superstructure. It would prove to be a fateful change.

When the battleship arrived at Singapore, she received another rapturous welcome from the colonial socialites. Henry Leach was a seventeen-year-old midshipman working as a plotter in the operations room of the naval headquarters. His father was John Leach, captain of the great battleship. Soon after his arrival, the two met for dinner. Sitting on a sofa, they finished writing a letter to Henry's mother, smoked and discussed the situation. After a bombastic comment from Henry, John replied: 'I don't think you have any idea of the enormity of the odds we are up against.'

The Japanese incursion into British imperial territory did not come unheralded. On 6 December 1941, troop convoys and warships were sighted heading for Indo-China, clearly preparing to attack Siam and Malaya, perhaps even Borneo and the Dutch East Indies. Early in the morning of 8 December, only a few hours after the raid on Pearl Harbor, a small group of seventeen bombers was spotted over Singapore. Searchlights picked them out but a half-hearted salvo of anti-aircraft fire from the *Prince of Wales* failed to trouble the formation, high up at 10,000 feet.

Later that day, Admiral Tom Phillips agreed to take *Prince of Wales* and *Repulse* along with the destroyers *Electra*, *Express*, *Vampire* and *Tenedos* – collectively termed Force Z – around the coast and northwards in an attempt to disrupt the Japanese landings further up the Malayan peninsula. As the ships left harbour in the evening, they were doused by heavy rain from a series of tropical storms. Continuing north the following day through more mist and rain showers, confirmation was received that they were now beyond the range of fighter protection. That evening, with the poor weather subsiding, Force Z was sighted by a Japanese submarine and reconnaissance aircraft, which were spotted in turn by lookouts aboard *Prince of Wales*. Once darkness had fallen, Phillips first decided to escape back towards Singapore, but then changed his mind after vague reports of enemy convoys near Kuantan on the Malayan coastline.

The 10th of December dawned with Force Z still lingering. 'It was a glorious day with the bluest of blue seas,' wrote Lieutenant Commander Kenneth Buckley, executive officer of *Repulse*. At 10 a.m. HMS *Tenedos*, since despatched to Singapore, reported an attack by Japanese aircraft. Soon afterwards, lookouts spotted another reconnaissance plane. On the upper deck of *Prince of Wales*, Graeme Allen and his gun crew made ready for action. Just after 11 a.m. the first wave of Mitsubishi bombers attacked, swooping towards the battleships in a line, before breaking off into groups of two or three, ignoring the 150 barrels firing at them. Flying through the flak, they hit *Repulse*. The next wave attacked *Prince of Wales*.

Directing his anti-aircraft gun, Graeme Allen was soon overwhelmed. The Japanese aircraft were extremely fast and manoeuvrable, and were armed with well-designed torpedoes which could be launched from distance and were four times more powerful than the British warheads used against the *Bismarck*. Allen's gun was out of range when the torpedoes were dropped, and was scarcely able to train as the Japanese bombers flashed past. The first torpedo strikes tore through bulkheads causing explosions and shuddering vibrations throughout *Prince of Wales*. Steering mechanisms were ripped apart, electrical power was lost and seawater gushed through the breaches, making the battleship start to list dramatically.

Captain Leonard Bell, part of Admiral Tom Phillips's staff, was on the admiral's bridge, just below the main upper bridge. 'We saw the first torpedo coming towards us and felt it hit,' he wrote to his wife soon afterwards, 'a nasty jar but very little noise in the midst of all our own anti-aircraft. This gave us a list to port. I remember the Fleet Gunnery Officer and I having quite an argument as to how many degrees of list we actually did have.' Below decks, the heat was rising as ventilation gave out, and gun crews above struggled to train their sights. More torpedoes hit the starboard side under Allen's gun, and 'a great wall of water' soaked him and his crew.

*Repulse* was next to suffer. After managing to avoid or fend off several torpedoes, the old battlecruiser was finally hit by four missiles, rolling to port as men scrambled up the deck. The captain broadcast the order to abandon ship, which reverberated from the loudspeakers. Kenneth Buckley rushed down to his cabin to retrieve his Gieves life jacket. 'It took me some time to find,' he wrote, 'as my tidy servant had put it on a coat-hanger in the cupboard.' By the time Buckley arrived back up on deck, the ship was at an acute angle. 'The port side of the ship, usually about 20 feet above the water, was just awash,' he wrote, 'and the starboard side correspondingly higher. Forward the boatswain was chucking wooden planks over the side, and aft of me an Australian midshipman was still madly firing his Oerlikon gun at an aircraft and blaspheming anyone who dared to foul his sight.'

As men began to abandon ship, *Repulse* continued to travel at some speed, propellers still 'churning up a huge race which was brown with the oil fuel that was pouring from a forward tank. As I watched, a stoker whom I knew well went in, and was quickly chewed up in that ugly race.' The boatswain, 'cool as a cucumber', encouraged men to leap over the high side of the ship. Buckley decided to try the opposite side, by now practically submerged:

> In a second I was tobogganing at high speed on my pants across the ship, and I met the water when the top guard-rail was about a foot below water. As I entered the water a strong backwash, which was flooding the port hangar, swept me back on board; I held on to the side of the hangar like grim death; but it was hard work and, as every second's delay lessened my chance of escape, I let go and was swept under

the door into the darkness within. I was travelling fast, all underwater, and bumping occasionally; at least one other was there too, as I was kicked by a boot from above. I was in a very bad temper at this turn of fate, and was just beginning to wonder what it would be like when I had to open my mouth, when the top of the hangar rolltop-desk door split open and I was spewed out into the blue sea again.

Aboard *Prince of Wales*, Graeme Allen watched in horror as HMS *Repulse* succumbed. 'She was several miles away and listing heavily,' he wrote. 'Then slowly, her bows came up into the air, she turned over, and disappeared. It was unbelievable, that a ship like that could be so quickly destroyed, and we all knew then that we could not last much longer.' Captain Bell echoed these sentiments: 'Although we had been hit ourselves it was really sickening to see that lovely ship *Repulse* with a bad list to port belching smoke and gradually heeling over until she disappeared and all we could see were a couple of her boats and a few rafts.'

The destroyers *Electra* and *Vampire* moved in to rescue survivors. With *Repulse* gone, the bombers could concentrate on *Prince of Wales*. 'The sky seemed full of these yellow bellies,' wrote Captain Bell. 'They did not seem to mind all the A.A. barrage which we put up against them. They came along like a solid steel rod straight for us and dropped their bombs. We fell flat on the deck and while lying there waited for the bombs to explode. I remembered having read in some A.R.P. pamphlet that one should put a pencil in the mouth which I did. The bomb that hit us was a big one possibly 1000 lb, and it burst about 200 ft. from us and made a hell of a noise.'

*Prince of Wales* listed dramatically to port once again. Men flooded onto the upper decks, and anything that would float was thrown overboard. The destroyer HMS *Express* came alongside, sailors throwing lines and nets between her and the stricken battleship. Some men crossed along the hawsers, hanging and moving hand over hand. Graeme Allen opted for the alternative, which was to leap into the sea and swim for the nets which had been lowered from the destroyer. As he clambered up, *Prince of Wales* began to keel over.

Lines from *Express* were cut and the ship manoeuvred astern of the

*Prince of Wales* to avoid her death throes. Bell told his wife that 'actually the ship was still secured alongside with wires when our ship turned over. Her Captain told me afterwards that he did not enjoy that part of it much.' Allen, wet and exhausted, was now a dumbfounded observer: 'We on the destroyer saw the terrible sight of the great ship turning upside down, with men running all over the ship's side and the bilges, before it all disappeared, leaving nothing but debris, oil, and the heads of men frantically swimming for their lives.'

One of the swimmers was Captain Bell. After receiving the order to abandon ship, he began to clamber down the first of six ladders that led to the main deck. On reaching the end of the first ladder, he found that the list was so extreme that one side of the flag deck, which should have been fifty feet above the waterline, was barely twelve feet from the sea:

I decided to jump on the low die. Before doing so, I jerked my binoculars, cap and shoes off; this could not possibly have taken more than two seconds but when I looked at the water again the 12 ft. drop had gone and I just stepped in, as one would go into a swimming bath in the shallow end. I swam like hell. I did not get very far away however when I was closely pursued by the ship's mast which hit me very slightly on the head and pushed me down under water for what seemed an eternity. However, I disentangled myself from the rigging and shot up like a piece of cork, as a result of my life belt being blown up. I just had time to get my breath (a very quick one) when a nest of guns from the other side of the ship came tumbling down and took me down in the depths again, this time I thought I was done for. But Providence was on my side, I bobbed up again, looked round to see if anything else was coming up to hit me and saw the old ship upside down and bottom up.

He managed to find an empty biscuit tin, which made a makeshift float until he was eventually hauled onto a raft with several other sailors. They could do little to help the others still in the water: 'Most of us were too weak to swim and rescue people, the only thing I could do was to talk to some of these men and by encouragement and gentle persuasion make them swim or drift slowly to the float.'

A group of RAF Brewster Buffalo fighters arrived overhead while the destroyers picked up as many swimmers as they could before making for Singapore. Bell and his fellow survivors were rescued just after 3 p.m., two hours after the sinking. 'I was in a shocking mess after my long immersion in a mixture of seawater and oil fuel,' he wrote, 'but my watch was still working perfectly!' He reached Singapore just after midnight, along with several hundred other men. 'What a party,' wrote Bell. 'I must admit that I had an incredible quantity of whisky which made absolutely no difference to one's head. One might have been drinking water; but it was very soothing.' Lieutenant Haruki Iki, one of the Japanese pilots who had participated in the attack, later flew back over the site of the sinkings and dropped wreaths of flowers to commemorate the dead.

A third of the men aboard *Repulse* had been killed, along with a quarter of those aboard *Prince of Wales*. Destroyers eventually rescued 796 men from *Repulse* and 1,285 from *Prince of Wales*, but Admiral Tom Phillips was not amongst them. When the survivors reached Singapore, many were in a parlous condition. 'Some did not at all resemble human beings,' recalled one nurse assigned to treat them. At the dockside was Henry Leach, who had come to look for his father. 'A great big man took me to one side,' Leach recalled, 'and he put his arm around my shoulder and said, "You'd best get back to your ship lad, there is nothing more you can do."' Back at his quarters, he met Lieutenant Commander Skipworth, executive officer in *Prince of Wales*, who told him what had happened: 'The Admiral, Tom Phillips, and his Flag Captain, my father, were standing alone above the bridge when the ship was pretty well in the final stages, and various people had gone up to them to try to persuade them to get away before it was too late, and the Admiral just stood there staring into the distance . . . Later my Father was seen in the water – very blue. He had evidently drowned by then.'

Captain Bell had nothing but praise for the ship's company. 'The discipline and the calmness of all the lads in the *P. of W.* was simply magnificent,' he wrote to his wife. 'Frightened? Yes of course I was frightened and yet I had keyed myself up for unpleasant events anyway, after that first torpedo, and so one did not sort of worry much . . . I think it was a miracle that a good many of us got away with it and I thank God for it.'

Around the world, sailors greeted the news with despondency. 'The most depressing news bulletin of the war came through during the lunch hour today,' wrote Midshipman Tom Dowling of HMS *Queen Elizabeth*. 'We have lost the *Prince of Wales* and *Repulse* in operations off Malaya. Both were sunk by air attack . . . the fighters which are so essential nowadays were lacking.' 'There is no further news about how they were sunk except that the Japanese say they were sunk by aircraft,' wrote Midshipman John Roberts of HMS *Renown*. '*Prince of Wales* had only arrived there last week with Admiral Phillips, as flagship of the Far East fleet. How they were sunk goodness only knows.' Able Seaman I. G. Hall of HMS *Glasgow*, operating in the Indian Ocean, was pessimistic: 'I suppose we shall soon be adding our name to the list of sunken ships.'

'In all the war I never received a more direct shock,' wrote Churchill, in one of the many famous passages in his later account of the war. On Boxing Day 1941, after parliamentary questions had probed the causes of the disaster, the midshipmen of HMS *Renown* pondered the issue. 'Who-ever ordained that the ships should go,' wrote J. B. T. Davies, 'was either mad or very courageous, but he has the satisfaction of knowing he severely shattered the British Eastern Fleet and enabled the Japanese to run their convoys in comparative safety, with the result that the Japanese are playing merry hell on Malay.'

Across the islands of south-east Asia, the Japanese advance precipitated self-inflicted carnage. Oil and rubber plants were sabotaged, reducing a crucial supply of the raw materials which the aggressors were anxious to acquire. In northern Borneo, workers and administrators on oil fields cooperated to destroy their sites. After this depressing job was complete, European managers were then evacuated to Singapore, leaving behind most of their Asian workforce. One employee of Shell Oil, R. G. Tyler, reflected on the task in his diary:

I was too busy mostly to give a thought to anything but the immediate job in hand, but there were moments when I could reflect on the pitiful nature of our work. The labour of years destroyed in a few hours. The brains, sweat and head-action that have gone into the establishment of this field, one of the most promising in the world with potentialities that nobody could estimate. All that now remains is a scene of complete destruction – fires everywhere and black columns of smoke reaching in every direction.

The Japanese attacked Hong Kong on 18 December. By Christmas Day, the sailors of a small flotilla of British motor torpedo boats were preparing to leave. They were to evacuate several senior officials to safety through Japanese lines to inland waterways leading to so-called 'Free China'. Christopher Meadows was leading telegraphist in one boat. In an account penned shortly after his escape, he wrote: 'As we were leaving Hong Kong, I read a signal from a small island asking us to take them off. I reported the signal and was told to make "sorry impossible". Grim as it was, we could do nothing to help.' Evading searchlights at top speed, the boats eventually made for a secluded bay, where the sailors stripped their craft of any equipment that could be donated to the Chinese, before sinking them and making for Rangoon under the protection of the guerrillas. Back in Hong Kong, the servicemen, medical staff and civilians who remained faced a terrifying ordeal under Japanese imprisonment. Some were treated humanely, many more were abused. Dozens of nurses were raped, tortured and murdered by Japanese soldiers.

Christmas in the Indian Ocean was spent under a cloud of anxiety. Aboard HMS *Glasgow*, Able Seaman I. G. Hall was discontented. 'I saw several sweating hands carrying the officers' turkeys down aft to the galley,' he noted in his diary on Christmas Eve. 'Funny thing that the higher-ups seem to see a distinct biological difference between the common herd, and officers. I believe that in the Japanese and Russian forces the officers live on more or less the same food. This life and world is an insult to basic decency.'

*Glasgow* spent Christmas Day off Ceylon and Hall, for one, had a miserable time. 'About the lousiest Xmas I've spent in my life,' he wrote. 'Came down [off watch] to a dinner of roast potatoes, ditto pork and peas. The pork which I had was uneatable and resembled in outward appearance a miniature octopus . . . The captain broadcast and remarked that we would all feel happy to be spending this Xmas on the high seas instead of in dock as we were last year. He ought to have asked the opinion of a few more people on this ship.'

With Japanese forces advancing down the Malayan peninsula towards Singapore, the first weeks of 1942 saw an exodus. Gladys Barnes, the wife of a rubber plantation owner – whom she had left in the city – was evacuated along with her young son on the passenger ship *Empress of Japan* at the end of January. In her diary, she described children and 'women of all sizes and shapes in all types of garments lying on mattresses on the floor, in every conceivable posture'. It was 'a queer, unreal atmosphere – tragic beyond words in spite of the humour one finds there, for nearly all these women have been used to luxury homes and the help of several servants'.

As British and local forces retreated across the Straits of Johore, they were joined by many survivors from the *Prince of Wales* and *Repulse*. Royal Marines from warships were given weapons and sent to join the army units defending the perimeter. Previously rigid barriers of class and culture crumbled in this grandest of colonial outposts. Subaltern Stephen Abbott reported that 'every able-bodied man they can lay their hands on had been given a rifle and attached to some unit or other. Malays are fighting shoulder to shoulder with Australians; Tommy with Gurkha.' He recorded the final days of the outpost in his diary: 'The city is in a shocking state. Buildings are down everywhere . . . The wounded are taken into the buildings all around, where the First Aid Posts and hospitals have been hastily established. There is no distinction between Civil and Military. British Officer lies beside Chinese coolie, Civil Servant by Indian Sepoy.'

The surrender came on 15 February, and over 100,000 people became prisoners of war. In the final chaotic days, men, women and children were evacuated on what ships remained – naval, merchant and civilian – across the Indian Ocean to Batavia, Australia and Ceylon, often under prolonged air attack. Several were sunk, with heavy loss of life. Some fortunate survivors were able to swim to small islands to await rescue. Other ships were captured, sailors and passengers alike condemned to imprisonment in squalid Japanese camps.

Nurse Phyllis Briggs was on board the *Mata Hari*: a slow ship, with no effective defensive weapons. Under air attack and surrounded by Japanese craft, the captain was forced to surrender, but not before ensuring that all charts and hand weapons had been thrown overboard. Men were ordered below, women and children to the upper deck. Briggs described the end:

> The Jap naval officer came on board, followed by two sailors carrying swords. Our captain, wearing a spotless jacket, met the Jap officer with a salute. For a few moments there was complete silence, and there was no panic. I remember feeling icy cold in spite of the heat on the deck. We heard that all the men were to be taken off the ship that morning and the women and children were to follow in the afternoon. A few of the elderly and wounded men remained with us. The Jap flag was run up, so now we were under the Rising Sun.

The fall of Singapore heralded a nadir in British morale. Mass Observation assessments of the spirits of Londoners registered their lowest scores in the entire war in February 1942. Just after Christmas 1941, its correspondents were asked how long they thought the war would last. One third believed that the conflict would be over within a year. After the surrender, only one in twenty were so optimistic. 'Good god,' wrote one MO diarist, 'are we NEVER going to begin to win this war?'

By this time Midshipman Graeme Allen, who had survived both the battle with the *Bismarck* and the sinking of the *Prince of Wales*, had been assigned to a new ship: HMS *Exeter*, one of the cruisers made famous for her part in defeating the *Graf Spee*. In the first weeks of 1942, *Exeter* operated around the Dutch East Indies, as part of a combined 'ABDA' (American, British, Dutch and Australian) force intended to prevent the Japanese from reaching the precious resources in Sumatra, Borneo and Celebes. Conditions were uncomfortable, cramped and hot. The gun room, where the midshipmen spent much of their time, was directly above the boiler room. Allen described how 'the black adhesive holding down the thick cortisone lino used to come bubbling through the cracks'.

In the sweltering heat, with morale diminishing and struggling to combine forces effectively, the Allies could do little to halt the Japanese advance. On 15 February, the day of Singapore's capture, *Exeter* was attacked by a Japanese bomber in the Bangka Strait, east of Sumatra. Allen was on the bridge, armed with a pair of binoculars. When he saw the payload released, he shouted 'bombs gone' and the captain ordered the helm hard over. Those on the bridge crouched for cover and waited for the bombs to hit the water. After the all-clear, Allen took a moment to commit the scene to memory: 'Palm-fringed islands on either side, a dead calm sea, and clear blue skies. It was a lovely place for a cruise, and the weather was perfect . . . it was all a bit unreal.'

In an attempt to prevent Japanese amphibious forces taking Java, a combined fleet under Dutch command set out on 27 February to attack the invasion convoy. *Exeter* was amongst them, the only ship in the group fitted with radar. In a confusing series of engagements, Japanese naval forces mounted a stout defence through the afternoon and evening. Eighteen-year-old Glaswegian William Climie was on the flag deck of *Exeter*, raising flags and signals for other ships. As the cruiser fired her salvoes, he took cover from the blast and the cordite fumes behind a locker. Then *Exeter* was hit:

> The deck beneath our feet suddenly shudders as if about to split asunder and a roaring white geyser of pressurised steam erupts from our for'ard funnel . . . 'Don't look down at the boat deck!' someone bawls above the uproar of escaping steam and we immediately do the opposite. There is a jagged hole in the four inch gun mounting below where the enemy shell scythed through and down into the heart of the ship. The strangely contorted bodies of some of the gun's crew lie around the point of entry in the deck . . . I swallow hard and look away.

A Japanese shell had ripped through the forecastle deck and through the bulkheads into a boiler room, smashing fans, oil and steam pipes and a generator. According to the ship's senior engineer, everyone died instantly except one petty officer, who was blown near to the door and managed to escape with only burns. Superheated steam was flushed into the enclosed space, making it too hot for a rescue party even to approach. Helped by the destroyer HMS *Electra*, which was sunk in the process, *Exeter* managed to escape under cover of a smokescreen, and retreated to Surabaya for running repairs. The following morning the temperature in the boiler room was still so high that it could not be reached, and a funeral for the fourteen dead had to be delayed until later in the day.

On 1 March, after being patched up, *Exeter* made for the Sunda Strait with two destroyers, *Encounter* and *Pope*. Underpowered and with a reduced armament, the aim was to avoid the enemy. Men remained at their action stations. 'We munch our corned beef sandwiches and sip "kye" interminably,' wrote Climie, yet the naval version of cocoa did little to quell the nerves of waiting sailors. Few were surprised when the ship was discovered by a strong Japanese naval force of four heavy cruisers and five destroyers. Once again, Climie experienced Japanese gunnery first hand: 'Inexorably their rounds creep nearer and nearer, then straddle and finally one again thunders its way down into our ship's vitals.'

Graeme Allen called it 'a curious sort of action, all carried out at rather long range'. It took two hours before the first shell hit *Exeter*, but soon all power had been lost, and shells and a torpedo rocked the cruiser from one side to the other. Captain Oliver Gordon ordered the ship to be scuttled before she was abandoned. 'I hear the instructions being issued to prevent any needless loss of life,' wrote Climie.

Every man is to see to himself . . . nothing more can be done . . . it is all over . . . It takes time for the realisation to percolate through to the mind and act . . . I stumble uncertainly along the port boat deck and pass the Commander strolling up and down with telescope tucked under his arm as if merely marshalling everyone aft to Sunday Divisions . . . 'Steady,' he calls, 'Steady . . .' My allocated Carley raft is already in the water and men are poising, one after the other at the ship's side then leaping outwards and plummeting into the sea.

Allen was up in the crow's nest, helping a Glaswegian lookout whose already broad accent had become incomprehensible with excitement and anxiety. He was unaware of the final order to abandon ship. 'Those on the bridge omitted to relay this information up the voicepipe to us in the crow's nest,' wrote Allen. 'I looked down at the bridge and was astonished to see that it was empty. I looked aft, and saw that men were throwing the Carley rafts over the sides, and I realised that it was time to go.'

Climie was joined by others racing up from below decks to the sound of explosions and shearing metal. He leapt from the ship's side:

> The noise changes to a roaring bubbling sound as I go down into the depths . . . I can see the light filtering through the greenness from the surface and wonder about the length of time it is taking to come up, when all at once, I am in the harsh garish light of the sun again and bobbing thankfully in the heavy swell, apparently alone, but unharmed. A wave carries me up and over and I momentarily sight countless heads of the ship's company bobbing about amid all sorts of floating debris . . . Several hours later we stagger gratefully up the lowered ladder of the rescuing destroyer . . . It's wonderful to feel the solid deck of a ship beneath your feet again, even though it is the ensign of the Rising Sun which flutters instead overhead.

Graeme Allen was also rescued by the Japanese, along with 800 others from *Exeter* and the two destroyers, both of which had also succumbed to Japanese guns. Survivors were taken to prison camps around south-east Asia. Allen was first taken to a former Dutch army barracks at Macassar in Celebes, before being moved to several other camps in Java. It was only after the war that the precise details of *Exeter*'s fate became known, when prisoners were repatriated and could provide reports to the Admiralty. The ship's captain, Oliver Gordon, had written his own testimony while imprisoned and kept it hidden in a tube of shaving foam.

With the remaining resistance broken, the Japanese advance reached west into Burma and threatened India, swept through the American-controlled Philippines, took Malaya and the Dutch East

Indies and finally reached New Guinea and the Solomon Islands. Japanese bombers were able to strike Darwin in northern Australia, now protected only by the American navy and the Antipodean naval forces. All across the world, sailors read each fresh report with growing incredulity. 'When are we going to stop these little yellow bastards?' wrote Frank Layard, in command of a destroyer in the Atlantic.

The onslaught was finally halted in early May 1942 with the Battle of the Coral Sea, the first decided entirely by carriers, in which the US Navy managed to prevent a Japanese landing near Port Moresby in the south of New Guinea. To the east, an attack by US Marines on the island of Guadalcanal eventually pushed the Japanese from the Solomons, and Australian and American forces fought back desperately in terrible conditions in New Guinea. Then, at the start of June, a decisive carrier battle at Midway would finally deliver the strategic initiative to the Americans.

By this time, with Japanese forces in control of Malaya and threatening the land border with India, the Indian Ocean had become the Royal Navy's frontier. Most of the Eastern Fleet was removed to Kilindini, the harbour adjoining Mombasa in Kenya, and to a secret base at Addu Atoll in the Maldives, leaving only a small force in Ceylon which included the cruisers *Cornwall* and *Dorsetshire*, several destroyers, and the aged aircraft carrier HMS *Hermes*.

Serving aboard *Hermes* was Charles Thomas, the acerbic critic of British class prejudice and the suffocating snobbery of colonial high society, who had witnessed the Japanese advance into China before the war. In March 1942, Thomas was homesick, frustrated and depressed, as he admitted in a letter to his sister:

You say that I take life too seriously. Life in the Navy is a negative existence which cannot be taken seriously. If I had taken life seriously during the past two and a half years I would not be writing this letter because I would have resorted to the very simple escape from this hideous phantasm which is contained in about two hundred aspirin tablets . . . You must realise that except for one unhappy month I have been cut off from normal society for five years, most of which has been spent in some of the worst climates in the world often under bad conditions and difficult circumstances.

Despite the depths of his despair, he retained his great hope for democratic and equal opportunity in the forces and society at large, which had previously been the cause of so much mockery on the messdeck: 'I have noticed that my theories on social, political and military reform which not many months ago were treated with contempt and derision are now respected and shared by many.' Later in 1942, this movement would find its most famous expression with the publication of the Beveridge Report, a blueprint for social insurance and the foundation of the post-war welfare state.

On 5 April 1942, Easter Sunday, Japanese bombers attacked Colombo, Ceylon's capital city, hoping to decimate the British fleet as they had done at Pearl Harbor. Thwarted by the Royal Navy's withdrawal across the Indian Ocean, they nevertheless sank *Cornwall* and *Dorsetshire* and several other ships as they tried to escape. Three days later, HMS *Hermes* was in harbour at Trincomalee when warning came through of another imminent Japanese air attack. The carrier's fighters were grounded ashore, and the ship was sent out to sea to avoid the bombardment, escorted by the Australian destroyer *Vampire* and the corvette *Hollyhock*. The following day, just as the Japanese carrier force prepared to retreat eastwards, a reconnaissance aircraft spotted *Hermes* returning to Ceylon. Dozens of bombers were sent to attack the defenceless carrier. Both the smaller ships were quickly destroyed. *Hermes* was devastated by bombs and plunged beneath the sea, sinking without a trace. Over 300 men were killed. Charles Thomas had written his last letter.

# 12. Dice Loaded

In June 1942, Lieutenant Richard Walker of HMS *Ledbury* was helping to prepare his ship for a voyage to Russia. As well as serving as an escort for convoy PQ17, the destroyer would be carrying four passengers to Murmansk, and they were entertained in the wardroom before the ship left harbour. 'Only one of them, Lieutenant Waterson, had been there and could speak Russian,' Walker wrote in his diary. 'Poor fellow, he was stammering with fright. To watch him drinking was pathetic, the glass clattering against his teeth and the relish he took in his last few pints of English beer.'

The Arctic convoys were a fearsome challenge and a supreme test of individual spirit and endurance. In the words of Admiral Sir Dudley Pound, First Sea Lord at their inception, they constituted 'a most unsound operation with the dice loaded against us in every direction'. Perpetual snow and ice strained even the most robust ships. In summer, daylight lingered around the clock and good visibility brought enemy aircraft from their bases in northern Norway. Fog and darkness caused navigational havoc and allowed submarines to pick off stragglers. For medical officer Harry Balfour, the convoys were 'the grimmest and most thankless task that the Navy had to carry out'. Alec Dennis of HMS *Savage* summed up the campaign: 'I felt that if Hell were to be cold, this would be a foretaste of it.'

Convoys to Russia were given the designation PQ, and those returning to Britain were labelled QP; later amended to JW and RA respectively. Murmansk in the Kola Inlet was the usual destination, with some ships travelling to Archangel in the White Sea during the summer when the icepacks allowed. Local escorts patrolled each terminus, swapping between outward and inbound convoys. The first group of six merchant ships left Iceland for Archangel in August

1941, protected by only three destroyers, three minesweepers and three trawlers.

The first Arctic convoys were little more than a gesture of solidarity with Russia, but freighters and tankers would eventually carry thousands of tons of tanks and trucks, aircraft and fuel, food and supplies to aid the Soviet war effort. But aside from representing moral and material support, the convoys were important to the British public. 'A premature peace by Russia would be a terrible disappointment to great masses of people in our country,' declared Winston Churchill in July 1941. 'As long as they go on it does not matter where the front lies. These people have shown themselves worth backing and we must make sacrifices and take risks, even at inconvenience, which I realise, to maintain their morale.'

British public opinion was unfailingly supportive of the Russian ally. In 1941, Mass Observation reported a widespread belief that 'Russia was basically sensible, kindly and ordinary'. While Americans were viewed with no small degree of suspicion and cynicism, there was genuine interest, sympathy and pride in the achievements, real or imagined, of the Russian people and Soviet regime. After joining HMS *Hornpipe*, Geoff Dormer discovered that the wardroom was decorated by a mural which included a portrait of Stalin alongside the usual images of mermaids and drunken sailors.

Iceland became the home base of the Arctic convoys: a staging post before the long, arduous voyage. It was not only a haven from the harsh conditions of the North Atlantic, but also from the war itself. 'Quite a change to see bright lights again undarkened,' wrote Syd Wallace as the minesweeper HMS *Harrier* approached harbour. 'Nearly all houses and buildings of corrugated iron painted mostly white with bright red roofs. No green grass and mountains all snow capped . . . Icelanders mostly Norse type with fair skin and hair and healthy looking.'

The island had been forcibly occupied by the British in May 1940 to prevent it falling into German hands and to exploit its crucial strategic position in the North Atlantic. Although the invasion was largely uncontested, Iceland was a neutral country and the government had protested before eventually accepting the military presence.

Over the summer of 1941, American troops began to take over garrison duties. 'Attitude to British is normally slightly hostile,' wrote Supply Assistant Wilfred Lambert of HMS *Ramillies* in July 1941. 'American Marines are more popular with residents. Shops sell Nazi literature, whilst various Swastikas are scratched and painted in different places . . . Preference always given to Icelanders, or Americans.' 'They are not in any way openly hostile to us, but I think they <u>are</u> suspicious and rather doubt our sincerity,' wrote Midshipman John Roberts. 'Once you know them personally they are very pleasant.'

Outside the capital, sailors usually received a warmer welcome than they did from the jaded population of Reykjavik. Geoff Dormer and the men of the trawler *Cape Argona* visited several of the smaller towns in late 1941. 'A ship's arrival is a sensation for the English in the wilds, at Akureyri or Seidisfjord, so the resulting party continues day and night,' he wrote. 'It is almost all night up here anyway, for we have seen the last of the sun till spring. It becomes twilight about 10 am, sunrise and sunset colours tint the sky until two o'clock, and by three it is dark again. Away from the Capital, the people are more friendly, but the language barrier is insurmountable.'

The Icelandic landscape was quite beautiful. 'In some parts the scenery is fantastic,' noted Dormer in his diary. 'When the moon, and the Northern Lights, are reflected by sea and snow, night is brighter than day. Only a poet could describe the weird beauty of the Aurora, which is almost beyond belief, as ribbons, streamers, curtains and search-light beams, of all the colours of the rainbow, weave about, over the whole sky.'

The British haven in Iceland was Hvalfjordur, a deep-water fjord which served as the main harbour for warships. The relative safety allowed for rowing-boat races and regattas. Keen fishermen were also well catered for. 'Thousands of small herring inhabit the fjord and can be very easily caught,' noted Midshipman Davies. 'The trout fishing inland is reported to be very good . . . our Captain received three very fine rainbow trout from the captain of *Victorious*.' Midshipman Dick Garnons-Williams of HMS *Belfast* described one sporting fixture in his journal: 'Eight of us went across to HMS *Biter* to play deck hockey. We lost 4–6. After the game, which was played

in thick snow, we had a battle with snow balls, *Belfast* v *Biter*.' Hvalfjordur was also home to American sailors, known to the British as
'the Gobs'. At the American Officers' Club visitors could sample, as
Richard Campbell-Begg noted, 'tinned salted pea-nuts which are a
great luxury'.

Too many home comforts could be counterproductive. In March
1942, the officers of HMS *Renown* were concerned about the possible
reaction to the announcement of the ship's imminent departure.
'Hand messages had to be taken to diverse ships in the harbour by the
drifter,' explained Midshipman Davies in his journal. 'The crew were
rather "bolshie" about being kept up so late at night, so a midshipman armed with an empty revolver was sent in the drifter to see they
did not run off to Reykjavik.' There was a good reason for such
measures: British battleships needed to be at peak efficiency if they
were to best their German counterparts.

By early 1942, the Arctic was the only region in which German
battleships might still emerge to attack convoys. *Tirpitz* had been
sent to protect Norway in January, and was joined the following
month by *Scharnhorst*. A potential confrontation with these last big
beasts of the Kriegsmarine obsessed senior officers. A strategy was
developed in which a small close escort accompanied each convoy,
with a distant escort of stronger warships which would be in a position to pounce should the enemy emerge to attack the merchant
ships.

Far from inspiring fear, a confrontation with the last remaining
German battleships was almost welcomed. A *Times* editorial claimed
of Admiral Tovey, the commander-in-chief of the Home Fleet, that
'he would probably much prefer to find them at sea than to know
that they continued to lurk in a lair so conveniently placed. If the
Russian convoys prove a magnet to draw them to sea, he will know
how to deal with them.'

The first time that ships and aircraft of the Home Fleet came close
to catching the *Tirpitz* was in March 1942. 'The rumours that the
*Tirpitz* was out were growing stronger all the time,' wrote Midshipman John Roberts of the battlecruiser HMS *Renown* on 5 March.
'The convoy consisted of twenty-six ships and therefore was a very

good bait. We had all to gain and nothing to lose if everything went to plan. If *Tirpitz* came out we should sink her; if she stayed in, a very valuable convoy got through.'

Two days later, reports based on intercepted signals came through from Britain suggesting that *Tirpitz* had left Trondheim with a small escort of destroyers. *Renown* and other battleships altered course to intercept. The following twenty-four hours proved tense but ultimately failed to produce an engagement. 'We were at action stations all through the night,' wrote Roberts, 'but nothing happened.' Only when back at Scapa did Roberts learn how close they had been to finding their prey.

Aircraft from *Victorious* had caught sight of the German ship and launched an attack. Charles Friend was a senior observer in one of the Albacore biplanes. 'We sighted *Tirpitz*, with one destroyer,' he wrote, 'and from our low approach height we climbed much higher to begin the attack. Ice began to form on our wings during the climb, which took us up into the cloud cover. The huge ship seemed to be there for hours as we crawled towards her, although it was only ten minutes from sighting to attack.' Two waves of attacks failed to score a torpedo hit: the result of both inexperience and bad luck. Friend recalled that when his squadron landed 'we received for our efforts and the loss of six men what can only be described in the naval slang of the time as a severe bottle'.

'People are apt to say it was a complete flop,' wrote Midshipman J. B. T. Davies of *Renown* in his journal. 'This is not true. The object-ive was to get the convoy through. This was achieved. The *Tirpitz* was a diversion which might have been a great naval success for us.' For John Roberts the incident served to diminish the aura of invinci-bility which *Tirpitz* had acquired. 'Apparently she was completely unprepared,' he wrote, 'and had not the slightest suspicion that the Home Fleet was anywhere near.' It would be another eighteen months before the British had a better opportunity to attack *Tirpitz*.

Without the prospect of a major engagement, convincing men of the importance of their convoys became increasingly necessary from the spring of 1942. Although the intricacies of global strategy did not meet with the interest or the comprehension of every sailor, belief in the mission helped to maintain morale. Aboard HMS *Norfolk*, the commander's noticeboard was used to provide information for sailors. Some posters described local wildlife or relayed anecdotes about the region. One notice stated that Nelson had visited the nearby island of Spitsbergen as a midshipman during a scientific expedition in 1773: 'It is recorded that he was attacked by a polar bear, and was saved by the coxswain of his boat, who drove it off with a long boat hook.'

During convoy duties, notices illustrated routes and provided assessments of risk. News of sinkings and casualty estimates were also posted. Some information included secret and confidential material, with strict warnings not to divulge sensitive information outside the ship. Officers and men were asked 'to make every effort to run to earth any leakage of information which may occur, and any person who may fail in his trust, by reporting the case without delay or fear'. This was an unusual and innovative system. 'We were certainly ahead of our time,' wrote Lieutenant Commander R. S. C. Langford, an officer in *Norfolk*, but he 'never heard of a case of this trust being betrayed'.

'Both the Russians and the Germans are now preparing for the summer campaign, which will open as soon as the spring thaw is over,' stated a notice in April 1942. 'This campaign may have a decisive effect upon the war in Europe and the Middle East. Therefore, the safe and timely arrival of war supplies for the Russians is of tremendous importance.' Other potential supply routes through the Pacific, the Persian Gulf or India were largely impassable, so the burden would fall on the Arctic. Warnings were stark: *Norfolk* and the rest of the Home Fleet 'must be prepared to fight the convoys through, if they are attacked'.

Confidence that their efforts were significant was even more important given the extreme climatic conditions under which sailors laboured. The Arctic was lonely and wild, and much of the burden of escort duties fell on destroyers and other smaller warships, which were ill-equipped for such extreme weather. 'There were long periods of fear untinged with any excitement,' wrote Surgeon Lieutenant Commander Harry Balfour. 'Those vast grey arctic seas dominated everything with a merciless threat to such a small Destroyer.'

Charles Hutchinson had recently joined the destroyer HMS *Intrepid* when she was sent to the Arctic in February 1942:

> Never seen anything like it. The ship was covered in ice, the sea terrible, the mess decks were a sight, almost unbelievable, inches thick in slime, consisting of food spilt, and sea water off oil skins, and tea, and as the ship rolled and pitched one chap grabbed hold of a large fire extinguisher to keep his balance, it came down and the darned thing went off spraying the whole mess deck and anyone in its way with the chemical fluid. I had an accident, slipped and cut my eye on some iron, have a large plaster on now, looking like Nelson.

'We had to halve the length of the watches,' recorded John Roberts. 'Two hours was all the body could stand before the limbs became numb and refused to work, the eyes so full of salt and tears that it was impossible to keep an efficient look out.' Special equipment was not always available. Sailors tended to make do as best they could with duffle coats and woollen hats and gloves, heavy boots and socks. Indeed, some resented the so-called 'all-gears', those men with an abundance of kit.

Jack Neale was navigation officer in the minesweeper HMS *Speedwell*. He recalled one particular piece of gear which helped with the cold: 'long underpants of very fine quality which were so thick they would almost stand up on their own'. He and many others also wore 'enormous leather boots several sizes too large in which could be worn three or four pairs of thick socks'. Some men made use of their own natural defences. *Speedwell*'s captain suspended the normal rule under which sailors had to obtain permission before growing a beard. 'A beard did give one's face some protection from the biting winds on watch,' wrote Neale. 'But one had to continually "open wide" to prevent one's breath freezing moustache to beard.'

Ships were 'Arcticized' by piping steam from the engines to heat the decks. This created an environment which might have been warmer, but was also far more humid, racked by condensation and even waterlogged. Many destroyers were sprayed liberally with asbestos before they began convoy duties in the Arctic. 'Measures that were taken were aimed not at habitability,' stated one senior medical officer of the light cruiser HMS *Scylla*, 'but at preventing the freezing up of gun mechanisms, technical machinery and the navigation instruments on which the ship's life depended.'

Lieutenant Commander John Mowlam was in command of the destroyer HMS *Matchless* during Arctic convoys in 1942 and 1943. 'Condensation occurred on all metal surfaces making everything dripping wet, in spite of the constant mopping up there was always an appreciable trickle of water,' he recalled. 'Every deadlight and hatch had to be battened down so that the only light was artificial. Although the ventilation fans pumped in hot damp air, there was no adequate exhaust, causing the air to become foetid, assisted by the reek of stale cigarette smoke and the lingering smell of cleared-up vomit.' Although he was on call permanently, ready for action twenty-four hours a day, Mowlam felt guilty about the relative level of comfort of his own quarters: 'I had a dry, warm, sea cabin to go to and could indulge in the luxury of privacy.'

Coder E. J. Marshall of the armed trawler HMS *Vizalma* described one winter convoy in his diary: 'It has turned bitter and a high wind off our port bow has increased our already hectic rolling. Spray has covered the deck, ladders, ropes etc. with a thick coating of ice.' Actions that would be easily manageable under normal conditions became feats of endurance. Even getting across the deck necessitated 'a very careful crawl hanging on like grim death to the frozen life-lines with leather seaboots slipping all over the ice and in the knee-deep sea and spray . . . After several hours, the head becomes dizzy and heavy, and muscles ache through constant tension.'

Ice was a menace to sailors and equipment, but it was a particular danger to small ships, where every man had to help with the constant chipping required to prevent the extra weight from proving fatal. 'We roll terribly and I was really rather scared,' admitted Marshall. 'Once we went heavily over to port and stayed there for five or six seconds (although it seemed like minutes). My throat went dry and my heart missed a beat.'

Storms in the Arctic seas could be terrifying. Vincent Shackleton of the minesweeper HMS *Salamander* described the conditions during one voyage to Britain from Russia:

> I know that there is no way that I can convey to others the awesome nature and power of those rolling mountains of water. There is no yardstick that can be used, no similes, no adjectives, no extravagance of metaphor that could convincingly impress on the most comprehending mind the scale of the fury . . . The sea was a boiling white mass almost permanently obscured by driving spray, massive waves that hung high over the bridge like apartment blocks before breaking in great avalanches over the bows . . . Continual noise and movement stretched the frayed nerves almost to breaking point, with no relaxation of tension by night or day . . . The bows rose high, borne aloft by the huge wave. As it passed beneath the hull the screws raced, then the bows crashed down with a hammer blow that shook every plate in the vessel.

Arctic convoy duty was as much a psychological challenge as a physical test. Surgeon Lieutenant Commander Harry Balfour, who served aboard the destroyer HMS *Middleton*, later admitted that it 'was to prove a test I nearly failed . . . When conditions were appalling we all, I suppose, buttoned up our personalities inside our duffle coats and I never quite managed to throw mine off even when conditions were reasonable.'

Balfour had graduated in medicine from Oxford and trained as a civilian doctor before joining the RNVR. On one occasion, a young rating was brought to the sick bay, 'hysterical with fear and cold and could take no more'. Balfour 'sedated him and warmed him in my cot for a while. This calmed him a little, but he remained totally disturbed and could not possibly be sent back to any form of duty.' Desperate for a pragmatic solution, Balfour attempted counselling: 'I tried my best to persuade him that he was able to overcome his fears,' wrote Balfour, despite the fact that at the time, the doctor's 'views about the whole position were not too far removed' from those of his patient. 'He talked out all his problems. After that he slept for a while and when he woke he was just about capable of carrying on.' At Scapa, the rating was quietly transferred to shore duties.

Every sailor knew that the chances of survival were slim for any man left stranded in the freezing Arctic waters. Jack Neale, of the minesweeper *Speedwell*, witnessed the torpedoing of the destroyer HMS *Matabele* during PQ8 on 17 January 1942: 'An enormous pillar of flame was ascending into the sky, ending in a large mushroom shape . . . It seemed to hang there and then large glowing objects fell back towards the sea.' Only two men from a ship's company of over 200 were rescued. Many, so it was said, slipped from the hands of potential rescuers because they were covered with oil.

So slender were the odds of survival that commanding officers in the Arctic were even less likely to attempt rescue than elsewhere. When HMS *Middleton* was under attack in rough seas, two men from the depth-charge team were lost over the side. 'Of course there was nobody on board who did not want to heave to, turn round and search,' wrote Harry Balfour, 'but there was no hope whatever of their surviving and there might well be danger in manoeuvring in these seas so the Captain with sensible courage never hesitated. There was nothing we could do. The longest a man could live in those waters was thought to be three minutes, so we just steamed straight on.'

Controlling damage and keeping a stricken ship afloat were of the utmost importance. In larger warships, there were various mechanisms for isolating damage and preventing catastrophic explosions. Ron Wood served aboard the cruiser HMS *London* in the Arctic. When the alarm for action stations sounded, he would don his blue overalls, white hood and forearm-covering gauntlets, all intended to give some protection from the 'flash' of a fire or explosion blast, and join a queue of men descending into watertight compartments above the magazines. 'The hatch in the deck of my compartment had already been secured on the men below in the shell handling room,' wrote Wood. 'As I settled down on my haunches in the corner of the compartment I heard the hatch above me clang shut, followed by the securing of the dog clamps.'

There were only two things in the space: 'a four inch valve set in a water pipe, and a telephone'. His task was simple: 'When the telephone rang I would be ordered to either open the valve and flood the compartment below, or to stand by to exit as the action was over.'

Wood never had to open the valve, much to his relief. 'Somehow being involved in these awful activities didn't register at the time,' he wrote. 'I was twenty and had been trained to obey orders, I was desperately tired, and terrified that I should fall asleep at my action station.' This was perhaps just as well, because there was a final dimension to his predicament: 'The compartment above me contained another man with a flooding valve and telephone.'

There were few better examples of the importance of damage control than the case of HMS *Edinburgh*. Nineteen-year-old John Kenny had volunteered for the navy in late 1941 and was posted to the cruiser, the flagship of Rear Admiral Stuart Bonham Carter, just before she was attached to convoy PQ14 in April 1942. Having lost one merchant ship to a submarine's torpedo and several more to the weather, the convoy reached the Kola Inlet on 19 April. Ten days later *Edinburgh* was assigned to cover the returning convoy QP11.

Before the ship left harbour, several dozen wooden boxes were carried on board under armed guard, and stored in a reinforced armoured room below decks. Inside was five tons of gold bullion, part of Russia's payments for the war supplies that were being transported across the Arctic seas. Kenny and his messmates were unaware of their cargo, but were eager to get back to Scotland as quickly as possible. 'Having a job inside the ship meant I had no special protective clothing when up on deck,' he wrote, 'and woollen sweaters sent from home had not arrived when we left Scapa.'

QP11 came under attack almost as soon as it left Russia. It was decided that *Edinburgh* would leave the convoy and its escort, as the cruiser would be more vulnerable travelling at such a low speed than she would be sailing alone. On the afternoon of 30 April, John Kenny was in his mess drinking tea. 'There was a terrific flash,' he recalled, 'and two tremendous bangs that almost merged into one and the lights went out. Time seemed to stand still – like a film stopped suddenly and in the dim light coming from the deck hatch I saw through the thick smoke a huge wide crack in the bulkhead which ran from the roof to the floor.'

After a moment of shock, the familiar routines took hold. Men who had been sleeping were roused by their shipmates, gear was gathered and all were accounted for. A queue was formed to ascend the ladder to the upper decks. Kenny's group had been fortunate. 'The messdeck next to us which had taken the full force of the explosion was a scene of absolute carnage,' he wrote. 'Many were killed outright, and perhaps they were fortunate for most of the rest fell into the oil tanks below and had lingering deaths.'

Two torpedoes from U-456 had hit *Edinburgh*'s forward boiler room and devastated her stern, mangling the quarterdeck. The rudder was useless, and although some power remained, movement was uncontrollable. A torrent of seawater had trapped many sailors below decks. The grim decision had to be taken to lock hatches near the affected areas to control the damage. 'A seventeen-year-old seaman was trapped in the telephone room with water all around,' recalled Kenny. 'He was in communication by voice pipe with the bridge. The Captain and others did their best to bolster his morale as long as possible by talking to him but he eventually succumbed.'

Damage control teams eventually managed to contain the flooding, but *Edinburgh* was some distance away from the nearest British ships, and another torpedo strike was feared at any moment. The cruiser was effectively helpless, and was starting to heel over. 'At that stage,' wrote Kenny, 'I quickly said a prayer and quickly joined in doing what I could to help move heavy things to the port side to balance the starboard list.' The long night was tense, uncomfortable and cold. Heating systems failed as the temperature plummeted.

'The Warrant Officers' baths were scrubbed clean and filled with hot soup and cocoa,' recalled Kenny, 'and this and hot sausage rolls and sandwiches were available at any time.' Cigarettes, chocolate and other luxuries were passed around. Sailors with spare dry clothes shared them with those who needed replacements. Kenny worked in the communications office to help coordinate the rescue vessels which were approaching. Two Russian destroyers began to tow the stricken cruiser back towards Murmansk, before three British minesweepers and the destroyer *Foresight* took over.

Confidential books, codes and ciphers were put in weighted bags in preparation for dumping over the side. First German torpedo-bombers and then destroyers attacked. From the communications office, Kenny could hear gunfire and the sounds of increasing activity. *Edinburgh*'s gun teams and the smaller ships managed to fend off the German destroyers, but then another explosion shook the ship, causing an instant dramatic list. A torpedo had struck, 'literally cutting the ship in half'.

Kenny and a fellow coder made their way up on deck and threw their weighted bags over the side. He discovered that the evacuation had already started: '*Edinburgh* had sunk to the extent that her deck was almost level with the decks of the minesweepers.' The wounded were taken off first, stretchers being passed across as the ships drifted dangerously apart. Others lined along the rails waiting for their moment to jump across towards the arms of sailors leaning over the side of the minesweepers. Kenny and several hundred others ended up aboard HMS *Gossamer* and HMS *Harrier*.

HMS *Edinburgh* was the largest ship to be lost by the Royal Navy during the Arctic convoys, along with the cruiser HMS *Trinidad* – damaged by one of her own torpedoes and later hit by a bomb as she returned to Britain just days after *Edinburgh*'s demise. It was testament to both the damage control teams and the morale of the ship's company that *Edinburgh* was kept afloat for three days after the initial torpedo hit. Without the immediate, heartbreaking decisions to seal off hatches, many more would have been killed.

May 1942 also saw the largest Arctic convoy to date set off for Russia. Of the thirty-six merchant ships which made up PQ16, nearly two-thirds were American. As the numbers of cargo vessels increased, so did the escorts. The chief danger in the twenty-four-hour daylight of an Arctic summer was air attack. John Lussey was a telegraphist in HMS *Alynbank*, a former tramp now converted into a dedicated anti-aircraft ship, which was at the head of one of the eight columns.

For two days, the escort's barrage helped to fend off attacks, although submarines still managed to pick off one merchant ship. On 27 May the bombers were more successful. 'Three merchant ships were badly damaged, two being on fire,' reported Lussey. 'Two of these were deemed hopeless cases and were sunk by torpedo from our own sub, *Trident*. The third, a Russian freighter, deserves special mention. The crew steadfastly refused help for the stricken vessel which blazed seriously for'ard. They kept their ship in line and by sheer determination brought the fire under control and resumed their convoy station.'

During the lull after this attack, the men of *Alynbank* took the opportunity to refuel. 'A temporary meal of corned beef sandwiches and jam bread had to be issued,' wrote Lussey. 'It tasted as good as a four course luncheon.' Soon, the convoy was under attack again. For several hours *Alynbank* attempted to protect her wards, with increasing desperation. 'We'd all had a good shaking up,' admitted Lussey. As soon as one raid was over, the convoy would attempt to regroup: 'Various rescue operations etc. were carried out and just when we believed we could call it a day another attack developed.' Yet PQ16 was a success. Eight merchant ships were lost, six to air attack and one each to a submarine's torpedo and a mine, but the remaining vessels arrived in Murmansk and Archangel at the end of May to much fanfare.

The next convoy, PQ17, would have the strongest warship escort yet assembled. The thirty-five merchant ships would be immediately protected by six destroyers, two anti-aircraft ships and eleven smaller corvettes, minesweepers and trawlers, and two submarines. Cover would be provided by four cruisers and four destroyers, two of each from the American navy. To guard against attacks by German battleships, a more distant force of battleships and cruisers would follow, led by the commander-in-chief of the Home Fleet, Admiral Jack Tovey, with another American battleship in attendance. No sailor was left in any doubt that strong resistance was anticipated. 'Captain cleared Lower Deck and told us of the dangers to be expected and when,' wrote Able Seaman Walter Edgley in his diary as the anti-aircraft ship HMS *Pozarica* was prepared to leave Iceland on 27 June 1942.

In the first days after the convoy had set off for Archangel, heavy ice damaged four merchant ships, which were forced to turn back. The expected maelstrom was yet to come, although reconnaissance aircraft were a constant annoyance. 'An uneventful day, if one forgets the eternal presence of our shadowing planes,' wrote signalman Vincent Shackleton of the minesweeper *Salamander* two days into the voyage. 'Every time one ventures close we go to Action Stations, and he generally picks the worst time of day or night to do so. I had no sleep on Wednesday night, and little last night, and the alarm bells are beginning to make my scalp prickle, which has been fairly often.'

'I don't think firing at shadows is worthwhile unless he is a sitting target,' wrote Lieutenant Richard Walker of the escort destroyer HMS *Ledbury* in his diary. 'Ammunition is too valuable especially in view of the torpedo and dive-bombers we expect to come.' On 2 July the first of the anticipated air attacks was launched. Walker had just settled down with a novel by the German expressionist writer Leonhard Frank: 'I had just come off the afternoon watch, and was enjoying a cup of tea over *Carl and Anna* when the bells rang and up we dashed to action stations. There appeared to be planes in all directions.' In poor visibility, German torpedo-bombers raided, as the air-defence gunners put up their barrage:

> They came zooming in at the convoy – Heinkel 115s – torpedoes splashing in all directions. Everyone opened fire furiously but they were 20 or 30 ft above sea-level and darting in and out of the fog, so spotting was difficult. Shells seemed to be bursting all round them but we saw none in flames . . . Not one ship in either convoy or escort was hit – a most extraordinary escape.

This unsuccessful air attack bolstered morale, relieving some of the fear of the unknown and replacing it with determination. 'The general effect of this engagement was most exhilarating,' wrote Walker, 'everyone feeling bucked, I think, at having "proved his metal in the face of the enemy" . . . We all felt happy and laughed and joked a lot and slapped each other's backs, full of bonhomie.' The following day, however, these high spirits were shaken by reports that two German battleships were at large and close by. 'News has come through that *Hipper* and *Tirpitz* are OUT, so we may expect them among our attendants,' wrote Walker. 'I hope to God C-in-C is somewhere near.'

In the first moments of 4 July, just after midnight, the American merchant ships suddenly took down their flags. 'This was puzzling,' noted Vincent Shackleton, 'until they all hoisted new, clean, battle size ensigns, and we realised the date – Independence Day. About twenty-five of our ships are Yankees, but they were not allowed very much celebration.' Not long afterwards, the convoy suffered the first of another series of forceful air attacks which continued all night and through the day. Merchant ships were hit, the American vessel *Christopher Newport* was torpedoed and the crew were taken off by a Russian ship before she was sunk. The fiercest attack came late in the afternoon. 'The aircraft flew through a vicious hail of fire,' wrote Shackleton. 'The first blew up after releasing his torpedoes, the second crashed, but the others continued to come through . . . Hardly had the first wave passed when in came the second, and so we were for five hours.'

Richard Walker witnessed it from the bridge of HMS *Ledbury*:

> The attack was wildly exhilarating, guns firing in every direction, planes flashing in the sun like swallows as they turned and twisted to attack, shells bursting just above the water, torpedoes dropping everywhere, tracer bullets, the Captain directing fire over the loud hailer: control, control, control, barrage, barrage, barrage, all the thrill of battle. I was staggered by the beauty and excitement of it all. There was no time to be afraid. It was a matter of engaging aircraft all over the place. At times they came so close that we could see the expression on the pilots' faces.

In the chaos it was difficult to register the damage to attacking aircraft, but several were hit by anti-aircraft fire and crashed into the sea in flames. An American merchant ship was struck by bombs, as was the Russian oil tanker *Azerbaijan*. 'The sea seemed to be littered with rafts, floats, ship's boats and wrecked planes,' noted Walker. John Beardmore, then a sub-lieutenant and navigating officer in the corvette HMS *Poppy*, recalled the aftermath of the hit on the *Azerbaijan*. 'As some of her crew abandoned ship the women gunners left on board turned a machine gun onto the departing lifeboat, fired a couple of bursts and forced the panicking crew back on board where they set to, fought and extinguished the fire and . . . caught up again with the convoy. How we cheered them!' The minesweeper *Salamander* passed close by the tanker, and her commanding officer passed his binoculars to Vincent Shackleton: 'I heard the skipper say "Can you see what I can see, Shackleton?"

Members of the crew were trying to round up and re-pen a number of pigs which were running around the upper deck.'

Not long after the final air attack, just after 9 p.m. on 4 July, new orders came through from the Admiralty. First the distant cruiser force was withdrawn. Then ten minutes later every ship in PQ17 was advised that 'owing to threat from surface ships, convoy is to disperse and proceed to Russian ports'. A final signal gave a simple instruction: 'Convoy is to scatter.'

On the bridge of HMS *Poppy*, officers were incredulous. John Beardmore recalled the first lieutenant saying to the captain, 'We can't just leave these poor sods to their fate and bugger off.' The implications of the order were not entirely clear. 'Good sleep, then forenoon watch,' recorded Walter Edgley on 5 July, still unaware of the precise reason for the new orders until the captain cleared lower deck 'and told us that an enemy force of *Tirpitz*, *Hipper* and eight destroyers was steaming in our direction, and we could expect an attack later at night or early next morning'. By 6 July, with no attack forthcoming, confusion reigned. 'There must be something more behind all this that we know nothing about,' wrote Richard Walker. 'All sorts of fantastic tales and excuses fly around – the invasion of England, peace has been declared, *Tirpitz* and *Hipper* have been sunk by Coastal Command, we are off to a German base in Norway.'

Merchant ships making their way independently to Russia suffered catastrophic punishment at the hands of U-boats and the Luftwaffe. Only the smaller escort vessels remained, but the anti-aircraft ships, minesweepers, corvettes and trawlers were ill equipped to protect the scattered merchantmen. On 5 July, the day after the order to scatter, six merchant ships were sunk by aircraft and six by U-boats. Over the next four days, ten more were lost. Others were forced to jettison their precious cargoes.

Escort vessels and aircraft from Russia searched for surviving ships, but only eleven of the thirty-five merchant ships managed to reach their destination and 153 merchant mariners lost their lives. Amongst the surviving crews, there were many terrible injuries, including severe burns and gangrenous feet. Not long afterwards, HMS *Salamander* transported casualties back to Britain. 'Particularly poignant was a boy who had lost part of all four limbs,' wrote Vincent Shackleton. 'He had his sixteenth birthday on passage and we all made a great fuss of him. He was adopted by the Seamen's Mess and never lacked company or a "steed" to gallop around the deck or take him to the bathroom.'

'Final result: 23 ships sunk,' stated a message posted on HMS *Norfolk*'s notice board on 19 July. 'Some of the remainder have reached Archangel; others still being rounded up by the minesweepers and corvettes and trawlers and aircraft.' In the cruiser, the reaction to the disaster was ugly. 'Charts and maps displayed for the benefit of the ship have been de-faced,' another notice stated. 'They will be replaced after cleaning.' Lieutenant Commander Langford was in no doubt that this represented 'an expression of the feeling on the Lower Deck at the decision to scatter the convoy. They did <u>NOT</u> approve!'

While the merchant crews struggled to survive, many of those in the escort vessels were also left scarred by the incident. Their guilt over PQ17 would contribute to the ardent defence of convoys to Malta the following month, with several of the vessels involved in the Arctic debacle immediately transferred to the Mediterranean to take part. Meanwhile, anger on the part of merchant sailors resulted in brawls with their Royal Navy counterparts in the pubs on the Clyde. First Sea Lord Admiral Dudley Pound's decision to order the scatter was the chief controversy. No guidance had been forthcoming from ULTRA intelligence, after changes to the German code mechanisms had thrown Bletchley into a new information blackout. Pound's personal circumstances in July were also difficult; whether his wife's recent death or his declining health contributed to a premature decision remained a matter of debate. Yet to most sailors involved, the decision was deeply flawed. Commander Jack Broome would later attest that he had noted in his diary at the time: 'My impression on seeing the resolution displayed by the convoy and its escort was that, providing the ammunition lasted, PQ17 could get anywhere.'

PQ17 led to the suspension of Arctic convoys until the autumn of 1942. 'Our "aid to Russia" is a waste of time,' wrote Midshipman John Roberts of HMS *Renown* in his training journal. 'Most of it is lost on the way, and the part that does get through is such a ridiculously small amount in proportion to the gigantic armies engaged on this 2,000 mile front, that it could be far more usefully employed by us.'

When PQ18 sailed for Russia in September 1942, it set yet another new record: forty merchant ships were involved – twenty of which were American – along with four auxiliary rescue and fuel ships. It was also the first to be joined by a dedicated aircraft-carrier escort, HMS *Avenger*, armed with Sea Hurricane fighters. Yet even with such protection, the experience for merchant sailors remained deeply traumatic. Jim Richardson was the convoy yeoman of signals in SS *Temple Arch*. It was an arduous voyage, during which he regularly spent twenty hours a day on the bridge. He watched as dozens of enemy aircraft approached:

> We had about 5 minutes to wait as they flew in, before they ran into the fire of our outer escort, and then they were amongst us, those that didn't turn away, and it was a hectic three minutes with torpedo planes all around us and every one firing away as hard as they could, with a few bombs coming down from dive bombers just to make it a little more interesting. One or two planes were shot down but I'm afraid not many . . . we lost eight ships.

Aboard the destroyer HMS *Intrepid* was the recently transferred Charles Hutchinson. 'Phew! Having a short break,' he scribbled in his diary. 'We have been attacked and attacked . . . Dive bombers, Ju88s, torpedo planes and high level bombers. The fighters are doing their best, but are hopelessly outnumbered . . . On one attack by torpedoes there must have been nearly fifty planes coming from everywhere, flying very low above the water.'

After the chaos of the attack, merchant ships were out of position and in various degrees of dishevelment. Jim Richardson recorded that 'one ship had gone up in a huge cloud of smoke'. It had been carrying explosives, which 'made me think a little when I remembered we had some 4,000 tons of TNT besides explosives'. Fighter cover from the carrier had not proved a panacea: 'Ships were stopped, sinking, listing and going down all around us – all done in three minutes. I've never seen such a devastating attack and don't particularly wish to again either. Somehow we squared the ships up again and made them look like a convoy again and hung on for the next blow.'

That night, another ship was torpedoed and abandoned. The following day, another air attack came at noon. This time, the fighter resistance was more effective, the barrage even more robust. Official reports claimed over forty enemy aircraft shot down, and the attack eased off. 'It was good to come through the attack without loss,' wrote Richardson, 'and to see one of the bastards catch fire and struggle through the air for a while before crashing in flames.'

'We got one,' recorded Hutchinson in *Intrepid*. 'It crashed into the sea right by the side of the ship. Saw the three Jerries trying to scramble out and standing up in the cockpits, they looked like any other human being and didn't seem to relish the idea of going down in the icy water, but the plane soon settled down and they followed it.'

Thirteen merchant ships were sunk in total from PQ18, including three lost in battles with submarines on the approach to Russia, during which two U-boats were also destroyed by escort vessels. Compared with the disaster of PQ17, it was a success – twenty-seven cargo ships arriving safely to disgorge their supplies – but the Arctic convoys remained a bloody war of attrition.

Soon after the arrival of PQ18, convoy QP14 set off from Russia for Britain. Edward Sullivan was part of a gun crew aboard the destroyer HMS *Somali*, part of an escort group which also included Charles Hutchinson's HMS *Intrepid*. On the evening of 20 September, *Somali* was torpedoed by a submarine, leaving the destroyer severely damaged, but still afloat. Unable to reach Britain alone, she was detached from the convoy and taken in tow by the destroyer HMS *Ashanti* along with three other destroyers, including *Intrepid*, and the trawler *Lord Middleton*.

Eighty-two men remained aboard *Somali* as the small flotilla made its way slowly through the freezing seas. Three days and 400 miles later, on the night of 23 September, a terrible gale began to develop. 'The seas were mountainous high and it was snowing,' wrote Charles Hutchinson in his diary. Shortly before 3 a.m. *Intrepid* received the signal that *Somali* was sinking, the strain on the hull having fractured the metal to breaking point. Hutchinson described the rescue attempt:

We increased speed and rushed over to where she was. I went down off the bridge to clear the scrambling nets for survivors to get hold of if there were any in the water. The seas were coming over and I was wet through and numb with cold, so how anyone could be expected to survive in that icy water and such seas, I don't know. She sank in two minutes, and when we got over the rest of the destroyers were there playing searchlights all over the water. All one could see at times were huge seas and blinding snow . . . We searched for about two hours and *Intrepid* never picked anyone up.

Edward Sullivan was in his action mess, level with *Somali*'s main deck. 'I was resting there when I was woken by a great cracking sound,' he wrote. 'It was of course the ship breaking up.' He rushed up to the forecastle at the prow of the ship and gripped the guard rails. 'I watched the after portion of the ship disappear into the sea and I was still clinging to the guard rails when the bridge went under. I was very fortunate because a Carley float, which had jammed near the ready-use shells, broke loose and I practically fell into it as I let go to enter the water.'

While Sullivan did his best to stay inside, a few other men managed to reach the float, each clinging to the ropes around the side. Some drifted away, others succumbed to the cold. *Ashanti* and *Lord Middleton* were the first rescuing ships to arrive, struggling to pick out survivors in the dark. When a ship neared Sullivan's float, some of the men clinging to the side were dragged under the keel and drowned. Eventually, a powerful lamp from the destroyer *Eskimo* was turned onto the float.

'I had lost the use of my right arm and my legs,' wrote Sullivan, 'but as we rose on the crest of a wave I managed to take my weight on the side of the Float and take a few loose turns round my arm on a heaving line dropped from the side of *Eskimo*. As I went down with the trough the line tightened round my left wrist and I was able to hold on just long enough to be hauled aboard. I remember trying to get a hold of the heaving line with my teeth because it was slipping from my grasp.'

Sullivan managed to maintain his grip, and was soon hauled on deck, wrapped in blankets and put into a cot. When he regained consciousness he discovered that only two of the men in his float had survived. In all, only thirty-five of the sailors who had remained aboard *Somali* were rescued.

Shortly after Edward Sullivan arrived back in Britain, he was summoned before an officer selection board at the Admiralty and passed the interview. After that, he attended *King Alfred* in Hove for training before being commissioned as a sub-lieutenant, RNVR. Yet the incident continued to haunt him. He searched out the mother of a fellow officer candidate whom he had known on *Somali*, and who had not managed to escape from the Arctic waters. 'She was heart-broken, poor woman, and kept saying what a strong swimmer her son had been. I hardly knew what to say.'

Despite such traumatic losses, PQ18 and QP14 demonstrated that the Arctic convoys could be fought through. PQ17 was a devastating defeat, but it was also exceptional. Greater numbers of defensive aircraft were helping to fend off bombers and improving escort tactics were enabling destroyers to hunt enemy submarines more successfully. Hunting *Tirpitz* and *Scharnhorst* remained an obsession of senior commanders, but December 1942 brought an engagement with smaller warships that would prove no less dramatic.

'Christmas Day in the Arctic,' wrote Donald Goodbrand, telegraphist in the destroyer HMS *Obdurate*, was spent 'watch-keeping, scrubbing decks, clearing up the mess of broken crockery, wet articles of food, clothing and vomit and odds and ends that swirled in sodden masses round the messdeck as water poured through ventilation shafts in the fetid fug provided by closed ports and deadlights, as the ship rolled and pitched in manic desperation.'

*Obdurate* was part of the escort for convoy JW51B, bound for Russia. A small group of six destroyers, two corvettes, a minesweeper and a trawler protected the fourteen merchant ships, led by Captain Robert St Vincent Sherbrooke in the destroyer HMS *Onslow*. Conditions were not much better aboard the cruiser HMS *Sheffield*, patrolling the Barents Sea as part of the response force along with the cruiser *Jamaica* and two destroyers. This group was under the command of Rear Admiral Robert Burnett, who had finished his pre-convoy briefing by telling his officers: 'No posthumous V.C.'s wanted or required.'

John Somers was an anti-aircraft gunner on *Sheffield*'s exposed upper deck. On New Year's Eve he was, as he had been for several days, at action stations: 'My feet are frozen. I stamp them trying to warm them up. I've been in the caboose (a deck shelter for the Oerlikon crews). It had a black heat radiant heater to no avail . . . I hope I don't get frostbite.'

In the gloom of the Arctic twilight, the cruiser sighted distant gunfire. It was the signal for *Sheffield* and *Jamaica* to investigate. 'Flashes are seen on the horizon,' wrote Somers. 'We go to full speed. The whole deck shudders with the force of the air being drawn down to power the boilers. Spray flies from the waves parted by the bows, spin drift flies everywhere freezing into the already ice laden superstructure, mast, yards and rigging. Close range weapons crews are ordered to take cover.'

Meanwhile, the convoy had been intercepted by the German heavy cruiser *Admiral Hipper* and the pocket battleship *Lützow* – known before the war as *Deutschland* – along with six destroyers. Sherbrooke ordered the British destroyers to attack. Donald Goodbrand and the other 'sparkers' remained in the small wireless telegraphy office of *Obdurate*, headphones over their ears, transposing the Morse signals into written messages. 'Had our imaginations not been restrained by the sinews of naval discipline,' wrote Goodbrand, 'we must have shuddered at the scenario . . . As it was we lost ourselves in the routine of the sea . . . we drank our kye subliminally, oblivious for the most part to what was going on in other parts of the juddering, lurching ship.'

Above them on *Obdurate*'s bridge, confusion reigned in the darkness. Few were completely sure of the ship's tactical position. Lieutenant Charles Owen later described the psychological effect of gunfire from the stronger German warships:

A salvo of 8-inch shells descended and we were neatly and completely encased by their splashes . . . I was certain the end of the world had come. I thought of the bombs I had survived both at sea and on land –

Norway, St. Nazaire, London, Portsmouth, Liverpool – and wondered why I had felt frightened then. This was my first taste of being at the wrong end of a naval broadside. I looked at the cold grey sea whose temperature was hovering around freezing point and tried to decide whether it would be better to discard my duffle coat and a couple of layers of thick clothes or whether I would prefer to drown well wrapped up. Morbid thoughts, but the ship was heaving and quaking with the explosions, and the air screaming with the deadly flight of metal.

For three hours, the small British ships held off the attackers. The minesweeper HMS *Bramble* was sunk, the destroyer *Achates* badly damaged, and *Onslow* hit by shells which injured Sherbrooke. In *Obdurate*'s wireless office, Donald Goodbrand and his fellow operators were beginning to worry that their destruction might be imminent. They waited in silence, until the senior petty officer 'jumped to his feet in excitement, exclaiming "It's the *Sheffield*! The *Sheffield*'s on its way!" And indeed the cruiser's call sign, a series of four letters constantly repeated, rang strength five round the confined cabin . . . The sighs of relief were audible.'

*Sheffield* and *Jamaica* had arrived unheralded, and immediately opened fire on *Admiral Hipper*. John Somers described the scene:

> The Battle Ensign of pure silk is now flying from the main mast. We twist and turn then *Sheffield* fires a broadside. The ship shudders under the recoil of 12 high velocity guns and crashing down about is ice. Tons and tons of ice shaken loose by the concussion. I watch the four tracer shells, one from each turret, sweep in. A great arc out across the twilight sky going, it seems, much too far to the right but by some magic they curve towards the left and start to drop . . . Another and yet another broadside. I lose count of how many.

The German destroyer *Friedrich Eckoldt* retreated towards what her officers believed was the *Admiral Hipper*. In fact, it was the *Sheffield*. From the gun deck of the British cruiser, it appeared to John Somers that the German vessel was mounting a suicide attack:

Said the lookout: 'There's a destroyer coming directly at us from dead ahead.' So there is . . . If something don't happen soon we will collide. 'Stand by to ram' . . . B turret fires. The shells smash into the destroyer . . . All guns are now firing at this stricken ship. We pass only a couple of hundred yards apart . . . Fire must have reached the magazine, she blows up in a display of fireworks. I will never forget. I turn to my oppo. 'Poor bastards,' I said, 'What a way to go. Either blown up, burnt or frozen to death.'

With the Germans in retreat, the merchant ships were gathered together and the convoy continued its passage to the Kola Inlet. Its redoubtable defence was a propaganda coup for Britain. Robert Sherbrooke was decorated for his Nelsonian bravery, a comparison enhanced by the fact that he had been blinded in one eye. The British lost 250 sailors along with *Bramble* and *Achates*, the Germans 330 men and a destroyer, but the consequences would be far-reaching. In the aftermath of the battle, Admiral Erich Raeder resigned his position as commander-in-chief of the German fleet. His replacement was Karl Dönitz, previously in command of the U-boat arm. Henceforth, the Kriegsmarine would focus its efforts on submarine warfare.

Despite such sacrifices, the quantities of supplies arriving in Russia were insufficient to impress Stalin, who constantly berated the Americans and British for their lack of commitment. Two more convoys would depart for Kola in January and February 1943, but the campaign was then suspended until November. In the meantime, the war on the Eastern Front had reached a turning point. 'Today came the great news that the Russians had taken Stalingrad and destroyed the last of the besieging army,' wrote Midshipman J. B. T. Davies of the destroyer HMS *Puckeridge* on 3 February 1943. 'At the outbreak of the great attack this army had numbered some 300,000 men. It was completely annihilated; 91,000 prisoners were taken including the army commander and 7 other generals. This will go down in history as one of the greatest military victories yet won in any war this world has yet experienced.'

By this time, the Arctic had taken its toll on even the sturdiest ships and the hardiest crews. Donald Povey was a telegraphist in the trawler HMS *Northern Pride*. He kept a diary of JW52, which left

Britain on 20 January 1943, recording the constant tension during the voyage through perpetual gloom, fending off enemy bombers and submarines. On the return trip there were daily submarine scares and several attacks amid floating ice and squalls. After a merchant ship was torpedoed, *Northern Pride* took on forty-two survivors, swelling the ship's complement. A dive-bombing attack and continual rough seas disrupted plans to transfer survivors to other ships. 'Life nowadays is unimaginable,' wrote Povey. 'Meals are a struggle and with nearly 100 men on board one seldom sees one's own bunk! Add this to the delay in progress and you can gather how <u>happy</u> we are.' Fresh water was in such short supply that washing was forbidden. *Northern Pride* made it back to the Scottish coast with all manner of mechanical defects and in a state of squalor. Povey found his cabin 'swilling in two inches of water'.

'The big moment at last,' he wrote on 16 March when the Outer Hebrides were sighted. 'The end of two months of Hell.' Yet little more than a fortnight later, the *Pride* was assigned to go to sea again. 'The spirit of the crew is lower at the commencement of this trip than I have ever known it,' wrote Povey. 'Officers and men have little faith in the ability of the ship itself to stand up to the ordeal ahead.' After the discovery of leaks below decks, and the refusal of the convoy commodore to allow the ship to return to port, the response of *Pride*'s sailors was fierce. 'MUTINY!!' wrote Povey in his diary. 'As one man, the lads refused to touch a rope.' *Northern Pride*'s commanding officer – 'white and trembling' according to Povey – told his men that 'either we obey orders or else get forced to do the job from an armed boarding-party'. Engineering experts came aboard from another ship and eventually the stand-off was resolved. 'After much to-do we are eventually ordered to return to base together with a note,' recorded Povey, 'that the ship should never have been sent out in such a condition.' The trawler crawled back to Belfast, the hold steadily flooding. Povey was triumphant: 'Victory to the mutineers!! Perhaps now the would-be murderers will realise that this blasted crate is sadly in need of an extensive overhaul.'

## 13. Fidelity

At the beginning of 1942 the British public were becoming disillusioned with the government's conduct of the war, as Petty Officer Edward Records noted in his diary at the end of January:

Up and down the country there is an undercurrent of dissatisfaction on how the war is being run. It isn't the loss of territory or the defeats we have had. It is the rackets that are being worked in every phase of the war effort for £ s d or power. People seem resigned to put up with it in most cases lest they retard the war effort, but are all saying after the war things will be different. One hears of so many unfairnesses and of mismanagement . . . Workers on aerodromes practically doing nothing then doing overtime. People in aircraft factories doing the same . . . People in factories making £14 a week and soldiers being paid 14 shillings. Meat rackets, fish rackets, clothing rackets, people buying safe jobs.

In the Atlantic, the precarious balance of merchant ship losses had been thrown into chaos by the official entry of the USA into the struggle. In January 1942, Dönitz had launched Operation Drumbeat. Long-range Type IX U-boats were sent across the ocean to bring the Atlantic war to America's doorstep – New York, the Carolinas, Florida, the Caribbean, the Gulf of Mexico – where, despite the admonitions of the British, no escort system or coastal blackout had yet been established. Although each submarine was armed with sixteen torpedoes at most, they were faced with an abundance of targets: tankers full to the brim with high-octane fuel, cargo freighters laden with raw materials and machinery. Between December 1941 and February 1942, Allied shipping losses quadrupled from 114,000 tons to 441,000 tons. It was the start of a second 'Happy Time' for German submariners.

Out at sea, the dry statistics of supplies and shipping capacity found visceral illustration: burning oil tankers engulfing merchant sailors in flame, cargo ships laden with steel or iron ore disappearing in mere moments beneath the waves. Such destruction exacerbated the tensions between the navy and the nation. In his wartime writing, corvette officer Nicholas Monsarrat criticized 'food-wasters, black-market buyers and thieves' and various other dishonest citizens, who undermined the efforts of merchant sailors and escort crews by their actions. But the conduct of the wider civilian workforce also caused animosity and, above all, it was strikes which proved most controversial.

'I've not been able to explain to questioners why,' wrote Monsarrat, 'of two men fighting the same war for the same clear stake of survival, one of them, enjoying home life, comparative security, and high-level wages, can refuse outright to work unless he is paid more: and the other, conscripted at a meagre wage and sent far from home and into danger, would be shot out of hand if he tried the same tactic.' Escort sailors often considered themselves to be an extension of the national workforce. Being so closely associated with merchant sailors and their cargoes, they felt that they were literally, as Monsarrat put it, 'fighting the same war' as workers at home. Any suspicion of unequal sacrifice could therefore be a serious threat to morale.

It was the dockyard worker, more than any other, who attracted the vitriol of sailors. Ships required repairs, and whether for a boiler clean or a refit, the dockyard was where the clash between the military and the civilian was most apparent. 'There was a nice big conspiracy between workers and employers,' wrote Derric Breen, reflecting a widely held belief, 'to spin each job out for as long as possible, boosting the cost and therefore upping the profit.' He recalled that 'my seamanship instructor, teaching us how to fix a ship, said, "Take a bearing on at least two immovable objects: dockyard maties will do splendidly."'

Geoff Dormer was first lieutenant of the minesweeper trawler HMS *Hornpipe* during a lengthy refit. He described 'daily arguments with dockyard supervisors', often as a result of incomprehensible union rules: 'Numbers of men would sit about, playing cards for hours, because a Hole-Borer wasn't there, to drill a few holes that anyone could have made in a few minutes.' Royal Navy sailors had a song, to the tune of 'Just like the Ivy on the Old Garden Wall': 'Dockyard Maties' children / Sitting on the Dockyard Wall / Just like their fathers / Doing fuck all. / When they grow older / They'll be Dockyard Maties too / Just like their fathers / With fuck all to do.'

Accusations of theft from ships by dockyard workmen were common. Regardless of their accuracy, such rumours reflected the general perception of civilian workmen within the navy. After the destroyer HMS *Sheldrake* sustained damage in a collision, she underwent repairs at the Royal Docks in London, with the ship's company granted fourteen days' leave. Engine Room Artificer Jim Fisher, a skilled mechanic, later wrote, 'When I returned I went down into the engine room and discovered the lock on my tool box had been forced and all my tools stolen . . . The lack of respect shown by dockers and [lack of] consideration for those who were actively engaged in the war at sea appalled me.'

Sailors relied on the civilian workforce for their very survival. Positive experiences, of course, inspired far less comment than complaints, but no matter how many efficient repairs were carried out, a poor job could be disastrous. C. C. Young, petty officer in HMS *Hartland*, described a boiler cleaning at Falmouth. 'They came aboard with their tool boxes, morning paper, and Billy Can for making tea,' he wrote, 'then sat down and read their morning papers and played cards until 5 p.m., when they started work, on overtime. Our remarks about us risking our lives and working long hours in order to keep Britain supplied with food and war supplies, fell on deaf ears . . . The outcome of this 10 weeks of slovenly, sickening work, was that off Freetown in West Africa, with submarines around, whilst escorting a convoy, one boiler went bust and had to be closed down and the ship reduced to half speed.'

Beyond the dockyards, however, the Royal Navy was a less immediate presence. Sailors in uniform were nevertheless recognizable representatives, and the imagery of warships remained potent, formed from the pages of magazines or the black-and-white newsreels and picture shows. But even if they had little direct contact with the Senior Service, the public was heavily invested on an emotional level with the idea of naval strength. That the Royal Navy could always be relied upon was an unspoken assumption. Never was this more explicitly illustrated than in February 1942, when the battleship *Scharnhorst*, along with the *Gneisenau* and the *Bismarck*'s former partner *Prinz Eugen*, managed to escape from Brest and scurry through the English Channel to the havens of German ports.

Despite being alerted by intelligence decrypts, a combination of bombing and mine attacks by RAF aircraft and Fleet Air Arm Swordfish, along with MTBs and a hastily assembled force of destroyers, failed to prevent this 'Channel Dash'. Sailors waited for the inevitable backlash. 'I expect there will be an uproar in the papers and in Parliament about the whole affair,' wrote Midshipman John Roberts of HMS *Renown* in his journal, 'and quite rightly so too.'

The episode was a striking reminder that the psychological prop provided by naval superiority was hard won and easily lost. 'Nothing more mortifying to the pride of sea power has happened in home waters since the seventeenth century,' proclaimed *The Times*. 'That this blow should be sustained at a time when our resources at sea are strained as never before is doubly lamentable.' Mass Observation recorded that the initial reaction of the public was furious, eclipsing even the fall of Singapore a few days later. But before long government intelligence reports were suggesting that, while criticism of the air force for its part in the failure remained outspoken, people seemed willing to forgive their sailors.

In March 1942, children from Barnsbury Central School in London composed a poem entitled 'Salute to the Navy' as part of their activities in aid of a local 'Warship Week' fund-raising appeal.

> Courageous are the men who guard our shores
> Or bring our food across the raging seas;
> Death lurks beneath, and high above them soars
> And never can they rest with minds at ease.
>
> They watch the waves, they scan the sky's vast space,
> They strain their ears to catch the deadly drone

Of 'plane or U-Boat. Eagerly they chase
The foemen who would rule the seas alone.

So we must help them in their gallant task.
That they may win, we'll save with all our might;
Supply for them whatever they may ask,
Give up those pleasures in which we delight,

To aid our men out fighting on the sea
That all the world may once again be free.

Throughout the spring of 1942, members of the public in towns
and cities across Britain took part in the Warship Week campaign,
orchestrated as part of the National Savings drive. Funds and gifts
amounting to hundreds of millions of pounds were raised over the
course of the war. Communities were given fund-raising targets
which equated to the cost of 'adopting' a ship. Smaller towns might
be allocated a destroyer; larger cities a battleship. Organizations also
took part: HMS *Warspite* was supported by the London Stock
Exchange. Sailors would receive gifts of luxuries, books, clothing or
other items, once the link had been established. Some of the money
raised was also set aside for local charities. Detachments of sailors
might be sent to visit their adopters, posing for photographs and giving interviews to the local newspapers, attending parties for children
and dances for adults.

HMS *Orwell* was adopted by Ipswich. Nineteen-year-old Midshipman Richard Campbell-Begg was particularly pleased when the
townspeople donated a 'sun-ray lamp'. 'I sat under it for some ten
minutes and came out as red as a beetroot and one mass of freckles,'
he wrote in his diary. 'Now it is all peeling off so I am due another
treatment.' John McGregor, a radar operator in the battleship *Duke of
York*, had managed to acquire a valuable memento during another of
Winston Churchill's voyages across the Atlantic in December 1941:
'One of his cigar ends, which some months later I sent to the Ilford
Council for their Warships Week and over £400 was realized on it.'

It was not only government programmes which brought sailors

and civilians together. Personal relationships could flourish if a ship remained in one place for some time. When HMS *Salamander* was based at Rosyth, Vincent Shackleton befriended a local artisan known as 'Jock' Hutton who had two young daughters. One of them suffered from polio and was confined to a wheelchair. Shackleton and his messmates 'adopted' her, taking her to watch her beloved Dunfermline Athletic and escorting her on afternoons out. Long-distance relationships were also possible. Aside from their normal correspondence with family and friends, sailors might receive letters from schoolchildren or gifts from members of the Women's Institute. Many female factory workers were eager to acquire pen-pals. One matelot reminisced that 'we had packs of cigarettes from South Africa containing at times young ladies' photos and addresses'. Others found notes secreted inside their life jackets by factory workers with messages such as: 'May this save the life of a Sailor. God bless you.'

An emotional link between sailors and civilians was at the heart of the Atlantic enterprise. At the beginning of the war, Frank Layard had felt guilty about remaining at his desk while his peers returned to sea. By 1942 he was commanding the destroyer HMS *Firedrake* in the Atlantic. Yet he remained as emotionally engaged with developments at home as those abroad. 'It was announced on the news that there had been a combined raid on St Nazaire by the Navy, Army and R.A.F. but no details,' he wrote in his diary on 28 March. 'London's Warship Week has raised £142,000,000. The King spoke on the wireless at 9.00. Most inspiring.'

The raid on St Nazaire was just as inspiring as the public's generosity or the King's speech. At the mouth of the River Loire, its docks were the only facilities on the French Atlantic coastline capable of servicing the German battleship *Tirpitz*, should she break out into the open ocean. In an attempt to pre-empt that possibility, a plan was formed to sabotage the dry docks by fitting the ex-American destroyer HMS *Campbeltown* with time-delayed explosive charges and crashing her into the lock gates. A small flotilla succeeded in fighting its way in through the gauntlet of shore batteries, passing the site of the *Lancastria*'s demise in 1940, and *Campbeltown* was set on course to career into the gates. Motor launches landed commandos at the dockside and fought a running battle with German guards.

After successfully infiltrating St Nazaire, only ten of the eighteen raiding craft remained in a fit state to escape. 'All hell broke loose,' wrote Frank Arkle, who was manning one of the motor launches. 'The British tracers were all orange in colour and the Germans' were all a blue and green colour.' After landing its troops, the motor launch picked up men from *Campbeltown* and made for the open sea at top speed. Before a smokescreen could be made, the boat was hit. 'Poor old Mark Rodier was standing exactly between me and the shell,' Arkle recalled, 'and he took the brunt of the whole explosion.'

Good fortune saved his life, but Arkle was injured: 'I felt my right eye on my cheek and I was convinced that my eye had been blown out of my head and was hanging down my cheek, and I felt that there was only one thing to do about this so I plucked it out and threw it overboard.' In fact, despite this gruesome feeling, Arkle's eye was intact and the wound only imagined. His left foot was truly hurt, however, and he limped below to snatch a bandage before abandoning ship. Rescued by a German trawler, he was landed ashore, taken prisoner, and given coffee. He and several others were photographed – an image which appeared in *Time* magazine three months later – and were being questioned as the delayed explosions tore through the dock gates. Arkle spent the rest of the war a prisoner in Marlag camp, near Bremen. In all, 215 raiders were captured and 169 killed.

Yet despite the audacious success, St Nazaire provided only a temporary tonic amid a general malaise. The spring of 1942 marked the nadir of the war for Britain. Since the turn of the year, the Battle of the Atlantic had once again become a gruelling war of attrition. From March 1942 onwards, monthly losses of merchant shipping in excess of 500,000 tons became the norm. More U-boats were now operational. A change in the Enigma cipher in February led to an intelligence crisis which lasted until the autumn. Convoys were finding it harder to avoid the growing wolf-packs. Singapore had been lost. North Africa was in the balance. Naval forces in the Mediterranean were severely depleted and Malta was isolated. It seemed that the British Empire did not have the strength required to defend itself. Government assessments of public morale recorded new lows.

All this despite the long-awaited entry of a new and powerful ally across the Atlantic Ocean. Securing American support had been a personal mission for Churchill, and many had shared his emotional investment in the New World. But the reality of the alliance produced a great deal of disillusionment amongst the British public. Wartime opinion polls consistently revealed cynicism about the American contribution. In June 1943, one Gallup survey asked respondents which of the Allies was making the single greatest contribution to winning the war. While 50 per cent named Russia and 43 per cent Britain itself, the USA trailed behind China with only 3 per cent.

From the outset of the war, sailors had formed the most direct link between Britain and America. Even before Pearl Harbor, the Royal Navy had been a source of some fascination to the American public. Richard Campbell-Begg arrived in New York aboard the liner *Empress of Asia* in September 1941. With him were veterans of the intense fighting around Crete and, as the ship entered New York harbour, press photographers asked for pictures of the servicemen before the Statue of Liberty. 'The newspaper men were being spun many a tale of daring do whilst the huge Movietone cameras filmed all and sundry,' wrote Campbell-Begg. 'War Heroes Talk of Beer and Jerry,' reported a *New York Times* headline. 'British Veterans Think Former Too Cold Here and Latter Will Be Licked.' Later, Royal Navy personnel would be sent on goodwill tours of America. Captain Angus Nicholl visited steel works and factories producing parts for destroyers, 'shaking hundreds of hands' as he travelled from New York to California, talking about his experiences and reassuring workers about the role they were playing in the Allied war effort.

British warships underwent repairs in American dockyards, a practice which became increasingly common as facilities at home were overwhelmed with demand and American capacity expanded. When the battleship *Queen Elizabeth* was being repaired at Norfolk, Virginia, in 1942, Midshipman Tom Dowling took the opportunity to explore. 'Outwardly,' he wrote, 'it is much like a modern English provincial town but it is very different in many ways. All large shops and cinemas are air-cooled . . . and when you enter one of these cinemas you feel quite chilly until you have stopped sweating and have got used to it.' He noticed several cultural differences: 'Their chemist shops are "Drug Stores" and very numerous . . . Their cinemas are one-price and are called "movies" . . . their petrol ("gasoline") is very cheap . . . Shorts are never worn even in this climate by boys or men . . . It seems quite done for the average American to drink coca-cola (more or less their national beverage) on the streets.'

In the summer of 1942, Vere Wight-Boycott, now a lieutenant commander, and a newly formed crew travelled to America in the troopship *Thomas H. Barry* to take command of the destroyer HMS *Ilex* at Charleston, South Carolina. En route, they called at New York, staying at the Hotel Barbizon Plaza 'on the King' with $4 a day allowance. Wight-Boycott visited the Radio City cinema, watching *Mrs Miniver*, and several Broadway plays, including an infamous show at the Winter Garden Theatre called *Sons o' Fun*, performed by Ole Olsen and Chic Johnson of *Hellzapoppin'* fame. 'Half the action takes place amongst the audience,' wrote Wight-Boycott. 'They are persuaded to undress in public for prizes, dance with the chorus in the aisles etc.'

Wight-Boycott was already familiar with America, having taken command in 1940 of one of the fifty ex-US destroyers given to Britain in exchange for military bases overseas. After his previous experiences, he decided to attempt to educate his new ship's company before the troopship reached harbour. 'I gave a "lecture" tonight on "What to do and say in America",' he wrote in his diary. 'It was a rehash of all I could remember of the booklet issued originally by the R.A.F. . . . It lasted half an hour and got a few laughs, so as it was only really intended to pass the time, I reckoned that was all right.'

Sailors were able to visit towns and cities across the east coast, and often enjoyed lavish hospitality. Surgeon Lieutenant Dunlop of HMS *Sheffield* took a trip to Boston later in the war. In a letter to his family, he described the distinctive wooden houses, the multi-storey buildings, the subway, the shoe-shine boys, and the red brickwork of Harvard University. But the material differences were not as significant to him as 'the people one met, and the way they looked on life'. He was charmed by the locals: 'If you walked into a shop the girls behind the counters would talk to you as if you were a friend.'

Hundreds of intelligence, signals and administrative staff travelled across the Atlantic over the course of the war, working behind the scenes to ensure that Britain was kept informed, organized and prepared in its dealings with the American military and political leaderships. Elizabeth Gibson had joined the WRNS at the start of the war and in 1940 worked in Washington, DC, ostensibly as one of the staff of the British Embassy, collating information about British ships in American ports and coordinating intelligence on German submarines. Initially, this was done in secret and in plain-clothes, but after Pearl Harbor Gibson and her fellow Wrens wore uniform and moved into air-conditioned offices in the Public Health Building on Constitution Avenue. Their unusual garb caused some initial confusion. Gibson later recalled that they were often 'taken for nurses or St. John's Ambulance and expected to give First Aid to people who fainted in theatres'. She and three others lived in a house in Georgetown, but had plenty of opportunities to explore the continent. They visited whaling settlements on Nantucket Island near Cape Cod, participated in a 'squaw dance round a bonfire' on a Navajo reservation in Arizona, and went duck shooting on the St Lawrence river in Canada.

Relations between the Royal Navy and its American ally were seldom straightforward. Admiralty reports on the US Navy disparaged its cumbersome bureaucracy and the 'mediocre ability' of its officers, who exhibited a 'defensive spirit and caution'. It took several months before the American admirals accepted the necessity for a system of coastal convoys and more rigorous organization. Admiral Ernest King, in particular, had a reputation for being vehemently anti-British – although this was perhaps the result of a generally stubborn personality – and the Admiralty was eventually forced to send some of its most respected men to Washington as liaison officers in an effort to exert some influence.

Personal rivalries developed quickly between British sailors and their upstart American counterparts. Leading Signalman Matthews of the destroyer HMS *Fame* attended a boxing tournament between men from a British escort group and a US Navy barracks. 'The result should have been foregone,' he recounted in his diary, 'with the Yanks looking so large and muscular – but we won – 3 points to 2. The big job was to get men to weigh up to the weight to fight the Yanks. They are a fine looking hefty race but we believe soft compared with the average Englishman.' At least in this case, the competition seemed to have spilled over elsewhere: 'There are plenty of fisticuffs in the U.S. Fleet Canteen every night and usually the under sized Englishman is on top. I like the Yanks, they are very generous, but some are "stroppy" to say the least.'

The British took great pride in such successes, clinging to the last vestiges of moral superiority over their wealthier associates. A famous anecdote about the relationship between the two navies told the story of a signal from an American ship to a British vessel asking, 'How does it feel to be the second largest navy in the world?' The British captain was said to have replied, 'How does it feel to be the second best?' Material inferiority was outweighed by a strong sense of superiority of spirit and tradition, as the ship's company of HMS *Penelope* reported in a book compiled by the ship's chaplain and published in New York:

> We were most impressed with the luxury and comforts of the American ships, and we all wondered how these delightful peace-time ships would get on in wartime . . . We were given ice-cream and fruit and magazines and lots of other welcome and rare things . . . one of our matelots was being treated to a magnificent sundae in the ice-cream parlour of an American battleship. His host asked, 'What do you serve out in your ship?', and he answered, 'Oh, just cordite and hot steel.'

'On paper they have a fine and powerful fleet,' wrote Midshipman J. B. T. Davies of HMS *Renown* in his training journal. 'The ships themselves are very comfortably fitted. Both officers' and men's quarters are furnished to a degree of comfort that would probably disgust the British sailor, for instance every man has a bunk.' There was, however, one particular feature of these ships which Davies felt moved to comment upon: 'All American ships are dry; whether this is a good thing or not is a moot point, I am inclined to think not. I imagine that a man who has had his daily pint for years, joins the navy, and has to sustain himself on Coca-Cola, will on his first shore leave try and make up for lost time, with disastrous results.'

Tensions became apparent as American servicemen began to flood into what had been exclusively British bases in Newfoundland, the Caribbean, and Ascension Island in the South Atlantic. It formed a precursor to the eventual 'American invasion' of Britain later in the war, when the civilian population would experience a similar influx. Trinidad was the home of the Royal Naval Air Station HMS *Goshawk*. Charles Friend served as an instructor at the base, and enjoyed the swimming pool and sports fields. He lived in wooden cabins surrounded by palm trees and humming birds, although he recalled that 'the hairy great coconut spiders scared me out of my wits'. When American troops began to arrive during 1941, the bars and cinemas in Port of Spain became the scenes of violent squabbles. 'When a large British ship was in harbour,' recalled Royal Navy officer Lieutenant R. Aitchison, 'the ranks of the Brits were increased enormously and fighting almost reached riot proportions.'

HMS *Ilex* spent several months under repair at Charleston, before the ship was ready to go to sea, during which time Vere Wight-Boycott became increasingly frustrated with what he perceived to be the disparaging attitude of his American equivalents. Sentries seemed haughty; officials appeared unduly obstructive. It was, he wrote in his diary, 'run by ignorant and assertive Ensigns who ought to have been serving at sea instead of sitting on their backsides in offices ordering sea-going officers about'. During engine trials in September 1942, immediately after leaving the hands of American dockyard workers, the first attempt to manoeuvre ended with the destroyer heading in entirely the opposite direction to the one intended. It was found that the steering gear had been connected the wrong way round. There was, wrote Wight-Boycott, a 'feeling of lease-lend'.

Working up in Key West, Florida, was far less troublesome. From here, *Ilex* continued to trial and train in the Caribbean. The islands had been thrust into the heart of the campaign by U-boat attacks on oil tankers in early 1942, and 270 ships would be lost in the area before the end of the year. The British West Indies provided thousands of volunteers for the RAF, but the Royal Navy relied on Jamaica, Barbados, Trinidad and Tobago, and their smaller neighbours, primarily for their amenities rather than their manpower. The American influence in the region perfectly illustrated the imperial tensions at the heart of the Anglo-American relationship. On her tour, *Ilex* visited Guantanamo Bay in Cuba. Vere Wight-Boycott explained its unusual status: 'This is one of the bases where the U.S. (who deprecate the system so much when exercised by Britain in China) have extra-territorial rights in a foreign sovereign state. It corresponds very much to Wei-Hai-Wei.'

From the Caribbean, *Ilex* travelled to Brazil in the style of a pre-war 'showing the flag' cruise, before sailing for the Cape Verde Islands and then to Freetown on the west coast of Africa. Since the start of hostilities in the Mediterranean, the importance of the African coast-lines – both east and west – had increased dramatically. With the critical shipping route through Mediterranean to the Suez Canal effectively closed, convoys were faced with a 10,000-mile detour. From Britain, ships sailed to Freetown and then on to South Africa, from there to proceed up the eastern seaboard of Africa to the Red Sea and the Middle East or into the Indian Ocean. This was an essential link between Britain and the resources of colonies and Commonwealth, and the contrast between the Royal Navy's status in America and Africa could not have been greater.

John Smith had turned seventeen in June 1940, while his ship HMS *Neptune* was based in the Mediterranean. From August to December 1940, the cruiser was sent from Suez to Aden and then around the African continent. The first stop was Mombasa in Kenya. 'The most beautifullest place I have ever seen,' wrote Smith in his diary. 'It has a jungle surrounding it, breakers along the coast and nice weather. All kinds of fruits grow wild. Also very modern in one part and natives in another. Things very dear including beer . . . Went ashore into jungle . . . Picked coconuts and other fruits, bathed on coral isle.'

The Eastern Fleet's retreat to Kenya after the Japanese attack on

Ceylon in April 1942 brought fresh strategic dilemmas. The following month, a strong force of Royal Marines supported by warships
took Madagascar, held by the Vichy French, in order to secure the
east African convoy routes. Able Seaman Alan Gould was serving in
the destroyer HMS *Lightning*, which supported the landings at Diego
Suarez. 'We have now captured the naval base and harbour,' he wrote
in his diary on 7 May. 'What a harbour!' Amongst his messmates
there was some sourness about the reporting of the operation. 'What
got under my skin about the news was what Churchill said,' wrote
Gould. 'He praised everyone bar the navy.' Another speech by
Churchill a few days later came during Gould's watch, 'but he gives
me the pip anyway so I didn't miss much. I don't need him to give me
moral support and if a vote was cast in the services for him he would
not be there anyway, the navy has a special dislike for him as we do
all his dirty work for him.'

Madagascar was hot and uncomfortable. 'I've just had a shower
and the sweat's running off me as if I were a miner,' noted Gould.
Diego Suarez was 'a rotten hole . . . but they have a nice type of
salad.' Sporting endeavours helped to alleviate this frustration. 'They
are keen on swimming here,' explained Gould, 'so I've started to run
a water polo team and at 4.30 we had our first game and were able to
pick some very promising players. It is shark-infested water so we
have a chap on lookout with a Tommy gun just in case.'

Whatever moderate appeal Madagascar might have held paled
in comparison with the ports of South Africa, which *Lightning* had
visited en route to Diego Suarez. Cape Town, Gould had written,
was 'a lovely sight with the Table Mountain and the city below it, the
lights beginning to come on, at night it was a city of lights'. Durban,
meanwhile, was 'as big I suppose as Brighton but a lovelier place
owing to the climate . . . You can imagine how we felt after a month
at sea and not seeing women from the time we left England, then
going ashore in Durban seeing the women in their summer frocks
also imagine nearly 50,000 troops on the loose.' As ships left Durban
harbour, many waited on deck to hear 'The Lady in White', who
stood at the quayside singing a song for every sailor.

The Union of South Africa was a British dominion, sharing the monarch but politically independent and rich in natural resources, minerals and precious metals. It was a society divided: the disenfranchised black majority and the ruling white Afrikaner elite had little inherent investment in the Allied cause, unlike the English-speaking and fervently pro-British white minority. Mobilization was equivocal and slow, although South Africa would eventually make a considerable contribution in both lives and raw materials. Maritime power represented the most visible imperial link. Some 13,000 ships were repaired in South African dockyards over the course of the war, and major ports became essential havens for the cargo ships, troop transports and warships of the 400 convoys which passed through.

Just as critical to the South Atlantic convoy system was British West Africa. The port of Freetown in Sierra Leone was both the most significant and the most unlikely naval base. Over the course of the war this former colonial backwater experienced rapid construction to transform it into a serviceable station. It was not a popular posting. Despite the grand beauty of Sugar Loaf Mountain and the Charlotte Falls, high temperatures and humidity gave it a reputation amongst British sailors as the 'white man's grave'. There was one redeeming feature. Lumley Beach was described by Midshipman Tom Dowling of the destroyer HMS *Beaufort* in August 1942: 'The surf is good even on calm days though the beach is a trifle too steep, and in consequence the runs in, when you were lucky enough to get a surf-board, were short. Tea at the golf course consisted of tea and peanuts. They had run out of bananas, the only other item on the menu.'

Dowling took a trip through Freetown and came across 'a very amusing little boy, naked, and with a great pail of water balanced on his head . . . He was only about four.' But above all else he was struck by the great cotton tree in the centre. 'The roots divide out at the bottom like angle irons,' wrote Dowling in his journal, 'and it was under this tree that the slave market [once] was. A very large proportion of the millions of negroes in the U.S.A. descend from those who passed under that tree.'

After arriving in the autumn of 1942, HMS *Ilex* remained at

Freetown for several weeks, contributing to convoy defence and undergoing piecemeal repairs and general maintenance. Without access to many of the more familiar luxuries and amenities, Christmas Day 1942 was an improvised affair. Wight-Boycott made his way up to the bridge in his tropical shirt and shorts, a monkey jacket and red slippers. The officers' lunch included a gaunt chicken, some tinned ham and 'a brave imitation of a Christmas pudding' with brandy sauce concocted from Cuban rum and tinned milk.

Also based at Freetown was the West African Escort Force, which provided extra cover for convoys travelling between Gibraltar and Cape Town, patrolling as far as Takoradi on the Gold Coast, and Lagos in Nigeria. John Smith visited Lagos as part of *Neptune*'s African tour. 'Customs buildings,' he noted in his diary. 'Coconut palms along shores. Native villages outside town in the bush.' Ashore, Smith once again joined a tour party as he had in Mombasa. 'Went in native village,' he wrote. 'I was frightened at first. Later went in bush to collect fruit.'

West African escort duty became known to sailors as the 'long-haul trade'. Few of the ships allocated to the area were modern. Sub-Lieutenant Philip Calvert served aboard the coal-fired trawler *Morris Dance*. He recalled that fuelling the ship by hand was 'a dirty, time-wasting business', which was conducted 'mostly by native women carrying the coal aboard in baskets on their heads, two or three pounds at a time, and our requirements were generally about two hundred tons'.

Derric Breen was a veteran of the African convoys. He recalled that he and his shipmates aboard the sloop HMS *Egret* became 'a real pirate crew', with uniform restrictions eased and wild beards grown to save fresh water. Like many other escort vessels, *Egret* made periodic visits to some of the remoter reaches of British influence, including a cruise upriver from Bathurst in the Gambia, to entertain tribal chiefs who provided reports on the Vichy French activity in the region. Local musicians performed on deck, with drums, bow violins and 'Kova' mandolins. African dignitaries were permitted to fire the ship's guns, and were presented with a polished shell-casing as a memento at the end of their visit. In America, British sailors represented fading imperial superiority. In Africa, they continued to play the role of imperial masters.

The assistance of the British Commonwealth came at a price. South Africa's military and political leadership took the opportunity to assert the Union's freedoms in London. The withdrawal of the Royal Navy from the Pacific put greater responsibility on the naval forces of Australia and New Zealand, and pushed the Dominions further towards the American sphere of influence. In the Atlantic, meanwhile, the Royal Canadian Navy became an essential and invaluable partner.

By the end of the war, Canada's navy had grown from thirteen small ships and around 2,500 men to the world's third largest maritime force. This expansion was cultivated by the Canadian government, eager to exploit its new-found status. By the end of 1942, Canadian forces escorted more than a third of all Atlantic convoys. Yet such a remarkable transformation was not without problems. In the second half of 1942, some sixty of the eighty merchant ships lost in the Atlantic were from Canadian-escorted convoys. That nearly twice as many Canadian-escorted convoys were discovered by U-boats than those with British escorts did little to placate the unease in Western Approaches. Reports were compiled which seemed to indicate that the Canadian escorts were not as 'efficient' at killing U-boats as they could be. The Canadians certainly had difficulty: partly the result of ship shortages and technological impairment – their destroyers were often last in line for new equipment – but their crews also suffered from truncated training. After being temporarily withdrawn for intensive working up in Britain at the turn of the year, Canadian escorts returned to the campaign with renewed purpose.

The Atlantic convoys were a truly multinational enterprise. From July 1940, efforts were made to bring Free French naval forces under the umbrella of the Royal Navy, along with their Polish, Czech, Dutch, Belgian and Norwegian counterparts. Official communications suggested that they should be welcomed because 'it is most necessary to give to the War which Great Britain is waging single-handed the broad, international character which will add greatly to our strength and prestige'. Sailors from an international coalition served with the Royal Navy, some in their own vessels and others in ships provided by the British. Many made distinguished contributions and earned reputations for brazen bravery. After the sinking of the *Bismarck*, there was much amusement at reports that the small Polish destroyer *Piorun* had been expressly forbidden to ram the German battleship.

There was one ship in the Royal Navy which epitomized the spirit of cooperation: HMS *Fidelity*. Originally the cargo vessel *Le Rhin*, she was commandeered at Marseilles in June 1940 by a motley crew of French and Belgian dissidents along with other misfits of various nationalities. That the Royal Navy agreed to bring both the ship and her crew into the service was largely due to the tireless efforts of the captain, a Corsican French patriot who had changed his name from Jacques Peri to 'Jack Langlais' after the collapse of the Republic. *Fidelity* was fitted out and worked up, and returned to the Mediterranean in the spring of 1941 as a 'Q-ship', disguised as a merchant vessel, to engage in secret operations off the coasts of Spain and France. After one disastrous operation she was brought back to Britain and integrated into Western Approaches.

Patrick Whinney, assigned as a liaison officer to monitor *Fidelity*, recalled that his task was made no easier by the fact that 'no-one on board spoke English'. 'Langlais' was a fiery character, fiercely loyal to the Royal Navy, but seldom adhering to its formal codes of discipline. His temper led to indiscretions ranging from shouting abuse at subordinates to solving disagreements by way of his fists and, on one occasion, chaining a young officer to the ship's boiler for twenty-four hours as a punishment. If this was not enough to worry Admiralty officials, *Fidelity*'s second officer was female: a fearsome and feisty Parisienne born Madeleine Bayard, who had Anglicized her name to Barclay after the WRNS commissioned her. In addition to being an intelligence agent, she also happened to be the captain's lover.

Despite this most irregular management, few who came into contact with the ship or her sailors could fail to be charmed. Frank Layard, commanding the destroyer HMS *Firedrake*, visited *Fidelity* at

Liverpool in February 1942. 'They are a nice crowd,' he recorded in his diary. 'The Captain, who is a tremendous character I believe, was unfortunately not there. They reckon they belong to the British Navy and they are intensely anti Free French and every other sort of French. They have a live pig on board which they call "Admiral Darlan".' Such high spirits convinced the Admiralty to allow Langlais and his unconventional crew to participate in convoy duties, but the ship was to have a tragic fate. Helping to escort a convoy off the Azores in December 1942, *Fidelity* was the victim of a submarine's torpedo and was lost with all hands.

Fidelity was indeed the essence of the Battle of the Atlantic. Britain's survival depended on harnessing the collective efforts of millions of people in several continents. But in the summer of 1942, shipping losses reached their greatest extent, and the Atlantic remained in the balance. 'The war is passing through one of the most critical phases, probably more critical than it has been since the Battle of Britain,' wrote Midshipman Tom Dowling in his training journal at the start of August 1942. 'Supposing the U-boat is defeated, then we could win the war by building up an Army and Air Force in Britain superior to the whole German Army and making a frontal attack, or possibly through the south of Europe, but the German army would still have to be fought. Alternatively, big bombers might conceivably turn the scales. But both methods would take years . . . Defensive or Offensive we are powerless to continue if they keep up last month's sinkings.'

# 14. The Land of the Living

In September 1941, almost exactly a year after the bombing of HMS *Kent*, George Blundell again had to fight to save his ship. This time he was in HMS *Nelson*, escorting a convoy to Malta, when Italian torpedo-bombers attacked. 'They came right over our screen which seemed to have no deterrent effect on them,' he wrote in his diary. 'There was simply nothing we could do . . . there was that horrid underwater thud, the whole bow rose and quivered, and the ship shook like a mighty animal.' *Nelson* was vulnerable, but rapid repairs sustained the battleship long enough to reach Gibraltar. Blundell was upset by the damage to the ship, but devastated by one particular casualty: 'I feel heartbroken about my 101lb Cape Town cheese, husbanded all these months in the Cold Room, waiting for the day I go on leave.'

By late 1941, a fierce war of convoys had developed in the Mediterranean. Axis transports to North Africa, supplying and reinforcing the German and Italian troops fighting under Rommel, were under attack from British ships, aircraft and submarines. Meanwhile, the Allies' routes to Malta – eastwards from Gibraltar and north-west from Alexandria – had become ferociously contested. Escort groups of ever-increasing numbers and strength were required to protect the merchant ships carrying troops, aircraft, fuel and supplies to the besieged island, and the German and Italian dominance of the skies was beginning to take its toll. U-boats, sent through the Straits of Gibraltar at high risk, were also beginning to have an effect. 'A blur of action – eat when you can, sleep when you can, fight and die with as little fuss as possible,' was how Able Seaman George Gilroy, gunner in the destroyer HMS *Lightning*, characterized the campaign.

On 13 November, the aircraft carrier HMS *Ark Royal* – one of the most famous ships in the navy – finally succumbed to a torpedo from a German submarine, 150 miles east of Gibraltar. 'The explosion blew a great cloud of dust up from various hatchways,' wrote Charles Friend, a Fleet Air Arm observer who had flown against the *Bismarck*. 'As the dust cleared I saw Swordfish which had already been parked with their wings folded hopping down the list to starboard, their oleo legs flexing in and out, looking for all the world like giant grass-hoppers dancing.'

Surgeon Commander William Scott was on *Ark Royal's* quarter-deck with the captain's secretary, attempting to work out how to reach the destroyer *Legion*, which had come alongside to take men off the crippled carrier: 'I was given the answer by a young midshipman. He uncoiled a hose and threw the end of it down to the destroyer, over the gap of twenty feet or so. Holding on to this, he pulled him-self down backwards, keeping his balance with his hands. Without his example, I would never have believed that this balancing act was possible. To my surprise, I found that the hose held me securely by the groin, and I was never in any danger of overbalancing into the sea.'

After fourteen hours of desperate efforts by repair teams to keep the *Ark* afloat, the carrier capsized and sank early the following morning. Her sailors had often delighted in Lord Haw Haw's regular premature reports of the *Ark's* demise; her final end was a shock to the public almost as great as the loss of the *Hood*. Yet more destruc-tion was to follow in the Mediterranean within a matter of days.

On the afternoon of 25 November 1941 Lieutenant Commander Arthur Prideaux was on the bridge of the destroyer HMS *Decoy*, screening the battleships *Queen Elizabeth*, *Valiant* and *Barham* off Egypt, to the north of Sidi Barrani. With little warning, an explosion engulfed *Barham* in smoke and a column of water. Prideaux described the sight in his diary:

When smoke cleared she was already heeling over . . . and was just being abandoned when she blew up, disappearing in a towering cloud of brown smoke hundreds of feet high. When smoke cleared, after considerable time, there was no sign of *Barham*. Four destroyers went back to pick up survivors but we remained on the screen. The whole affair a most harrowing sight and everyone was very subdued at dinner in the wardroom, with Guns showing signs of slight 'bomb bewilderment'.

Three torpedoes fired by the German submarine U-331 had struck in quick succession, and *Barham*'s magazine had ignited, causing a devastating explosion which tore apart the battleship. Over 860 men were killed, but 450 were eventually rescued: an outcome seen by many of those who had witnessed the incident as a minor miracle.

At the start of December, Admiral Cunningham wrote to First Sea Lord Dudley Pound expressing his fears about further battleship losses: 'I must keep them rather in cotton wool as it won't do to get another put out of action.' Such concerns were only reinforced a week later, when *Prince of Wales* and *Repulse* were sunk off Malaya. But very soon British naval forces in the eastern Mediterranean would suffer yet more losses, this time in the space of only a few hours.

In the evening of 19 December 1941 Force K, a strong group of cruisers and destroyers based at Malta, was on its way to intercept a convoy resupplying Axis forces near Tripoli. It was a stormy night and the squadron strayed into a freshly laid Italian minefield with terrible consequences. HMS *Neptune*, at the front of the group, suffered debilitating damage from two mines. HMS *Kandahar* hit a mine which blew away her stern and killed seventy-three men. *Aurora* and *Penelope* were also hit but managed to escape the field, after Captain Rory O'Conor, commanding officer of *Neptune*, had signalled 'Keep Away'. 'It was a heartbreaking situation,' wrote Captain Angus Nicholl of *Penelope*. 'To leave a stricken ship without trying to save her or to rescue survivors runs against all the traditions of the Royal Navy and indeed against every instinct of a sailor.'

*Neptune*, meanwhile, hit a third and then a fourth mine, after which she capsized and sank quickly, taking nearly all 765 hands with her. One hundred and fifty were New Zealanders. Amongst those killed was eighteen-year-old Ordinary Seaman John Smith who, just a year earlier, had filled his diary with tales of coral isles and African villages.

A group of little more than thirty men managed to escape and congregate in and around a lifeboat, including Captain O'Conor. Several died shortly afterwards, the victims of their injuries and of the all-encompassing oil. One by one, the other survivors succumbed to the conditions. After several days had passed, only a handful remained. These included Norman Walton, a twenty-year-old able seaman who had spent three days swimming around the raft waiting for space to become available. Only four men remained on the fourth day. The captain died in Walton's arms.

The fifth day was Christmas Eve, by which time only one man, Price, remained alive with Walton. 'I saw an aircraft,' he recalled, 'waved to it and an hour later an Italian torpedo boat came alongside and threw me a line. I collapsed when I got on board and woke up on Christmas Day in a Tripoli hospital. They told me Price was dead.' Walton had a serious leg injury, was suffering from exposure and had been blinded by the smothering oil. 'Still,' he said, 'apart from my broken leg I was almost back to normal by New Year's Day, when I was put on a ship bound for Italy full of German and Italian troops going on leave.' He was taken to a prisoner-of-war camp, where he remained until the summer of 1943, when he was released as part of a prisoner exchange. After returning home and enjoying a few weeks of leave, he was reassigned and later served in a frigate on Russian convoys.

Only a matter of hours after *Neptune* had struck the first mine, Midshipman Tom Dowling was asleep aboard the battleship HMS *Queen Elizabeth*, berthed in Alexandria harbour. 'In the middle of the night,' he wrote in his journal, 'the commander broadcast that midget enemy submarines were supposed to have got into the harbour. This seemed like a dream. Later through the length of the night we heard smaller and greater explosions – which we accepted as being depth charges. The last and greatest explosion caused us junior midshipmen to jump out of our hammocks and run round in small circles.'

Two Italians had managed to infiltrate the harbour in single-man underwater craft, avoiding the anti-submarine defences, and had attached limpet mines to the hulls of *Queen Elizabeth* and *Valiant*.

Both were crippled. At first, it was feared that the attack might be only the first strike of a wider offensive. 'It may be the preliminary to a sea or air or both bombardment of Alexandria,' wrote Dowling. 'In any case it seems improbable that this move is not part of a plan: we must, I think, expect more.'

The sabotage in fact proved to be an isolated attack, but it caused considerable consternation. Extraordinary attempts were made to hide the extent of the damage from the enemy. *Queen Elizabeth* was refloated, righted and patched up in case reconnaissance aircraft passed overhead. Admiral Cunningham continued to use the ship as an administrative hub. It did little to alleviate the general anxiety. A few weeks later, Dowling described another casualty: 'Ordinary Seaman H. Smith lost his life while playing with his rifle on sentry duty on the pom-pom deck. It is thought that the shot ricocheted back.'

In early 1942, with no major battleships operational, precious little air cover, Malta's force of cruisers decimated, and no reinforcements available, the British position in the eastern Mediterranean was precarious. No risks could be taken until repairs were completed and replacements found. While the Japanese took Singapore and German battleships dashed through the English Channel, the Mediterranean Fleet did its best to avoid any further losses. Optimism was in short supply.

In March 1942, twenty-year-old Sub-Lieutenant John Carter was given a new posting. The former teenage merchant sailor had been promoted to junior officership, before spending several months in 1941 at Mersa Matruh, helping to supply Tobruk, and had since commanded a tug in Alexandria harbour. 'At last I am back where I wanted to be,' he wrote to his parents on 14 March after receiving his orders to report for duty aboard HMS *Kingston*. 'Yes, destroyers, and a beautiful ship too . . . it felt like coming home to be back on board again.' There was hot and cold running water, a 'luxurious' shared cabin and, most importantly, a chance to see some real action.

He did not have to wait long. On 22 March, *Kingston* was escorting convoy MW10 as it attempted to reach Malta. It was set upon by several Italian warships including the battleship *Littorio*, and the escort of small cruisers and destroyers led by Admiral Philip Vian mounted a vigorous defence in what became known as the Second Battle of Sirte.

Vian's tactics were to engage the enemy aggressively, and John Carter was in the thick of things. While undertaking a torpedo attack, *Kingston* was hit by a shell which passed through the bulkheads before exploding. The damage was serious, the ship dead in the water. The escort group managed to fend off the aggressors, but most ships were left short on ammunition and fuel, and returned to Alexandria. Others joined the merchant vessels continuing to Malta.

Despite the bold defence of the convoy, air attacks over the following days decimated the cargo ships in harbour, and the casualties included the precious oil tanker *Breconshire*. After repairs at sea, *Kingston* was also able to struggle on to Malta. But it was too late for John Carter. He had succumbed to grievous wounds sustained during the battle. Before joining the ship he had visited a shop in Alexandria with his girlfriend. 'I bought Schubert's "Unfinished Symphony" the other day in a fit of extravagance,' he had written to his parents in his exuberant last letter home. 'It is a most beautiful work – I do wish he had finished it.'

'Entering Malta,' wrote Midshipman Dowling, aboard HMS *Beaufort*, 'was [one] of the most pleasant experiences I have enjoyed for some time. In the first place it was far safer than the sea outside but the picturesqueness of the place and the sight of an entirely white population, and their cheers as we passed all added to the effect.' Yet the island was by no means a secure hideaway. The Malta blitz continued to bring death and devastation to locals and servicemen alike. Sailors mostly slept ashore, often in the large caves which served as bomb shelters. Even amid such an onslaught, the citizens of Malta continued to support and sustain the Royal Navy. The staff at the Union Club in Valletta and the Sliema Club worked hard to refresh officers. In the 'Gut' – the most notorious street in the Mediterranean – baser entertainments continued unabashed. Yet for the sailors of ships operating from the island, or of those vessels undergoing repairs in the dockyards, the heavy air raids continued to exact a considerable psychological toll.

For the small squadron based at Malta, there was little respite. The most famous ship of Force K was the cruiser HMS *Penelope*, already a veteran of several months in the eastern Mediterranean. Captain Angus Nicholl kept a close eye on the morale of his men during *Penelope*'s stay. He later attributed much to the maintenance of every-day amenities, including the daily tot and the hot food served from the ship's galleys. The messes were habitable, at least until the ward-room was damaged by a bomb. The lack of mail was a serious problem, but routine was kept up, the ship was frequently cleaned, and officers' rounds continued as normal. Groups of sailors were also sent away to a glorious sandy beach at the secluded cove of Ghajn Tuffieha, ten miles from Valletta in the north-west of Malta, to swim, picnic, and rest for a few days.

Nicholl recounted only two occasions on which individuals snapped. The first involved a stoker who had deserted his post for the sick bay during the Battle of Sirte. Following examination by the ship's medical officer, the man was sent back to the engine room, but returned soon. 'I asked the doctor for his opinion,' wrote Nicholl, 'and he said that the stoker was merely frightened.' Hauling the stoker into his office, Nicholl warned him that his family would suf-fer financially while he was incarcerated: 'Evidently your duty to your Country and your shipmates is not enough to overcome your fears but I hope that the thought of your wife and family will succeed in doing so.' The sentence would be suspended, the stoker was told, but any further transgression would result in it being enacted: 'Now, carry on with your job and think of your wife and children.'

The second incident involved a young rating who was part of a gun's crew, and had deserted his post during an air raid a few days later. 'He was a nice young man,' wrote Nicholl, 'and I knew that he had been at a famous public school before his call-up. I sentenced him to thirty days in the detention quarters on shore.' Before sending him away, Nicholl explained that the man's privileged background meant that it was 'impossible for me to show you leniency or to suspend your sentence' for fear of any suspicion of class favouritism.

As the Easter weekend approached, preparations were being made for *Penelope* to leave Malta for Gibraltar. On the same day as Japanese aircraft bombed Ceylon, Malta was subjected to its own devastating raids. Gun crews on *Penelope*'s upper decks had to be rotated, with sailors usually employed elsewhere taking turns at the trigger. Ammunition parties had to remain, along with fire fighters and first aiders, and a small group of officers. But by limiting the numbers defending the ship, Nicholl minimized casualties. Only one officer and three ratings were killed as a result of air raids, with thirty-four men injured. Meanwhile, dockyard workers and the ship's artisans worked around the clock on repairs, welding plates to the battered hull of the cruiser. A special air-raid siren warned them of incoming aircraft, and men often continued to hammer, drill and cut until the very last moment before haring for nearby shelters.

The voyage to Gibraltar would be perilous, and *Penelope*'s guns were nearly worn out. Black patches were painted on the upper decks in an attempt to fool reconnaissance aircraft into overestimating the damage. An Italian flag was found to use in an emergency. Wounded men were left behind. Then on 8 April, the day the cruiser was due to depart, seven air raids caused huge damage. Nicholl was injured. The gunnery officer was killed when one of his own worn-out guns blew up. The ship ran out of ammunition. An appeal had to be made by loudspeaker across the dockyards for assistance in bringing aboard more shells. Sailors from other ships, soldiers from the shore garrison, dockyard officials and civilian workers all helped to shift the munitions as quickly as possible and before long *Penelope* was steaming out of the harbour. It was a hair-raising voyage back to Gibraltar, under attack from torpedoes and high-level bombing, but *Penelope* managed to survive to widespread public acclaim. It was found that the ship's cat had given birth to three kittens, which the sailors named Bomb, Blitz and Blast.

In Gibraltar, Midshipman J. B. T. Davies of the battlecruiser HMS *Renown* observed the new arrival. 'In the next dock to ourselves was *Penelope*,' he wrote in his journal. 'She was greatly smashed about, but she looked far worse than she really was. A near miss . . . has filled her hull abreast of the bridge full of small holes and dents.' *Penelope* became famous, due in no small part to photographs which showed the state of the hull and amply illustrated why the sailors had nicknamed her 'HMS *Pepperpot*'.

Malta was not only a base for surface ships. It was also the hub for the 10th Submarine Flotilla, from which boats operated across the Mediterranean. Just as enemy U-boats threatened Allied convoys, British submarines attacked and disrupted Axis supply lines to North Africa. Over the course of the Mediterranean campaign, British submarines sank over 280 enemy vessels, equating to more than a million tons of shipping. As they returned to harbour, submarines would fly a skull-and-crossbones flag, with symbols denoting their victims. Yet despite such bravura this was an exhausting and terrifying business, and extremely dangerous. A total of forty-five boats would be lost in the Mediterranean by the end of the war.

The most celebrated was HMS *Upholder*, commanded by Lieutenant Commander Malcolm Wanklyn. He was awarded the Victoria Cross in 1941 for sinking the 18,000-ton liner *Conte Rosso*, loaded with Italian troops, after dodging destroyers and surviving a two-hour hunt and dozens of depth-charge attacks. Soon after *Penelope*'s departure in April 1942, *Upholder* was reported missing and never returned.

Submarines also played a vital role in supplying Malta. Joe Brighton, chief petty officer and torpedo specialist, served in HMS *Porpoise*, which carried out supply runs between Alexandria, Haifa and Malta as well as laying mines and attacking Italian convoys. The boat was always full of mailbags, stuffed in every conceivable receptacle, and ferried all manner of precious military and civilian stores. It was a dangerous task and coming under attack from depth charges was a harrowing experience, as Brighton recalled:

> The poor old girl lurched and bounced. The depth gauges and the hydrophone listening gear went out of action and the main port motor blew its fuses. The torpedo hatch in the fore-ends was taking in water . . . Gauge glasses shattered. The whole structure of the boat was under terrific strain. Such structural strain transmits itself to the human body almost as an electric shock, causing the same kind of vibration.

In the spring of 1941, Lieutenant Godfrey Darling had been in Lazaretto waiting to take the reins of his new command. He sent a letter to his parents on 25 March expressing his delight at taking control of the submarine HMS *Usk*. 'I am very pleased,' he wrote. 'As you know I have been aching to get into the fight, as victory may mean a new and better world.' To emphasize the point, he quoted T. E. Lawrence:

'We were wrought up with ideas inexpressible and vaporous but to be fought for. We lived many lives in those whirling campaigns, never sparing ourselves good or evil. Yet when we achieved and the new world dawned, the old men came out again and took from us our victory and made it in the likeness of the former world they knew.'

Darling finished by explaining to his mother and father that, in the event of his capture by the enemy, he would use a coded letter to inform them and the Admiralty of his fate. The opening 'My dearest Mother & Daddy', for instance, would mean that the submarine's confidential books and ASDIC had been destroyed. Signing off 'Best love, Godfrey' would mean that the boat had been sunk by depth charges. 'Love, Godfrey' would mean that the boat had been sunk by a mine. *Usk* sailed on 19 April for a patrol off the north-west coast of Sicily. She was reported missing on 3 May 1941 and was never seen again.

The clear waters and unpredictable currents of the Mediterranean meant that while submarines were able to sink thousands of tons of supply shipping and enemy warships, life for the submariners of every country was fraught with peril. Clifford Simkin served in the engine room of the sloop HMS *Flamingo*, and later described his own feelings on the underwater enemy:

The mental reaction experienced by each and every one involved in the attacking and sinking of a submarine must vary from man to man, and it must be remembered you cannot see the submarine (unless it is on the surface). You only have a mental picture of her and the various movements and actions her crew will take. My reaction I can describe because it was always the same. When the attack started I would become aware of my heart-beat, it would be heavy but normal rate, then when we increase speed, the prelude to dropping depth charges,

my heart would increase speed until it raced with mad excitement.
Then when it was all over I felt a certain amount of remorse and I
would always have the same thoughts, 'Some of the poor bastards
were probably better citizens than I will ever be'.

The Atlantic was defined by the struggle with the U-boats but in
the Mediterranean, air attack was just as often the predominant concern. Enemy pilots were viewed with a mixture of hate and curiosity.
In late April 1942, HMS *Beaufort* was sailing from Tobruk to Alexandria with a convoy when a German reconnaissance plane was shot
down by a Hurricane overhead. The destroyer picked up the para-
chutist who had baled out. Midshipman Tom Dowling reported that:

> I could not see him myself as everyone in the crew was lining the side,
> some shouting wisecracks. There was much difference of opinion as
> to how to treat him . . . He is to be treated as a social outcast; and is
> not to be given any luxuries but is to be kept locked up, only the
> interpreter and interrogator being allowed to speak to him. He was
> put in the bathroom as soon as we got him onboard and he there
> changed into survivor's kit. Without his spectacles and flying kit he
> looked ten years younger, quite a normal young man in fact . . . he
> insisted he had never been on a bombing raid . . . and was apparently
> quite scared of us taking reprisals there and then.

Geoff Dormer was first lieutenant of the minesweeper *Hornpipe*
when, off the North African coast, an Italian torpedo-bomber
crashed after clipping its wing in the sea attempting to bank. After
the wreckage had been brought aboard, wrote Dormer in his diary,
'we inspected, with mixed emotions, the remains of the fellow who
had so nearly got US. A little dark chap, somewhat bruised and battered. I wonder who he was? Then we had a booze-up, to celebrate.'

For the civilians of Malta, the aerial torment continued. By the
summer of 1942 the island was in desperate need. It had been subjected to a sustained bombardment of scarcely imaginable proportions.
Twice the tonnage of bombs was dropped on Malta in March and
April 1942 than fell on London during the entire period of the Blitz.

Fuel and ammunition were running low. Spare parts for the small squadron of Spitfires based on the island were needed. Food was becoming scarce and civilians were on draconian rations.

Malta was a precious stronghold because it remained the Allies' last bastion in the Mediterranean Sea and was a vital base from which the supply lines to North Africa could be threatened. But it also had a symbolic value which drove efforts to maintain its supplies. For the Royal Navy, the defence of Malta was a matter of pride. For the crews of merchant ships, meanwhile, the Malta run was a terrifying prospect. They knew that enemy aircraft and submarines would be targeting their vessels above all others and, particularly for those working around huge quantities of ammunition or fuel oil, the stakes could not have been higher.

In June 1942, a two-pronged convoy run attempted to reinforce the island. One group was sent from Gibraltar, designated Operation Harpoon, and another travelled from Alexandria, called Operation Vigorous. The Harpoon convoy soon came under heavy attack from aircraft and Italian warships, causing serious damage to several of the British escort vessels. Only two of the six merchant ships from Gibraltar made it to Malta. After leaving Alexandria, the Vigorous convoy fared even worse, and was forced to turn back by the Italian fleet and heavy air attacks. Midshipman Dowling of the destroyer HMS *Beaufort* witnessed the torpedoing of HMS *Hermione* in the middle of the night:

> The flash shot about 600 ft into the air, dwarfing the cruiser . . . We immediately swept outwards dropping charges every five minutes but obtained no contact, so we returned to where the cruiser had been. The final sinking must have been extremely quick . . . there were so many navy calcium floats, and yet there was a lot of yelling to start with. It was the most tragic noise I have ever heard and more high pitched than one would expect but it died down as we got into the midst of them.

The Allied campaign in North Africa was reaching a moment of crisis. The campaigns in the desert had gone back and forth since

1940, and sailors had played a key role in supplying Tobruk from the base of Mersa Matruh and from Alexandria. Billeted alongside the soldiers, they were frequently ungrateful guests at the army's table. 'Just one grouse,' wrote Petty Officer Wesley Barker at Mersa Matruh, 'the food is P.B.A. [Pretty Bloody Average] as we are under the Army for victualling, but we do get our spirit issue, thank heavens'.

Tobruk was by now a devastated city. Midshipman Dowling had recently visited. 'I walked round the town and found it extremely interesting,' he wrote in his journal. 'The only buildings with stair-cases are the buildings along the front, a hotel or two and administrative buildings . . . Every building was damaged almost without exception; there was not a pane of glass remaining. The church was almost intact but was out of bounds as the roof may come down.'

Rommel's forces attacked again at the end of May 1942, and as Harpoon struggled towards Malta, the Battle of Gazala was going badly. Wesley Barker was amongst those preparing to withdraw from Mersa Matruh. 'Have started to lay my demolitions in the docks, piers and lighters,' he wrote, 'and am using depth charges for the purpose so there will be some sweet bangs when the time arrives.' By 10 June, he was unstrapping dead gunners from motor torpedo boats returning from the front line.

Tobruk fell on 21 June 1942, and British and Commonwealth forces had to fight hard to halt the Axis advance in July. Cairo was thrown into a state of panic. Evacuation was already underway at Alexandria. The naval base was temporarily abandoned, and signs were erected warning that the punishment for looting was death. Elsewhere around the city, swastikas could be seen hanging from windows. Some ships were withdrawn to Port Said; others went to Haifa in Palestine. 'Such a lovely place,' wrote Wilf Morris of HMS *Zulu* in a letter home. 'It's very expensive, but even so I prefer it to any place in Egypt. From here I have been able to visit such places as Nazareth, Samaria and Jerusalem. Jerusalem is a fine place, altogether different from what I expected. It's a real modern city that's very interesting to visit.'

With Allied naval forces pushed back all the way to Suez and Palestine, Malta was in an even more desperate situation. Sending supplies from Alexandria was now impossible. So, at the start of August, a new plan was formed for a convoy from Gibraltar. It would include a squadron of Spitfires, all manner of civilian and military stores and, crucially, fuel. Denys Barton had been sent to Greenock to join the tanker *Ohio*, American-owned and recently requisitioned by the British, as a naval liaison officer advising the ship's master during the voyage. 'We weren't told where we were going,' he wrote to his mother soon afterwards, 'but when I got there and saw a loaded tanker – obviously a fast ship and with a lot of extra guns – it was pretty obvious to me where we were off to!'

This latest attempt to resupply Malta would be the most dangerous to date. Several escort ships were brought to the Mediterranean directly from the Arctic to assist, including Richard Walker's HMS *Ledbury* and Charles Hutchinson's HMS *Intrepid*. For the destroyer men, remorse over the fate of convoy PQ17 merely strengthened their desire to protect the vulnerable merchant sailors. It was proposed that the tanker *Ohio*, along with thirteen other merchant vessels, would proceed from Gibraltar with a strong escort. At the end of the second day, the merchant ships would pass through the dangerous Skerki Channel, between Sicily and North Africa, with only a small force of cruisers and destroyers for protection. It was too great a risk to send capital ships all the way. Lieutenant Commander George Blundell, executive officer in the battleship HMS *Nelson*, described the scheme in his diary: 'I read the orders for the operation which is called "Pedestal", or for short "Ped". It makes me sweat reading the bit about the poor convoy getting through the last bit. Otherwise it is just one of our usual club runs through the Med., leaving the poor blighters at the Skerki Channel.'

Initially, at least, the escort would be immense. 'The biggest that has ever escorted a convoy,' wrote Denys Barton, 'two battleships, three aircraft-carriers, a large number of cruisers and a whole swarm of destroyers.' As *Nelson* took her station in preparation to begin the passage from Gibraltar, George Blundell was confident. 'We looked quite a formidable force today,' he wrote. When the ship's chaplain suggested a communal prayer before the convoy sailed, Blundell was less impressed: 'Our new parson is as wet as a flat fish. He wanted to broadcast a service before the Battle. I can't imagine anything more calculated to remind the troops of death!'

'We left Gib early Monday morning,' wrote Able Seaman Alan Gould of the destroyer HMS *Lightning*. He was keeping a daily diary of his experiences, addressed to his wife: 'I'm not very happy darling as things have started a lot too soon this time. We have been at action stations since one this afternoon when we had a concentrated attack by submarines. It was B. awful.' There had already been an early casualty. A German submarine had torpedoed the aircraft carrier HMS *Eagle* early in the morning of 11 August. 'I saw it go,' wrote Gould. 'She just rolled on her side and disappeared. What an awful feeling it gives you in the pit of your stomach. Torpedoes and subs were bobbing up all around. We stand a much better chance in a destroyer but that doesn't stop you from being frightened.'

'She was struck by four torpedoes,' wrote Graham Lumsden of the cruiser HMS *Phoebe*, 'and presented a terrible sight as she heeled over, turned bottom up and sank with horrible speed. Men and aircraft could be seen falling off her flight deck as she capsized.' George Blundell had been watching from the bridge of *Nelson*. 'One moment there was a serene blue sea with peaceful ships and hardly a cloud in the sky,' he wrote in his diary, 'next moment there were some billows of smoke from *Eagle* . . . and she had gone in eight minutes. I've never before seen such a thing. It makes one tremble.'

Although the death toll was less than first feared – more than 900 of the 1,160 on board were eventually rescued – the sinking deprived the convoy of some of its desperately needed fighter cover, and was a severe psychological blow. In HMS *Lightning*, Alan Gould decided to take some precautions. 'I've got my wallet in my pocket with £4.15 and a door key in,' he noted. 'Also I carry this pen around with me; of course I always wear my watch.' In *Nelson*, Blundell was planning to address the ship's company to bolster morale but, he wrote, 'It was not to be, for at 20.30 we sounded off, "Alarm to Arms", followed by the alarm rattlers.'

As the light faded at the end of the first day, the guns of the warships produced a sheet of fire. 'Did we put up a barrage or did we,' wrote Gould. 'Talk about blitz over London. The sky was black all over the convoy. I think our fighters broke them up before they got in.' Denys Barton, on the bridge of the tanker *Ohio*, was impressed: 'I have never seen anything so colossal as the barrage the ships put up – it really seemed impossible that planes could come through it and get away.' George Blundell described the attack as

> two of the most exciting hours in my life. Bombs fell all over the
> place . . . the barrage put up by the fleet and its screen was aesthet-
> ically one of the weirdest and most wonderful and beautiful I have
> ever seen . . . It was the purple sea, the black sky, and the Red in the
> West, and the pearls and rubies of the tracer necklaces, lurid bursts in
> the sky, and the dark little ships putting up this miracle display . . .
> People who had seen it all had a look on their faces as if they'd seen a
> vision – the sort of look a man would have on his face just after he'd
> looked on the Almighty.

The following day brought little respite. 'I'm just about all in,' wrote Alan Gould late on 12 August. 'They gave us twelve hours of it today. I've had no dinner, tea or supper – I'm sure glad to be alive sweet.'

Torpedo-bombers attacked in waves, followed by dive-bombers and planes equipped with armour-piercing explosives. Sea Hurricanes, Fulmars and Martlets engaged them. As the afternoon progressed, submarines were fought off by destroyers. One Italian submarine was rammed. In the early evening, another wave of bombers attacked. 'It was a beautiful day but just hazy,' wrote Gould, 'so they flew very low and you just couldn't see them till they were on top of you.' The aircraft carrier *Indomitable* was hit by three bombs but emerged from the smoke with guns still firing, before later being forced to withdraw.

At the appointed time, the main part of the escort, including Gould's HMS *Lightning* and Blundell's HMS *Nelson*, turned back for Gibraltar, leaving the merchant ships with an escort of just four cruisers and twelve destroyers. Gould made a final entry in his diary for his wife:

I'm writing this at action stations as we are remaining at them all
night. What I would like is a nice bath and go to bed! Our ammo is
very low, we could just about stand four or five attacks but no more.
The state of our guns are bad, one of the 4" HA is useless worn out
and the left gun of 'A' turret is worn out also, it could almost take a 5"
shell now. My eyes are very sore darling so I'll say goodnight to you
my precious.

As the convoy entered the Skerki Channel there was barely an
hour of peace before another devastating attack. At almost the same
instant, Italian torpedoes struck the cruiser flagship *Nigeria* and blew
the stern off the cruiser *Cairo*. 'I saw great bits flying about 400 yards,'
wrote Denys Barton on the bridge of the tanker *Ohio*. 'And then
while we were still looking at *Cairo*, there was a tremendous sheet of
flame just abaft our bridge – and we too had been torpedoed.'

A huge petrol fire roared from the tanker, the flames fifty feet high.
Preparations were made to abandon ship, but sailors managed to
bring the fire under control with the aid of seawater and chemical
extinguishers. 'There was a big hole in the side where the torpedo hit
us,' wrote Barton, 'and it had also torn up the deck nearly halfway
across the ship, the engines had stopped but otherwise there wasn't
very much wrong, so the engineers set about getting the engines
going again.'

As they made the repairs, the rest of the convoy continued, increasingly disorganized. Those on the upper deck of *Ohio* could see attacks
from the air on the horizon and the red and white flashes of tracer
shell careering across the sky. Two merchant ships were sunk and
others were damaged. E-boats armed with torpedoes sped towards
the convoy from hiding places along the Tunisian coast. The cruiser
*Manchester* suffered a crippling blow, and four straggling cargo ships
were sunk.

*Ohio*'s compass had been rendered useless, but steering had been
salvaged, albeit from a makeshift position. 'A destroyer came up and
told us to follow him,' explained Denys Barton, 'which was much
better as our navigation would have been pretty hit or miss and we
knew there were minefields all over the place.' Aided by a pale blue

light from HMS *Ledbury*, the tanker gradually caught up with the convoy the following morning, 13 August, but still the dive-bombers came. One was shot down and crashed into *Ohio*'s deck. 'It didn't do any damage,' wrote Barton, 'but bits of it were all over the ship.'

Nearby, the merchant ship *Waimarama* was hit by bombs which ignited ammunition and petrol below decks, causing an enormous explosion. 'I think that was one of the grimmest things I have ever seen,' wrote Barton. Charles Hutchinson felt the same way. 'It was the most terrible sight I've seen so far,' he wrote in his diary. 'There was an indescribable flash and the ship blew to atoms . . . Although no one on board would know anything about it, it was a terrible sight, made me feel sick. Gosh, I could hardly keep my legs from knocking together.'

'She appeared to go up in a great sheet of flame followed by a huge pall of smoke,' wrote Anthony Hollings, first lieutenant of the destroyer HMS *Ledbury*, all of a mile away. 'We could feel the heat of the flames and did not imagine anyone could live through it.' Following close behind, *Melbourne Star* could not avoid the blaze and passed through the flames. Men on her open deck leapt for their lives into the sea. *Ledbury* moved to rescue survivors, but only eighteen men were brought on board from *Waimarama*, along with twenty-four who had leapt from *Melbourne Star*.

Later in the morning, near misses from another bombing raid finally crippled *Ohio*'s engines. 'So we were in rather a plight,' wrote Denys Barton, 'as we now had no power or light in the ship, we couldn't even steer, and we were 100 miles from Malta.' Meanwhile, in the early evening of 13 August, three merchant ships – *Port Chalmers*, *Melbourne Star* and *Rochester Castle* – entered Valletta's Grand Harbour, to be joined later by *Brisbane Star*, and began disgorging their 32,000 tons of food and supplies.

*Ohio* languished off Malta along with *Dorset*, another disabled merchant ship, until brought in tow by the destroyer *Penn* and pulled onwards. Another bombing raid sank *Dorset* and hit *Ohio* once more. 'We all thought she was going to sink then and so abandoned ship in the lifeboats,' wrote Barton, but the bedraggled tanker merely settled even lower in the water and struggled on. Early on the following day, 14 August, a destroyer was lashed on either side and a skeleton crew went on board. As *Ohio* was dragged towards Malta, Barton was in a motor launch. 'I couldn't do any more liaison work with a destroyer each side in charge,' he wrote, 'and anyway it wasn't a very healthy prospect.'

It was not until the morning of 15 August that the battered hulk of *Ohio*, barely afloat but still carrying her precious cargo, was finally dragged into Grand Harbour, guided by a flotilla of tugs and mine-sweepers. It was a national holiday, the Feast of Santa Marija, and crowds lined the docks and the ramparts of the ancient fortifications. Bands played both the British and American anthems. As the wreck was secured, huge pipes were attached and the process of pumping out the 10,000 tons of fuel began. Some young Maltese children were heard to shout 'We want food, not oil!'

'What a tragic failure the convoy has been!' wrote George Blun-dell of HMS *Nelson*, back in Gibraltar. 'Nine ships out of the fourteen lost and great damage and loss to warships . . . The convoy and their light forces escort going through the Skerki Channel had a terrible time, submarines doing most of the damage. *Cairo* was sunk, *Manchester* got sunk, *Nigeria* and *Kenya* were torpedoed and 8 of the merchant ships were destroyed. Only *Port Chalmers*, *Brisbane Star*, *Melbourne Star*, *Rochester Castle* and *Ohio*, though torpedoed, got into Malta. What a price to pay!'

The price was indeed great, but the arrival of the merchant ships proved vital to the survival of Malta. Operation Pedestal came to be seen as one of the greatest achievements of the naval war. *Ohio* served to epitomize the sacrifices and courage of the merchant sailors, ultimately responsible for delivering their precious cargo. She was saved by the Herculean efforts of an international group of gunners and crewmen who re-boarded the tanker when all seemed lost, Spit-fire pilots from Malta and Fleet Air Arm fliers who fended off air attacks, the men of the destroyers which were lashed alongside for the final push, the Malta tugs and minesweepers which helped to drag her into Grand Harbour, and her merchant crew led by Captain Dudley William Mason, who was duly rewarded with the George Cross.

None of those who took part in Pedestal would ever forget it, including Charles Hutchinson:

It's a grand feeling to be still in the land of the living. I found that the worst thing of all is the waiting for what you think will be a certain hit, and watching everything around you go up, and wondering who will be next on the list. But when actually in action firing, you forget it all, and just crack away. I know at times I felt rotten, but it was soon over when there was anything to do, in fact when we were in local firing and I was laying on one of the torpedo planes and firing the gun myself, I didn't worry two hoots what else was coming at us, I was enjoying myself.

Desmond Dickens was an apprentice in the merchant ship *Dorset*, sunk just before she reached Malta. A few months later he attempted to express his feelings about the ordeal. Addressing an imagined readership amongst British public, he wrote:

Imagine to yourselves what we felt like sitting on top of aviation spirit, which even one spark from a cigarette would light in a flash. Think too what _we_ feel like when we come home and see the wicked waste of petrol which goes on today and that some petrol may have come by the very blood of sailors – this is no idle thought; it is stark reality.

Pedestal did not mark the end of Malta's trials, but by the autumn of 1942 the defence of the island was more adequately assured. It continued to come under air attack, and convoys remained a difficult proposition, but the island's role gradually changed from a bastion in enemy territory into a launch-pad for offensive operations. The defence and supply of Malta between the summer of 1940 and the end of 1943 cost the lives of some 1,600 civilians and 700 soldiers on the island itself and 900 RAF personnel along with over 700 aircraft. Two hundred merchant sailors were killed. Amongst the Royal Navy's losses in defence of Malta were one battleship, two aircraft carriers, four cruisers, thirteen destroyers and minesweepers, and forty submarines. A total of 2,200 warship sailors and 1,700 submariners lost their lives.

★

In North Africa, with the Axis advance halted, the Allies were preparing their own offensives. On 14 September 1942 British ships took part in a raid on Tobruk, now held by German and Italian forces, called Operation Agreement. Royal Marines and soldiers were landed from the destroyers *Sikh* and *Zulu*, which then covered their assault. Unfortunately, they disembarked on the wrong beach, directed by pathfinders who had themselves lost their way. German resistance was stern, and of the 400 Royal Marines who began the assault, 300 were killed, wounded or captured. Another 150 Allied soldiers were also lost but, in contrast, only sixteen defenders were killed. As the ships attempted to withdraw, they came under heavy fire from shore batteries.

'We landed the troops and then the fun started,' wrote Wilf Morris of HMS *Zulu* in a letter home. 'I felt sure that Jerry knew that we were coming, thanks to the Fifth Columnists. It wasn't long before they scored a direct hit on our sister ship, the *Sikh*. They had put her steering out of commission and so she was helpless. We made our way to her and attempted to get a tow-line across to her. All the while this was going on we were being pounded by the coastal guns. We had been hit twice and shrapnel was falling like rain and causing a lot of casualties.' The attempts to bring *Sikh* in tow failed, and *Zulu* was finally ordered to withdraw. 'So we started to retire,' wrote Morris. 'It was a sad sight to see our chaps on the *Sikh*, unable to move, a standing target, and yet she was still blazing away with all guns.' *Zulu*'s captain sent a signal to the stricken *Sikh*: 'Sorry to leave you. Good luck. Goodbye, and God Bless You All.'

Meanwhile, the escorting cruiser HMS *Coventry* had suffered critical damage from air attack and had to be scuttled by *Zulu*. On her way back to Alexandria, overloaded with rescued sailors, *Zulu* was attacked from the air near Mersa Matruh. 'The strain was beginning to tell on us all,' wrote Morris. Finally, a bomb struck the engine room, the ship was rendered helpless, and the sailors were transferred onto a rescue ship.

In total, more than 700 men had been killed in the disastrous operation and many more wounded or taken prisoner. One of the sailors aboard HMS *Sikh* was John Evans, who had witnessed the Japanese attacks on China from a Yangtze gunboat before the war. He survived the sinking, but was captured and became a prisoner of war in the Italian camp PG51. He wrote to his wife in November 1942:

> I am quite well although not as fit as usual due mainly to the lack of food – the B.R.C. [British Red Cross] keep us alive with their most welcome parcels. We are still living in tents although the weather is extremely cold and damp. We expect to be home in about 6 months time, the sooner the better. I'm looking forward to those eggs and bacon and roast beef, potatoes etc. and apple pudding!! I have not yet received a letter from you but live in hopes of one any day now.

His was a relatively quiet incarceration, although not without its hardships, and he was released six months later, in March 1943, as part of a prisoner exchange. Back in British hands, he wrote to his wife: 'This is the most wonderful day of our lives! At 1030 this morning I was set free from P.O.W. life, from starvation, filth and misery. I have now had a decent bath, a clean change of clothes, eaten like a civilized being and am looking forward to sleeping in a nice clean bed tonight!'

Only a matter of weeks after the debacle of Operation Agreement, a British-led offensive began at El Alamein in the Western Desert under the direction of Lieutenant General Bernard Montgomery. Sailors were also expecting action. On the day before the Alamein offensive began, Midshipman John Roberts commented in his journal that something seemed to be afoot:

> There is a certain amount of tenseness in the air at the moment as a result of all the bombardment practice which *Rodney*, *Nelson* and ourselves have been doing; Dakar is the most popular answer. Certainly, French North Africa has been 'in the news' lately, and any form of second, or more correctly fifth, front would have a terrific effect on the morale of the United Nations.

A week later, Montgomery's forces had broken through the Axis lines and were pushing onwards towards a decisive victory.

Meanwhile, on the morning of 6 November 1942, HMS *Renown* was sailing along the North African coast escorting a task force which was to land Allied forces in Operation Torch. The main objectives of the landings were Casablanca, Oran and Algiers, and resistance from the Vichy French defenders was not expected to be strong. Casablanca was the responsibility of the American Western Task Force, bringing soldiers directly across the Atlantic into French Morocco. The Algerian coast was the responsibility of two combined British and American task forces. Lieutenant M. Freer Roger, a soldier in the Argyll and Sutherland Highlanders, described the approach to the Mediterranean from the deck of a troopship: 'We passed through the Straits at midnight. The lights of Tangiers twinkling close on the starboard beam, and the little Moorish Felukkas could be seen dodging in and out of the convoy in the starlight. Next day we sailed close to the Spanish coast, the snows of the Sierra Nevada sparkling white in the sunshine.'

Within a matter of days, Operation Torch was successfully completed. It was a boost for the naval planners who were still developing the art of mass amphibious landings. 'I've never had to deal with so many ships before,' wrote Commander Manley Power, one of the British officers responsible for designing the offensive. 'It must have run to nearly a thousand all told I should think.' He was also happy with the new American commander-in-chief who was overseeing the campaign: 'Eisenhower is a decent old boy and easy to get on with.'

Power might have been pleased with the results, but the operation itself was far from perfect. The landings were occasionally chaotic – disembarkation points were missed, sandbanks were hit, timings went awry – and some soldiers and sailors met unexpectedly stern resistance from elements of the Vichy French forces. By far the most difficult task proved to be the direct assaults on Oran and Algiers, undertaken by Royal Navy ships flying American flags in a half-hearted attempt to diminish anti-British sentiment amongst the defenders.

At Oran, a plan had been devised to capture the port intact before the Vichy defenders were able to respond. HMS *Walney* and

HMS *Hartland*, former cutters of the US Coastguard, were to land soldiers inside the harbour who would rapidly secure strategic points. It was a risky tactic which proved costly. Shore guns and French ships guided by searchlights ruthlessly targeted the small vessels, reducing them to burning wrecks and causing severe casualties.

Petty Officer C. C. Young was in HMS *Hartland*. The cutter sustained a casualty rate of over 50 per cent: more than thirty were killed and a hundred wounded. All those who made it ashore were captured. As the ship was being abandoned amid gunfire and shelling, Young rowed a lifeboat and rescued wounded men from the water. 'In those moments of hot action,' he recalled, 'all fear was gone, only the impulse to do your best and help the others.' Of the 400 men assaulting Oran, 183 were killed, with a further 157 wounded and subsequently taken prisoner. Of the dead, 113 were from the Royal Navy. The garrison surrendered to Allied land forces only a few days later, but not before the harbour had been wrecked.

A similar assault was attempted at Algiers. Lieutenant Commander Frank Layard was in command of the destroyer HMS *Broke*, flying an American flag with US troops on board ready to seize the port before it could be sabotaged. It was another costly endeavour. Commandos went ashore in the wrong place, and failed to capture shore batteries which then turned their fire on *Broke* and her accompanying destroyer HMS *Malcolm*. When the latter was forced to fall back, it was left to Layard to push on, smash *Broke* through the boom and enter the harbour.

Frank Layard had worried about his capacities since the outbreak of war. 'I don't think I'm nearly brave enough,' he had written in his diary before the sinking of the *Rawalpindi*. Yet escorting convoys he had shown himself to be more than capable, and at Algiers he proved himself wrong once again. *Broke* entered the harbour to what he described as 'not much more than machine gun opposition' and 'desultory sniping'. All the ship's Oerlikon guns were blazing – 'God knows what at' – and the American troops had to be shooed ashore. Layard was far from impressed by his American contingent:

I was furious and disgusted. The sailors were all a bit worked up and it was difficult to stop them firing at absolutely nothing. I thought there was rather an unnecessary tendency to fall flat every time a rifle went off. I was delighted to find I didn't want to [take cover] myself. I was simply overjoyed at finding I was able under fire to at least conceal any feelings of fright but of course with so much to do and think about it was comparatively easy not to be windy.

The soldiers eventually captured the power station and several other strategic points, but by then *Broke* had come under heavy fire for several hours from inland artillery. Layard was eventually forced to take the destroyer back out to sea, where she promptly sank while under tow.

Once the Torch landings were complete, there was a campaign to be fought. Continued supply was critical. For many of the sailors responsible for transporting men, equipment, munitions and victuals to the armies, the logistical task was tough. 'Life doesn't get much easier,' wrote Manley Power to his wife later in November. 'This is a big show and isn't all over with the shouting. Our part is not spectacular and anyhow we discourage the press. But the importance you can realise when I tell you we have delivered over two million tons of shipping to North Africa and <u>without loss</u>. I think we can claim a big success and it will lead to great things as long as that mercurial P.M. of ours doesn't get restless and start some new enterprise elsewhere before we have cleaned up this one. I mistrust that man profoundly.'

The Vichy French navy had troubled the British only occasionally since 1940: bombarding Gibraltar briefly on one occasion, and causing some anxiety in the eastern Mediterranean off the Syrian coast. Yet even during Torch it had remained mostly in port in southern France. 'On the news this evening it was announced that the Germans have broken their promise to keep out of Toulon, and as a result the French fleet there is scuttling itself,' wrote Midshipman John Roberts in his journal on 27 November. 'The most vivid stories have been coming through about how one after another, all the battleships and cruisers blew themselves up, the French sailors fighting the Germans until the destruction was complete.' It was a poignant coda for Britain's first ally.

It took some time for the Allies to rectify the damage done to the North African ports. After visiting Mers-el-Kébir, Midshipman Davies of *Renown* described its condition in his journal: 'Very little to entice the prospective shopper or even sightseer. The population are friendly and very hungry. There is an abundance of filth of every description, picked out here or there by a neat whitewashed house built after the Moorish style. No, M.E.K. will not make a good impression upon the horde of empire builders who will descend upon N. Africa after the war.'

As the Allied imperialists continued to arrive in the early months of 1943, there were mounting problems of discipline, mail and morale. Censorship reports revealed widespread discontent amongst British personnel. Letters were not being delivered, conditions were poor, work was hard. Worst of all, the Americans appeared to be installed in the best hotels, spending their generous wages at will, and receiving the adulation of the British newspapers. 'They never seem to do any work,' wrote one man in a censored letter. 'You can see our Tommies tramping about with all their kit while the blasted Yanks ride around all day in cars and when the war is over I expect they'll say they've won it again.'

In March, Midshipman John Roberts contemplated the problem of inebriated and belligerent soldiers and sailors ashore at Algiers. 'A few nights ago there was a large-scale fight between some of the Black Watch and a crowd of Americans,' he wrote. 'Several people were hurt on both sides, they had to go to hospital and consequently twenty or thirty able men were unnecessarily out of action; and about a hundred and fifty men probably have a grudge. Well, if this sort of thing goes on every night, it is bound to affect our much advertised "war effort".' Roberts had his own way of dealing with the Americans: 'I find that as long as you take their boasts about winning the war with a pinch of salt, they are extremely nice indeed.'

At sea, the Mediterranean continued to be a battleground. Able Seaman George Gilroy served as a gunner in the destroyer HMS *Lightning*. In February and March 1943 the ship was on escort duty by day and attacking enemy convoys by night. 'We were at action stations almost constantly and rarely got any sleep,' he recalled. 'This was the lowest ebb of my life.' Long hours were spent at action stations. Food supplies were limited. Gilroy had a gum infection and lost some teeth: 'We did not realise it at the time but we were gradually getting physically and mentally worn out.' One night off the Algerian coast *Lightning* was struck by a torpedo fired by an enemy E-boat and sank within ten minutes. Forty-five men were lost, but 183 managed to survive. After they had been rescued, the survivors were each given a pre-prepared airmail letter to send home stating merely that they had been transferred to HMS *Hannibal*. They were taken back to Britain aboard a large troopship. 'The men from *Lightning* spent most of the time on the upper deck,' admitted Gilroy, 'in case they had to abandon ship again in a hurry.'

Victory in the desert was proclaimed in May 1943, and the Mediterranean was gradually brought under control. Losses of merchant ships continued to average around eleven per month over the course of the year; eighteen vessels were lost in December. But this was offset by the huge quantities of material which could now be sent through the Straits of Gibraltar and on to the Suez Canal. 'Super convoys' could reach Egypt from Britain up to six weeks more quickly than before, and over the summer of 1944 around 12,000 merchant ships passed through with negligible damage.

As convoys began to run more freely, supplies improved. By the summer of 1943, Wight-Boycott judged Gibraltar 'much better off for goods than any port'. There were still shortages and high prices, but 'the food situation seemed better' and, he reported, 'I dined once at the Bristol, Victoria, and Yacht Club'. Before *Ilex* left, he and his fellow officers stocked up on sherry. They were disappointed to learn that they 'could only get one dozen gin out of Saccone's. It is becoming increasingly hard to find.'

There was, however, one Gibraltar luxury which the war could not diminish. Richard Walker and his friends were advised by a medical officer that sunbathing 'will atrophy your brain'. They took little notice: 'We lay until the top of the Rock made pointed shadows on the sand,' he wrote in his diary.

Meanwhile, Malta remained in a devastated condition. In June

1943 the naval authorities were confident enough of the island's security to sanction a visit by King George VI. Valletta was in ruins. Vere Wight-Boycott described the scene shortly after the royal visit:

It is a sad sight. There seems to be hardly an undamaged building standing. The opera house, Governor's Palace, Cathedral were among the damaged ones. I went to look for Gieves, but only found a rubble heap . . . Even the little watchtower on the parapet of the bastion on Senglea Point, which used to have an eye sculpted on one side and an ear on the other and where the knights of old kept watch as part of their novitiate has been knocked clean off into the harbour.

In the sunshine on the morning of Sunday 20 June, King George sailed into Grand Harbour aboard the cruiser HMS *Aurora*. Church bells rang. Crowds cheered. The monarch stood on a specially constructed platform in front of the bridge and took the applause.

## 15. Getting the Goods Home

June 1942 brought the worst monthly shipping losses of the Atlantic war. Some 131 ships were sunk, equating to more than 650,000 tons. May had ended with the first of Bomber Command's mass raids and a blitz on Cologne, lauded throughout Britain as justifiable aggression. 'Well dearest the news of 1000 planes over Germany for the last couple of days is rather cheering,' wrote Alan Gould of HMS *Lightning* to his fiancée. 'But just now I really thought of it and what it meant and it means one hell of a lot of suffering for some innocent people.'

Officials within the Admiralty felt that they, too, were suffering from the enthusiasm with which the large-scale bomber offensive was embraced. Throughout the war, the Admiralty fought a 'battle of the air' with the Air Ministry over strategic priorities and aircraft resources. Ever since the RAF had grudgingly relinquished control over naval aviation, the Fleet Air Arm had struggled with obsolete aircraft and limited production. Even the RAF's own Coastal Command, vital to the protection of ocean convoys, was regarded by Arthur Harris, the architect and most vociferous advocate of the bomber offensive, as an 'obstacle to victory'.

Yet air power was a vital factor in the Atlantic. From the moment that Allied aircraft became established in Newfoundland and Iceland, U-boats began to gravitate towards the mid-ocean 'air gap', beyond flying range. By the summer of 1942, this was the chief battleground. Long-range bombers and reconnaissance planes would be essential components in the defence of shipping and, as far as the Admiralty was concerned, the strategy pursued by Bomber Command was to the detriment of the Atlantic campaign: hoarding resources which were vital in securing Britain's essential seaborne supplies. Nevertheless, the bombing campaign matched the mood of the nation: eager for retaliation, not retrenchment.

By the summer of 1942 public pressure was also mounting for an offensive in Europe. In Britain and America mass rallies demanded a 'Second Front Now!' The most influential patron in Britain was Lord Beaverbrook, who, after visiting the Soviet Union, had become convinced of the need for a major Allied assault in western Europe. Midshipman John Roberts of HMS *Renown* agreed:

> The only thing to do is to start a second front. The phrase 'second front' should really be fourth, since we are already fighting in Russia, Egypt and India, but what is meant is an invasion of France or another of the occupied countries . . . The question of where we should actually strike is immaterial from the point of view of relieving the pressure on Russia . . . In my opinion we have just about reached the crisis of the war; we can win, but we can lose quite easily if mistakes are made.

On 19 August, only a few days after the conclusion of Operation Pedestal in the Mediterranean, the largest incursion yet into German-occupied territory took place at Dieppe. Since 1940, the British Combined Operations Headquarters had been developing tactics and technology for amphibious operations, mounting several small-scale commando raids from Norway to St Nazaire. Under the leadership of freshly promoted Lord Louis Mountbatten, a plan code-named Operation Jubilee was formed for a frontal assault on Dieppe and its surrounding beaches, ostensibly to test the enemy defences and destroy key installations. Five thousand soldiers of the 2nd Canadian Infantry Division formed the core of the force, along with 1,000 Royal Marine commandos and fifty US Rangers. Support from sea and air was strong: eight destroyers accompanied over 200 landing craft, and dozens of RAF fighter squadrons were attached.

Jubilee was a disaster. The task force was spotted in the English Channel, eliminating any element of surprise. Poor intelligence had failed to identify the strength and position of German forces and the landings were confused and ineffective. Sea walls and shore batteries combined to repel the beach assaults, and the commandos fared little better in the harbour itself. Destroyers, the largest warships that could be risked in the Channel, proved inadequate against strong artillery attacks. Captain Derry Turner was the bombardment liaison officer in the destroyer HMS *Garth*, but he was forced to spend more time sheltering from the enemy's shells than helping to direct British fire. 'These air bursts of the enemy were hellish,' he wrote soon afterwards, 'bursting about 15 feet above us with a sharp crack and then the whine and whirr of flying shell fragments and then nothing but little puffs of smoke were left hanging in the air.'

A fug of smokescreens combined with the smoke from British guns to make visibility minimal. Any judgement on accuracy and direction was impossible; Turner could barely discern the origin of enemy fire. A lull amid the chaos brought a visitor to the upper deck:

Old Knight, the wardroom steward, appeared on the bridge carrying a large tray of hot cups of tea, smiles all over his face! I was glad of that tea and drank half my cup and gave the rest to my signaller and asked if he would like some whisky in it. He said he would like some – he looked as if he needed it – and I gave him a large measure. The Hun's shells began bursting all around us again and we ran behind our screen again.

An explosion rocked the bridge shelter in which Turner was standing, with shrapnel flying across the flat.

I felt an extraordinary numb bang on my fingers on my left hand, and heard the loudest noise I've ever heard – a short sharp scream of metal. I looked at my fingers. My index finger was hanging nearly off and I felt no pain. I then felt the back of my right leg with my right hand and felt nothing but hot rawness but again, no pain . . . I held my finger between my centre finger and thumb. I saw the side of the bridge. It was splattered with blood and there was a piece of meat about the size of a large mouthful sticking to some woodwork and slipping down. I looked round to see if anyone else had been hit – they hadn't – and that meat was a bit of me! I heard the Captain shout down a voice pipe, 'Doctor to the bridge!'

Turner was taken below to a cabin, his shattered leg treated first. Then came the finger: 'I asked him to cut it off, but he took one look at it and said, "You'd better keep it . . ." And so he pulled out his pencil and tied it on with a long bandage. He then gave me some brandy from his flask and left me to attend to others.' The patient was plied with regular alcohol until *Garth* withdrew, then injected with copious quantities of morphine and spent the Channel crossing delirious. Almost as soon as he was conscious, he recorded his experiences in his journal.

By far the worst casualties at Dieppe were suffered by the Canadian forces, of whom 900 were killed and nearly 1,900 taken prisoner. There were 275 casualties amongst the commandos, and the Royal Navy suffered 550 casualties. German losses, in comparison, amounted to 314 killed and 37 captured. One Royal Navy destroyer was sunk, along with 33 landing craft, and a total of 99 Allied aircraft was lost: one of the most costly days for the RAF in the war, and worse than any day during the Battle of Britain.

Yet such was the desire for success that there was initially great reluctance to accept the scale of the catastrophe. John Adams, first lieutenant of the destroyer HMS *Cleveland*, operating in the English Channel, reported the news in his diary: 'We landed a strong force on the French coast and kept them there all day with the destroyers offshore and fighters overhead . . . HMS *Berkeley* lost by bombing and I fear a lot of Canadian troops – but it's just the stuff for everyone's morale.'

Despite the disaster at Dieppe, there was an inexorable momentum behind amphibious warfare. For many young sailors, the Royal Marine commando held a particular fascination. A month later, in September 1942, a group of midshipmen from the battlecruiser HMS *Renown* attended a training day at Greenock on the banks of the Clyde to learn about the commando force. Midshipman John Roberts described the morning's activities:

The first thing we had was a lecture from one of their officers about their history and uses . . . After that, and after we had examined one of their notorious daggers, we marched through the town and up on to a desolate patch of moor; by this time it had begun to rain which made standing about in the long wet grass uncomfortable to say the least of it. Up there we saw the latest type of hand grenade being thrown at a small hut, and then how to cut steel girders with explosives. The next item on the programme was the demonstration of 'Tommy Guns', Bren guns, anti-tank rifles and several mortars. By then it was nearly 1300 and we went back to the town to eat our sandwiches in a Y.M.C.A. hall.

In the afternoon, the group went to Commando HQ, 'where we first of all played about with their collapsible boats and canoes, and then ran round the easier of their two assault courses'. Midshipman J. B. T. Davies described the difficulties of using the canoes, each of which could hold two men and their equipment: 'Our efforts succeeded in getting most of the men very wet, especially the canoeists. I happened to be one of them and in our haste to withdraw to the sea, our canoe capsized. However everyone enjoyed themselves very much.'

The Royal Marines underwent a transformation over the course of the war. From being predominately based aboard ships and used for the occasional foray in land expeditions, they became a key component of British amphibious warfare and established as one of the world's elite fighting forces. In December 1942, ten Royal Marines in five canoes were deposited in the mouth of the Gironde estuary and made their way upriver towards Bordeaux. In one of the most daring feats of the war, they placed limpet mines on several ships in harbour, four of which were damaged by the ensuing explosions. Only two of the 'Cockleshell Heroes' survived, escaping with the help of the French resistance. Two were drowned, and six were captured and executed.

By the start of 1943, the struggle with the U-boats in the Atlantic was reaching its apogee. Dieppe provided further evidence that an Allied invasion of occupied Europe would require huge resources of materials and men. These could only be provided by ocean convoy routes. During Operation Torch, Allied troops had been delivered directly across the Atlantic to North Africa, but this had required such a quantity of protective escorts that merchant shipping suffered significant losses in their absence. There were now 212 operational craft in the U-boat fleet, more than double the total of the previous January. After the record month of June 1942, when over 650,000 tons of merchant shipping was sunk, an average of 550,000 tons was lost each month in the North Atlantic. A meeting of the Allied leaders at Casablanca in January 1943 recognized that the ocean routes had to be secured before any major offensive could be contemplated. Regardless of the impact of the bomber offensive, the Atlantic would be the true heart of Allied strategy.

Seafarers of all nations enjoyed a fraternity which the war did not entirely eliminate: mariners in need should be assisted regardless of the colour of the flag under which they sailed. But as the stakes increased in the Atlantic, so did the ferocity of the struggle. The nature of U-boat warfare sometimes created a psychological distinction between the warship sailors and enemy submariners. On occasion, the traditional maritime camaraderie broke down entirely. Nicholas Monsarrat, writing after the war in *The Cruel Sea*, his semi-autobiographical novel, described the reaction of escort sailors to rescued U-boat survivors: 'No heroes, these: deprived of their ship, they were indeed hardly men at all . . . They were people from another and infinitely abhorrent world – not just Germans, but U-boat Germans, doubly revolting.'

There was often little enough opportunity to rescue Allied warship or merchant sailors, let alone the enemy's. Evelyn Chavasse was in command of the destroyer HMS *Broadway*, defending a convoy, when an attacking U-boat was hit by supporting aircraft. As it sank, German submariners scrambled onto the outer deck, waving to be rescued. Before he could act, however, Chavasse received a request from another escort vessel for assistance. 'I had clear evidence of a further U-boat threat ahead of the convoy, and the safety of the convoy was my job,' he wrote. 'I needed <u>all</u> my escorts around the convoy. I deliberately condemned those Germans to death, and said No.'

One of the most controversial episodes of the Atlantic war occurred in September 1942, after the liner RMS *Laconia* was torpedoed by

U-156 off the West African coast. Aboard were 2,771 passengers and crew, including 1,800 Italian prisoners of war and 300 British and Polish soldiers. Men, women and children were rescued from the wreckage by the U-boat crew, some helped into lifeboats which were taken in tow. Flying Red Cross flags, the submarine attempted to rendezvous with Vichy French ships in order to transfer its passengers, but was attacked in error by an American B24 Liberator bomber operating from Ascension Island. The commander of U-156, Werner Hartenstein, reluctantly left the survivors to their fates, setting the lifeboats adrift and leaving hundreds stranded in the water. More than half of those aboard *Laconia* were lost during the torpedo attack and its aftermath. A thousand fortunate survivors were eventually rescued by French ships; others reached the African coast after many days adrift.

The incident persuaded Admiral Dönitz to order his submariners to abandon any rescue attempts in future. It was a departure from previous practice, because although submarines were too cramped to accommodate large numbers of prisoners, it had not been unknown for U-boat crews to provide basic medical supplies to stranded survivors. Indeed, this continued on occasion even after the new guidelines, but the *Laconia* provided another example of the ruthlessness demonstrated by both sides during the Atlantic campaign. Far from being a cold matter of shipping accountancy, this was a ferocious battle.

On 16 October 1942, the destroyers of B-6 Escort Group were protecting convoy SC104. 'Teeming with rain,' wrote Leading Signalman C. L. R. Matthews of HMS *Fame* in his diary that morning. 'Having had no sleep and soaked to the skin everyone on the bridge was very bad tempered.' *Fame* was in the vanguard. Just as those on watch were about to enjoy a well-earned rest, the ASDIC operators reported a contact. A pattern of depth charges was dropped, and Matthews described the outcome:

As the sea astern shivered, flattened and then rose in great fountains, the black bow of a U-boat rose into the air. As we turned, she levelled out and was probably going to dive again. The skipper gave the order, 'stand by to ram'. This was shouted over the ship and we went at the U-boat full ahead. We hit her a glancing blow, just forward of her conning tower. She slewed round and her conning tower scraped down our starboard side tearing a hole in our ship's side.

The German submarine had come off worse. Aboard *Fame*, damage control parties did their best to make temporary repairs, while others prepared for another attack. 'The U-boat was almost as big as we were,' wrote Matthews. 'As we came round again some of the Jerries came out of the conning tower and made a run for the gun on her forward deck. Every gun we had opened fire at her and everyone aboard was cheering like mad.'

*Fame* had been fortunate. U-353 was sinking. Documents were seized and prisoners brought aboard the British ship before the submarine vanished beneath the waves. After attempting to patch up the damage to the destroyer, the decision was taken to return to Liverpool. Contrary to the predictions of some pessimists amongst her crew, *Fame* reached the Mersey, but delays to preparations on shore meant that she was forced to wait for a berth. 'We sat in the river in a sinking condition,' wrote Matthews, 'with the skipper biting his nails and saying, "Wouldn't it be awful if we sank?"' He was happy to record for posterity that they did not.

Two weeks later, in the eastern Mediterranean, a similar success was achieved which would have lasting ramifications for the Atlantic, but at a tragic cost. U-559 was detected by aircraft between Port Said and Haifa, and was pursued by several Royal Navy destroyers. After a hunt which lasted ten hours, the submarine was damaged and forced to the surface. As German sailors abandoned their boat, a botched attempt at self-sabotage by flooding the diving tanks left it on the surface, slowly taking on water.

Aboard HMS *Petard*, a boarding party was hastily formed while an advanced group of four men made their way across to the submarine. Tony Fasson, first lieutenant of *Petard*, was the first down the conning tower, followed by Able Seaman Colin Grazier, ASDIC operator Ken Lacroix and sixteen-year-old canteen assistant Tommy Brown. German sailors were by now attempting to clamber up ropes thrown over the side of the destroyer. 'One had terrible stomach wounds and got stuck on the ropes,' wrote wireless engineer Reg Crang. 'He slipped off and drifted away.' Crang hauled one man aboard: 'I was thrilled to get a German in my hands, and felt like shaking him to bits.'

Tommy Brown later described the scene that greeted him inside the submarine. The gloom was disrupted only by Fasson's torch, as he used a machine gun to smash open cabinets in the rising water. Brown was handed piles of books and papers to take up the conning tower to the boarding party's boat. As he returned below, he saw that 'there was a hole just forward of the conning tower through which the water was pouring. As one went down through the conning tower compartment, one felt it pour down one's back . . . The water was getting deeper and I told First Lieutenant that they were all shouting on deck. He gave me some more books from the cabin.'

Brown continued to take the material up, until Gordon Connell, the officer in charge of the recently arrived rescue boat, decided that the 'pinch' was becoming too dangerous. Warnings were shouted into the gloom. Lacroix appeared and clambered into the boat. Tommy Brown remained at the top of the tower, calling down to the remaining two men. Grazier and Fasson appeared at the bottom of the hatch, and Brown repeated his warnings. But it was too late. 'They had just started up,' Brown recalled, 'when the submarine started to sink very quickly.' He was hauled into the boat as U-559 slipped beneath the waves, taking Fasson and Grazier with it.

Since February 1942, British cryptographers had been unable to read the U-boat 'Shark' cipher, but the documents recovered from U-559 enabled Bletchley Park to break it once again, helping to reduce the heavy shipping losses in the North Atlantic by the end of the year. Both Fasson and Grazier received a posthumous George Medal – their bravery not enacted in the face of the enemy and therefore ineligible for a military award. Tommy Brown, the sixteen-year-old galley hand, also received the medal, but was nevertheless removed from the navy because he was under-age. He returned to his family in North Shields but would die in 1945, attempting to rescue his four-year-old sister Maureen from a domestic fire which destroyed their home.

The intelligence breakthrough which followed HMS *Petard*'s 'pinch' helped to recover some of the initiative which had been lost, but alone it was not enough to nullify the submarine threat. Another alteration in the Enigma cipher produced a temporary ULTRA blackout which instantly threw the convoys back into danger and resulted in some of the heaviest losses of the war. In March 1943, the last great crisis of the Atlantic campaign began.

George Treadaway was a merchant sailor in the *Empire Bunting*, part of convoy SC121 travelling from Newfoundland to Britain with a cargo of rice, copper and high explosives. For three days, amid fierce Atlantic squalls, seventeen U-boats stalked the convoy, picking off merchant ships one by one. 'All hell breaks out starting at 8 p.m.,' wrote Treadaway in his diary. 'A ship on the starboard column is torpedoed. I was on lookout when I saw the flash and saw rockets. The wind was blowing and heavy sea running. I pitied the men aboard her.'

By midnight, he had returned to his bunk, only to be woken by another alarm before racing to the upper deck. 'The sky was alight with star shells sent up by the escort,' he wrote. 'In no time the starboard column had gone. The blasties were in the centre of the column evidently.' *Empire Bunting*'s steering gear had broken, and the ship was drifting away from the group. 'As the convoy continued I felt a tear at my heart,' admitted Treadaway, 'and yet a curious feeling of jubilation to leave the convoy, the U-boats had it marked.'

SC121 lost thirteen ships, its escorts failing to sink a single U-boat in retaliation. After emergency repairs and help from a Canadian corvette and an American cutter, *Bunting* got back underway and eventually reached Loch Long safely. Along the way, Treadaway was exasperated by one amateur photographer: 'A guy on the escort kept taking pictures of us. I'd like to have one, maybe it would show the different expressions on our faces as we tried desperately to get her ropes aboard, our minds dwelling all the time on the TNT below decks.'

A few days later, the largest convoy battle of the war began. Between 16 and 20 March, two converging convoys – HX229 and SC122 – were attacked by some thirty-eight U-boats over a wide expanse of sea south of Greenland. The two sets of escort ships tried in vain to prevent the submarines wreaking havoc amongst the merchant vessels. On the first night, twelve were hit or sunk. As the convoys came together, the eighteen escorts worked with shore-based bombers to sink one U-boat before the submarines were withdrawn on 20 March. A total of twenty-one merchant ships were lost, along with 368 of their sailors and passengers – a quarter of the total carried in the two convoys. In all, ninety-seven ships had been lost in the Atlantic in the first three weeks of March.

What helped to sustain the Atlantic convoys at this time was a process of evolution in anti-submarine warfare, which was beginning to bear fruit even in the spring of 1943. Western Approaches had continued to develop under Admiral Max Horton, who had replaced Percy Noble in November 1942. Dedicated support groups were established in order to supplement the escort vessels protecting convoys. Operating independently to hunt U-boats, they benefited from new tactics and dynamic leadership, cutting-edge technology, effective weapons, and well-drilled sailors in teams of modern vessels. Escort group commanders such as Peter Gretton and Frederic 'Johnnie' Walker became known as U-boat hunting 'aces', scoring multiple 'kills' during their patrols.

Air cover was a vital component of the improving scenario. By the spring of 1943, the gap between the areas covered by RAF Coastal Command and the Royal Canadian Air Force was becoming smaller. Greater numbers of long-range aircraft equipped with advanced radar and weaponry were becoming available. At the start of March 1943 there were no support groups at sea, but by the start of April there were six, including one formed of American vessels, of which three included a dedicated escort carrier. By the end of 1943 the Royal Navy had forty escort carriers in operation, each carrying up to twenty aircraft, and the US Navy had sixty-five. July 1942 saw the sinking of the first U-boat destroyed by a bomber fitted with a Leigh Light – an extremely powerful searchlight combined with radar. Air power proved crucial in the Atlantic: over the course of the war, shore-based aircraft sank nearly as many U-boats as did the escort groups.

Escort vessels themselves were also improving. New Loch-class frigates and Castle-class corvettes were a marked improvement on previous uncomfortable iterations. Shipboard technology was in a continual process of development. An array of electronic gadgetry proliferated. Complementing the ASDIC sonar system for detecting submarines underwater, radar evolved over the course of the war, enabling escorts to detect U-boats on the surface. The Type 271 system began to be mounted on destroyers throughout 1941 and 1942, and by 1943 similar technology in patrol aircraft helped them to track and attack submarines more effectively.

The other major development was radio-direction finding, which detected the high-frequency radio signals broadcast by U-boats when coordinating an attack. Known as HF/DF, or 'Huff-Duff', this combined with shore-based plotting to help re-route convoys or coordinate hunter groups. Weapons also improved. Depth charges, previously deployed by a relatively straightforward launcher over the back or sides of an escort, became more effective thanks to innovations such as the 'Hedgehog' system, which launched the explosives in a wider pattern around and ahead of the ship and helped to avoid disruption of ASDIC tracking.

New technology was not always welcomed unconditionally by sailors. There were countless examples of faulty or malfunctioning equipment causing serious damage and even death. For every successful innovation, there were many short-lived failures, such as 'Holman's Projector', a drainpipe-like mortar tube which used compressed steam to launch grenades from the deck. Any problem with the steam pressure sent the grenade unpredictably back onto the ship, leaving only a few seconds to make it safe. 'We disposed of that one very quickly,' recalled one corvette sailor. 'It was very good for firing potatoes out of. They went for miles in the air.'

Suspicion and superstition were common. Graham Lumsden recalled the reaction of sailors in HMS *Keith* to the introduction of degaussing equipment in 1940, which protected the ship against magnetic mines by using an electrical field to eliminate the ship's magnetism: 'Someone speculated that this field would have a serious effect on a man's powers in bed. Within hours there was serious

unease throughout the ship.' Even ASDIC was viewed with scepticism by some crews when it was first introduced. 'Among the many
myths surrounding this magic instrument was one to the effect that
close contact with it rendered the operator sterile,' wrote Nicholas
Monsarrat, 'a rumour so widespread that it had to be countered by an
official pronouncement that there was no ground for any such fears.'

Complex equipment was seldom infallible, and this was sufficient
to unsettle many crews. False readings on RDF or ASDIC systems
could be particularly troublesome, particularly during long and
stressful convoys on which attacks might come at any moment. As
this equipment was new and constantly developing, very few on
board – even those with the relevant training – were completely cog-
nizant of its technicalities. This lent a further air of unease to
erroneous readings. 'We must have got an echo on a temperature
layer or something,' recorded Frank Layard in his diary after one false
alarm. 'Bad for the nerves that sort of thing.'

Weaponry and technology were only as effective as their operators. By 1943, most escort vessels were manned by a mixture of old
hands and new, regulars and reservists, with temporary sailors dom-
inating. Above all, it was the influx of RNVR officers which enabled
the expansion of the escort fleet. When John Mosse was given command of the frigate HMS *Mermaid*, his fellow officers were a typical
mixture of characters:

> Dixon, a first class navigator, was a businessman. Danskin was an
> accountant, wardroom clown and piano player. Of the two Sub Lieu-
> tenants, Oakley the Gunnery Control Officer was a chemist, whilst
> the all important Anti-Submarine Control Officer was one Caughey
> Gauntlett, a practising Salvationist . . . There were also two midship-
> men: Scanlon who eventually became a doctor, and Freeman. With
> the Doctor, that made ten of us . . . The sailors numbered about one
> hundred and eighty, of whom eighty per cent were Hostilities Only.

The Atlantic campaign began as a battle between a German elite
and British and Allied reservists or inexperienced volunteers. But as
escort crews became increasingly experienced, the rate of attrition

amongst U-boat crews wore down the numbers of veteran submariners. Training programmes had improved the coordination, tactics and effectiveness of escorts. In particular, the strict regime under 'Monkey' Stephenson at HMS *Western Isles* and the anti-submarine school of Captain Gilbert Roberts had gradually turned the Royal Navy's escort force into a far more effective fighting organization than it had been in 1941. By the early summer of 1943, despite the crisis of the spring, anti-submarine warfare had begun to reach its full potential.

No fewer than 113 U-boats were destroyed in the first half of 1943, with 41 alone lost in what became known to German submariners as 'Black May'. Such a heavy toll was unsustainable. Dönitz temporarily withdrew his U-boats from the North Atlantic. By 24 May, he would later write, 'we had lost the Battle of the Atlantic'. It was not the end of the struggle by any means. Some U-boats were relocated south of the Azores, some to the Indian Ocean, making these convoy routes for a time the more threatened. But although the total number of U-boats available continued to rise – from 331 in the second half of 1942 to 436 at the start of 1944 – losses continued to mount. In the second half of 1942, 66 U-boats had been sunk. Nearly twice as many were sunk in the first half of 1943 alone, with another 124 in the second half of the year. Not only did this represent the loss of valuable weapons, but it also meant the deaths or capture of irreplaceable crews, with fewer and fewer experienced submariners active. Of the 1,170 U-boats commissioned over the course of the war, 630 were destroyed in action and another 81 in harbour. Some 30,000 German submariners lost their lives.

This was not the end of the war against the U-boats, which continued until the very last night of the conflict, but it marked the end of the threat to the Atlantic lifeline. By June 1943, shipping losses in the North Atlantic were down from 206,000 tons in May to only 30,000 tons. Thereafter, they would only rarely rise beyond 50,000 tons, the equivalent to barely a dozen ships per month and a mere fraction of the regular monthly losses in excess of 500,000 tons experienced during 1942.

*

The Battle of the Atlantic epitomized Britain's war. It was a long struggle of industrial attrition, in which success depended on many things. The support of a multinational coalition of allies provided the means for victory. Improving technology and invention, and the ingenious exploitation of hard-won intelligence became a British forte. The people of Africa and the Americas formed just as important a part of the campaign as the ocean between them. The resilience of British civilians, burdened by rationing and short-age, was matched by the steadfastness of the merchant sailors who manned the freighters which nourished both industry and citizenry.

Although the number of red chalk marks on the 'score board' in Derby House continued to increase, the pattern of the campaign was less apparent to those at sea. Sailors manning the small groups of escort ships on the front line of the struggle against the U-boats sim-ply continued to do their jobs. Evelyn Chavasse was the commanding officer of the rickety Lend-Lease destroyer HMS *Broadway*:

> Our primary job was not to sink U-boats. It was to get the convoys and their vital cargoes safely and quickly to their destinations. It was drummed into us, almost *ad nauseam*, that our only object was enshrined in the very simple and quite memorable phrase: 'The safe and timely arrival of the convoy' . . . In fact our little ships were not cut out for blood, we were out for getting the goods home; and if I had any clue where a U-boat might be lurking, my first concern was to dodge them, run away in fact, instead of charging straight at them, as we so much wanted to.

'In many ways, we enjoyed the Battle of the Atlantic,' wrote Sid France. 'We did know at the time that ships were being sunk and men were dying, but we only had thoughts for our own ship and blotted out everything else.' In command of an escort destroyer in July 1942, Frank Layard once again worried that he was not doing his bit: 'Whenever I hear of first hand accounts of any particularly tough bit of bombing or fighting,' he wrote in his diary, 'it makes me feel somehow that I'm not having my share of hardship.' In fact, his turn would come soon enough: his convoys were attacked and HMS *Fire-drake* was torpedoed.

Atlantic convoys were a matter of routine and tension. Battles with U-boats were extraordinary, not the norm. This presented a particular problem when it came to rewarding sailors for their efforts in protecting the merchant ships. After a speech by First Lord of the Admiralty A. V. Alexander in early 1943, Derric Breen was riled by the praise apparently reserved for the escort 'aces' such as 'Johnnie' Walker, who sank U-boats but also seemingly sacrificed many ships in the process. 'Feelings were running high between the escort groups where those who sank submarines were given media adulation and showered with decorations despite their losses,' he wrote. 'Given twenty Walkers our losses would be such that we would lose the war . . . There was acrimony and a lot of bitter feeling.'

Vere Wight-Boycott totted up the efforts of HMS *Ilex* at the end of 1942. He calculated that the ship had been at sea for seventy-three of ninety-seven days between September and December, and had steamed 19,668 miles. It was a record of which he was proud.

We have no positive results to show for our hard work, no U-boats sunk nor aircraft shot down – yet – but that does not mean we have not made a valuable contribution to the war effort. We have not lost a ship in convoy, we cannot tell that we have not scared off U-boats, and it should be remembered that if we had not been available for the duties we have carried out, either merchant ship sailings would have been delayed, or other H.M. ships would have to have been taken off other jobs to take our place.

The Atlantic took its toll on the escort sailors. Young men ended their service with tired eyes and weatherbeaten faces. Fatigued veterans retired for the second time. Even those most lauded for their achievements found little respite from the harsh conditions. Twenty-year-old Acting Third Officer Charlotte Dyer was working in the signals office for Western Approaches in Liverpool. One day in March 1944, she and a friend were amongst a crowd of well-wishers at the docks welcoming Walker's 2nd Escort Group back home. She described the scene in her diary: 'The first ship to come in was the *Starling*, with Captain Walker standing up on the bridge, he acknowledged the cheers with a salute. According to the paper the cheering was loud and continuous, but we thought it was very feeble and at times there was absolute dead silence.' The procession of ships continued: *Wild Goose*, *Magpie* and *Wren*. Dyer decided to get a better vantage point: 'Joyce and I broke ranks as soon as possible and went right to the dockside and had a very [good] view of the *Starling* and of Captain Walker, who was standing high on the bridge, he has a very nice, bronzed face, a typical seaman.'

Four months later, Frederic 'Johnnie' Walker was dead at forty-eight, the result of a stroke brought about by exhaustion.

# 16. A Hell of a Battering

On 22 September 1943, in the deep natural harbour of Kaafjord in northern Norway, a small submarine was stuck in a net. Little more than fifty feet long and five feet in diameter, X-7 carried four sailors and two mines. In command was twenty-two-year-old Lieutenant Godfrey Place. Each man had volunteered for service in the cramped midget submarine, known as an X-craft, and their mission was to attack the German battleship *Tirpitz*.

X-7 was one of six submarines attempting to infiltrate the fjords as part of Operation Source: an effort to disable the *Tirpitz* and her fellow battleships *Scharnhorst* and *Lützow*. The craft had been towed all the way across the Norwegian Sea by larger submarines before being released. It was a highly dangerous endeavour for these vulnerable miniatures. Before they had even reached Norway, X-9 had sunk with all hands and X-8 had been damaged beyond repair. X-10 would develop mechanical problems and return to its transport before reaching its objective. After being sighted on its way to the fjord, X-5 was never seen again.

X-6, commanded by Lieutenant Donald Cameron, and Godfrey Place's X-7 both managed to reach the fjord, each making its own lonely way without the ability to communicate with the other. 'The water was like a sheet of turquoise stained glass,' wrote Place of the approach, 'the steep sides of the fjord luxurious in browns and greens emphasised by the bright sunlight and the Norwegian fishing boats, picturesque enough for even the most blasé traveller'. By the time X-7 reached the first of the anti-submarine defences, the weather had turned overcast and windy, helping the X-craft to hide.

Lookouts watched the harbour and a devious maze of mines, underwater nets and wires protected the battleship. X-7 became entangled several times, and only considerable skill and ingenuity on the part of its crew combined with a slice of luck freed it from the traps before it finally emerged in the shadow of the *Tirpitz*. Place slid his submarine underneath the battleship's hull and released his charges before making the frantic dash to safety before the hour-long fuses expired, or the mines of another craft detonated.

Navigation was difficult, and oxygen was running out. X-7 became entangled in yet more netting, Place and his crew trying every desperate measure to free their tiny vessel. They ran out of time. 'The explosion came,' wrote Place, 'a continuous roar that seemed to last whole minutes.' Charges from X-7 and from Cameron's X-6 had detonated, tearing through the battleship's hull and mangling her rudders and steering gear.

X-7 was also damaged by the explosion – lights had exploded and the depth gauges were rendered useless – but the hull remained intact. Most importantly, it had been shaken free of its binds. But oxygen was by now reaching critically low levels, too little to mount an escape, and so Place and his team accepted that they would have to surrender. The submarine surfaced next to a target used for gunnery practice, and Place emerged waving a white sweater. As he stepped out onto the platform, X-7 began to sink rapidly. Only one of the three men remaining inside would escape, and was later discovered by the Germans floating barely conscious in the water.

*Tirpitz* had been crippled, and would not be ready for service until the spring of 1944. Place was captured, along with the crew of X-6, all of whom were taken on board the damaged German battleship and plied with schnapps. Cameron and Place would later be awarded the Victoria Cross for their efforts. It was a remarkable achievement, and the handful of future X-craft operations would never quite match the significance of the first. Once verified intelligence confirmed that *Tirpitz* was out of action, the Arctic convoys, which had been suspended over the summer of 1943, could resume.

Now only one of Germany's battleships remained. The *Scharnhorst* had lingered in the Norwegian fjords since the spring of 1943, after a year of repairs and trials following the 'Channel Dash' of February 1942. Forays into the open sea had been rare, but the Admiralty remained on high alert. In December 1943 the code breakers of

Bletchley Park learned that the *Scharnhorst* had been ordered to attack a convoy bound for Russia.

On Christmas Day of 1943 Revd Ken Mathews, the chaplain of HMS *Norfolk*, led a prayer service for the ship's company. 'Bring light and warmth and hope, we humbly pray Thee,' he said on behalf of his congregation, 'to all whose Christmastide is dark and cold and sad. Bind us close in spirit to all for whom we deeply care, and grant that they and we, for all the bleakness of our circumstance, may catch something of the Christmas joy, for the sake of him whom no ill fortune could daunt.'

*Norfolk* was in Arctic waters, near the North Cape at the tip of Norway, along with fellow cruisers HMS *Belfast* and HMS *Sheffield*, providing close cover for convoy JW55B as it made its way to Murmansk. A few days earlier at Scapa Flow, the ship's company of *Belfast* had been addressed by the commander of the 10th Cruiser Squadron, Rear Admiral Robert Burnett. He had a striking red beard and an exuberant manner, and his role in the Battle of the Barents Sea had helped to build a reputation for action. John Wilson, a trainee officer serving his mandatory spell on the lower deck, was amongst the ratings in the audience:

> His speech was a remarkable one. He told us bluntly that he was going to seek an engagement with the enemy if he could possibly manage it . . . 'Unless I can strike a blow against the enemy, this will be my last voyage. I shall be retired. I intend, therefore, to do my damnedest to bring about an action' . . . This admiral who wanted to sink the enemy in order to get promotion and a K.B.E., and said so, was a figure from another century. We sailors took a fairly gloomy view of his speech. 'Fuck this for a lark' was the prevailing opinion on the messdecks.

Despite this dour response, Burnett's three cruisers were amongst the best-run and most efficient ships in the navy, with the experience of four years of war. *Norfolk* and *Sheffield* were veterans of the *Bismarck* chase. Nor were they alone: providing distant cover was Admiral Bruce Fraser's flagship, the modern battleship HMS *Duke of York*, sister ship of *Prince of Wales* and one of the most powerful in the

Royal Navy. Fraser was joined by the cruiser HMS *Jamaica* and several destroyers: *Savage*, *Scorpion*, *Saumarez* and *Sword*, along with the Norwegian *Stord*.

As Boxing Day dawned, the loudspeakers of the cruisers related the news that the German battleship *Scharnhorst* was believed to be nearby, and that all should prepare for an engagement. In *Sheffield*, recalled Stanley Walker, everybody was 'on the alert at once' as the captain stated that 'should we have the good fortune to meet her, and it was the Admiral's intention to do so, we would engage her notwithstanding her superior armament, armour and speed'. John Wilson of HMS *Belfast* wrote that after the initial tension, a certain relaxation took over. 'It was hard to believe that we were really going to meet an enemy more substantial than a U-boat or an aeroplane,' he wrote. 'On the lower deck few of us really expected to meet the *Scharnhorst*.'

The following hours proved to be a tense and tiring endurance test, in which sailors remained at action stations without a break. Nineteen-year-old Alan Tyler had already spent three gruelling days on long watches. 'We were all pretty tired and dirty,' he admitted. But when the news came through that the *Scharnhorst* had finally been located, all was forgotten: 'We bucked up to full efficiency when we knew there was something doing.' Tyler was in charge of two medium-sized 8-inch guns on the forward turret of HMS *Norfolk*. He would spend fourteen hours at action stations, with only two bars of chocolate and two packets of chewing gum for sustenance, along with a copy of the Bible and a poetry anthology. 'I never had a long enough lull to read them,' he wrote. 'I only realised afterwards that I forgot the brandy flask.'

Boxing Day had brought a gale which whipped up the Arctic wind and swirling snowstorms. At nine o'clock, more than an hour before dawn, *Scharnhorst* was sailing north-east towards the convoy, along with five destroyers splayed out in a search formation. Meanwhile, guided by radar, Burnett's cruisers were positioning themselves to intercept. John Wilson was at action stations aboard HMS *Belfast*. His post was in the air-defence position, immediately behind the bridge, which controlled twelve 4-inch guns. He described his main task – directing the guns under orders from a junior officer – as 'twiddling some knobs and following markers with pointers on two or three dials'.

Just before 9.30 a.m., the opening salvoes finally came. They were met with incredulity rather than adrenaline for Wilson. 'We had fired the first shots and the action had begun,' he wrote, 'but most of us had little idea what was going on. I myself did not realise that we were engaging *Scharnhorst*, and I remember thinking that we must be investigating some fishing boats or establishing the exact position of the convoy.'

*Scharnhorst* was also caught cold. Without warning amid the snow and darkness, a star-shell exploded high in the sky and began to descend, bathing the battleship in a pale glow. Such was the distance from the cruisers that the boom of the British guns was heard only after the alarm bells had started ringing in response. Yet once alerted, the German battleship was a daunting enemy. Even though the cruisers enjoyed the numerical advantage, *Scharnhorst* could outgun them all. As the British guns opened up, Graham Lumsden, navigation officer in *Sheffield*, found that he had unconsciously placed himself behind the metal casing which held the ship's compass: 'I took up a strategic position behind the binnacle, which offered some psychological protection: others similarly fooled themselves that the front of the bridge offered some cover against 11-inch shells!'

The sailors loading and operating the guns of the British ships entered into the routine for which they had been trained. For Alan Tyler, in the forward gun turret of *Norfolk*, a single-minded euphoria descended. 'It is astonishing what a drug and intoxicant action is,' he wrote in a letter shortly after the battle. 'One barely noticed the shattering thud of recoils as the guns kept running back, and we did not feel or notice as their shells hit and fell around us. It was all so exciting that everyone almost automatically did their jobs correctly with clear heads.' Below decks, meanwhile, men only had limited awareness of what was transpiring. Surgeon Lieutenant J. C. H. Dunlop was a medical officer in HMS *Sheffield*. 'We spent most of our time in the Sick Bay just waiting and listening,' he wrote soon afterwards, 'lying flat on our bellies and feeling rather frightened.'

The initial engagement lasted only fifteen minutes. After making a smokescreen, the German ships retreated. While the German destroyers moved away to the south-west, *Scharnhorst* turned away to the south-east. The cruisers had made an impression: shells from *Norfolk* knocking out the battleship's forward radar and causing some damage below decks. Aboard the German battleship Rear Admiral Bey contacted his headquarters to inform his superiors of the confrontation and was ordered to continue with his mission by Dönitz himself. *Scharnhorst* now headed north to intercept the convoy. Meanwhile, Burnett took a calculated gamble on their enemy's likely bearing, informed by his impeccable instincts, and ordered his cruisers to the north in order to intercept *Scharnhorst* as she turned back towards the convoy from the north-east.

Soon after noon, in the half-light of the day, Burnett's cruisers made long-distance radar contact once again. For the second time, the British guns opened fire from seven miles away. But on this occasion *Scharnhorst* had the better of the shooting. *Norfolk* took several hits: a turret was smashed and a hit amidships sent flames into the sky. *Sheffield* was straddled by shells. Burnett decided to hold back as *Scharnhorst* escaped once again, this time to the south. By now, what light there had been had faded and the seas were once again in total darkness.

Aboard the cruisers, confined to shadowing at distance, rations and refreshments were distributed. Aboard *Sheffield*, Stanley Walker received 'a cup of hot soup, a pie and two bars of chocolate'. Meanwhile, it was left to *Belfast* to maintain contact with the fast German ship. 'What a chase,' wrote Bill Withers soon afterwards. 'We were nipping along like hell, I don't know how many knots we were doing but the admiral told us after the action she did more speed that day than she'd ever done in her life.' According to radar operator George Burridge, this chase 'frightened the life out of us, because we knew we were completely outgunned and outclassed . . . Everyone was as tense as could be.'

But *Belfast* was not alone. Heading east at top speed was Admiral Fraser's *Duke of York*, along with the cruiser *Jamaica* and the destroyers, on an intercept course. Ernie Heather was in the transmitting station of *Duke of York*, conveying data on the movements of the target to the guns. 'We had confidence in the ship we were sailing in,' he recalled, 'confidence in our officers and – though nobody would ever speak about it – confidence in each other that, should we come into contact with the enemy, then we were going to do our utmost and our level best to *annihilate* it.'

Sub-Lieutenant Henry Leach was at action stations inside the foremost gun turret of *Duke of York*. 'I am up in the front part of the turret between the two centre guns,' he recalled, 'where I had a tiny little periscope, usually completely misted up with salt or ice or spray, and a little chair and a range receiver and voice pipe for communications.' As the British battleship closed in on *Scharnhorst*, he watched 'the range counters just alongside my head gradually ticking down . . . The guns ready, just for the triggers to be pressed, and all we needed was the order "open fire", and then it came.'

Just before five o'clock, with star-shell explosions covering the seas with an eerie twilight glow, the heavy guns of *Duke of York* and the *Scharnhorst* opened up. Paul Chavasse, who had survived the sinking of his minesweeper in 1940, was now serving as torpedo officer of HMS *Jamaica*. He wrote to his wife shortly afterwards:

This gun action was most exciting and *Scharnhorst*'s shooting good. We were near missed several times. Of course a single salvo of her heavy stuff would have put us out. However we were lucky though a lot fell uncomfortably close. Some of her stuff burst on impact with the water. This caused an unpleasant number of splinters to fly. Others, armour piercing stuff, burst deep. One of these fell <u>just</u> abreast B turret. This put up a column of water 100–150 feet high which fell on the bridge and simply soaked us. It was rather an amazing scene. Calm sea, very dark night with these frequent blinding flashes from gun fire and shell burst.

*Scharnhorst* attempted to escape once again, this time to the east. In his gun turret aboard *Duke of York*, Henry Leach watched as 'the range counters, instead of ticking down, steadied and started to tick up'. The British guns were now barely in range. Icy waves crashed over the bows of the destroyers while down in the engine rooms of the British ships, stokers strained every sinew to maintain speed. 'After all we had been through what an awful damp squib this was turning out to be,' recalled Leach. 'One felt really very saddened and frustrated. And then suddenly the ticking range counters steadied and they started to tick down again.' *Scharnhorst* was slowing, her engine room damaged. Led by *Duke of York*, the British ships moved in for the kill.

Lieutenant Bryce Ramsden, at his station directing the guns of HMS *Jamaica*, could see the unfolding action. 'Dead ahead were the signs of a furious engagement,' he wrote. 'Star-shell flared high, guns flashed, red beads of pom-pom fire ran out in livid streams.' *Jamaica* fired into the dark, then Ramsden caught a glimpse of the *Scharnhorst* in the red glow of gunfire:

> 'She's hit! My God, we've got her!' I was yelling like one possessed . . . All over the ship a cheer went up, audible above the gun-fire. I had risen half standing in my seat as the wild thrill took hold of me . . . Great columns of water stood out clearly in the brief instant of light, and I could see smoke hanging above her. I was mad with excitement until I realised that my ravings must be an incoherent babble of enthusiasm to those below as the telephones were still hanging round my head.

*Duke of York*'s shells had finally struck the telling blow. Burnett and Fraser pressed their advantage. *Belfast* moved in and opened fire once again. 'There were flashes all around,' wrote John Wilson. 'It was an extraordinary sight to see these stately flights of luminous shells, and the whole scene, with the northern lights playing above the clouds, the star-shell flares – our own yellow, and the enemy's a sort of cold, electric blue – casting their unearthly radiance over the sea, and the tracer shells following each other in ordered flights, was beautiful and fantastic.'

From *Duke of York*, Henry Leach had a front-line view: 'We closed right in to literally point blank range and then you could see things and very unpleasant they were. In the glare of the raging fires of the *Scharnhorst* you could actually see silhouetted figures leaping over the side to escape the flames.' The battleship was disabled, but still firing. 'Streams of red and green pom-pom tracer shells and bright red flashes lit up the sea, while the star-shells flared balefully above,' wrote Wilson. He was able to provide his colleagues with some idea of what was unfolding: 'My guns were constantly asking me what was happening, and I had long since settled down to give them a running commentary on the scene in the intervals when we were not firing ourselves.'

Some might have preferred not to see the battle for themselves. Leading Seaman Bob Thomas, part of the crew of a forward gun on *Duke of York*, recalled that 'when the action began, the darkness soon filled with indescribable noise, the stench of cordite and flash. But more than anything else it was the approach of the red and yellow tracer that made me so very frightened. Fear was mounting [so much] that if I could have escaped from the scene I would have bolted like a rabbit.'

While the battleships had been exchanging fire, British destroyers were manoeuvring into position for a torpedo attack. 'It was as black as pitch now,' wrote J. N. Rodwell of HMS *Scorpion* to his girlfriend soon afterwards. '*Duke of York* opened fire with all her big guns, the *Scharnhorst* returned the fire for a while . . . The whole world seemed to have opened up with fire.'

On either side of *Scharnhorst*, the destroyers made ready: *Savage* and *Saumarez* on the starboard side, *Scorpion* and *Stord* to port. 'She was massive and we were like a tugboat alongside her,' explained Rodwell. 'It was dangerous because she could blow us out of the water with one salvo. As we moved in closer the *Scharnhorst* opened fire and changed her course to head straight towards us, the *Scorpion* and *Stord*. It was then that our Captain put on all speed and went straight for her letting go our eight torpedoes when we were 2,000 yards away, at the same time bashing away with our guns.'

From *Jamaica*, Paul Chavasse watched the destroyer attack unfolding. 'This was carried out with amazing guts,' he wrote afterwards, 'and they pressed in to deliver their attack though going through hell from *Scharnhorst*'s secondary armament and close range weapons.' Soon, the British task force had caught up and continued their barrage, while the destroyers retreated. 'The guns thundered, the wind howled, and great flashes marked the salvoes,' recalled Alec Dennis, first lieutenant of the destroyer HMS *Savage*. 'All in all, a splendid sight, especially as they weren't firing at us.' Huge explosions rocked the *Scharnhorst* as the torpedoes and shells struck. One sailor in HMS *Belfast* described the battleship 'on fire from bow to stern – literally just a mass of flames'. 'What a sight,' wrote Rodwell. 'It was like November the 5th.'

*Jamaica* was ordered to move in and fire more torpedoes. 'Gosh, that gave me a kick,' wrote Paul Chavasse. As the cruiser closed at speed, German close-range armament continued to fire, 'like streams of red tennis balls pouring out of her side'. When *Jamaica* was within range, Chavasse gave the orders to fire: 'I got two torpedoes into her guts which exploded with the most glorious clashes.'

Aboard *Belfast*, there was some disappointment that *Jamaica* had received the order to attack first. Any animosity was short lived, as *Belfast* was instructed to attack soon afterwards. 'We had to fire from just outside 6000 yards and that's rather long to be certain of hitting,' wrote torpedo officer Lieutenant E. 'Andy' Palmer to a former shipmate soon afterwards. 'However, we got one hit, and turned to fire the port tubes, but by the time the sights came on she'd sunk . . . We're painting a swastika on "X" tube, from which the hitting torpedo came.'

*Scharnhorst* and her 2,000 sailors went down firing. British ships converged with searchlights to illuminate the scene, as destroyers attempted to rescue survivors. John Wilson could see only a few men: 'poor devils swimming round in the ice-cold water, with oil all over them, and sleet beating down on them'. Bill Withers emerged from his gun turret and saw the carnage: 'I thought how lucky we were as it might have been us . . . I was shivering with cold and I was dry.' Picking up swimmers from the icy water was a difficult proposition in the heavy weather. 'It was a ticklish job owing to a pretty rough sea,' wrote J. N. Rodwell of *Scorpion*, 'but we managed to get 28, the water killed a lot – it was absolutely freezing and a man couldn't stop more than a few minutes in it. Another ship picked up eight so that made 36 which isn't many.'

After the sinking had been confirmed to the crew of *Sheffield*, the reaction was a combination of exhilaration, relief and melancholy. 'The excitement on board had to be seen to be believed,' wrote Stanley Walker. 'It seemed incredible that all that was left of a 26,000 ton ship was some 36 survivors and a few pieces of shrapnel. One couldn't help feeling a little sorry for those who had perished. It was a cold, dark night with little chance of survival in those icy waters. However it might just as easily have been one, or indeed all of us.' Henry Leach expressed similar sentiments: 'I certainly personally experienced a feeling of real sadness because we had killed a lot of people and we had sent a very fine ship to the bottom . . . But the overwhelming feeling of course, was exuberance that we had succeeded.'

'It's the thought of those poor miserable wretches that makes the whole thing rather nauseating,' wrote Surgeon Lieutenant Dunlop of HMS *Sheffield* soon afterwards. 'We "spliced the mainbrace" next day to celebrate the action, but . . . I must admit that the edge was taken off one's enjoyment by the personal tragedies behind it all.' He was under no illusions about the difference between success and defeat, between life and death: 'It <u>might</u> have been us.' John Wilson echoed this view: 'We were lucky whereas the *Scharnhorst* was not.'

Bill Withers of HMS *Belfast* reflected the general sense of respect felt by most British sailors towards their enemy. 'I've got to hand it to Jerry,' he wrote, 'he went down fighting and her for'ard turret was still firing when she went down so the gunmen must have been drowned, they were either damned good sailors or else they were locked in and couldn't get out. The *Scharnhorst* was all she was boasted to be and she gave us all a run for our money and it took a lot to sink her and we had our hands full doing it even if we were a crowd. She took a hell of a battering.'

The destruction of the *Scharnhorst* was a famous victory for the navy. Of the major German warships only the *Tirpitz* remained, disabled and confined to her fjord. Those who took part were justifiably proud, and those who missed out were equally disappointed. One junior officer had been transferred off the *Duke of York* just before the battle. It was 'heartbreaking . . . I felt miserable for a day about it,' he wrote in his journal. 'How I hated everyone!'

The Battle of North Cape would be the final engagement between capital ships without air support, armed only with their guns and supporting vessels. It was, as one historian put it, the 'last battle of the dinosaurs'. It was a triumph of intelligence, of technology, of organization, of efficiency and seamanship. In a letter to his mother, Bill

Withers was honest about the psychological challenge: 'Everybody was calm and cool during the action, well they were calm on the outside but they were a bit ruffled inside but they didn't show it, and the whole show went off a treat. I had a few "thoughts", so did everybody else, but they kept them to themselves.'

The destroyer HMS *Saumarez* had lost eleven men during the torpedo attack. 'The behaviour of the ship's company throughout was magnificent,' reported her commanding officer, Lieutenant Commander Eric Walmsley. 'The majority had never been under fire before and many had never been to sea six months ago. Before, during and after the action, the morale and "guts" of the officers and men were never for a moment in doubt.' *Norfolk* suffered seven casualties; her damage control teams undoubtedly prevented more. Aboard *Belfast*, wrote Bill Withers, there were only two injuries he knew of: 'One chap had a cordite case drop on his head and he only saw a few stars, the other chap was me (trust me to be in it when there's trouble about). I caught my finger in the door of the turret and fetched the skin off and bruised it, it's nothing serious but it's very sore.' In fact, there was one other notable casualty in *Belfast*. The Admiral's reindeer, a present from Russia, had gone mad in its hangar during the battle and had been put down.

After the battle there were prayer services, as Bill Withers put it, 'in thanks for our good fortune and lucky escape. As the buzzes go we nearly "got it" twice so we'd got plenty to be thankful for.' Then sailors set about writing letters to their family and friends. Many were eager to describe their own particular part in the battle. After a BBC radio broadcast described the action, several were keen to put right inaccuracies, particularly aboard *Belfast*, where there was some irritation at the suggestion that *Jamaica* had fired the decisive torpedo. 'I shall never forget it,' wrote Paul Chavasse to his wife. 'After it was over I felt as if I had run 20 miles though felt quite fresh during the action. I sustained myself from time to time with your Xmas toffee. At the end of it most of us had the most acute thirsts, reaction I suppose. It was some time before we could get a drink as our fresh water system had been smashed.'

Surgeon Lieutenant Dunlop explained the victory in a letter home:

'The essential thing in naval warfare is to make sure that you have got a superior force concentrated at the right place and at the right time – and it is by no means easy; and I reckon that our organisation at the Admiralty deserves high praise for getting the whole thing to run like clockwork; and it's been working up to this for a long time now, of course.' J. N. Rodwell reported the reception for HMS *Scorpion*: 'When we arrived back in this country all the ships in the harbour had their decks lined with their crews who gave us a terrible cheer as we steamed in. That is the end of a menace to our shipping and all we need now is a little peace and quietness and we hope some leave.'

'That's another Jerry off the list,' wrote Able Seaman Eddie Gould of HMS *Belfast* to his aunt Emma, before informing her that 'we had corned beef sandwiches for our Christmas lunch'. Because of the initial alert, Christmas aboard *Belfast* had been postponed. 'We had our xmas in the turret, eating biscuits,' wrote Bill Withers, 'but we are having our big eats at a later date to make up for it.' The belated Christmas menu, when it came a few days later, was some compensation: coffee, bacon, sausage, egg, rolls and marmalade for breakfast; for dinner, a starter of tomato soup followed by roast turkey, stuffing, boiled ham, bread sauce, runner beans and roast potatoes; the obligatory Christmas pudding and custard for dessert; Christmas cake at teatime, and cold roast pork and pickle for supper.

As HMS *Belfast* approached the Kola Inlet shortly after the battle, Admiral Burnett gave another speech to the ship's company over the loudspeaker. Before the battle, many of the ratings had baulked at his overt aggression but, as John Wilson recalled, his words now emphasized their collective achievement: 'I shall get a good deal out of this, and you will get nothing. But I want you to know that, in reality, anything given to me is given to the ship and to the squadron. Thank you all for your help.' The sailors were magnanimous. Here, wrote Wilson, was 'an honest man who put things in an honest way'. Fraser and Burnett received the accolades, save for a handful of awards for individual sailors, but there were few who begrudged them their rewards. After all, wrote Wilson, 'none of us had done anything but twiddle his particular knob and hope for the best'.

*

While the sailors of the victorious ships were recovering and writing letters home describing their exploits, Richard Walker was in Scotland preparing to join the newly built destroyer HMS *Wakeful*. After the necessary checks had been completed, *Wakeful* was commissioned, resurrecting the name of a destroyer sunk at Dunkirk, and the ship's company spent February working up. It was a peaceful time. In his diary, Walker described a trip to Loch Long near Arrochar: 'A glorious day and the narrow loch with high mountains on either side and the little white winding road running along the shore, looked as remote from the war as anywhere we could wish.' While conducting torpedo exercises in the Clyde, sailors took the opportunity to 'play football, climb the Cobbler, dance in the village hall, ring up home and our girl-friends, walk to Tarbert on Loch Lomond for lunch at the pub . . . in short, have the most delightfully unwarlike time'.

Only a few weeks later, *Wakeful* was in northern waters and Walker was on morning watch with two other men. 'Heavy snow squalls all day, temperature 29° F. Fog in patches,' he recorded in his diary on 1 April 1944. 'Discuss question of breakfast with great intensity and decide on porridge, kippers, fried eggs on bread, bacon, mushrooms and tomatoes, washed down with good strong coffee – actual breakfast was sausage and v. salty bacon! Crossed Arctic circle during afternoon watch.' *Wakeful* was part of the protective escort for a group of six aircraft carriers and fifteen Fleet Air Arm squadrons which were the strike force for Operation Tungsten. Barracuda torpedo-bombers would fly along with American-built Hellcats, Wildcats and Corsairs, Seafires and Swordfish to destroy the last of the Kriegsmarine's great battleships.

'Attack on *Tirpitz* during morning watch,' wrote Walker on 3 April. 'The aircraft took off three-quarters of an hour apart, and flew off in two strikes to bomb *Tirpitz*. It was a beautiful clear morning with a light breeze and calm sea. We could see the snow on the Norwegian mountains about sixty miles off to the south.' Four aircraft were lost during the attack, but the battleship had been hit fourteen times. Her armour had prevented more serious damage, but a further three months of repairs would be required. The commander-in-chief of the Home Fleet sent a message to the strike force: 'All congratulations. I could not be more pleased. There is no place for the Wicked when the Righteous set about them.'

The Fleet Air Arm made several further attempts to finish the job, but without success. In September 1944 RAF Lancaster bombers flying from Russian airfields made their first attack on *Tirpitz* using enormous 'Tallboy' bombs which, weighing 12,000lb, were ten times more powerful than the Fleet Air Arm's ordnance. Only one bomb hit its target through a defensive smokescreen, but this was enough to cause irreparable damage. *Tirpitz* was moved to Tromsø, where she was subjected to more RAF bombing attacks. On 12 November 1944, bombs from a final Lancaster strike penetrated the heavy armour and caused explosions which tore through the hull, causing the battleship to capsize. More than 1,000 men were trapped. Rescue teams cut through the upturned hull, but only eighty-six sailors were saved.

With *Tirpitz* incapacitated and *Scharnhorst* destroyed, greater numbers of merchant vessels could be escorted to the Arctic from early 1944. The convoys nevertheless remained a dangerous proposition. Enemy submarines continued to pose a constant threat, and the weather remained vicious. Rescuing men from stricken ships was as difficult as ever. John Roberts, now transferred from the battlecruiser *Renown* to the destroyer HMS *Serapis*, witnessed the torpedoing of the destroyer *Mahratta* in February 1944. Heavy snowstorms reduced visibility and confused radar. *Mahratta* had already been hit once when another strike caused a magazine to explode and the destroyer to sink rapidly. 'The state of the sea made it impossible for another destroyer to go alongside her,' noted Roberts in his journal. Only sixteen of the 236 men on board survived.

Over the course of the war more than 16 million tons of supplies were sent to the Soviet Union by Britain and the USA, nearly 4 million tons of which were transported by Arctic convoys. Nearly half were sent via the Pacific, the other quarter through the Persian Gulf. Britain convoyed all of its aid through the Arctic. Some £300 million worth of war supplies and another £120 million worth of raw materials, food and medical supplies was sent. This included more than 5,000 tanks, 7,000 aircraft, 9,000 bazookas, guns, rifles and automatic weapons, and 4,000 radio sets amongst other equipment. Fourteen minesweepers, ten destroyers, four submarines and a battleship were transferred to the Russian navy over the course of the war. This represented a substantial commitment, although it was eclipsed by the sheer scale of the American effort: nearly 15,000 aircraft, over 375,000 trucks, thousands of railway carriages and half a million tons of rails, a million miles of telephone cable, millions of tons of petrol and 15 million pairs of boots.

The Royal Navy lost eighteen warships and 1,944 men in the Arctic between 1941 and 1945. Ninety-eight merchant vessels were lost, with 829 deaths. Losses in the German navy were comparable, with one battleship, three destroyers, thirty-two submarines and numerous aircraft destroyed. Judged simply by relative casualty rates, this was the most dangerous convoy route, but the human cost went further. Physical and psychological trauma continued to take their toll long afterwards. While the participants of the other major convoy campaigns were decorated, there was no British medal for veterans of the Arctic.

Convoys to Russia continued long after the Soviet armies had begun to advance on Germany. Yet even in the final stages of the war, the Arctic convoys remained a dangerous and arduous task. On 5 February 1945 HMS *Campania* left Scapa to help escort convoy JW64 to Murmansk. Almost immediately upon reaching open water, it came under attack from a Junkers 88, which was destroyed by anti-aircraft fire. 'Lt Smythe was killed in the attack,' wrote Lieutenant Peter Cockrell in his diary. 'We heard the whole affair on the wardroom loud speaker in between Beethoven's 7th Symphony.' After fending off further air attacks, the convoy reached its destination a week later. As they entered the Kola Inlet, men from *Campania* witnessed the sinking of a former British destroyer, only recently donated to the Russians, as it patrolled outside Murmansk. Cockrell recorded the incident: 'Russian destroyer *Churchill* (ex USA) came out to meet us and was torpedoed with very heavy loss of life outside Kola Inlet.'

A few days later at Murmansk, a group of Norwegian refugees from the island of Soray were embarked. 'The menfolk of the island had killed the German garrison there and the Germans had destroyed everything and burnt the houses,' explained Cockrell. 'Russians refuse to accommodate the refugees so they are all coming with the convoy back to England, including an old lady of 81 and a baby of 2. We are also bringing back some British escaped prisoners of war and five American lunatics (where they come from, I don't know).' The bedraggled refugees were spread amongst several ships preparing to leave for Britain in convoy RA64. Before it left, the Russians performed a concert for the sailors and their passengers in an aircraft hangar, complete with choir, orchestra and folk-dancing.

When the convoy left on 17 February, a series of devastating attacks by enemy submarines sank two ships. Several traumatized Norwegian women and children were rescued, some picked up by HMS *Bluebell*. Cockrell described the subsequent events in his diary: 'At 3.30 in the afternoon *Bluebell* was literally blown to pieces in a blast of smoke and flame. One survivor out of a ship's company of 200 . . . I went for a rather twitchy three hours rest before my watch thinking of the rocket magazine and 52,000 gallons of aviation spirit directly below my cabin.'

The following day brought some respite, and medical officers set about the task of treating wounded civilians. 'The ship is crowded with Norwegians in chairs and camp beds,' wrote Cockrell. 'Some of the refugees are injured including a mother and her little boy and Doc Williams is very busy in the sick-bay.' Over the following days, hurricane-force winds made for uncomfortable conditions in the destroyer, but also helped to fend off enemy submarines. There was one blessing at the height of the storm: 'Baby son born to refugee on ship No. 93. Both well.'

A week later, the convoy had nearly reached Britain. Cockrell was relieved, but there was further tragedy: '100 miles to Faroes. Very cold but an <u>English looking</u> sky. The baby refugee aged 2 died of pneumonia – all flags half-masted.' A few days later *Campania* reached Greenock. 'Tied up at Tail o' the Bank at 1700,' noted Cockrell in his final diary entry. 'Ashore and to the Officer's Club for a bath and a real long sleep.'

# 17. Jack in Joe's Land

Eighteen-year-old George Hadden's first time at sea was aboard the cruiser HMS *Glasgow* escorting a convoy to Russia in January 1943. He spent most of the voyage at action stations in a small communications post next to the engine room, surrounded by ammunition stores and oil tanks. He and his fellow telephone operators remained there for three or four days at a time, using a bucket in the corner to relieve themselves, eating bully-beef sandwiches, and trying to ignore their perilous prospects should the ship be hit by a torpedo. When *Glasgow* finally neared the Russian coast, Hadden rushed to the upper deck at the first opportunity, eager to see their destination. 'It was about the most dismal place that I had ever seen,' he wrote, 'nothing but snow, ice and some dark fir trees and that was about it.'

British sailors travelled the world, experiencing diverse cultures and climates, sampling local cuisine and customs, exploring every kind of landscape from great cities to isolated tropical islands. Veterans could help novices seek out the best leisure activities wherever they happened to be, even in the absence of bright lights and easy amusement. Arctic Russia was different. The Royal Navy's most recent experience of the region was in 1919, when troops had been landed to support the anti-Bolshevik forces in the Russian Civil War. Murmansk and Archangel presented sailors with uncharted territory: a run ashore like no other.

Sailors from the warships and merchant vessels of incoming convoys usually stayed in Russia just as long as it took to unload and join a return convoy. If they were unfortunate, they might have to wait for a period of some weeks depending on sailing schedules. Others remained in Russia for longer. Survivors from ships sunk during their passage were stranded until space could be found for them on homeward-bound vessels. After the PQ17 disaster in 1942, some sailors remained for five months, from June to November, waiting for transport back to Britain. There were other long-term visitors. A modest fleet of British naval and civilian ships was eventually stationed in the ports to assist with harbour duties, minesweeping and anti-submarine work. A small RAF squadron flew from a makeshift airstrip in the barren hills. But the most permanent residents were those hardy few assigned to a small communications staff ashore.

In January 1942, nineteen-year-old William Johnston took the early-morning train known as the 'Jellicoe Special' from London to Thurso, from where sailors were shuttled to Scapa Flow. He boarded the cruiser HMS *Trinidad*, about to escort convoy PQ8 to Russia. On arrival, he made his way to the embryonic British wireless communications office at Polyarnoe. For the next eighteen months, this would be his home.

Johnston was one of around forty British officers and ratings posted to the wireless office. Polyarnoe was the main headquarters of the Red Fleet in the Kola Inlet, up the coast from Murmansk, the destination for most of the Arctic convoys. Leslie Sullivan arrived at the Polyarnoe station soon after William Johnston, in February 1942. His initial impressions were that it was 'very bleak. Very very bleak indeed. And very very cold.'

The men of Naval Party 100, as the group was designated, were the navy's main representatives in the Russian ports. They called themselves 'The Legion of the Lost'. Their number gradually expanded over the course of the war, but this did little to alleviate the feeling that they were at the very edge of the world. They were led by Rear Admiral Ernest Archer, the senior British naval officer (SNBO), who oversaw British operations in the region. 'This isolation has got to be experienced to be believed,' wrote Archer in September 1943. 'I have been struck by the reaction of those who pass through Russia for the first time and their unanimous remark: "Good God, do the people at home know about this state of affairs?"'

Polyarnoe was little more than a sparse collection of wooden huts, the Red Fleet Club, and another large brick building, known as Navy House, where the British contingent was based. The wireless station was on the top floor, with living quarters below. Russian sentries stood guard at the door. 'The atmosphere there in that wireless station was very very strange,' recalled Alexander Downing, who arrived in January 1943. 'It was an extraordinary place to be, at the time of year I went up there it was total darkness for 24 hours. No light at all.'

The chief duties of Naval Party 100 were to organize incoming and outbound convoys, and to manage coded signal traffic from ships around the Kola Inlet. They organized berths and anchorages, held briefings and conferences, arranged escort groups, provided stores and equipment, and monitored enemy signals. Power failures were frequent, and even the specialist coders and telegraphists struggled with the unique climatic conditions which garbled messages and scrambled chatter.

Some took shifts in Murmansk, the primary destination for incoming merchant ships. Bombed frequently by German planes flying from the nearby Finnish border, it was little more than the shell of a town. Most of the inhabitants lived in low huts which stood alongside the few larger brick buildings, the majority of which were dilapidated and damaged. 'At a rough estimate,' stated a British report in June 1944, 'one third has been entirely demolished, one third is not fit for habitation and not one single building has a half of its full complement of glass.'

Murmansk was said to have derived its name from the local Saami dialect, meaning 'the edge of the earth'. To Donald Povey, telegraphist aboard the trawler *Northern Pride*, it was simply 'a hole'. Joffre Swales, arriving aboard HMS *Norfolk*, was similarly unimpressed: 'I went into one eating house . . . Bare tables. Just pictures of Stalin and Lenin. And before every diner was just one plate of beetroot.' Most British visitors spent their time at the demure, dimly lit halls of the International Club or the Intourist Hotel. Living quarters for the wireless staff varied from the top floor of a grim block of flats in Stalin Prospekt to a small cottage beside the fish docks. 'We had a Russian housekeeper, who reported twice a week to the secret police,' recalled William Johnston, 'and we had a cook, and a Russian servant girl who kept the place tidy.' Phones were inevitably tapped. But because of the eccentricities of Russian wiring, attempts to contact Polyarnoe might easily result in hearing 'the news in Russian from Murmansk or a wild Slavonic symphony'.

Across the Kola Inlet from Murmansk lay Vaenga, which became a holding area for incoming escort ships. 'The surrounding country is made up of low rolling hills, the sides of which are covered with trees which look like silver spruce,' reported Midshipman Dick Garnons-Williams of HMS *Belfast* in his journal. 'I was scanning the shore with a pair of binoculars, and saw men ski-ing and also a horse drawn sledge moving along what appears to be the one and only road.'

John Wilson, arriving aboard HMS *Belfast* in 1942, was disheartened. 'The only presentable building in the place was the Red Army club,' he wrote, 'a gloomy establishment decorated exclusively with huge photographs of Stalin and the other Soviet leaders. We returned feeling that we had exhausted the possibilities of Arctic Russia.' Others found their way to the 'House of Culture', which displayed permanent exhibitions of Soviet propaganda. Loudspeakers in the street broadcast speeches or military marches. By 1944 a British auxiliary naval hospital had been established, one of only three brick buildings. Geoff Greenfield was posted there as a medical assistant, arriving with a foot of snow on the ground: 'The impression I got of Vaenga was that it was just a village dumped in a lot of mud and snow.'

The Kola Inlet was a militarized zone, with the Red Army fighting a fierce campaign nearby against combined Finnish and German forces. Murmansk was only a few miles from the front, and the flashes of gunfire could be seen at night over the hills. Joffre Swales watched 'little sledges or sleighs pulled by reindeers, carrying letters, post and mail to the Finnish front'. Russian soldiers patrolled the area constantly, establishing roadblocks, enforcing curfews and conducting incessant identification checks. William Grenfell passed by a camp housing captured German soldiers. 'They were just like animals,' he recalled. 'The ground was wet. They were in rags and tatters. And as far as I could see, their food was in a slop bucket, and was thrown into a wooden trough, and they squatted round this trough and just grabbed the food out with their hands . . . We felt sorry for them.'

William Johnston recalled an evening spent watching the Northern Lights: 'It was like somebody had a huge bowl of steaming liquid, and there were just bands of colour weaving all over the sky, every colour you could think of, and the stars dotted in between. And of course the snow lying underneath it reflected it back – it was beautiful. And in the middle of it all we had an air raid.' British ships used their advanced radio detection equipment to help provide early warnings of raids. Percy Price of HMS *Pozarica* witnessed the more old-fashioned response of the local authorities: 'There was a bloke who went round on a horse ringing a bell and shouting "Air Raid" in Russian round the villages.'

Archangel lay further around the coast to the south-east, on the estuary of the River Dvina in the heart of the White Sea. The surrounding area was sparsely populated, even by Russian standards. 'It was a poor place,' wrote J. R. Stuart White, a dental officer in HMS *Norfolk*, of the approach to Archangel in November 1941, 'just a couple of wooden huts by the river with a small boy soldier with a rifle on every corner.' Trains which ran between Murmansk and Archangel were old wood-burning locomotives which had to stop every so often to load up with fresh fuel. The 400-mile journey took around five days.

Unlike Murmansk, which benefited from the Gulf Stream and remained open all year round, Archangel was frozen and ice-bound for months at a time. The summer thaw brought mosquitoes and nauseating odours. It was nevertheless a popular posting for those wireless staff seconded to the town, designated Naval Party 200, largely because it lay beyond the range of German bombers. 'Polyarnoe was just a submarine base, with a few buildings dotted about in the snow in the hills,' recalled Leslie Sullivan. 'But Archangel was a proper town, with wooden sidewalks, and trolley buses running through.'

Into this impoverished region came a swarm of British and Allied sailors. Most were accommodated aboard their own ships, venturing into Murmansk or Archangel only occasionally. But over the course of 1942, as the numbers of ships sunk during Arctic convoys began to rise, hundreds of survivors were deposited ashore. They were housed in makeshift camps and wooden huts with little more to eat than black bread and grass soup. Often without proper clothing, they were dependent upon the material generosity of other sailors.

John Kenny, a survivor from HMS *Edinburgh*, was amongst those housed in a Soviet army barracks in the hills above Murmansk in May 1942. The buildings were unheated, furnished only with wooden bunks and straw mattresses. There were no toilets, so the sailors made makeshift trenches. 'A number of people had dysentery type stomach disorders,' wrote Kenny, 'and there were numerous crises in the early morning when it was found that overnight the Russians had taken all the toilet rolls to make paper bags to put in a type of tobacco seed to smoke.'

Bob Collins survived the sinking of the merchant ship *Empire Lawrence*. 'The washing facilities were really crude,' he recalled. 'It consisted of a trough . . . above this trough was a pipe, and along this pipe were holes, and in each of these holes was a six inch nail . . . so you pushed the nail up, got a bit of water in your hands and splashed your face . . . most of the survivors during their stay in the camp at Murmansk got crabs and body lice.' Things improved when they were moved to a schoolhouse outside Archangel. The survivors spent their time scrounging bread, cigarettes and cups of tea from the crews of the ships in dock, many of whom had just survived the PQ17 convoy.

The men of Naval Party 100 did what they could to help survivors but the increasing numbers of men stranded in Russia meant that it was impossible to provide adequate care, particularly after PQ17. 'We could never build up big enough stocks for the survivors,' explained William Johnston. 'At one time we had almost a thousand survivors living ashore in North Russia, off the *Edinburgh*, the *Trinidad* and merchant ships. We went through our kit and gave away as much of our clothing as we could afford to give. We gave up packs from our cigarette ration to send to the hospital, or wherever they were stationed. We tried to help them as much as we could, but we didn't have all that much.'

Medical care was the most pressing need. In July 1942 the Soviet authorities refused permission for the British to establish their own dedicated facilities near Murmansk. The local Russian hospital was a converted school, and enthusiastic staff could do little to make up for overcrowding and inadequate equipment. 'This place is incredible,' stated one British report in 1941. 'It is stuffy and badly ventilated, it looks unclean, the beds are crowded together, the nursing staff vary but in many the white coat they wear is insufficient to hide their uncleanliness.'

Once the Soviet authorities finally relented, a rudimentary treatment centre was established to deal with injured men arriving with convoys, transported in a battered old van. Sick Berth Attendant Geoff Greenfield described the facilities: 'We had two wards, which held about twelve patients each, and two single rooms, in case we needed those for special care. We had an operating theatre, which was extremely basic.' Cases of frostbite were common, and there were several amputations of feet, hands and even lower legs. But most harrowing for the medical staff were the psychological casualties, particularly those rescued from the sea. 'They were in a hell of a state, mentally,' recalled Greenfield. 'We had no psychiatrist or anything like that. The doctors just had to do the best they could, and we kept them quiet with drugs, and sent them home as quickly as we possibly could. But we had to wait for convoys to come up to transport them back. But they were traumatised, those poor young men.'

Both the permanent British staff and temporary visitors struggled to find food. Local shops had empty windows and bare shelves. Staples such as eggs, potatoes and green vegetables were in short supply. Royal Navy officials travelling by railway between Moscow and Archangel were frequently accosted by local children trading wild strawberries for bread. One British report in the summer of 1942 predicted that the Russian convoys would soon be carrying only food.

Naval Party 100 relied on incoming convoys to replenish their provisions. Although supplies were unpredictable, there were usually sufficient quantities of preserved rations to feed them. 'Our food was pretty stodgy,' explained William Johnston. 'Everything was in tins . . . The Russian black bread was very sour, and if you didn't eat it that day it went as hard as concrete . . . A lot of us suffered from constipation because we weren't getting a lot of roughage.' Sailors and shore staff alike were given vitamin pills and lime juice to help prevent scurvy. For the men of convoy ships docked in the Kola Inlet or Archangel, basic rations often had to be endured without enhancement. 'We were down to bully beef and biscuits,' recalled Jack Seal of HMS *Pozarica* of the ship's arrival after the disastrous PQ17 convoy. 'The Russians gave us some yak meat, which was so tough nobody could eat it.'

Survivors housed in the military camp at Vaenga shared facilities with the Red Army soldiers. 'It was dreadful,' recalled William Grenfell. 'Three times a day, a sort of green soup, vegetable soup, sometimes you had a small piece of meat in it.' There was one local delicacy, however, which met with his approval: 'Pine needle tea . . . it really tasted good.' Bob Collins recalled similar meals: 'Couple of slices of rye bread for breakfast, for lunch you got a sort of cabbage-type soup with little bits and pieces floating around which could have been yak or goat or something.'

Alcohol was far more readily available than food. The men of Naval Party 100 looked forward to deliveries of cans of British beer, but were forced to wait before their treat could be enjoyed. 'They had been standing on the jetty for a while,' explained Alexander Downing. 'They were in tins, and it said "Chill Before Serving", but in fact you had to stand it on a stove before you could actually make it liquid enough to drink.'

Vodka was the local staple. Russians adhered to a strict social etiquette which prohibited them from public displays of inebriation. This led many sailors to underestimate the potency of the substance. When Charles Hutchinson went ashore from HMS *Intrepid* in June 1942, he was warned not to drink the vodka. Inevitably, some of his messmates ignored the warnings and ordered shots in long-stemmed glasses. 'They just tilted their heads back, down it went, and then they just slithered off the chairs down on to the floor,' wrote Hutchinson in his diary. 'They withered away like icicles in front of a fire, no power over their legs and then they started hollering and lashing out at anything, and slashing themselves about, and then all the drink was stopped, even the wine.'

Beyond the austere drinking halls, distractions normally ubiquitous elsewhere in the world were all but absent. In the Russian ports, everyday existence sometimes seemed as bleak as the winter land-scape. For the permanent staff of Naval Party 100, boredom was a real threat to morale. 'Our entertainment,' recalled Geoff Greenfield, 'consisted of walking, skiing when permitted, and indoors we had table tennis and two pairs of boxing gloves, with which we used to knock each other out.'

Organized sport depended entirely on weather conditions, but some activities were possible. Alec Dennis recalled skiing near Pol-yarnoe in an area known as 'Death Valley'. He was, he wrote, 'put to shame by little Russian boys on what looked like barrel staves, rush-ing down the slopes with broad grins and great élan'. Football was also a popular pastime. A team consisting of British merchant sailors entered the local league at Archangel, calling themselves Inter-Club. After the tournament had ended the Archangel Town Committee of Sport and Physical Culture posted the final table: '1st D.K.A., 2nd Kiselyova, 3rd Dynamo, 4th Belozertseva, 5th Inter-Club'. Despite having gained the most points, the British team were placed last as they did not hold Soviet citizenship.

Every week a film in English would be shown at the Russian Navy Club in Polyarnoe. Each convoy brought with it new reels, eagerly anticipated by the wireless staff. In the periods when operations were suspended, however, they had to endure repeat showings of what-ever picture happened to have been delivered last. A dull romance about Johan Strauss called *The Great Waltz* was ingrained into the memory of any man who spent the summer of 1943 in Russia.

Newspapers and magazines such as *Picture Post* would occasionally be delivered, and officers arranged for quizzes, talks and lectures on topical issues such as the Beveridge Plan. The shore staff compiled their own home-made magazine called 'Northern Light', which fea-tured short items of news on the progress of the war and contributions of stories, poems, jokes and song lyrics written by officers and rat-ings, often under pseudonym. There were also pieces on local news and events. 'On the evening of May 11th, a scratch soccer match was played between a Russian eleven and an eleven from the Hospital staff,' reported one article. 'The Russians won by 9 goals to 4. One of our team is now in hospital.'

A concert party was formed to sing on Sundays and to perform to visiting ships and Russian officers. Lieutenant James Bold had worked as a producer for the BBC before the war and was the catalyst for the highlight of the war in Polyarnoe: an all-singing, all-dancing satirical pantomime, complete with costumes and sets made by the shore staff. 'It was based on Jack and the Beanstalk,' explained William Johnston. 'Because Stalin was the boss-man, we called it Jack in Joe's Land – we being the Jacks and he being the Joe.'

Personal relationships between British sailors and Russians were complicated by climate, culture and commissars. 'The Russians themselves are a mixed lot,' wrote Midshipman R. W. Herbert Smith of HMS *Belfast* in his training journal in March 1943. 'Some are surly and won't talk to you at all while others are very friendly and helpful. They are all very confident in a Russian victory and nearly everybody wears a uniform of sorts.' On a personal level, British sailors and Russian matelots often shared a mutual affinity. 'The Russian sailors were marvellous people,' recalled Downing. 'At the Fleet Club we were all Jack Tars together . . . They taught us to sing Russian songs.' The International Club in Archangel, recalled Bob Collins, 'was overflowing with vodka. You never bought anything because the Russian soldiers used to buy everything for you. You'd sit down at a table, and you'd have to drink to keep up with them.'

Alexander Downing was part of a small naval delegation which travelled to Moscow in the autumn of 1943 to deliver confidential documents to the British Embassy. He visited the Bolshoi and watched a performance of *Swan Lake*. In the streets, his bell-bottomed trousers attracted crowds of Russians, who recognized the uniform from the dubbed version of *In Which We Serve*, showing in the capital's cinemas. 'They would pat us on the back and touch our shoulders,' he recalled. 'They were extremely nice to us.'

Barter was a constant social medium. Murmansk operated on an exchange economy. Cigarettes and chocolates were the de facto currency of the ports. Locals would offer trinkets, brooches and badges, in exchange for these luxuries. Russian servicemen offered military knives and second-hand clothing. 'I bought a Russian fur hat complete with a red star,' wrote E. J. Marshall of a run ashore in January

1943. 'It was only later that I discovered that the hat had a patch over a large hole and I wondered about the fate of the previous owner.'

Most of the female population of the Russian ports were older women employed in labouring, farming and dock work. Younger women were often either well-educated interpreters, briefed and monitored by Soviet commissars and wary of over-familiarity, or hostesses in the clubs, eager to gain custom and with sufficient experience to fend off advances. The dance was the quintessential opportunity for fraternization all over the world, but opportunities for British sailors to attend with Russian women were limited, particularly in the early years. Unsupervised contact remained minimal, but organized events had become more frequent by 1945. Nevertheless, some of the young women who did approach British sailors had ulterior motives. Ratings recalled dances attended by Russian girls who attempted to extract information from their partners: 'How many destroyers have you got?' 'How many million barrels of oil do you produce in England?'

Relationships between British sailors and Russian women were always problematic. 'The Soviet authorities like nothing so much as to manufacture a complaint against the British personnel in North Russia,' stated one official report. 'Buzz is that they have orders to shoot if they see one speak to a woman,' recorded Peter Cree, a junior officer in HMS *Venus*, in his journal in January 1944. 'Better one still – two matelots here doing 325 years prison sentence for asking a woman the time. Atmosphere is unfriendly to say the least.' There were several occasions upon which Soviet officials refused to ratify exit visas for British sailors and accused them of, as the official language had it, 'putting a girl in the family way'.

Soviet authority was widely perceived to be draconian. When nearing Murmansk, the crew of HMS *Norfolk* was told that 'Russian officers and sentries must be obeyed promptly. Sentries are liable to fire instantly if not obeyed, without regard to language difficulties.' Tales of brutality were widespread. Sailors from HMS *Trinidad*, under repair in Murmansk in April 1942, reported seeing Russian guards shoot dead two elderly local men caught pilfering from the ship's cargo, one of whom had stolen a jar of jam. Another story concerned a wardroom party held aboard a British ship during which a Russian officer had taken one drink too many. The Royal Navy host, so it was said, had accepted the apologies of a commissar the following day and informed him that the officer in question was welcome to return anytime. He was told that the Russian had been shot that morning for his indiscretion.

British shore staff laboured under a catalogue of bureaucratic hurdles, political machinations and administrative inertia. Visas were refused for additional staff, which made it impossible to organize relief for men who had been in Russia for months and sometimes years. Strict customs regulations were seemingly invented at will, and private mail was seized for censorship. Movement between the British offices was restricted, and surveillance on British personnel became more stringent and increasingly explicit.

'The situation can be summed up very briefly,' wrote Rear Admiral Archer. 'Our life is akin to that of a concentration camp but with the difference that those in one of those establishments at least know who their wardens are and what to expect.' In late 1943, the British inadvertently obtained the instructions for the Liaison Department of the Soviet Fleet at Polyarnoe. 'It directs how to keep an eye on the British,' reported Rear Admiral Archer to his superiors at the Admiralty, 'with particular reference to their tastes as regards wine, women and song, how to extract information and what was wanted . . . The reference to women is rather superfluous as we never meet any.'

Archer's tenure as SBNO encompassed the most challenging period for Anglo-Russian relations during the long convoy suspensions of 1943. Hundreds of unoccupied and dispirited men roamed the ports in search of entertainment. Admiral Arseny Golovko, the senior Russian naval officer, and Soviet officials in Moscow demanded that the British government act to prevent sailors 'running amok' and 'maltreating Soviet citizens'. For its part, the Admiralty was adamant that conduct had been 'admirable', and that 'considering the incessant indignities to which our sailors are subjected in North Russia, it is amazing that so few incidents have occurred'.

The case of one Sergeant Ryan, an anti-aircraft gunner aboard the SS *Pontfield*, was typical of many similar incidents. In June 1943, he was identified after a disagreement involving a hostess at the International Club in Murmansk. Promptly arrested by local militia, he appeared to have accepted his fate until, according to a British report, 'Ryan objected strongly to being marched through the streets in uniform in daylight followed by as he termed it a b ----- procession with a crowd of f ---- Russians who in any case were no f ---- use.' He finally managed to get back to his ship, after which protracted negotiations took place when the Soviet authorities demanded his surrender. Eventually, the British took unilateral legal action. As Rear Admiral Archer reported, 'I have inflicted the heaviest possible punishment on him, namely that he never again should set foot on Soviet Russian soil.'

Much of the trouble ashore was caused by merchant sailors. The Ministry of War Transport was frequently warned by the Admiralty to impress upon merchant seamen that 'Soviet Authorities take a very strict view of brawling offences ashore, and that men may get into serious trouble for what in England might be regarded as a comparatively minor offence'. Of five major incidents reported by the local authorities in July and August 1943, four involved men from the merchant ships. These generally involved charges of 'hooliganism' and crimes such as 'smoking in a prohibited area' and 'disparaging remarks against the Soviet regime'. Most charges of violence involved abuse of Soviet officials, usually found to have been the arresting parties. Aside from these cases, there were regular scuffles between locals and sailors and a handful of more serious crimes, including a murder, along with several suicides and 'mental cases'.

The British response was as pragmatic as ever. Once in Soviet courts, sailors were in danger of receiving draconian sentences, such as two years' imprisonment if caught smoking where forbidden, and five years for striking an official. Although a number of British ratings and merchant sailors were held in Soviet captivity for short periods, at most three months, the majority of troublemakers were taken quickly to naval brigs, out of the hands of Soviet militia. They were usually swiftly returned to Britain. This was largely achieved through the prompt actions of captains and commanders of individual vessels and the SBNO, who dealt arbitrarily with as many cases as possible.

Despite these isolated problems, discipline was remarkably good amongst the British naval and merchant crews in Russia. Morale was maintained through a combination of the efforts of individual ships' captains and the shore-based administration. Drills and exercises were frequent, and competitive sporting activities encouraged. Some films and concerts were provided. Throughout the Arctic campaign, deliveries of charitable gifts including playing cards, games, newspapers and magazines were vital in supplementing the existing provisions. In June 1942 the Overseas League provided 50,000 cigarettes and the RN War Amenities Fund sent 1,000lb of chocolate.

The relationship between navy men and merchant sailors was also crucial. Although the Royal Navy was not officially responsible for merchant sailors, from the summer of 1943 all British provisions in north Russia were pooled, and canteen supplies, clothing and other stores were distributed amongst merchant ships. The two sets of sailors shared leisure activities, establishing a joint football league. A. J. Clarke, quartermaster of minesweeper HMS *Jason*, was a particularly keen player. He kept a journal recording the results of various tournaments which took place during eight months in 1943. An HMS *Jason* XI took part in a joint naval and merchant seamen's competition, the 'RN and MN North Russian Championship'. On the anniversary of the formation of the Russian Fleet on 25 July 1943, a match took place between a combined team of British sailors and the Russian champions, watched by an estimated 2,500-strong crowd including 'all the Russian Admirals and "big nobs" . . . it was quite a do'. Despite losing the match 3–2 it was, for Clarke, 'one of the big moments of my existence up here'.

Whatever reservations they had about the authoritarian commissars, those who served in north Russia often left the region with a vivid impression of the character of the ordinary Russian people: their spirit, their hardiness and their indefatigability. Sidney Taylor served aboard HMS *Seagull*, a minesweeper sent to the White Sea to demonstrate her methods to the Russians. Taylor was shocked to discover that the Red Navy vessels used hand grenades to set off mines. They might not have had the necessary equipment, the implacable traditions or the well-practised skills of the British, but their strengths lay elsewhere:

I got the feeling that they could take anything, the Russians, and dole it out as well I may add, but they were as tough as old boots. Really tough people . . . The winters they had to endure, and the way they wrapped themselves up, and the way they rolled cigarette tobacco in old newspapers to smoke. They had to rough it, no doubt about that.

Communism was one of the great fears of the Admiralty, and so the exposure of British sailors to the Russian people and Soviet propaganda was the cause of some concern. Yet those who witnessed the responses of sailors to the reality of life in Murmansk and Archangel attempted to reassure their superiors. In the opinion of SBNO Rear Admiral Archer in August 1943, it would soon shatter any political illusions, even amongst merchant crews: 'There is no doubt what the personnel of these ships think of our Allies – even the reddest of the red . . . have altered their views of Communism.' Official reports stated that 'no one who has served here could ever again attach any importance to the Communist bogey – that is a system which just would not work in Britain'.

There were some, nevertheless, who retained sympathies for the ideology, if not the practical implementation, of communism, but many sailors echoed the official statements. 'I had a hatred of Russia,' stated Jack Seal. 'I know they were in an immense struggle, but I just didn't like what I saw there. I felt there was more class distinction than I'd seen anywhere in the world. The commissars and their wives seemed to have the shopping baskets with nice food in it. The peasants sat on the kerbside with their tins.' 'If we did take any Communists to Russia,' wrote Vincent Shackleton, 'we certainly did not bring any back.'

'Anglo-Russian relations are something like a game of snakes and ladders,' reported one diplomat to the Joint Intelligence Committee in June 1943. 'So far we have spent much time on the snakes.' Naval Party 100 knew this better than anyone. By November 1943, the Soviet authorities began to relax their strict bureaucratic demands. Greater numbers of visas were permitted, allowing replacements to be arranged for tired staff and expanding their numbers. By 1944, the group numbered over 300. Their efforts were undoubtedly of great value to the organization, administration and morale of the British sailors who arrived with the Arctic convoys. Their task was one of the most thankless of the war, and yet it was critical to the success of the entire endeavour. What occupied them above all else, however, was an issue which was commented upon time and again by the SBNO and his colleagues: the problem of 'prestige'.

In September 1943, Rear Admiral Douglas Fisher, of the British Naval Mission in Moscow, reported: 'Mr Stalin made a particular point by saying that there would never have been any difficulties put in the way of British Service personnel entering Russia had it not been for the patronising manner of the British sailors there toward the Russians.' In October, Foreign Secretary Anthony Eden echoed this when he informed the Prime Minister of Stalin's statement that 'if only our people in North Russia had treated his people as equals, none of these difficulties would have arisen'.

British officers unquestionably felt themselves to be superior to their Soviet counterparts. Most of the Royal Navy officials based in north Russia were older men, often former commanders brought out of retirement at the start of the war, but it was thought that 'however long retired any officer who comes out here may be, and however much he has forgotten, he still remembers more about the sea than his Russian companion has ever known or is ever likely to know'.

British assessments of the quality of the Soviet Navy were disparaging, highlighting a reliance on rigid doctrine and proscriptive training which produced little collective spirit. One report concluded that 'no "camaraderie" exists in the Red Navy . . . Soviet officers in conversation with their British colleagues have said that no social life exists aboard Soviet warships in the U.S.S.R.' Amongst the Russian officers there was thought to be a 'general low standard in intellect', a lack of responsibility and a poor standard of professional conduct. They were 'slovenly, dirty and untidy both in themselves and in their general manner in dealing with the ratings'. The Russian sailors, although the vast majority were inexperienced, were at least hardworking: 'They are very keen and work at their various duties from 0630 to 2230 daily and appear to be perfectly happy in so doing.'

What proved most unsettling to the officers of Naval Party 100 was that Britain's naval superiority and reputation, maritime power and imperial credibility seemingly counted for little in the face of Soviet bureaucratic obstruction. The Royal Navy was simply not accustomed to such treatment. The Russian attitude was, according to one report, an attempt at 'humiliating' Britain, and the result of Soviet ambitions to be treated as a 'first class power'. Furthermore, the apparent disdain displayed by Soviet officials towards the British was in sharp contrast to their dealings with the US Navy liaison officers. To the naval exiles of north Russia, the decline of British prestige and influence appeared palpable. They seemed to be witnessing at first hand the end of Britain's predominance.

Most of the personnel serving with Naval Party 100 were eager to return home as soon as their period of service was complete. Those sent to the British station at Polyarnoe generally served no more than eighteen months before their posting expired and they were due home leave. The minesweeper HMS *Jason* was in Russia between February and October 1943. 'We all thought we were going to be left up here to rot,' wrote a relieved A. J. Clarke in his diary as *Jason*'s stay came to an end. 'Eight months in this joint is enough to drive anyone screwy.'

Those marooned in Russia by the sinking of their ships were taken back to Britain as quickly as possible. Some, however, faced an indefinite stay. Space aboard returning vessels was limited. Convalescents had priority; any remaining places were allocated by lottery. John Kenny, the survivor from HMS *Edinburgh*, missed out in the draw for a place on HMS *Trinidad* in May 1942, two weeks after he had arrived in Russia. *Trinidad* was sunk during the voyage to Britain after being attacked by German bombers. In June 1942 he again thought himself unlucky after the draw for convoy QP13. Most of his friends from *Edinburgh* departed on HMS *Niger*, leaving only twenty behind. In bad weather, the convoy strayed into an Allied minefield off Iceland. *Niger* struck a mine and sank, killing nine officers and 140 ratings, including all the *Edinburgh* men. It was 5 July, and Kenny had been celebrating his twentieth birthday. Shaken and demoralized after hearing the news, he finally made it safely back to Britain in August 1942.

George Hadden returned to Russia as part of the last ever Arctic convoy, JW66, in April 1945. Now twenty, he had been made a junior officer in the small anti-submarine frigate HMS *Goodall*. Just before the ship was due to return to Britain, she was ordered to look for several U-boats which were suspected to be lying in wait around the bay in a desperate last stand. *Goodall* went out to sweep the area and was hit by a torpedo which exploded the main forward gun magazines. Hadden found himself clinging to a rail above the freezing sea: 'I couldn't hang on any longer and just had to let go and smashed myself against the side of the ship and fell into the water and I thought well that's the end and I'm now going to die, but strangely enough this didn't perturb me.'

*Goodall* sank, killing 98 of the 156 men aboard. The submarine responsible, U-286, was immediately hit by depth charges, killing all 51 of its crew. Hadden survived, scrambling onto a life raft before passing into delirium. He regained consciousness in the Soviet army hospital in Polyarnoe, with severe frostbite and a jaw broken in five places. He remained in the dark, dank ward for several days, enduring both the stench and the staple meal of semolina. Before long he was declared well enough to be transported to the British Naval Mission, where the other survivors were based. By the time he returned to Britain, Germany had been defeated. Hadden was amongst the last survivors to leave Russia, but his war was not over. 'I got a bit of leave,' he wrote, 'and went out to the Far East in a minesweeper.'

# 18. City of Ships

In June 1943, there was keen debate amongst the midshipmen of HMS *Kent* about the next strategic development of the war. Richard Campbell-Begg explained in his journal: 'Bombing raids against Germany and Italy have gained momentum and an "invasion sweep" has been organised on where our next landings will be in the Mediterranean. I have drawn Crete.' The sweepstake prize pot reached £10, but Campbell-Begg was to be disappointed.

Lieutenant Commander Vere Wight-Boycott, commanding officer of HMS *Ilex*, was also eager to learn about the imminent landings. The destroyer had spent most of June near Bizerta on the Tunisian coast, the base for operations around Sicily and Sardinia. 'A gloomy place it is,' he wrote in his diary. 'Before the First Army drove the Germans out, they systematically went through the town and made it unliveable. As a first step they destroyed all the sanitary arrangements, down to breaking lavatory pans and washbasins with a hammer. As a final Hunnish act they left the mark of the beast all over walls and floors . . . The civilian population has left and the city to all intents and purposes is dead.'

*Ilex* took part in the bombardment of Pantelleria, a small island to the west of Malta. It was a valuable strategic asset but the 11,000 Italian defenders surrendered with minimal resistance. 'Rather like throwing apples at a lame vicar,' was Wight-Boycott's verdict. It turned out to be the first stage of the imminent invasion of Sicily. 'On 6 July we received an order to open the secret envelopes and charts we have been carrying round for some time now,' he wrote in his diary. 'Soon afterwards we got a signal that told us that the first boats should run ashore at 0245 on the 10th July ("D" Day as it is called).'

*Ilex* would help to protect the Allied landings in what was termed

Operation Husky. The British contingent would form the Eastern Task Force, under the command of Admiral Bertram Ramsay, the mastermind of the Dunkirk evacuation. It would land troops on the south-east coast of Sicily, aiming to capture Syracuse and move inland. The Western Task Force, landing on the south-western sea-board, would be the responsibility of the Americans. The operation would begin with airborne troops landed by gliders, and a bombard-ment would pre-empt the main landings. Naval escorts would protect both task forces, and the entire operation would be covered out at sea by the warships of Force H. Enemy submarines were a particular concern as were enemy air forces, outnumbered but with the advan-tage of proximity. Allied submarines, battleships and destroyers attempted to cover every potential threat to the landing route. The invasion armada was overwhelmingly British: of the 279 warships taking part, only 68 were American and 12 from other Allied navies. Another 200 merchant ships carried supplies.

German commanders had no more knowledge of the plan than *Kent*'s midshipmen and, hoodwinked by a complex Allied deception, sent reinforcements to the Balkans and Sardinia. Yet the Italian and German defenders of Sicily were still expected to prove a stern test, not least for the 2,000 landing craft which had to be shepherded towards the beachhead. Since 1940, dozens of different types of trans-port had been developed for Combined Operations. Some could travel directly from port to beach; others arrived offshore and loaded their passengers into smaller craft. Merchant ships, from ferries to tankers, were converted into landing ships which could unload troops and tanks down ramps from open bows. Each variation had a differ-ent designation: Landing Ship or Landing Craft – LS or LC – followed by Infantry (I) Tank (T), Mechanised (M), Rocket (R), Gun (G), and several other variations. First-wave troops were delivered in Landing Craft Assault (LCA).

Commander George Blundell, executive officer of the battleship *Nelson*, was expecting the worst. 'It is blazing hot,' he wrote in his diary the day before the invasion. 'The sea gently ruffled blue, sky cloudless. It is as pretty and splendid a picture as one could see. It seems strange that hundreds of men will be dying on the beaches tomorrow.' Later, in the midst of an unseasonable storm, he added: 'It is at times like this that I'm glad I'm a sailor and not a soldier. Just think of the poor devils huddled in landing craft, wet with spray, feeling seasick, waiting to land in the grey of dawn on an unknown beach, having just spent fourteen days in cramped, blazing hot transport.'

Though they were removed from much of the visceral intensity of infantry combat, many sailors were nevertheless deeply conscious of their duty of care over the soldiers in the front line. Nowhere was this felt more keenly than at the helm of a landing craft. There were many shared emotions between navy and army men. Lieutenant Dennis Brown was in command of a flotilla of landing craft. 'The grim preamble and anticipation,' he wrote, 'was always the worst part of it all. The ritual loading of my revolver, putting on my lifebelt and steel helmet, making my way to my boat.' During the approach to the beach, he admitted, 'my mind was in something of a turmoil'. But, in common with every other man, his aim was to 'never let anyone see that you might be concerned'.

Brown had to ensure he deposited his soldiers in the right place, as well as holding position to organize the rest of his flotilla. A single-minded focus was a necessity. Dozens of gliders attempting to land in advance of the seaborne forces had crashed into the sea. 'I heard many desperate cries for help coming from the water,' wrote Brown. 'One's every instinct would be to go to their aid, whoever they might be . . . but, against my every such instinct I had to ignore them. I had to. I could not stop, I dare not stop. I could well have completely buggered up the entire operation in my sector . . . It was all very heart-rending.'

Others were fully exposed to the dangers of the front line. Ken Oakley belonged to a Royal Naval Commando unit, part of the vanguard to ensure organization on the beaches. He landed at Avola, in the centre of the British zone, and described his experiences in his journal:

Tat-Tat-Tat-Tat, Bren guns began to speak and then 'Crunch', 'Down Door' and we were there. A sapper began to cry, plead and cling to the floor-boards, swearing he would not move. We left him (his nerve was gone) and dived into about three feet of water to wade fifty yards to the shore. The shrill whine of bullets speeded us on and at last we went to earth at the water's edge.

Oakley and the other commandos set up lights around the area to guide the second wave, then tracked back across the beach to mark other favourable spots, 'directing the avalanche of men ashore'. After an hour, a nearby landing craft was shelled and beached. Oakley waded out to encourage soldiers to escape down ladders into the water:

A few jumped and I steadied them as they fell and then it came. A terrific explosion and I felt myself fading away into oblivion. I came to under the water. I felt numb and shocked . . . then I felt someone clutch my legs and drag me down again. I lost my reason and kicked like mad until I was free and shot to the surface. A body floated by, its limbs still kicking, it must have been the man who clutched me. The water had become a sea of blood and limbs.

HMS *Ilex* was tasked with helping to screen the invasion forces from submarines. Soon after dawn, an ASDIC contact was made nearby. *Ilex* was despatched with another destroyer, *Echo*, and given an hour to hunt. They struggled to find the submarine, dropping depth charges but without success. 'By this time it was broad daylight,' wrote Wight-Boycott, 'and we were only 20 miles from the south coast of the toe of Italy.' The hour was up, and he was preparing to inform his superiors that they had failed: 'I was shouting to the yeoman to pass my signal when a U-boat popped up like a jack in the box on *Echo*'s wake.'

Both ships attacked immediately. The first shots were wild – 'about three miles over', estimated Wight-Boycott – but then shells smashed through the submarine's hull, just below the conning tower. Soon, only a handful of survivors were left in the water. Boats from *Echo* set about rescuing them. There was some disgruntlement on *Ilex*'s upper deck. 'Everyone on board was so obviously desperately disappointed that we should have nothing to show for it,' wrote Wight-Boycott, 'that I eventually closed in and picked up six men.'

Attacks by the Luftwaffe proved the most effective enemy resistance. Telegraphist D. A. Hibbit was serving in the supply ship *Ennerdale*, supporting the invasion. At dawn on 10 July, the support group had arrived off the coast, before the landing craft were released to make their way inshore. At that stage, wrote Hibbit in his diary, 'everything was fairly quiet'. He and three signalmen had slung their hammocks in the open under the bridge. Not long afterwards, he awoke to the sound of gunfire:

> Suddenly the whole ship shook violently from stem to stern and our anti-aircraft guns opened fire on the several twin-engined bombers passing overhead. As I fell out of my hammock a stick of heavy bombs just missed us on our starboard beam sending up columns of water and shrapnel, and my hammock and the signalmen's hammocks were swamped with water . . . From that moment onwards we hardly had a moment's peace.

The tanker came under frequent, determined air attack. For the crew of a supply ship, this was a particular concern. 'We had to fuel plenty of ships with oil, petrol and water,' wrote Hibbit. 'All I wanted was to get out of this place – it was getting too hot.' After several days of nerves, the tanker was withdrawn on 14 July, much to Hibbit's relief: 'Thank goodness. We had sustained 22 near misses out of 20 air-raids through a period of the four worst days I have ever known.'

Despite such air attacks, over 80,000 men and 7,000 vehicles were landed on Sicily in the space of three days, and with far less bloodshed than had been feared. Submarines were unable to break the Allied perimeter: four German and three Italian boats were sunk. Shore batteries were effectively silenced by ferocious shelling from warships. Notable by their absence throughout were the powerful Italian warships. George Blundell, who had been so pessimistic beforehand, commented in his diary the day after the first landings:

> I believe all these Continental countries are scared of the sea, and have an inferiority complex about the Royal Navy . . . There were no enemy reports and no RDF contacts. RDF is now called Radar to

conform with the Yanks . . . Brief reports started to come through: the Commandos had captured their beaches, 44 beach was captured, Amber and Red beaches were captured . . . At dawn we had a splendid view of Etna, 92 miles away and also to the North we could see the toe of Italy. It was a simply wonderful golden morning.

'It was almost unreal,' wrote Admiral Ramsay to his wife, 'to find oneself off Sicily with Etna looking down on the scene of the landings. Hundreds literally of ships of the largest size down to the smallest and one had to pinch oneself to make sure one was not in a dream. The coast looked so sleepy and peaceful.' Within a few days of the landings, the area was safe enough for commander-in-chief General Dwight D. Eisenhower to tour the beaches. He observed the American zones before coming aboard the destroyer HMS *Petard* for a meeting with Montgomery and a tour of the British invasion beaches. 'On our way round the coast an enemy gun fired three rounds at us,' wrote Petty Officer Reg Crang in his diary. 'Each shot fell very short so there was no danger but it made the General jump.' Several British sailors asked Eisenhower for his autograph. When *Petard*'s first lieutenant noticed the gaggle of fans, recorded Crang, 'he stamped on it straight away'.

Later that month, on 26 July, Vere Wight-Boycott recorded the news that Mussolini had been ousted by King Victor Emmanuel and his own Fascist colleagues. *Il Duce*'s whereabouts were unknown, he noted, but he recognized that this was a significant development: 'This seems the first and most important step in neutralising Italy's war effort, though I imagine Italy will become just another occupied country very shortly though who will be the occupier is not absolutely certain as yet.'

It was the German army which seized control, occupying Rome after the Italians officially capitulated on 8 September. This coincided with the next Allied invasion at the Gulf of Salerno, some thirty miles to the south of Naples. In a hastily arranged plan, British and American forces would be landed in two sectors, ten miles apart. Salerno proved a far more difficult proposition than Sicily. The beaches around the bay were enticing enough, but the olive groves of the plains inland were skirted by mountain ranges which provided perfect vantage points for German artillery. Furthermore, in an attempt to achieve surprise, there was no prior bombardment of the shore defences.

Many of the Combined Operations forces were by now veterans of two major landings, North Africa and Sicily, and had well-developed routines. 'We hoisted our battle ensign at the gaff, test-fired our guns, checked our ammunition deck lockers to the brim, cut sandwiches, filled our Thermos flasks and positioned our tin hats and medical kits for immediate use,' wrote Geoffrey Hobday, in command of a motor gunboat. Activity was intended to reduce tension, but the moments immediately before the start of the operation were the most important. 'I had purposely held back the rum issue until this moment and it was now distributed, together with sandwiches and hot drinks,' wrote Hobday. 'I went the rounds of the ship, having a cheery word with everyone and making encouraging remarks.'

Landing craft managed to put ashore their troops and vehicles without too much trouble just as dawn was breaking, but the assault troops found sterner and better-organized resistance than in Sicily. The beachheads soon became, as one British soldier put it, 'one hell of a shambles'. Artillery, tanks and Luftwaffe bombers created chaos. Subsequent waves of troops and tanks were scattered. Bodies and smouldering vehicles littered the beaches.

Warships lying offshore were called upon to provide support for the pinned-down troops, and to cover the subsequent waves of landing craft. Destroyers exchanged fire with Panzers and shore batteries. The failure to capture a nearby airfield meant that air attack remained the chief danger for the naval forces. Before the landings, George Blundell had worried about 'weak threads in our plans' but once the operation was underway, he was less concerned about the plight of the troops than the confusion of anti-aircraft cover. 'We had a terrific night,' he explained. 'Torpedo planes, we believed were ordered to attack the transports, came at us instead, and one of them came down our port side in a mass of flame.'

Several aircraft carriers had been assigned to protect the landings. 'We are not getting things all our own way,' wrote Kenneth Wilson, in the escort carrier HMS *Attacker*. 'One plane crashed this evening with its cannon still firing. I was on deck seeing to the aerials and the cannon shells hit the bulkhead very close to me, a near do . . . It is now 24 hours since I had any sleep and no wash or meal since leaving Malta. Living on coffee and sandwiches.' Crash landings seemed depressingly common. Few aircrew were enamoured of the Seafires: converted Spitfires that struggled to match the performance of the original version. 'We started the operation with 110 Seafires between us,' wrote Wilson, 'but now only 38 are serviceable.' They were not just dangerous for pilots: 'One of our flight deck crew was killed at 0800hrs when he walked into a Seafire propeller. He was more or less chopped to pieces. We buried him over the side.'

A few days after the first Salerno landings, K. B. Huntbatch, a coder in the minesweeper HMS *Circe*, recorded his thoughts in his diary:

This place certainly looks beautiful; a long sandy beach, the town set at the foot of the mountains and buildings straggling up the mountainside . . . This first glance has certainly aroused in me once again the desire to visit and live for a while in European towns and villages and have a good look around . . . I'm afraid I want to do too many things, I am too moody. My greatest desire is to be a farmer in England but I sometimes wonder if I shall be able to stick in one spot day after day, year after year. I have only seen small parts of the English countryside and there are still hundreds of places there which I want to visit besides these foreign countries . . . Another thing to consider is marriage. I am now approaching the age where I shall want to take a wife and raise a family . . . A good steady job and income is of primary importance. There is someone else to consider and work for and there can be no getting fed up with things around you and taking it in your head to see places you have always wanted to see. No saying 'I'm fed up, where's my bag, I'm going to Italy!'

Ashore, the offensive had resulted in stalemate. Some objectives had been captured but others remained out of reach and, critically, the two beachheads had not been linked. A German counter-attack resulted in days of gruelling fighting. Allied naval and air forces were called upon to provide support for infantry troops struggling to consolidate their positions. Warships lying offshore were exposed to attacks by German radio-controlled bombs launched from 19,000 feet. Two American ships were hit and HMS *Uganda* was seriously damaged. On 16 September, HMS *Warspite* was struck, only a day after arriving off Salerno. The famous battleship had to be unceremoniously towed back to Malta.

While the Allied armies were struggling to quell stern German resistance ashore, ships of the Italian navy made their way to Malta to conclude their formal surrender. They were attacked en route by radio-guided bombs launched by their former allies, one of which sank the *Roma*. While the Salerno landings remained in the balance, there was little opportunity to celebrate the first surrender amongst the Axis powers. 'It might have been paraded for our men's benefit,' wrote George Blundell in his diary. 'After all, it's their Victory: even a dog gets shewn the kill at a foxhunt. One day we'll realize we can do without Admirals and Commanders but not without sailors and stokers!'

The opportunity to celebrate properly came at the end of the month, after German forces had finally withdrawn from Salerno towards their prepared defensive lines to the north. On 29 September, the 'Armistice between the United Nations and Italy' was officially signed and concluded on board HMS *Nelson*, lying in Valletta's Grand Harbour. Resplendent in their white uniforms, officers and men formed a guard of honour to welcome the dignitaries, ferried by barge from the pier to the battleship. George Blundell recorded that the Mediterranean commander-in-chief, Andrew Cunningham, wore medals borrowed from the vice-admiral based in Malta 'as he had mislaid his own'. Cunningham was Britain's hero of the hour, soon to be made First Sea Lord, the most senior role in the navy, after the death of Dudley Pound. Cunningham stood to attention at the top of the gangway, while he was piped aboard *Nelson*. The ship's band played 'Rule Britannia'. 'A.B.C. has a red rim to his right eye,' noted Blundell, 'which makes him look rather like a bloodhound.'

Following Cunningham was the Allied commander-in-chief, General Eisenhower, accompanied by the British army and air force representatives General Alexander and Air Marshal Tedder, and those Blundell described as 'hangers-on', such as Harold Macmillan. Blundell had arranged for a bodyguard patrol ashore, which proved fortunate: 'A mob of Maltese women broke though the police cordon shouting and demonstrating.' Last to arrive was the Italian delegation, led by interim leader Marshal Badoglio. 'He looked most decrepit,' wrote Blundell, 'all of his 72 years, very worn and white, and his uniform looked as if it had come out of a screwed up bundle.'

While supply convoys flowed into Italy to support the Allied armies in their struggle of attrition, a new campaign began to develop in the Aegean Sea. The seizure of Rhodes and the Dodecanese archipelago was a long-cherished scheme of Churchill's and, despite the absence of American support, plans to move on the Greek islands went forward soon after the Italian surrender. A force consisting largely of the plucky irregulars of the Special Air Service, Special Boat Squadron and the Long Range Desert Group was formed to seize them. Meanwhile, however, German troops quickly supplanted the unwarlike Italian incumbents on the vital island of Rhodes, despite the extraordinary efforts of George Jellicoe, son of the famous First World War admiral, who parachuted onto the island and attempted in vain to organize resistance. Control of Rhodes gave the Luftwaffe a critical advantage. Without adequate air cover and operating at an uncomfortable stretch from its Mediterranean strongholds, the Royal Navy soon found the campaign for the Aegean to be one of the most demoralizing experiences of the war.

The Dodecanese became known as the 'Destroyers' Graveyard'. Reg Crang, petty officer in HMS *Petard*, witnessed a fellow destroyer attacked by a Stuka: '*Panther* was hit amidships by two bombs. She was going fast at the time and just drove herself under the water like a submarine making a dive. It was a truly terrible sight.' Only a few days later, *Petard* was sailing close behind HMS *Eclipse*, which was carrying 200 soldiers of the Royal East Kent Regiment, on their way to reinforce the garrison on Leros. *Eclipse* steamed straight into a minefield. 'She blew up with an appalling explosion, no more than 200 yards ahead of us,' wrote Crang in his diary. 'Within seconds she was gone.' Over 130 soldiers were killed along with 120 sailors, half the ship's company.

Many of the ships operating in the Dodecanese were small motor gunboats, torpedo boats and launches. In the feisty narrow waters under autumnal weather their crews suffered a gruelling experience. Geoffrey Hobday was in command of MGB 643. 'As we were severely rationed for water, rarely had any cooked food or hot drinks and were confined to our ship day in and day out, we found that life became progressively more intolerable,' he recalled. 'There was nothing to look forward to and tempers became very frayed. It became increasingly difficult to maintain discipline and good spirit, vital ingredients in any recipe for survival.'

Despite a brave effort by British Special Forces, soldiers and over-stretched RAF pilots, along with the local Greek defenders, the Allies were unable to hold the islands. Defeat on Leros in November 1943 was one of many disappointments. Air and sea forces failed to disrupt German landings, and the poorly led garrison surrendered a few days later. Hundreds of wounded had been evacuated in a scratch armada of small boats, and another rapid retreat followed with 3,000 British, Greek and Italian soldiers pre-emptively removed from nearby Samos.

For sailors, the Aegean formed a brief but unwelcome reprise of the catastrophe in Greece and Crete in 1941. The British and Greek navies suffered six destroyers sunk and four damaged, four cruisers damaged, and ten smaller coastal craft and minesweepers lost. Of the 5,000 personnel involved in the Aegean campaign between September and November 1943, 1,500 were killed. Of these, 745 were from the Royal Navy, with 422 soldiers and 333 RAF pilots and aircrew.

Shortly after the fall of Leros, Doreen Drax was aboard the battle-cruiser HMS *Renown*, steaming across the Mediterranean. She was part of a contingent of Wrens working as communications staff for Winston Churchill as the British Prime Minister made his way to a conference in Cairo, and thence to Tehran to meet President Roosevelt and Marshal Stalin. Drax was excited. 'It was fun standing right in the stern,' she wrote in her diary, 'where the vibration was terrific and the noise of the screws deafening, and the sea below was churned up into a turmoil of foam which spread out into a long brilliant blue and emerald streak behind us'. Churchill strode around the deck and the Wrens took photographs with their personal cameras. 'He stood in characteristic attitude,' wrote Drax, 'his hands in his pockets and the inevitable cigar stuck in the corner of his mouth.'

*Renown* called at Malta en route to Egypt. The island still bore the scars of the devastation inflicted upon it over the previous years. 'It was all a pathetic sight,' wrote Drax in her diary. 'Vast bomb craters, ruins and desolation everywhere; the people bustled about or sat on their doorsteps, haggard drawn expressions on their faces, their clothes tattered, torn and filthy, the children dirty, half-clothed, emaciated and under-nourished crawled about the streets or sat huddled together in the gutters.'

Once their official duties had been completed, Doreen Drax and her fellow Wrens toured the Holy Land. From Haifa, they travelled to Bethlehem and Jerusalem. In the latter, she wrote in her diary, 'the shop windows displayed all the latest western fashions which looked peculiarly out of place in the East. Large modern cinemas showed the newest film productions and the majority of people looked very little different from their counterparts in the modern world . . . Many of the women appeared in public heavily veiled in black chiffon headdress and long black skirts looking strangely incongruous in such modern surroundings.'

At Cairo, and later at Tehran, Churchill would persist in promoting the idea of an offensive in the Aegean as a route to the Balkans and towards eliminating Romania and Bulgaria from the war. Despite American impatience with the Mediterranean campaign, the Prime Minister feared the potentially devastating casualties inherent in the planned invasion of France. The risk of failure was great. From the earliest discussions, it was accepted that thousands of deaths, possibly tens of thousands, were a possible consequence of a head-on assault. On 11 November 1943, Vere Wight-Boycott was in Gibraltar. 'Armistice day,' he wrote in his diary. 'This means nothing to anyone here, but I have not seen anyone, service or civilian, without a poppy. The "local memoranda" covering the sale of emblems asks everyone to return their poppies as otherwise next year they may be in very short supply.'

Landings at Anzio in western Italy in January 1944, code-named Operation Shingle, proved that the Allies were becoming increasingly skilled at both organizing and conducting combined operations. 'D-Day evening,' noted Geoff Dormer of the trawler HMS *Hornpipe* on 21 January 1944. 'Things have been very quiet, and it has been a lovely, calm, sunny day, with almost cloudless blue skies. The multitude of ships off the beaches look more like a Review than an Invasion Fleet.' But Anzio was also a salutary lesson that successfully landing an army did not guarantee victory. The bridgehead was heavily defended and the Allied advance was stopped in its tracks. Initial plans had anticipated that resupply from the sea would be necessary for two weeks, but four months of gruelling stalemate ensued.

Monte Cassino, the focus of the greatest battle of attrition on the Italian Front, would only be taken in May 1944, with Rome falling on 4 June, and German forces in northern Italy would not be finally conquered until April 1945. During this long and costly campaign, Allied armies were supplied entirely by the merchant convoys which continued to deliver food and fuel, munitions and medical supplies from America and Britain, protected from the continuing threat of U-boats and bombers by escorting warships. As preparations continued for the invasion of France in early 1944, it was clear that landings were a beginning, not an end.

In March 1944 the destroyer HMS *Serapis* had just completed her second stint on Russian convoys. Midshipman John Roberts recorded in his journal the increasingly frequent appearance of the phrase 'Operation Overlord'. A dedicated bombardment liaison officer was attached to the ship, which was issued with special charts and sent for long-range bombardment exercises. When the destroyer flotilla was transferred to Portsmouth, 'we thought it was the real thing but it turned out to be only an exercise. There were hundreds of landing craft all around the Solent and the exercise landing was carried out near Hayling Island; from our point of view it was very dull, although it gave everybody some idea of what an invasion looked like.'

During the initial planning stages of the invasion of Normandy, First Sea Lord Admiral Andrew Cunningham was said to have proclaimed: 'I have already evacuated three British armies in the face of the enemy and I don't propose to evacuate a fourth.' Operation Neptune, the naval element of the invasion, was the culmination of years of experience in planning, conducting and learning from amphibious landings and retreats, developing tactics and technology. Like the evacuation from Dunkirk, the Normandy landings would rely on a gargantuan effort of bureaucracy. If the Royal Navy struggled with material poverty, it enjoyed an abundance of administrative expertise.

Overlord was eventually set for June 1944, and would be under the command of General Eisenhower and SHAEF, the Supreme Headquarters Allied Expeditionary Force. The Allied navies would land the invasion forces on five beaches: Utah and Omaha in the American sector under the Western Task Force, Gold, Juno and Sword in the British and Canadian sector under the Eastern Task Force. After the initial landings, the beachhead would have to be secured and, critically, even larger numbers of men and greater quantities of supplies delivered over the following days and weeks in order to consolidate the operation.

Training had been underway for months: warships practised shore bombardment, Combined Operations teams drilled for the embarkation and disembarkation of troops and equipment, RNVR officers and landing craft crews took on assault courses and mountain hikes in Scotland. Wrens flooded into plotting rooms and planning offices. Miscreants from the naval detention barracks at Portsmouth were assigned to a special unit dedicated to clearing beach obstacles and sent for demolition training. 'In this two-week period,' recalled Rene Le Roy, then a young midshipman in charge, 'they progressed to blowing up anything you could think of, including trees and safes.'

Every angle of the operation was discussed, and every possibility explored. At one stage, it was envisaged that up to 30,000 French civilians displaced by the fighting might have to be evacuated from the invasion area shortly after the landings, to be rehoused in a camp in Shoreham. Emergency treatment centres were established all across the south coast, many organized by Wrens, which prepared to receive the thousands of servicemen expected to be wounded during the operation.

There was no better illustration of the importance of proper planning and protection than a disastrous training incident at the end of April 1944. Exercise Tiger, at Slapton Sands in Devon, was already going badly, with practice landings disrupted by confused timings and positioning. Then, on the night of 27 April, German E-boats attacked a group of landing craft in the low mist of Lyme Bay. Two were sunk and another damaged, with 638 American soldiers killed and dozens injured. 'It was just breaking dawn,' recalled John Capon of the destroyer HMS *Obedient* of the following morning, 'and I looked around and you couldn't see anywhere without a body, without a Yankee turned upside down, dead. There was hundreds and hundreds of bodies.'

Admiral Bertram Ramsay, architect of the evacuation from Dunkirk in 1940 and commander of the British task force at Sicily, was now Allied Naval Commander Expeditionary Force and in control of Operation Neptune. It would be undertaken by a mighty armada of almost 7,000 ships and landing craft and 195,000 sailors. Although it was an international maritime effort – with American, Polish, Dutch, Greek, Norwegian and French vessels amongst the many nations represented in the Allied naval and merchant fleet – the British and Canadian navies provided 80 per cent of the 1,200 warships involved. Neptune would carry 130,000 soldiers, 12,000 vehicles, 2,000 tanks and thousands of tons of supplies to the beaches of Normandy.

Landing craft and ships of all sizes congregated off the south coast of England, many crowding the waters around Southampton and the Isle of Wight, from Netley to the Needles. 'The scene in the Solent at this time,' wrote Midshipman John Roberts of the week before the invasion, 'was extraordinarily peaceful when one considered how close the Germans were.' The first four days of June brought glorious sunshine. 'In a matter of hours we acquired a tan worthy of any Riviera beach inhabitant,' wrote Roberts. 'The soldiers looked a bit apprehensive, and they were entitled to . . . they were rather like cows being driven to the slaughter house.'

Surgeon Lieutenant Graham Airth was a medical officer in

LST 302, a specially equipped landing ship designed to treat and evacuate the wounded. On 2 June, it was moored in a designated area off Ryde on the Isle of Wight. 'To what a world did we wake,' he wrote in his diary, 'larties [latrines], bathrooms, wardroom, solid with khaki. Queues everywhere . . . We have four meals a day and the army only three, so we have managed to get the table to ourselves now and then; but they sit and <u>watch</u> us eat that fourth meal; disgusting people the army!'

Airth was perplexed by the peacefulness of the mooring zone. 'Last night passed uneventfully, why Jerry is leaving us alone I can't imagine; there is a huge concentration of shipping here . . . Every square yard of sea, allowing for the swing of ships with the tide, is filled with war craft.' Great efforts had been made to mislead the enemy about the precise nature and aims of the massing force, both through deception and disguise. 'There is a cruiser, lying not far away, that looks particularly unreal,' noted Airth, 'a single glance gives one the impression that a large buoy is there; one needs field glasses – even at such short distance, to just see the rest of the ship!'

On 4 June 1944, the day before the invasion was due to commence, the captain of HMS *Warspite* broadcast a message to the ship's company. 'The Allies were about to invade France,' recalled cook R. B. Buckle, 'the Operation must succeed whatever the cost. Everyone listened quietly as the Captain told the men what our particular task would be, and that if we should be hit and likely to sink, he intended to steam for the beach. Here, he concluded, we would continue to fire our main armament to the last. With this comforting thought we turned in to an uneasy rest.'

In the Solent, the landing ships and small craft were experiencing difficult conditions in deteriorating weather. 'The ship has a terrific roll – we are experiencing a really good channel swell,' wrote medical officer Graham Airth in his diary on 5 June. 'It would appear that today was planned as D-Day, but weather would not permit . . . Have now been confined to the ship for almost five days – no one but ourselves and the army types to look at . . . There are rows and rows of people "lining the railings" – they may just be looking out at the sea, but there is a tortured look in their eyes.'

The invasion was postponed because of the adverse weather, and D-Day became 6 June. Off Juno and Sword beaches, the midget submarines X-20 and X-23 had already been waiting for two days to guide the invasion force in with their flashing green lights, signals and radio beacons. The delay meant more tense hours underwater, with finite oxygen supplies. Lieutenant Commander George Honour recalled watching German soldiers playing with a beach ball and paddling: 'I thought, "I hope there are no Olympic swimmers and that they don't swim out a mile from shore and find us".'

The following day, as the naval forces prepared to launch, Admiral Ramsay sent a message to every ship which formed a corollary to General Eisenhower's more famous communication sent to all the invasion forces wishing them luck on 'the Great Crusade'. Ramsay's letter laid bare the operational priorities: transporting the armies, establishing a bridgehead, securing it and consolidating the invasion with rapid logistical support:

> It is to be our privilege to take part in the greatest amphibious operation in history – a necessary preliminary to the opening of the Western Front in Europe which in conjunction with the great Russian advance, will crush the fighting power of Germany . . .
>
> Our task in conjunction with the Merchant Navies of the United Nations, and supported by the Allied Air Forces, is to carry the Allied Expeditionary Force to the Continent, to establish it there in a secure bridgehead and to built it up and maintain it at a rate which will outmatch that of the enemy.
>
> Let no one underestimate the magnitude of this task . . . I count on every man to do his utmost to ensure the success of this great enterprise which is the climax of the European war.
>
> Good luck to you all and God speed.

Donald Povey of the trawler *Chasse Marie*, converted into a fuel carrier for the operation, was excited. 'By all appearances, the moment for which we have waited so long, is now at hand,' he wrote in his diary. 'Personally, I am amazed at the pessimism prevailing on board; but my guess is half of the jargon ("Cheers, it was nice to have met you" and so on) is in fun.' Povey was confident, and patriotic: 'The British Lion is unleashed!!'

Despite the magnitude of the armada, one of the least glamorous branches of the navy provided the most critical foundation. In the evening of 5 June, minesweepers made a final clearance of ten lanes across the Channel. While this dangerous work was conducted, airborne forces which would provide the vanguard of the invasion made their way towards France. 'During the hours of darkness we heard our aircraft passing overhead,' wrote Lieutenant J. W. Main, of the minesweeper HMS *Fraserburgh*. 'Many were towing gliders.'

Behind the minesweepers came the landing ships and infantry transports, protected by coastal forces and small craft, and the warships which would bombard the enemy coast in preparation for the landings. Junior officer John Pelly was serving in the destroyer HMS *Eglinton*. He wrote to his parents soon afterwards, telling them that 'if you can imagine visibility of ten miles and not being able to see water for ships – you've got the invasion in a nutshell'. Pelly's ship was at the vanguard of the naval force:

We – the *Eglinton* – were the very first ship in of the whole invasion – a very great honour. It was the most terrific sight and experience . . . I felt rather excited and a little frightened too – dressing up like a Christmas tree with life jacket, revolver, hundreds of rounds (we had instructions to beach the ship if necessary and go on fighting), a knife, whistle, money wrapped up and watertight and so on – and of course steel hat.

We passed the endless landing craft, large and small, transports, landing craft carriers, all crammed with tanks and waving soldiers . . . and finally took up our position in the lead. All night we slowly crossed the Channel with nothing happening and then as it grew light early on the morning of 6th June 1944 we saw ahead the coast of Normandy, and behind one sea of shipping.

It was expected that the slow convoys would come under attack from German E-boats, submarines and aircraft. In the event, naval forces provided stout protection. The major casualty was the Norwegian destroyer *Svenner*. John Roberts was watching from the destroyer *Serapis*:

> A quarter past five, and the time had come; with a dozen other destroyers and innumerable small craft we closed the shore. The first signs of dawn were already in the sky, and the faint outline of the French coast was soon visible ... Suddenly the ship shuddered; we knew instinctively that it was an underwater explosion of some sort; a mile on our port side a destroyer was stopped, smoke and steam rising into the air ... After a minute her back began to break, her middle slowly sinking beneath the waves. The bow and stern rose high into the air to form a colossal 'V'.

'Fear,' wrote John Pelly in his letter home. 'I remember that, just after seeing the destroyer so close to us go down and sensing that this was a very unpleasant welcome so early on, I felt a fear of uncertainty that I'd never before known – before it had just taken the usual form of excitement and an effort to appear calm in speech; but for a few seconds on this occasion I couldn't get a sound from my mouth.' Most of the Norwegian sailors were picked up, and a handful of other E-boat attacks came to nothing. Yet despite the overwhelming superiority of the invasion force, many of the sailors continued to feel vulnerable. John Roberts described the feeling when the warning came of torpedoes approaching his own ship: 'It was too late for us to do anything, except bend one's knees and hang on to something. Nothing happened anyway. By now everybody was thoroughly keyed up – torpedoes and mines already, anything might happen, all I had heard about secret weapons came back to me with a rush.'

Sailors watched Allied bombers unleashing their payloads on the coastal defences. 'It was all one mass of flame right the way down the coast,' recalled Petty Officer Edward Rose of the cruiser HMS *Diadem*. 'In the distance, on our right Cherbourg, on our left Le Havre, were given away by the twinkling of heavy flak bursting amongst our bombers,' wrote John Roberts of HMS *Serapis*, 'and everywhere ahead streams of coloured tracer crossed the sky, green and red flares fell slowly through the clouds, and the continuous flashes of gunfire vainly opposed the loads of bombs raining down on the German defences.' Despite the fearsome bombardment, and the continued dominance of the British and American air forces throughout the day, the blitz succeeded more in shaking defenders than destroying defences, many of which were left intact.

At the appointed time, the first thunderous broadside was unleashed from the monitors and battleships. Such was the intensity of the firing aboard the cruiser HMS *Belfast* that light bulbs blew out below decks. The destroyers were able to get closer inshore. 'We were so close one could plainly see people opening windows, cycling etc.,' wrote John Pelly, 'and it was with sadistic delight that we knocked things down.' *Eglinton* had been assigned a stretch of coast-line around two miles long, the main settlement in which was Luc-sur-Mer, a small village near Courseulles, with clusters of houses and structures just inland. Pelly described the bombardment:

> Finding hardly any opposition and thus probably few gunsights, the Captain chose his own targets and we were so close that we couldn't miss. Down came a water tower, the top of the gasworks went for six, any German who ran out of a house up the street had four four-inch shells overtaking him. In fact we had the time of our lives – all point-ing out targets and shooting up anything that took or didn't take our fancy – like the green house that the Captain thought to be an eye-sore.

Meanwhile, the trawler *Chasse Marie* lagged behind in the Chan-nel. Donald Povey was becoming increasingly frustrated. 'Wherever we're going we're not getting there very fast,' he wrote in his diary for 6 June. 'We have the unenviable job of rounding up stragglers: and there are many of them. These small crafts, to me appear to be the fly in the ointment. Their speed is slow at best, and frequent breakings-down made it a day of towing for us . . . Long before dusk we have lost sight of our convoy; three times tow-ropes snapped and one landing barge is filling with water. Thank god the whole inva-sion isn't as poorly executed as this department.'

Many of the smaller craft were victims of the weather before they even reached the Normandy coast and had to be evacuated: some were waterlogged, others smashed against the sides of larger ships and were irrevocably damaged. A total of 258 Royal Navy landing craft were sunk by the weather or by obstacles before they reached their destination. Others were sunk or broken on the beaches. Every craft lost had to be accounted for. The senior surviving crew member was required to undergo questioning back at base about the precise circumstances of the loss, the casualties sustained, and any other information about the operation that he could provide. 'The weather beat us,' admitted one sailor from a sunken craft. 'Wish we had had a compass – we would have done it then,' suggested another. 'It was a sheer waste of time so far as we were concerned,' reported one man on a landing vessel damaged during the crossing, 'all we did was to hang about and get smashed up by our own craft.'

Landing craft reaching their designated zones found defences largely intact. 'Beach thick with mines and obstacles of all sorts,' reported one Royal Marine. 'I don't know how we got ashore. We touched one or two but they didn't go off.' Another described strong resistance: 'We had a hot reception from Mortars and M/G and snipers and the beach, which we were told would be clear, was thick with obstacles, mines and traps of all kinds.' Not every sector matched the intensity of Omaha Beach, made immediately infamous by its combination of difficult landing conditions, the fearsome natural barrier formed by steep embankments, and stern resistance from undamaged defensive installations. But nowhere was the experience a pleasant one for the first waves of assault troops. John Pelly observed the proceedings as HMS *Eglinton* patrolled offshore:

We had a grandstand view of the first landings . . . We watched the bitter fighting and the masses of material being landed and the tanks getting ashore and fighting in the fields above the beaches . . . We watched one or two ships get hit and sometimes sunk . . . I had awful qualms at times about the land fighting. I'll never forget the chaos and awfulness of landing craft returning out of control full to almost sinking with a red mixture of blood, water and oil fuel with legs and heads sticking out. One or two came alongside and we hauled the wounded out, mostly Canadians and Marines, and placed them in their awful suffering along the upper deck, doing what little we could.

Although the number of casualties on D-Day did not match the most pessimistic predictions, the hard-fought foothold in France cost British forces 3,300 men killed, wounded or captured. The Canadians lost 1,000, the Americans 6,000. Medical officer Graham Airth summed up the first day in his diary:

This has indeed been D-Day; Dawned-day, Death-day, Destruction-day, Disappointment and Disillusion-day. I have seen men die suddenly, horribly. I have twice been very near death myself, so near that I desperately wish to forget, but will probably never do so.

Sailors piloting the landing craft which had delivered infantry troops into the face of the enemy machine guns felt responsible for the fates of their passengers. In those sectors where strong resistance was encountered, the experience was traumatic. Jimmy Green was a junior officer commanding a landing-craft flotilla at Omaha Beach. Every man who left his craft was killed. 'I can still see those fresh-faced boys getting out of the boat,' he recalled many years later. 'It comes back to me from time to time, that I was a link in their death. I know I had to do my job, they had to do their job, but I was in some way responsible for putting them there and it does haunt me from time to time. It does haunt me. I still see their faces.'

In the British sectors alone, over 75,000 soldiers, more than 6,000 trucks and tanks, and 4,000 tons of supplies were landed on the first day. Royal Navy beachmasters organized, navigated and directed as they had in Sicily and Italy. Landing craft continued to disgorge troops, tanks and equipment. Bottlenecks were identified and contingencies were made. Reports began to be sent to the Admiralty. Sailors watching from warships frequently commented on the impressive barrage of fire from the newly developed rocket barges. From the beaches, the perspective was rather different. 'Rocket Ships astern were firing short when landing on French Coast,' reported one soldier. 'We were hit.' Another stated that 'rockets from our own ships were more dangerous than the Germans'.

For those guarding the perimeters, there was a certain sense of detachment from the action. The destroyer HMS *Savage* had been tasked with patrolling the eastern section of the bridgehead to prevent attacks from torpedo boats operating out of Le Havre. It was a role not without danger, as the sinking of *Savage*'s Norwegian sister ship *Svenner* illustrated, but Alec Dennis judged the threat to be 'a pin-prick against our enormous armada'. After the event, he felt disappointed about his own role: 'The whole operation from our point of view was, after the initial approach, a huge anti-climax. One had been expecting mayhem but it hadn't come our way. We never saw a hostile aircraft and nobody shot at us. The main worry was the pressure mines.'

Donald Povey, in the trawler *Chasse Marie*, finally reached the French coast on 7 June. 'A sight hard to credit was presented,' he wrote. 'There were literally thousands of ships of every type and all signs: seeing this alone convinces me of the certainty of victory. Battleships and destroyers close inshore were firing broadsides over the red cliffs, and everywhere there was movement and an exhilarating atmosphere of a job well done.' While the trawler lay offshore, Povey surveyed the shoreline through his binoculars: 'The beach is laden with craft discharging vast quantities of men and equipment, towns and villages are in ruins, our aircraft dominate the sky, and ships lie around in their hundreds . . . On the second day of invasion, my summary of events is that on the beaches all is as quiet as we <u>didn't</u> expect.'

While continuing to deposit ever more men and materiel on the Normandy beaches, naval forces were also called upon to evacuate casualties. 'The sea is covered with oil and debris,' wrote Leading Signalman C. L. R. Matthews of HMS *Fame*. 'Bodies are floating around, some face up, some face down, clad in life jackets.' Povey described one of the sights he had witnessed: 'A Canadian killed during the initial landing was lying on the beach, and a tank net was laid over him. Each time a tank stormed up the beach, blood spurted out from the mutilated corpse! Is that human?'

One of the most important tasks was the treatment of injured men returning to the beaches from the front line. Surgeon Lieutenant Graham Airth remained in his converted landing ship on Juno Beach, busy dealing with the stream of wounded. Not until six days later, on 12 June, did he find time to record his thoughts in his diary:

There were some ghastly injuries. Some of the men had taken 48 hours to reach us; morphia had been plentiful, but treatment non-existent . . . our wide open tank door faced hostile guns, and my fear was that someone would lob a lucky shot straight into the ship. But it didn't happen . . . The most massive effort was for an amputation through the thigh for gas gangrene. But the poor fellow was too far gone; despite several pints of blood, he did not rally. Another was quite the opposite – blood was life-saving – he sat up after the first pint, came on board the colour of paper.

While the soldiers and pilots fought their way out of the bridge-head in Normandy, it was the sailors' task to secure the supply routes that were vital to the consolidation of the invasion. Artificial harbours were constructed, most notably the famous 'Mulberry' at Arromanches. Steamers and coasters which had spent much of the war dodging bombers and E-boats to deliver vital supplies around Britain now helped to supply the Allied armies, escorted and aided by battered destroyers and minesweepers. Monitors and warships continued their directed salvoes. On one occasion, HMS *Rodney* hit a target all of seventeen miles inland. From the outset, the Normandy beachhead represented a mighty maritime achievement. After Churchill visited the area on 12 June, he sent a message to Stalin: 'It is a wonderful sight to see this city of ships stretching along the coast for nearly fifty miles and apparently safe from the air and the U-boats which are so near.'

A defensive perimeter – called the 'trout line' – was established, and had to be patrolled to protect the constant stream of cargo vessels. 'There were many rumours of secret weapons and other fearful things which might be tried by a desperate enemy,' wrote John Wilson, serving in MTB 248. One night, strange radar readings were reported before a swarm of tiny boats were sighted, whizzing out of the darkness towards the perimeter. Each had a distinctive pair of red and green lights which provided bright targets for machine guns. Around forty were destroyed by the defenders. 'These were explosive motor boats,' wrote Wilson, 'fast radio-controlled speed boats which we later found looked like the little boats you drive round the pond in Regent's Park.'

U-boats continued to probe Allied defences, and destroyer flotillas were also fought off. Mines remained a perennial problem, deposited from the air into shipping lanes. Confrontations with enemy coastal forces based at Le Havre became far more intense after D-Day than they had been during the initial landings. *Eglinton* acted as a rearguard for Allied motor torpedo boats. The destroyer was, as John Pelly put it, a 'mortuary ship'. He described how the small craft 'came alongside us in the early hours and transferred their dead and dying. How well I remember unstrapping dead gunners from their Oerlikon guns.' Even two months after the initial landings, attacks continued to pester the supply lines. Early one morning in August, 'human torpedoes', so-called because they were guided by divers, were sighted near the 'Gooseberry' makeshift harbour at Sword beach. 'Approximately eighteen torpedoes were accounted for,' an official report stated, 'including nine shot up by the R.A.F.' Seven prisoners were taken, and only one blockship was hit.

Between 19 and 21 June terrible storms destroyed the artificial harbours in the American sector, and damaged the British 'Mulberry' harbour. 'Today brings us relief from four days I shall never forget not even want to repeat,' wrote Donald Povey on 23 June. High winds and heavy squalls had caused damage to his trawler, which meant that it could not anchor properly. 'Being unable to effect repairs, we then proceeded to stooge around, doing so throughout a stormy, nerve-racking, sleepless night . . . Never before, not even in Russia, have I been so desperate as on this night.' Back in Britain a few days later, a disconsolate Povey attempted to sum up his experiences. 'The most boring period of my service so far,' he wrote. 'Had I known that the naval part in this invasion was to have been such a walk-over, I wouldn't have taken the trouble to have started this diary.'

For many sailors, the aftermath of 'D-Day' during every invasion

– from North Africa to Sicily, Italy and now Normandy – had been similar: a logistical role which was utterly essential to the success of the land operation, but which rarely brought a strong sense of mutual involvement or particular appreciation. The commanding officer in one landing craft beached at Arromanches at the end of June reported that, while living in the small vessel for days following the Normandy landings, 'difficulty was found in washing, sleeping and feeding adequately'. But most importantly, 'the men were quick to notice that our presence from "D" Day onwards was of little value, and that no-one appeared to be very interested in us. They accordingly lose interest in proceedings and became more difficult to handle.' Before long, landing craft which had disembarked Allied infantry on D-Day were being used to transport German prisoners back across the Channel.

Graham Airth continued to provide medical care for injured soldiers as they were evacuated. After minimal front-line treatment and with a lengthy journey to reach hospitals in Britain, his was a vital service. Operating on severe wounds under the unpredictable conditions at sea took great skill. 'Am about to remove piece of shrapnel from man's lower eyelid,' wrote Airth in his journal. 'Am frankly windy of this, as the ship has a 20° to 30° roll, has been worse and may become worse again, when I'm in the middle of it and can't stop.'

Between 6 June and the official close of Operation Neptune at the end of the month, Allied naval and merchant ships landed 850,000 men, over 150,000 vehicles and 570,000 tons of supplies. By 5 July a million men had been transported across the English Channel. Operation Overlord was the pinnacle of Allied cooperation and planning. Victory ultimately relied on the bravery and resilience of airborne and infantry soldiers. Only a few sailors experienced the front-line assault. But the naval effort provided a foundation for success. Sailors planned the mission and helped to scout the beaches, prepared the ground and transported the troops, protected the perimeter and supplied the bridgehead. Ahead was a bloody struggle to break through the German lines, a campaign which would again rely on maritime supply routes.

Graham Airth's surgery was a success. 'A close shave indeed,' he wrote in his journal. 'Sewed up the wound with superfine silk, and sewed only the deep parts of the skin together, so that there were no "stitches" to leave marks . . . No afterpain, and there should be no scar.'

'Because it all went so smoothly it may seem to some people that it was all easy and plain sailing,' wrote Admiral Ramsay in his small private pocket diary. 'Nothing could be more wrong. It was excellent planning and execution.' Ramsay was the ultimate unsung hero: highly respected amongst his peers but with a modest public profile. He would continue to work alongside Eisenhower as the campaign in north-west Europe progressed through the autumn and winter of 1944. On 2 January 1945, the Admiral was on his way to a conference of Allied commanders when his plane crashed on take-off from a snowy runway outside Paris. There were no survivors. Ramsay was buried six days later at St-Germain-en-Laye.

## 19. A Routine for Everything

'He had run away from his gun,' wrote George Blundell in his diary. 'If proven, the penalty is to be shot.' On 11 August 1943, a court martial had been held on board HMS *Nelson*, anchored at Valletta, to hear the case of a sailor from *Uganda* who stood accused of cowardice. 'It was for us, the members of the Court, a most difficult and painful case,' explained Blundell. 'The man had been sunk in the *Kelly*, was then in the *Queen Elizabeth* when she was damaged at Alex, and he admitted to being afraid when, during an air attack on *Uganda*, he had refused to man his pom-pom. I hoped for him to have detention only, but the Court gave him one year's imprisonment and dismissed him from the Navy.'

The psychology of the individual sailor often appeared subservient to rigid discipline. 'The Navy lives under the dominion of the past; it is far too robust to bother about a sailor's nerves,' wrote Lord Moran in his 1945 treatise *The Anatomy of Courage*. 'Every rating is a mechanic, there is purpose in each day; he is intelligent rather than imaginative, he thinks rather than feels about things.'

There were undoubtedly those within the Admiralty who were more interested in machinery than men. But, as George Blundell's attitude proved, compassion was not entirely absent, and the service was often far more sensitive than Moran suggested. 'It is the men who fight, and hold on, and decide the issue for us,' stated Captain Alfred Duckworth in a lecture for junior officers. 'Strange new and peculiar weapons multiply weekly, but it is always the men who operate them who count for most.' An anonymous naval officer, in an article submitted to the *Naval Review* in 1944, agreed: 'The finest ships and the finest weapons are only as good as the men who have to handle them.'

'Every man is not by nature a hero,' argued RNVR Surgeon Lieutenant Commander Edward Benson McDowall in a paper concerning sailors' morale written in 1942. 'He must be made into a fighter by training him to such a pitch that he is able and eager to overcome all instincts of self-preservation and to carry out his job to the limits of his mental and physical capacity – and this in situations in which he may be dead next minute.'

Trained in psychiatry, McDowall had witnessed the traumatic effects of the war at sea first-hand when his ship HMS *Terror* had been sunk by German aircraft in the Mediterranean in February 1941. He had subsequently won the Distinguished Service Cross while serving in the destroyer HMS *Nubian* during the evacuation of Crete. His work became an officially sanctioned analysis, issued as a confidential battle order to the Mediterranean Fleet in December 1942.

McDowall emphasized that heroism consisted of devotion to duty, efficient and reliable conduct, and collective effort. The nature of naval warfare required courage on the part of the average sailor, to be sure, but this took the form of steady and efficient activity, rather than gallantry. Everything about service in the navy, McDowall suggested, should reinforce one idea above all else: 'I am a British sailor. The British sailor has always been the best seaman, the finest fighter, the hero of the people. Therefore I am a hero.'

At the heart of McDowall's message was leadership. 'The behaviour of officers,' he argued, 'is the keystone of the whole structure of morale.' Sailors should feel that their welfare mattered. Everyday considerations were important: mail, leave, information, recreation and comforts. Officers should exhibit 'the personal touch' in dealing with worries about home. Sailors needed self-respect, generated through smartness, cleanliness, pride in the ship and education about their role and mission: 'The man's whole training and surroundings should create in him such a personal pride that failure to do his duty becomes unthinkable.'

Every successful officer took an interest in the welfare of his subordinates. The formal decrees of the wartime *King's Regulations and Admiralty Instructions* advised that officers 'kept in close and constant touch with their men. Officers should be responsible for the work, training and advancement of their men and for their general wellbeing. They should study their men's interests sufficiently to be well

acquainted with their conditions of life both on board and ashore.'
These conditions included many of the everyday aspects of life which
could have a profound effect on spirits: accommodation, washing
facilities, food, or leisure activities. If faced with troubles of any
kind, ratings were advised to talk to their divisional officers or, in a
larger warship, to see the commander. An influential pre-war guide
by Rory O'Conor, who would later lose his life on one of HMS *Neptune*'s lifeboats, suggested that commanders should literally have an
open-door policy.

Operational necessity meant that designated tours of duty and
crew rotation were not the norm in the Royal Navy. Morale at sea in
the long term therefore depended greatly on leave, which in turn was
subject to the requirements of the service and local operational conditions. Aside from emergency compassionate leave, there were
essentially three types: shore leave, awarded at the discretion of commanding officers, and lasting an evening, an afternoon or a day; home
leave, which allowed sailors to take a lengthier break from the ship;
and survivors' leave granted to men whose ship had been sunk or
seriously damaged and who required a period of recuperation while
arrangements were made for redrafting.

A 'run ashore' was at the heart of the sailor's psychology. There
was naturally a great variation in facilities and hospitality between
places as diverse as New York and Newfoundland, Ceylon and Sierra
Leone, Egypt and Iceland. In certain ports and bases, Amenities
Liaison Officers coordinated leisure activities: providing information
on recreation facilities; helping to obtain luxuries and equipment;
supervising canteens, clubs and hostels; organizing dances, sports,
concerts and films, and ENSA events. In Britain, the streets and pubs
of sailors' towns such as Portsmouth, Plymouth and Liverpool were
invariably filled with drunken ratings at liberty.

Although the presence of British sailors in foreign territories
tended to create its own norms of behaviour – enhancing the market
for prostitution and illegal liquor, instantly increasing the potential
for violence – efforts were usually made to conform to local custom.
When the cruiser HMS *Nigeria* was sent to Simonstown in South
Africa for a refit in 1944, Captain Henry King addressed the ship's

company before they were allowed ashore. He explained South Africa's political status, and that sailors should behave like guests, not proprietors. Ratings were not to associate with black locals: 'As far as you are concerned, you'd better leave them alone – particularly the women. It is the law of the land that it is an offence for a white man to go with a coloured woman . . . Do your best not to let the side down by letting coloured people see a white man disgracing himself in public.' Finally, he provided a blunt recommendation of contraception: 'You'll all have heard what the Padre has had to say. You've all heard what the Doctor has had to say and all I want to add is my advice to do nothing which you'll regret afterwards . . . So, if you can't be good, be damned careful, both for your own sakes and for the sake of the girlfriend or wife at home.'

Relationships between sailors and local women sometimes developed into something more than a brief affair. Legislation on servicemen's marriage meant that a letter from the commanding officer was often required for an officer or rating to wed, a safeguard which provided an opportunity for intervention. In August 1943 the parents of a young stoker based at Malta wrote to the Admiralty with troubling news of an 'impending tragedy'. They had learned of his apparently imminent marriage to a young local woman after receiving a letter from the girl's widowed mother. The return address was De Micoli's macaroni factory, her place of employment, and she had informed the prospective in-laws that the young man was 'willing to Marry my daughter Lily. On my part I am rather pleased as I think that the boy is genuine . . . Hoping that you will not find no objection as I don't wish to disappoint these young Couple which I think that they are very much in Love.'

The parents complained to the Admiralty that they had received no mail from their son for three months, and that he had not been home in over two and a half years. Both worked at a factory making engines for torpedoes, but complained that they could not 'settle down' to their work, such were their worries. They had been in Coventry during the Blitz, they explained, but 'we can assure you that our mental agony and suspense are far greater now than then'. The stoker was subsequently drafted away from Malta in November 1943, returning to Britain the following month and, according to the senior officer on the island, 'as far as can be ascertained he did not marry before he left Malta'.

Despite the popular image of heavy-drinking, womanizing Jack, many sailors valued comfort, warmth, good food and a chance to rest above all else. Domesticity was a priceless luxury after the discomforts of the sea. Invitations to eat or even sleep in civilian houses were not uncommon, particularly for officers but also occasionally for ratings. 'Ashore, matelots were usually far less interested in getting their leg over than in getting their feet under the table,' claimed one sailor. 'A few hours round the fire in a normal comfortable house were prized.'

For sailors on foreign service, prolonged absence from home was a given. Shortly after the outbreak of war, Douglas Woolf had written to his younger brother, who had recently volunteered for the navy: 'Hope you are doing alright wherever you are – stick it out Old Boy – we'll have a grand party after the war's over.' The brothers saw little of each other before Peter Woolf, a signalman in HMS *Wild Swan*, died in the Atlantic in June 1942. Wren Charlotte Dyer, working at Western Approaches, spent an afternoon with her brother in the summer of 1943. He was a sub-lieutenant in a motor launch, about to leave for Algiers. 'We bid each other a cheerful goodbye,' she wrote, 'and said "See you in a couple of years' time" and that was that.'

Worries about domestic affairs were the most common welfare concern. Family Welfare Centres had existed since 1935 in the main base ports of Portsmouth, Devonport and Chatham, and during the war more were established in Rosyth, Liverpool, Lowestoft, Glasgow, Belfast and London. Staffed by dedicated and professional social workers, the centres represented an extension of the responsibilities of the Admiralty. They became primary agencies for working with sailors' families, alongside charities such as the Soldiers, Sailors and Airmen's Families Association, and dealt with an array of domestic issues, from investigating family problems to organizing housing for bombed-out wives and children.

Keeping in touch with home by letter was the best way of allaying anxiety. Mail was of vital importance to the morale of every serviceman, and sailors were no exception. Receiving a letter was often a boon for flagging spirits, even if the content was banal. For the more articulate, writing could be a cathartic process, a crucial psychological coping mechanism, and an opportunity to digest events by constructing a personal narrative. Even for the less eloquent, writing letters was a regular relaxation activity.

Correspondence was deemed to be so important that men were sometimes ordered to write more regularly to friends and family, on pain of extra work. But letters also caused problems. When sailors received a bundle of mail, they would invariably read the most recent letter first, in case there was bad news: the breaking-off of an engagement, the death of a loved one, details about bomb damage. There were also particular logistical challenges in delivering mail to sailors. Sacks of letters and parcels might arrive in a port after several weeks of transit, but their intended recipients might already have sailed for another destination. It was a problem that the navy worked hard to overcome. 'Nothing upsets a ship's company more than mishandling of mails,' wrote George Blundell.

Censorship was a necessary evil in wartime. Responsibility was usually devolved to the officers of individual ships or bases, who would use scissors to cut offending passages from letters. Unacceptable content was clearly defined: there should be no references to locations, movements, operations, casualties, the conditions of ports, ships or morale. Nor were men to make any 'criticisms of war operations or any statement harmful to the reputation of H.M. fighting forces'.

Nevertheless, censors were able to exercise considerable discretion. Vere Wight-Boycott, as commanding officer of HMS *Ilex* in September 1943, was confronted with a conundrum after mail deliveries had been postponed: 'The Doctor as censor officer asked my opinion as to the rights of a man to inform his correspondent that he had had no mail owing to "bloody incompetence" somewhere. Strictly this is "bringing the Service into disrepute" but I thought it better to let it go.' Some officers were lax. Surgeon Lieutenant Terence Barwell of HMS *Express* admitted that he 'used to skim them and anyone who wanted to pass on a little information could easily have done so'. Others were impeccably diligent. 'I was very conscientious,' wrote Geoff Dormer, 'and quite often cut bits out of my own letters.'

'The troops hate the censoring, of course,' wrote George Blundell. 'It would be better, I consider, if censoring officers were ones who did not know the men whose letters they were reading.' Surgeon Commander William Scott, a medical officer in *Ark Royal*, recalled that he 'learnt much about the ratings' view of life from their letters, but would never discuss them with anyone else'. His junior colleagues were less tactful, 'sub-lieutenants laughing among themselves at some of the off remarks and phrases they read'.

Official guidelines suggested that censorship should be invisible, and carried out 'in as private a place as possible'. Officers were warned not to use information gleaned in this way to punish minor indiscretions, unless evidence was found of crimes against civilian law. Wherever possible, censorship duties were assigned to medical officers and chaplains, who were more associated with welfare than discipline.

Over 500 RNVR chaplains were recruited over the course of the war, mostly from the Church of England, but also from other denominations. All larger warships had a dedicated padre, usually with a compulsory Sunday prayer service. The system was more flexible on smaller ships, where the captain would recite the prayers, and smaller ships or escort groups often shared a chaplain between them.

During battle, official advice was that chaplains should resist the temptation to tend to men on the upper decks, and take up a position with the medical officer below: 'In doing this you will come across the ratings who in actual fact most need your presence, because very many of them are under the strain of merely waiting until the ship is hit. A cheerful word here, a word of encouragement there, will steady many an inexperienced youngster, and ensure that he does the right thing when the time comes.' Nevertheless, several chaplains were decorated for their bravery.

While they may have whispered a quiet prayer in the heat of battle, many sailors had an ambivalent response to organized religion. Communal services were a fixture throughout the war. George Blundell was appreciative of Sunday prayers in HMS *Kent*: 'It is quite a moving sound to hear 400 or more saying the simple, direct words of the Lord's prayer together.' On the messdeck, however, pious sailors were often derided as 'bible thumpers' or 'Holy Joes'.

Pastoral care was often more important than spiritual advice, the chaplain turning from preacher to counsellor. Chaplains were outside of the normal officer hierarchy, and most chose to wear officer uniform without the marks of rank. This lent them a detachment which was appealing for men with worries to discuss. 'Received another card from Hilda which confirmed my suspicions,' wrote Signalman H. Osborne in his diary. 'I was knocked sick by the news – wrote four letters, all I could do was write today. Am more fed up than ever. Decided to see the Padre.'

The other individual on board ship whose role was specifically to care for the well-being of sailors was the medical officer. Compared to the other armed forces, the navy's medical organization was small. There were fewer than 400 permanent medical officers in September 1939 and this increased to 2,610 by the end of the war. Of the final total, 85 per cent were temporary RNVR commissions, making the naval medical branch overwhelmingly 'civilian' in nature. But despite these new recruits, the increasing numbers of personnel throughout the service meant that the ratio of medical officers to men actually decreased. From the peacetime target of four doctors per thousand men – a level lower than in the American or German navies – the Royal Navy only had three per thousand by 1945.

The Royal Navy had a particular appeal for medical professionals, with a reputation for excellence and the opportunity to play a full role as part of a fighting unit aboard ship. For many civilian doctors, this was an opportunity to see real action. Terence Barwell applied to join the navy soon after qualifying as a doctor in late 1939, and recalled that 'I did not want to go into the army, and I did not like the idea of the RAF where others went off flying and the MOs were always part of the ground staff'. Surgeon Lieutenant Commander Harry Balfour 'dismissed the Army and the Air Force as it seemed likely that I might be stuck in some hospital or base camp away from all action. The Navy was the obvious answer.'

Serving at sea meant that naval medical officers had to contend with situations very different from those in the other armed forces, in which highly trained professionals tended to operate behind the lines rather than at the heart of the action. Surgeon Commander T. N.

D'Arcy described scenes for which no amount of formal medical education could compensate: 'Lights are out, wounded are crawling about in dark corners, cries for help come from bottoms of ladders, where twisted and torn metal make investigations terribly difficult, and urgent requests for the doctor arrive from several parts of the ship at the same time.'

Before the war, medical officers had been distributed sparingly: three to each battleship, one shared between each flotilla of up to ten destroyers. During the war, doctors were provided for as many smaller ships as possible, and from 1942 new escort ships were each assigned a medical officer as standard. Dedicated hospital ships were rare – only five in total until 1942, and eleven thereafter – and although sometimes attached to fleets or shore bases, they were most commonly used to transport casualties between ship and shore.

Medical officers therefore had a great deal of independence, and were allowed to follow whatever practices best suited their own particular circumstances. As the war progressed, greater numbers of specialists became available to advise on and treat specific health problems. Dental officers, for example, served aboard larger ships, providing emergency treatment for teeth smashed against railings, relief for disease-ridden gums or the extraction of rotting molars. But senior medical officers were wary of over-specialization. Any ship's doctor, it was felt, should be able to deal with whatever challenges he might face. Ultimately, the aim was to preserve the operational efficiency of the warship. 'Our one duty as naval medical officers,' wrote Vice-Admiral Sheldon Dudley, the Admiralty's medical director-general, 'is to keep as many men at the guns for as many days as possible.'

The ship's doctor also fulfilled an important pastoral role. The relationship between the medical officer and the lower deck could be extremely important. 'Big ships and barges had their padres,' explained Harry Balfour, 'but destroyers had only doctors . . . I began to learn the great value of listening. The anxieties were always present . . . many men were frightened . . . Sometimes there was positive action I could take to help a problem but mostly it was allowing them to talk which was of value.'

The Admiralty encouraged medical officers to talk to sailors about the psychological and physiological responses to combat. 'The most common cause of anxiety is the fear of the individual that he might be a coward,' stated one expert. The advice to doctors was to tell men that: 'To be afraid is natural – to run away is cowardly. If you are efficient in your job you need have no fear of your behaviour in an emergency. Admitting your worries to a friend makes it easier. In nine cases out of ten he will be feeling exactly the same.'

A sailor's psychology was built on routine, efficiency and collective effort. Under normal conditions, an individual's natural survival instinct was channelled into carrying out his own duties and trusting that all around him were doing the same. Continuing to do one's job was usually the safest option. But when a ship sustained damage, this carefully constructed mental state came under threat.

Damage control was an essential part of a ship's operations. It was rare for a torpedo or a bomb to sink a warship quickly; the speed with which *Hood* or *Barham* vanished contributed greatly to the shock of their loss. There was often an opportunity at least to assess the damage, and often to attempt to isolate it – sealing hatches, putting out fires, performing quick repairs – before a decision was made to abandon ship. Warships could potentially be kept afloat for days, or at least long enough for rescuing ships to come alongside.

While damage control teams set about their work, it was important that other sailors continued with their jobs. Training aimed to remove the natural instinct for self-preservation or flight in the face of danger, but confidence in officers was essential to maintaining order in the event of a crisis. Donald Crabbie was first lieutenant of HMS *Cowdray* when the destroyer was torpedoed during the Torch landings near Algiers in 1942. 'I raced forward to try to assess the damage,' he recalled. 'The ship had stopped immediately, but it never occurred to me that we might sink. I was met by a rush of one officer and several ratings descending from the bridge and a gunnery director unit in panic. I stopped them in their tracks and sent them back to their posts.' The ship was held together long enough to beach in Algiers Bay.

Once sailors were stranded in the water, their chances of survival began to diminish rapidly. Even those who managed to reach lifeboats still might have to endure the open sea for days on end. Unless they were found quickly, they had little hope of salvation. Stories like that of Norman Walton – the sole survivor from HMS *Neptune* – were all too rare. The testimonies of survivors were studied intently by medical staff in an attempt to distil the essence of their endurance. One study of the aftermath of the sinking of HMS *Glorious* analysed the hallucinations of sailors stranded in lifeboats – visions of distant ships and battles, dockyards and trees – arguing that their collective nature illustrated a 'psychic contagion', the result of the continued strength derived from the ship. Even once the physical structure had gone, one witness stated, 'he felt always in communication with something and that he could not be lost; in short he had, to a considerable extent, assimilated the ship into his personality'.

An emotionless order had to be maintained on life rafts, where dead men were ditched and hangers-on waited for their turn to be hauled aboard. If there was a danger of overloading, men in the water had to remain there. Nicholas Monsarrat vividly described this terrible fate in *The Cruel Sea*: '[T]hey swam round and round in the darkness, calling out, cursing their comrades, crying for help, slobbering their prayers. Some of those gripping the ratlines found that they could do so no longer, and drifted away.'

Ultimately, survival on the open sea depended not only on individual endurance but also on good fortune, and on any number of variables, from the temperature of the water to the amount of nearby debris. The rescue of survivors was rarely an immediate priority for nearby ships: convoys had to maintain their speed; escorts had to search for U-boats; aircraft had to be fought off. Swimmers might be left to fend for themselves or, worse, subjected to the effects of depth charges launched by escorts in the heat of battle. Sailors were often deeply troubled if they felt their rescue efforts to have been inadequate. It was often the faceless cries of desperate swimmers that remained most prominent in their memories. One corvette rating recalled many years later that 'the thing that always went through your mind was some people who cried out for help, by the time you got to them, [they] weren't there any longer. And I think that that's something that sticks a bit with you.'

Fortunate survivors might be found by designated rescue vessels, or picked up by destroyers in the lull after combat. Once aboard, they would be clothed, warmed and treated for oil-filled lungs, bodily wounds and exposure. Some were remarkably upbeat. Frederick Bushell, a chief petty officer on HMS *Express*, reported that a 'youngster sitting on a mess table and shivering with cold after his dip was lighting a cigarette and said "Any how we will get fourteen days leave."' But many more survivors were traumatized, often refusing to go below decks.

An Admiralty committee to consider the problem of survival at sea was established in October 1941, but its main reports were not officially published until mid-1943. Initial studies focused on the physiological condition of euphemistically termed 'shipwrecked' personnel, and an interim report in March 1942, based on interviews and reports from 151 British survivors, illustrated the limitations of contemporary medical knowledge concerning even the most straightforward physical challenges. A pamphlet guide was produced in 1943, providing advice on the basics of survival: from preparations on board ship to behaviour in life rafts or the sea, including medical advice and guidance on the distribution of provisions and water. 'With knowledge, foresight and initiative,' it opened, somewhat optimistically, 'the chances of survival can be increased, bodily discomforts reduced, spirits cheered and morale maintained during exposure and the general condition on rescue improved.'

Practical measures were outlined for hydration, sustenance and physical repair. Once again, it was 'the bearing and conduct of the officer in charge' which was highlighted. 'A confident, calm officer, who can assume responsibility,' stated the report, 'goes further towards bringing his lifeboat into safety than any single factor.' Perpetuating proper organization and discipline would always help, even if the methods were unusual: 'A difficult individual should be hit over the head rather than be allowed to upset all the others.'

If physical wounds could be easily identified, the psychological effects of 'shipwreck' were more difficult to discern. After HMS *Valiant* was damaged in the Mediterranean, she refitted at Durban between April and June 1942. To make up the complement, over 600 new personnel – more than half the ship's company – were assigned from a pool of survivors from other sunken ships such as *Prince of Wales*, *Repulse*, *Dorsetshire*, *Cornwall*, *Naiad*, *Lively*, *Jackal* and *Barham*. Most of these men had been overseas for more than a year. Those from *Dorsetshire* had spent only three weeks in Britain in three years.

As the ship was working up over the summer, *Valiant*'s medical officer, Surgeon Lieutenant C. R. G. Howard, became gravely concerned about morale and the psychological state of the ratings. There was disciplinary trouble, increasing complaints about anxiety, and 'an indefinable air of mistrust of officers'. Censorship revealed a great deal of discontent: 'I'm chocker', 'this ship is lousy, I'm fed up', 'I advise you not to join the Navy'.

Howard made efforts to remedy the situation, and morale improved once *Valiant* had sailed for Mombasa to join the Eastern Fleet. He subsequently wrote a report for the Admiralty based on his observations, recommending measures to rehabilitate survivors which were later adapted into official guidelines. These aimed to minimize 'self-pity' and promote renewed confidence and morale by balancing sympathy with rehabilitation. A short period of rest should be followed by routine and work, with officers taking a personal role in providing fresh kits and uniforms. No verbal promises of any kind should be made, and examining medical officers should avoid asking suggestive questions such as 'Are your nerves all right?' The standard period of fourteen days survivors' leave should be followed by reassignment into a well-led new ship's company into which men could invest their pride.

As the war continued, there were few in the navy who did not experience trauma in some form. Each of the armed forces struggled to deal effectively with the mental health of servicemen, and the navy was no exception. On 11 November 1942, Armistice Day, HMS *Ilex* was en route to the Cape Verde islands to join a convoy travelling south across the Atlantic. Commanding officer Vere Wight-Boycott was worried about the mental state of his ship's company. 'It is a distressing fact that the number of so-called Neurotics in the Navy seems to be increasing,' he wrote in his diary, recalling incidents in his previous ships:

In _Delight_ one stoker went mad, and during the Narvik campaign the Engineer Officer 'could not take it'. In _Roxborough_ two Coxswains had to be relieved and finally a signalman became suicidal and had to be locked up. In this ship already we have landed a stoker with homicidal tendencies, and the Doctor tells me there is a leading stoker who is practically useless, a Stoker Petty Officer who had a weeping fit the other day, a Newfoundland seaman who wanders round the deck all night for fear of being torpedoed, and the Supply Petty Officer nearly persuaded himself that he had Spotted Fever. This last the Doctor thinks he has cured psychologically by injections of pure water.

Breakdown amongst sailors was certainly not uncommon. Derric Breen of HMS _Egret_ recalled an incident at Takoradi on the Gold Coast in December 1944. One popular leading seaman, a 'gentle giant', was discovered on the upper deck brandishing a machete, threatening anyone who came near him. Breen was able to calm him before moving closer and convincing him to drop the weapon. 'Serenely,' wrote Breen, 'he handed it over and broke down . . . We took him ashore, that great splendid man, weeping like a child and pushing against me for comfort.'

Psychiatry was a controversial issue. Desmond Curran, the navy's chief psychiatric consultant, was reluctant to accept 'operational strain' as the chief cause of neurosis and breakdown, preferring to blame inherent psychological weaknesses. Although his opinions were not universally accepted, specialist psychiatric care was nevertheless only cautiously adopted. 'The great danger for psychiatry is to become a special cult,' wrote Curran. 'The great danger for a special psychiatric hospital is to obtain the reputation of a "loony bin" the entry to which is a prelude to invaliding.'

Curran was concerned that inexperienced medical officers might encourage psychosomatic disorders or hypochondria by being overly zealous. This was illustrated by the debate over 'effort syndrome', an ambiguous condition widely thought to be the result of the shock to a sedentary, untrained civilian who was thrust into a regimented military environment. It was regarded as a potential 'epidemic' if not dealt with in a certain way. '"Back to duty" as soon as he can do a reasonable day's work must be your constant aim', stated one medical expert. 'There is no reason why the ship's medical officer, even if he has had no psychiatric training, should not deal effectively with the simpler cases,' argued another. 'He may be the means of preventing a recurrence and . . . the loss of a man to the Service. Admission to hospital is usually best avoided in many such cases.'

Combat stress amongst pilots in the Fleet Air Arm was a particular challenge. First Sea Lord Andrew Cunningham complained that the navy's pilots were 'getting contaminated by the RAF and want leave after so many operational hours'. He was adamant that 'the Medical Officer's duty was to keep them flying and not make reports that whole squadrons were suffering from operational fatigue'. Surgeon Commander Scott, of the carrier *Ark Royal*, viewed the problem in terms of the effect on the entire ship's company:

> Had we grounded aircrew on the first suspicion of stress this would have severely affected general morale, from the suspicion that all that was needed to secure release from dangerous activities was to produce symptoms for the Medical Department. In the *Ark Royal* I never had cause to doubt the reality of physical complaints produced by any officer or rating, and had more difficulty in persuading the manifestly unfit to remain off duty than to return to it those who had recovered.

Shore-based specialists were housed exclusively in depots and other establishments, rather than in 'forward' positions aboard ships themselves. By the end of 1943, the army had 227 neuropsychiatric specialists, the navy only 36. Only three were based outside Britain: in Alexandria, Durban and Colombo. Treatment in these shore establishments employed a series of 'filters' to ensure that relatively minor symptoms did not deteriorate through the misplaced actions of doctors or exposure to other patients with graver conditions.

The role of the psychiatrist on shore, according to a 1942 paper, was 'to render the maximum number of patients fit for sea in the shortest time'. This was evident in the work of the few dedicated auxiliary hospitals, such as Cholmondeley Castle in Cheshire, which sought to preserve an attachment to naval routine through discipline, training, occupational therapy and psychotherapy. HMS *Standard*, a naval 'pioneer corps' established in February 1942, had transferred 680 of its 842 members to 'useful service employment' by July 1945.

Kenneth Rail was serving in the battleship HMS *Nelson* in 1943 when he suffered a breakdown. He had been in *Cossack* at Narvik, and had survived when the destroyer was sunk by a torpedo in October 1941. After a period of survivors' leave and several months in shore jobs, he was redrafted to *Nelson* and was made a gun loader. 'One finds it difficult to adjust after two years on a small ship,' he wrote. 'Although feeling good physically, I had bouts of nervous tension.' In July 1943, during a training exercise, 'I started to shake, an uncomfortable feeling.' He was taken to sick bay, and then to a hospital ship the next morning and eventually to a psychiatric hospital at Knowle in Hampshire.

'The doctors were kind and sympathetic,' Rail recalled, 'the ten day narcotics treatment rather unpleasant, but there was plenty of occupational therapy, which included working on a nearby farm for two days a week for a month or so.' After seven months at Knowle, he was judged 'no longer fit for further service' and discharged in February 1944. His pension only lasted three years, something about which he remained bitter for many years. 'Apparently if one is wounded with shrapnel it's different,' he wrote, 'so it seems that the mental state does not count.'

The fear of such an outcome contributed to the scepticism with which some sailors viewed psychiatric interviews and shore-based experts. 'I do not trust him and I am suspicious of his sympathy,' as one sailor put it. 'He hasn't been to sea, he hasn't seen a boy with his head on the mess-table sobbing quietly after prolonged action and no sleep.' But for others the experience was positive. Philip Rambaut was a senior engineering officer in the destroyer HMS *Grenville* during 1943, when the ship was almost constantly employed sweeping the Channel and the Bay of Biscay. By early 1944, he was becoming worn out. 'The strain of four years of war was beginning to have its effect on me,' he wrote. 'I was able to perform my duties satisfactorily but our doctor noticed that I was unable to relax, walking up and down a great deal and showing irritability.' The destroyer was running well, which paradoxically meant 'too much time contemplating dangers, so anxiety ensued'. After a nearby destroyer was sunk by a torpedo, Rambaut suffered a breakdown and the medical officer decided to send him ashore. A relief was arranged, and he was sent on leave before being given a staff job in Liverpool. Within a few months, he felt well enough to apply for sea service again, and was assigned to the destroyer *Ulysses* which left for the Far East in June 1945.

Some forward-thinking officers developed their own methods. Courtney Anderson was a veteran captain of motor torpedo boats, who had seen action from the Channel to Crete and Tobruk. After returning to Britain in 1943, he was eventually given command of the old destroyer HMS *Wivern*. 'I had a doctor who was a psychiatrist from Glasgow,' he recalled, 'and he got me interested in psychiatry and we worked out a system together.' Any defaulters and men in breach of discipline would be assessed by both of them, and the medical officer's suggestions for psychiatric treatment would be taken up wherever appropriate.

'The system worked so well,' Anderson explained, 'that in 36 ships in the Rosyth escort force any sailor who was punished by warrant . . . was automatically sent to *Wivern*, and with this combination of naval discipline and psychiatry . . . I won't say we made good sailors out of them, but they never got into trouble again and they were useful hands on board.' In nearly every case, a satisfactory outcome was reached: 'We had virtually no discipline troubles at all. It was a very happy ship.'

Medical officers knew from personal experience the psychological effects of battle stress, long convoys and intense bombardments. But with only limited means of treating patients at sea, some felt unable to deal adequately with the problems. 'It was no good recognizing the existence of such conditions as battle fatigue, fear neurosis or being bomb happy,' wrote one medical officer. 'There was nowhere to go to get away from it all so you just had to get on with the job. Probably most people had some degree of these conditions.' Most believed that the best method of supporting the mental health of sailors was not a separate and extensive system of psychiatric specialists, but simply taking good care of sailors on an everyday basis.

'Contrary to general belief,' wrote Sheldon Dudley, the navy's medical director-general in 1943, a medical officer's duties 'are not primarily concerned with the care of the sick and wounded. The first and main duty of the medical service is the maintenance of health and fighting fitness. The most important work in this connection is the maintenance of mental health, i.e. happiness, contentment, and morale.'

Cowardice and mental disorders were uncomfortable issues. The navy was not unique amongst the armed forces in struggling to adapt to the challenge of caring for its men, but it was influenced above all by operational concerns. While the army and air force were operating at limited capacity for much of the war, the navy had to maintain maximum effort from the outset. Although the outcome of the court martial heard by George Blundell was regrettable, the aim of the navy's approach to morale, welfare and medical care was to prevent such instances from happening in the first place. Even if it failed on occasion to care adequately for every man, the navy simply could not afford to ignore the psychology of the sailor.

In Nicholas Monsarrat's *Cruel Sea*, Able Seaman Gregg is absent without leave for seventeen days and misses sailing. He is revealed to have been in London dealing with an adulterous wife. His captain reflects perfectly the service culture in domestic matters: he tells Gregg that it is part of the responsibility of officers to help under such circumstances, and that special leave could have been arranged:

Just remember that the Royal Navy has a routine for *everything*, whether it's going into battle, or for taking a shell out of a gun when it's jammed and may explode, or for helping in domestic trouble like yours. It's usually the only workable routine there is, the best available, because the Navy looks after its own.

## 20. Jimmy the Bastard

In June 1942, the destroyer HMS *Lightning* was at Madagascar, in the aftermath of the successful operation to seize the island from Vichy French forces. Able Seaman Alan Gould had been looking forward to the calm of a few days in harbour. Yet work continued unabated, directed by the first lieutenant. There seemed to be nothing the ratings could do to satisfy his demands, as Gould explained in a diary he was keeping for his wife: 'He's so exact that he doesn't realize what his madness causes and no one works hard enough for him.' After confronting his despised taskmaster, Gould's opinion was merely confirmed:

> We spent most of the afternoon talking and I came to the conclusion that he is two faced and not fit to be in charge of men. He suffers from nerves I'm sure as he has eaten or picked his fingers and fingernails to pieces. We went to sea on Sunday night. I was very miserable and longed for you so much as the conditions aboard disgusted me so much more than usual. I only hope it will not spoil my future life, I hope I shall forget the navy and the bitterness it has given me.

At night, Gould worked his way through A. J. Cronin's *The Stars Look Down*: 'It is a very sordid book, but I suppose true to life, he has a bit of a go in his books does Cronin.' The tale of inequality and poverty in a north-eastern mining community between the wars seemed to strike a chord. Gould confessed that he had 'noticed lately that no matter how much is said or written about the injustice or unfairness it never gets very far and it is only an outlet for one's bitter feelings. I may be wrong, I hope so, but I know what it is like in the navy if you kick up a stink. They let you go so far, then when you are getting at the root of the evil you find that you have got a shift.'

Battleships and larger warships were run by a commander, some-times in charge of several dozen officers, but in destroyers and smaller ships it was the first lieutenant who acted as executive officer and second-in-command. 'Jimmy the One' – as he was called in naval slang – could easily be cast as the villain by discontented matelots.

In October 1943 Geoff Dormer was 'Jimmy the One' aboard the converted trawler HMS *Hornpipe*, which was minesweeping off the Italian coast in the aftermath of the Salerno landings. 'Trouble with the crew,' he wrote in his diary. 'The starboard watch refused to turn to in the afternoon, although they had been off all morning.' Caught between the petty officers and the captain, there was little he could do except attempt to deal with the situation personally: 'The Cox-swain is incapable of exerting any authority, so I have to be on deck 16 hours a day, to get anything done at all. Meanwhile the CO com-plains that I don't work the men hard enough.'

*Hornpipe* spent the autumn working around the bay of Naples as Allied troops struggled to push German forces inland. The docks were infested with unexploded bombs and shrouded in rubble. In the city itself, reported Dormer, 'some streets were still carpeted with broken glass' and inhabited by 'swarms of prostitutes and pimps'. The presence of American forces exacerbated the ill feeling. 'Food scrounging is a popular midnight pastime now,' wrote Dormer in November. 'The quays of Naples are piled high with American rations, and their sentries are often looking the other way, so our diet is sometimes varied with unexpected delicacies . . . We are beggars, looking through a rich man's windows.'

By December, relations between the lower deck and the officers of *Hornpipe* had deteriorated yet further. Sailors wrote letters addressed to one another, merely so that they would be read by Dormer in the course of his censorship duties: 'They tell each other what they think of "Jimmy the Bastard".' The contempt was mutual. 'The morning passes in my usual round of slave driving,' wrote Dormer in his diary. 'Some of them are a useless lot of bastards. I can only keep my tem-per by regarding them as beneath contempt . . . the other slouching rats, who can't even pick their feet up as they shamble round the deck, are the type who'd live on the dole for choice.'

Sailors were more often workers than warriors. Officers became their managers. The war at sea was largely an industrial experience, not far removed from the essence of the factory: the nurtured machinery of the engine room; the organized procedures of the wireless telegraphy office; the drilled routines of the gun, depth-charge or torpedo teams; the choreographed process of the aircraft launch; the bureaucracy of the bridge. Ships were governed according to a culture of mechanical efficiency with production-line values. Whether he was firing shells, cooking meals, navigating rough seas or unloading stores, an individual was invariably effective only as part of a team.

The ubiquitous mantra of the Royal Navy was 'fighting efficiency'. The goal of the average sailor was not to commit extraordinary acts of personal bravery but rather to achieve a perfect working process. For sailors, unlike soldiers or airmen, the concept of the 'battlefield' was largely redundant. There was no 'behind-the-lines' at sea. Sailors therefore had to be efficient workers at all times, whether in combat or not. Similarly, the best officers were often the most effective managers. This was an important part of the institutional fabric of the Royal Navy, even if officers sometimes fell short of the ideal. The aims of naval discipline were to inculcate the values of the service, and to ensure that the war machine worked as smoothly as possible through paternalism, pragmatism and, above all, efficiency.

By 1943 fears were growing about the potential breakdown of this carefully cultivated ideology. The buzzword was 'dilution'. Over the course of the war, the navy recruited 40,000 temporary officers and over half a million 'Hostilities Only' ratings. Their training emphasized the institutional ethos but there was only so much that could be done in a truncated schedule. Experienced officers fretted that their youthful juniors would fail to uphold traditional values, and that the hordes of men drawn from civilian employment would further dismantle years of tradition. The Admiralty wrote to senior officers in September 1943 warning them about 'the lack of knowledge and experience of certain Reserve Officers in the matter of Naval discipline' and recommending that they arrange for additional instruction to be provided 'for the benefit of officers who have little or no experience of exercising disciplinary control'.

Alfred Duckworth, a senior officer in HMS *Warspite* and an expert on naval law, gave a lecture to junior officers at Gibraltar a few months later. His themes were the importance of self-discipline and mutual respect. 'What we have to show, unmistakably,' he told his younger colleagues, 'is that we are *fit* to be officers, and know how to behave as such.' Everything from their appearance to their demeanour would be noticed, and the reaction of their men adjusted accordingly. They should set an example: 'If you appear to evince no great interest in your job you must expect the men to follow your example, and they too will all too readily adopt the pose of being "fed up" with their work.' Discipline was not, Duckworth suggested, simply 'a mere matter of "offences" and "punishments"'. He emphasized the necessity for officers to understand their men's concerns, interviewing them and keeping abreast of their domestic circumstances. Welfare was the foundation of warfare.

Every seagoing sailor wanted to serve in a 'happy ship'. This meant good morale, an efficient and effective ship's company and a fair and transparent system of discipline. The advice given to new officers by Captain John N. Pelly, in charge of the RNVR training base HMS *King Alfred*, was that 'a ship is either efficient, smart, clean and happy, or none of these things. They go hand in hand, or not at all.' Yet there was no foolproof blueprint for achieving such a state. Every ship in the navy was different, and what worked in one was not guaranteed to do so in another. It was important to keep busy and to have a taste of action; inactivity could foment unrest. Cohesion amongst the ship's company was invaluable: bonds between messes and departments, a strong sense of identity within the ship, an attachment to the traditions of the navy and a belief in the value of the mission. But discipline was vital. Sam Lombard-Hobson recalled the advice given to him by a veteran petty officer: '"You will not have a happy ship's company if you *ever* let up on discipline."'

Individual officers played a crucial role in deciding the tone and character of discipline within their ships. The Naval Discipline Act and *The King's Regulations and Admiralty Instructions* formed the official code, but they were best enforced with discretion, pragmatism and flexibility. Formal bureaucratic procedures were not always practical or preferred. The court martial was a relatively little-used tribunal, a result of both the logistical difficulties inherent in a disparate and mobile organization and an institutional dislike of its cumbersome and time-consuming proceedings. There were only 40 trials of naval personnel by court martial in 1939, rising to 1,134 in 1945. The rate was, both numerically and proportionally, considerably lower than in the other services: in 1945 the RAF held 3,868 trials and the army 49,113.

More serious offences were referred ashore, and could lead to the removal of good conduct badges and their related pay bonus, demotion or incarceration. But for the petty offender, justice was best served through imposing extra duties, docking pay and stopping leave. These were not simply soft options. George Blundell noted that the potential humiliation of forgoing such basic privileges could be a very effective deterrent: 'It acted as a disgrace rather than a punishment.' An article in the *Naval Review* in 1944 offered guidance to young commanding officers: 'Summary justice, if sympathetically and intelligently wielded by the captain, can be the fairest form of justice . . . Rule One is: see to it that your summary justice is utterly fair and impartial. On your success in this rests the discipline and morale of your ship.'

One of the consequences of a happy ship was that discipline remained light; conversely, a long warrant sheet recording minor offences was often a symptom of poor morale. Drunkenness was probably the most common transgression, but was barely noticeable in official records because it was largely dealt with summarily. Men coming aboard drunk after shore leave were tolerated, as long as they were on time. 'All altercations with excited and drunken men are to be avoided,' stated *The King's Regulations and Admiralty Instructions*. Officers were expected to prevent inebriated ratings from committing more serious offences such as insubordination or assaulting a superior. It was the duty of the patrol or the petty officers to accost drunks, not the supervising officer. John Wilson recalled that he sometimes had to go to great lengths to avoid 'fighting drunks' returning to HMS *Oribi* after shore leave: 'Occasionally I had to dodge round the deck or even take to my heels while a petty officer pursued the delinquent.'

Venereal disease was one of the most pervasive problems the navy faced. Known as 'CDA', an acronym for both the Contagious Diseases Act and the fact that a man 'caught disease ashore', it was both a medical concern and a disciplinary issue. But in common with practice in parts of the army, concealing an infection was far more severely punished than contracting one. Having to confine men to 'Rose Cottage' – a dedicated mess for sufferers – was an inconvenience, but far better than risking the spread of a disease and the decimation of a ship's company. A strategy of education and exhortation was preferred to punitive punishment. Official figures suggested that levels of venereal disease had been reduced to a third of their pre-war level by 1943.

It was often left to the judgement of officers and medics to provide guidance to men and to develop their own approach, tailored to the nature of the ship and its operational environment. Free contraception was often distributed to sailors. The medical officer of HMS *Hood* broadcast a message on the subject to the ship's company in November 1940, advertising his wares and advising them that failing to take advantage would be 'really against your finer judgement and the best interests of the Service. It is well known that for protection the Soccer player wears Shin Guards, the Cricketer large pads and gloves.' Harry Balfour, who served in destroyers on east-coast convoys, recalled the occasion when his ship docked at Grimsby for repairs: 'One of the first men aboard was the local Padre who obviously had a very practical and progressive attitude to life for he presented me with a list of those "houses" which had a very bad reputation for V.D. and those which were said to be better run.'

Brothels were known to sailors as 'Bag Shanties'. The most notorious, such as those in the area of Valletta known as the Rag, were officially prohibited. But even here, a nearby clinic was established to treat men who had contracted a sexually transmitted infection. While he was at Bombay in 1945, Lieutenant Commander Alex Hughes noted that although most of the local brothels were firmly out of bounds, an exception was made for an establishment exclusively for officers by the name of Madam Andree's: 'Not only is it in bounds but is officially approved – the telephone number is in the official direc-

21. HMS *Belfast* in the Arctic, November 1943. A sailor in winter gear stands below a gun turret.

22. Charles Thomas in naval uniform.

23. Sailors writing home from the destroyer HMS *Garth*, 1944.

24. Officers censoring letters in the wardroom.

27. Following a depth charge explosion, a sailor from an escort vessel retrieves dead fish, which will be cooked and eaten later.

28. A band plays on the deck of a destroyer at sea off the coast of Britain, November 1942.

29. Uckers. A group of sailors in fancy dress enjoy the ubiquitous naval game, using a wooden barrel to roll the dice.

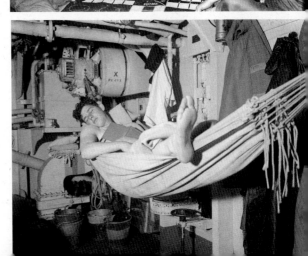

30. A sailor asleep in his hammock on board HMS *Anson*, August 1942.

31. 'Crossing the Line' aboard the troop transport SS *Empress of Australia*, August 1941. An initiate is thrown into the dunking pool by the 'bears' after being shaved by King Neptune's barber.

32. A boxing match held under the shadow of the guns on board HMS *Rodney*, 1943.

33. A Swordfish flies low over the aircraft carrier HMS *Indomitable*, June 1942. On deck a game of hockey is in progress, next to the opening of the hangar lift.

34. Firefighters at work with foam and water after a kamikaze strike on HMS *Formidable* during the Okinawa campaign, May 1945.

35. Wrens bring a torpedo along the dockside at HMS *Dolphin*, Gosport, in preparation for loading onto a submarine, September 1943.

36. Female visitors aboard the submarine HMS *Trump* at Adelaide, September 1945. The stork symbol in the lower left corner of the flag denotes the four babies born to the wives of the submariners while they have been away from home.

37. Early morning exercises on the flight deck of HMS *Indomitable* during the passage home from the Far East, October 1945. The instructor stands on a platform and the Royal Marine Band provides the music.

38. Aboard HMS *Ruler*, children recently released from Japanese prison camps play with toys made by the ship's carpenter, who stands behind them.

tory for the Services . . . How the powers that be get away with it I don't know but they are to be congratulated – it is a pity there isn't a similar establishment for the men – whose needs are at least as great.'

Homosexuality was another disciplinary challenge which produced a pragmatic response. A confidential fleet order in April 1940 reiterated the official legislation on 'Unnatural Offences'. It was extremely explicit, providing uninhibited advice and details for medical officers on how to identify whether certain activities had been undertaken either by consent or force. Yet it was notable also for being the one and only official wartime communiqué from the Admiralty on the subject. Official regulations were strict but the navy's approach appeared far less proscriptive than those of the American navy and the British army.

Veteran rating Leonard Harris only ever witnessed the reading of two warrants for such offences in his career. On the first, the commanding officer spoke of 'evil men', but on the second, the captain was more sympathetic, referring to 'these unfortunate men, victims of being packed together almost like sardines in a tin'. It could be an emotive subject. Able Seaman Donald Butcher of HMS *Nelson* wrote in his diary in February 1942: 'Met my first homosexual, felt disgusted with Man.' Yet the chief cause for censure was not personal inclination but predatory behaviour. As Able Seaman I. G. Hall of HMS *Glasgow* wrote in his diary: 'I say nothing of the purely voluntary and clandestine arrangement between two parties, which perhaps harms no one. The attempt at enforced compulsion and endeavour to take advantage of a person under the influence of drink is different.'

'Private' matters were not, as a rule, interfered with unless they affected morale and efficiency. Standards of behaviour were more effectively enforced by peer-group pressure than by Admiralty decree. Denunciation and punishment awaited sailors who were seen to have committed crimes against their shipmates, put them in danger, compromised the efficiency and morale of the collective, or otherwise acted in ways likely to prove detrimental to the ship or the service. Above all, crimes committed by sailors against their shipmates were seen as the most serious form of offence. Cheating, scamming, stealing and deceit may not have been absent, but they were severely punished. Pilfering was the ultimate taboo. 'Theft on board was a cardinal sin,' wrote former Chief Petty Officer Ken Nodder, 'and any thieves were never brought up on charge but were dealt with by their own messmates. I recall only one case and he was pretty badly beaten up.'

Pragmatic discipline only went so far. As Alfred Duckworth emphasized, a happy ship was built on mutual respect. When this broke down, collective discipline was at risk. Mutiny was the most inflammatory word in the navy. Almost as famous as the Royal Navy's glorious victories were those infamous occasions on which officers were overthrown by their subordinates, such as the Spithead Mutiny of 1797 or the ignominious events aboard HMS *Bounty*. The end of the First World War had produced devastating mutinies in Germany and Russia, and even Royal Navy officers had at times struggled to control dissatisfaction aboard ships operating in the Baltic in late 1919.

Yet it was the so-called Invergordon Mutiny of September 1931 which dominated the mindsets of most officers in the Second World War. It was not a 'mutiny' in the traditional sense, but rather a refusal of duty by sailors in several ships of the Home Fleet, sparked by government-enforced changes to pay which were not adequately explained or understood. Invergordon was a national scandal which shocked the money markets and helped jolt Britain off the international exchange system of the Gold Standard.

'It was a nightmare of a time, a feeling of brooding unrest everywhere,' wrote Casper Swinley, an officer in HMS *Repulse* at Invergordon. Yet his description was more reminiscent of the picket line than Captain Bligh: 'I remember my Midshipmen coming back to the ship and reporting that everywhere down the line they had been "booed" in their boats and called "Yellow Bellies" and "Blacklegs".' It was, in essence, not a mutiny but a strike. Although triggered by pay, it was also the result of wider problems, most notably a fracture between officers and men. The lesson drawn by many young officers, such as Andrew Cunningham, was that their superiors had become disconnected from the sailors, ignorant of their needs and problems. He refused to euphemize: 'A mutiny it certainly was. It has no other name. We were all to blame.'

A raft of reforms in the 1930s attempted both to placate ill feeling and to prevent future problems. Some improvements in living conditions were made and new welfare machinery was established, including a new dedicated Department of Personal Services at the Admiralty. Meanwhile, a secret Admiralty document was drawn up entitled 'Notes on Dealing with Insubordination'. Officers were advised on how best to isolate troublemakers, when and whether force was necessary, and the tactics to be employed should violence erupt. But these were measures of last resort, and the importance of preventing problems developing was constantly emphasized. Sailors were to be made aware of the procedures for airing their grievances, and officers should ensure that the process was seen to be fair and reliable.

Invergordon was a watershed because it illustrated an increasingly cohesive and politically organized industrial workforce. Although the terminology of 'mutinous behaviour' remained, further incidents in the late 1930s confirmed this pattern. In 1936 twenty men in HMS *Guardian* refused to carry out their duties because of poor living conditions, and in 1937 a group protest took place on HMS *Warspite* which was eventually quelled by Marines. In the aftermath of these incidents, an Admiralty report recognized the semantic problem, preferring the term 'mass indiscipline' for events which seemed 'more analogous to the civilian strike than to the mutinies of the earlier days'.

This formed the background to wartime disciplinary policy. Official advice followed several straightforward principles: prevention was better than cure; minor grievances should not be allowed to develop into active disobedience; potential ringleaders should be monitored; good management was the key. 'It should be impossible for a good Captain of a ship to be unaware of the mentality of his ship's company,' wrote First Sea Lord Admiral Chatfield after the *Warspite* incident.

Many incidents of what would be officially called 'mutinous behaviour' took place during the war. Most were resolved quickly and never officially reported or recorded. Examples such as Bill Crawford's description of discontent aboard HMS *Hood* in 1940, or Donald Povey's jubilation at the 'victory to the mutineers' in HMS *Northern Pride* in 1943, illustrate how far insubordination could

go before it reached formal disciplinary procedures. Even major incidents could be kept quiet. In January 1944, when the cruiser
HMS *Mauritius* was preparing to leave Plymouth after a short refuelling stop, a large group of sailors refused to fall in for duty. The ship
had been away for seventeen months and shore leave had been refused.
According to Chief Engine Room Artificer William Lewis, the
stokers told him that they were 'on strike'. Eventually, petty officers
had to get the ship underway. After several ringleaders were removed
from the ship at Malta, the ship returned to operational duties and no
official report of the incident was made.

That so few incidents reached the level of official investigation was
testament partly to such pragmatism, and partly to the motivational
powers of regular operational activity, but it was also a result of the
overwhelming success of officers – even those inexperienced reservists
– in managing their ships and of the willingness of ordinary sailors to
put up with discomfort in the name of duty. Those episodes which
were subject to Admiralty boards of enquiry invariably involved similar patterns: petty grievances over such matters as leave, food or leisure
which were allowed to escalate into more widespread discontent; and
officers unaware of their subordinates' concerns or incapable of placating them, exacerbated by personality clashes or inexperience.

In late 1942, sailors started leaving the minesweeper HMS *Llan-
dudno* and failing to return. An enquiry found the ship's reservist
officers to be 'backward', failing to keep in touch with their men or
to communicate with them effectively. In 1943, HMS *Manxmaid* was
found to be an 'unhappy ship' largely because of her 'very hot tempered' commanding officer who abused his colleagues, most of
whom were reservists. When a group of ratings aboard the destroyer
HMS *Beaufort* refused to fall in for duty in the autumn of 1944, the
Admiralty found that the grievances were entirely familiar: an
unpopular and poorly implemented change in routine, and the cancellation of the normal 'make-and-mend' relaxation time. The ship's
first lieutenant, while honest and hard-working, was thought to be
'unusually lacking in the "human touch", in understanding and sympathy for his men and their weaknesses'.

The investigation into the *Beaufort* incident also highlighted another issue. 'The ship's company is typical of what is met in these days,' stated the Admiralty report, 'being largely composed of young ratings who have been in the Service only a year or two and have been brought up from childhood to think that it is right and honourable to "strike" when pressed beyond what is considered just and reasonable . . . Only the older Petty Officers are imbued with Service tradition.' By the end of the war, all but the most intransigent of senior officers recognized that the very concept of 'mutiny' had changed. 'It is not surprising,' stated the Admiralty report of another incident in 1945, 'that men who are accustomed in civil life to seek redress by means of strikes should feel that similar action in the Navy simply represents a forceful method of expressing their grievances and does not compare with mutiny.'

Discipline was a matter of management, leadership and of collective effort. Such was the variety of ships, sailors and conditions within the navy that there could be no certain method of achieving a 'happy ship'. The only certainties were the factors which made for 'unhappy ships'. But by the spring of 1944, another threat to discipline had emerged which eclipsed even those long-standing fears about the 'dilution' of the service and the changing nature of the lower deck: the defeat of Germany.

In March 1944, the new Second Sea Lord, Vice-Admiral Algernon Willis, instigated a wide-ranging series of proposals intended to counteract the threat of a general crisis of discipline. 'We have seldom got through a major war without some breakdown of morale varying from serious mutiny down to vociferous expressions of dissension and dissatisfaction,' he wrote. 'Some of the ingredients which go to make trouble . . . seem likely to exist when the Germans are defeated and full realisation that for the Navy this will mean an even greater effort in order to defeat Japan is brought home to the personnel.'

An updated version of the official guidelines written after Invergordon was prepared, now called 'Notes on Dealing with Mutiny or Massed Disobedience'. It again provided detailed advice on suppressing mutinies, but began by emphasizing the importance of prevention. Poor conditions, bad food or disruption to routines should be explained, and the cancellation of expected leave without notice should be avoided at all costs. Most dangerous were discrepancies in the delivery of mail or the payment of wages. Officers had ultimate responsibility for preventing minor grievances from developing into widespread discontent.

It did not take long for the Admiralty's fears to come to fruition. Just before the publication and dissemination of the new version of the 'Notes', the most serious mutiny of the war took place. In the afternoon of 1 September 1944, the converted merchant vessel HMS *Lothian* was berthed at Balboa, at the southern end of the Panama Canal. On the jetty was a small group of sailors who were refusing to return aboard. Watching them were a guard of Royal Marines armed with loaded rifles.

Previously known as the MV *City of Edinburgh*, the ship had been converted in 1943 into what was known as a Landing Ship Infantry Headquarters, intended to serve as a communications hub for amphibious operations. *Lothian* had sailed from the Clyde at very short notice the previous month and embarkation leave had been cut short. Many men felt inadequately prepared, with domestic arrangements left unsettled. As the ship crossed the Atlantic it was announced that *Lothian* was destined to join the British Pacific Fleet in Australia. They would be away from home for some time.

Conditions were uncomfortable. In addition to the usual complement of 500 or so sailors, there were several hundred RAF personnel and Royal Corps of Signals specialists on board: 'passengers' as the matelots called them. Messes were cramped and overcrowded, water supplies were limited and the standard of food rapidly deteriorated. Soon the ship had become dirty and disorganized, with detritus on the upper deck and fetid air down below. When *Lothian* docked at New York, sailors were desperate for shore leave. Yet there was work to be done, preparations to be made, and stores to be loaded. While the 'passengers' remained at liberty, sailors toiled in the searing heat of an east-coast summer. Several responded by breaking out of the ship and pilfering NAAFI stores.

As *Lothian* continued her voyage, disgruntlement continued to grow. Sailors began to call their ship 'HMS *Unsanitary*'. Inexperienced officers appeared to be incapable of placating them, and minor infringements of discipline went unpunished. A few ringleaders began to discuss the possibility of refusing duty on the messdecks. One sailor was heard to say, 'It would be a good job if we had a mutiny . . .' Fuelled by rum and recrimination, the voices of discontent grew louder as the ship passed through the Panama Canal.

When orders were piped on the afternoon of 1 September, *Lothian* entered a state of utter confusion. Some men refused to fall in for duty. Petty officers were despatched to intervene. As the congregation barricaded itself on the messdeck, the crowd grew larger. The first lieutenant addressed the malcontents, warning them of the penalty for mutiny and attempting to identify the ringleaders.

Then one sailor was reported to be in possession of a rifle. More rumours suggested a small-arms cache had been raided. Within a moment, wilful disobedience had escalated into something potentially far more serious. Below decks, the heat was becoming unbearable. A swarm of seamen forced their way to the upper decks past half-hearted guards and began to gather at the forecastle. A detachment of Royal Marines was armed and told to prepare for a confrontation. The captain spoke to the crowd, but a group of thirty sailors broke out of the ship past a couple of confused gangway sentries and gathered alongside on the jetty. A stand-off emerged. Some of the would-be mutineers had second thoughts and returned aboard before being put under arrest. A hard core of around twenty men continued to hold out in the evening heat.

Sergeant J. C. E. Prentice, part of the contingent of soldiers aboard, was called to the upper deck and informed of the situation. There seemed by now to be no sign of any weapons, but none of the officers could be sure. The ship's officers were reluctant to send in the armed Royal Marines and risk the ignominy of internecine fighting, so Prentice was ordered to take a detachment of his army signals staff ashore to retrieve the mutineers. 'Nothing I had been taught or had learned so far in my service had prepared me to handle the type of situation that I now found myself facing,' he recalled. 'Something that in a lifetime of soldiering one would not expect to encounter, especially involving the Royal Navy.'

Twenty-two soldiers marched down the gangway with loaded rifles and lined up opposite the sailors. Prentice ordered them to 'fire a volley over the heads of the mutineers if they showed any sign of resistance and tried to attack us . . . I had decided <u>not</u> to fix bayonets as I considered my men might hesitate to use them on British sailors, even under attack.' But by now the stress and the heat had taken their toll. After a brief discussion, the men agreed to come back aboard. In order to prove to *Lothian*'s watching officers that they were quitting peacefully, in the hope of lenient treatment, the mutineers agreed with Prentice that he would assign 'a small, bespectacled, Scotsman as escort to the tallest sailor' before sending them up the gangway. This did little to placate the waiting guards, however, and the mutineers were unceremoniously bundled into confinement as soon as they stepped on board.

As *Lothian* continued her passage to the Antipodes, the post-mortem began. Sailors and soldiers alike were threatened with severe punishments if any information about the incident was leaked. Even before the ship reached its destination, warrants were drawn up and court martial enquiries began. Senior officers in crisp white tropical uniforms and ceremonial swords attended secret hearings. Sergeant Prentice was not invited to give evidence. In the Board of Enquiry minutes, the involvement of soldiers was only referred to in a short statement of the chronology of events: 'Extra guard of army ranks is ordered to fall in.'

'As a mutiny this was a very feeble affair,' wrote the Second Sea Lord after reading the official verdict on the incident. 'It was not pre-meditated or organised; and had the situation been properly handled from the start there would have been no need to bring a charge of mutiny at all.' *Lothian* was a perfect example of the failure to follow the lessons of the war. 'Apart from the ringleaders,' stated the report, 'the majority of mutineers were very young seamen who had only recently left civil life. They appear to have regarded the outbreak in the nature of a "strike".'

But *Lothian* also illustrated what might happen if sailors were not convinced about the importance of the war against Japan. According to mutineer Bill Glenton, he and his fellow discontents suffered above all from a 'lack of belief in our mission'. Although sailors could usually be relied upon to defend themselves in action, the problem with the Pacific campaign was getting them there in the first place.

Eighteen months before the *Lothian* incident, in February 1943, Alfred Duckworth of HMS *Warspite* had written a letter to the Admiralty. 'It appears to have escaped general lower deck notice that there will still remain Japan to be dealt with,' he stated bluntly, 'and I suggest we ought to be thinking out how to remind the sailor tactfully, and in good time, that he will not ipso facto be free to go home the moment the European conflict has been got under control.'

In fact, plans about dealing with the so-called 'two-stage' end of the war had begun as far back as 1942. Because the navy would provide the essential logistical role, it was felt within the Admiralty that the war in the Far East was in some ways 'of even greater concern to the Navy than to the other Services'. There were other problems too: an extensive reorganization would be required to supply a new Pacific Fleet, tricky geopolitical questions would have to be resolved, and the process of demobilization would overshadow the efforts of those required to stay on. It was feared that the average sailor 'was not really keen' about the war in the Pacific, and 'would almost certainly react unfavourably to the prospect of continuing the struggle against Japan after Germany had been defeated'.

Sailors were regarded as part of the national community. Throughout its discussions, the Admiralty conceived the challenge as a matter of national will, referring to 'the national war effort', 'machinery to effect the education of the Services and the nation', and the views of the 'average man'. 'National education on the subject is necessary,' wrote the Director of Personal Services, arguing that the problem 'concerns the whole nation'. A committee involving each of the armed forces was established to liaise with the Ministry of Information and the wider government to help deal with the national problem of morale and the Far East.

It would be important to ensure that those at home understood what was happening to sailors. 'It cannot be too strongly stressed,' wrote one senior officer to his Admiralty superiors, 'that the reactions of personnel to a Far Eastern draft, particularly after the end of the war in Europe, will be largely influenced by the reactions of their wives, mothers and sweethearts, who appear to be profoundly ignorant of the fact that the Japanese war has any direct bearing on their own lives or on the interests of Great Britain.'

The joint committee proposed that a propaganda drive should be organized to sell the war in the Far East. The mission was to be emphasized through books and magazines, media coverage, radio programmes, displays and exhibitions organized by the services and Ministry of Information. Key themes were established: that the war was 'one war' and Japan was just as criminal as Germany; that there was an 'inextinguishable debt' to the Dominions to fulfil; that this was not merely 'America's War', because British raw materials and territory had to be reclaimed in order to ensure the 'standard of life of the whole British commonwealth'. The overarching message would be that the war against Japan was 'a campaign in the cause of freedom and of a decent way of life, both for ourselves and for our Dominions and Allies . . . It is only by a complete defeat of the nations guilty of aggression that we shall prevent another war in a few years' time.'

Meanwhile, in a departure from its carefully cultivated image as the 'Silent Service', the navy began to expand its own propaganda efforts. 'When the war with Germany is ended,' wrote one prominent naval commentator, 'there will be an opportunity for reconsidering the whole subject of naval news in terms of the War with Japan. Let us hope . . . that the British public at last may come to realise the full extent of the debt they owe to their naval forces.' A new Department of the Chief of Naval Information was established within the Admiralty, aiming to ensure self-confidence and morale within the service. As the first incumbent put it, the aim was to 'sell the British Navy to the British public' and throughout the world, particularly in America, but the ultimate goal was 'to sell the British Navy to itself'.

Sailors would fight as citizens. It was widely accepted that motivation for the war in the Far East was inextricably linked to education programmes which emphasized national community and citizenship. 'Upon the effectiveness with which this is put into practice will depend the morale of all engaged in the ordeals ahead of the Navy,' stated an Admiralty letter to officers. 'The Adult Education scheme comprising education on current affairs, citizenship, post-war reconstruction etc. is so closely bound up with morale as to be inseparable from the necessity for education about Japan.' Aside from lectures, one of the central activities would be discussion groups: organized group conversations under the supervision of an officer in which sailors could explore political, social and cultural questions.

Discussion groups had been running in some ships for some time, largely dependent on the initiative of forward-thinking officers. After voicing his concerns about the Japanese campaign to the Admiralty, Alfred Duckworth organized a programme of discussions of topical issues aboard *Warspite*. Far from simply attempting to explain the Far East mission, he dealt with all manner of citizenship themes. The question for the first meeting was 'What are we to do with Germany after the War?', and later sessions included a wide variety of social, political and economic issues, such as 'State Control vs Private Enterprise', 'Education', 'Security of Employment', 'What is the use of the House of Lords?', 'Is the British Press really free?' and 'In our eagerness to make a "new world" after the war are we moving too fast and in danger of discarding too readily the lessons and traditions of the past?'

Many discussion groups also covered the practicalities of post-war life. Reports from across the fleet on sessions in the autumn of 1944 revealed that sailors wanted information about the process of demobilization. Post-war employment was by far the most important issue within the armed forces, and the navy was no different. Men wanted to know about the order of priority for demob, the status of 'reserved jobs', the policies of the other armed forces and the position of women in the workforce. But questions of politics and citizenship were also frequently raised. One senior officer reported that 'the power of the vote' was of interest to his men, and that there was an intense interest in questions of post-war planning, housing, education and social services, but with a 'lack of confidence that the proposed schemes will ever be carried out. Mistrust, not of any particular government, but of politicians in general.'

★

As the end of the war in Europe drew closer, sailors became increasingly embroiled in political conflicts. Communism was the great fear of the military authorities. While socialism was relatively respectable, concerns about a Red mist on the messdecks remained potent. Around Europe, left-wing movements were stirring. Greek forces had mutinied in April 1944 in support of the communist-inspired National Liberation Front. The Greek navy was a substantial presence in the Mediterranean, and resistance aboard several ships in Alexandria had to be quelled by force. In time, the power struggle in Greece would result in a civil war. Throughout the eastern Mediterranean, the Royal Navy had to operate in highly politicized environments.

In the Adriatic, British sailors were caught between the last remnants of German forces and communist partisans scrambling for political influence in Yugoslavia. Geoffrey Hobday was in command of MGB 643, operating with other British coastal forces from the island of Vis in support of partisans led by Marshal Tito. It was a swashbuckling campaign. 'We decided to take a leaf from the partisans' book and forget about conventional methods of warfare,' he explained. Carrying a detachment of Royal Marine commandos, they performed actions reminiscent of naval warfare in the age of sail: concentrating fire on the enemy bridge and engine room, sweeping the decks with machine guns, crashing alongside, boarding and seizing control, then transferring prisoners across and sinking the ship. 'The atmosphere at Vis was exhilarating,' wrote Hobday. 'Here the odds were still stacked against us, but . . . we couldn't help but be inspired by the daring and fervour of the partisans.'

Between November 1944 and March 1945, HMS *Delhi* was assigned a peacekeeping role at the Croatian port of Split. Captain Ridley Waymouth described it as 'four months of mental struggle, during which *Delhi* had sailed only twenty-seven feet'. He was most concerned about morale. *Delhi* had been away from Britain for three years. Many of the sailors were young 'Hostilities Only' ratings. Mail was sporadic and fresh food was hard to come by. Waymouth was concerned that the highly politicized environment might cause even greater problems: 'The Partisans were doing their best to spread division, alarm and despondency.'

Humanitarian work helped. The sailors of *Delhi* held a Christmas party for 500 local children in a seafront hotel. Lights were powered by the ship's generators, as was the cinema equipment brought ashore. Ratings had spent weeks making toys and collecting food and treats. On the evening of the party, wrote Waymouth, 'we watched from the ship columns of children marshalled by the Partisans, singing revolutionary songs and carrying banners with Communist slogans, converging on the hotel'. Inside were sailors in fancy dress, the most rotund dressed as Father Christmas. They played games and watched a Mickey Mouse movie. 'When the children left, hugging their toys, they came out not as Communist revolutionaries, but as normal, happy children. It was a party that neither the hosts nor the children are likely to forget.'

But Waymouth attributed the maintenance of morale and the avoidance of a crisis of discipline to discussion groups. In such a febrile political atmosphere, citizenship education was not merely an academic exercise. Organized by a group of officers and senior ratings, each mess would hold a weekly session to discuss current affairs. On Fridays the ship's company would congregate to hear the summary of each group's conclusions. 'At first the men were suspicious that something was being put over them,' wrote Waymouth, 'but after a few weeks more and more men got interested and spontaneous discussions went on all over the ship at unexpected times and places.' When passing the heads, one officer had overheard 'the voice of a well-known scallywag floating out through the scuttle with the forbidden cigarette smoke in the middle of working hours saying, "Well, all I can f . . . ing well say is I f . . . ing well wouldn't want to live in one of those f . . . ing council houses if I f . . . ing well was paid to." Not a very elevated discussion but that chap was still thinking about something four hours after the official discussion!'

## 21. By Hook or by Crook

In the spring of 1944, the aircraft carrier HMS *Indomitable* was at Norfolk, Virginia, refitting and working up in preparation for service in the Indian Ocean and the Pacific. Commander Robert Parker, the ship's senior engineering officer, had a great deal of paperwork to do. 'Getting bored with it,' he wrote in his diary. *Indomitable*'s boilers were in a sorry state, causing arguments and recriminations amongst the engine-room staff and the civilian dockyard workers. Tempers began to fray. 'Had a pistol held at my head for the third time in the last seven days,' recorded Parker on one occasion. 'Getting tired of it. Shall be rude soon. Feel very like Hitler.' He kept a daily record of his drinking habits: whisky, rum, beer and a troubling over-consumption of Pepsi-Cola. Not every sailor was so restrained: *Indomitable*'s officers were on the alert for drunkenness. In a nearby British ship, a sailor had recently died from alcohol poisoning: 'Broke open rum store and killed himself!'

As the engineering specialist, Parker was responsible for ensuring that the carrier's engines were in proper working condition, but as the scheduled date for *Indomitable*'s departure approached, there seemed to be little prospect of the work being completed. 'These damned Yanks sleep all the time instead of working,' he wrote. On 20 March, the ship was the scene of 'chaos', with Parker again blaming American workers: 'A hundred men and no room to move. Typical of these people, leaving everything till the last minute, then thinking they're super if they make the date.' Soon afterwards, however, a fatal accident put this bickering into perspective. Parker reported that a rating had 'killed himself in bomb lift. Cocktail party cancelled. Nasty sight, happened to see it just afterwards.'

Finally on her way to the Pacific, *Indomitable* steamed through the Mediterranean, bound for the Suez Canal. Fleet Air Arm exercises were conducted en route, training for launching and landing aircraft. Several proved utterly catastrophic. Parker recorded that two Barracudas 'broke up in air during dive bombing exercise. Saw them both, horrible sight . . . Nobody saved. Wings pulled right off at bottom of dive.' Not long afterwards, a 'Corsair dived into the sea, pilot lost'. The problems were not confined to the flight deck. Parker had to deal with constant engine trouble, causing much antagonism amongst the ranks. He became increasingly frustrated with stokers he referred to as 'dumb', 'dull' and 'half asleep'.

Not every ship travelling east was quite so troubled. Indeed, the vistas of the Indian Ocean were spectacular enough to inspire even the most cynical seaman. Signalman Ivor Turner of HMS *Durban* described a convoy from Mombasa to Bombay in his diary: 'The dawns and sunsets out here are said to be the most beautiful in the world and I can quite believe it after the few I've seen. The colours are so bright and when you're by yourselves in the middle of such a vast ocean it seems that nature is putting on a show just for your benefit.'

HMS *Petard* helped to escort a convoy to the naval base at Addu Atoll, at the southern edge of the Maldives. A deep turquoise lagoon was enclosed by a shallow shelf of sand and several narrow islands. 'The sand is dazzling white,' wrote Reg Crang in his diary, 'and the coconut palms dotted around the shore give it an exotic appearance.' He described how the men from *Petard* traded cigarettes for coconuts and watched the barracuda in the lagoon. They saw flying foxes and, inevitably, it was not long before someone 'shot one of these in flight and proudly brought it into the Mess'.

Yet the Indian Ocean remained a battleground. In February 1944, the Japanese submarine I-27 attacked a convoy of five troop transports south-west of the Maldives as they made their way towards Ceylon. The SS *Khedive Ismail* was hit by two torpedoes and sank within minutes. There were more than 1,500 people on board, with soldiers and nurses alongside sailors. Nearly 1,300 lost their lives. That the submarine was sunk after being depth charged, rammed and finally torpedoed by the destroyers *Paladin* and *Petard* proved little consolation after one of the highest death tolls from a single incident in the war at sea.

After the Japanese attack on Ceylon in April 1942, the British East

Indies Fleet had retreated to Kenya, with Addu Atoll serving as a forward sea base. It was the American navy which bore the brunt of the war against Japan in the Pacific. In the Battle of the Coral Sea in May 1942, Australian ships and aircraft contributed to the American task force which halted the Japanese advance. While the US carrier force defeated the Japanese at Midway, and US Marines began to fight an island campaign from Guadalcanal, Australian and New Zealand ships were largely responsible for the defence of their homelands.

After its protracted absence, the Royal Navy finally returned to Ceylon in strength over the course of 1944. Convoys transported service personnel and supplies from South Africa and Suez to the island in preparation for a renewed campaign against Japanese forces in south-east Asia, initially in Burma, Malaya and Indonesia. Ultimately, it was anticipated that a British Pacific Fleet would join with the Americans in a final offensive against Japan itself.

Reg Crang arrived at Colombo in early 1944. In his diary, he described the city as 'a clean and somewhat select sort of seaside town, with wide promenades planted with palm trees. It has a very nice Fleet Club, set in beautiful grounds, but with very little beer in its bars . . . The long stretch of beach reminded me of Torquay and made me sigh for home.' Trincomalee, in the north-east, was very different: 'a naval anchorage beside a native village. There is no western civilization such as is to be found in Colombo but the sand there is almost white.'

Those who travelled inland discovered jungle temples and tamed elephants. Alex Hughes visited Diyaluma Falls and Arugam Bay on the south-east coast. 'I had never – seeing only Colombo-Jaffna – imagined there was anything so beautiful as these hills,' he wrote in his diary. 'Today looking down all the smaller hills and foothills were blue – wonderful breathtaking unpaintable view.' Lieutenant Richard Walker toured the jungle near Trincomalee, describing 'flamboyant butterflies (red swallowtails, milkwort fritillaries), kingfishers, flying squirrels, tortoises . . . queer landcrabs with a single white claw and evil sluggish movements'. On returning to the town, he found 'small Ceylon children with pot bellies and angelic faces – "me hungry, money, money", they cry'.

Some were not enamoured of Ceylon, particularly those posted to the naval base of Trincomalee. One sailor described it as 'Scapa with palm trees'. An anonymous rating from HMS *Phoebe* expressed a similarly jaundiced view in the lower deck's self-produced newsletter:

The swaying palms and thundering surf? Yes, and the red ants, the mosquito, the crabs, jelly fish and barracuda. And the ear diseases. The stars and the sun? And the prickly heat, toe rot, sunburn. The flies, smells and everlasting lassitude. The cruises, with lazy hours lounging in deck chairs beneath a tropic sun, and swimming in a sparkling blue sea? The weary sweltering hours in turret, boiler room and Action Stations . . . There we have the exotic East – a la East Indies Fleet. There isn't as much glamour in two years in the Far East as there is in two hours in the East End.

'This place seems to have an unlimited capacity for absorbing Wrens,' wrote Lieutenant Hooper of Colombo's naval intelligence station, HMS *Anderson*, in February 1944. 'Large crowd of new Wrens appeared this morning and were gradually distributed . . . There are a few winners in the new bunch, but most of them have the generous proportions proper to their kind. Our allocation was one only, a short girl with well-groomed features, a deep voice, and plenty of body.'

One group of Wrens was transported to Ceylon in the armed merchant cruiser HMS *Chitral*, a converted passenger liner. They were treated like the lowliest ratings: sleeping in hammocks, washing the decks and cleaning the heads. There was only one crucial exception: they were ineligible for a daily tot of rum. A delegation of Wrens made representations to the captain, who finally relented. 'Very few of us enjoyed the rum,' recalled Mary Sturt, 'but we were out to make a point, so stomach it we did!'

After arriving in Ceylon, Carol Wilson was eager to describe Colombo to her parents. In a letter home, she mentioned the 'red splodges on the pavement' caused by the betel nuts chewed and spat out by the locals, the jewellery shops and famous carved wooden elephants of Hospital Street, but was most enthusiastic about the Sundae Tearooms: 'Lovely fruit salads there consisting of pineapple, banana, water melon and so on. Also they have lovely fruit drinks, lime, orange or passion fruit with great lumps of ice in them. Absolutely "lush"!'

Her first few weeks of service involved a great deal of socializing. 'I am doing my duty towards the poor lonely boys,' wrote Wilson. 'It gets a bit complicated when one has to cope with so many though! We Wrens really work hard when we go to dances because so many invitations come in a day. When we get to the dance hall we find there are about ten men to every girl and as the band plays nearly all "excuse me's" it gets a bit warm.'

Many Wrens were employed in the headquarters of South East Asia Command (SEAC), which oversaw all Allied efforts in the region. After the appointment of Lord Mountbatten to Supreme Commander of SEAC in late 1943, the base of operations was moved from Delhi to Kandy. Elizabeth Gibson had already served as a cipher officer in Washington, DC, and at the Allied conferences at Quebec and Cairo, before being transferred to Mountbatten's private office in March 1944.

Initially, the staff lived in the Queen's Hotel, 'overlooking Kandy lake and the Temple of the Tooth and grappled with mosquitoes, disgusting bed bugs, constant theft of underwear, booze etc.' They were later moved to a collection of bamboo huts near Peradeniya, which offered better hygiene and food, if not such dramatic views. The Supreme Commander's reputation as a ladies' man inevitably had an effect on the conduct of female assistants. In the run-up to D-Day, secretaries were required to fly to London for consultations with Admiralty staff. 'To avoid malicious gossip,' wrote Gibson, 'I or female staff did not fly in the same plane as Lord Louis, except on the rare occasions when Lady Louis was present.'

Racial and religious problems were never far from the surface in south-east Asia. In Ceylon, this took the form of the perceived contrast between the Tamil and Sinhalese populations. 'These Tamils are good people,' wrote Alex Hughes in his diary, 'they are fairly honest and very hard working. The Sinhalese live mainly in the south of Ceylon and want to be rid of the Tamils who migrated from Southern India.'

Hughes described the festivities on Wesak Day, as he put it 'the Buddhist Christmas':

The town was gaily decorated with flags and streams and lights . . . ships and aeroplanes made of wood and paper about 15 feet long [and] an enormous Chinese lantern with smaller ones hanging from it. In the evening there were various processions . . . a cart decorated and with the figure of Buddha inside then about 12 boys dressed in the traditional Kandyan costume – brass bracelets and medallions, fuzzy wigs and red colouring on the cheeks and an orchestra with drums and wind instruments.

Ceylon was once again the hub for the Royal Navy's efforts in the Indian Ocean, but bases in India itself were also developing rapidly. Some British sailors were already well acquainted with the country. Back in May 1941, after the destroyer HMS *Kelvin* was damaged during the evacuation from Crete, she was sent to Bombay for repairs. While the work was carried out, a group of sailors were taken on a tour of northern India, 'showing the flag'. They visited Delhi, Rawalpindi and then the city of Peshawar. Able Seaman A. Andrews reported in his journal that 'crowds literally lined the streets and at every corner detachments of troops presented arms'.

As guests of honour, the sailors were treated to lavish meals. 'Curried rice, several chickens, fish, sausages, spinach, roast meats and many kinds of sweetmeats were eaten from one plate,' wrote Andrews. 'Green tea and cigars completed the repast.' There was a visit to the Khyber Pass, including photographs with tribal leaders – 'bearded, fine looking fellows' – who presented the naval officers with goats. The party stopped at the border with Afghanistan, taking a moment to observe the road to Kabul. As they returned, they visited a British encampment in the mountains. 'The British soldiers there,' wrote Andrews, 'begged us to let the people back home know they were "doing their bit" too in the war, and pointed out that they were often in danger from snipers in this wild, untamed region, where marauding tribesmen sought plunder.'

Ships regularly called at Bombay. 'This certainly is a colourful city,' wrote Signalman Ivor Turner of HMS *Durban* in January 1943. 'There are so many different races and castes.' The arrival of American servicemen was already beginning to transform the previously unparalleled position of the British military. '2000 Yanks came in yesterday,' wrote Turner. 'How I hate those guys. If they could only fight instead of yap.' On 26 January, many in the city marked 'Independence Day': the anniversary of the adoption in 1930 of Gandhi's demand for self-rule – the Declaration of Independence – by the Indian National Congress. 'Although there were a few disturbances nothing serious happened,' wrote Turner. 'Arrests are made almost daily of saboteurs. It reminds me of the IRA in Birmingham when they were active with home made bombs.'

By the spring of 1944, the East Indies Fleet was ready to launch its first air strikes against Japanese targets in Sumatra. Oil refineries at Sabang were targeted in eight operations beginning in March and continuing until October. Yet these were hardly indicative of a mighty naval power. Discord developed at the highest political level about the precise nature of the Royal Navy's participation in the Japanese campaign. Churchill preferred to focus on south-east Asia, aiming to recover lost territory and consolidate British imperial influence. His chiefs of staff pushed for a greater role alongside the Americans in the Pacific against the Japanese home islands. Without this, they felt, any ambition of British imperial recovery would be undermined. In August 1944 James Somerville was sent to America and replaced by Admiral Bruce Fraser, who would officially become commander-in-chief of the new British Pacific Fleet in November. By this time, however, victory in the Battle of Leyte Gulf had merely confirmed the fact of American ascendancy.

As Second Sea Lord Algernon Willis had anticipated, British sailors began to question their mission. In October 1944 Alex Hughes – part of a Combined Operations reconnaissance team based in Ceylon – had a conversation with an army colonel over a cup of tea. 'We discussed Nationalisation pros and cons at length,' Hughes wrote in his diary. 'He in common with many feels that there is a spiritual lack in the world.' Hughes disagreed. At thirty years of age, he was involved in the Common Wealth Party, a socialist coalition of left-wing thinkers and liberals founded two years previously. His analysis was rather more pragmatic: 'Spiritual values can mean little to a man economically oppressed by the self styled adherents of these values – when the leaders have no regard for the people but continue to talk of spiritual matters the bottom dog rightly becomes cynical.' Wren Carol Wilson was also interested in the post-war settlement, but in rather more practical terms. 'Education and schools should be improved after the war,' she wrote. 'The principal subjects being mathematics, history, political debates – if children were trained for this they would not be uninterested or too frightened to demand their rights from their MPs when they became Citizens.'

Aboard ships operating in the Indian Ocean, as elsewhere, citizenship could be a useful practical means of sustaining morale. In the autumn of 1944 there were several minor disciplinary incidents aboard the destroyer HMS *Wakeful*, which for several weeks had seen little action. 'Capper, I think, wants a full investigation to find out what is wrong in general,' noted navigation officer Richard Walker in his diary. 'He thinks there is not enough Spirit of Fraternity aboard . . . To remedy this we are to have an orgy of football and water polo, games during the forenoon, inter-part competition spirit.' After this failed to stop rumblings of discontent, another tactic was adopted while *Wakeful* was travelling from Trincomalee to Bombay.

'To pass away the time,' noted Walker, 'or perhaps to ward off complete mental stagnation, each officer is to make a speech on any subject, during the last dogwatches. No. 1 led off with "Why we need to fight Japan", with ample quotations from a pamphlet of that name and boiling down to a general retreat to the status quo.' After another presentation on tropical storms, 'Doc came next with a spirited dissertation on "Town and Country" and the necessity for proper planning and rehabilitation (vile word) after the war, not only in Europe but also at home. This was a very good speech and several of the ship's company have said to me how important they think it is and how unlikely it is that anything even basic will be done.'

Not every officer was convinced of the efficacy of lectures and discussion groups. Before taking command of the destroyer HMS *Valorous* in late 1944, Alec Dennis attended several training courses. 'There was a Current Affairs course,' he recalled, 'which was a waste of time and can only have been insisted upon by the politicians. Its whole tenor was socialist, run by the Army Bureau of Current Affairs who might have been better employed in the front line. We were encouraged to start "discussion groups" in our ships, and reports were to be made. I doubt if many active ships did anything about it. I certainly didn't.'

By the end of 1944 sailors were contributing to the campaign in Burma, where Lieutenant General Sir William Slim's forces were fighting a gruelling campaign against the Japanese in the jungle. British ships were increasingly able to supply and land troops in occupied territory. A coastal campaign similar to that being fought off the Dalmatian coast of Yugoslavia developed, in which small ships and boats fought short, intense battles against the Japanese.

Lieutenant Commander Alex Hughes was part of COPP 3, based in Ceylon. This was one of the navy's Combined Operations Pilotage Parties, reconnaissance canoeists whose role was to infiltrate and scout enemy beaches in preparation for invasion forces. The groups were formed after a trial mission at Rhodes in April 1941, in which two men paddled a canoe from a submarine and swam ashore, making surveys of the beach and tides, using a condom to take samples of the sand in order to ensure it was sufficiently compacted to bear the weight of vehicles and tanks. Beach reconnaissance had since played an important role in Sicily, Italy and Normandy, and in the autumn of 1944 Hughes and his team were preparing for missions along the coast of Burma.

Each canoe was manned by an officer and a paddler. Some craft were also fitted with a sail and outriggers. Most of the personnel were from the Royal Navy, but there were also army experts, mostly Royal Engineers. Aside from their personal equipment, infiltrators carried a 'blood chit'. This was a message written in local dialects and English requesting the help of civilians: 'Dear friend, I am an Allied fighter, I did not come here to do any harm to you who are my friends, I only want to do harm to the Japanese and chase them away from your country as quickly as possible. If you will lead me to the nearest Allied Military Post, my Government will give you a good reward.' Yet despite the very real danger of death or capture, Hughes was pleased by the positive attitude of his men. 'They are all so keen,' he wrote in his diary soon after the formation of the team. 'They worry more about no beer or – worse – no mail than about any Jap. They haven't met him yet of course but it is the right spirit.'

Christmas 1944 was spent preparing for a mission to be undertaken at the turn of the year. Before embarking on the operation, there was an opportunity for the COPP team to enjoy a belated festive meal. They had been keeping a goose for the occasion. Hughes had been concerned that some of the men had been getting too attached to it: they had named it Jasper. He need not have worried. 'Christmas Day went very well,' he wrote in his diary. 'We had Jasper for dinner plus lots of wine. After dinner there was a punch mixed in a huge cooking dish – 5 bottles of rum, 1½ gin, 1 brandy, 2 port, 1 cherry brandy, two beer and 6 oranges. Strong but good – amongst 8 men . . . The sunlight was a bit strong next morning.'

On New Year's Eve, two canoes – each carrying two men – were towed by motor launches to an area near Akyab, the capital of the Arakan region of Burma. Once darkness had fallen, the canoes were launched into the Mayu river to observe the area. 'We landed on a rock about a mile from the Jap defence positions to investigate possibilities of laying up there,' wrote Hughes in his journal. 'We carried out the recce then hauled the canoes on to the rock and camouflaged them then settled down . . . And so 1944 was ushered out and 1945 crept quietly in – no celebration – no Auld Lang Syne – no clock chimes – just darkness and quiet.'

Two weeks later, the COPP team was assisting a flotilla of motor launches in an attack near Myebon. Early in the morning, they set off as RAF aircraft, a cruiser and several sloops and destroyers bombarded the target beach. 'The Japs gave us a hot reception with medium MG fire and mortars,' wrote Hughes, 'that awful weapon which arrives alongside with a plop, spitting dirt all over the place.' Once ashore, the fighting was face-to-face. Hughes described how one British commando 'flinging down his rifle ran after the last Jap and caught him round the throat – in about two seconds the Commando was flat on his back and the Jap choking the life out of him until he was rescued by the other Commandos'. The conclusion was that the Japanese were 'nasty customers at close quarters with ju-jitsu'.

On 8 March 1945, Hughes led a COPP mission to the coast near

Phuket, in what was called Operation Baboon. Hughes was joined by Lieutenant Ian 'Canada' Alcock, a Canadian volunteer officer, and Captain W. E. F. 'Johnny' Johns, of the Royal Engineers, along with their paddlers. They had surveyed the beach they would be infiltrating through the periscope of a submarine, and at nightfall the canoes were towed to within three miles of the coast before being released.

On the way to the beach, Hughes and Alcock lost sight of Johns's canoe in the darkness, but continued with the mission, paddling gently towards the shore, illuminated only by twinkling lights from nearby buildings. They dragged their canoes slightly up the sand and wriggled towards their targets:

> There were a few huts with – I think – coast watchers in them, [they] were rather frightening as the occupants kept coming out and wandering around flashing white torches. Lying on a sandy beach one feels terribly naked. When one sentry passed I tried to dig myself in but the sand was coarse and hard – I gave up and lay praying. He passed some yards away with torch flashing but took no interest in the sand outside him.

The recce complete, Hughes sneaked back to his canoe and made for the rendezvous point with the submarine *Torbay*. 'We had to paddle 5 miles back and I felt a bit played out when I got on board,' he wrote. 'We had been paddling steadily for 6½ hours except for ½ hour I spent crawling on a beach – hardly relaxation.' He was met by Alcock, but Johns had not returned. The submarine dived, and Hughes slept.

They returned the following night to search for their missing comrade. As the submarine approached the shore, Hughes was worried: 'Not a light – complete blackout – that was suspicious – then the Asdic reported transmissions to the south of us. That decided the captain that something was wrong.' The submarine retreated. Over the following days, *Torbay* returned to the designated rendezvous point but no canoe was found. 'I am worried about Johnny,' Hughes admitted. 'His "dark" sense is so bad particularly at sea or on a beach . . . he tends to panic when left alone.' So, on 12 March, Hughes returned to the beach with Alcock to complete their scouting mission and to search for any sign of their missing canoe:

> I have seldom felt more scared than I did leaving the submarine that night. However we paddled in and with Canada 50 yards off I crept in – I watching through binoculars, with my Tommy at the ready, Turner paddling gently, gently. At 30 yards I saw a sentry – stop – then on again, quiet, slowed to 10 yards then we went slowly along the full length of the beach – the sentry was walking in the same direction with [his] back to us. He turned and we stopped. He was I suppose about 30 yards from us but as we were lying as low as we could and no movement he passed us. My fingers were on the trigger and I shook like a leaf and – once again – swore 'Never! Never again.'

When the coast was clear, they moved in to search: 'I went ashore across the beach twice – in fear and trembling as patrols could be seen on the beach and it was obvious that they were "on guard".' He acquired his samples, but there was no sign of the lost canoe. Depressed and fatigued, Hughes tried to relax in the submarine, writing up his experiences in his diary. As he was putting his thoughts in order, there was a new threat:

> We have just had to dive in barely enough water – an enemy ship just appeared. Don't know what kind yet. This on top of everything else is definitely enough. We have just switched off all ventilation and engines in case they give away our position. My stomach is somewhere down in my boots – my hair slightly on end and I can feel all my muscles tense. Canada sitting beside me is white as a sheet. We are so near the coast we can take no real avoiding action – we can't go deep in fact we must wait and hope the enemy is either a merchant ship or, if a man o' war, can't find us. I can hear the whir of her propellers – quite close now. This may be not unusual in a submariner's life but with my limited knowledge and experience it is the most frightening thing. Not a sound – orders in whispers – everything, – everyone tense and expectant – what will she do?

Eventually, the ship passed overhead, and the submarine was able to slink away. Hughes was forced to come to terms with the fact that his friend 'Johnny' Johns was lost, along with two other men. He wrote down all the possible explanations, but the mystery remained, along with a sense of disbelief:

It is difficult to think of chaps as close as they were just 'gone'. Although it has always been an ever present possibility I have never considered it a personal one – 'it can't happen to my party'. Even now I don't fully believe it has happened . . . If one sees a man shot and lying there one becomes aware immediately of the tragedy but when someone just doesn't come back the realisation is slow and painful . . . in this war – there is so little to hope for – I pray that Johnny has been killed – it will save him so much – COPPs are not regarded with favour by our 'honourable' foe.

As the Burmese campaign continued, British submarines and surface ships attempted to engage Japanese forces in the waters around Malaya and Indonesia. Able Seaman John 'Lofty' Mills was an ammunition loader on 'A' gun of the destroyer HMS *Volage*. On 19 March 1945, searching for enemy shipping around the Andaman Islands, *Volage* came under fire in Stewart Sound while going to the aid of two other destroyers, *Saumarez* and *Rapid*. The latter had been hit and, as Mills put it, was 'making a terrific noise as steam was belching out of her torn pipes'. A dozen aboard had been killed and *Saumarez* was towing her out to sea stern first. The captain of *Volage* decided to go beyond both and lay a smokescreen close to the shore. Mills was called into action:

I remember 'A' Gun opening fire, with Gunlayer Eric Gates shouting out that the shore battery's guns were elevating to reload. I was waiting to load the gun tray with another cartridge. Geo Evans was standing beside me, witnessing a shell bursting the water ahead to starboard – a pretty sight, green and spraying out on striking the water – then there was a crash as another shell seconds later burst close to 'A' Gun, hitting the ship's side at about three feet down from the upper deck. Geo Evans went down mortally wounded, then another shell crashed into the ship, landing in the upper aft of the bridge.

Only the prompt action of a nimble petty officer prevented *Volage* from beaching, when he connected the emergency steering system in the nick of time. Turning into the smokescreen, the destroyer escaped back through Stewart Sound with three dead and eight wounded.

The incident did much to shape the reaction of the destroyer's sailors to their next encounter with the Japanese. A week later, *Volage*, along with other destroyers *Vigilant*, *Virago* and *Saumarez*, was patrolling the Andaman Sea in search of Japanese convoys. The flotilla came across a large enemy troopship, guarded by a handful of smaller escorts. As the British began to fire, a Liberator bomber appeared. Mills watched as the plane approached and dropped its payload, then 'hit the ship's mast and blew himself and the ship up'.

*Volage* lowered her scramble nets to rescue survivors. When it was found that the men in the water were refusing help, the first lieutenant ordered two ratings to pull them out. Mills estimated that there were perhaps eighty Japanese sailors in the water, and around a dozen were hauled aboard. One swimmer was spotted at the stern, hitting the hull with what appeared to be a shell. He was shot at by the chief engineer before the captain ordered the starboard propeller to be fired up, which 'sucked the culprit under the stern not to be seen again'. With anxiety increasing about the prospect of another would-be saboteur, the destroyer made off for Trincomalee, leaving the remaining survivors in the water. Those who were rescued remained defiant in the extreme. Mills reported that before the ship reached harbour, one prisoner had jumped overboard and another had managed to hang himself in the bathroom with a bandage.

While the Bay of Bengal and the waters around Malaya remained battlegrounds, British ships sent to the Pacific islands initially saw rather less action. The destroyer HMS *Wakeful* was one of a group of Allied ships attached to a task force at the Admiralty Islands in March 1945. 'Manus is fantastic,' wrote the ship's navigation officer Richard Walker. 'It may be a small island, but the harbour is enormous, about twice the size of Windermere, and packed with craft of all kind from huge battleships . . . to hundreds of skimmers and dinghies.' A direct comparison between the Royal Naval vessels and their US Navy counterparts was unavoidable. 'American voices are everywhere, heard over loud speakers and tannoy systems,' complained Walker. 'The British presence is almost insignificant and we wonder if they really want us.'

'All feeling very gloomy and depressed,' wrote Commander Robert Parker of the aircraft carrier HMS *Indomitable*, now in the Pacific and ready for action. 'Quite evident Yanks won't let us do anything. Out for exercises next week if you please!' On 16 March, Parker described an incident which illustrated the potential for serious disciplinary breakdown:

> Row over troops' dinner (curry) and sailors refused duty, amounted to mutiny really but was not treated as such. Commander very weak and ineffective. Sailors have something in their grouse I think, Pay[master] takes very little interest in their food. Unpleasant atmosphere all round. Told Captain I thought lot of discontent due to conduct of young aviators in wardroom, drunk every night.

Part of the problem was inactivity. Aside from further air strikes against Palembang in Sumatra in January 1945, there had been little for Royal Navy aircraft carriers to do. The British Pacific Fleet had been designated Task Force 57 and put under American command. Admiral Chester Nimitz was notoriously antagonistic towards the British, and the sheer weakness of the Royal Navy presence compared with his own forces did little to impress him. Although the British Pacific Fleet would eventually expand to become the largest in the Royal Navy's history, in March 1945 Task Force 57 consisted of two battleships, five cruisers, eleven destroyers and four precious aircraft carriers. This corresponded to barely half the strength of the American Task Force 58. Indeed, by one reckoning, excluding convoy escorts and focusing solely on the critical carriers and capital ships, the entire Royal Navy was weaker than Task Force 58.

The British Pacific Fleet was also hampered by technical and logistical weaknesses. Its gunnery systems were not tachymetric, relying on manual sightings which proved far less efficient than the automated American systems. Supplying and refuelling the fleet at long range from Australia with a 'fleet train' was an anachronistic practice which severely reduced its ability to conduct effective operations. Conditions in many ships were uncomfortable, with limited refrigeration facilities and erratic air conditioning.

Nevertheless, the start of Operation Iceberg in March, an American-led offensive against Okinawa, saw Royal Navy carriers contributing to the campaign for the first time, helping to strike targets in the Sakishima Gunto archipelago. Although the British contribution totalled 218 carrier aircraft, a small force compared to over 1,200 American-flown planes, it was a significant effort for the sailors and pilots involved.

Okinawa was defended ruthlessly. While US Marines struggled ashore in terrifying and gruesome combat, Mitsubishi Zero fighters – known as 'Zekes' to the Allies – targeted the giant warships and aircraft carriers out at sea. Just as Japanese soldiers attempted to repel the invaders with banzai charges of suicidal intensity, so their aerial counterparts adopted the most extreme tactics. Since the autumn of 1944, the kamikaze had become a serious threat to Allied warships. At Okinawa, the campaign reached its most desperate, as hundreds of kamikaze aircraft attempted to break through the defences of the Allied fleets. Early on the morning of 1 April 1945, Easter Sunday, British carriers came under attack.

By this time, Fleet Air Arm squadrons relied on American-designed fighters and bombers in their carrier operations – Hellcats, Corsairs, Avengers – but there was one veteran British plane which could still hold its own. The Seafire, the naval version of the Spitfire, remained in service, defending ships against aerial attack. Lithe and manoeuvrable, despite their flaws, Seafires were used for combat air patrols to intercept low-flying enemy raiders.

Sub-Lieutenant Dick Reynolds was in 894 Squadron, based aboard HMS *Indefatigable*. His Seafire was scrambled when Japanese fighters were detected approaching British warships. 'I got on the tail of a Zeke after he had already dived on *King George V*,' recalled Reynolds.

'He pulled up, I got on his tail again and managed to give him a burst. I clipped his port wing, he rolled over on his back and dived straight into a carrier which was enveloped in smoke and flames. I thought, you poor bastards. What I didn't realise was that it was my ship.'

Reynolds went on to shoot down two more Zeros, both of which crashed into the sea. When he eventually returned to *Indefatigable*, he witnessed the damage: 'This blackened flight-deck with a bloody great hole . . . The sight on deck was unbelievable.' Fourteen men had been killed and another sixteen wounded. The upper decks of Royal Navy carriers were famously more robust than their American counterparts, with extra armour which helped to mitigate much of the potential destruction, and well-drilled damage control teams played a vital part in limiting casualties. Yet this did little to remedy the personal losses. 'Our Lord's resurrection,' wrote N. B. Gray of *Indefatigable* in his diary. 'At sea south of Japan. S.B. [suicide bomber] hits us. Casualties. 3 pals died.'

The danger to British carriers would continue. 'Strike at Sakishima again,' wrote Robert Parker of *Indomitable* on 4 May. 'About mid-day several Zekes (suiciders) attacked. One hit *Formidable*, made hole in flight deck . . . One landed on our flight deck, shot up by our gunfire first, and bounced over side where it exploded. Another shot out of control in vertical dive missed ship by few feet and landed off starboard bow, exploding in water. Lucky escapes and good shooting.'

Again, there were casualties: eight men were killed and forty-seven were wounded aboard *Formidable*, fires were started and several parked aircraft destroyed. *Indomitable* and *Formidable* would be hit again only a few days later. But, most significantly, British ships were able to control the damage and resume their operations within hours. American carriers, meanwhile, suffered far greater damage and were out of action for weeks if not months. Nevertheless, kamikaze attacks proved a harrowing experience for many. 'I helped to bury two dead comrades,' wrote N. B. Gray after one strike. 'My nerves bad.'

This was very much a campaign for aircraft carriers and their support vessels. Those British ships not involved often found themselves left in rather more quiet surroundings. In the spring of 1945, sailors from the destroyer HMS *Wakeful* were given leave to explore New

Zealand. Richard Walker fished in Ohau Channel, visited hot springs, picnicked at Okahu, cooked sausages and crumpets on an open fire at Lake Tikitapu, played golf and attended church. He later noted that during this idyllic Antipodean interlude, Europe saw the execution of Mussolini, the German surrender in Italy and the death of Hitler in his Berlin bunker. The most notable incident to befall the men of *Wakeful* was an infamous drinking session in Auckland, after which 'several bodies had to be carried home'.

\* \* \*

While the Pacific war continued unabated, the war in Europe was coming to an end. In the first week of April 1945, Able Seaman Sid France was serving in the destroyer HMS *Evenlode*. The ship had just left Liverpool to escort a convoy bound for Gibraltar. France was called to the captain's cabin. Even many years later, he could perfectly recall the conversation: '"Sit down, France. Would you like a cigarette?" He didn't need to say any more. I knew.' The ship had received a signal that France's son, Alan, had died at the age of three months. He had been suffering from a rare condition known as pyloric stenosis, a stomach problem which meant that he was unable to eat properly. It was untreatable at the time, so he 'had to simply waste away and die'.

France was distraught. *Evenlode* was still in sight of land, and he was so addled that he pleaded with the captain to let him swim back. But the best that could be done was to arrange for emergency leave as soon as the ship returned to Britain. Alan France died on 4 April, but *Evenlode* did not arrive back until over a month later. Almost as soon as his feet touched dry land, France raced for a train to take him home to his wife. It was 8 May, which would become known as VE Day.

Surgeon Lieutenant Graham Airth was a medical officer in the cruiser HMS *Dido*. On 7 May the vessel was part of a large convoy slowly making its way towards Denmark. There was a choice to be made, as Airth explained in his diary: 'At present we are in straggly lines, owing to mines popping up all around us. Decision on whether we go in to Copenhagen . . . [or] convoy the carriers back to Rosyth, and go straight back on leave.' There were German ships in the Danish capital, ready to surrender to Allied forces. 'Am torn between desire to get back,' wrote Airth, 'and even greater desire to be in at the death of the German navy.'

It was not until the following day that a final decision was made. 'So this is VE Day,' wrote Airth. 'Marvellous day with clear blue sky, a few wispy white clouds, and a flat greenish-grey sea. Very warm on upper deck. Morning announcement by Captain that we are going in to Copenhagen. Mines are still all over the place . . . Incredible sight is numbers of German and British aircraft stooging around the sky and not firing at each other.'

As *Dido* approached the Langelinie, Copenhagen's famous quay-side, Airth was somewhat underwhelmed: 'First sight of enemy warship – mastheads of *Prinz Eugen* – first seen at 1130. Masses of German small craft – minesweepers and E-boats, all with standards hauled down – no flags whatever flying . . . Very small crowd; Danish, British, American flags . . . Everybody very well fed, very fit look-ing . . . A few cheers . . . People looked genuinely glad to see us, but not in need of us.' But two days later, the celebrations were in full swing: 'Midnight Copenhagen – Wow!! What an incredible city, suddenly plunged into "occupation" five years ago, and as suddenly freed now. Wild and enthusiastic crowds ashore.'

German naval forces surrendered across Scandinavia and the North Sea coasts. Alec Dennis, in command of the destroyer HMS *Valorous*, was at Kristiansand in southern Norway to witness the surrender of a U-boat flotilla. 'I walked around some of them and was tremen-dously impressed with their equipment, their cleanliness and the high morale of the officers and men,' he recalled. 'They wanted to join us to fight the Russians whom they regarded as barbarians.'

For some, the war with Germany continued until the very last moment. On the evening of 7 May the men of the anti-submarine trawler *Leicester City* had rigged a radio on deck, anticipating a news broadcast announcing the end of hostilities in Europe. Although they would have preferred not to have been escorting a convoy between the Firth of Forth and Belfast, the mood was good. They had caught fish for tea. 'Altogether there was a feeling of buoyant excitement,' wrote the first lieutenant, Philip Calvert, 'perhaps slightly tinged with thoughts of being drafted to the Far East.'

After finishing his watch, Calvert went to bed. His captain had suggested taking the opportunity to sleep in pyjamas, but he decided to keep his clothes on, as he had done every other night of the war while at sea. Not long after falling asleep, he was woken by an alarm. One of the freighters in the convoy had been torpedoed and, as Calvert reached the upper deck, another was hit. *Leicester City* immediately carried out her attack routine with depth charges. 'We fired as deep a pattern as we dared,' wrote Calvert, 'but even so the resulting five explosions almost lifted us out of the water and blew all the main electric fuses.'

With no sign of the submarine, the next priority was to search for survivors from the merchant ships. A dozen were brought over the scrambling nets. One man 'had a big hole in his back, screamed when we took hold of him, and fortunately passed out. Another was covered in blood, and another stark naked, having been blown clean out of the bath into the sea.' The trawler was too small to carry a medical officer, so Calvert improvised with tea and blankets. At 4 a.m. they disembarked the wounded at Methil and then went back out to sea to search for the U-boat.

'The C.O. had been on the bridge for nine hours continuously and myself six hours and we were both very tired,' wrote Calvert. By breakfast time, he was close to collapse. In the wardroom, the steward had prepared a boiled egg: 'He had to feed me the egg on a spoon like a baby.' *Leicester City* continued to search all day until the signal was received to 'splice the mainbrace'. The traditional naval toast, in which every man would be given a tot of rum, would take place on British ships around the world to celebrate the defeat of Germany.

For most sailors, the prevailing sensation was relief. Yet VE Day was not an enjoyable experience for all. Angus Nicholl, now captain of the battleship *Duke of York*, was part of a court martial hearing the case of a marine accused of murdering a brothel mistress in Catania, Sicily. The man was found guilty and sentenced to death by firing squad, a sentence later reduced to life in prison. In Scapa Flow, leading seaman Walter Edgley worked in the mail room of the aircraft carrier HMS *Vindex*. 'Very miserable spliced mainbrace,' he wrote in his diary. 'Trip at night for mail, plenty of work. Listened to Prime

Minster's speech at 15:00, and the King's speech at 21:00. Pictures at night. Red Skelton and Eleanor Powell in "By Hook or By Crook".'

Some ships were already on their way to join the Pacific campaign. On VE Day the submarine HMS *Stubborn* was passing through the Suez Canal. Junior officer Patrick Mullins described 'British troops lining the bank and cheering themselves hoarse. They shouted "You're going the wrong way," jerking their thumbs in the approximate direction of home.'

In the evening of 8 May 1945 the ships of the Eastern Fleet received the signal to 'splice the mainbrace'. This was followed by instructions for the festivities to be held the following day, for 'Thanksgiving and rejoicing to celebrate the Unconditional surrender of Germany'. Commanding officers were to ensure that their ships were dressed with flags, and that men were brought together on deck as if for Sunday service. Captains would say a few words, followed by prayers, 'including a prayer for re-dedication of Service towards Victory in the Far East'.

The Admiralty sent a congratulatory message to every ship in the navy:

> For the second time since the Battle of Trafalgar, sea power has preserved and sustained our nation and commonwealth and led to the decisive defeat of Germany and her European associates. The Board of Admiralty congratulate all officers and men upon their share in this great victory, confident that the fortitude, skill and tenacity which has made it possible will be displayed with the same distinction and effect in the task yet to be completed in the Far East.

In the Eastern Fleet, this was followed by a bombastic message from the commander-in-chief:

> Germany forced this war on us when we foolishly were unarmed. She thought she had beaten us and called on her accomplices to hasten our destruction. However, since 1942 the world has seen the strength of the British Empire and that of our allies, each of our insignificant enemies thrashed, and now Germany on her knees with the Japanese Nation awaiting destruction.

For these tremendous events we must be profoundly thankful, and as an Empire we can also be proud of the major part we have played in a world war. To achieve victory has meant a vast undertaking with much anxiety and suffering. Similar efforts lie ahead if we are to replace evil with good and no individual will for very many years be able to lead a life of his own choosing.

It was deemed that sailors were then to be given 'a specially good dinner'. But both during and after these celebrations, it was emphasized, 'War routine against Japan must proceed.'

'Everyone is full of excitement getting ready for their marvellous celebrations tonight,' wrote Wren Carol Wilson to her parents, 'and where am I? I am in Sick Bay with a cold!!!' She was working at the wireless telegraphy station HMS *Anderson* in Colombo, and had made the mistake of mentioning to the medical officer that she had a sore throat. After a recent diphtheria outbreak, the doctor took no chances. 'I shall be discharged the day after tomorrow just when the excitement has finished,' she wrote. 'Ugh!!!' To compensate for missing the festivities, each woman in the ward was given a bottle of beer.

'Thank God!' wrote Able Seaman Donald Butcher, of the frigate HMS *Halladale*. 'The war in Europe is over, now I know that my loved ones are safe . . . By golly it is hard to believe, but I guess it will not make much difference to us!' *Halladale* was operating around the island of Ramree, off the coast of Burma. Butcher was eager to leave. 'No mail for me or anyone today,' he wrote on 15 May in his diary. 'Won't we be glad to get somewhere back into civilization again as we are all getting on each other's nerves.' Such a mood was not helped by the climate in the Bay of Bengal: hot and humid, with frequent violent storms. 'I had to get up very early as a big thunderstorm broke and nearly washed me out,' wrote Butcher two days later. 'Oh! how fed up I am, no proper food not much sleep, and worst of all no mail, by golly I do not know how much longer I will be able to stick this existence. Today we are receiving a double allowance of messing in place of the V.E. celebrations at home, HA! HA!'

Aboard HMS *Paladin*, the end of the war in Europe brought about considerable upheaval. In early June, Richard Campbell-Begg commented:

All is going well here and every-one is hoping that we will now get 'stuck in' and end this war soon. Most of the South Africans on board have opted to exercise their prerogative to return home now the war with the Germans has ended. By doing this we will be losing a number of very highly trained people and will have to start off training new recruits. It does seem rather tough to me that the poor long suffering Britisher will be expected to carry the brunt of the fighting now.

In the Pacific, air strikes continued unabated against Okinawa. 'Official end of war with Germany announced,' wrote Robert Parker of *Indomitable* in his diary. 'Sounds good to hear of public holidays etc. at home! Heard a piece of Churchill's speech.' There was, however, no holiday at sea:

Strikes on islands as usual . . . strong attack by suiciders. *Victorious* hit twice . . . neither causing serious damage. *Formidable* hit again on flight deck, large fire in aircraft park, but got under control. Another shot down just short of *Howe*. Altogether not so pleasant, but effects on ships less than *Formid*'s previous hit. Fighters intercepted the little swine, but went off after one, leaving four to get through. Withdrew to oiling area in late evening. Meantime we hear over American radio of rejoicing in Europe, end of war, etc., also masses of congratulatory speeches by everyone. Rather peeving – wish I was home instead of fighting Japs!

Alex Hughes in Ceylon was looking further forward:

We have waited so long and it has been a weary hard struggle. There is only heartfelt relief that at least part of it is over – that we can start rebuilding somewhere. When one considers even the daily problems that confront us now – the feeding of two million prisoners and all the liberated people and the German civilians. The top priority now, of course, is shipping, ought to be food for Europe, hundreds of ships into Hamburg, Copenhagen, Antwerp, Bremen, every possible port. Feed those people before there is trouble and disease and suffering. God knows they have suffered enough even in these last five months . . . Now we can make a peace which will stand for ever – now in these next weeks and months.

In prisoner-of-war camps around Germany, servicemen waited for their release. Lieutenant Commander Charles Coles had been captured after his motor launch was sunk off Algeria in February 1943. He was taken to the prison camp Marlag O, between Bremen and Hamburg in northern Germany. By the autumn of 1944 it housed around 300 British naval officers, along with seventy ratings who had volunteered to act as their orderlies, and several other officers from the RAF and the army, and from France, Greece, Holland, Norway, South Africa and New Zealand.

Coles kept a scrapbook in which he collected the signatures of each naval officer along with their date and place of capture. There were men from every form of naval service: destroyers, submarines, coastal forces, the Special Boat Service, the Fleet Air Arm. Denis Dugdale had been sunk with the *Rawalpindi* in November 1939. Sam Beattie had commanded HMS *Campbeltown* in the raid on St Nazaire in 1942. Twenty-nine men had been captured around Crete, fourteen at Dieppe, twenty-three at Tobruk. Forty-five were from submarines and X-craft. Coles recalled the sheer range of locations: 'on an island in the Adriatic', 'ashore at Spitzbergen', 'beach reconnaissance in Italy', 'in a Beaufighter over the Med'.

As former prisoners prepared for repatriation, there were other exiles to be transported home. Surgeon Lieutenant Dunlop of HMS *Norfolk* described the return of King Haakon to Norway in early June 1945:

Almost every boat in Oslo and the whole neighbourhood must have been out that day – hundreds of them, literally – decked with flags from stem to stern, many of them decorated too with flowers and shrubs . . . bands playing in the pleasure steamers as well as on our quarterdeck . . . foghorns and sirens blowing off in every direction . . . It was truly an amazing sight. The King and the Royal Party were on our quarterdeck acknowledging the cheers (the Crown Prince's little son of eight so exhausted after five or six hours of the excitement that all he could do was to lean against the guard rails and let his hanky flutter).

Across northern Germany, British ships helped to secure ports and naval bases. Sailors worked to restore damaged facilities, bring in supplies, commandeer or decommission equipment, and maintain order. At the same time, many were able to enjoy themselves. In July 1945, John Wilson was at Lübeck with HMS *Oribi*. As he told his parents in a letter home:

Our stay in Germany has been very interesting and great fun. Everyone lives like millionaires. *Oribi* has acquired a large steam launch, a speed boat, three cars, a six cylinder Mercedes, an auto Union and a Fiat, and numerous other things. Tennis, riding, swimming and yachting are laid on and from the farms one can buy delicious fresh peas, new potatoes, strawberries etc. We even have five minute little girls who come down to the ship and sing 'Lili Marlene' to us and are entirely sweet.

There was one problem – Wilson happened to be writing from an army hospital bed:

One slight fly in the ointment is that I have been shot in the leg by an enthusiastic sentry while I was driving some Army types home at 2 a.m. It was nobody's fault and luckily has done little harm, merely taking some flesh and a bit of bone off my knee.

Before the accident, Wilson and some friends had driven to Hamburg. One of the grand Hanseatic ports, it had been targeted by Allied bombing raids in July and August 1943 which were later estimated to have killed 46,000 people, in the firestorms which tore through the city. Wilson wrote: 'Except for a small section by the river and the suburbs, the entire city of two and a half millions is wrecked, an amazing scene of devastation. For miles not a house is standing.'

## 22. Even Japan Is Beautiful

On VE Day, HMS *Phoebe* was berthed at Rangoon. The captain gathered his men on deck. 'Very many of you will shortly be going back to Civvy Street,' he told them, 'and we who stay on in the Navy envy you that home life of which we see so little. But the Navy must go on if England is to live . . . This time we have got to make sure that the sacrifices of the men and women of the Empire are not thrown away . . . <u>All of us</u> must make certain that only men who are pledged to ensure our security should get into Parliament . . . Remember that if we don't look after our own island and Empire we shall not gain peace and without peace there'll be no Beveridge plan, no social security, no pensions – old age and others – no trade and therefore no jobs . . . each one of us has a responsibility and a duty to use that vote and use it properly. If we fail in this we shall have fought the war in vain.'

Not everyone shared an interest in the intricacies of political, economic and social reconstruction. One of *Phoebe*'s sailors preserved a clipping from a letter to the *Sunday Express* newspaper, and sent it to the editors of the ship's self-produced magazine to be printed with the title 'Our War Aims': 'Surely our best War Memorial would be a Statue of Liberty on Dover Cliffs showing Mr Churchill facing Europe with folded arms, cigar and all, the cigar to be lit at night. And we should make the Germans build it with marble supplied by the Wops.'

Elsewhere, *Phoebe*'s magazine – called 'Full Moon' – reflected a keen awareness of the political ramifications of the end of the war. Cartoons by the resident artist were light-hearted in style but in content they were dark, even morbid. In a hand-drawn sketch entitled 'Two Sides of a Question', a group of servicemen watch a businessman brandishing the club of 'Fascism' striding into a voting hall. In another, a man whispering 'liberal' suffers a grotesque woman clutching a handful of 'gratuity' banknotes screaming 'Labour' in his face.

Two Sides of a Question

Other cartoons illustrated a pronounced sense of isolation and frustration. Above the caption 'V. Day?', the grim reaper towers above soldiers wearing torn and tatty jungle uniform, while a tiny ship sails upriver towards a camp from which figures escape. Over the horizon, revellers celebrate 'European Peace', conspicuously swigging from bottles.

In the waters between the Indian Ocean and the Pacific, around the Malayan peninsula and the Indonesian archipelago, British ships continued to fight against Japanese naval forces. Only a week after VE Day, British destroyers discovered the cruiser *Haguro* along with her supporting destroyer *Kamikaze* in the Malacca Strait, attempting to carry supplies to the beleaguered Japanese garrison on the Andaman Islands and to evacuate soldiers to Singapore. In command of the 26th Destroyer Flotilla was Captain Manley Power, back at sea after planning the invasions of North Africa and Sicily, with his flag in HMS *Saumarez* alongside *Vigilant*, *Venus*, *Verulam*, *Virago* and *Volage*.

Just after 1 a.m. on the morning of 16 May, the flotilla made radar contact and prepared to attack. Heavy rain showers pounded the sea and the sky was illuminated by lightning. It was, wrote Power to his wife shortly afterwards, 'the maddest ten minutes of my life'. As the destroyers closed, they fired their guns, hitting *Haguro* almost instantly. *Saumarez* passed behind the cruiser and fired on the destroyer *Kamikaze* while Power waited to give the order to fire torpedoes:

> The sea was spouting with shell splashes all round us. We were drenched to the skin with near misses and water streaming everywhere as we closed the range. Our guns still firing rapid broadsides into the destroyer and hell's delight going on with enemy salvoes screaming over the ship. Before I got to my chosen range we got hit in the boiler room. There was a roar of escaping steam and clouds of smoke and steam. A lot of instruments went out of action and the way started to come off the ship. I smacked the helm over to get the fish away before we stopped or sank (which appeared on the cards). Off they went, while the enemy continued to throw everything he'd got. The Engine room, by magnificent work got the engines going almost without a pause . . . we turned away under smoke, enemy salvoes still cracking down at rapid intervals . . . Then, astern, through the fumes of our smoke screen, three enormous pillars of flame and spray went up (like a Prince of Wales' feathers) as the torpedoes struck home. The enemy never fired again.

Torpedoes from the British destroyers stopped the *Haguro*, and they proceeded to pound their sitting target with gunfire before more torpedoes finally sank the beleaguered Japanese cruiser. Meanwhile, the *Kamikaze* was damaged but escaped, and returned to the scene the following day to rescue around 300 survivors. Some 900 Japanese sailors had died. Aboard *Saumarez*, returning to Ceylon victorious, two men had been killed and three injured in the boiler room.

Aboard HMS *Phoebe*, news of the sinking of the *Haguro* was met with disappointment by some who felt that they had missed out on a valuable opportunity for glory. On 22 May 1945 the captain broadcast a message to the ship's company informing them of the situation in the Andamans, and warning them of complacency: 'I am keeping as relaxed as possible . . . [but] you never quite know what is going to pop up around the next island . . . if you want to get back to Civvy Street, don't let yourselves be lulled into a false sense of security.'

Danger remained around the coastline of Malaya and in the East Indies. Minesweepers were damaged, causing several deaths, while operating off the coast of Japanese-occupied Siam. On 25 July, near Phuket, the East Indies Fleet suffered its only kamikaze attack of the war. One of the ships targeted was minesweeper HMS *Vestal*. Richard Campbell-Begg watched from nearby HMS *Paladin*. 'There was a tremendous explosion and when the smoke and flames had died away there was the *Vestal*, still afloat with the remnants of this plane perched on its upper-works,' he wrote in his diary. Fifteen men were killed and the ship had to be sunk. A second Japanese plane was hit by anti-aircraft fire before it could strike. To Campbell-Begg, it 'appeared to disintegrate in a mass of smoke and flame'.

The conflict between America and Japan was supremely violent, driven by racial antagonism, fear and propaganda. US Marines and their foes fought, as one historian put it, a 'war without mercy'. While Australian sailors occasionally exhibited racial hatred, British ratings – most of whom were far less familiar with the Japanese – rarely went beyond commonplace insults such as 'little yellow bastards' or 'yellow devils'. In the earliest discussions on the Far East deployment, evidence had been presented to the Admiralty of the 'spirit of hatred' displayed by Australian, American, Indian and British soldiers fighting the Japanese. Reports suggested that this made them 'more formidable as a fighting force than any other not so inspired'.

But few senior officers were convinced that such material would necessarily be good for morale. 'It is notoriously difficult to arouse the average Englishman to hatred by long-range propaganda,' wrote one senior official, 'and an attempt to do so by means of atrocity stories may possibly have the opposite effect of merely making the men concerned more reluctant to take part in the campaign than they otherwise would be.' Furthermore, it was argued that such propaganda would be 'less likely to be effective when addressed to men who will not normally come to close personal grips with the Japanese, such as sailors and airmen'.

Thereafter, official education and propaganda efforts for the Royal Navy in the Far East tended to focus on a positive message of duty, commitment and honour, rather than revenge. Throughout 1944 and 1945, large orders were placed for books, paid for by the Ships' Libraries Grant, to explain the campaign. Alongside familiar works such as *How the Jap Army Fights* and *The Japanese Enemy* were political, geographical, anthropological and historical texts, such as: *The Pageant of Japanese History*, *The Far East in World Politics* and *Japan and the Modern World*.

But if British sailors were not motivated by racial hostility of the same intensity as soldiers, they were far from sympathetic when coming into direct contact with their enemies. In July 1945, the submarine HMS *Stubborn* was patrolling the Java Sea when she came across a Japanese patrol vessel in the Lombok Strait. Officer of the watch was Sub-Lieutenant Patrick Mullins. He described the moments after torpedoes had been fired:

> We had a full three minutes to wait and they seemed interminable in that hot, taut atmosphere as we tried to look anywhere but at each other. When it seemed that all hope of success had gone, there was a heavy thud, clearly heard throughout the boat, followed almost at once by another . . . 'Got her, blown her bloody stern off' [the captain] shouted exultantly. There was a subdued cheer . . . The skipper remained glued to the periscope, giving a running commentary on the dissolution of the destroyer, until he most surprisingly stepped back and said, 'Anyone want to see?'

Men jostled to look through the periscope: 'A positive queue of people lining up to see the sight, for all the world like Clacton Pier. For about twenty seconds there was near chaos.' *Stubborn* surfaced, still some distance from where the destroyer had been.

> I could see wreckage in the water, which was discoloured and was dotted with the heads of survivors. It took us several minutes to reach the scene and nose in quietly among them, the stench of oil being almost overpowering. By any moral standards it must have been – it was – a distressing sight, but honesty compels me to say that that was the last thought in our minds. We were jubilant, laughing and shouting.

Mullins and his fellow officers had a plan:

> We wanted one Japanese prisoner, no more, for intelligence purposes and to show off to our flotilla . . . The survivors had no intention of being rescued and swam away . . . One man deliberately went under when our people tried to reach out to him and another seized a floating bucket and inverted it over his head.

Then a lookout thought he saw a plane, and the submarine dived in 'near panic . . . leaving the survivors to their fate'.

While the Eastern Fleet continued to eliminate Japanese forces around the East Indies, the sailors and pilots of the British Pacific Fleet continued to operate alongside their American counterparts. Meeting stern and suicidal resistance, US Marines had taken Iwo Jima and landed on Okinawa. Preparations were underway for the final assault against the Japanese home islands. Their material contribution may have been relatively small, but the sailors and airmen of the British carriers and their support ships worked hard. Vigilance had to be sustained, gun crews ready to fend off attack, and pilots ready to scramble. Even on days when aircraft were not being flown, every man had a full roster of duties to attend to. Aboard HMS *Indefatigable*, N. B. Gray's diary entry on 2 June summed up his experience: 'Worked like a bastard.' Even after the ship had returned to Sydney, his mood remained sombre. 'Fed up to my eyebrows,' he wrote. 'Got thoroughly drunk.'

In June 1945, Audrey Goulden wrote to a friend to tell her the latest news from the Pacific. Their husbands were both serving in aircraft carriers; Goulden's husband Lindsay was aboard HMS *Victorious*. In their correspondence, the women discussed the latest newsreel footage and compared notes on their spouses' susceptibility to prickly heat. They joked about their plans for home life after demobilization. Lindsay Goulden had told his wife that he planned to eat a steak-and-onion dinner in a year's time. 'Where they'll get the steak from they never say!' wrote Audrey. 'Just like a man!' He had also told his wife about kamikaze attacks. 'He mentions that they're thrilling to watch,' wrote Audrey, 'or so he believes (he himself always gets out of the way when they're around!) but not so dangerous as one is given to think. From what he can see, the pilots either bale out or shoot themselves before they crash. Maybe he's just putting the best side of the thing to us.'

There were also grumbles. Lindsay had told his wife that, aboard *Victorious*, a divide was forming between the regular, career sailors and their volunteer counterparts – particularly those due to return home in the first 'A' category of demobilization. 'There is a strong feeling of R.N. regulars versus the R.N.V.R. men, especially the "A" boys,' she wrote. 'It sets Lindsay very mad, because he says if it wasn't for the R.N.V.R. men, the Navy would be of little help in the war – especially the Air Arm which is almost entirely made up of R.N.V.R. men. Apparently the *Illustrious* had nothing of the feeling at all.'

Any such divide between civilian and career sailors was partly influenced by the pace of political change at home. A general election was due to be held on 5 July 1945, which would have practical consequences for both groups. Merely holding the election was controversial. Richard Campbell-Begg believed that the war against Japan would last another year. 'Pity about the U.K. elections having to be held now,' he wrote in his diary. 'It would be better, surely, to have the present Government carry on till the war is finished. I can't see that there is anyone else amongst them with half the personality of Churchill or his ability either.' The Prime Minister would have agreed on both counts.

Absentee ballots were distributed amongst the 'floating voters' aboard British warships. Not everyone was interested. Able Seaman John Mills described the atmosphere aboard the destroyer HMS *Volage* in Trincomalee: 'Elections in the UK for Parliament with war over in Europe, talked about on the mess deck (myself not 21, not eligible). One of our killicks (Leading Seaman) a sea lawyer by choice and an ardent Labour supporter, had lots to shout about, few took notice.'

Others were genuinely inspired by political rhetoric. In early June, Alex Hughes and his COPP canoeists were preparing for yet another infiltration of a Malayan beach. While they prepared their diving suits and sharpened their knives, the men listened to *Words for Battle*, compiled by film-maker Humphrey Jennings. Beginning with Shakespeare and continuing with Milton, Blake, Browning, Kipling and Churchill, the collection finished with Abraham Lincoln's Gettysburg Address. 'That great, clear, exposition of the fundamental principles of democracy – and, naturally, how apt today,' wrote Hughes in his diary. 'We must fight, not only the powerful vested interests whose goal is power and money, not only the people who believe that there are two types in the country, the leader's class and the people's class, but we must also fight that great section of the population who are politically apathetic, who believe that "we are getting better everyday" and "that things aren't too bad and we have a lot to be thankful for".'

Over the summer of 1945, the prisoners of war in a camp near Mukden, Manchuria, had been kept up to date with the latest political developments by Chinese newspapers smuggled in the false heels of a pair of workman's boots. Maurice Bennett, formerly a junior officer in HMS *Exeter*, described the reaction to the results of the election in his secret diary:

We had all taken it for granted that Mr Churchill would be re-elected and the success of the Labour Government was a real shock for us. It was most amusing to see the British senior officers walking around the camp with long faces expressing their doubts and disapprovals in muttered semitones. We, the younger officers, less worried by capital and invested incomes, mostly thought it good to have the change and that a Labour government would make more of the opportunities for reconstruction without the Tory tendency to slip back to the old ways as we did after 1918.

HMS *Wakeful* received breaking news of the election result at an oiling station in the Pacific. 'Overwhelming Labour victory, Clement Attlee in Charge,' wrote navigation officer Richard Walker. The following week, the full details of the election result came through. Walker considered that it was 'not altogether a shock as the feeling on this ship, fairly representative, I suppose, has been that Labour would get in'. He characterized the general response as mixed: 'They can hardly make a worse hash of things than the Conservatives, and yet we hope they will not try some hare-brained schemes which will ruin what good work has been done.' The officers on the bridge amused themselves by forming hypothetical cabinets, before work started again in earnest. 'More pressing business is at hand,' wrote Walker. 'We have returned to the Honshu coast and the first strike flew off at 0445 this morning.'

'We met the American 3rd fleet,' wrote N. B. Gray of HMS *Indefatigable* on 16 July 1945. 'A grand sight of Anglo-American sea power.' Preparations continued for strikes against the Japanese home islands at the end of the month, hitting coastal shipping and an airbase at Yokoshima. Then, at 8.15 a.m. on 6 August, an American B29 bomber known as 'Enola Gay' dropped a nuclear weapon called 'Little Boy' on Hiroshima. Exploding just under 2,000 feet above the city, it obliterated every wooden structure within 1.2 miles and destroyed nearly two-thirds of all the city's buildings, damaging many more. An estimated 120,000 civilians died in the blast or succumbed to their injuries within a year.

Aboard HMS *Indefatigable*, preparations continued for more air strikes. 'A new atomic bomb dropped on Japan,' wrote Gray in his diary. 'News good. A little chocker.' On 9 August, while more air strikes on airfields took place, a second atomic bomb called 'Fat Man' was dropped on Nagasaki, killing 74,000 people and injuring a similar number. After refuelling at Manus, *Indefatigable* and other Royal Navy ships continued with small-scale strikes on airfields and installations for several days. Meanwhile, the Japanese were preparing to surrender.

On Wednesday 15 August, HMS *Vindex* was at Sydney. 'Announced at 09.00 (midnight at home) that the war is over!' wrote Leading Seaman Walter Edgley in his diary. Half an hour later he was one of thousands in the city centre: 'Crowds and crowds cheering, dancing and singing. The city went wild – paper streamers from all buildings and it was just like a snowstorm.' He and his friends had trouble finding anything to drink, but nevertheless only returned aboard in the early hours. 'Marvellous time,' he wrote, 'and above all it is PEACE.'

HMS *Indomitable* was preparing to leave Sydney for Hong Kong. 'Peace declared but we have to sail at 1445 just the same,' wrote Commander Robert Parker. 'Large crowd of women came to see us off, many drunks and absentees, several of them stokers I regret to say. Spliced mainbrace, more drinking, dressing up etc. on the lines of Xmas, but it might have been much worse.' 'Victory over Japan announced. The world rejoices,' wrote N. B. Gray of HMS *Indefatigable*. 'Rear Admiral Vian came aboard. Prayers on the flight deck. Captain spoke. A lovely day. Splice the mainbrace.'

On 14 August 1945 the commander-in-chief of the East Indies Fleet had sent a message to the ships under his command, preparing them for the imminent end of hostilities. He informed captains that the day of the announcement would be known as VJ Day. All ships would splice the mainbrace, and an extra rum ration and beer could be issued. Where appropriate, ships' companies would be permitted to stand down after the announcement, and, where operational conditions permitted, could be given two days' leave.

Yet, as after the defeat of Germany, there was also a note of caution. 'There will be deep thankfulness and much rejoicing,' the message read. 'Nevertheless everyone must realise that the end of hostilities will by no means end the navy's commitments and Their Lordships have reminded me by signal of the immense task that lies ahead of us on this station when the Japanese surrender.' It was emphasized that the navy had a particular role to play:

I want you all to remember that the navy can move so much faster than the army or R.A.F. because we carry our own essential stores. Consequently we may have to occupy very rapidly a number of the ports recently in Japanese hands. We must bring help to our prisoners of war quickly. We must maintain order amongst peoples who have been under but are now released from Japanese domination . . . Celebrations in connection with victory are right and proper but in many instances we shall be hard at work and unable to take part.

At HMS *Fledgling*, a Fleet Air Arm shore base in Staffordshire, Wren cipher officer Audrey Deacon was roused from her bed by 'shouts and whistles and whatnot' after Prime Minister Attlee's announcement at midnight. 'We had been preparing a bonfire for VJ day itself,' she wrote in her diary, 'but someone set light to it now, and it began to blaze. It was a wonderful bonfire. There was an effigy of Tojo (or Hirohito?) which was duly burned. The wardroom piano was carried out onto the grass, and we sang songs and vaguely rushed round the fire for an hour or so. A barrel of beer was broached, and we retired to the wardroom for drinks.'

Sore heads the following morning were placated by a reduced Sunday routine. There was another breach of protocol, as the Wrens spliced the mainbrace. Deacon wrote that it was 'my first taste of rum, which I didn't like much. Strictly speaking, WRNS personnel are not entitled, but one doesn't win a war every day. I had only half a tot, and had to disguise that with orange in order to drink it.' She contemplated the strangeness of the moment after six years of graft – 'it's very hard to take in the fact' – but noted optimistically that 'the Chinese have had eight years of war – it must be even more wonderful for them'.

On the evening of 1 September, the British battleship HMS *Duke of York* was anchored in a small bay near Tokyo. The next day a Japanese delegation would attend the nearby USS *Missouri* to complete the formal surrender. The commander-in-chief of the British Pacific Fleet, Admiral Bruce Fraser, stood on the *Duke of York*'s quarterdeck with Captain Angus Nicholl. As the two men watched the sunset, Fraser leant over and quipped: 'The setting of the Rising Sun.'

'It seems hardly believable,' wrote Richard Campbell-Begg of HMS *Paladin*. 'I never thought for a moment that the end would come so suddenly. It came as a wonderful surprise. There will still be a lot of clearing up to do in this part of the world before things are

straightened out but that isn't worrying me.' On 10 September 1945
*Paladin* arrived at Georgetown, on the island of Penang, to the north-
west of Singapore. It was, wrote Campbell-Begg, 'a lovely little town
but has been completely spoilt by the Japanese'. The locals were 'very
pleased to see us. They hated the Japs,' he stated, adding that local
Malay children 'are a most attractive lot and would follow us around
in large numbers. At one time we had about fifty in our retinue.'

Two days later *Paladin* was at Singapore, where the formal surrender ceremony for the Japanese forces in Malaya was taking place.
Thousands gathered around the Municipal Chambers to witness the
delegates arriving, chief amongst them Lord Louis Mountbatten.
Campbell-Begg was in the crowd:

> The Japanese top Brass then appeared, each man having two senior
> British Officers as guards, one on each side. They were marched into
> the building to the jeers of the crowd. Then, suddenly, there was a
> burst of what sounded like machine-gun fire on the outskirts of the
> crowd and, for an awful moment, we thought that the Japanese mili-
> tary had had a change of mind . . . it turned out that the 'musketry'
> was only fire crackers being let off by the jubilant Chinese! After the
> signing the Japanese were led away and Lord Louis appeared and gave
> a very spirited and apt speech.

The spectators saluted as a Union flag was raised before the building. Brass bands from each of the forces played 'God Save the King'
followed by the national anthems of each of the Allies. *Paladin*'s sailors then got back to the business of reconstruction work. Within a
few days, they had helped themselves to the Japanese equipment that
was widely available, including oilskins, binoculars and even a motor
boat. Campbell-Begg noted that 'we have the appearance rather of a
Japanese ship with so many of the crew wearing those funny little
Japanese khaki caps and other bits and pieces'.

The streets of Singapore were full of recently released prisoners of
war. 'All are as thin as rakes,' wrote Campbell-Begg, 'hardly any flesh
left on them to speak of. They have had a dreadful time and are to be
sent home as soon as possible.' Camps in the East Indies had begun to

be liberated several months before VJ Day, but the abrupt surrender meant that plans for the repatriation of thousands more former prisoners were incomplete. At short notice, British ships were converted for passenger duties in a process known as Operation Ethelred.

Keeping track of released prisoners was a considerable bureaucratic challenge. A standardized process of interrogation, medical examination and debriefing had to be developed. Sick and wounded had to be transported to Australia or America. In such a fast-moving and confusing scenario, it was easy for individuals to be misplaced. In one case, an able seaman had been released from a camp in Luzon by American forces in January 1945 and, at least according to the navy's records, promptly disappeared. He was eventually discovered amongst ratings in the Royal Naval Barracks at Sydney in March having, as the official report of the incident put it, 'hitch-hiked his way from Lingayen via Leyte and Hollandia in British and American ships'.

Some of the last prisoners to be liberated were those in Japanese territory in China and on the home islands themselves. Maurice Bennett's camp in Mukden, Manchuria, housed around 1,250 men. They had been spared some of the worst atrocities of the Japanese prison camps elsewhere, but had survived only on limited rations: 'two small buns per day, one pint of Indian corn mush for breakfast, and a pint of thin soup at midday and night'.

The prisoners had been kept informed of the progress of the war by their smuggled newspapers. They learned of the 'tremendous bombing of Jap cities' and where the main Allied forces were. On 16 August rumours circulated that Chinese workers were saying the war was over. Then prisoners saw supplies and parachutists in the sky. A squad of American paratroopers had been sent to negotiate the liberation of the camp from the Japanese commandant. That night, the truth became clear, as Bennett recorded in his diary:

It was a hot night and . . . all found it too hot and exciting to sleep. Gradually conversation became louder until, everyone off his bed, was smoking, playing poker and talking so loudly that, had the war not been over, the Nips would have played hell. As it was, no guards were to be seen, save one, who at about 0300 sauntered through our barracks smiling, indifferent to the gross disobedience of orders going on around him. This was final proof.

Red Cross parcels with food and kit were delivered. Most of the prisoners were weak and emaciated, with dozens seriously ill. The first priority was to treat the most pressing cases. Authority within the camp entered a period of transition. The Japanese guards remained, but took on an alternative role. 'The Nips all wanted to leave the camp immediately,' wrote Bennett, 'but we, having no arms, must have some sort of guard to keep off the Chinese who, though friendly to us, we did not want inside the camp.' Fences had now become barricades. 'This night we hear a lot of shooting in Mukden – Chinese murdering Nips we suppose.'

'It would be impossible to recount all the new thrills as they come upon us,' wrote Bennett on 19 August:

> The joy of smoking whole cigarettes knowing that there are plenty more, the pleasure of finishing a good meal without having to lick the plate and still feel hungry. The joy of being left alone with no guard every half hour through the barracks to annoy us and make us stand to salute him. I am now beginning to wonder how I ever did it.

The following evening, a 'victory concert' was performed by the camp orchestra. Three national anthems were played – Russian, British and American – 'the first time we had heard them for 3½ years'. A Russian officer and an American interpreter addressed the audience. 'The speaker first told us that from now on we were free. The crowd roared.' The ex-prisoners lined the parade ground to witness the formal surrender of the Japanese officers and guards. They emerged, dropped their rifles and swords, and 'bowed low and long to us'. The Russian officer presented the senior American prisoner with a pistol 'and told him that the Nips were our prisoners now'. A guitar band played a concert in the parade ground, and as Bennett lay on a blanket listening, 'the full realisation of my deliverance first came over me. I turned in at midnight and slept like a log.'

After their liberation, the prisoners were forced to stay in their camp until their repatriation could be organized. Japanese supplies were looted, including a depot from which former prisoners and Chinese locals made off with Leica cameras, swords, watches, pens and other luxuries. Recent editions of photo-journalism magazines such as *Life* and *Time* were acquired. Bennett was astounded by 'pictures of the end of the war in Europe. Photographs of all sorts of war equipment we had never heard of. What a hell of a cost this war must have been.'

The former prisoners continued to reside in their crowded quarters. Forty-eight men slept alongside Bennett. Fresh clothing was delivered and unceremoniously dumped in piles. Crates of beer looted from a Japanese brewery were everywhere. The floor was covered with papers, cigarette ends, bags of sugar, bicycles, suitcases and food. 'When meals came up,' wrote Bennett, 'now requiring six or eight buckets instead of the previous meagre two, there was such a scrum of eating and plate carrying men that the place literally became a pig sty, and we, British officers, the pigs around a trough.' After months and years of back-breaking work, it was hardly surprising that chores were unpopular. Still, there was now an alternative. 'It was amusing to see our former guards working in the camp for us every day,' wrote Bennett. 'We had them as slaves now, and they were most useful for doing the dirty jobs.'

The Royal Navy's residents were eager for news of the role played by their fellow sailors in the defeat of Japan. 'Our Fleet has been out here but has done little compared with the American task forces,' wrote Bennett. The balance of power within the camp ran along similar lines. 'We strongly dislike having to be administered by Americans but we must get used to it, because although we have saved our "faces", and can still sing "Rule Britannia", we no longer lead the world in importance. That is a fact, and the sooner we realise it without too much regret the better.'

While those still residing in their former prisons waited to be transported to the coast, where they would be organized for their return home, ships began to prepare for the enormous logistical task of ensuring that adequate supplies of food, clothing and medicine would be available in the departure depots. Only two days after VJ Day, Red Cross supplies began to be loaded onto HMS

*Vindex* in preparation for transport from Sydney to Hong Kong. The voyage was uncomfortable. 'Felt pretty bad,' wrote Walter Edgley on 6 September. 'Ship's company and passengers are going down sick like flies with the heat.' *Vindex* docked at Hong Kong the following day, and Edgley and his shipmates worked for twenty-two hours straight unloading the urgently needed supplies under difficult conditions: 'Tons of stores got out. Snipers about while we were unloading.'

Over the coming days, there would be little respite. Edgley had been relieved at 2 a.m., and was at work again the following morning, from just after 9 a.m. until 11.30 p.m. 'Everyone is fed up and grumbling,' he wrote after another long shift, 'but for most of us it means about six hours off (for meals) and four hours sleep in the last 48 hours, and there are scores in the Sick Bay. Talk about being grim, we are just like slaves . . . It has been murder even though it is Red Cross Stores.'

The next task was to prepare the ship to embark survivors of the Japanese prison camps. 'Ex-Prisoners-of-War came aboard,' wrote Edgley on 15 September, 'about 70 Australians so far and we have more people to come aboard on Monday to take back to Sydney.' Amongst the prisoners were 126 officers and men of the 8th Division of the Australian army, who had been captured on the island of Ambon in the East Indies in 1942. Edgley gave them their mail, reported in the press at the time as their first for forty-four months. Nearly 1,100 Australian troops had originally been sent to the island as the 'Gull Force'. Only 300 saw the end of the war.

The following day, 16 September, another official surrender ceremony took place in Hong Kong. *Vindex* fired a twenty-one-gun salute to celebrate, and the ship's company spliced the mainbrace. In the evening, wrote Edgley, 'all searchlights were put on and left in shape of a V in the sky. Then they followed the *Duke of York*'s lights all around and then circled about in the sky, then suddenly swept down to the water. Then the fireworks started. Red, white, and green rockets, Very lights etc. and it was marvellous for almost an hour.'

As the carrier made her way back to Sydney, sailors relaxed a little. They played deck hockey. A variety show was staged in the hangar by the 'Vindex Vagabonds'. An Abbott and Costello film was shown. Some activities, however, lasted longer than others. 'Football on Flight deck in afternoon,' wrote Edgley, 'until ball went over the side.'

Lieutenant John Pelly, who had been in the vanguard of the Normandy landings, was in Formosa helping to repatriate prisoners aboard the destroyer HMS *Tyrian*. He sent a letter to his parents describing the conditions he had witnessed:

> I hate to tell you more because I never knew I would see anything so ghastly. The number that died of starvation and slave driving can't be estimated and the survivors are terribly emaciated, so weak they can't walk – thinner than the most awful pictures you saw – and riddled with disease . . . If you read about this cruelty you wouldn't believe it . . . The sight has brought home the fact that war must never be glamorised to our children – but stories of this sort of thing – the result of war – must be made known to all.

For the prisoners, it was a long voyage home. Repatriated passengers on board the aircraft carrier HMS *Indomitable* at the end of September 1945 were provided with a booklet containing an illustrated map of the route from Hong Kong via Manus to Australia, then across the Indian Ocean to Ceylon, past Aden through Suez to the Mediterranean, and from Gibraltar to Spithead. By the time they arrived back in Britain, a month later, they had been treated to a programme of concerts, shows and entertainments – mostly provided by the ship's company – including a skit called 'The Third World War'.

Not everyone was in such a hurry to return to Britain. Denys Barton, who had been aboard the oil tanker *Ohio* during her epic voyage to Malta in 1942, was now serving in the cruiser HMS *Cleopatra*. In September 1945 he was in Colombo, ruminating on the possibility of returning to Europe. 'Rumours are very strong that we shall go back to the Med,' he wrote in a letter to his sister-in-law. Barton was perfectly content to stay in the East: 'We might as well stay here until they stop paying Jap campaign pay – I see no reason to give away £7 a month for a slightly better climate!' Alexandria would be acceptable, he admitted, despite its high cost of living, and it had the advantage of excellent night clubs: 'London's seem like sordid hovels in comparison and of course the climate is superb.'

Despite the extra remuneration, however, most sailors were all too eager to get back. HMS *Halladale* spent much of September and October in Cape Town. November and December were spent in Ceylon. 'Everyone is fed-up,' wrote Donald Butcher in his diary. There was no sign of the long-awaited orders to return home. On Christmas Eve, at Colombo, he and his messmates were thoroughly miserable. 'Still waiting for draft and I am getting fed up with it,' he wrote in his diary. 'There is no feeling of Xmas on the lower deck but the officers are pretty drunk already, and they have their sluts aboard. It is pouring with rain and a thunder storm is on. What a life!'

Meanwhile, HMS *Vindex* continued to ferry stores and passengers. On Armistice Day, 11 November 1945, the ship was at Manila. 'Embarked 45 Indian collaborators in afternoon,' noted Walter Edgley in his diary, adding euphemistically: 'Marines "looked after" them.' By late November, morale had sunk to a new low. 'Dinner was bad and complaints were made,' noted Edgley one day. 'Unrest and trouble aboard. "Sit-down Strike" . . . Maxie put in cells for trying to start a mutiny!' *Vindex* spent Christmas in Australia: 'Xmas Day and DUTY AGAIN! Up 06.00 and served breakfast – tons of work.'

The sailors of HMS *Nigeria* spent much of September and October 1945 at Sabang in Indonesia, where the cruiser was acting as a guardship. Ratings formed working parties to aid in the reconstruction of damaged infrastructure: constructing latrines, fixing roofs and working on hospital buildings. Free time was spent sailing, fishing and playing hockey or football. Some young sailors were caught in a local house and charged with looting. Captain Henry King reported that 'all the accused pleaded in mitigation that they "thought it was a Japanese house"'.

Several British ships were sent to Japan. HMS *Wakeful* visited the fishing town of Shiogama in September 1945. 'We wandered everywhere,' wrote Lieutenant Richard Walker in his diary, 'through the streets, up the hill to the temple courtyards, looked at the prayers they had tied to the fir tree branches, into the shops, bartered our cigarettes, soap and chocolate, for little oddments like china cups, hats, magazines and postcards.' He was quite taken by the small children who followed the party around, 'heads on one side and shy smiles'.

In China, meanwhile, HMS *Tyrian* was sent up the Yangtze. Lieutenant Pelly wrote to his parents describing the scene:

> A week ago we turned up the Yangtze Kiang as the first ship (allied) to do so since Dec 1941 and then down the fifteen miles of the Whangpoo to Shanghai – all the Chinese were mad with joy and made it very difficult to get upriver with thousands of sampans and junks and steam ferry boats hooting, all flying huge Chinese flags and all very excited, while all the people of the villages on the river bank were yelling and letting off fireworks etc. As we reached Shanghai . . . the scene was terrific and the Bund (the Front) was covered with people.

After a short period of shore leave, the work began again. Pelly and his comrades in the *Tyrian* and similar vessels were at the forefront of the efforts to re-establish the British presence in the lucrative Chinese market:

> And so back on board again. Everything tightening up and peace time routine which is rather irksome, but we've got to impress the Chinese if we are going to get their trade – of course there are thousands of Yanks here, buying the place up and trying to out our interests – and so we the Navy have got to keep our end up – and thank god I'm an Englishman – the way they appear and slop around is revolting. The Chinese National Army (Chiang Kai-Shek) is moving in – the Communists just outside and the Japs in barbed wire – all most complicated.

★ ★ ★

Douglas Woolf had been a junior officer during the Abyssinian crisis. During the Spanish Civil War he had befriended German sailors from the *Graf Spee* and later fought them when serving in the cruiser *Ajax*. After the Battle of the River Plate he was appointed to a shore job, on a minelayer base in Scotland, followed by various other administrative posts and positions from Alexandria to Africa. In the summer of 1946, now with the rank of lieutenant commander, he was sent to the Far East to serve as secretary to a senior British admiral in the Pacific Fleet.

Woolf travelled to Sydney by aeroplane. The fuelling stops along the way echoed the navy's eastern war: Sicily, Cairo, Basra, Bahrain, Karachi, Calcutta, Rangoon, Penang, Singapore, Surabaya, Darwin. He found the journey rather depressing, as he wrote in his diary shortly after arriving in Australia:

Well I can't say I've been frightfully impressed with what I've seen of the countries I've passed through. Everyone has trouble and unsettlement. The Japs have left Burma and Malay in a mess . . . the Indonesians are still fighting the Dutch and we were only allowed a few yards from the landing place for fear of snipers . . . Now the whole of the Dutch East Indies is in a state of war . . . Australia seems to be torn by strikes – in fact after India I realised that I think England is as well off as any – though the days of our empire as we knew it before the war are numbered. Even in Singapore the people I talked with are not at all happy about the future of Malaya – where outside the towns and up country the Malays are giving trouble and demanding their independence.

From Australia, Woolf travelled to Hong Kong, now reclaimed by the British. He toured the Chinese countryside, which he found 'quite lovely' and 'not dissimilar to North Wales'. But it was the people who made the biggest impression. 'What strikes one first about the Chinese is how friendly and polite they are,' he wrote. 'They have an atmosphere of happiness about them that one would find quite difficult to equal anywhere else in the world . . . With their terrible privations during the Japanese occupation and the cruelties they undoubtedly suffered, it is quite amazing.' From his billet, he could watch elderly men congregate for their evening games, much as they always had done, 'seated round a table sucking their pipes playing "Mah jong" and what a performance! Right on till the early hours one could hear the continuous shuffling of the bricks.'

In the daylight, Woolf found Hong Kong 'in a pretty parlous state – practically every European house was looted – everything from the doors to the window panes have been removed – mostly for firewood during the cold weather'. The dockside and harbour housed 'a mess of old wrecks of Jap ships'. Woolf commented on the absence of animals, attributing this to the necessities of diet during the occupation. He noted the 'particularly odious building' which had housed prisoners of war. At the time, war-crimes trials were being conducted. Woolf was told that the criminals 'are being despatched pretty swiftly either by hanging or shooting depending on whether they are service or civilian'.

Soon, Woolf was on his way to his final destination: Japan. 'Coming through the inland sea which is dotted with innumerable small islands,' he wrote, 'we passed some wonderful scenery – mountains combined with the vivid green of the rice fields growing in terraces up their sides was a new experience and one cannot help saying – even Japan is beautiful.' Then he arrived at the capital city.

> Tokyo itself is in a worse state than London ever was. The Japs however haven't taken long to put up their wooden paper houses which are dotted about amongst the ruins. Yokohama harbour and the sea-roads leading up to it and the whole of Tokyo Bay are littered with the wrecks of battleships, carriers, cruisers and destroyers. The amenities ashore are nil and food is very scarce. The population quite respectful and submissive. As you pass them they bow and scrape as if we were Gods. Though there is some fraternisation with the Geisha girls which is considerably discouraged by the Military Police, on the whole they meet with a cold reception from their victors. The children though are treated differently and it would be hard to be otherwise – they look so cute in their native dress and wave to any soldier or sailor who passes.

'The descriptions in the newspapers were not exaggerated,' he wrote of Hiroshima, 'and even after a year, the place is in a frightful state . . . Amongst the ruins the only things to be seen above six feet are the scorched and deadened trunks of the trees.'

# 23. Epilogue

Maurice Bennett had been a junior officer in *Exeter*, and a prisoner of the Japanese for three and a half years. When he arrived home in May 1946, he transcribed the diary he had kept of the last weeks of his incarceration, signed and dated it, and added a postscript:

> One more word: to those of you who are at all apprehensive about the future, take it from someone who was out of the country for five years – that we did win the war, and behind all the queues, government controls, and rationing, we still have the same, the greatest little country in the world, and going to be better than ever just as soon as we can get things straightened out.

But few of the old certainties endured. The Royal Navy remained in strength in the Indian Ocean and the Far East, where violence had erupted in the colonial territories of the Dutch East Indies. British rule in India came to an abrupt end, while communist guerrillas began an insurgency in Malaya. Within five years of VJ Day, British forces were again involved in a major international conflict in the Far East, after the outbreak of the Korean War in 1950. In this, the first armed confrontation of the Cold War, Britain fought as part of an American-led United Nations coalition, fighting communist forces backed by the Soviet Union and Maoist China.

Career sailors continued to serve. Those young midshipmen who had recorded their wartime development in training journals would begin to rise up the ranks, and by the 1960s they were leading the navy. John Roberts, who had started as a 'snotty' in the battlescruiser *Renown*, would eventually command the new HMS *Ark Royal*, also a wartime veteran having been laid down in 1943, but now carrying jet fighters armed with heat-seeking missiles.

Many would continue to travel across the globe. After a short stint as commander of the Royal Naval College, Dartmouth, Vere Wight-Boycott would go on to serve in the USA and Canada, then in the Middle East. Douglas Woolf returned to bases in Bermuda and the West Indies – the scene of his 'slight incident with a shark'. John Evans, away from his wife for so long in China before the war and then in an Italian POW camp, spent a few years ashore at Rosyth before departing once again for several years at Trincomalee, Port Said and Alexandria. When they eventually retired, many would find other employment in city firms or family businesses, in civil service or schools, some using their service contacts, others establishing their own companies. When George Blundell left the navy in the late 1950s, he joined a motor components manufacturer, using his experience of electrical engineering in a civilian capacity.

Reservists and volunteers had already returned to civvy street. Lieutenant Richard Walker of the destroyer HMS *Wakeful* received his discharge papers in the summer of 1946. 'On the occasion of your release from Naval Service,' they stated, 'I am commanded by My Lords Commissioners of the Admiralty to convey to you an expression of their recognition of your services in the Royal Navy during the war. The good wishes of Their Lordships go with you on your return to civil life.'

Some sailors would never return home. Ian Anderson, John Carter and Charles Thomas were amongst the 50,758 Royal Navy personnel killed during the war. More than 7,400 endured the deprivations of imprisonment, and 14,663 were registered wounded. The merchant navy also suffered greatly: 30,248 mariners were lost. Beyond the official figures, however, many others who served at sea continued to suffer for many years, traumatized and exhausted by their efforts.

Charles Hutchinson returned to East Yorkshire, where he and his wife found a cottage in the small seaside village of Hornsea. As with many sailors, the war had taken a severe toll on his health. He never spoke of his experiences, nor did he continue to keep a diary. His wife did not learn of the existence of his wartime journal until many years later. Hutchinson still enjoyed the occasional trip out to sea, but in a fishing boat rather than a warship.

Commander John Mosse had captained the frigate HMS *Mermaid* in the Arctic and the Atlantic in 1944 and 1945, and had helped to sink two U-boats. After the war he worked in the Tactical and Staff Duties Division at the Admiralty until 1955. His retirement was followed by that of his ship. *Mermaid* was sold to the West German Bundesmarine for use as a training vessel. She was renamed *Scharnhorst*.

Several years later, *Scharnhorst* called at Portsmouth and Mosse travelled to the south coast with his wife to visit his old ship. He was welcomed on board and given a tour, standing once more on the bridge and sitting in his old cabin. 'We were very hospitably received,' he wrote. The Germans had made a few noticeable alterations, including the installation on the bridge of 'a long teak shelf with recesses for beer tankards'. Afterwards, a party went to the Queen's Hotel in Southsea for lunch. Mosse sat next to an ex-submariner who had commanded a U-boat during the war. 'We discussed tactics,' he recalled, 'and fought a friendly convoy battle with knives, forks and salt cellars.'

# Acknowledgements

My first debt is to the men and women whose diaries, letters, memoirs and recollections inspired this book. I would like to express my sincere gratitude to every veteran, relative or family friend who granted permission for personal papers to be quoted. Special thanks are due to Rear Admiral John Roberts for allowing me to make use of his Midshipman's Journal, a document written in youth which marked the start of a distinguished career.

It has been an uncommon privilege to speak with, and to receive letters from, many of the witnesses on whose words I have drawn, or to talk to their partners, children or grandchildren. Every effort has been made to reach copyright holders, but in a few cases this was not possible. Correspondence is welcomed by the author and the relevant archives in any such instance.

Many archivists and librarians helped to make my research more effective as well as more pleasurable. Chief amongst them was Roderick Suddaby of the Department of Documents at the Imperial War Museum in London, who went far beyond the call of duty in providing invaluable assistance and guidance. The staff of the Department of Documents, as well as their colleagues at the departments of Printed Books, Sound, and Photographs, were unfailingly patient and helpful. I am particularly grateful to Sabrina Rowlatt, who processed an enormous number of correspondence requests, and to Thomas Eaton, Ian Proctor and Richard Hughes.

At the National Museum of the Royal Navy in Portsmouth, Matthew Sheldon offered a great deal of helpful advice at both the start and the end of the research process, as did the staff of the museum's library. At the Second World War Experience Centre, now located in Wetherby, Cathy Pugh was a welcoming and enthusiastic guide to the collections under her care, and the volunteers at the centre generously shared their workspace with me. The automated ordering system at the National Archives is a great help to researchers, but there are times when people are better than computers, and fortunately the staff at Kew were always willing to help. Thanks also to John Parton at Curtis Brown and Dan Parry at Dangerous Films, who responded swiftly to copyright requests. For access to their material, I am grateful to the Trustees of the Imperial War Museum and the London Metropolitan Archives; Mass Observation material is reproduced with the permission of Curtis Brown on behalf of the Trustees of the Mass Observation Archive.

The idea for this book emerged from research originally conducted for a D.Phil. at Oxford University. Professor Hew Strachan was a sage and supportive supervisor, and provided much-valued counsel at the outset of this project. Professor N. A. M. Rodger and Professor Jose Harris encouraged me to develop my work further. Although the final outcome takes a different form, I hope that much of the essence of the earlier material remains.

Annabel Merullo at Peters Fraser and Dunlop took a chance on a new writer, and could not have found the book a better home than Viking. Eleo Gordon has been as encouraging and judicious an editor as an author could want. Her infectious enthusiasm was always invigorating. Ben Brusey, Keith Taylor and Lesley Hodgson provided sterling assistance at crucial points. Trevor Horwood was a superb copy-editor, casting a meticulous eye over the manuscript. Douglas Matthews compiled the index with great care. It has been a pleasure to work with the entire publishing team.

For invitations to speak to exacting audiences, I am grateful to Saul Dubow, Ian Gazeley and Pierre Purseigle. For the provision of sofas and spare rooms, offices and internet connections during the process of research and writing, I owe many favours to Nick Badger and Rachael Holmes, Catherine Will and Tom Counsell, Paul Betts, Elizabeth Nolan, Michael Perks, Kathryn Ward, Jaishan Rajendra, Michael Francis and James Toop. Gerhard Wolf helped out with his camera at short notice and to good effect.

I could not wish for a more supportive family. Bob and Audrey Barron have given me another place to call home. Cleo Barron and

Chris Prior always help to keep me smiling. Dewi and Meirion Prysor, my brothers, are a source of immense pride and much-needed perspective. Richard Williams and Anne Warwick, my parents, deserve greater praise than these few words can offer. They inspire me far more than they imagine.

This book is dedicated to Hester, my wife. I could not have faced the task of writing it without her. She is my anchor.

# Notes

## *Abbreviations*

*DBFP*: *Documents on British Foreign Policy 1918–1939*
IWM: Imperial War Museum, Department of Documents
IWM SA: Imperial War Museum, Sound Archive
LMA: London Metropolitan Archives
MO: Mass Observation Archive, University of Sussex
NMRN: National Museum of the Royal Navy, Portsmouth
SWWEC: Second World War Experience Centre, Wetherby
TNA: The National Archives, Kew

## *1 Introduction*

pp. 1–2 'Hell's pandemonium started . . .', IWM Hutchinson, 3 May 1940.

pp. 2–3 'This has caught hold of me now . . .', IWM Hutchinson, 10 May 1940.

pp. 3–4 'an anonymous and efficient organisation . . .', MO File Report 886–7, 'Civilian Attitudes to the Navy compared with R.A.F. and Army', 30 Sept. 1941.

p. 4 'I don't think anyone could realise . . .', NMRN Hall, 10 Dec. 1939.

p. 4 'You may think . . .', Mallalieu, *Very Ordinary Seaman*, p. 277.

## *2 Flashes of Fire*

p. 8 'I don't want to frighten you darling . . .', IWM Evans, 20 Sept. 1935.

p. 8 'We are as ready as we can be . . .', IWM Wight-Boycott, 7 Sept., 16 Oct. 1935.

p. 9   'Everything possible should be done . . .', *DBFP*, 2nd series, XIV, no. 431, pp. 470–71.

p. 9   'touching off . . .', Chatfield to Fisher, 25 Aug. 1935; quoted in Marder, *From the Dardanelles*, pp. 68–9.

pp. 9–10   'Today was the hottest . . .', IWM Manisty, 6–7 Oct. 1935.

p. 10   'I feel perfectly safe . . .', IWM Evans, 13 March 1936.

p. 10   'I am in charge . . .', IWM Woolf, undated letter.

p. 10   'I say in all seriousness . . .', IWM Woolf, 25 Oct. 1935.

p. 10–11   'The situation is still grim . . .', IWM Evans, 16 Oct. 1935.

p. 11   'The modern Italian . . .', Chatfield to Fisher, 25 Aug. 1935; quoted in Marder, *From the Dardanelles*, pp. 77, 79.

p. 11   'the matelots are still . . .', IWM Woolf, 25 Oct. 1935.

p. 11   'The Navy's description . . .', IWM Thomas, 30 Sept. 1938.

p. 11   'that he was going to visit . . .', IWM Evans, 4 Nov. 1935.

p. 11   'Armistice Day . . .', IWM Manisty, 11 Nov. 1935.

p. 11   'the two minutes silence . . .', IWM Woolf, 13 Nov. 1935.

p. 11   'Cowboys and Abyssinians . . .', IWM Evans, 11 Nov. 1935.

p. 11–12   'Pray hard . . .', IWM Evans, 7 Nov. 1935.

p. 12   'The rest say . . .', IWM Wight-Boycott, 28 Oct. 1935.

p. 12   'We don't think much . . .', IWM Thomas, 17 Oct. 1935.

p. 12   'We must build a bigger navy . . .', IWM Evans, 27 Sept. 1935.

p. 12   'The town itself . . .', IWM Thomas, 17 Oct. 1935.

pp. 12–13   'a most motley crowd . . .', IWM Woolf, 10 Nov., 1 Dec. 1935.

p. 13   'The International Sporting Club . . .', IWM Clay, 15 Sept. 1935.

p. 13   'I served and promptly hit him . . .', IWM Wight-Boycott, 20 Oct. 1935.

p. 13   'We must thank our lucky stars . . .', IWM Evans, 9 Dec. 1935.

p. 13   'mosaic work . . .', IWM Thomas, 11 May 1936.

p. 14   'I think we are going to fight . . .', IWM Wight-Boycott, 9 Dec. 1935.

p. 14   'Every ship flies Christmas trees . . .', IWM Thomas, 27 Dec. 1935.

p. 14   'my visits to many parts . . .', IWM Carew-Hunt, 22 Jan. 1936.

pp. 14–15 'the Geneva pacifists . . .', Marder, *From the Dardanelles*, p. 83.

p. 15   Plans for war . . . , TNA ADM 116/3476, 'History of the Italian–Abyssinian Emergency'.

p. 15   'The crews are made up . . .', IWM Evans, 11 May 1936.

p. 15   'I do not attach any importance . . .', IWM Evans, 15 March 1936.

pp. 15–16 'It was too much to expect . . .', IWM Carew-Hunt, 12–13 March 1936.

pp. 16–17 'My first impression . . .', IWM Misc. 3 (12), 'Brief narrative'.

p. 17 'Judging from the posters . . .', IWM Thomas, 7 Feb. 1936.

p. 17 'As usual . . .', IWM Woolf, 15 May 1936.

pp. 17–18 'We knew little . . .', IWM Haslam, 3 Aug. 1936.

p. 18 'crowded with refugees . . .', IWM Woolf, 3 Feb. 1937.

p. 18 'As well as Britishers . . .', IWM de Winton, p. 46.

p. 18 'babies, slung in canvas cots . . .', IWM Swinley, p. 127, 'Report of Proceedings, 27 Feb. 1937'.

pp. 18–19 'It is pathetic . . .', IWM Woolf, 14 Feb. 1937.

pp. 19–20 'We are being diverted . . .', IWM Wright, 'HMS *London*'.

p. 20 'I do think . . .', IWM Larios, 18 July 1936.

pp. 20–1 'It's a grim spot . . .', IWM Haslam, 3 Aug. 1936.

p. 21 'hot coffee . . .', IWM Swinley, W. E. Wilson: 'Evacuation . . . 17th September 1936'.

p. 21 'He shot two men . . .', IWM Wight-Boycott, 16 Jan. 1937.

p. 22 'They are called the Celta . . .', IWM Wight-Boycott, 4 Feb. 1937.

p. 22 'I don't see why . . .', IWM Thomas, 28 Sept.–14 Oct. 1936.

pp. 22–3 'quite content whichever side wins . . .', IWM Woolf, 3 Feb. 1937.

p. 23 'not to speak . . .', IWM Thomas, 6 and 24 Oct. 1936.

p. 23 'He was a pleasant . . .', IWM de Winton, p. 47.

p. 23 'Before kicking off . . .', Wardle, *Dive Navy*, p. 24.

pp. 23–5 'Perhaps the one visit . . .', IWM Woolf, 3–26 Feb. 1937.

p. 25 'Personally I feel . . .', IWM Carew-Hunt, 11–12 Dec. 1936.

p. 26 'It has been my privilege . . .', IWM Swinley, p. 125, and TNA ADM 1/9045, 'The Gracious Message of His Majesty King George VI to the Fleet on his Accession'.

p. 26 *Asigara* . . . , IWM Ross, p. 313.

pp. 26–7 'At the present moment . . .', see Roskill, *Naval Policy*, vol. 2, pp. 349–50; TNA ADM 178/140.

p. 27 'Before I came to China . . .', IWM Evans, 16 July 1937.

p. 27 'The struggle seems . . .', IWM Carew-Hunt, 11 July 1937.

p. 28 Contemporary statistics . . . , Louis, *British Strategy in the Far East*, p. 8.

p. 28 'We are always rather sitting . . .', Haggie, *Britannia at Bay*, p. 22.

p. 28 'Gunboats are very convenient . . .', Osterhammel, 'China', p. 651.

p. 28    'could not imagine . . .', *DBFP*, 2nd series, XXI, no. 291, p. 377.

p. 28    'We cannot foresee the time . . .', *DBFP*, 2nd series, XIX, no. 316, p. 513.

p. 29    'With regards . . .', IWM Evans, 19 Dec. 1937.

p. 29    'a strange sort of twilight war', IWM Mowlam, 'Letter to Mr Rennison'.

p. 29    'officious and suspicious . . .', IWM Carew-Hunt, 27 April, 7 Aug. 1937.

pp. 29–30   'There seems to be considerable unrest . . .', IWM Carew-Hunt, 27 April, 19 July, 9 and 14 Aug. 1937; see TNA ADM 116/3682 for details.

p. 30    'Nanking is in a state of panic . . .', IWM Evans, 5 Dec. 1937.

p. 30    'After the usual air-raid warnings . . .', IWM Holt, 4 Dec. 1937.

pp. 30–32   'The air was littered . . .', IWM Evans, 2–9 and 17 Dec. 1937.

pp. 32–3   I put on my protest face . . .', IWM Holt, 19 Dec. 1937.

pp. 33–4   'naturalist's paradise . . .', IWM Thomas, 8 May, 10 July, 6 and 14 Aug., 3 Sept., 27 Oct. 1937.

p. 34    One in five . . . , IWM Wight-Boycott, 20 Nov. 1938.

pp. 34–5   'I don't think the average Englishman . . .', IWM Evans, 12 June 1937.

p. 35    'Things are being tightened up . . .', IWM Thomas, 5 Jan. 1938.

p. 35    'If Hong Kong was attacked . . .', IWM Thomas, 6 Aug., 29 Oct., 28 Nov. 1937.

pp. 35–6   'with much fuss and pomp . . .', IWM Anderson, 14 Feb. 1938.

p. 36    'The naval base at Singapore . . .', IWM Wight-Boycott, 12 April 1938.

p. 36    'The situation ashore . . .', IWM Wight-Boycott, 17 June 1938.

p. 36    'the Japanese flag flew proudly . . .', IWM Anderson, 30 May 1938.

p. 36    'Their army is quite mad . . .', IWM Holt, 2 Feb. 1938.

p. 36    'A disgusting and uncivilised order . . .', IWM Anderson, 30 May 1938.

pp. 36–7   'the Chinese are being used . . .', IWM Evans, 14 Jan., 8 Feb. 1938.

p. 37    'I expect you are listening . . .', IWM Wight-Boycott, 25 Sept. 1938.

p. 37    'During the past week . . .', IWM Thomas, 30 Sept. 1938.

pp. 37–8   We are living here . . .', IWM Anderson, 2 Oct. 1938.

p. 38    'It is the duty . . .', IWM Thomas, 15 Oct. 1938, 17 June 1938.

p. 38    One event . . . , Roskill, *Naval Policy*, vol. 2, p. 432.

p. 38    'In spite of headlines . . .', IWM Wight-Boycott, 17 April 1939.

p. 38 'The Japs know that . . .', IWM Haslam, 21 June 1939.

p. 39 'I think the trouble is . . .', IWM Wight-Boycott, 4 Sept. 1938.

p. 39 'occupied by the Japs . . .', IWM Holt, 10 Nov. 1938.

p. 39 'A harmless gunboat . . .', IWM Evans, 19 March 1938.

## 3 Total Germany

p. 40 'Tonight I am visiting . . .', IWM Thomas, 24 Aug. 1939.

p. 41 'When the Prime Minister . . .', MO DR 1061, reply to Sept. 1939 Directive.

p. 41 'the men are very cheerful . . .', IWM Blundell, 2–3 Sept. 1939.

p. 42 'It is difficult to believe . . .', NMRN Layard, 3 Sept. 1939.

p. 42 'A very stupid thing . . .', NMRN Layard, 4 Sept. 1939.

p. 43 'One rating in his excitement . . .', SWWEC Adams, 4 Sept. 1939.

pp. 43–4 'Our bows went into . . .', SWWEC Adams, 11–12 Sept. 1939.

p. 44 'Last night it was black . . .', NMRN Records, 13 Sept. 1939.

p. 44 'I got a look at her . . .', NMRN Records, 14–15 Sept. 1939.

p. 45 'a lack of that indefinable . . .', Maiolo, *Royal Navy and Nazi Germany*, pp. 128–9.

p. 45 'only demonstrate that it knows . . .', Tooze, *Wages of Destruction*, p. 326.

p. 46 'Learnt that *Courageous* . . .', IWM Blundell, 18 Sept. 1939.

p. 46 'So many rumours . . .', NMRN Records, 23 Sept. 1939.

p. 46 'I think I ought to record . . .', NMRN Hall, 20 Oct. 1939.

p. 46 'The news of the *Royal Oak* . . .', IWM Woolf, 27 Oct. 1939.

p. 47 'a marvellous bit of work . . .', NMRN Layard, 17 Oct. 1939.

p. 47 'an amazing performance . . .', IWM Anderson, 19 Oct., 27 Sept., 11 Nov. 1939.

p. 47 'Another Armistice day . . .', NMRN Hall, 11 Nov. 1939.

pp. 47–8 'The water is covered . . .', IWM Walker, 16 Jan., 25 Feb. 1940.

p. 48 'Binoculars, barometers . . .', IWM Walker, 21 Nov. 1939.

p. 48 'The whole ship's company . . .', IWM Walker, 8 March 1940.

pp. 48–9 'She never had a chance . . .', IWM Anderson, 10 Jan. 1940.

p. 49 'We heard about the *Rawalpindi* . . .', IWM Wight-Boycott, 25 Nov. 1939.

p. 49 'I have never seen him so happy . . .', Kennedy, *Sub-Lieutenant*, p. 27.

p. 49 'They must have known . . .', Kennedy, *Sub-Lieutenant*, p. 37.

p. 50 'I cannot help feeling . . .', Colville, *Fringes of Power*, 28 Nov. 1939.

pp. 50–51 'We are having our own . . .', IWM Wight-Boycott, 25 Nov., 4 Sept., 4 Oct. 1939.

p. 51 'We have heard . . .', IWM Wight-Boycott, 25 Nov. 1939.

p. 51 'No doubt we will soon . . .', IWM Thomas, 4 Oct. 1939.

p. 51 'I found it a fascinating place . . .', IWM Dennis, pp. 10–12.

pp. 51–2 'We spent a dismal few hours . . .', IWM Dennis, pp. 23–4.

p. 52 'most of us are getting fairly fed up . . .', NMRN Hall, 15–19 Oct., 15 Nov., 5–14 Dec. 1939.

p. 52 'Sitting in an office ashore . . .', NMRN Layard, 11 and 14 Sept. 1939.

p. 53 'Apparently Jolly in the *Mohawk* . . .', NMRN Layard, 19 Oct. 1939.

p. 53 'I hope I'm not required . . .', NMRN Layard, 26 Oct., 9 Nov., 28 Nov. 1939.

pp. 53–4 'The Navy is used . . .', NMRN Lumsden, pp. 2–3.

p. 54 'HAPPY RETURNS . . .', IWM Woolf, 28 May 1938; telegram 7 July 1938.

p. 55 'There was something terribly pathetic . . .', IWM Woolf, 27 Oct., 25 Sept., 27 Oct. 1939.

pp. 56–7 'To have really felt the fear . . .', IWM Woolf, 18 Dec. 1939.

p. 57 'The *Graf Spee* has been given . . .', NMRN Hall, 15 Dec. 1939.

pp. 57–8 'even greater strain . . .', IWM Woolf, 18 Dec. 1939.

p. 58 'From the accounts . . .', IWM Thomas, 16 Dec. 1939.

p. 58 'I wonder what Drake and Nelson . . .', SWWEC Turner, 15 Feb. 1940.

pp. 58–9 'I've never seen . . .', IWM Blundell, 25 July, 26–9 Aug., 4 Oct., 4 Nov. 1939; 19 Jan., 11 Feb. 1940.

p. 59 'We are still ignored . . .', IWM Anderson, 7 Sept., 20 Oct. 1939.

pp. 60–61 'interrogate the natives . . .', IWM Anderson, 6 Nov., 3 Dec. 1939; 10–16 Jan., 7 and 10 March 1940.

p. 61 'They say the destroyer was *Cossack* . . .', NMRN Hall, 17 Feb. 1940.

p. 61 'The wireless has just given us . . .', IWM Wight-Boycott, 17 Feb. 1940.

p. 62 'I took my wireless up to the bridge . . .', SWWEC Adams, 7 April 1940.

p. 62 'Words absolutely fail me . . .', IWM Carter, 13 April 1940.

p. 62 'Any number of wild rumours . . .', IWM Blundell, 10 and 11 April 1940.

pp. 62–3 'What a world . . .', IWM Haslam, 12 April 1940.

p. 63 'The upper deck had been sprayed . . .', IWM Middleton.

p. 64 'Suddenly the door . . .', IWM Chavasse, P. M. B., 21 May 1940.


## 4 Daniel and the Lions


p.65 'Heavy snow and rain . . .', NMRN Robertson, 31 March–2 April 1940.

p. 65 'We begin to wonder . . .', NMRN Robertson, 3–7 April 1940.

p. 66 'I felt a little proud . . .', IWM Wight-Boycott, 19 April 1940.

pp. 66–7 'we were going in . . .', IWM SA Auffret; Arthur, *Forgotten Voices*, pp. 35–6.

p. 67 'a giant among giants . . .', Brennecke, *Hunters*, pp. 52–3.

p. 67 'What we'll do there . . .', NMRN Hall, 12 April 1940.

pp. 67–8 'formed in a semi-circle . . .', NMRN Robertson, 24 April 1940.

p. 68 'German snipers . . .', NMRN Robertson, 25–8 April 1940.

pp. 68–9 'You can't see the path . . .', IWM Hutchinson, 20 April 1940.

p. 69 'sunk herself . . .', NMRN Robertson, 7 May 1940.

p. 69 'I think most of us . . .', NMRN Hall, 10 April 1940.

p. 69 'I must say . . .', SWWEC Adams, 24 May 1940.

p. 70 'our Lewis gunners . . .', NMRN Robertson, 18 April 1940.

p. 70 'We went in . . .', SWWEC Adams, 30 April 1940.

p. 70 'I've never seen . . .', IWM Hutchinson, 30 April, 1 May 1940.

pp. 70–71 'I could see the bombs . . .', SWWEC Adams, 4–5 May 1940.

p. 71 'The ship's company's nerves . . .', SWWEC Adams, 20–21, 23 and 27 May 1940.

p. 71 'We were ordered . . .', NMRN Robertson, 31 May 1940.

p. 71 'We trudged home . . .', SWWEC Adams, 19 June 1940.

p. 72 'a flood of humanity . . .', Winton (ed.), *War at Sea*, pp. 38–40.

p. 72 'I should have loved . . .', IWM Williams, B. R., 1 May 1940.

p. 73 'They didn't have two heads . . .', Ballantyne, *Warspite*, p. 103.

p. 73 'mental strain . . .', NMRN Hall, 13 April 1940.

p. 73 'you knew this was definitely . . .', IWM Earridge, p. 28.

p. 73 'Guess the saying . . .', NMRN Hall, 8 July 1940.

p. 73 'Events have been happening . . .', SWWEC Adams, 12 and 23 May 1940.

p. 74 One man was shot . . . , Lombard-Hobson, *A Sailor's War*, pp. 86–7.

p. 74 'It was a bitter experience . . .', NMRN Lumsden, p. 7.

p. 75 'little holiday steamers . . .', J. B. Priestley, 'Postscripts', in Calder, *People's War*, p. 109.

p. 75 'Piles of French dead . . .', IWM Leach.

p. 75 'like some mighty ant heap . . .', Hadley, *Third Class to Dunkirk*, p. 127.

p. 75 'Down on the beach . . .', 'Gun Buster', *Return via Dunkirk*, p. 245.

pp. 75–6 'My first reaction . . .', IWM Johnson, A. F.

p. 76 'The first thing I noticed . . .', IWM Adams.

p. 76 'Never was a prayer . . .', IWM Brabyn.

p. 76 'the unfortunate soldiers . . .', Hichens, *Gunboat Command*, p. 71.

p. 76 'It was rather a desperate business . . .', IWM Hewett, 22 June 1940.

pp. 76–7 'I saw lots of men . . .', Atkin, *Pillar of Fire*, p. 213.

p. 77 'When it came to my turn . . .', IWM Vollans.

p. 77 'In the blackness . . .', IWM Brodie.

p. 77 'Everyone in the boat . . .', IWM Engler.

p. 77 'He ordered one man . . .', IWM SA Howard.

p. 77 'My instructions are . . .', Gates, *End of the Affair*, p. 111.

p. 78 'Refuse them embarkation . . .', Atkin, *Pillar of Fire*, p. 186.

p. 78 'made a rush . . .', IWM Brodie.

p. 78 'Some difficulty experienced . . .', IWM Hewett, 'Narrative of events'.

p. 78 'a French officer . . .', IWM SA Wells.

p. 78 'They just got hold . . .', IWM SA Love.

p. 79 'The ship's dog . . .', IWM McSwiney.

p. 79 'The ship kept vibrating . . .', IWM Blaxland.

p. 79 'though whilst we were waiting . . .', IWM Doll.

p. 79 'The bomber swooped . . .', IWM Cannon.

pp. 79–80 'career along at full speed . . .', IWM Boys-Smith, pp. 31–4.

p. 80 'I was lying on deck . . .', Atkin, *Pillar of Fire*, p. 177.

p. 81 Of the thirty-eight destroyers . . ., Barnett, *Engage the Enemy*, p. 161.

p. 81 'They were fine fellows . . .', IWM Hewett, 22 June 1940.

p. 82 'The success is mostly due . . .', Barnett, *Engage the Enemy*, pp. 161–2.

p. 82 'We grudged the time . . .', Wells, *The Royal Navy*, p. 179.

pp. 83–4 'She had just embarked . . .', IWM Mosse, pp. 20–21.

p. 84 'When the last Allied soldier . . .', IWM Thomas, 30 May 1940.

p. 84 'ITALY DECLARES WAR . . .', NMRN Hackforth, 10 June 1940.

p. 84 'Today's news . . .', IWM Wight-Boycott, 10 June 1940.

p. 84 'I suppose the news . . .', IWM Baylis, 25 June 1940.

p. 85   'After the first shock . . .', IWM Blundell, 18 and 24 June 1940.

pp. 85–6   'Hostilities at that range . . .', NMRN Hackforth, May–June 1940.

p. 86   'French ships in harbour . . .', IWM Smith, 3 July 1940.

p. 86   'We have seen our first action . . .', IWM Williams, B. R., 21 July 1940.

p. 86   'What a bombardment! . . .', IWM SA Coles.

p. 86   'Blue, green and yellow . . .', IWM de Winton, p. 56.

p. 86   'Things got a bit warm . . .', IWM Williams, B. R., 21 July 1940.

p. 87   'For a while . . .', IWM Crawford, W. M., 13 July 1940.

p. 87   'I must admit . . .', IWM Williams, B. R., 21 July 1940.

p. 87   'It was a fine sight . . .', IWM de Winton, pp. 56–9.

p. 87   'We all feel . . .', Smith, *England's Last War*, p. 87.

p. 88   'general relief', 5 July 1940; Addison and Crang (eds.), *Listening to Britain*, pp. 192–3.

p. 88   'To many of us here . . .', IWM Thomas, B. R., 9 July 1940.

p. 88   'We steamed down . . .', IWM Williams, B. R., 21 July 1940, pp. 2–3.

p. 88   'May the Itie's . . .', IWM Crawford, W. M., 13 July 1940.

pp. 88–9   'Tonight we sail . . .', IWM Anderson, 4 June 1940; letter, 19 May 1940.

## 5 *The Sea Will Run Red*

p. 90   'All one discusses . . .', IWM Hutchinson, 18 June 1940.

p. 90   'Here is where we come . . .', Hansard, HC Deb. 18 June 1940, vol. 362, cols. 51–64.

p. 90   'There are a few Jonahs . . .', IWM Hutchinson, 18 June 1940.

pp. 90–91   'I expect that . . .', Hansard, HC Deb. 18 June 1940, vol. 362, cols. 51–64.

p. 91   'Only Britain left . . .', SWWEC Adams, 19 June 1940.

p. 91   'I do hope . . .', IWM Thomas, 24 June 1940.

p. 91   'I wish to hell . . .', IWM Carter, 8 Aug. 1940.

p. 91   'I pondered . . .', IWM Waymouth, vol. 2, p. 70.

p. 92   'Schemes for Baffling . . .', TNA CAFO 3669/39, 'War – Suggestions from the Fleet'; IWM Duckworth, 'Ideas, Proposals, Schemes . . .', 20–21 June 1940.

pp. 92–3   'infra-red ray cameras . . .', TNA ADM 199/687, 'Invasion Countermeasures'.

p. 93   'Those four weeks . . .', IWM SA Apps.

p. 93   'determination to challenge . . .', 11 July 1940; Addison and Crang (eds.), *Listening to Britain*, p. 217.

pp. 93–4   'I got up . . .', IWM SA Walsh.

p. 94   'Between his bursts . . .', *London Gazette*, 3 Sept. 1940.

pp. 94–5   'We were well pleased . . .', IWM Wight-Boycott, 'The End of HMS *Delight*'.

p. 96   'Why I volunteered . . .', SWWEC Turner, 10 Aug. 1940.

p. 96   'We went after them . . .', SWWEC Turner, 13 Aug. 1940.

p. 96   'Four ships from here . . .', SWWEC Turner, 14 Oct. 1940.

p. 96   'lined with blackened . . .', SWWEC Dormer, 25 July 1940.

pp. 96–7   'I pressed the Alarm Bells . . .', SWWEC Dormer, 11 Aug. 1940.

p. 97   'trip wires with bells . . .', TNA ADM 199/687, 'Report of Night Landing Exercise . . .'

p. 97   'I have heard . . .', RNM Hall, 14 Sept. 1940.

p. 97   'We were waiting . . .', SWWEC Breen, pp. 11–12.

p. 98   'and the last Wren', SWWEC Duvall.

p. 98   'Directly above me . . .', Perry, *Boy in the Blitz*, p. 111.

p. 99   'the skeletons of dead ships . . .', SWWEC Breen, p. 23.

p. 99   'The best bomb shelter . . .', IWM Somers, p. 6.

p. 99   'It is pleasant . . .', IWM Thomas, 18 July 1940.

p. 100   'I guess you are having . . .', IWM Evans, 19 Aug. 1940.

p. 100   'The last news . . .', IWM Haslam, 10 Sept. 1940.

p. 100   'courage and patience . . .', TNA ADM 1/24362, 'Welfare Services'.

p. 100   'relief services . . .', TNA ADM 182/106, AFO 2133/41; ADM 182/115, AFO 3520/43.

p. 101   'You will never know . . .', IWM Lawrence, 3 Feb. 1941.

p. 101   'The other day . . .', Coward to Wilson, 28 July 1941, in Day (ed.), *Letters of Noël Coward*, pp. 436–7.

pp. 101–2   'It is thoroughly unpleasing . . .', IWM Walker, 25 Feb., 28 April 1940.

p. 102   'Our links . . .', SWWEC Breen, p. 25.

p. 102   'profound depression . . .', SWWEC Dormer, pp. 7–9.

p. 103   'I would sit down there . . .', SWWEC Kennedy.

p. 103   'He stressed the fact . . .', IWM Davies, 10 Oct. 1942.

p. 104    'Painting superstructure . . .', IWM Crawford, W. M., 10–12 and 24 Dec 1940.

p. 105    'I find myself on deck . . .', RNM Bowman, 21–22 Aug. 1941.

pp. 105–6   'Sometimes we would go . . .', IWM Gillett, pp. 14, 17.

p. 106    'We had been expecting . . .', SWWEC Adams, 14 July 1942.

p. 106    'like R.A.F. bombers . . .', IWM Moran, p. 99.

pp. 106–7   'A mock invasion . . .', SWWEC Pippard, 27 Sept. 1942.

p. 107    'Apparently we are still . . .', NMRN Records, 27 April 1941.

## 6 Working Up

p. 108    'How nice it would be . . .', SWWEC Dormer, 9, 17, 23–5 and 27 Sept. 1938.

p. 109    'If we meet . . .', SWWEC Dormer, p. 5.

p. 109    'The Royal Navy . . .', Connelly, 'Battleships'; Harrington, '"Mighty Hood"'.

p. 109    'both the personal . . .', TNA INF 1/293, 5 Dec. 1941.

p. 110    'selection is a search . . .', Moran, *Anatomy of Courage*, p. 170.

p. 110–11   'It is a great change . . .', IWM Carter, 23 Sept. 1939.

p. 111    'The ship's company . . .', IWM Thomas, 4 and 7 Aug. 1939.

p. 111    'The large mess . . .', IWM Waymouth, vol. 2, p. 68.

p. 112    ten applicants . . ., Lavery, *Hostilities Only*, p. 226.

p. 112    In July 1940 . . ., TNA CAB 141/95.

p. 112    'snob appeal', SWWEC Hodges, p. 28.

p. 112    'We lived . . .', IWM Dunkley, p. 2.

p. 112    'lousy with W.R.N.S. . . .', SWWEC Adams, 24 Nov. 1939.

p. 113    'The office job . . .', SWWEC Campbell-Begg, p. 2.

p. 113    'spent in drawing . . .', Roberts, Midshipman's Journal, 20 Oct. 1941, 9 Jan. 1943.

p. 114    'a prudent desire . . .', NMRN Prideaux, pp. 1–5.

p. 114    'very efficient . . .', Hobday, *Harm's Way*, p. 13.

pp. 114–15   Officer candidates . . ., TNA CAB 21/2548, Curran Report, p. 4.

p. 115    'The officers are the ones . . .', IWM Moran, p. 59.

p. 115    'intelligent men . . .', TNA ADM 182/132, CAFO 460/42; ADM 182/113, AFO 1163/43.

p. 116 'The administration . . .', IWM Thomas, 15 Oct. 1938.

p. 116 'to get a movement going . . .', IWM Thomas, 20 Aug. 1938, 11 Jan. 1939.

p. 117 'the newest additions . . .', IWM France, p. 4.

pp. 117–18 'We came together . . .', IWM Shackleton.

p. 118 'Wisdom it is strength . . .', IWM Rail.

p. 118 '14 collapse . . .', NMRN Bowman, 7 Sept. 1940.

p. 118 'Any difference . . .', IWM Moran, p. 56.

p. 119 'We had to master . . .', IWM Mullins, p. 62.

p. 119 'mock-up cockpits . . .', IWM Friend, pp. 6, 9.

p. 119 'test menu . . .', IWM Buckle, pp. 15–16.

p. 120 '5th rate . . .', IWM Moran, p. 55.

p. 120 ice-cream vendors' tricycles . . . , Hobday, *Harm's Way*, p. 14.

p. 120 'Life is frightful . . .', IWM Moran, Feb.–April 1944.

p. 120 'exactly what I had joined . . .', SWWEC Dormer, p. 12.

p. 120 'A long line . . .', IWM Somers, p. 5.

p. 121 'a large consignment . . .', SWWEC Hodges, pp. 28–9.

p. 122 'I was disgusted . . .', IWM France, p. 8.

p. 123 'At last we commissioned . . .', Roberts, *Midshipman's Journal*, Oct. 1943.

p. 123 'from the messdeck . . .', NMRN Young, p. 50.

pp. 123–4 'It was assumed . . .', IWM Davies, 12 Oct. 1942.

p. 124 'The damage control . . .', Roberts, *Midshipman's Journal*, 1 March 1942.

p. 124 'he'd allocate a ship . . .', Bailey, *Battle of the Atlantic*, pp. 12–13; see also Baker, *Terror of Tobermory*.

p. 124 'When displeased . . .', SWWEC Dormer, vol. 2, p. 13.

p. 125 '[Y]ou're disciplined . . .', Bailey, *Battle of the Atlantic*, p. 141.

p. 125 'The tragedy . . .', IWM Blundell, 29 May 1940.

p. 125 'The first two weeks . . .', NMRN Nodder, vol. 1, p. 2.

## 7 Memor Es Tuorum

p. 126 'In my eyes . . .', IWM Nicholl, p. 64.

p. 127 The famous bell-bottoms . . . , Colville, 'Jack Tar and the Gentleman Officer'.

p. 127    'These RNVR officers . . .', IWM Blundell, 9–11 Nov. 1940.

pp. 127–8    'I think that some of these permanents . . .', IWM Hughes, 7 Oct. 1944.

p. 128    'only concerned with . . .', IWM Nicholl, p. 64.

p. 128    'Naval wardrooms . . .', IWM Hooper, 12 Feb. 1944.

p. 128    'a poor crowd . . .', IWM Osborne, pp. 13–14.

pp. 128–9    'a rub up . . .', IWM Anderson, 15 Nov. 1939.

p. 129    'I have no faith . . .', IWM Thomas, 15 March 1941.

p. 129    'What I've seen . . .', IWM Hutchinson, 18 Aug. 1940.

p. 129    'It seems that all the elite . . .', NMRN Records, 24 Jan. 1942.

p. 129    'one is the father . . .', Graham, *Random Naval Recollections*, p. 265.

p. 129    'we resembled . . .', Hobday, *Harm's Way*, pp. 143–4.

p. 129    'family feeling', Bailey, *Battle of the Atlantic*, p. 143.

pp. 129–30    'One sometimes made . . .', NMRN Harris, p. 99.

p. 130    'there was friendship . . .', IWM Balfour, p. 127.

p. 130    'No sooner am I . . .', IWM Sear: Weir journal, 16 July 1941.

p. 130    'People didn't talk much . . .', IWM Goodbrand, pp. 26–7.

p. 131    'I have no friends . . .', IWM Thomas, 14 Aug., 26 Dec. 1940.

p. 131    'The chief drawback . . .', IWM Walker, 3 Sept. 1944.

p. 132    'One of our nicest . . .', SWWEC Dormer, 5 June 1942.

p. 132    'the absolute trust . . .', NMRN Young, p. 28.

p. 132    '"We are bound . . ."', IWM Blundell, 20 Feb. 1941.

p. 132    'we entertained . . .', SWWEC Kennedy.

pp. 132–3    'A remarkably abstemious body . . .', King, *Rule Britannia*, p. 119.

p. 133    'portioned out . . .', IWM Goodbrand, p. 23.

pp. 133–4    'The steward . . .', SWWEC Campbell-Begg, 4 Oct. 1942.

p. 134    'You can't help spending . . .', NMRN Hall, 10 Nov. 1939.

p. 134    'where electrical ovens . . .', Morton, *Atlantic Meeting*, p. 74.

pp. 134–5    'Horace is now installed . . .', SWWEC Campbell-Begg, 13 June, 2 July 1943.

p. 135    'did not really . . .', NMRN Harris, pp. 95–8.

p. 135    'Little Nazi', SWWEC Campbell-Begg, pp. 190–91.

p. 135    'lovely little thing . . .', NMRN Hackforth, 15 March 1940.

p. 136    'Crown and Anchor . . .', NMRN Harris, pp. 62–4.

p. 136    'The great game . . .', IWM Anderson, 13 Nov. 1939.

p. 136    'What excitement you can have . . .', IWM Somers, p. 24.

p. 137    'fancy dress . . .', SWWEC Breen, p. 65.

p. 137    'five muscular seamen . . .', SWWEC Campbell-Begg, 30 March 1945.

p. 137    'I thought that was . . .', SWWEC Pippard, 23 Feb. 1944.

p. 138    'whistled and stamped . . .', IWM Mullins, p. 20.

pp. 138–9    'a Royal Marine . . .', SWWEC Ditcham, p. 61.

p. 139    'beautifully clean sheep . . . ,' IWM Wight-Boycott, 21 May 1943.

p. 140    'Crossed the line . . .', NMRN Butcher, 2 July 1942; K., 'Crossing the Line in Wartime'.

pp. 140–41    'an excuse for a brawl . . .', IWM Walker, 5 Sept. 1944.

p. 141    'The Navy makes me . . .', IWM Carter, 24 Nov. 1940.

p. 141    'There's no doubt . . .', IWM Hutchinson, 25 March 1940.

p. 141    'haunted by Nelson', Morton, *Atlantic Meeting*, pp. 54–5.

p. 141    'Naval history . . .', Tunstall, *World War at Sea*, pp. 16–17.

p. 141    'Let us not ignore . . .', IWM Duckworth, 'Notes on Discipline', p. 4.

## *8 A Long and Hazardous Journey*

p. 142    'When we was having milk . . .', *Life*, 14 Oct. 1940.

p. 142    'Dear Mum and Dad . . .', *Sunday Express*, 14 April 1985.

pp. 143–5    'We were literally shaken . . .', IWM Walder, 1 Oct. 1940.

p. 145    'The Atlantic is the vital area . . .', TNA PREM 3/163/3.

p. 145    'If we lose the war at sea . . .', TNA CAB 69/4, quoted in Barnett, *Engage the Enemy*, p. 440.

p. 146    'We made sure . . .', IWM Pragnell.

pp. 147–8    'We knew from the start . . .', IWM Morry.

p. 148    'had spent some thought . . .', IWM Wight-Boycott, 27 Nov. 1940.

p. 148    'The U.S. trades . . .', *Life*, 16 Sept. 1940, p. 19.

p. 149    'an American NO . . .', IWM Wight-Boycott, 27 Nov. 1940.

p. 149    'The pact with America . . .', IWM Haslam, 10 Sept. 1940.

p. 149    'Icy rain flew . . .', IWM France, pp. 17–18.

p. 151    'Three tankers . . .', IWM Potts, 28 April 1941.

p. 151    In the summer of 1938 . . . , Bennett and Bennett, *Survivors*, p. 26.

p. 151    By 1941 . . . , Lane, *Merchant Seamen's War*, p. 27.

p. 152    'We can crack on . . .', Monsarrat, *Three Corvettes*, pp. 55–6.

p. 152    'We know the merchant men . . .', IWM Hutchinson, 8 July 1940.

p. 153   In Port Said . . . , Billy and Billy, *Merchant Mariners*, p. 24.

p. 153   'This mortal danger . . .', Churchill, *Second World War*, vol. 3, pp. 106–7.

p. 154   'It seemed you could . . .', IWM France, p. 24.

p. 154   'There was in fact . . .', IWM Chavasse, E. H., p. 1.

p. 155   'cork bouncing about . . .', IWM Walker, 28 Oct. 1941.

pp. 155–6   'There was no pattern . . .', SWWEC Breen, pp. 27, 31.

p. 156   'One creeps along . . .', SWWEC Campbell-Begg, pp. 190–91; 20 Oct. 1943.

p. 156   'Gosh, what a life . . .', IWM Hutchinson, 7 Jan. 1942.

p. 156   'no escape . . .', SWWEC Breen, pp. 33–4.

p. 157   'A two bar electric fire . . .', IWM Matthews, p. 23.

p. 157   'One would have to walk . . .', IWM Gardner.

p. 157   'The food was pretty awful . . .', IWM Matthews, pp. 23–4.

p. 158   'Don't mind this weather . . .', IWM Matthews, 14 Aug. 1943.

p. 158   'a thick white . . .', IWM Wight-Boycott, 5 May 1942.

p. 158   'all the dope. . .', IWM Matthews, 1 Aug. 1943.

p. 158   'In those horrid waters . . .', IWM Chavasse, E. H., p. 29.

pp. 158–9   'Saturday night . . .', IWM Matthews, 31 July, 8 Aug., 12 Sept. 1943.

p. 159   'After booking in . . .', IWM France, pp. 34–5.

p. 159   'very dull . . .', SWWEC Dowling, Oct.–Nov. 1942.

p. 159   'it is much easier . . .', IWM Wight-Boycott, 5 May 1942.

pp. 159–60   'The cold is unbearable . . .', NMRN Bowman, 15–23 Jan., 4–10 Feb., 5–10 March, 28 April 1941.

p. 161   'Our ship trembles . . .', IWM Matthews, 18 Aug. 1943.

p. 161   'This was always . . .', IWM France, p. 25.

pp. 161–2   'Wasted an hour . . .', SWWEC Dormer, 1 March 1942.

pp. 162–3   'I was near to despair . . .', Macintyre, *U-Boat Killer*, pp. 35–9.

p. 163   In May, convoy HX 129 . . . , Barnett, *Engage the Enemy*, p. 265.

p. 164   'It was a sunny day . . .', IWM Balme, pp. 17–18.

pp. 164–5   'As they came aboard . . .', IWM Funge-Smith, letter to Stephen Roskill, 23 Dec. 1957.

pp. 165–6   'Going down bottom first . . .', IWM Balme, pp. 19–21.

p. 166   'to be treated . . .', IWM Funge-Smith, signal from C-in-C WA, 10 May 1941.

pp. 166–7   'He had fought . . .', IWM Fairrie.

pp. 167–8   'missionaries from Japan . . .', IWM Boyce, 7 July 1941.

p. 168   'She staggered . . .', Creighton, *Convoy Commodore*, pp. 144–5.

pp. 168–9   'War brings to a soldier . . .', Morton, *Atlantic Meeting*, pp. 71–2.

p. 169   'I thought . . .', Kennedy, 'The Enemy Within', in Kerr and James (eds.), *Wavy Navy*, p. 127.

p. 169   'I think we were all . . .', Monsarrat, *Three Corvettes*, p. 89.

p. 169   'Properly done . . .', IWM France, p. 25.

p. 170   'Like any new ship . . .', Lombard-Hobson, *A Sailor's War*, p. 54.

p. 170   'I think because we were . . .', Bailey, *Battle of the Atlantic*, p. 140.

p. 170   'Often one had . . .', NMRN Young, p. 47.

pp. 170–71   'Although this job . . .', IWM Scott, H. G., 22 Jan. 1942.

## 9 Terrible Punishment

p. 172   'We are cruising . . .', IWM Walker, 22 May 1941.

pp. 173–4   'Dearest Mum . . .', IWM Crawford, W. M., 18–23 March 1941.

p. 174   'We were drinking . . .', IWM Collett.

p. 174   'We whipped up . . .', IWM Smith, B. W., pp. 2–3.

pp. 174–5   'They were sighted . . .', IWM Collett.

p. 175   'illuminated table . . .', IWM Allen, pp. 13–14.

p. 176   'She was still engaged . . .', IWM Wake-Walker, p. 3.

p. 176   'We must sink *Bismarck* . . .', IWM Flory, 24 May 1941.

p. 176   'We must avenge . . .', IWM Franklin.

pp. 176–7   'I had been standing . . .', IWM Collett.

p. 177   'hot sausages . . .', IWM Smith, B. W., p. 4.

p. 177   'She appeared . . .', IWM Collett.

p. 177   'We could see . . .', IWM Smith, B. W., p. 4.

p. 177   'I saw the flash . . .', IWM Collett.

p. 177   'We made our thanks . . .', IWM Smith, B. W., p. 4.

p. 178   'The bodies were sewn up . . .', IWM Allen, pp. 13–14.

p. 178   'The weather was getting worse . . .', IWM Swanton.

p. 178   'I was told to attack . . .', IWM Stewart-Moore, p. 6.

p. 178   'The waves were so high . . .', IWM Friend, p. 97.

pp. 178–9   'This made landing . . .', IWM Stewart-Moore, p. 5.

p. 179   'awesome in the extreme . . .', IWM Friend, p. 97.

p. 179    'After we had been going . . .', IWM Stewart-Moore, p. 6.

p. 179    'One after another . . .', IWM Swanton.

p. 179    'The rest continued . . .', IWM Stewart-Moore, p. 7.

p. 180    'animated, but lessons were learned', IWM Swanton.

p. 180    'We ran into . . .', IWM Stewart-Moore, p. 11.

p. 180    'In a 4 ship formation . . .', IWM Swanton.

p. 180    'a rather forlorn attack . . .', IWM Stewart-Moore, p. 11.

p. 180    'I pushed the "tit" . . .', IWM Swanton.

p. 180    'dodging like snipe as we went . . .', IWM Stewart-Moore, p. 11.

pp. 180–81    'a series of flashes . . .', IWM Swanton.

p. 181    'a sorry tale . . .', IWM Stewart-Moore, p. 12.

p. 181    'Vesper Jesu . . .', IWM Flory, 25–26 May 1941.

pp. 181–2    'We could see the fall . . .', IWM Morry.

p. 182    'I am going to put . . .', IWM Franklin.

p. 182    'By jove . . .', IWM Flory, 26–27 May 1941.

pp. 182–3    'High seas . . .', SWWEC Kennedy.

p. 183    'The binoculars . . .', IWM Morry.

p. 183    'The battle finished . . .', IWM Franklin.

p. 183    'She put up . . .', IWM Collett.

p. 183    'For a moment . . .', IWM Flory, 26–7 May 1941.

p. 184    'a retinue . . .', Colville, *Fringes of Power*, 3 Aug. 1941; Hastings, *Finest Years*, pp. 191–2.

p. 184    'We crammed in . . .', IWM Allen, p. 15.

p. 185    'Churchill's first draft . . .', IWM Middleton.

pp. 185–6    'O Eternal Lord . . .', Morton, *Atlantic Meeting*, p. 103.

p. 186    'hoisted up to the roof . . .', IWM Allen, p. 16.

p. 187    Admiral Dönitz had recognized . . ., Tooze, *Wages of Destruction*, p. 398.

## 10 Mare Nostrum

pp. 188–90    'It is extraordinary . . .', IWM Blundell, 15 Aug., 1, 3, 4, 17, 18, 19 and 20 Sept. 1940.

p. 191    'the sort of cold . . .', Spector, *At War at Sea*, pp. 166–7.

p. 191    'You will have seen . . .', IWM Power, 13 Nov. 1940.

p. 191    'There is a saying . . .', IWM Thomas, 10 Dec. 1939.

p. 192    'pull a skiff . . .', IWM Friend, p. 64.

p. 192    'It seems to me . . .', letter of 5 Jan. 1941, in Ball, *Bitter Sea*, p. 74.

p. 193    'was hit on the spine . . .', IWM Misc. 223 (3208), 3 March 1941.

p. 194    'one great cloud . . .', IWM Nicholls, 16–19 Jan. 1941.

p. 194    'It was not nice . . .', IWM Blois-Brooke, pp. 89–90.

pp. 194–5    'My worst job . . .', IWM Misc. 223 (3208), 3 March 1941.

p. 195    'Just back from Genoa . . .', IWM Larcom, 11 Feb. 1941.

pp. 195–6    'Immorality is very rife . . .', IWM Hutchinson, 14 March 1941.

p. 196    'Bars, restaurants . . .', IWM Dennis, p. 148.

p. 196    'muttering "King Farouk" . . .', IWM Mosse, p. 44.

p. 197    'Suddenly a hoarse yell . . .', IWM Ruck Keene, 28 March 1941.

pp. 197–8    'We had a most terrific show . . .', IWM Power, 1 April 1941.

p. 198    'The Battle Fleet . . .', IWM Ruck Keene, 28 March 1941.

p. 198    'We collected . . .', IWM Power, 1 April 1941.

p. 198    'when the lads . . .', IWM Hutchinson, 9 April 1941.

pp. 199–200    'the finest lot of fellows . . .', IWM Hutchinson, 27 and 28 April 1941.

pp. 200–201    'I was hardly prepared . . .', IWM Barker, May 1941.

p. 201    'Wherever you looked . . .', IWM Hutchinson, 22 May 1941.

pp. 201–2    'the equivalent of saying . . .', IWM Sear: Manders, 'An Adventure at Crete'.

p. 202    'After leaving the *Gloucester* . . .', IWM Stocken, Owen letter.

p. 202    'No praise . . .', IWM Sear: Manders, 'An Adventure at Crete'.

p. 202    'I lay down . . .', IWM Stocken, Owen letter.

p. 202    'We could almost walk . . .', IWM Sear: Manders, 'An Adventure at Crete'.

pp. 202–3    'with which I had taken . . .', IWM Stocken, Owen letter.

pp. 203–4    'The devils started . . .', IWM Hutchinson, 22 May 1941.

p. 204    'was discovered to be in possession . . .', IWM Stocken, Owen letter.

p. 204    'I was in overalls . . .', IWM Sear: Manders, 'An Adventure at Crete'.

pp. 204–5    'The ship stopped dead . . .', IWM Gardner.

pp. 205–6    'To see those awful sights . . .', IWM Ruck Keene, 22–3 and 24 May 1941.

p. 206    'Once again we have . . .', IWM Speakman, May 1941.

p. 206    'As soon as it was light . . .', IWM Brooks, 12 Feb. 1943.

p. 206    'the soldier has to find . . .', NMRN Lumsden, p. 15.

pp. 207–8   'Ammunition parties . . .', IWM Speakman, May 1941.

p. 208    'We are living . . .', IWM Barker, May 1941.

p. 208    'We spent the night . . .', IWM Hutchinson, 22 May 1941.

p. 208    'I cannot possibly begin . . .', IWM Ruck Keene, 23 May 1941.

pp. 208–9   'There were plenty . . .', Ballantyne, *Warspite*, p. 117.

p. 209    'a most welcome rest.', NMRN Prideaux, p. 41, 7 Dec. 1941.

p. 209    'The anxieties were always present . . .', IWM Balfour, p. 46.

p. 209    'The most common cause . . .', Silvester, 'A Provocative Dose',
          pp. 371–2.

p. 209    'Because you have a fine ship . . .', Winton, *Cunningham*, pp. 215–
          16.

p. 210    'the navy had never yet . . .', Lambert, *Admirals*, p. 404.

p. 210    'A mighty crash . . .', IWM Ruck Keene, 8 June 1941.

p. 210    'British troops reached . . .', IWM Ruck Keene, 23–30 May 1941.

p. 211    'You had an absolute . . .', IWM Dennis.

p. 211    'I hate the desert . . .', IWM Carter, 6 Oct. 1941.

p. 211    'One of my mess-mates . . .', IWM Simkin.

p. 211    'Mrs Miniver . . .', Arthur Kelly, Vice President of United Artists,
          16 Oct. 1942, in Day (ed.), *Letters of Noël Coward*, p. 479.

p. 212    'The nervous strain . . .', IWM Carter, 9 Oct. 1941.

## 11 Under the Rising Sun

p. 213    'Daddy, in his last letter . . .', IWM Haslam, 29 Nov. 1940.

pp. 214–17   'Our ship then gets . . .', IWM Clarke, W. S., May 1941.

p. 218    'The view was terrific . . .', IWM Somers, pp. 11, 14–15.

p. 219    'Persons are allowed . . .', IWM Thomas, 1 Oct. 1940.

p. 219    'In the early morning . . .', IWM Davies, 7 Dec. 1941.

p. 219    'Japan has attacked . . .', Roberts, Midshipman's Journal, 8 Dec.
          1941.

pp. 219–20   'We have only . . .', TNA ADM 205/10 and PREM 3/163/325:
          25 and 29 Aug. 1941.

p. 220    'We had an inflated idea . . .', IWM Allen, p. 22.

p. 220    'I don't think . . .', SWWEC Leach.

p. 221    'It was a glorious day . . .', Buckley, 'A Personal Account', pp. 197–200.

p. 222    'We saw the first . . .', IWM Bell, 17 Dec. 1941.

p. 222    'a great wall of water', IWM Allen, p. 23.

pp. 222–3  'It took me some time . . .', Buckley, 'A Personal Account', pp. 197–200.

p. 223    'She was several miles away . . .', IWM Allen, p. 24.

pp. 223–4  'Although we had been hit . . .', IWM Bell, 17 Dec. 1941.

p. 224    'We on the destroyer . . .', IWM Allen, p. 24.

pp. 224–5  'I decided to jump . . .', IWM Bell, 17 Dec. 1941.

p. 225    Lieutenant Haruki Iki . . . , Marder et al., *Old Friends*, vol. 2, p. 508.

p. 225    'Some did not . . .', Tyrer, *Sisters in Arms*, p. 76.

p. 225    'A great big man . . .', SWWEC Leach.

pp. 225–6  'The discipline and the calmness . . .', IWM Bell, 17 Dec. 1941.

p. 226    'The most depressing news . . .', SWWEC Dowling, 12 Dec. 1941.

p. 226    'There is no further news . . .', Roberts, Midshipman's Journal, 10 Dec. 1941.

p. 226    'I suppose we shall . . .', NMRN Hall, 11 Dec. 1941.

p. 226    'In all the war . . .', Churchill, *Second World War*, vol. 3, p. 620.

p. 226    'Who-ever ordained . . .', IWM Davies, 26 Dec. 1941.

pp. 226–7  'I was too busy . . .', IWM Tyler, R. G., 8–18 Dec. 1941.

p. 227    'As we were leaving . . .', IWM Meadows, 25 Dec. 1941.

pp. 227–8  'I saw several sweating hands . . .', NMRN Hall, 24 and 25 Dec. 1941.

p. 228    'women of all sizes . . .', IWM Barnes, 2 Feb. 1942.

p. 228    'every able-bodied man . . .', IWM Abbott, 14 Feb. 1942.

p. 229    'The Jap naval officer . . .', IWM Briggs, p. 5, 15 Feb. 1942.

p. 229    Mass Observation assessments . . . , MO FR 2332, 'War Morale Chart', 1946; FR 1101, 19 Feb. 1942.

p. 229    'Good god . . .', MO D 5447, 13 Feb. 1942.

pp. 229–30  'the black adhesive . . .', IWM Allen, pp. 26, 28.

pp. 230–31  'The deck beneath our feet . . .', IWM Climie, pp. 4–11.

p. 231    'a curious sort . . .', IWM Allen, p. 30.

p. 231    'I hear the instructions . . .', IWM Climie, p. 12.

p. 232    'Those on the bridge . . .', IWM Allen, p. 30.

p. 232    'The noise changes . . .', IWM Climie, pp. 13–14.

p. 233   'When are we . . .', NMRN Layard, 10 March 1942.

pp. 233–4   'You say that I . . .', IWM Thomas, 7 March 1942.

p. 234   'I have noticed . . .', IWM Thomas, 27 March 1942.


## 12 Dice Loaded


p. 235   'Only one of them . . .', IWM Walker, 24 June 1942.

p. 235   'a most unsound . . .', Woodman, *Arctic Convoys*, p. 9.

p. 235   'the grimmest . . .', IWM Balfour, p. 138.

p. 235   'I felt that if Hell . . .', IWM Dennis, p. 227.

p. 236   'A premature peace . . .', Gilbert, *Churchill: A Life*, p. 703.

p. 236   'Russia was basically . . .', Calder, *People's War*, p. 75.

p. 236   After joining . . . , SWWEC Dormer, p. 16.

p. 236   'Quite a change . . .', IWM Wallace, April 1943.

p. 237   'Attitude to British . . .', IWM Lambert, 20 July 1941.

p. 237   'They are not . . .', Roberts, Midshipman's Journal, 24 July 1942.

p. 237   'A ship's arrival . . .', SWWEC Dormer, 15 Dec. 1941.

p. 237   'Thousands of small herring . . .', IWM Davies, 8 June 1942.

pp. 237–8   'Eight of us . . .', IWM Garnons-Williams, 24 April 1943.

p. 238   'tinned salted pea-nuts . . .', SWWEC Campbell-Begg, 6 Sept. 1942.

p. 238   'Hand messages . . .', IWM Davies, 2 March 1942.

p. 238   'he would probably . . .', *The Times*, 4 April 1942.

pp. 238–9   The rumours that the *Tirpitz* . . .', Roberts, Midshipman's Journal, 5 March 1942.

p. 239   'We sighted *Tirpitz* . . .', IWM Friend, pp. 124–6.

p. 239   'People are apt to say . . .', IWM Davies, 11 March 1942.

p. 239   'Apparently she was . . .', Roberts, Midshipman's Journal, 10 March 1942.

p. 240   Aboard HMS *Norfolk* . . . , IWM Langford, noticeboard cuttings, 1942.

p. 240   'We were certainly . . .', IWM Langford, 'Author's Coversheet'.

p. 240   'Both the Russians . . .', IWM Langford, noticeboard cuttings, 12 April 1942.

p. 240   'There were long periods . . .', IWM Balfour, p. 127.

p. 241   'Never seen anything . . .', IWM Hutchinson, 8 Feb. 1942.

p. 241   'We had to halve . . .', Roberts, Midshipman's Journal, JW57 1944.

p. 241    'long underpants . . .', IWM Neale, pp. 127, 135.

pp. 241–2    'Measures that were taken . . .', Coulter, *Royal Naval Medical Service*, vol. 2, p. 420.

p. 242    'Condensation occurred . . .', IWM Mowlam, p. 68.

p. 242    'It has turned bitter . . .', IWM Marshall, 27–31 Dec. 1942, 1 Jan. 1943.

p. 243    'I know that . . .', IWM Shackleton.

p. 243    'was to prove a test . . .', IWM Balfour, pp. 128–9.

p. 243    'An enormous pillar . . .', IWM Neale, p. 127.

p. 243    'Of course there was nobody . . .', IWM Balfour, p. 140.

pp. 244–5    'The hatch in the deck . . .', IWM Wood, p. 6.

pp. 245–7    'Having a job inside the ship . . .', IWM Kenny, pp. 3–7.

pp. 247–8    'Three merchant ships . . .', IWM Lussey, 23–7 May 1942.

p. 248    'Captain cleared Lower Deck . . .', IWM Edgley, 29 June 1942.

pp. 248–9    'An uneventful day . . .', IWM Shackleton, PQ17 diary.

p. 249    'I don't think firing . . .', IWM Walker, 2 and 3 July 1942.

pp. 249–50    'This was puzzling . . .', IWM Shackleton, PQ17 diary.

p. 250    'The attack was wildly exhilarating . . .', IWM Walker, 5 July 1942.

p. 250    'As some of her crew . . .', IWM Beardmore, p. 5.

pp. 250–51    'I heard the skipper say . . .', IWM Shackleton, PQ17 diary.

p. 251    'owing to threat . . .', Woodman, *Arctic Convoys*, pp. 211–12.

p. 251    'We can't just leave . . .', IWM Beardmore, p. 7.

p. 251    'Good sleep . . .', IWM Edgley, 5 July 1942.

p. 251    'There must be something more . . .', IWM Walker, 6 July 1942.

pp. 251–2    'Particularly poignant . . .', IWM Shackleton, PQ17 diary.

p. 252    'Final result . . .', IWM Langford, 19 July 1942, 'PQ17'.

p. 252    'My impression on seeing . . .', Broome, *Convoy Is to Scatter*, p. 167.

pp. 252–3    'Our "aid to Russia" . . .', Roberts, Midshipman's Journal, 2 Aug. 1942.

p. 253    'We had about 5 minutes . . .', IWM Richardson, Sept. 1942.

p. 253    'Phew! . . .', IWM Hutchinson, 14 Sept. 1942.

pp. 253–4    'one ship had gone . . .', IWM Richardson, Sept. 1942.

p. 254    'We got one . . .', IWM Hutchinson, 14 Sept. 1942.

pp. 254–5    'The seas were mountainous . . .', IWM Hutchinson, 24 Sept. 1942.

pp. 255–6    'I was resting there . . .', IWM Misc. 200 (2930).

p. 256    'Christmas Day . . .', IWM Goodbrand, p. 17.

p. 257    'No posthumous V.C's . . .', IWM Mowlam, p. 60.

p. 257    'My feet are frozen . . .', IWM Somers, p. 37.

p. 257    'Had our imagination . . .', IWM Goodbrand, p. 37–8.

pp. 257–8    'A salvo of 8-inch shells . . .', BBC 'London Calling', 28 March 1943.

p. 258    'jumped to his feet . . .', IWM Goodbrand, p. 38.

pp. 258–9    'The Battle Ensign . . .', IWM Somers, p. 37.

p. 259    'Today came the great news . . .', IWM Davies, 3 Feb. 1943.

p. 260    'Life nowadays is unimaginable . . .', IWM Povey, 1–18 March, 8 and 9 April 1943.

## 13 Fidelity

p. 261    'Up and down the country . . .', NMRN Records, 24 Jan. 1942.

p. 262    'food-wasters . . .', Monsarrat, *Three Corvettes*, pp. 119–22.

p. 262    'There was a nice . . .', SWWEC Breen, pp. 41, 201.

pp. 262–3    'daily arguments . . .', SWWEC Dormer, 'HMS Hornpipe'.

p. 263    'When I returned . . .', IWM Fisher, p. 9.

p. 263    'They came aboard . . .', NMRN Young, p. 51.

p. 264    'I expect there will be . . .', Roberts, Midshipman's Journal, 12 Feb. 1942.

p. 264    'Nothing more mortifying . . .', *The Times*, 14 Feb. 1942.

p. 264    But before long . . . , TNA INF 1/292, 18 and 25 Feb. 1942.

pp. 264–5    'Courageous are the men . . .', LMA LCC/EO/PS/11/011, March 1942.

p. 265    'I sat under it . . .', SWWEC Campbell-Begg, 22 Nov. 1943.

p. 265    'One of his cigar ends . . .', IWM McGregor, 16–26 Oct. 1942.

p. 266    'adopted . . .', IWM Shackleton.

p. 266    'we had packs . . .', IWM Rail.

p. 266    'May this save . . .', IWM Buckle, p. 121.

p. 266    'It was announced . . .', NMRN Layard, 28 March 1942.

p. 267    'All hell broke loose . . .', SWWEC Arkle.

p. 268    In June 1943 . . . , Hastings, *Finest Years*, p. 371.

p. 268    'The newspaper men . . .', SWWEC Campbell-Begg, 5 and 13 Sept. 1941.

p. 268    'War Heroes Talk . . .', *New York Times*, 7 Sept. 1941.

p. 268    'shaking hundreds of hands', IWM Nicholl, p. 121.

pp. 268–9   'Outwardly, it is much like . . .', SWWEC Dowling, 9–19 Sept. 1942.

p. 269   'Half the action . . .', IWM Wight-Boycott, 21–2 July 1942.

p. 270   'the people one met . . .', IWM Dunlop, 3 Sept. 1944.

p. 270   'taken for nurses . . .', IWM Dunkley.

p. 270   'mediocre ability . . .', Marder et al., *Old Friends*, vol. 2, pp. 33–4.

p. 271   'The result should have been . . .', IWM Matthews, 7–8 Aug. 1943.

p. 271   'We were most impressed . . .', Palmer, *Our Penelope*, p. 21.

pp. 271–2   'On paper they have . . .', IWM Davies, 26 Dec. 1941.

p. 272   'the hairy great coconut . . .', IWM Friend, pp. 172–3.

p. 272   'When a large . . .', IWM Aitchison, p. 57.

p. 272   'run by ignorant . . .', IWM Wight-Boycott, 28 Oct. 1942.

p. 273   'This is one . . .', IWM Wight-Boycott, 28 Oct. 1942.

p. 273   'The most beautifullest . . .', IWM Smith, J., 26 Aug. 1940.

p. 274   'We have now captured . . .', IWM Gould, C. A., 7, 11, 13 and 24 May 1942.

p. 274   'a lovely sight . . .', IWM Gould, C. A., 1–2 May 1942.

p. 275   'The surf is good . . .', SWWEC Dowling, 21 Aug. 1942.

p. 276   'a brave imitation . . .', IWM Wight-Boycott, Dec. 1942.

p. 276   'Customs buildings . . .', IWM Smith, J., 16 Nov. 1940.

p. 276   'a dirty, time-wasting business . . .', IWM Calvert, p. 41.

p. 276   'a real pirate crew . . .', SWWEC Breen, p. 55.

p. 277   By the end of the war . . . , Milner, *North Atlantic Run*, pp. 129, 190–92.

pp. 277–8   'it is most necessary . . .', TNA ADM 178/211, 12 July 1940.

p. 278   'No-one on board . . .', IWM Whinney, p. 4; ADM 199/1320, 'War History of HMS Fidelity'.

p. 279   'They are a nice crowd . . .', NMRN Layard, 13 Feb. 1942.

p. 279   'The war is passing . . .', SWWEC Dowling, 1 Aug. 1942.

## 14 *The Land of the Living*

p. 280   'They came right over . . .', IWM Blundell, 27 Sept. 1941.

p. 280   'A blur of action . . .', IWM Gilroy, p. 9.

p. 281   'The explosion blew . . .', IWM Friend.

p. 281   'I was given . . .', IWM Scott, W. I. D., p. 80.

pp. 281–2   'When smoke cleared . . .', NMRN Prideaux, 25 Nov. 1941.

p. 282   'I must keep them . . .', letter of 4 Dec. 1941, in Ball, *Bitter Sea*, p. 122.

p. 282   'It was a heartbreaking situation . . .', IWM Nicholl, p. 80.

p. 283   'I saw an aircraft . . .', *Daily Telegraph*, 10 May 2005; *The Times*, 17 May 2005.

pp. 283–4   'In the middle of the night . . .', SWWEC Dowling, 19 and 20 Dec. 1941, 18 Jan. 1942.

pp. 284–5   'At last I am back . . .', IWM Carter, 14 March 1942.

p. 285   'Entering Malta . . .', SWWEC Dowling, 23 March 1942.

p. 286   'I asked the doctor . . .', IWM Nicholl, p. 109–18.

p. 287   'In the next dock . . .', IWM Davies, 23 April 1942.

p. 288   'The poor old girl . . .', IWM Brighton, p. 14.

p. 289   'I am very pleased . . .', IWM Darling, 25 March 1941.

pp. 289–90   'The mental reaction . . .', IWM Simkin.

p. 290   'I could not see him . . .', SWWEC Dowling, 29 April 1942.

p. 290   'we inspected . . .', SWWEC Dormer, 15 July 1943.

p. 291   'The flash shot . . .', SWWEC Dowling, 16 June 1942.

p. 292   'Just one grouse . . .', IWM Barker, 23 March 1942.

p. 292   'I walked round . . .', SWWEC Dowling, 21 April 1942.

p. 292   'Have started to lay . . .', IWM Barker, 7 June 1942.

p. 292   'Such a lovely place . . .', IWM Morris, Sept.–Oct. 1942.

p. 293   'We weren't told . . .', IWM Barton, 1 Sept. 1942.

p. 293   'I read the orders . . .', IWM Blundell, 3 Aug. 1942.

p. 293   'The biggest that has ever . . .', IWM Barton, 1 Sept. 1942.

pp. 293–4   'We looked quite . . .', IWM Blundell, 9 Aug. 1942.

p. 294   'We left Gib early . . .', IWM Gould, C. A., 11 Aug. 1942.

p. 294   'She was struck . . .', NMRN Lumsden.

p. 294   'One moment there was . . .', IWM Blundell, 11–14 Aug. 1942.

p. 294   'I've got my wallet . . .', IWM Gould, C. A., 11 Aug. 1942.

p. 294   'It was not to be . . .', IWM Blundell, 11–14 Aug. 1942.

p. 295   'Did we put up . . .', IWM Gould, C. A., 11 Aug. 1942.

p. 295   'I have never seen anything . . .', IWM Barton, 1 Sept. 1942.

p. 295   'two of the most . . .', IWM Blundell, 11–14 Aug. 1942.

pp. 295–6   'I'm just about . . .', IWM Gould, C. A., 12 Aug. 1942.

pp. 296–7   'I saw great bits flying . . .', IWM Barton, 1 Sept. 1942.

p. 297   'It was the most terrible sight . . .', IWM Hutchinson, 15 Aug. 1942.

p. 297   'She appeared to go up . . .', IWM Hollings, 1942 account.

pp. 297–8   'So we were in . . .', IWM Barton, 1 Sept. 1942.

p. 298   'We want food . . .', Woodman, *Malta Convoys*, p. 454.

p. 298   'What a tragic failure . . .', IWM Blundell, 11–14 Aug. 1942.

p. 299   'It's a grand feeling . . .', IWM Hutchinson, 15 and 17 Aug. 1942.

p. 299   'Imagine to yourselves . . .', IWM Dickens, 1942 account.

p. 300   'We landed the troops . . .', IWM Morris, Sept.–Oct. 1942.

p. 301   'I am quite well . . .', IWM Evans, 17 Nov. 1942, 21 March 1943.

p. 301   'There is a certain amount . . .', Roberts, Midshipman's Journal, 24 Oct. 1942.

p. 302   'We passed through . . .', IWM Freer Roger, Dec. 1943.

p. 302   'I've never had to deal . . .', IWM Power, 12 Nov. 1942.

p. 303   'In those moments . . .', NMRN Young, p. 54.

pp. 303–4   'not much more . . .', NMRN Layard, 8 Nov. 1942.

p. 304   'Life doesn't get much easier . . .', IWM Power, 21 Nov. 1942.

p. 304   'On the news . . .', Roberts, Midshipman's Journal, 27 Nov. 1942.

p. 305   'Very little to entice . . .', IWM Davies, 30 Nov. 1942.

p. 305   'They never seem . . .', TNA ADM 1/13058, 'Morale of Naval Personnel in North Africa'.

p. 305   'A few nights ago . . .', Roberts, Midshipman's Journal, 18 March 1943.

pp. 305–6   'We were at action stations . . .', IWM Gilroy, pp. 32–8.

p. 306   'much better off . . .', IWM Wight-Boycott, 20 June 1943.

p. 306   'will atrophy your brain . . .', IWM Walker, 2 Aug. 1944.

p. 307   'It is a sad sight . . .', IWM Wight-Boycott, 15 July 1943.

## 15 *Getting the Goods Home*

p. 308   'Well dearest . . .', IWM Gould, C. A., 2 June 1942.

p. 308   'obstacle to victory', Barnett, *Engage the Enemy*, p. 469.

p. 309   'The only thing to do . . .', Roberts, Midshipman's Journal, 2 and 9 Aug. 1942.

pp. 310–11   'These air bursts . . .', IWM Turner, 16 Sept. 1942.

p. 311   'We landed a strong force . . .', SWWEC Adams, 22 Aug. 1942.

p. 312   'The first thing . . .', Roberts, Midshipman's Journal, 22 Sept. 1942.

p. 312    'Our efforts succeeded . . .', IWM Davies, 22 Sept. 1942.

p. 313    'No heroes, these . . .', Monsarrat, *Cruel Sea*, p. 237.

p. 313    'I had clear evidence . . .', IWM Chavasse, E. H., p. 42.

pp. 314–15    'Teeming with rain . . .', IWM Matthews, 16 Oct. 1942.

p. 316    'One had terrible . . .', SWWEC Crang, 30 Oct. 1942.

p. 316    'there was a hole . . .', Sebag-Montefiore, *Enigma*, pp. 220–21.

p. 317    'All hell breaks out . . .', IWM Treadaway, 10 March 1943.

p. 319    'We disposed of that one . . .', Bailey, *Battle of the Atlantic*, p. 52.

pp. 319–20    'Someone speculated . . .', NMRN Lumsden, p. 4.

p. 320    'Among the many myths . . .', Monsarrat, *Monsarrat at Sea*, p. 294.

p. 320    'We must have got . . .', NMRN Layard, 7 Sept. 1942.

p. 320    'Dixon, a first class . . .', IWM Mosse, p. 57.

p. 321    'we had lost . . .', Dönitz, *Memoirs*, p. 341.

p. 322    'Our primary job . . .', IWM Chavasse, E. H., p. 25.

p. 322    'In many ways . . .', IWM France, p. 25.

p. 322    'Whenever I hear . . .', NMRN Layard, 7 July 1942.

p. 323    'Feelings were running . . .', SWWEC Breen, p. 56.

p. 323    'We have no positive . . .', IWM Wight-Boycott, 'H.M.S. Ilex', 1942.

p. 324    'The first ship . . .', SWWEC Pippard, 22 March 1944.

## 16 A Hell of a Battering

pp. 325–6    'The water was like . . .', Place, 'The Midget Attack on Tirpitz', in Winton (ed.), *War at Sea*, pp. 288–95.

p. 327    'Bring light and warmth . . .', IWM Warner.

p. 327    'His speech was a remarkable one . . .', IWM Moran, p. 66.

p. 328    'on the alert . . .', IWM Dunlop: Walker, 'Personal Account', p. 1.

p. 328    'It was hard to believe . . .', IWM Moran, pp. 70–71.

p. 328    'We were all . . .', IWM Tyler, A. J. L., 29 Dec. 1943.

pp. 328–9    'twiddling some knobs . . .', IWM Moran, pp. 68–9, 71–2.

p. 329    'I took up . . .', NMRN Lumsden, p. 38.

p. 329    'It is astonishing . . .', IWM Tyler, A. J. L., 29 Dec. 1943, pp. 2–3.

p. 329    'We spent most of our time . . .', IWM Dunlop, 'Scharnhorst Action', p. 5.

p. 330   'a cup of hot soup . . .', IWM Dunlop: Walker, 'Personal Account', p. 2.

p. 330   'What a chase . . .', IWM Withers, 29 Dec. 1943.

p. 330   'frightened the life . . .', IWM SA Burridge.

pp. 330–31   'We had confidence . . .', in Winton, *Death of the Scharnhorst*, p. 46.

p. 331   'I am up in the front . . .', SWWEC Leach.

p. 331   'This gun action . . .', IWM Chavasse, P. M. B., 30 Dec. 1943.

pp. 331–2   'the range counters, instead . . .', SWWEC Leach.

p. 332   'Dead ahead were the signs . . .', Ramsden, 'Sinking the Scharnhorst', p. 349.

p. 332   'There were flashes . . .', IWM Moran, p. 76.

p. 332   'We closed right in . . .', SWWEC Leach.

pp. 332–3   'Streams of red . . .', IWM Moran, pp. 75–7.

p. 333   'when the action began . . .', in Kemp, *Convoy!*, p. 178.

p. 333   'It was as black . . .', IWM Rodwell.

p. 333   'This was carried out . . .', IWM Chavasse, P. M. B., 30 Dec. 1943.

p. 333   'The guns thundered . . .', IWM Dennis, p. 235.

p. 334   'on fire from bow . . .', IWM SA Burridge.

p. 334   'What a sight . . .', IWM Rodwell.

p. 334   'Gosh, that gave me . . .', IWM Chavasse, P. M. B., 30 Dec. 1943.

p. 334   'We had to fire . . .', IWM Palmer, 27 Dec. 1943.

p. 334   'poor devils swimming . . .', IWM Moran, p. 78.

p. 334   'I thought how lucky . . .', IWM Withers, 29 Dec. 1943.

p. 334   'It was a ticklish job . . .', IWM Rodwell.

pp. 334–5   'The excitement on board . . .', IWM Dunlop: Walker, 'Personal Account', p. 5.

p. 335   'I certainly personally . . .', SWWEC Leach.

p. 335   'It's the thought . . .', IWM Dunlop, 'Scharnhorst Action', pp. 3–4.

p. 335   'We were lucky . . .', IWM Moran, p. 80.

p. 335   'I've got to hand it . . .', IWM Withers, 29 Dec. 1943.

p. 335   'heartbreaking . . .', IWM Cree.

p. 335   'last battle of the dinosaurs', Winton (ed.), *War at Sea*, p. 306.

p. 336   'Everybody was calm . . .', IWM Withers, 29 Dec. 1943.

p. 336   'The behaviour of . . .', IWM Walmsley, 28 Dec. 1943.

p. 336   'One chap had . . .', IWM Withers, 29 Dec. 1943.

p. 336   'I shall never forget . . .', IWM Chavasse, P. M. B., 30 Dec. 1943.

p. 337    'The essential thing . . .', IWM Dunlop, 'Scharnhorst Action', p. 4.

p. 337    'When we arrived . . .', IWM Rodwell.

p. 337    'That's another Jerry . . .', IWM Gould, E. R., 4 Jan. 1944.

p. 337    'We had our xmas . . .', IWM Withers, 29 Dec. 1943.

p. 337    Christmas menu . . . , IWM Misc. 225 (3231).

p. 337    'I shall get . . .', IWM Moran, pp. 79–80.

pp. 338–9   'A glorious day . . .', IWM Walker, 19–28 Feb., 1–3 April 1944.

p. 339    'The state of the sea . . .', Roberts, Midshipman's Journal, 1944.

pp. 339–41   'Lt Smythe was killed . . .', IWM Cockrell, 6–27 Feb., 1 March
1945.

## 17 Jack in Joe's Land

p. 342    'It was about . . .', IWM Hadden, pp. 4–5.

p. 343    'very bleak . . .', IWM SA Sullivan.

p. 343    'This isolation . . .', TNA ADM 119/1104, 'Report of Proceedings,
1 to 31 August 1943'.

p. 344    'The atmosphere there . . .', IWM SA Downing.

p. 344    'At a rough estimate . . .', TNA ADM 119/1104, 'Murmansk'.

p. 344    'a hole', IWM Povey, 20 Jan. 1943.

p. 344    'I went into one . . .', IWM SA Swales.

pp. 344–5   'We had a Russian housekeeper . . .', IWM SA Johnston.

p. 345    'The surrounding country . . .', IWM Garnons-Williams, 26 Feb.
1943.

p. 345    'The only presentable building . . .', IWM Moran, p. 69.

p. 345    'The impression I got . . .', IWM SA Greenfield.

p. 345    'little sledges . . .', IWM SA Swales.

p. 345    'They were just like animals . . .', IWM SA Grenfell.

p. 346    'It was like somebody . . .', IWM SA Johnston.

p. 346    'There was a bloke . . .', IWM SA Price.

p. 346    'It was a poor place . . .', Stuart White, *HMS Norfolk*, p. 22.

p. 346    'Polyarnoe was just . . .', IWM SA Sullivan.

p. 347    'A number of people . . .', IWM Kenny, p. 7.

p. 347    'The washing facilities . . .', IWM SA Collins.

p. 347    'We could never build up . . .', IWM SA Johnston.

p. 348   'This place is incredible . . .', TNA ADM 199/1104, 'Report of Proceedings 26 July–31 Aug. 1942', 10 Oct. 1942, p. 5; TNA ADM 199/606, 'General Survey of the Situation at Murmansk', 26 Aug. 1941, p. 2.

p. 348   'We had two wards . . .', IWM SA Greenfield.

p. 348   One British report . . . , TNA ADM 119/1104, 'Murmansk', part 2, p. 3.

p. 348   'Our food was pretty stodgy . . .', IWM SA Johnston.

p. 349   'We were down to bully beef . . .', IWM SA Seal.

p. 349   'It was dreadful . . .', IWM SA Grenfell.

p. 349   'Couple of slices . . .', IWM SA Collins.

p. 349   'They had been standing . . .', IWM SA Downing.

p. 349   'They just tilted . . .', IWM Hutchinson, 23 June 1942.

p. 350   'Our entertainment . . .', IWM SA Greenfield.

p. 350   'put to shame . . .', IWM Dennis, p. 222.

p. 350   '1st D.K.A . . .', TNA ADM 199/1104, '25th Monthly Report', 3 Oct. 1943.

p. 350   'On the evening . . .', TNA ADM 199/1104, 'Northern Light', no. 2, May 1943.

p. 351   'It was based . . .', IWM SA Johnston.

p. 351   'The Russians themselves . . .', IWM Herbert Smith, 1 March 1943.

p. 351   'The Russian sailors . . .', IWM SA Downing.

p. 351   'was overflowing with vodka . . .', IWM SA Collins.

p. 351   'They would pat us . . .', IWM SA Downing.

pp. 351–2   'I bought a Russian fur hat . . .', IWM Marshall.

p. 352   'How many destroyers . . .', IWM Hadden, p. 15.

p. 352   'The Soviet authorities . . .', TNA ADM 178/319, Fisher Report, 12 Sept. 1943.

p. 352   'Buzz is that . . .', IWM Cree, 28 Jan. 1944.

p. 352   'putting a girl . . .', TNA ADM 119/1104, '25th Monthly Report', 3 Oct. 1943.

p. 352   'Russian officers . . .', IWM Langford.

pp. 352–3   Tales of brutality . . . , Woodman, *Arctic Convoys*, pp. 112–13.

p. 353   'The situation can be summed up . . .', TNA ADM 199/1104, '21st Monthly Report', 31 May 1943; 'Report of Proceedings', 7 Sept. 1943.

p. 353   'It directs how . . .', TNA ADM 199/1104, 'Report of Proceedings, 22 Nov.–26 Dec. 1943', p. 5.

p. 353   'running amok . . .', TNA ADM 1/13144, DNI, 30 Dec. 1943.

p. 354 'Ryan objected strongly . . .', TNA ADM 199/606, 'Vexatious Formalities in North Russia', 16 Sept. 1943; ADM 119/1104, '25th Monthly Report', 3 Oct. 1943.

p. 354 'Soviet Authorities . . .', TNA ADM 1/13144, 12 Jan. 44.

p. 354 'hooliganism . . .', TNA ADM 199/1104, 'Report on Proceedings', 7 Sept. 1943.

p. 355 Overseas League . . . , TNA ADM 199/604, SBNO to Admiralty, 12 June 1942.

p. 355 Although the Royal Navy . . . , TNA ADM 199/1104, '25th Monthly Report', 3 Oct. 1943.

p. 355 'all the Russian Admirals . . .', IWM Clarke, A. J., 25 July 1943.

p. 356 'I got the feeling . . .', IWM SA Taylor.

p. 356 'There is no doubt . . .', TNA ADM 199/1104, 'Report of Proceedings, 1st to 31st August 1943', 7 Sept. 1943.

p. 356 'no one who has served . . .', TNA ADM 199/1104, '30th Monthly Report of Proceedings', 31 March 1944.

p. 356 'I had a hatred . . .', IWM SA Seal.

p. 356 'If we did take any . . .', IWM Shackleton.

p. 356 'Anglo-Russian relations . . .', TNA ADM 199/604, 'Some Aspects of British Relations with the U.S.S.R.', 16 June 1943.

p. 357 'Mr Stalin made . . .', TNA ADM 178/319, 12 Sept. 1943.

p. 357 'if only our people . . .', TNA ADM 199/606, 22 Oct. 1943.

p. 357 'however long retired . . .', TNA ADM 199/605, Archer, 'Murmansk Convoy Season 1943/44', 31 Jan. 1944.

p. 357 'no "camaraderie" exists . . .', TNA ADM 199/605, 'Archangel', 19 Sept. 1944; DNI, 28 Sept. 1944; BNLO report, 12 Sept. 1944, p. 7.

p. 358 'humiliating . . .', TNA ADM 199/604, 'Russian Obstruction to Operation of Northern Convoys', 26 Feb. 1943.

p. 358 'We all thought . . .', IWM Clarke, A. J., 10 Oct. 1943.

p. 359 'I couldn't hang on . . .', IWM Hadden, p. 10.

## 18 City of Ships

p. 360 'Bombing raids . . .', SWWEC Campbell-Begg, 21–6 June 1943.

p. 360 'A gloomy place . . .', IWM Wight-Boycott, 5 June, 9 July 1943.

pp. 361–2 'It is blazing hot . . .', IWM Blundell, 9 July 1943.

p. 362 'The grim preamble . . .', IWM Brown, p. 140.

pp. 362–3 'Tat-Tat-Tat-Tat . . .', IWM Oakley, 10 July 1943.

p. 363 'By this time . . .', IWM Wight-Boycott, 15 July 1943.

p. 364 'everything was fairly quiet . . .', IWM Hibbit, 10–14 July 1943.

p. 365 'I believe these . . .', IWM Blundell, 10–11 July 1943.

p. 365 'It was almost unreal . . .', 11 July 1943, in Barnett, *Engage the Enemy*, p. 644.

p. 365 'On our way round . . .', SWWEC Crang, July 1943.

p. 365 'This seems the first . . .', IWM Wight-Boycott, 26 July 1943.

p. 366 'We hoisted our battle ensign . . .', Hobday, *Harm's Way*, pp. 143–4.

p. 366 'one hell of a shambles', IWM Williams, J. E., 9 Sept. 1943.

p. 366 'weak threads in our plans . . .', IWM Blundell, 9 Sept. 1943.

pp. 366–7 'We are not getting things . . .', IWM Wilson, K., 9 Sept. 1943.

p. 367 'This place certainly looks . . .', IWM Huntbatch, 12 Sept. 1943.

pp. 368–9 'It might have been paraded . . .', IWM Blundell, 12 and 29 Sept. 1943.

pp. 369–70 '*Panther* was hit . . .', SWWEC Crang, 12 and 26 Oct. 1943.

p. 370 'As we were severely rationed . . .', Hobday, *Harm's Way*, p. 161.

pp. 370–71 'It was fun . . .', IWM Drax, 18 Nov., 1 Dec. 1943.

pp. 371–2 'Armistice day . . .', IWM Wight-Boycott, 11 Nov. 1943.

p. 372 'D-Day evening . . .', SWWEC Dormer, 21 Jan. 1944.

p. 372 'we thought it was the real thing . . .', Roberts, Midshipman's Journal, 1944.

p. 373 'I have already evacuated . . .', Hastings, *Finest Years*, pp. 385–6.

p. 373 'In this two-week period . . .', IWM SA Le Roy.

p. 373 French civilians . . . , TNA ADM 199/1653, 'Possible evacuation of refugees . . .'

p. 374 'It was just breaking dawn . . .', IWM SA Capon.

p. 374 'The scene in the Solent . . .', Roberts, Midshipman's Journal, 1944.

p. 375 'To what a world . . .', IWM Airth, 2 and 3 June 1944.

p. 375 'The Allies were about . . .', IWM Buckle, p. 120.

p. 375 'The ship has a terrific . . .', IWM Airth, 5 June 1944.

p. 376 'I thought . . .', IWM SA Honour.

p. 376 'It is to be our privilege . . .', Special Order of the Day, 31 May 1944, reproduced in *Naval Review*, 82, 2 (1944).

pp. 376–7  'By all appearances . . .', IWM Povey, 5 June 1944.

p. 377  'During the hours . . .', IWM Main.

p. 377  'if you can imagine . . .', IWM Pelly, 12 June 1944.

p. 378  'A quarter past five . . .', Roberts, Midshipman's Journal, 1944.

p. 378  'Fear . . . ,' IWM Pelly, 12 June 1944.

p. 378  'It was too late . . .', Roberts, Midshipman's Journal, 1944.

pp. 378–9  'It was all one mass . . .', IWM SA Rose.

p. 379  'In the distance . . .', Roberts, Midshipman's Journal, 1944.

p. 379  'We were so close . . .', IWM Pelly, 12 June 1944.

p. 379  'Wherever we're going . . .', IWM Povey, 6 June 1944.

p. 380  'The weather beat us . . .', TNA ADM 199/1650, 'Interrogation Reports'.

pp. 380–81  'We had a grandstand view . . .', IWM Pelly, handwritten account, p. 7.

p. 381  'This has indeed . . .', IWM Airth, 6 June 1944.

p. 381  'I can still see . . .', IWM SA Green.

pp. 381–2  'Rocket ships astern . . .', TNA ADM 199/1650, 'Interrogation Reports'.

p. 382  'a pin-prick . . .', IWM Dennis, p. 257.

p. 382  'A sight hard to credit . . .', IWM Povey, 7 June 1944.

p. 382  'The sea is covered . . .', IWM Matthews, 8 June 1944.

p. 382  'A Canadian killed . . .', IWM Povey, 8 June 1944.

p. 383  'There were some ghastly . . .', IWM Airth, 12 June 1944.

p. 383  'It is a wonderful sight . . .', Hastings, *Finest Years*, p. 489.

pp. 383–4  'There were many rumours . . .', IWM Moran, pp. 111–13.

p. 384  'mortuary ship . . .', IWM Pelly, handwritten account, p. 9.

p. 384  'Approximately eighteen . . .', TNA ADM 199/1652, Report 171440/August 1944.

p. 384  'Today brings us relief . . .', IWM Povey, 23–5 June 1944.

p. 385  'difficulty was found . . .', TNA ADM 199/1651, Sillitoe, LCS (M) 74.

pp. 385–6  'Am about to remove . . .', IWM Airth, 3 Aug. 1944.

p. 386  'Because it all went so smoothly . . .', Barnett, *Engage the Enemy*, p. 837.

## 19 A Routine for Everything

p. 387    'He had run away . . .', IWM Blundell, 24 Aug. 1943.

p. 387    'The Navy lives . . .', Moran, *Anatomy of Courage*, pp. 100–101.

p. 387    'It is the men . . .', IWM Duckworth, 'Notes on Discipline', p. 1.

p. 387    'The finest ships . . .', 'Quirt', 'Man or Machine?', pp. 241–3.

pp. 387–8    'Every man is not . . .', McDowall, 'Morale', pp. 19–22.

p. 389    Amenities Liaison Officers . . . , TNA ADM 1/24362, 'Welfare Services', pp. 1–2; Blacklock, 'Welfare Services of the Navy', p. 169.

p. 390    'As far as you are . . .', IWM King.

pp. 390–91    'impending tragedy . . .', TNA ADM 178/292, 'Objection to proposed marriage . . .', 5 Aug. 1943.

p. 391    'Ashore, matelots . . .', IWM Booth, p. 38.

p. 391    'Hope you are . . .', IWM Woolf, 25 Sept. 1939.

p. 391    'We bid each other . . .', SWWEC Pippard, 3 June 1943.

p. 391    Family Welfare Centres . . . , TNA ADM 1/24362, 'Welfare Services', p. 4; ADM 182/110–121: AFOs 2028/42, 2746/42, 1798/44, 2587/44, AFO 133/45.

p. 392    'Nothing upsets . . .', IWM Blundell, 17 May 1940.

p. 392    'criticisms of war operations . . .', TNA ADM 234/4, 'Censorship', pp. 11–12.

p. 392    'The Doctor as censor . . .', IWM Wight-Boycott, 7 Sept. 1943.

p. 392    'used to skim them . . .', NMRN Barwell, p. 53.

p. 392    'I was very conscientious . . .', SWWEC Dormer.

p. 393    'The troops hate . . .', IWM Blundell, 10 Sept. 1939.

p. 393    'learnt much about . . .', IWM Scott, W. I. D., p. 71.

p. 393    'in as private . . .', TNA ADM 234/4, 'Censorship', p. 4.

p. 393    'In doing this . . .', IWM Warner, circular letter, 30 Aug. 1940.

p. 393    'It is quite a moving sound . . .', IWM Blundell, 2 June 1940.

p. 394    'Received another card . . .', IWM Osborne, p. 100.

p. 394    navy's medical organization . . . , Coulter, *Royal Naval Medical Service*, vol. 1, p. 3.

p. 394    'I did not want to go . . .', NMRN Barwell, p. 41.

p. 394    'dismissed the Army . . .', IWM Balfour, p. 9.

p. 395    'Lights are out . . .', D'Arcy, 'The Casualties of War', p. 117.

p. 395   'Our one duty . . .', Dudley, 'The Prevention of Venereal Disease', p. 253.

p. 395   'Big ships and barges . . .', IWM Balfour, p. 46.

p. 396   'The most common cause . . .', Silvester, 'A Provocative Dose', pp. 371–4.

p. 396   'I raced forward . . .', IWM Crabbie, p. 20.

p. 397   'he felt always in communication . . .', Anderson, 'Abnormal Mental States in Survivors', pp. 361–77.

p. 397   '[T]hey swam round . . .', Monsarrat, *Cruel Sea*, pp. 285–6.

p. 397   'the thing that always . . .', in Bailey, *Battle of the Atlantic*, pp. 74–5.

p. 398   'youngster sitting on a mess table . . .', NMRN Bushell, 18 May 1940.

p. 398   'With knowledge . . .', TNA FD 1/7025, Medical Research Council: Committee on Care of Shipwrecked Personnel; ADM 298/78, 'Personnel Research in the Royal Navy 1939–1945', pp. 2–3; FD 1/7025, Critchley, 'Interim Report Based on Survivors' Stories', 11 March 1942, pp. 1–4; FD 1/7025, 'A Guide to the Preservation of Life at Sea after Shipwreck', pp. 1–3.

p. 399   'an indefinable air . . .', TNA ADM 1/27768, 'Observations on Morale in a Battleship' and 'The Management of Survivors'.

pp. 399–400   'It is a distressing fact . . .', IWM Wight-Boycott, 11 Nov. 1942.

p. 400   'Serenely, he handed it over . . .', SWWEC Breen, pp. 162–3.

p. 400   'The great danger . . .', Curran, 'Functional Nervous States', p. 220; see also Curran, 'Operational Strain: Psychological Casualties in the Royal Navy', p. 233; Jones and Greenberg, 'Royal Naval Psychiatry', p. 200.

pp. 400–401   '"Back to duty" . . .', Danson, 'The Effort Syndrome', p. 109; Forbes, 'Effort Syndrome', p. 169.

p. 401   'There is no reason . . .', Anderson, 'Hysteria in War-Time', pp. 147–8.

p. 401   'getting contaminated . . .', Winton, *Cunningham*, p. 361.

p. 401   'Had we grounded . . .', IWM Scott, W. I. D., p. 64.

p. 401   Shore-based specialists . . . , TNA CAB 21/2548, 'Neuropsychiatry – Royal Navy', Appendix II; Coulter, *Royal Navy Medical Service*, vol. 1, pp. 154–5; TNA ADM 1/12067, 'Organization for Handling Nervous and Mental Diseases in the Royal Navy', p. 1.

p. 401   'to render the maximum . . .', Garmany, 'Psychiatry under Bar-
         racks Conditions', p. 164.

p. 402   'useful service employment', Forbes, 'The Rehabilitation of
         Neuropsychiatric Cases at a Royal Naval Auxiliary Hospital', pp. 206–
         14; Coulter, *Royal Naval Medical Service*, vol. 1, p. 154.

p. 402   'One finds it difficult . . .', IWM Rail.

p. 402   'I do not trust him . . .', Knight, 'Now I Know', in Winton (ed.),
         *War at Sea*, pp. 268–9.

pp. 402–3  'The strain of four years . . .', IWM Rambaut, p. 37.

p. 403   'I had a doctor . . .', SWWEC Anderson, p. 17.

p. 403   'It was no good . . .', Wallis, *Two Red Stripes*, pp. 72–3.

pp. 403–4  'Contrary to general belief . . .', TNA ADM 116/5559, MDG
         memo, 10 June 1943.

p. 404   'Just remember . . .', Monsarrat, *Cruel Sea*, p. 138.

## *20 Jimmy the Bastard*

p. 405   'He's so exact . . .', IWM Gould, C. A., 22 May, 2 and 26 June 1942.

p. 406   'Trouble with the crew . . .', SWWEC Dormer, 16 Oct., 22 Nov.
         1943, 17 Jan. 1944, 12 Dec. 1943.

p. 407   'the lack of knowledge . . .', IWM Duckworth; Admiralty Letter
         11957/43, 22 Sept. 1943.

p. 408   'What we have to show . . .', IWM Duckworth; 'Notes on Dis-
         cipline', 2 March 1944.

p. 408   'a ship is either . . .', Pelly, 'Officer's Aide Memoire', p. 17.

p. 408   '"You will not . . ."', Lombard-Hobson, *A Sailor's War*, p. 154.

p. 409   The court martial . . . , Sears, 'Discipline', pp. 40–44; Lavery,
         *Churchill's Navy*, pp. 118–19.

p. 409   'It acted as a disgrace . . .', IWM Blundell, 'Naval Anecdotes', 7 and
         8.

p. 409   'Summary justice . . .', 'G. H. S.', 'Some Advice to a Young
         Destroyer Captain', p. 214.

p. 409   'fighting drunks . . .', IWM Moran, p. 123.

p. 410   'CDA . . .', *King's Regulations*, Articles 1387–8, 1585–6; TNA AFO
         2739/44, 'Venereal Diseases – Guidance for Lectures On', 25 May 1944.

p. 410   Official figures . . . , Mellor (ed.), *Medical History*, p. 15.

p. 410 'really against your finer . . .', TNA ADM 101/565, Fourth Quarter 1940, 1 Oct. to 31 Dec.

p. 410 'One of the first men . . .', IWM Balfour, p. 70.

pp. 410–11 'Not only is it in bounds . . .', IWM Hughes, 5 April 1945.

p. 411 'Unnatural Offences', TNA ADM 182/127, CAFO 648/40, 25 April 1940.

p. 411 Official regulations . . . , Costello, *Love, Sex, and War*, pp. 156–71.

p. 411 'evil men . . .', NMRN Harris, pp. 119–20.

p. 411 'Met my first . . .', NMRN Butcher, 28 Feb. 1942.

p. 411 'I say nothing . . .', NMRN Hall, 5 Nov. 1941.

p. 412 'Theft on board . . .', NMRN Nodder, vol. 1, p. 7.

p. 412 'It was a nightmare . . .', IWM Swinley, p. 104.

p. 412 'A mutiny it certainly was . . .', Winton, *Cunningham*, p. 52; see also Bell, 'Royal Navy and the Lessons of the Invergordon Mutiny'.

p. 413 'Notes on Dealing with Insubordination', TNA ADM 178/133.

p. 413 'more analogous to . . .', TNA ADM 178/180, Report, 26 Oct. 1936; Carew, *Lower Deck*, p. 214; TNA ADM 178/190 and 178/191; ADM 1/10277, 'Mass Indiscipline', Feb. 1938, p. 1.

p. 413 'It should be impossible . . .', TNA ADM 1/10277, 8 Sept. 1937, pp. 3–4.

p. 414 'on strike . . .', Connell, *Jack's War*, pp. 174–6; Lavery, *Churchill's Navy*, p. 121.

p. 414 'backward', TNA ADM 178/298, 24 Nov. 1942, 8 April 1943.

p. 414 'unhappy ship', TNA ADM 178/349, Report, 7 Sept. 1944.

pp. 415–15 'unusually lacking . . .', TNA ADM 178/364A, Board of Enquiry, 11 Dec. 1944.

p. 415 'It is not surprising . . .', TNA ADM 178/238, Director of Service Conditions, 1 Nov. 1945.

p. 415 'We have seldom . . .', TNA ADM 1/22967, 16 March 1944.

p. 415 'Notes on Dealing . . .', TNA ADM 1/22967, 'Morale in the RN', 'Notes', p. 3.

pp. 416–17 HMS *Lothian* . . . , TNA ADM 178/237: Board of Enquiry; ADM 116/6423, ADM 178/258B and ADM 178/259: Courts Martial.

pp. 417–18 '<u>Nothing</u> I had been taught . . .', IWM Prentice, p. 4.

p. 418 'Extra guard . . .', TNA ADM 178/237: Board of Enquiry.

p. 418 'As a mutiny . . .', TNA ADM 178/237, memo 8 Feb. 1945.

p. 418 'Apart from the ringleaders . . .', TNA ADM 178/237, FOIC Force X Report, p. 1.

p. 419 'lack of belief . . .', Glenton, *Mutiny in Force X*, pp. 226–8.

p. 419 'It appears to have escaped . . .', IWM Duckworth, 'Japan', 8 Feb. 1943.

p. 419 'of even greater concern . . .', TNA ADM 1/13143, Director of Plans, 26 Jan. 1943; Minutes, 11 March 1943; Director of Personal Services, memo, 7 Feb. 1943.

pp. 419–20 'It cannot be too strongly . . .', TNA ADM 1/18872, 'Adult Education in Far Eastern Affairs, Remarks . . .', FONAC, docket 5 Sept. 1944.

p. 420 'one war . . .', TNA ADM 1/16807, MISC First Interim Report, p. 3.

p. 420 'When the war with Germany . . .', Tunstall, *Ocean Power Wins*, pp. v–x.

p. 420 'sell the British Navy . . .', TNA ADM 1/19195, Report, p. 17.

pp. 420–21 'Upon the effectiveness . . .', TNA ADM 1/18872, Admiralty letter, 30 March 1944.

p. 421 'What are we to do . . .', IWM Duckworth, 'Discussion Group', 9 Dec. 1943.

p. 421 'the power of the vote . . .', TNA ADM 1/18872, 'Dover Command', FO/C Dover, docket 1 Nov. 1944.

p. 422 'We decided to take . . .', Hobday, *Harm's Way*, pp. 181–8.

pp. 422–3 'four months of mental struggle . . .', IWM Waymouth, vol. 2, pp. 92–101.

## 21 By Hook or by Crook

pp. 424–5 'Getting bored with it . . .', NMRN Parker, 18 Feb., 6–7 and 19–20 March, 3 April 1944.

p. 425 'The dawns and sunsets . . .', SWWEC Turner, Jan. 1943.

p. 425 'The sand is dazzling . . .', SWWEC Crang, 9 Feb. 1944.

p. 426 'a clean and somewhat . . .', SWWEC Crang, 9 Feb. 1944.

p. 426 'I had never . . .', IWM Hughes, 20 Nov. 1944.

p. 426 'flamboyant butterflies . . .', IWM Walker, 13 Oct. 1944.

p. 427    'Scapa with palm trees', in Ballantyne, *Warspite*, pp. 154–5.

p. 427    'The swaying palms . . .', IWM Pollard, 'Trincomalee: A Drip'.

p. 427    'This place seems . . .', IWM Hooper, 22 Feb. 1944.

p. 427    'Very few of us . . .', IWM Pratt, p. 9.

pp. 427–8    'red splodges on the pavement . . .', IWM Wilson, C. A., 25 April 1944.

p. 428    'overlooking Kandy lake . . .', IWM Dunkley, pp. 6–9.

pp. 428–9    'These Tamils . . .', IWM Hughes, 13 Oct. 1944; 28 May 1945.

p. 429    'crowds literally lined . . .', IWM Andrews, 'Journal of a tour made in India, from August to September 1941'.

pp. 429–30    'This certainly is . . .', SWWEC Turner, 12, 15 and 29 Jan. 1943.

pp. 430–31    'We discussed Nationalisation . . .', IWM Hughes, 5 Oct. 1944.

p. 431    'Education and schools . . .', IWM Wilson, C. A., 10 March 1945.

p. 431    'Capper, I think . . .', IWM Walker, 23 Oct., 19 Nov. 1944.

pp. 431–2    'There was a Current Affairs . . .', IWM Dennis, p. 268.

p. 432    'Dear friend . . .', IWM Hughes.

pp. 432–3    'They are all so keen . . .', IWM Hughes, 3 Oct., 29 Dec. 1944; 5, 14 and 21 Jan. 1945.

pp. 434–6    'There were a few huts . . .', IWM Hughes, 9 March–5 April 1945.

pp. 436–7    'making a terrific noise . . .', SWWEC Mills, sections 15–16.

pp. 437–8    'Manus is fantastic . . .', IWM Walker, 7 March 1945.

p. 438    'All feeling very gloomy . . .', NMRN Parker, 10 and 16 March 1945.

p. 438    Indeed, by one reckoning . . . , Barnett, *Engage the Enemy*, p. 879.

pp. 439–40    'I got on the tail . . .', in Arthur, *Lost Voices*, p. 513.

p. 440    'Our Lord's resurrection . . .', IWM Gray, 1 April 1945.

p. 440    'Strike at Sakishima . . .', NMRN Parker, 4–5 May 1945.

p. 440    'I helped to bury . . .', IWM Gray, 9 May 1945.

p. 441    'several bodies . . .', IWM Walker, pp. 194–6, 217.

p. 441    '"Sit down, France" . . .', IWM France, p. 87.

pp. 441–2    'At present we are . . .', IWM Airth, 7–10 May 1945.

p. 442    'I walked around . . .', IWM Dennis, pp. 291–2.

pp. 442–3    'Altogether there was a feeling . . .', IWM Calvert.

pp. 443–4    'Very miserable . . .', IWM Edgley, 8 May 1945.

p. 444   'British troops lining . . .', IWM Mullins, p. 82.

p. 444   'Thanksgiving and rejoicing . . .', IWM Pollard, Signal: 2155, 8 May 1945.

p. 444   'For the second time . . .', IWM Pollard, Signal: 1540, 9 May 1945.

pp. 444–5   'Germany forced . . .', IWM Pollard, C-in-C EI, 9 May 1945.

p. 445   'Everyone is full . . .', IWM Wilson, C. A., 8 May 1945.

p. 445   'Thank God . . .', NMRN Butcher, 8, 15 and 17 May 1945.

p. 446   'All is going well . . .', SWWEC Campbell-Begg, 4 June 1945.

p. 446   'Official end . . .', NMRN Parker, 8–9 May 1945.

pp. 446–7   'We have waited . . .', IWM Hughes, 6 May 1945.

p. 447   'on an island . . .', SWWEC Coles.

pp. 447–8   'Almost every boat . . .', IWM Dunlop, 13 June 1945.

p. 448   'Our stay in Germany . . .', IWM Moran, 8 July 1945.

## 22 Even Japan Is Beautiful

p. 449   'Very many of you . . .', IWM Pollard, 'Broadcast Talk to Ship's Company'.

p. 449   'Our War Aims . . .', IWM Pollard, extracts from 'Full Moon'.

p. 451   'the maddest ten minutes . . .', IWM Power, 20 May 1945.

p. 452   'I am keeping . . .', IWM Pollard, 'Captain's Broadcast'.

p. 452   'There was a . . .', SWWEC Campbell-Begg, 24–5 July 1945.

p. 452   'war without mercy', Dower, *War Without Mercy*.

p. 452   'little yellow bastards . . .', Stevens, 'The Faceless Foe'.

pp. 452–3   'spirit of hatred . . .', TNA ADM 1/13143, 'Propaganda . . . Morale of Forces', Director of Plans memo, 26 Jan. 1943; ADM 1/16807, MISC First Interim Report, 20 June 1944, p. 4.

p. 453   'How the Jap Army Fights . . .', TNA STAT 14/1858.

pp. 453–4   'We had a full three minutes . . .', IWM Mullins, pp. 90–93.

p. 454   'Worked like a bastard . . .', IWM Gray, 2 and 20 June 1945.

p. 455   'Where they'll get . . .', IWM Misc. 20 (376), 14 June 1945.

p. 455   'Pity about the U.K. elections . . .', SWWEC Campbell-Begg, 3 July 1945.

p. 456   'Elections in the UK . . .', SWWEC Mills.

p. 456   'That great, clear exposition . . .', IWM Hughes, 6 June 1945.

pp. 456–7   'We had all taken it . . .', IWM Bennett, 'Diary of Events of August 1945'.

p. 457   'Overwhelming Labour victory . . .', IWM Walker, 19 and 28 July 1945.

p. 457   'We met the American . . .', IWM Gray, 16 July, 8 Aug. 1945.

p. 458   'Announced at 09.00 . . .', IWM Edgley, 15 Aug. 1945.

p. 458   'Peace declared . . .', NMRN Parker, 15 Aug. 1945.

p. 458   'Victory over Japan . . .', IWM Gray, 16 Aug. 1945.

pp. 458–9   'There will be deep thankfulness . . .', IWM Pollard, Signal 14 Aug. 1945.

p. 459   'shouts and whistles . . .', IWM Deacon, 14 and 15 Aug. 1945.

p. 459   'The setting . . .', IWM Nicholl, p. 143.

pp. 459–60   'It seems hardly believable . . .', SWWEC Campbell-Begg, 16 Aug., 10, 12 and 27 Sept. 1945.

p. 461   'hitch-hiked his way . . .', IWM Crawford, M. D. S. B.

pp. 461–3 'two small buns . . .', IWM Bennett, 'Diary of Events of August 1945'.

pp. 464–5   'Felt pretty bad . . .', IWM Edgley, 6–7, 8–9 and 15–16 Sept., 23 Sept.–3 Oct. 1945.

p. 465   'I hate to tell you . . .', IWM Pelly, 11 Sept. 1945.

p. 465   'The Third World War', IWM Gelling, 'The Voyage in His Majesty's Ship *Indomitable*'.

pp. 465–6   'Rumours are very strong . . .', IWM Barton, 19 Sept. 1945.

p. 466   'Everyone is fed-up . . .', NMRN Butcher, 24 Dec. 1945.

p. 466   'Embarked 45 Indian . . .', IWM Edgley, 11 and 26 Nov., 25 Dec. 1945.

p. 466   'all the accused . . .', IWM King, 'Report of Proceedings 9 September to 13 October 1945'.

pp. 466–7 'We wandered everywhere . . .', IWM Walker, pp. 254–5.

p. 467   'A week ago . . .', IWM Pelly, 24 Sept. 1945.

pp. 468–9 'Well I can't say . . .', IWM Woolf, 4 June, 7 Sept. 1946.

## 23 Epilogue

p. 470   'One more word . . .', IWM Bennett, 'Diary of Events of August 1945'.

p. 471   'On the occasion . . .', IWM Walker, p. 262.

p. 472   'We were very hospitably received . . .', IWM Mosse, p. 75.

# Personal Sources

## *Imperial War Museum, Department of Documents*

Abbott, S. S. (89/15/1)

Adams, F. C. M. (67/254/1)

Airth, G. R., Surgeon Lieutenant RNVR (05/63/1)

Aitchison, R., Lieutenant DSC RNVR (91/7/1)

Allen, G. P., Lieutenant RIN (96/6/1)

Anderson, I. M., Lieutenant RN (PP/MCR/17)

Andrews, A. (01/39/1)

Balfour, H. M., Surgeon Lieutenant Commander RNVR (95/23/1)

Balme, D. E., Lieutenant Commander DSC RN (02/2/1)

Barker, W. (04/35/1)

Barnes, G. E. (99/25/1)

Barton, D. E., Commander MVO DSC RN (86/11/1)

Bates, N. W. J. (P188)

Baylis, L. G. (98/23/1)

Beardmore, W. T. J., Lieutenant RNVR (92/45/1)

Bell, L. H., Captain CBE RN (98/1/1)

Bennett, N. J. M., Lieutenant RN (97/41/1)

Blaxland, W. G., Major (83/46/1)

Blois-Brooke, M. S., Lieutenant Commander RD RNR (95/5/1)

Blundell, G. C., Captain CBE RN (98/38/1)

Booth, J. W., OBE (91/17/1)

Boyce, Mrs V. I. (93/18/1)

Boys-Smith, H. G., Captain DSO DSC RD RNR (99/5/1)

Brabyn, Revd F. J. (87/59/1)

Briggs, P. M. (82/24/1)

Brighton, J. C., DSM (94/6/1)

Brodie, W. C., MBE (83/48/1)

Brooks, J. E. (84/13/1)

Brown, D. F. (92/45/1)

Buckle, R. B. (P188)

Bywater, Miss S. (05/62/1)

Calvert, P., Lieutenant RNVR (84/36/1)

Cannon, L. W. (79/27/1)

Carew-Hunt, G. H., Rear Admiral CBE (P422–423 and P423A)

Carter, J. E. N., Sub-Lieutenant RNR (92/45/1 and Con Shelf)

Chavasse, E. H., Commander DSO OBE DSC RN (81/49/1)

Chavasse, P. M. B., Captain CBE DSC RN (81/49/1)

Clarke, A. J. (87/15/1)

Clarke, W. S. (84/12/1)

Clay, R. G. R., Lieutenant Commander MBE RN (92/17/1)

Climie, W. (P138)

Cockrell, P. S., Lieutenant RNVR (92/45/1)

Collett, C. T., Commander OBE RN (95/5/1)

Crabbie, D., Lieutenant DSC RN (02/30/1)

Crawford, Miss M. D. St B. (86/26/1)

Crawford, W. M. (92/27/1)

Cree, P. B., Lieutenant Commander RN (PP/MCR/315)

Darling, G. P., Lieutenant RN (05/63/1)

Davies, J. B. T., Lieutenant RN (92/33/1)

de Chair, H. G. D., Commander DSC RN (P314)

de Winton, F. S. W., Captain RN (85/44/1)

Deacon, Mrs A. D., MBE (89/17/1)

Dennis, J. A. J., Commander DSC RN (95/5/1)

Dickens, D. A. G., Captain (85/24/1)

Dixon, Revd G. W., MA RN (83/9/1)

Doll, Sir W. R. S. (99/63/1)

Drax, Miss D. (92/30/1)

Duckworth, A. D., Captain RN (76/207/3)

Dunkley, Mrs E. W. (02/36/1)

Dunlop, J. C. H., Surgeon Lieutenant RNVR (82/13/1)

Durnford, J. W., Vice-Admiral (PP/MCR/C10)

Earridge, F. W. (85/35/1)

Edgley, W. (94/32/1)

Engler, K. (87/48/1)

Evans, J. W., Lieutenant MBE RN (99/8/8)

Fairrie, C. J. (04/2/1)

Fisher, J. (08/59/1)

Flory, E. H. (87/46/1)

France, S. (82/27/1)

Franklin, A. E. (01/39/1)

Freer Roger, M. (P382)

Friend, C., Lieutenant RN (86/37/1)

Funge-Smith, V., Captain DSO RD RNR (81/49/1)

Gardner, F. S. (96/22/1)

Garnons-Williams, R. L., Captain RN (98/1/1)

Gask, J., Surgeon Lieutenant RNVR (99/6/1)

Gelling, Mrs E. (06/82/1)

Gillett, G. W. (02/56/1)

Gilroy, G. J. (94/32/1)

Goodbrand, D. S. (91/17/1)

Gould, C. A. (02/56/1)

Gould, E. R. (96/22/1)

Gray, N. B. (05/80/1)

Hadden, G. C. L., Sub-Lieutenant RNVR (04/2/1)

Haslam, W. H. (74/134/1)

Herbert Smith, R. W., Lieutenant Commander RN (92/5/1)

Hewett, W. G., Lieutenant Commander, DSC RNVR (94/43/1)

Hibbit, D. A. (89/3/1)

Hollings, H. A. J., Commander
MBE DSC RN (85/24/1)

Holt, R. V., Vice-Admiral CB
DSO MVO (P186)

Hooper, H. F., Lieutenant RNVR
(95/5/1)

Hughes, A. I., Lieutenant Commander DSC RNR (93/1/1)

Huntbatch, K. B. (01/39/1)

Hutchinson, C. E., RNVR
(66/62/1)

James, A. D. (96/21/1)

Johnson A. F. (80/42/1)

Kenny, J. A. P. (92/27/1)

King, H. A., Captain CBE DSO
RN (90/23/1)

Lambert, W. (04/2/1)

Langford, R. S. C., Lieutenant
Commander RN (86/61/1)

Larcom, C. A. A., Captain DSO
RN (99/5/1)

Larios, Hon. Mrs J. E. (94/42/1)

Lawrence, Revd C. P. (01/2/1)

Leach, S. H. (98/3/1)

Lean, E. C. M., Lieutenant RNVR
(01/23/1)

Lehmann, H. F., Lieutenant
Commander RN (99/75/1)

Lussey, J. (92/27/1)

Main, J. W., Lieutenant RN
(66/274/1)

Manisty, P. F., Captain MBE DSC
RN (92/46/1)

Marshall, E. J. (94/32/1)

Matthews, C. L. R. (08/59/1)

McGregor, J. (06/127/1)

McSwiney, J. M., Major DSO MC
(97/36/1)

Meadows, C. (91/14/1)

Middleton, R. G., Lieutenant
Commander DSC RNVR
(94/43/1)

Moran, Lord KCMG (92/45/1)

'Morgan Report' (Miscellaneous 3
(12))

Morris, W. (06/127/1)

Morry, R. J. (05/6/1)

Mosse, J. P., Commander DSC RN
(90/23/1)

Mowlam, J., Commander DSO
RN (92/4/1)

Mullins, J. P., Lieutenant RNVR
(92/27/1)

Neale, J. K., Lieutenant Commander DSC RNVR (98/1/1)

Nicholl, A. D., Rear Admiral CB
CBE DSO (77/122/1)

Norsworthy, L. R., Surgeon
Commander RN (82/13/1)

Oakley, K. G. (96/22/1)

Osborne, H. (87/15/1)

Palmer, E., Captain (85/44/1)

Pelly, J. G., Lieutenant RNVR
(91/15/2)

Phillips, O. W., Rear Admiral CBE
(PP/MCR/153)

Pollard, Revd W. G. (93/9/1)

Potts, A. (06/50/1)

Povey, D. R. (04/35/1)

Power, Sir M., Admiral KCB CBE
DSO (P87)

Pragnell, P. R. (02/30/1)

Pratt, Mrs M. (99/37/1)

Prentice, J. C. E. (94/50/1)

Rail, K. F. W. (03/14/1)

Rambaut, P. M., Lieutenant DSC RN (95/5/1)

Richardson, P. J. (96/21/1)

Rodwell, J. N. (01/39/1)

Rose, E. S. J., Lieutenant RN (99/42/1)

Ross, G. C., Rear Admiral CBE (86/60/1)

Ruck Keene, T., Lieutenant RN (90/24/1)

Scott, H. G., Captain DSC RN (06/127/1)

Scott, W. I. D., Surgeon Commander RNR (99/12/1)

Sear, G. (91/17/1)

Shackleton, V. (96/22/1)

Short, D. G. (02/2/1)

Simkin, C. (91/17/1)

Smith, B. W., Lieutenant Commander RN (85/44/1)

Smith, J. (87/15/1)

Somers, J. W. (05/6/1)

Speakman, H., DSM (91/17/1)

Stewart-Moore, J. A., Commander RN (91/29/1)

Stocken, C. M., Lieutenant Commander DSC RN (02/56/1)

Swanton, F. A., Commander DSO DSC RN (92/5/1)

Swinley, C. S. B., Captain DSO DSC RN (83/44/11, 11A and 11B)

Terry, W. E. (85/24/1)

Thomas, C. R. (79/13/1 and Con Shelf)

Treadaway, G. (89/5/1)

Turner, D. H. H., Captain (01/4/1)

Tyler, A. J. L., Lieutenant Commander RN (96/56/1)

Tyler, R. G. (88/8/1)

Vollans, L. (82/14/1)

Wake-Walker, Sir F., Admiral CBE (88/55/1, 1A and Con Shelf)

Walder, Miss B. (91/37/1)

Walker, R. J. B., Lieutenant RNVR (04/31/1)

Wallace, S. W. (02/2/1)

Walmsley, E. N., Lieutenant Commander DSC RN (05/63/1)

Warner, Revd C. R. (93/9/1)

Waymouth, G. R., Captain CBE RN (87/16/1)

Whinney, P. F., Commander DSC OBE RNVR (78/50/1)

Wight-Boycott, V. A., Captain OBE DSC RN (96/59/6)

Wilkins, W. G. R. (01/2/1)

Williams, B. R. (92/27/1)

Williams, J. E., Captain (03/2/1)

Wilson, Miss C. A. (Con Shelf)

Wilson, K. (67/12/1)

Withers, D. (04/35/1)

Wood, R. J. (89/3/1)

Woolf, D. C., Captain RN (05/10/1 and Con Shelf)

Wright, N., Rear Admiral CB OBE (PP/MCR/364 and P161)

## Imperial War Museum, Sound Archive

Apps, R. (21581)

Auffret, D. V. (10681/4)

Burridge, G. (25217)

Capon, J. (30008)

Coles, V. (13422)

Collins, R. (20612)

Downing, A. (10936)

Green, J. (28401) (Copyright
    Dangerous Films)

Greenfield, G. (20965)

Grenfell, W. (15450)

Honour, G. (9709)

Howard, L. (6837)

Johnston, W. (12259)

Le Roy, R. (20332)

Love, S. (6728)

Price, P. (20817)

Rose, E. (13301)

Seal, J. (12719)

Sullivan, L. (12549)

Swales, J. (15108)

Taylor, S. (19532)

Walsh, R. (27308)

Wells, J. P. (12370)

## National Museum of the Royal Navy, Portsmouth

Barwell, T. (2001.44)

Bowman, S. (1996.195)

Bushell, F. (2004.55/2)

Butcher, D. (2002.39/1)

Hackforth, H. (1998.36/1)

Hall, I. G. (1995.119)

Harris, L. (1999.102)

Layard, A. F. C. (1990.271)

Lumsden, G. (1990.222)

Parker, E. W. (2003.113/1)

Records, E. (2004.40/5)

Robertson, W. (2002.9)

Young, C. C. (1992.63)

## Second World War Experience Centre, Wetherby

Adams, J. H. (2000.617)

Anderson, C. C., Rear Admiral
    (2001.1252)

Arkle, F. W. M. (2005–2803)

Breen D. A. (2001.1275)

Campbell-Begg, R. (2007.446)

Coles, C. (2001.927)

Crang, R. J. (2003.2017)

Ditcham, A. G. F. (2005.2799)

Dormer, Lord G. H. (2003.2423)

Dowling T. B. (2001.957)

Duvall, C. H. (2003.2006)

Hodges, E. M. (2001.1372)

Kennedy, L. (1999.320/321)

Leach, Sir H., Admiral
    (2003.1863/1985)

Loram, Sir D. V., Admiral (2003.2344)

Mills, J. S. (2006.143)

Pippard, C. F. (2002.1507)

Turner, G. I. (2007.639)

## *Private Papers*

Roberts, Rear Admiral J., Midshipman's Journal

# Select Bibliography

## Contemporary Publications

### Articles and Chapters

Note: *JRNMS* is the *Journal of the Royal Naval Medical Service*

Anderson, E. W., 'Abnormal Mental States in Survivors, With Special Reference to Collective Hallucinations', *JRNMS*, 28 (1942), 361–77

——, 'Hysteria in War-Time', *JRNMS*, 27 (1941), 141–9

Blacklock, R. W., 'Welfare Services of the Navy', *Journal of the Royal United Services Institution*, 90 (1945), 169–78

Buckley, K. R., 'A Personal Account of the Sinking of HMS Repulse', *Naval Review*, 30, 3 (1942), 197–200

Curran, D., 'Functional Nervous States in Relation to Service in the Royal Navy' (April 1943), in Tidy (ed.), *Inter-Allied Conferences on War Medicine*, pp. 219–24

——, 'Operational Strain: Psychological Casualties in the Royal Navy' (Feb. 1944), in Tidy (ed.), *Inter-Allied Conferences on War Medicine*, pp. 233–8

D'Arcy, T. N., 'The Casualties of War', *JRNMS*, 26 (1940), 116–22

Danson, J. G., 'The Effort Syndrome', *JRNMS*, 28 (1942), 108–18

Dudley, S., 'The Prevention of Venereal Disease in the Royal Navy' (March 1944), in Tidy (ed.), *Inter-Allied Conferences on War Medicine*, pp. 251–4

Forbes, H. S., 'The Rehabilitation of Neuropsychiatric Cases at a Royal Naval Auxiliary Hospital', *JRNMS*, 30 (1944), 206–14

Forbes, J. R., 'Effort Syndrome', *JRNMS*, 30 (1944), 163–70

'G. H. S.', 'Some Advice to a Young Destroyer Captain', *Naval Review*, 32 (1944), 214–16

Garmany, G., 'Psychiatry under Barracks Conditions', *JRNMS*, 28 (1942), 160–64

'Junior-Senior' [A. D. Duckworth], 'Naval Efficiency and Discipline', *Naval Review*, 32 (1944), 137–46

'K.', 'Crossing the Line in Wartime', *Naval Review*, 29 (1941), 62–6

McDowall, E. B., 'Morale', *Naval Review*, 53 (1965), 19–22

'Quirt', 'Man or Machine?', *Naval Review*, 32 (1944), 241–3

Ramsden, B. B., 'Sinking the Scharnhorst: 26th December 1943', *Black-wood's Magazine*, Nov. 1944, 343–51

Silvester, H. G., 'A Provocative Dose', *JRNMS*, 27 (1941), 371–4


### Books

Anon., *The Royal Navy Today* (London, 1942)

*Appendix to the Navy List* (1939–1945)

Chatfield, A. E. M., *The Navy and Defence: The Autobiography of Admiral of the Fleet Lord Chatfield*, vol. 2: *It Might Happen Again* (London, 1947)

Kennedy, L., *Sub-Lieutenant: A Personal Record of the War at Sea* (London, 1942)

King, C., *Rule Britannia* (London, 1941)

*The King's Regulations and Admiralty Instructions for the Government of His Majesty's Naval Service, Volume I – Articles – 1943* (London, 1944)

Knock, S., *'Clear Lower Deck': An Intimate Study of the Men of the Royal Navy* (London, 1932)

Mallalieu, J. P. W., *Very Ordinary Seaman* (London, 1944)

Monsarrat, N., *Three Corvettes: Comprising H.M. Corvette, East Coast Corvette, Corvette Command* (London, 1945)

Moran, C. M. W., *The Anatomy of Courage* (London, 1945)

Morton, H. V., *Atlantic Meeting* (London, 1944)

O'Conor, R., *Running a Big Ship on 'Ten Commandments'* (Portsmouth, 1937)

Palmer, J. E. I. (anon.), *Our Penelope* (New York, 1942)

Pelly, J. N., 'An Officer's Aide Memoire' (1943); reproduced in B. Lavery (ed.), *The Royal Navy Officer's Pocket Book, 1944* (London, 2007)

Scott, P., *The Battle of the Narrow Seas* (London, 1945)

Tidy, H. L. (ed.), *Inter-Allied Conferences on War Medicine, 1942–1945: Convened by the Royal Society of Medicine* (New York, 1947)

Tunstall, B., *Ocean Power Wins* (London, 1944)

———, *World War at Sea* (London, 1942)

# Official Histories

Central Statistical Office, *Fighting With Figures: A Statistical Digest of the Second World War* (London, 1995; updated version of *Statistical Digest of the War*, London, 1951)

Coulter, J. L. S., *The Royal Naval Medical Service*, 2 vols. (London, 1954–6)

MacNalty, A. S. and W. F. Mellor (eds.), *Medical Services in War: The Principal Medical Lessons of the Second World War* (London, 1968)

Mellor, W. F. (ed.), *Medical History of the Second World War: Casualties and Medical Statistics* (London, 1972)

Roskill, S. W., *The War at Sea, 1939–1945*, 4 vols. (London, 1954–61)

# Secondary Sources

## Articles, Chapters and Theses

Bell, C. M., 'The Royal Navy and the Lessons of the Invergordon Mutiny', *War in History*, 12 (2005), 75–92

Colville, Q., 'Jack Tar and the Gentleman Officer: The Role of Uniform in Shaping the Class and Gender-Related Identities of British Naval Personnel', *Transactions of the Royal Historical Society*, 13 (2003), 105–29

Connelly, M., 'Battleships and British Society, 1920–1960', *International Journal of Naval History*, 3 (2004)

Goddard, A. H., 'Operational Fatigue: The Air Branch of the Royal Navy's Experience during the Second World War', *Mariner's Mirror*, 91 (2005), 52–66

Harrington, R., '"The Mighty Hood": Navy, Empire, War at Sea and the British National Imagination, 1920–1960', *Journal of Contemporary History*, 38, 2 (2003), 171–85

Jeffery, K., 'The Second World War', in J. M. Brown and W. R. Louis (eds.), *The Oxford History of the British Empire*, vol. 4: *The Twentieth Century*, pp. 306–32

Jones, E. and N. Greenberg, 'Royal Naval Psychiatry: Organization, Methods and Outcomes, 1900–1945', *Mariner's Mirror*, 92 (2006), 190–203

Osterhammel, J., 'China', in J. M. Brown and W. R. Louis (eds.), *The Oxford History of the British Empire*, vol. 4: *The Twentieth Century*, pp. 643–66

Prysor, G., 'Morale at Sea: Personnel Policy and Operational Experience in the British Navy, 1939–1945', D.Phil. thesis, Oxford University, 2008

Sears, J., 'Discipline in the Royal Navy, 1913–1946', *War and Society*, 9 (1991), 29–60

Stevens, D., 'The Faceless Foe: Perceptions of the Enemy in Modern Naval Battle', in J. Reeve and D. Stevens (eds.), *The Face of Naval Battle: The Human Experience of Modern War at Sea* (Crow's Nest, Aus., 2003), pp. 263–84

Summerfield, P., 'Education and Politics in the British Armed Forces in the Second World War', *International Review of Social History*, 26 (1981), 133–58


## Books

Addison, P. and J. A. Crang (eds.), *Listening to Britain: Home Intelligence Reports on Britain's Finest Hour – May to September 1940* (London, 2010)

Allport, A., *Demobbed: Coming Home after the Second World War* (New Haven, 2009)

Arthur, M., *Forgotten Voices of the Second World War* (London, 2004)

———, *Lost Voices of the Royal Navy* (London, 2005)

———, *The Navy, 1939 to Present Day* (London, 1997)

Atkin, R., *Pillar of Fire: Dunkirk 1940* (Edinburgh, 2000)

Bailey, C. H., *The Royal Naval Museum Book of the Battle of the Atlantic. The Corvettes and their Crews: An Oral History* (Annapolis and London, 1994)

Baker, R., *The Terror of Tobermory* (Edinburgh, 1999)

Ball, S., *The Bitter Sea: The Struggle for Mastery in the Mediterranean, 1935–1949* (London, 2009)

Ballantyne, I., *Warspite* (London, 2001)

Barnett, C., *Engage the Enemy More Closely: The Royal Navy in the Second World War* (London, 1991)

Beevor, A., *The Battle for Spain: The Spanish Civil War 1936–1939* (London, 2006)

———, *D-Day: The Battle for Normandy* (London, 2009)

Bell, C. M., *The Royal Navy: Seapower and Strategy Between the Wars* (Basingstoke, 2000)

Bell C. M. and B. A. Elleman (eds.), *Naval Mutinies of the Twentieth Century: An International Perspective* (London, 2003)

Bennett, G. H. and R. Bennett, *Survivors: British Merchant Seamen in the Second World War* (London, 2007)

Billy, G. J. and C. M. Billy, *Merchant Mariners at War: An Oral History of World War II* (Gainesville, FL, 2008)

Brennecke, J., *The Hunters and the Hunted* (London, 1958)

Bridgland, T., *Waves of Hate: Naval Atrocities of the Second World War* (London, 2002)

Broome, J., *Convoy Is to Scatter* (London, 1972)

Brown, J. M. and W. R. Louis (eds.), *The Oxford History of the British Empire*, vol. 4: *The Twentieth Century* (Oxford, 1999)

Bull, P., *To Sea in a Sieve* (London, 1956)

Burn, A., *The Fighting Commodores: The Convoy Commanders in the Second World War* (London, 1999)

Calder, A., *The Myth of the Blitz* (London, 1992)

———, *The People's War: Britain 1939–45* (London, 1969)

Carew, A., *The Lower Deck of the Royal Navy 1900–1939: The Invergordon Mutiny in Perspective* (Manchester, 1981)

Chalmers, W. C., *Full Cycle: The Biography of Admiral Sir Bertram Home Ramsay* (London, 1959)

Churchill, W. S., *The Second World War*, 6 vols. (London, 1948–54)

Colville, J., *The Fringes of Power: Downing Street Diaries, 1939–1955* (London, 2004)

Connell, G. G., *Jack's War: Lower-deck Recollections from World War II* (London, 1985)

Connelly, M., *We Can Take it! Britain and the Memory of the Second World War* (Harlow, 2004)

Cooter, R., M. Harrison and S. Sturdy (eds.), *War, Medicine and Modernity* (Stroud, 1998)

Costello, J., *Love, Sex, and War: Changing Values, 1939–45* (London, 1985)

Crang, J. A., *The British Army and the People's War, 1939–1945* (Manchester, 2000)

Creighton, K., *Convoy Commodore* (London, 1956)

Cunningham, A. B., *A Sailor's Odyssey: The Autobiography of Admiral of the Fleet, Viscount Cunningham of Hyndhope* (London, 1951)

Day, B. (ed.), *The Letters of Noël Coward* (London, 2007)

Dear, I. and M. R. D. Foot (eds.), *The Oxford Companion to World War II* (Oxford, 2001)

Dönitz, K., *Memoirs: Ten Years and Twenty Days* (London, 1990; first published 1958)

Dower, J. W., *War Without Mercy: Race and Power in the Pacific War* (London, 1986)

Elphick, P., *Singapore: The Pregnable Fortress – A Study in Deception, Discord and Desertion* (London, 1995)

Farrell, B. P., *The Defence and Fall of Singapore, 1940–1942* (Stroud, 2005)

French, D., *Raising Churchill's Army: the British Army and the War against Germany, 1919–1945* (Oxford, 2000)

Gates, E., *End of the Affair: The Collapse of the Anglo-French Alliance* (London, 1981)

Gilbert, M., *Churchill: A Life* (London, 1991)

Glenton, B., *Mutiny in Force X* (London, 1986)

Graham, A. C., *Random Naval Recollections, 1905–1951* (Cardross, 1979)

Gray, E., *Operation Pacific: The Royal Navy's War against Japan, 1941–5* (London, 1990)

Griffiths, W., *My Darling Children: War from the Lower Deck* (London, 1992)

Grove, E. J., *The Royal Navy Since 1815: A New Short History* (Basingstoke, 2005)

'Gun Buster', *Return via Dunkirk* (London, 1940)

Hadley, P., *Third Class to Dunkirk* (London, 1944)

Haggie, P., *Britannia at Bay: The Defence of the British Empire against Japan, 1931–1941* (Oxford, 1981)

Harding R. (ed.), *The Royal Navy 1930–2000: Innovation and Defence* (London, 2005)

Harrison, M., *Medicine and Victory: British Military Medicine in the Second World War* (Oxford, 2004)

Hastings, M., *Finest Years: Churchill as Warlord 1940–45* (London, 2009)

Hawkins, I. (ed.), *Destroyer: An Anthology of First-hand Accounts of the War at Sea, 1939–1945* (London, 2003)

Herman, A., *To Rule the Waves: How the British Navy Shaped the Modern World* (London, 2005)

Hewitt, N., *Coastal Convoys 1939–1945: The Indestructible Highway* (Barnsley, 2008)

Hichens, A., *Gunboat Command* (Barnsley, 2007)

Hill, J. R. (ed.), *The Oxford Illustrated History of the Royal Navy* (Oxford, 1995)

Hobday, G., *In Harm's Way: An RNVR Officer at War, 1940–1944* (London, 1985)

Hough, R., *Former Naval Person: Churchill and the Wars at Sea* (London, 1985)

———, *The Hunting of Force Z: The Sinking of the Prince of Wales and the Repulse* (London, 1963)

———, *The Longest Battle: The War at Sea, 1939–45* (London, 2001)

Jackson, A., *The British Empire and the Second World War* (London, 2006)

Jackson, R., *The Royal Navy in World War II* (Shrewsbury, 1997)

Jullian, M., *H.M.S. Fidelity* (London, 1957)

Kemp, P., *Convoy! Drama in Arctic Waters* (London, 1993)

Kennedy, P. M., *The Rise and Fall of British Naval Mastery* (London, 1976)

Kerr, J. L. and D. James (eds.), *The Wavy Navy: By Some who Served* (London, 1950)

Laffin, J., *Jack Tar: The Story of the British Sailor* (London, 1969)

Lambert, A., *Admirals: The Naval Commanders who Made Britain Great* (London, 2008)

Lane, T., *The Merchant Seamen's War* (Manchester, 1990)

Lavery, B., *Churchill's Navy: The Ships, Men and Organisation, 1939–1945* (London, 2006)

———, *Hostilities Only: Training the Wartime Royal Navy* (London, 2004)

———, *In Which They Served: The Royal Navy Officer Experience in the Second World War* (London, 2008)

Levy, J. P., *The Royal Navy's Home Fleet in World War II* (Basingstoke, 2003)

Lombard-Hobson, S., *A Sailor's War* (London, 1983)

Louis, W. R., *British Strategy in the Far East, 1919–39* (Oxford, 1971)

Macintyre, D., *The Naval War against Hitler* (London, 1971)

———, *U-Boat Killer* (London, 1956)

Mackay, R., *Half the Battle: Civilian Morale in Britain During the Second World War* (Manchester, 2002)

Mackenzie, S. P., *British War Films, 1939–45: The Cinema and the Services* (London, 2001)

———, *Politics and Military Morale: Current-affairs and Citizenship Education in the British Army, 1914–1950* (Oxford, 1992)

Maiolo, J. A., *The Royal Navy and Nazi Germany, 1933–39: A Study in Appeasement and the Origins of the Second World War* (London, 1998)

Marder, A. J., *From the Dardanelles to Oran: Studies of the Royal Navy in War and Peace, 1915–1940* (London, 1974)

Marder, A. J., M. Jacobsen and J. Horsfield, *Old Friends, New Enemies: The Royal Navy and the Imperial Japanese Navy*, 2 vols. (Oxford, 1981 and 1990)

Marriott, E., *Claude and Madeleine* (London, 2005)

Mawdsley, E., *World War II: A New History* (Cambridge, 2010)

McKee, C., *Sober Men and True: Sailor Lives in the Royal Navy, 1900–1945* (Cambridge, MA, and London, 2002)

McLaine, I., *Ministry of Morale: Home Front Morale and the Ministry of Information in World War II* (London, 1979)

Mearns, D. and R. White, *Hood and Bismarck* (London, 2001)

Middlebrook, M. and P. Mahoney, *Battleship: The Loss of the Prince of Wales and the Repulse* (London, 2001, first published 1977)

———, *Convoy: The Battle for Convoys SC.122 and HX.229* (London, 1976)

Milner, M., *Battle of the Atlantic* (Stroud, 2003)

———, *North Atlantic Run: The Royal Canadian Navy and the Battle for the Convoys* (Toronto, 1985)

Monsarrat, N., *The Cruel Sea* (London, 2002; first published 1951)

———, *Monsarrat at Sea* (London, 1975)

Neidpath, J., *The Singapore Naval Base and the Defence of Britain's Eastern Empire, 1919–1941* (Oxford, 1981)

Norman, A., *HMS Hood: The Pride of the Royal Navy* (London, 2002)

Overy, R. J., *Why the Allies Won* (London, 1996)

Perry, C., *Boy in the Blitz* (Stroud, 2000)

Plevy, H., *Battleship Sailors: The Fighting Career of HMS Warspite Recalled by Her Men* (London, 2001)

Poolman, K., *The British Sailor* (London, 1989)

Reeve, J. and D. Stevens (eds.), *The Face of Naval Battle: The Human Experience of Modern War at Sea* (Crow's Nest, Aus., 2003)

Roskill, S. W., *HMS 'Warspite': the Story of a Famous Battleship* (London, 1974)

———, *Naval Policy Between the Wars*, 2 vols. (London, 1968)

———, *The Navy at War, 1939–1945* (London, 1960)

Ruge, F., *Sea Warfare, 1939–1945: A German Viewpoint* (London, 1957)

Sebag-Montefiore, H., *Dunkirk: Fight to the Last Man* (London, 2006)

————, *Enigma: The Battle for the Code* (London, 2000)

Shephard, B., *A War of Nerves: Soldiers and Psychiatrists, 1914–1994* (London, 2000)

Simpson, M. (ed.), *The Cunningham Papers: Selections from the Private and Official Correspondence of Admiral of the Fleet Viscount Cunningham of Hyndhope*, vol. 1 (London, 1999)

Smith, C., *England's Last War Against France: Fighting Vichy, 1940–1942* (London, 2009)

————, *Singapore Burning: Heroism and Surrender in World War II* (London, 2005)

Smith, G., *The War at Sea: Royal & Dominion Navy Actions in World War 2* (London, 1989)

Spector, R. H., *At War at Sea: Sailors and Naval Warfare in the Twentieth Century* (London, 2001)

Stephen, M., *The Fighting Admirals: British Admirals of the Second World War* (London, 1991)

Stuart White, J. R., *HMS Norfolk and Other Ships, 1940–1946: The Wartime Diary of a Dental Officer* (Leeds, 1995)

Taverner, N., *A Torch among the Tapers: The Life and Career of Captain Rory O'Conor, RN* (Bramber, 2000)

Taylor, G. C., *The Sea Chaplains: A History of the Chaplains of the Royal Navy* (Oxford, 1978)

Thomas, H., *The Spanish Civil War*, 4th edn (London, 2003)

Thompson, B., *The Arctic Convoys* (London, 1977)

Thompson, J., *The Imperial War Museum Book of the War at Sea: The Royal Navy in the Second World War* (London, 1996)

Tooze, A., *The Wages of Destruction: The Making and Breaking of the Nazi Economy* (London 2006)

Twiss, F., *Social Change in the Royal Navy, 1924–1970: The Life and Times of Admiral Sir Frank Twiss*, ed. C. H. Bailey (Stroud, 1996)

Tyrer, N., *Sisters in Arms: British Army Nurses Tell Their Story* (London, 2008)

Van der Vat, D., *Standard of Power: The Royal Navy in the Twentieth Century* (London, 2000)

Wallis, R. R., *Two Red Stripes: A Naval Surgeon at War* (London, 1973)

Wardle, H., *Dive Navy: Memoirs, 1935–58* (Hayling Island, 2002)

Wells, J., *The Royal Navy: An Illustrated Social History, 1870–1982* (Stroud, 1994)

Williams, A., *The Battle of the Atlantic* (London, 2002)

Willmott, H. P., *Grave of a Dozen Schemes: British Naval Planning and the War against Japan, 1943–1945* (Shrewsbury, 1996)

Winton, J., *Carrier Glorious: The Life and Death of an Aircraft Carrier* (London, 1986)

———, *Cunningham* (London, 1998)

———, *The Death of the Scharnhorst* (London, 1983)

———, *The Forgotten Fleet: The British Navy in the Pacific, 1944–45* (London, 1969)

Winton, J. (ed.), *The War at Sea, 1939–1945: An Anthology of Personal Experience* (London, 1967)

Woodman, R., *The Arctic Convoys, 1941–1945* (London, 1994)

———, *Malta Convoys, 1940–1943* (London, 2000)

Ziegler, P., *Mountbatten* (London, 1985)

# Index

NOTE: Ranks and titles are generally the highest mentioned in the text

# He just wanted a decent book to read ...

Not too much to ask, is it? It was in 1935 when Allen Lane, Managing Director of Bodley Head Publishers, stood on a platform at Exeter railway station looking for something good to read on his journey back to London. His choice was limited to popular magazines and poor-quality paperbacks – the same choice faced every day by the vast majority of readers, few of whom could afford hardbacks. Lane's disappointment and subsequent anger at the range of books generally available led him to found a company – and change the world.

*'We believed in the existence in this country of a vast reading public for intelligent books at a low price, and staked everything on it'*
**Sir Allen Lane, 1902–1970, founder of Penguin Books**

The quality paperback had arrived – and not just in bookshops. Lane was adamant that his Penguins should appear in chain stores and tobacconists, and should cost no more than a packet of cigarettes.

Reading habits (and cigarette prices) have changed since 1935, but Penguin still believes in publishing the best books for everybody to enjoy. We still believe that good design costs no more than bad design, and we still believe that quality books published passionately and responsibly make the world a better place.

So wherever you see the little bird – whether it's on a piece of prize-winning literary fiction or a celebrity autobiography, political tour de force or historical masterpiece, a serial-killer thriller, reference book, world classic or a piece of pure escapism – you can bet that it represents the very best that the genre has to offer.

**Whatever you like to read – trust Penguin.**

read more
www.penguin.co.uk